THE
KENNEDYS

THE
KENNEDYS

Peter Collier
David Horowitz

SECKER & WARBURG   London

First published in England 1984 by
Martin Secker & Warburg Limited
54 Poland Street, London W1V 3DF

Copyright © 1984 by Peter Collier and David Horowitz

ISBN 0-436-10551-9

Printed in the United States of America

CONTENTS

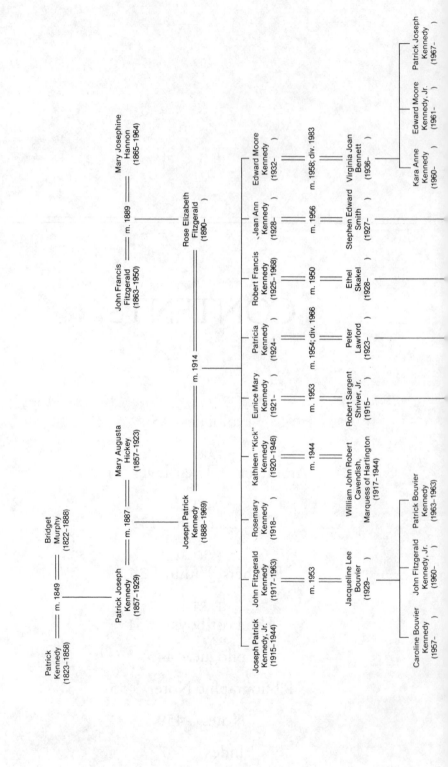

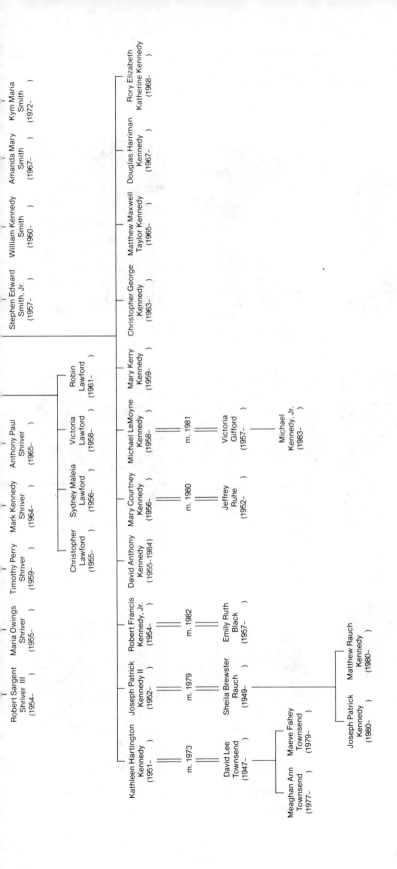

ARCHITECT OF THEIR LIVES

Patrick Joseph
Kennedy

Mary Augusta Hickey
Kennedy

John Francis Fitzgerald
("Honey Fitz")

Mary Josephine
Hannon Fitzgerald

Joseph Patrick
Kennedy

Rose Elizabeth
Fitzgerald Kennedy

Joseph Patrick
Kennedy, Jr.

John Fitzgerald
Kennedy

Rosemary Kennedy

Kathleen Kennedy
("Kick")

Eunice Mary Kennedy

Patricia Kennedy

Robert Francis
Kennedy

Jean Ann Kennedy

Edward Moore
Kennedy

Joseph Patrick
Kennedy

Rose Elizabeth
Fitzgerald Kennedy

Gloria Swanson

THE STAND-IN

Joseph Patrick
Kennedy, Jr.

John Fitzgerald
Kennedy

Inga Arvad

K. LeMoyne Billings

Rosemary Kennedy

Kathleen Kennedy
("Kick")

William John Robert
Cavendish, Marquess
of Hartington

Lord Peter Fitzwilliam

Eunice Mary Kennedy
Shriver

Robert Sargent
Shriver, Jr.

Patricia Kennedy
Lawford

Peter Lawford

Jean Ann Kennedy
Smith

Stephen Edward Smith

Robert Francis
Kennedy

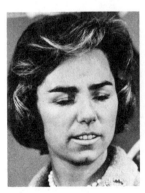

Ethel Skakel Kennedy

Edward Moore
Kennedy

Virginia Joan Bennett
Kennedy

BROTHERS WITHIN

John Fitzgerald
Kennedy

Jacqueline Lee
Bouvier Kennedy

K. LeMoyne Billings

Eunice Mary Kennedy
Shriver

Robert Sargent
Shriver, Jr.

Edward Moore
Kennedy

Jacqueline Lee
Bouvier Kennedy

Joseph Patrick
Kennedy

Rose Elizabeth
Fitzgerald Kennedy

THE LOST BOYS

K. LeMoyne Billings

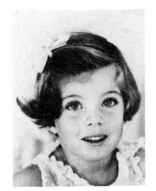

Caroline Bouvier
Kennedy

John Fitzgerald
Kennedy

Joseph Patrick
Kennedy, II

Robert Francis
Kennedy, Jr.

David Anthony
Kennedy

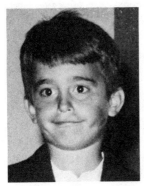

Robert Sargent
Shriver, III

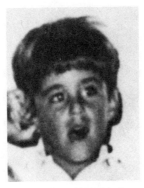

Christopher Kennedy
Lawford

Caroline Bouvier
Kennedy

John Fitzgerald
Kennedy, Jr.

Joseph Patrick
Kennedy, II

Robert Francis
Kennedy, Jr.

David Anthony
Kennedy

Robert Sargent
Shriver, III

Kim Kelly

Pam Kelly

Edward Moore
Kennedy, Jr.

Christopher Kennedy
Lawford

PROLOGUE: APRIL 1938

*I*T WAS A MOMENTARY PLATEAU IN Europe's long slide toward war. Hitler had absorbed Austria and was eying Czechoslovakia. Roosevelt, having abandoned any hope of convening a peace conference in Washington, was looking for a coherent policy. British Prime Minister Chamberlain had suffered setbacks in his appeasement strategy, but continued to believe that rational men will agree to go along if the deal offered them is sweet enough. Joseph P. Kennedy was on his way to Windsor Castle to visit the King and Queen.

It was less than a month since he had walked out of the embassy in top hat and cutaway, climbed into the ornate ceremonial coach, and ridden to Buckingham Palace to present his credentials as the new American Ambassador to the Court of St. James's. In the intervening weeks he and his family had taken England by storm. His brashness even more than his truculent isolationism had made him the talk of the diplomatic community. His wife, Rose, had been taken up by London society, sweet revenge for someone who'd often felt the sting of being excluded by the proper Bostonians back home. And the nine winsome Kennedy children had been photographed and written about as if they were some remarkable, very American experiment in genetics. In one breathtaking move the Kennedys had become America's first family abroad. The invitation to spend a weekend with the King and Queen was final proof that they had indeed arrived.

As their limousine pulled into Windsor Park, Joe and Rose drank in the royal details like tourists. The park looked like a forest in some old English ballad; the castle itself had an intentional magnificence unmatched by anything they'd ever seen in all their travels. As they were shown inside, they saw vaulted ceilings, furniture upholstered in red damask, gold ornaments, and liveried servants moving with silent precision down the long hallways. Their suitcases were deposited in a suite they later learned had once been Queen Victoria's private chambers. The peruked footman attending them looked like a relic from the British Museum.

Dinner itself was the kind of occasion Joe Kennedy liked—a banquet of anecdotes and impressions that could be passed on to his children like the hand-written notes of commendation he solicited from President Roosevelt and photographs of himself posed beside the famous. Prime Minister Chamberlain and his wife were there, along with the new Foreign Minister, Lord Halifax, and his wife, and the Queen's relatives Lord and Lady Elphinstone. When someone mentioned the painting of Victoria wearing the Garter, the royal couple discussed the origins of the motto of the Order: *Honi soit qui mal y pense*. Later, Kennedy gossiped with the Queen about American movies while the King swapped insights with Rose about child rearing. Eventually the King began to give the Queen significant looks that an imposing floral centerpiece prevented her from catching, which forced him to make a joke of the royal nod that traditionally signaled that dinner was over. After the ladies withdrew to a sitting room, the gentlemen remained behind with brandy and cigars, allowing their talk to turn to war. Prime Minister Chamberlain still believed the conflict could be avoided and Kennedy agreed with him; the King hoped they were right.

Later on, after everyone else had retired, Rose Kennedy lay in the canopied bed so high off the floor that a stepstool was required to climb up into it. She listened as the Windsor tower clock tolled eleven and the guard changed in the courtyard below her window. Feeling like an American Cinderella, she tried to fix the details of the evening in her memory; yet the moment was so special, such a dramatic caesura in the rush of their lives, that she could hardly force herself to realize she was really there: "I thought I must be dreaming that I, Rose Kennedy, a simple young matron, am really here at Windsor Castle, a guest of the Queen and two little Princesses." Although not given to sentimental backward looks at his life, Joe Kennedy too had experienced something like this sudden sense of perspective when they were dressing for dinner, although he expressed it with his usual directness: "Well, Rose, this is a hell of a long way from East Boston."

Indeed, the distance the Kennedys had come in half a lifetime was almost incalculable. Their grandparents had fled Ireland for America in steerage; they returned to England in first class, official representatives of an even greater power. Their grandparents had arrived in the New World anonymous and poor; they returned to Europe wealthy and famous. Yet the distance they had come involved more than history or geography. Character was also important, character and ambition. That they had gotten anywhere at all, Rose would have been the first to acknowledge, was because of her husband, one of the most talked-about men in America.

Not yet fifty years old, Joe Kennedy had already gone through several careers, always moving forward, pushing toward the center of things, grasping for more. He had been an operator on Wall Street, a self-made man who accumulated one of the largest private fortunes of the twenties. He had gone to Hollywood and become one of the first tycoons, making movies and engineering some of the mergers that transformed the film world from a colony into an industry. He had entered politics and become one of the most controversial personalities of the New Deal, a power in the Democratic Party and a friend of the President. Rumors of numerous extramarital affairs, illicit business dealings, and even ties to crime only added a piquant touch of mystery to his reputation and made him seem all the more romantic, Gatsbyesque.

Contemplating this remarkable rise, *Fortune* magazine had written: "The legends of Joe Kennedy make him at once the hero of a Frank Merriwell captain-of-the-nines adventure, a Horatio Alger success story, an E. Phillips Oppenheim tale of intrigue, and a John Dos Passos disillusioning report on the search for the big money. The truth makes him the central character of a picaresque novel of a sort not yet written."

Picaro: the hero of a picaresque novel; a rogue or adventurer who lives by his wits, working his way through various strata of society, worrying less about morality than mobility; part of everything but ultimately belonging nowhere. In many ways the definition fit. Joe Kennedy's whole life had been one of restless movement, an attempt to transcend ethnic assumptions while striking out into terra incognita where no Irish Catholic had yet been. For some other East Boston boy, the Court of St. James's might have been the culmination of ambition—minister to the nation that had oppressed his forefathers, occupant of America's leading social and diplomatic position abroad. But even as he spent this foggy April weekend at Windsor, the picaresque tale was continuing to unfold as Kennedy intrigued to position himself as a candidate for the White House if Roosevelt decided against a third term.

Always on the lookout for opportunity, he was more than a ruthless opportunist, as some had called him during his rise to prominence; more than an Irish Sammy Glick, as he would be called later on, after he had returned from England with the career that had seemed limitless now in shambles. If anything, Joe Kennedy was a homegrown Faust, willing to venture whatever he had in exchange for a chance to move closer to the heart of the American dream. It was a pact that implicated not only himself but his family too. Not long after the visit to the King and Queen, Kennedy was asked once again how he would keep from confusing the interests of the United States with those of England, as previous United States ambassadors had done. It was easy, he replied; he had a special stake in the future of his country. "After all"—he flashed his famous grin—"my wife and I have given nine hostages to fortune."

Hostages to fortune: the phrase would acquire a melancholy resonance in the years to come. When the saga he began had unraveled its skein, Joe Kennedy's triumph was that fortune did smile on him, making the Kennedys *the* American story. His tragedy was that in the final accounting, the hostages he gave would be taken one by one, and even those who survived would never be free.

PART 1

ARCHITECT OF THEIR LIVES

What is character but the determination of incident? What is incident but the illustration of character?

—HENRY JAMES

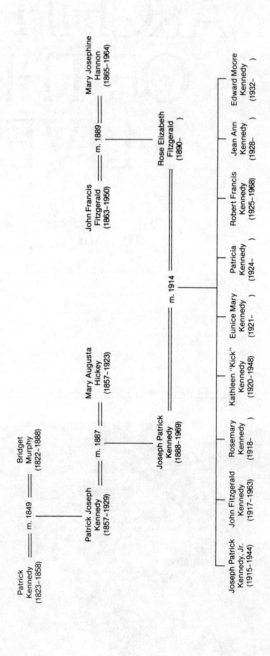

1.

$\mathcal{E}$XACTLY HOW MUCH AN IRISH
tale his story was, how much a metaphor for the rise of the American Irish
in general, Joe Kennedy himself would never acknowledge. In the middle of
his life, when a Boston newspaper referred to him as an ''Irishman'' one
time too many, he exploded: ''Goddamn it! I was born in this country! My
children were born in this country! What the hell does someone have to do
to become an American?'' He surrounded himself with tough-talking Boston
Irish, yet he had little patience with the easy tears and fusty rhetoric of the
stage Irishman who blamed all his woes on discrimination. A self-made,
indeed, a self-created man, he was fiercely protective of the individual nature
of his accomplishment and had to believe that it was due to temperament, to
his own will and philosophy, to what he liked to call ''moxie,'' and not to the
sharp and tragic rejection his people had experienced from the time they
first set foot on American soil. Those who knew him best, however, saw Joe
Kennedy as Irish to the core—a logical outcome of the undeclared war that
went back at least two hundred years before his birth to the day when a
woman named Goody Glover was hanged as a witch on Boston Common
because she'd knelt in front of a statue of the Blessed Virgin while telling
her beads in the ''devil's tongue'' of Gaelic.

The saga of the Irish in America—a history Joe Kennedy rarely mentioned but never forgot—was part history and part parable. The first federal
census, in 1790, had listed only 44,000 persons of Irish birth, most of them
Ulstermen (''Scotch-Irish,'' they called themselves) who, as skilled workers
and small businessmen, had become outriders for the conquest of the American frontier. Over the next few decades immigration increased, but in 1845

the history of Ireland and America was altered forever when Irish farmers discovered a "blight of unusual character" during the early stages of the potato harvest. The crop had been unreliable for several years, but now freshly dug potatoes turned rotten in hours, decomposing into a gelatinous black ooze with a putrescent smell. Livestock fed on the potatoes died; people hungry enough to eat them became violently ill. As the blight spread, the Crown convened boards of inquiry whose learned men theorized that the disease was perhaps caused by steam emitted from the locomotives recently introduced into Ireland, by sea-gull droppings the farmers used as fertilizer, or even by "mortiferous vapours" rising up from "blind volcanoes" deep in the earth. But if the causes were mysterious (it would later be discovered that the blight had been transmitted by a fungus that traveled to Ireland from America), the effects were clear enough. Over the next ten years, the period of the Great Hunger, a million Irish died and another million left their homeland, most of them heading across the sea.

The only parallels for this exodus were the plagues and persecutions of the Old Testament. Packet ships following the example of the Cunard Lines offered fares as low as twelve dollars between Londonderry or Liverpool and New York or Boston; often the tickets were purchased by absentee English landlords anxious to be rid of their starving peasants. The Irish squeezed onto the "coffin ships," floating pest houses of typhus and other diseases, and undertook a voyage as close as any white man ever came to experiencing the dread Middle Passage of the African slave trade. As much as 10 percent of a shipload were likely to die at sea. In 1847, the most disastrous year of all, an estimated 40,000, or 20 percent of those who set out from Ireland, perished on the trip. "If crosses and tombs could be erected on water," wrote a U.S. commissioner for emigration, "the whole route of the emigrant vessels from Europe to America would long since have assumed the appearance of a crowded cemetery."

Until 1840, Boston had been little more than a debarkation point for immigrants moving on to Canada and the interior of New England. In 1845, in fact, the city's foremost demographer confidently asserted that there could be no further increase in the city's population. But over the next ten years, a tidal wave of newcomers—Boston's harbor master claimed to be able to identify another shipload of them as far away as Deer Island just by the smell—piled off their ships, swarmed into Boston, and stayed, a quarter of a million of them. Called "famine Irish" to distinguish them from their predecessors, they were too poor to pay the tolls and fares that would take them out of the waterlocked city; they packed into the reeking Paddyvilles and Mick Alleys, as many as thirty or forty crowding into one tiny cellar, prey to accident and disease that made their death rate as high as it had been in Ireland at the height of the hunger. By 1850 they comprised a third of the city's population. Gravid with their sudden weight, Boston was about to give birth to the first American immigrant ghetto.

Construction companies from all over the country sent to Boston for Irish contract laborers, transporting them to new destinations in railway cars with sealed doors and curtains nailed across the windows. Those who stayed behind became coal heavers and longshoremen, "muckers" and "blacklegs" who dug canals and cleared marshes, remaking the face of the city and giving it an opportunity for unparallelled growth and expansion. (When tourists remarked on the beauty of the cobblestones on Beacon Hill some Irishman was sure to remark, "Those aren't cobblestones, those are Irish hearts.") Yet they remained a people apart, exempt from New England traditions of transcendental humanism and social uplift which pitied southern Negroes but not their own white slaves. By the 1850s, the infamous NINA—No Irish Need Apply—signs began to appear in Boston, as the antagonisms that culminated in the Know-Nothing Party and other nativist movements reached a dangerous simmer. Boston's Brahmin elite retreated from the Irish as if from contagion, dividing the city into two cultures, separate and unequal. Mayor Theodore Lyman spoke for those who intended to keep it that way, labeling the Irish "a race that will never be infused with our own, but on the contrary, will always remain distinct and hostile."

This was the atmosphere that twenty-six-year-old Patrick Kennedy found when he arrived in Boston in 1849. He was the third son of a prosperous farmer; the Kennedys of Dugganstown, New Ross, in County Wexford, had eighty acres on which they grew barley and raised beef, and their county was one of the areas least affected by the famine. Unlike the other immigrants, who were literally fleeing death, Patrick had undertaken the journey to improve his fortunes. He left his parents behind, a brother, James (the oldest son, John, had died in the battle of Vinegar Hill), and a sister, Mary. He would never see them again; they would never see America.

A handsome, muscular man of medium build, with reddish brown hair and bright blue eyes, Kennedy was not alone when he stepped off the *Washington Irving* at Noddle's Island, a strip of land in Boston Harbor that eventually became East Boston after Irish labor had joined it to the mainland. On board he had met Bridget Murphy, also a refugee from County Wexford, and begun his courtship at once. They were married on September 26 of the year they arrived, in the Holy Redeemer Church, by Father John Williams, later to become Boston's archbishop.

The Kennedys went no farther than East Boston, possibly because, like many of their compatriots, they couldn't afford the two pennies it cost to take the ferry across the bay. Patrick sat with other Irishmen on the piers in the shadows of the Cunard liners hoping a short-handed stevedore could use him, and, along with other newcomers, walked the crooked streets winding up from the docks looking for work in the warren of small shops. After a while he was able to establish himself as a cooper, fashioning yokes and staves for the Conestoga wagons heading west in the great Gold Rush to California and making whiskey barrels destined for the waterfront saloons where the Irish met to exercise their natural sociability and drown their sorrows.

At a time when Americans were beginning to move to cities to escape the smothering traditions of farms and villages, the Irish reaffirmed the conservative values of their recent rural past in the new urban setting. The tenement apartment, like the Irish farm, was a place where the generations stayed together; the family was the primary unit of emotion and survival. As the New World yielded less to their efforts than they had expected, the Irish turned inward to their kin for support, accenting the "clannishness" the Brahmins found so primitive. Like other immigrants who had left one family behind, Patrick and Bridget Kennedy quickly started another—four children in rapid succession, Mary, Margaret, Johanna, and, on January 14, 1858, a son, Patrick Joseph.

Whatever the fanciful tales told back in the Old Country, there were few rags-to-riches stories for this first generation of Irish. The streets of East Boston were not paved with gold. Instead of a material legacy, they left a sweat equity in America for their children and grandchildren to capitalize on. On November 22, 1858, ten months after the birth of his son, Patrick died of cholera, leaving behind no portraits or documents, just a family. He had survived in Boston for nine years, only five less than the life expectancy for an Irishman in America at mid-century. The first Kennedy to arrive in the New World, he was the last to die in anonymity.

Her husband's death forced Bridget Kennedy to look for a paying job, and she clerked in a notions shop near the ferry building which, through hard saving, in time became hers and the main support for her family. In an era when Irish ambivalence about America was intense—some Irishmen would soon riot against the draft at the same time that others were serving with distinction in campaigns against the Confederacy—Bridget Kennedy had no doubts about her adopted home. Realizing that the boy Patrick Joseph (known in the neighborhood as "Pat's boy" until they gave him the grown-up nickname "P. J.") was the key to the family's future, Bridget and her daughters pampered him and tried to keep him out of trouble. For a while he went to a school run by the Sisters of Notre Dame and helped his mother in the shop. But by the time he was a teenager, he was working on the docks as a stevedore. Over the next few years, as his sisters married, P. J. saved his money, looking for a way to solidify his family's tenuous hold on respectability. Not long after his twenty-second birthday, he heard of a run-down saloon for sale in a dilapidated section on Haymarket Square. With loans from his mother and sisters, he bought the place and went into business for himself.

P. J. Kennedy had the most important qualification of a saloonkeeper: he was a good listener. What he heard from the other side of the bar during the

first years he was building his business had less to do with the tragic hope-
lessness of Ireland than with questions of power in Boston. When the Irish
first arrived, the Brahmins, eloquent theorists about democracy, had tried to
blunt their impact by statute—attempting to extend the residency requirement for voting from five to twenty-one years. When this maneuver and
others like it failed, they had sought to keep the Irish quarantined in shanty
towns. But it was this enforced closeness, combining with their Old World
heritage of clandestine organization for self-defense, that made the Boston
Irish political in a way that was unrivaled by any other immigrant group.

Politics for them did not result from abstract theories about representative
government or the perfection of human nature; it was a strategy of survival.
By the 1870s they had begun to form barroom associations which took over
and systematized the chaotic political behavior in the streets. Building on
family friendships and neighborhood loyalties, going street by street and
ward by ward, they began moving into the local Democratic Party structures, taking them over by sheer numbers and nerve—that "moxie" Joe
Kennedy would prize so highly—and turning them into something like a
parallel government, a "machine" that had to be built because existing civic
institutions did not serve their needs for jobs, for protection against unscrupulous landlords, employers, and other social predators. In New York the
machine was Tammany; in Boston it was a network of political clubs spread
throughout the city's wards, each with a "boss" bound to his people by a
web of mutual loyalty and self-interest, brokering power for himself and his
constituents.

The first great boss in Boston was Martin Lomasney, a stubby, cigar-
chewing man in a derby whose father had been a tailor in Ireland. Known
as the "Mahatma," Lomasney met immigrants at the wharves and herded
them to his headquarters at the West End's Henricks Club. The deal he
offered showed the beautiful simplicity of the machine, a synchronicity of
moving parts that made it the political equivalent of perpetual motion. In
return for help getting them settled, Lomasney asked only that the newcomers register as Democrats and vote as he told them to. (And for those uncertain about the mechanics of the franchise he had "electoral aids" to help
them, the most famous of which was a "fine-tooth comb" with the teeth cut
out in a pattern that, when superimposed on a ballot, showed exactly how to
vote.) With their votes he got patronage which he used to find them employ-
ment. He sold his services effectively : "Is somebody out of a job? We do our
best to place him and not necessarily on the public payroll. Does the family
run in arrears with the landlord or the butcher? We lend a helping hand. Do
the kids need clothing or the mother a doctor? We do what we can, and sure,
as the world is run, such things must be done. We keep old friends and make
new ones."

There was a perverse integrity in Lomasney and his system, as muckraking

journalist Lincoln Steffens discovered when he came to Boston to do a damning article on the Mahatma and found him far from defensive. "Who do you
think you're kidding?" Lomasney challenged him. "You get paid for muckraking and I get paid for creating what you call the muck . . . Look, you walk
your side of the street and I'll walk mine." The two men ultimately became
friends and later on Steffens said that it was Lomasney, more than anyone
else, who had made the Boston Irish "players in the game."

For an ambitious young man like P. J. Kennedy, this game offered excitement as well as rewards. Although just into his twenties, he cut an imposing
figure—a large man with a full face, thick red hair, and piercing blue eyes
that almost seemed larger than the Teddy Roosevelt glasses. He had already
established himself as trustworthy and responsible, "old beyond his realistic
years," as a customer said, and had been successful enough to buy a second
tavern across the street from the East Boston Shipyards where he had once
worked. Having seen the dangers of drink up close, he was that rarest of
Irishmen, a teetotaler, relaxing his rule only on the most festive occasions,
when he allowed himself a single shot glass of beer. As the saloons made
money, he looked for other opportunities, buying into a partnership in a
well-known Boston hotel called the Maverick House, and in 1885 opening his
own liquor-importation business, P. J. Kennedy and Company, located at
numbers 15 and 17 High Street. His major product was Haig and Haig
scotch, which he supplied to some of Boston's best hotels and restaurants.

Political by nature, he found that politics came naturally to him. In 1884
he had been elected to the Democratic Club of Ward Two. (He publicized
both his careers at once, handing out to everybody wood-handled corkscrews
inscribed "Compliments of P. J. Kennedy and Co., Importers.") Because
East Boston lacked a strong leader of Lomasney's stature, he moved rapidly
into the ward's hierarchy. In 1886, the year that children of Irish immigrants
first outnumbered those of the native born in Boston, P. J. and his allies took
control of the Democratic Committee of Ward Two and he was elected to the
State Senate.

At the same time he was choosing a political life, Kennedy began courting
Mary Augusta Hickey ("Mame" he called her). A handsome, physically
imposing woman (larger than P. J. himself), she was the daughter of James
Hickey, a prosperous businessman. Mary Augusta later told her children
how she had watched the young legislator passing the parlor window of the
Hickey home at 144 Saratoga Street on his morning route, and "set her cap
for him." It was a good match for Kennedy because the Hickey family was
more settled and more "comfortable" than his own. One son, John, had
graduated from Harvard Medical School, among the first Irishmen to do so.
Another son, James, Jr., was moving up through the ranks of the Boston
police force toward an eventual captaincy. A third, Charles, was a funeral-
parlor owner in Brockton, where he also dabbled in politics on the way to

becoming the city's mayor. The Boston Irish community might have considered the Kennedys beneath the Hickeys, but P. J. himself did not. On Thanksgiving Eve, 1887, he and Mary Augusta were married at Sacred Heart Church.

The couple moved into a three-story house at 165 Webster Street. Set on the crest of a hill, its back lawn sloping towards Boston Harbor, its front yard facing the city skyline, No. 165 was one of the most modest dwellings on a block which was rapidly becoming known as the Beacon Street of the Irish community. The following year, P. J.'s mother, Bridget, died in her home at 25 Borden Street at the age of sixty-seven. She had lived long enough to see "Pat's boy" establish himself in the new world where she had struggled to survive. She had also lived long enough to see his first child, Joseph, born into it on September 6, 1888.

That year was significant for P. J. in another way: the party organization chose him to go to the Democratic National Convention and give a seconding speech for Grover Cleveland. It was a year when Boston's Irish elected their first mayor, Hugh O'Brien, and were climbing the greasy pole of political ambition with a vengeance. But while enjoying the official success of their assault, they had also gotten a feel for the severity of the struggle ahead. Evicted from City Hall, Boston's Brahmins had retreated to their Back Bay brownstones, grasping the levers of economic power all the more tightly and drawing social lines with a sharper edge. The message was clear: the Irish could be policemen, civil servants, settlement-house workers, even mayors; they could have the thankless task of assimilating and controlling a new wave of Catholic immigrants from lands where English was a foreign language. But they could not expect acceptance or a partnership in the complex arrangements by which ultimate social power was exercised.

During three terms in the Massachusetts Senate, P. J. did not distinguish himself as a particularly innovative or energetic legislator. In the entire 1892 session, for instance, he introduced only two bills—one mandating the clerk to supply daily magazines to the legislators and the other to put two more men onto the payroll of the Boston Fire Department. For him, the East End had the only action worth being involved in. While at the State Capitol, he tightened his hold over Ward Two, emerging as its most powerful figure. It was a sign of how far he had come that in 1898 he was able to battle Martin Lomasney for control of the city's Democratic nominating convention. Playing by the rules of the day, P. J. had his troops put up blockades around the convention site. They kept rivals out until the Mahatma disguised his delegates as a funeral procession and smuggled them through Kennedy's lines in a hearse.

After his years in the Senate, P. J. spent his days holding forth in a private room in one of his two saloons. He had patronage positions like Elections Commissioner, Wire Commissioner, and for a time Acting Fire Commissioner, all the while tending the pastures of Ward Two—listening to supplicants, arranging job interviews, addressing recommendations. In a gray-bound volume, carefully numbered and indexed in an ink script, he saved blue and purple carbons of the typed originals.

Letter #44, March 14, 1904:

Dear Dick,
    ...I have a matter now that I would like to have you assist me in. I have a young man, a friend of mine, who is a graduate of our schools and also of Harvard College, and is taking an extra course to fit him for teaching; yet under the rules as they prevail at the present time in the School Committee of Boston he is obliged to go outside of Boston to get a place. I do not think that any other city in the Commonwealth has such a rule as that. You may see that under these conditions it is hard for one of our young men to get a start, as instead of Boston boys being in a position to benefit by having been born here, it seems as though that is the very thing that works against them. It is particularly hard on one of our kind (I mean by this the Catholic boy) because there are very few cities in the Commonwealth that I know of that will give one of our boys a position if they know that he is Catholic....I thought if you folks did not happen to have any young man in your section, that was an applicant, possibly this young man might get an opportunity there....

In 1907, P. J. had gotten enough distance from his origins to undertake a sentimental journey to Ireland, visiting the New Ross farm of his ancestors in County Wexford, collecting keepsakes from the surviving relatives with whom he had kept in touch, and making the pilgrimage to Vinegar Hill, where his grandfather had fought and his great-uncle had died. "It was with a great deal of pleasure," he wrote to his Irish cousins after returning to Boston,

that I showed to my children and my sisters and the friends gathered around when I arrived home, the copy book my father used when he went to school. My children were particularly interested in it, and you know how pleased I was...the fact that I had never seen my father to remember him...so one of the pleasures of my whole trip was bringing that copy book back home.

He had had his motto engraved on a plaque which he hung above his desk, its sentiments capturing the Irish feel for the evanescence of life that he had inherited from his father, but also containing the core of a ward boss's political wisdom: "I shall pass through this world but once. Any kindness I can do, or goodness show, let me do it now—for I shall not pass this way again."

By the early 1900s P. J. had brokered his way up from being just another of twenty-five ward bosses to being one of the four members of the so-called Board of Strategy, which had outflanked Lomasney to become the center of power in Boston. Along with Kennedy, the weekly noontime meetings in Room 8 of the Quincy Hotel had a seat for "Smiling Jim" Donovan of the South End, Joseph Corbett of Charlestown, and the member of the quartet P. J. liked least, the North End's John F. Fitzgerald.

"Fitzie," as he was known (the nickname "Honey Fitz" would come later, in the sentimental afterglow of his active political career), was P. J.'s opposite—loud and pugnacious, something of a philanderer, a histrionic politician, reveling in a public display of his considerable gifts. He was short and slight, although an outstanding athlete; he was always smiling in his photographs but had a heavy-browed, brooding look when crossed, an expression he affected more often after someone said it made him look a little like Napoleon.

While P. J. Kennedy had plotted a steady and patient climb to power, working behind the scenes and calculating his opportunities carefully, John F. Fitzgerald was a gate crasher by nature, and his assault on Brahmin institutions had made him something of a legend in the North End while he was still a young man. As a boy he had insisted on going to Boston Latin School, a venerable Boston institution whose alumni included such figures as Cotton Mather, Ralph Waldo Emerson, and Henry Adams. After graduation, he went on to Harvard Medical School for a year, but he had to leave to take care of his six brothers when his father died. He worked in the insurance business and took up the Brahmin game of polo, playing in matches throughout New England.

But it was always clear that Fitzgerald had "the gift" and that politics would be his life. He became active in neighborhood affairs and caught the eye of Lomasney himself. Soon he was apprentice to the sorcerer of Boston politics, attending every dance and caper, distributing turkeys at Christmastime, keeping a card file of people who needed jobs, scanning the newspapers for obituaries each morning so he'd know what wakes to attend that night. His energy and high spirits had soon made him the dominant figure in the North End, which he so habitually evoked as "the dear old North End" that his followers became known as the "dearos." It was said that Fitzie was the first and most accomplished practitioner of the "Irish switch"—shaking the hand of one person while talking to another. But his greatest gift was the gift of gab. His ability to talk nonstop for hours helped inspire a popular verse later on: "Honey Fitz can talk you blind/on any subject you can find/Fish and fishing, motor boats/Railroads, streetcars, getting votes..." A word for it entered the lexicon of Boston politics: *Fitzblarney*.

He was elected to the State Senate in 1892, serving alongside P. J. Kennedy there and recognizing him as a probable future rival for power. He went on to a term in Congress, where his kinetic personality once prompted Ohio Representative Henry Grosvenor to yell from the House floor, "You are like a monkey on an organ grinder's rope, always jumping around and shouting!" Concerned with power rather than issues, Fitzgerald did rise to the occasion once, when he led the opposition to a bill which would have required potential immigrants to be able to pass a test that included being able to read the Constitution. After President Cleveland had vetoed the legislation, Fitzgerald was cornered by Senator Henry Cabot Lodge. "You are an impudent young man," the imperious Yankee began. "Do you think Jews or Italians have any right in this country?" Fitzie didn't miss a beat. "As much right as your father or mine," he replied. "After all, it's only a difference of a few ships."

But for someone raised in the dear old North End, national office was like serving in a foreign embassy. The only place that mattered was Boston; the only office that counted was mayor, a sort of Irish presidency. Having become moderately wealthy after leaving Congress by publishing a Boston newspaper, the *Republic* (and using his political clout to insure large advertising revenues), Fitzgerald made his move in 1905, even though it meant running against the opposition of his old allies on the Strategy Board. He waged the kind of campaign which until then had not been seen in Boston, making up to thirty speeches a day and mobilizing his "dearos" into a force that snaked through the city chanting his slogan: "The people not the bosses must rule! Bigger, Better, Busier Boston!"

When Fitzgerald won, he became the first mayor whose parents had been born in Ireland. In his victory speech, he said that he wished only that his mother and father were present: "It would have been a great delight to them, for they were natives of a country where democracy could not be exercised freely due to English dominion." On the night of his election he journeyed to the headquarters of Ward Two to make peace with Kennedy. While there he couldn't resist plunging into that crowd too. As P. J. watched the little man pressing flesh, he shook his head in wonder: "He knows them all. I don't know half of them, even though they are in my district." Then the new Mayor came to him and said: "Now that the fight is over, Pat, let's get together." As the two of them shook hands, small and large, it was a historic moment in the immigrants' rise and a first hurrah for the dynasty to come.

2.

*J*F P. J. HAD BEEN ABLE TO HAVE his way, Joe Kennedy would have been named Patrick Joseph Kennedy III. But at the last minute Mary Augusta decided he should be Joseph Patrick. The reason she gave to outsiders was that she ''wanted no 'little P. J.s' running around the house,'' but to the family she said that this version of the same name sounded ''less Irish,'' and they realized it was a way of indicating that she wasn't keen on the boy's following in his father's footsteps.

Joe's two younger sisters, Loretta and Margaret, treated their brother like an Irish prince. Margaret, the younger of the two and so attractive and lively that she was later called the Kennedys' ''It Girl,'' said of him later on: ''I thought he was a god. I'd be thrilled even if he asked me to put something away for him—anything, just as long as he noticed me.'' Loretta was always struck by the authority he assumed in the family, even as a child. She later told a newspaperman eager for an anecdote how she'd undergone a crisis of belief one Christmas when she came downstairs and saw the exact doll house she'd wanted but realized that it was too large for Santa Claus to have brought it down the chimney. When she questioned P. J. he shrugged and looked away. Joe immediately jumped up and told her that Santa had a magic wand which he used to make objects larger or smaller at will, thus preserving her faith for another year.

It was Mary Augusta who dominated Joe's youth. Calling him ''my Joe'' and possessively monopolizing his time, she quizzed him about his school work and reminded him that his Uncle John had been to Harvard. It was her stern stare of disapproval—''the Hickey look'' as the rest of the family referred to it—that spurred him to do better. And it was she who established his ambivalent attitude toward his Irish past. She was proud of the status in the community that P. J.'s political activity brought, yet aware that for "proper" people—the Bostonians who'd moved away from the Irish as if fearing contagion—politics had become a faintly disreputable profession. She wanted Joe to "be somebody" in a way that her husband—whatever his place in the hierarchy of Irish Boston—was not. Responsive to her ambitions, he came running home from the local parish school every noon to have lunch with her. "He missed me," Mary Augusta reminisced happily later on, after he had established himself as one of the leading young men of the city. "He missed me and wanted to hurry home and see me again."

Yet however ambivalent Mary Augusta may have been, politics continued to be the central reality of the Kennedys' lives and as much a part of Joe's early experience as the air he breathed. His growing up was an endless round of musicales and marriages, wakes and ward meetings—those grounds where campaign and community met. There was a constant flow of supplicants to 165 Webster. "Tell them we're eating," Mary Augusta would say in the early days when knocks sounded on the door. But P. J. would shake his head and stand, carefully wiping his moustache: "No, I'll see them now." After he had gone to the door, there would be hushed talk in the hallway and then he would stick his head into the dining room again as he was putting on his coat and hat: "You'll have to go on without me." Later she would see to it that fresh clothes were laid out for him in case he had to go out for an evening appointment, and she would make sure the cook prepared a large bowl of clam chowder surrounded by crackers ready for him when he came home. Sometimes Joe went with his father on his rounds. For the rest of his life, he remembered one election day when they were walking down the street and a Kennedy lieutenant dashed up and proudly reported that he had already voted 128 times.

The bosses were like an Irish family—feuding and maneuvering for advantage and obsessed with each other's doings and undoings, yet so close that they even vacationed together. One of the photographs Mary Augusta kept showed her husband, rotund with authority, on horseback next to little Fitzie, both of them incongruously attired in jodhpurs and hunting coats, ready to run the foxes during a junket to North Carolina. Another snapshot remained from one of the outings at Orchard Beach the Democratic Party of Boston staged every summer. It showed Joe as a light-haired, squinting boy, sitting a few feet from the Mayor's skinny daughter Rose.

Later on, Joe Kennedy tried to make his amazing accomplishment even greater than it was by implying that he had known poverty as a boy. In fact, his father's intertwined businesses of liquor and politics had produced a comfortable life, and enough of a surplus for investments in a local coal company and in Boston's only Irish-controlled bank, the Columbia Trust.

P. J. was well enough off to have a staff of maids and cooks to help Mary Augusta, to winter in Palm Beach when he chose, and to purchase a sixty-foot yacht, the *Eleanor*—skippered by a retired admiral—which he used for pleasure cruises in Boston Harbor as well as summertime meetings of the Board of Strategy. When the time came for his daughters to marry, he was able to stage impressive weddings for them: Margaret and her husband exchanged vows before hundreds of friends in an immense tent erected in the back yard of the Webster Street house, and Loretta had an elegant reception at the Copley Plaza Hotel. Brahmins living on trusts from the great New England fortunes in shipping and textiles might fret over the moral obligations of wealth, but P. J. and his Irish-American friends found such problems difficult to imagine. Money was not associated with guilt; it was the highly combustible fuel for their rise upward.

If Joe Kennedy always had enough, however, he always wanted more. An almost excessively wholesome boy—he had freckles, red hair a shade or two lighter than his father's, and P. J.'s shockingly blue eyes—he was what his era called a go-getter. It was Mary Augusta who started him on his career, deciding when he turned twelve that he should have a job and arranging one for him at a high-class millinery shop delivering hats to Brahmin ladies. No ordinary delivery boy, he carried his merchandise in a horse-drawn carriage with a liveried driver, taking the hats inside the grand houses and waiting to see if they fit. "If you are asked your name," Mary Augusta instructed him, "answer 'Joseph.' " There was no need to emphasize his Irish heritage.

After his millinery job, Joe branched out on his own. He sold candy on the harbor excursion boat *Excelsior*. He hawked papers at the ferry building close to the spot where his grandfather had stepped off the *Washington Irving* half a century earlier. He worked as a "Sabbath goy" lighting stoves for Orthodox Jews on their days of worship. When he heard that the Larkin Soap Company was sponsoring a contest, he got his friends to canvass the neighborhoods of East Boston and he won first prize—an oak bookcase on which he stacked the works of Horatio Alger that his sister Loretta remembered him reading avidly.

Making money was a way of exercising one's God-given talents, of using the world for a gymnastics of self. He grew up not only on the lookout for opportunities but also calculating their marginal returns. Mae Duanne, the rawboned Irish girl Mary Augusta hired to chaperone him around town, was struck by this aspect of his character. Once they went to Revere Beach in the middle of a Boston heat wave. Joe's dilemma for the day was that he had enough money either to rent a bathing suit or to have a tintype picture taken, but not to do both. "I think I'll choose the tintype," Duanne remembered him saying after long consideration. "When the day is over that'll be the end of swimming and I'll have nothing to show for it. The picture will last a long time."

When not wondering how to make money, Kennedy was exploring ways to shape his world. He directed plays in the back yard, assigning parts and collecting admission fees at the gate. (In one show he put on an Uncle Sam costume and read an essay he had written on "What America Means to All of Us" while "Columbia the Gem of the Ocean" was played in the background.) He organized a group of teenage friends into a military drill team to march in the Memorial Day parade. He became an accomplished athlete, recognizing sports as one of the few places ruled by an aristocracy of talent. Organizing a neighborhood baseball team called the Assumptions, he appointed himself first baseman, coach, and business manager, buying uniforms with money from his newspaper job, scheduling games with teams from other neighborhoods and then passing the hat to spectators who'd stopped to watch. Some of his teammates complained that they were functioning as second fiddles in a one-man band. Kennedy's sister Margaret, to whom he tossed his glove to put away when he came home from a game, always remembered his response: "If you can't be captain, don't play."

He had started off at a school run by the Christian Brothers, but Mary Augusta felt that while Catholic schools like those she and her husband had briefly attended might be theologically sound and socially safe, they also tended to isolate students from the larger world and stunt their ambitions. And so in 1901 she enrolled Joe in Boston Latin, the elite school that Mayor Fitzgerald had attended years earlier. He was aggressive and popular— president of his class; colonel on the drill team that won the city-wide competition; a good enough baseball player to win the Mayor's Cup (presented by Fitzie himself) for having the highest batting average in the city his senior year. In a valedictory mood he later called Boston Latin "a shrine that somehow seemed to make us all feel that if we could stick it out we were made of just a little bit better stuff than the fellows our age who were attending what we always thought were easier schools." It was the place where he first saw that he could not only compete with but outdo students who were otherwise regarded as more American than he.

The next step was Harvard. If the university had ceased to be the special preserve of the Cabots and Lowells and other families who talked only to each other and to God, it was still a purposefully intimidating experience for what were regarded as the lower social orders. Boston's crusty Cardinal O'Connell tried to steer the young people in his flock to Boston University or Holy Cross, both run by the Jesuits; but some Irish Catholics persisted in choosing Harvard, traveling back and forth between Cambridge and their own neighborhood every day by trolley car knowing that behind their backs they were referred to as "untouchables."*

---

*As late as 1922, one Boston newspaper, reporting on doings inside Harvard Yard, wrote: "The Irish not the Jews present the real problem. The new plan of class selection will cut down the number of Irish as well as Jews ..."

Joe Kennedy insisted on living in Harvard Yard, but even he went home on weekends to the seaside home P. J. had bought at 97 Washington Street in Winthrop, next door to his austere brother-in-law, Dr. Hickey, who lived there with his spinster sister Kate. Joe would bring some of his college friends with him, and they would spend Sundays walking along the beach in their blue trousers and blazers and then go in to feast on his mother's baked ham and baked beans. After dinner they would all go into the parlor. First there would be the ritual of trying to stump Mary Augusta at spelling. Joe would have prepared his schoolmates, challenging them earlier to find difficult words in the dictionary. Sometimes they would come up with scientific and technical terms that she didn't understand, but she still managed to spell them. And then Joe would beam: "No one can stump my mother!" Afterward, with Loretta accompanying on the piano, Joe would lead the songs: "Peg o' My Heart," "Danny Boy," and, of course, "Fair Harvard."

As son of a saloonkeeper and, even worse, grandson of one of the famine Irish, Joe Kennedy should have found university life difficult. But he shrugged off slurs against his background: when one door was slammed in his face he immediately knocked on the next one. He looked for openings, putting the onus on others by making them show prejudice in rejecting him, rather than taking himself out of the running in advance to avoid being hurt.

"Joe sucked up to 'important' people quite ingloriously and without scruple," says one classmate. "He tried to get some reflected glory by selecting roommates who were All-American football players and the like." Although he failed to make one of the good "final" clubs like Porcellian or Fly, he was chosen for Hasty Pudding, a significant accomplishment for someone from his background.

One episode that summarizes his technique occurred on the baseball diamond. His fine line-drive hitting had earned Kennedy a starting position on the Harvard freshman team, but he had never developed his fielding or base running, and by his senior year he was riding the bench. He would not have won a letter except that team captain and pitcher "Chick" McLaughlin asked the coach to put him in the game against Yale in the ninth inning. On the last play of the game, McLaughlin fielded a grounder to the mound and tossed the ball to Joe for the put-out. Instead of giving the ball back to McLaughlin, who'd earned it as a trophy, Kennedy stuffed it in his pocket and left the field. McLaughlin later admitted that he'd asked for Kennedy to be put in the game for a reason. His ambition was to open a movie house after graduation, and shortly before the game he had been visited by some anonymous men who pointed out that given P. J. Kennedy's influence at City Hall it would be much easier for McLaughlin to get the required business permits for his venture if Joe Kennedy got his letter.

On the whole, Kennedy's Harvard balance sheet after four years was

mixed. He was not a particularly good student. ("I did so poorly in a course
in banking and finance," he said after *Fortune* had estimated his wealth at
$250 million and he could savor the irony, "that I had to drop out of it after
one semester.") Nor was he particularly successful with the matrons of
Beacon Hill, whose deb balls, dances, and weekends destroyed the modest
attempts of Harvard officials to encourage democracy among their students.
But he was fairly well liked by those not bothered by his social climbing.
And he did establish himself as prime suitor of Rose Fitzgerald, lace-curtain
daughter of the Mayor.

At the time he graduated he was still very Irish—brash, feisty, determined
to get into everything. Rather than educating these qualities out of him,
Harvard had paradoxically shown their value. He still wanted everything
that those who proposed themselves as his social betters had; but he also saw
their hypocrisy, the emptiness of prerogatives that had little to do with talent
or real achievement. Envious and scornful, he emerged thinking he was as
good as anyone else in the Class of 1912, and he set out to complete the
journey to America his grandfather had begun half a century earlier.

While at Harvard, Kennedy had worked part-time as a tour-bus operator,
getting his father to persuade the Mayor to award him a choice route and
going into partnership with a friend who did the driving while he delivered
a spiel through a megaphone about the great Boston landmarks of American
history. He had put $300 into the business and it had netted him $5000
during his college years; that was a considerable sum in those days, but upon
graduation he was looking for far bigger money. He decided to go into
banking because it was the "basic profession" on which all others depended.

Joe Kennedy did not begin his career as a teller or junior executive, like
some of his classmates, who defined a career as patient upward movement to
the top of an institution. He got himself appointed a state bank examiner, a
job that allowed him to travel throughout the eastern part of Massachusetts
looking at bank records and books, learning how the banks made their money
and how they were connected to other businesses. In less than a year he saw
the opportunity he wanted. The Columbia Trust was about to be taken over
by a "downtown" bank, the First National. The merger was seen as a threat
by the Irish community, whose exclusion from the banking fraternity—
before the Columbia was founded—made the takeover a charged issue.* Joe
decided that if anybody was to take over the Columbia, he should be the one.

Joe borrowed to the hilt, lining up support and playing a game of bluff

---

*One of the stories about Mayor Fitzgerald involved a confrontation with a member
of an old WASP banking family. "You have plenty of Irish depositors," Fitzie had
said. "Why don't you have some Irishmen on your board of directors?" The banker
replied uneasily that some of the tellers were Irish. "Yes," Fitzgerald replied in
disgust, "and I suppose the charwomen are too."

that finally forced First National to give up. When the merger was called off, the Columbia directors rewarded him with the top job. At twenty-five he had become the youngest bank president in the country. In the press attention that followed, a local newspaper reporter asked exactly what he wanted out of life. Kennedy's reply came without hesitation: "I want to be a millionaire by the age of thirty-five." At the same time he secured his position in banking, Joe was making his move in other areas too, notably with Rose Fitzgerald.

Her father had established the family in a large and expensive home in Dorchester, complete with scrollwork porch, mansard turret, and stained-glass insert in the front door portraying what Fitzie insisted was the family's coat of arms. He had seen that his daughters were as well "finished" as any Beacon Hill heiress, with lessons in French, piano, and voice.

An Irish aristocrat at home ("greenbloods," the Brahmins sneeringly called people with such pretenses), Fitzie was a showman in office, a glad-hander and fancy man whose liaison with a shapely blond cigarette girl at the Ferncroft Inn named "Toodles" Ryan was one of the poorest-kept secrets in Boston. The city's number-one uninvited guest, he would go to parties with spare collars wrapped in a handkerchief in his back pocket so that he could dance all night and still look fresh. He was indefatigable, celebrating his fiftieth birthday by sprinting a hundred yards at seven o'clock in the morning, running a quarter-mile at nine, wrestling at noon, and boxing at one.

His wife, Mary Hannon Fitzgerald, a small, trim, withdrawn woman with dark Irish good looks and a piety some regarded as excessive, was not interested in politics and begrudged the long stretches of time the Mayor was absent. (Once when he was at home organizing his six children for a group photograph to be used in a campaign, she told him, "John, it does indeed seem refreshing to have you here. I'm not sorry you are to have photographs to mark the evening. I'm going to frame one and place a card over it on which I will write—'Taken on his one evening at home.'") Because Mary Fitzgerald refused to get involved in politics, the role of hostess and greeter fell to Rose, Fitzie's firstborn and favorite, who had grown up defending her father from charges of graft and explaining why his administration had developed such new civil service positions as Tea Warmer, Tree Climber, and Rubber Boot Repairman. When he campaigned, she was beside him. She played the piano for him when he broke into an Irish tenor, and introduced him to "Sweet Adeline," which became his theme song.

Rose had hoped to go to Wellesley after graduating from Dorchester High. But the Mayor insisted she attend one of the Sacred Heart convent schools that had become the pinnacle of Catholic education for women. The nuns came from the wealthiest Catholic families, endowing the institutions with their inheritances. As part of their training, the girls learned the proper ways to address servants and deport themselves at dinner parties. French was emphasized as the second language of the well-bred. The religious instruction taught "the child of the Sacred Heart" the feminine virtues of "tact, quiet courage, and the willingness to subordinate her will to another's gracefully and even gaily," and to model herself "on the ideal of womanhood found in the Mother of God."

In the summer of 1908, the Mayor sent Rose off to Europe for a grand tour. Once she was abroad, he enrolled her and her sister Agnes in a convent school in Holland for further study of languages and of "domestic science," which would prepare them to run a household.

"I am an angel," Rose wrote home after a few months at the school. "I arise at six o'clock (fifteen minutes earlier than the others) and go to meditation nearly every morning. So you see my piety is increasing. If I am extremely angelic, I may become an aspirant for the Children of Mary; later I may become a Child of Mary . . . the highest honor a child of the Sacred Heart can receive."

While letters filled with chatter about clothes, religion, and glimpses of European royalty diverted her parents, Rose kept up a secret correspondence with young Kennedy. As much as she missed him, however, she liked the devotional ritual and routine of the school. One of her fellow students recalled her zeal: "I used to be behind her in confession. My God, I used to have to wait an hour for her to come out . . ." Before the year was over, she received her medal as a Child of Mary.

After returning home, Rose attended the Sacred Heart Convent in New York for a year. When she got back to Boston for her debut, she could feel she was the equal of any young woman. After all, what other deb had a coming-out party attended by four hundred people, including two congressmen, the Governor, and the entire City Council, which declared the day a holiday in her honor? Yet she was also conscious that she was not invited to join any of the fashionable women's clubs of proper (and Protestant) Boston, and was not on the visiting list of the better families.

Feeling that a marriage into the Kennedy family would be a backward step for the Fitzgeralds, the Mayor tried to interest Rose in other suitors. She remained committed, although she and Joe had to meet on the sly. Sometimes she could persuade the chauffeur to stop and let her out for a secret street-corner rendezvous. Occasionally she donned a black veil and went figure skating with Joe on one of Boston's neighborhood ponds, her disguise fooling almost nobody. She cooperated with Kennedy when he thought up ruses to monopolize her attention, such as filling in her dance cards with fictitious names so that nobody else could reserve a dance. He used bluff as creatively in the courtship as in his business career. When he sailed to Europe for a vacation, he rented the imperial suite so that he could entertain Samuel Rea, president of the Pennsylvania Railroad, and his daughter Ruth, knowing that word would get back to Boston and raise his stock with the Fitzgeralds. Sometimes, as in this particular case, he went too far in his plots, and Rose would become so angry that she turned his picture face down on her dresser.

In 1914 Fitzie was up for reelection and his chief opponent was James M. Curley, the one Irish politician in Boston with even greater charisma than the Mayor. P. J. Kennedy and the Strategy Board supported Fitzgerald as the lesser of two evils. When the campaign began to get rough, Curley announced that he would give a series of public lectures. The first one, "Graft in Ancient Times and Modern," embarrassed Fitzie by calling attention to nepotism in various city departments. When Curley announced the title of the second lecture, "Great Lovers from Cleopatra to Toodles," Fitzie hurried to bow out of the race. Curley's victory was assured, and Fitzgerald's power and that of the Strategy Board was broken forever.

At the same time old-fashioned ward politics was becoming obsolete, Joe Kennedy was beginning his exploration of a larger world. His success at Columbia Trust made it difficult for the former Mayor to maintain that a match with his daughter would be disadvantageous, and in the summer of 1914 Joe slipped a flawless two-carat diamond on Rose's finger. It was characteristic of the velocity of his forward march on all his life fronts that Rose could never quite remember when he gave her the ring or whether he actually asked her to marry him. "I don't think he ever *did* ask me, not just straight out," she later recalled. "It was less a matter of 'Will you marry me?' than of 'When we get married ...' "

On October 7, they said their vows before Cardinal O'Connell, striking everyone as a handsome couple—she with agate eyes embedded in a narrow, fine-featured face terminating in a heavy chin; he tall and with the clear and open good looks women regarded as dazzlingly handsome. The wedding party was sumptuous. Not long after they returned from their honeymoon in White Sulphur Springs and settled down in a modest wood frame house on Beale Street in the Protestant suburb of Brookline, Rose was expecting.

The following summer the Kennedys rented a seaside cottage at Hull, where Rose had vacationed during her girlhood until her father offended the city elders and they had the Department of Public Works dig a five-foot-wide trench around his rented house. She and Joe spent the first part of July walking near the ocean and listening to George M. Cohan perform at the Hull Music Hall. The press speculated that their child, if a boy, would be named after Rose's father. No one who knew Joe Kennedy was surprised when the baby, who arrived later that month, was immediately christened Joseph Patrick Kennedy, Jr.

Over the next few years Boston papers came to rely on Kennedy for good copy. Articles began to appear portraying him as a no-nonsense, up-and-coming executive working in shirtsleeves and taking a quick noontime snack of milk and crackers at his desk. At home he was the family man, taking his son for walks and encouraging Rose to hire a maid to help her with the housework. When they finally found a young Italian girl, Rose spoke pidgin French to her and gave her a kitten when she wept with loneliness in her room.

From his desk at Columbia Trust, Kennedy set his sights on the next step up. By 1917, the year his second child was born—a son Rose was allowed to name John Fitzgerald after her father—he had enough of a reputation as a young man on the rise that Bethlehem Steel chairman Charles Schwab asked him to become general manager of the company's huge Fore River shipyards in Quincy, a job overseeing the work of two thousand employees and paying $20,000 a year. Not the least of its attractions was the fact that this position involved him in the war effort, although at a safe distance from the front. (Ralph Lowell, a classmate of Kennedy's at Harvard, later observed that the Class of '12 ''took pride in not waiting to be drafted and they didn't appreciate a man not going into the war, as, for instance, in the case of Joe.'')

Kennedy poured himself into the job, and soon the Fore River yards were smashing production records, turning out thirty-seven destroyers between the time he took over and Armistice Day. The only blemish on Kennedy's record with Bethlehem resulted from a run-in with then Assistant Secretary of the Navy Franklin D. Roosevelt over a pair of battleships on order by Argentina which he was holding until he received payment. Roosevelt wanted them released immediately so they could be used in the war effort. Kennedy refused, daring the government to use force. After Roosevelt had called his bluff by sending in armed troops and tugboats, Kennedy publicly called him a ''smiling four-flusher'' and privately admitted that meetings with this man had left him so frustrated that he had sometimes broken down and cried.

By the end of the war, there was another Kennedy—Rosemary was born in 1918. Kathleen arrived a little over a year later, and Eunice followed in 1921. Rose added a nurse to the household, although on pleasant days she took the children out by herself, wheeling the babies in a carriage with the two little boys toddling beside it. She usually found time to drop into a church because she wanted the children ''to form the habit of making God and religion a part of their daily lives.'' She tried to be ''scientific'' in her child-rearing techniques. When the family moved to a larger and more elaborate house in Brookline, she designed a series of partitions on the porch so the children could play with no danger of accidentally hurting each other. She kept a card index for each child on which she noted certain data— immunizations, shoe sizes, childhood diseases, growth rates, and so on. Although he was not with the children as much as Rose, Joe was emotionally more available in the time he did spend. When three-year-old Jack contracted scarlet fever, for instance, Joe spent days in prayer at church, pledging to give half of what he possessed to charity if the child recovered. After a long siege the boy's condition finally improved, and Kennedy made out a check for $3700 to the Guild of St. Apollonia.

Every Sunday he would pile all the children into his Ford sedan and drive out to visit his parents, sometimes leaving Rose behind for rare moments of solitude. As they all trooped into the kitchen of the Winthrop house, Mary Augusta would look them over and shake her head : ''Good Lord, Joe, one of these days you'll need a bus.'' After lunch, he would walk on the beach with P. J., gesturing and talking, the older man nodding and occasionally making a brief reply. On his way back home after the visit, he sometimes stopped at the old Meridian Street house where P. J. had been born, parking and staring at it in silence as he contemplated how far he had come and how far there was yet to go.

If his generation's time was coming, the old guard's was passing. Mayor Curley (prototype for Frank Skeffington in Edwin O'Connor's *The Last Hurrah*) had centralized Boston's power in his own hands, destroying the old ward system with an efficiency undreamed of by any of the city's municipal reformers. Martin Lomasney had become a mythic character of the past ; the Board of Strategy had broken up. In 1918 P. J. had been one of the first to feel the impact of the shift, losing an election—for Street Commissioner —for the first time. (''I am extremely sorry in your defeat,'' wrote his friend and political ally Richard Sullivan. ''It looked to me, with both organizations in your favor, like a sure thing. I was astounded by the results. No doubt you take it in your usual philosophical way but as a friend I can't take it that way.'') With his defeat P. J. retired to Winthrop as an elder statesman, out of liquor as well as politics because of Prohibition.

Honey Fitz had also stepped into the background. He had run for Congress in 1918, defeating incumbent Peter Tague primarily because Tague had not honored a commitment to vote for the United States to enter World War I only if Ireland's independence was recognized. Fitzgerald attended a session of Congress but was unseated when it was determined that his election had been accompanied by a degree of voter irregularity unusual even for Boston. The former Mayor would keep on running for office but never again be elected. He sold his home in Dorchester and moved into a suite in the Bellevue Hotel, spending time at the zoo and at Red Sox games and becoming a character around town. The balance of power had definitely shifted in his struggle with his son-in-law. The old man would come to visit, peering in the screened back porch to see if ''Big Joe'' was home before knocking. Kennedy sometimes teased his wife in a cutting way about the days when he had not been good enough to marry a Fitzgerald. ''Rose, were you lying when you said your father didn't like me? I met him today and he told me what a hell of a fellow I am.''

During the spring of 1923, Mary Augusta checked into New England Baptist Hospital in Boston, where diagnostic surgery disclosed an inoperable stomach cancer. After her release, P. J. took her to the seaside, at Sagamore, for a last family vacation. Joe and Rose visited, bringing Joe Junior, Jack, Rosemary, and two-year-old Eunice. In early summer she was readmitted to the hospital for her final battle. When it was over, a diminished P. J. took their daughters to Europe along a route that embraced the extremes of their family saga—a visit to the humble homestead in Ireland and a special audience in the Vatican with Pope Pius X.

Joe Kennedy had no time for travels. Head of his own growing family, and the guardian now of all their futures, he was working to achieve his great expectations. While trying to convert the Fore River shipyards to peacetime production, he had approached Galen Stone, who was not only a fabulously successful investment banker but also the force behind the President Lines. He didn't manage to sell Stone any ships, but he did sell himself. Kennedy jumped at the opportunity when Stone offered to teach him the stock business. His salary would be half what Bethlehem paid him, but Stone was exactly what Kennedy wanted to be—his own man.

When he moved into his office in the Hayden-Stone building in 1922, the sign on his door said simply, *Joseph P. Kennedy, Banker.* Under Stone's tutelage he learned to use inside information to minimize risk and maximize return. In one case Stone informed him that the Pond Creek Coal Company was about to be sold to Henry Ford. Borrowing heavily, Kennedy bought fifteen thousand shares at $16 a share, and later sold the stock at $45 a share. It was speculation without extreme risk, a distinction to which Kennedy attached particular importance. ''I think the primary notion back of most gambling is the excitement of it,'' he later said. ''While gamblers naturally want to win, the majority of them derive pleasure even if they lose. The desire to win, rather than the excitement involved, seems to me the compelling force behind speculation.''

The desire to win was something Joe Kennedy had in abundance. ''It's easy to make money in the market,'' he told another investor. ''We'd better get in before they pass a law against it.'' He became savvy at market maneuvers others considered shady and even illicit. One of his favorites was the stock pool, in which a few big traders got together to buy blocks of an inactive stock, creating the appearance of a boom, trading their shares back and forth until this ''churning'' had drawn in less sophisticated investors. When the price of the stock had risen to an agreed-upon level, they took their profits and left the others holding the bag as the stock sank back to its true market value. But while Kennedy might briefly join other lone wolves in a stock pool, he was never responsible to anyone other than himself. One acquaintance compared his mode of operation to the moves of a billiards player —constantly shifting his position around the table, taking tricky carom shots, always playing the angles rather than hitting the object straight on. He began to evolve a business philosophy : ''Never meet anybody after two for lunch. Meet in the morning because you're sharper. Never have long lunches. They're not only boring, but dangerous because of the martinis.''

By the early twenties he was in the money. His biggest score—the one that separated him from other go-getters—came in 1924. After going to bed early one night because of a bout of neuritis, he was awakened by Hearst editor Walter Howey, whom he had gotten to know during one of Honey Fitz's campaigns, knocking at his front door. Howey asked Kennedy for help in fending off a bear raid on the Yellow Cab Company, in which he was a large stockholder. Yellow Cab had gone down thirty-five points in a month, Howey explained, and company president John Hertz had raised $5 million to shore up its value.

Kennedy immediately left for New York, where he set up a command post in a suite at the Waldorf-Astoria with a ticker tape and a battery of phones, and began a complicated pattern of buying and selling to stabilize Yellow Cab at the best possible price. After weeks of round-the-clock deals his campaign was a success. When he returned to Boston his five children were waiting to greet him. All of them, including three-year-old Eunice, were yelling as the train pulled in : ''Daddy! Daddy! We've got another baby.'' It was Patricia, already a month old, whom he hadn't seen yet. Having missed her birth was worth it. Kennedy emerged from the Hertz deal, as he later said, ''a very wealthy man.'' Just past his thirty-fifth birthday, he had made good on the boast he made when first entering the business world by becoming a millionaire several times over.

On the edge of middle age, Kennedy was still broad-shouldered and athletic in the three-piece pin-striped suits he'd worn since he began at Columbia Trust. The sandy red hair was thinning, and the years had pulled the center of gravity of the freckled face from the forehead toward the jaw, although he was still left with that boyish and open look, the horn-rimmed glasses giving him something of Harold Lloyd's quizzical innocence. People who underestimated him on the basis of his appearance, or his ability to flatter when he felt it necessary to ingratiate himself, soon changed their minds when they met him up close and found him to be electric and vital, blunt and profane, with a temperament which gave off a feel of danger. There was something about his eyes—a gelid blue, generally exempt from the quick smile, able to hold and freeze the object of his stare. Joe Kennedy was a paradox. He wanted all the outward signs and perquisites of belonging, yet he didn't want to give up the freedom of being a lone wolf. Rather than being debilitated by this conflict, however, he drew power from it.

He had enough money but continued to make more, seeing wealth as a breakwater that would protect him and his family from the tidal flow of tragedy that had been so much a part of the Irish experience. His wealth came not from an institution but from his own intelligence and daring. He did not use it to build philanthropies, estates, or other monuments meant to commemorate his achievements in the future. He was his own future; he accumulated money as an instrument of survival and a transit to freedom.

He would always be on the lookout for targets of opportunity like the Hertz deal. But according to the rumors that swirled around him in the middle of the frenzied 1920s, he was not always wholly scrupulous in his involvements. He was often away from home for long periods of time, living with his cronies in a hotel somewhere and involved in unspecified negotiations. Later on, one of the gangster Meyer Lansky's associates claimed that some of Lansky's New York "East Side boys" had once tried to hijack a shipment of bootleg Irish whiskey, which Kennedy and others had financed, and that the Boston Irish guards of the small convoy of trucks had put up such a strong resistance that at the end of the bloody gunfight there were eleven men dead. And just before his own death nearly fifty years later, mob leader Frank Costello confided to *New York Times* writer Peter Maas that early in his career he had been a "partner" of Joe Kennedy's in the illicit liquor trade.

But the question was not so much the source of Kennedy's wealth as the uses to which it could be put. Upper-class New Englanders had reacted to the immigrant tide by creating caste institutions—exclusive prep schools and social clubs—which even respectable Boston Irishmen, about whom there were no rumors, couldn't buy their way into. Even in Cohasset, where the Kennedys rented a summer place and drove around in a plum-colored, chauffeured Rolls, there was discrimination, no longer devastating perhaps, but annoying enough when Brahmins found little ways to make it clear that they subscribed to J. P. Morgan's credo: you do business with anyone, but you can only sail with a gentleman. Rose was snubbed by the Cohasset matrons, and Joe was blackballed when he applied for membership in the Cohasset Country Club. ("Those narrow-minded bigoted sons of bitches barred me because I was an Irish Catholic and son of a barkeep," he said many years later, the memory still rankling. "You can go to Harvard and it doesn't mean a damned thing. The only thing these people understand is money.")

Such treatment did not go well with Kennedy's sense of his net worth. In any case the path to great wealth had already taken him far from the constrictive social atmosphere of Boston. And so in 1926 he completed the break by packing his family into a private railroad car and heading for New York, the archetypal open, multiethnic city. He later claimed that he made the move because he feared his sons would find their prospects curtailed in

Boston and his daughters would not be invited to the proper debutante parties when they came of age; that Boston was ''no place to raise Catholic children.'' But the transition was for himself more than for them. He had gotten a taste of what the larger world had to offer and wanted more.

Not long before he left, a friend asked him: ''What is it you really want?'' Kennedy looked at him, waiting a moment to reply as light hit the lenses of his glasses and made them reflective discs. ''Everything,'' he said.

3.

JOE KENNEDY INSTALLED THE family in Riverdale, in Upper Manhattan. They stayed in a leased manor with a view of the Hudson while he looked for a place to buy. With so many children—another son, Robert, had been born just before they left Brookline —the specifications kept changing. ("Kennedy can't use a residence," one of the real-estate agents involved in the search complained. "He wants a hotel.") Finally a permanent home was found in Bronxville, in Westchester County, some seventeen miles from New York City: a twenty-room red-brick colonial originally built for Anheuser Busch which came with five heavily wooded acres and cottages for the gardener and chauffeur. When the Kennedys took possession, they arrived in a convoy of limousines that disgorged children, nurses, governesses, and the heavy-jawed, squared-bodied Irishman who functioned as Joe Kennedy's handyman. The neighbors watched from behind drawn curtains, as fascinated as if it were Daddy Warbucks himself.

If leaving Boston was a breakout for Joe Kennedy, arriving in New York was an opportunity to plunge both hands deep into the American dream. He suddenly became a familiar if somewhat mysterious figure on Wall Street, joining other realists who believed that the great bull market of the twenties couldn't last forever. He also rented an elegant suite of offices in a Broadway skyscraper and set out to make a name for himself in the world of motion pictures.

The film industry was the perfect place for him at this point in his life. He saw that the business was disorganized, chaotic, ripe for someone like himself with an eye for the bottom line; he also understood the role movies would play in the life of the country as a result of their power to manipulate realities and create a mass culture that blurred class and ethnic lines. "Take Boston," he said to film star Gloria Swanson during one of their first meetings. "The Cabots and the Lodges wouldn't be caught at pictures, or let their children go. And that's why their servants know more about what's going on than they do. The working class gets smarter every day, thanks to radio and pictures. It's the snooty Back Bay bankers who are missing the boat."

He had first become interested in films while he was still president of Columbia Trust. After examining the books of a New England motion picture exhibiting company with an eye to possible purchase, he looked at a business associate in amazement: "We must get into the picture business. This is a new industry and a gold mine. In fact it looks like another telephone industry." By the time he was working at Hayden-Stone, he had bought a small chain of theaters of his own and was looking for an opportunity to become involved in production and distribution as well. "Look at that bunch of pants pressers in Hollywood making themselves millionaires," he said to a colleague at the brokerage house. "I could take the whole business away from them."

Hearing that a production company, Film Booking Office of America, was in trouble, Kennedy got in touch with the English owners about selling it. Although prepared to offer only a million dollars for a property they valued at seven times that much, he got enough encouragement to sail to London late in 1925 to negotiate in person. When he failed with the bankers who controlled F.B.O., Kennedy noticed in a newspaper article that the Prince of Wales, whom he had once met on a receiving line in Boston, was in Paris. Hurrying across the Channel (as he told the story later on), he went to the Prince's favorite restaurant and bribed the maître d' to seat him near the royal table. At the appropriate moment Kennedy introduced himself, mentioning that they'd met in America, and when the Prince asked what he was doing in Paris said, "Oh, just having a little fun before I go over to finish some banking in London tomorrow." "Anything I can do to help you?" the Prince inquired. "Oh no, thank you very much," Kennedy answered in such a way as to make it clear there was. The next morning a letter of introduction on the Prince of Wales's letterhead arrived by messenger at his hotel room.

Even with this endorsement, Kennedy could not swing the deal and returned home in agony from the ulcers that would bother him for the rest of his life. (So concerned about his boy that he did not catch the pun, P. J. told a friend that he feared "Joe has bitten off more in England than he can chew.") A few weeks later, however, sitting with friends at New York's Harvard Club while preparing to go to Florida to look into some land deals, he got a message from the agent for F.B.O., who was in town and wanted to see him. He dashed out and returned half an hour later. "Sorry, fellows," he said, grinning at his friends. "Guess you'll have to go to Florida without me. I've just bought a motion picture company." (Back home, the irrepressible Honey Fitz leaked the news, inflating the company's price to $10 million and managing to insinuate himself into the center of events so that the story in the next day's *Boston Post* was headlined: "John F. Fitzgerald Latest Movie Magnate.")

F.B.O. was nothing like M-G-M, Columbia, and the other dream machines the furriers and pants pressers had put together. And although he was better educated and more sophisticated than this first generation of film moguls, Kennedy was even less interested in film as an art. Instead of producing epics like *Ben Hur* or *The Ten Commandments* and developing stars like Pickford and Chaplin, F.B.O. under Joe Kennedy turned out titles like *Red Hot Hooves* and *The Dude Cowboy*, featuring unknown actors or over-the-hill stars or famous names from other fields, like Red Grange, whom he paid on a per diem basis to accommodate budgets that never exceeded $30,000. Kennedy was an avid movie fan who would watch films others found boring or banal. Yet he walked out of his top-grossing movie, *The Gorilla Hunt*, after five minutes. If F.B.O. films often didn't make it to New York, however, they did good business in Iowa and Kansas. While other producers fought to get their works onto Broadway, he was content to have a monopoly on Main Street. Under his guidance, Film Booking Office began to make money.

Kennedy could easily have stayed on the periphery of the film world, running his F.B.O. from his New York office while dabbling in stocks and other opportunities on the side. But while he had a sort of contempt for Hollywood insiders, he saw them as the aristocracy of the industry and compulsively sought their acceptance. In 1927 he hit on an ingenious stratagem and approached the Harvard Business School with a proposal to stage a seminar on this new and hitherto ignored aspect of American business. When his alma mater agreed to put up the money, Kennedy invited twelve of the giants of the movie world—Marcus Loew, Adolph Zukor, Harry Warner, and others—to appear as speakers. These men, many of whom hadn't finished high school and had never been in a college classroom, were flattered at the chance to appear at the nation's leading university and indebted to Kennedy, who made the affair a smashing success. By the time he sent each of them a calf-bound volume of the book he compiled from the proceedings (and grandly titled *The Story of the Films*), he had been accepted as one of them; his name would henceforth appear alongside those of Hollywood's great tycoons in statements of filmland policy. His new colleagues saw him as a fresh face in an industry wracked by bad publicity. Will Hays, former Postmaster General under Harding who'd been brought in as Hollywood's morals czar after the Fatty Arbuckle scandals, called him "a man who, in his business ideals and concepts as in the fine character of his home life, would bring to the industry much it has lacked in the past."

In his own comments at the Harvard seminar, Kennedy had called for "consolidation." Looking at the film industry with a businessman's eye, he saw what others didn't: that there was no resisting such innovations as sound; that there must be "vertical integration" of production, distribution, and exhibition into one enterprise; and that movie wildcatting must be ended and power centralized in the hands of a few great studios. Kennedy rented a large house on Rodeo Drive in Beverly Hills and began two and a half years of train commuting back and forth between his F.B.O. offices in New York and his field headquarters in Hollywood.

Rose Kennedy, who had grown up watching her mother deal with the Mayor's prolonged absences, now faced a similar experience of her own. While Joe was spending much of his time in Hollywood she did what she could to elevate the family's standing. New York was less parochial than Boston, socially less ossified; but it was still a hard town to crack, especially for someone trying to break into the Irish version of high society. The First Irish Families, as they were known, did not regard status based on prominence in the ward politics of another town as transferable. Their attitude toward the Kennedys seemed to prove the truth of Dr. Johnson's observation: "The Irish are a fair people—they never say anything good of one another."

"They copied us by coming here in the first place," said a member of the socially dominant McDonnell-Murray clan later on. The feeling was that the Kennedys were so *nouveau* that when Rose paid a call on Mrs. Anne McDonnell at Southampton, she must be there to find out how to set a table or fill a vase—how to *do things right*. One of the Murray women later told a story about Rose: "She and her daughters were being snubbed terribly in New York, so she'd gone to Auntie Anne [McDonnell] for some advice ... My mother was there and came back and said, 'Rose Kennedy—such a lovely person, but what a dreadful voice she has.' "

Rose kept on trying for acceptance. (Years later, when her son Jack was at Harvard, she turned to one of his friends and suddenly asked her celebrated question: "When *will* the nice people of Boston accept us?") But increasingly she turned inward, concentrating on her God and her children. Working through a small army of governesses, nurses, housekeepers, and cooks, she tried to organize the Kennedys in much the same way her husband was organizing the film industry.

She put clocks in every room so that the children would have no excuse to be late for meals; she coded the brood with different-colored bathing caps to keep track of them when they were swimming; she ordered clothes and household items by lots, making space in the high walk-in closets for boxes of shoelaces, toothbrushes, combs. She employed an orthodontist who traveled like a circuit rider to their various boarding schools to deal with problems that resulted from having Kennedy teeth in a Fitzgerald jaw.

She was didactic, lecturing the children on a variety of arcana—why the days got shorter in wintertime; how All Hallows Eve became Halloween; why there was a holiday for Thanksgiving. She initiated the parlor games for which they all retained a lifelong affection, though during her reign they all had to have a utilitarian value. One of her favorites was ''Snakes,'' a game involving extemporized math problems: ''Five times three, add one, divide by four, times eight, take any two, divide by three, divide by two. What's the answer?''

Borrowing a habit of her father's, she walked around the house with notes pinned to the bib of her dress listing the day's important chores. She communicated through written messages—notes taped to the walls reminding the boys to turn off the lights, notes pinned to the pillows telling the girls to be sure and wash off their lipstick before going to bed lest the pillowcases be stained. The trouble she had associating names and faces stood in marked contrast to Joe's ability to internalize in seconds relevant data about each person in a roomful of people. The boys had one friend whom they introduced to Rose so often that they finally made a game of it, using a different name each time he came home with them and once introducing him as a Parisian, knowing that their mother would look at him with sudden interest and begin speaking to him in French.

When the family began to spend their summers on Cape Cod, in 1928, she had her own little house on the beach at Hyannis where she retired to do her devotional reading. She played golf alone. Yet although inward herself, she concentrated on externals with the children, insisting that they be out and doing, constantly assaulting their surroundings. She wanted them to know God but also to be muscular Christians. It was she who began the ritual lessons—golf, tennis, swimming—who hired Mr. Swinnerton, the physical education instructor who had everyone out on the lawn at seven in the morning doing calisthenics. It was a regimen that abhorred weakness and tolerated no slackers. The children learned that her apparent distraction was protective coloration for a character that was actually iron-willed and durable.

When asked what Joe did, Rose airily answered: ''Business.'' Once, told the size of the Kennedy fortune, she responded with surprise: ''I didn't know we had *that* much.'' In truth, her husband made so many moves so quickly that his doings would have been hard to follow even if he had been more open about financial matters than he was. This was especially true of his years in Hollywood.

His daughter Eunice was exaggerating when she later said, ''My father built his financial empire with a secretary and a telephone.'' But Joe Kennedy did perfect a highly personal style of operation during his Hollywood years. When he bought up another film company, he brought his own staff with him—legal experts, accountants, and moneymen who were also cronies. Chief among them was Eddie Moore, a fey Irishman who had once been an aide to Honey Fitz and who eventually became Joe Kennedy's private secretary, valet, babysitter; the utility man and confidant who smoothed awkward situations created by Kennedy's abrasive manner and occasionally annoyed his boss by helping himself to what he considered worn-out suits and ties. Arthur Poole, whom Kennedy met during his Harvard seminar, became a controller for many of his private ventures as well as these film companies. Arthur Houghton, whom he found in the Hays Office, was in charge of supplying Kennedy with salacious gossip. ("He would not only tell Joe who was sleeping with whom," another aide says, "but also give graphic details, such as the case of the famous star who came home one day and found his wife *in flagrante* on a piano bench with a stunt man.") When Kennedy traveled back and forth between New York, where the banks were, and Hollywood, where the film companies were, these men traveled with him as his entourage. Able to set up a field headquarters in a small hotel room or in a corporate boardroom from which regular employees were excluded, they formed a sort of mobile executive apparatus, loyal only to Joe Kennedy.

His mystique augmented by this eccentric style and by the fact that he never stayed long in one place, Kennedy cut a wide swath through the film industry. In 1929 he was approached by R.C.A. chief David Sarnoff, who was worried because the Western Electric Company, a competitor of the R.C.A. affiliate General Electric, had managed to tie up contracts to supply sound equipment for most of the studios making a transition to talkies. In a deal concluded in a New York oyster bar, Sarnoff agreed to buy a large block of Film Booking Office stock, thus gaining access to a production company which would use G. E. technology.

Kennedy's next step was to begin raising nearly $5 million and use it to buy the huge Keith-Albee-Orpheum chain of theaters. Drawing a salary of $6000 a week as chairman of the F.B.O. and Keith-Albee boards, he worked to engineer a complete consolidation between those companies and R.C.A. The result was the future Hollywood giant, R.K.O. Studios. In addition to seeing his stock options for Film Booking Office and Keith-Albee zoom upward, Kennedy received a fee of $150,000 for engineering the merger that produced R.K.O.

All these negotiations were conducted with great speed in a typical Kennedy offensive. And in the middle of all this work, he was involved in a transaction even more demanding and complex—his famous romance with Gloria Swanson.

Although she was not the first movie actress to receive $1 million a year, Gloria Swanson was the first one who turned this sum down. She had been involved in films most of her life, outlasting Mary Pickford and others whose careers languished once they had outgrown ingenue roles. She had hit her stride in the late twenties largely as a result of her steamy portrait of Somerset Maugham's Sadie Thompson, and by the time Kennedy met her, she was Hollywood's reigning sex goddess and the most powerful woman in the industry.

If Kennedy was attracted to her because she was considered one of the most desirable women in the world, one of those symbols he had grappled for all his life, Swanson sought him out because of his growing reputation as one of the shrewdest money men in the film world. A strong-willed woman with a keen business sense, she was anxious to buck the studio system and set up her own production company. Infatuated with her from the beginning—with the idea of her as well as the fact—Kennedy not only gave her advice but smothered her with attention, bringing in his men to help her set up an independent company, Gloria Productions, personally taking over management of her tangled affairs, and working to insinuate himself into the center of her life.

It was not long after they met that he invited Swanson and her husband, the out-of-pocket nobleman Henri de la Coudraye, to join him in Palm Beach. As Swanson later described their arrival, Henri was arranging their luggage when Kennedy came charging down the corridor of the coach car, pushed her back into her drawing room, said a few excited words, kissed her twice, and then stood up to his full height, scraping his head on an overhead rack and dropping his glasses, then scrambling down onto his hands and knees to retrieve them, his mouth smeared with her lipstick. As she began to laugh, he stood up and said, ''I missed you and I wanted you to know.''

The consummation came after Kennedy had sent Henri off on a deep-sea fishing trip with a Kennedy aide. Buying so many orchids that her hotel suite was transformed into something close to a florist's shop, he showed up himself after Swanson had unpacked, looking boyish and Ivy League in white flannel trousers and an argyle sweater. What then took place between them was like a scene from one of Swanson's movies. As she later wrote in the breathless accents of a movie scenarist: ''He just stood there . . . staring at me a full minute or more before he entered the room and closed the door behind him. He moved so quickly that his mouth was on mine before either of us could speak. With one hand he held the back of my head. With the other he stroked my body and pulled at my kimono. He kept insisting in a drawn-out moan, 'No longer, no longer, now!' He was like a roped horse, rough, arduous, rearing to be free. After a hasty climax, he lay beside me, stroking my hair. Apart from his guilty, passionate mutterings, he had still said nothing coherent.''

In the following weeks, Kennedy got rid of Swanson's husband more permanently by giving him a lucrative job as head of Pathé's operations in Paris. After that, Kennedy began spending more and more time in Hollywood, protecting his reputation as a family man by having one of his aides pick Swanson up in the evening, bring her to the rented Beverly Hills mansion, and then, in the early morning hours, take her home. Working by day on his mergers and consolidations, and spending his nights with Swanson, Kennedy began to think about a project that would commemorate their relationship, something that would establish him as the greatest producer of the day just as she was the greatest actress. He commissioned a script by the celebrated Erich von Stroheim, who would also be the director. He intended the project, originally called ''The Swamp,'' to rank with the great epics of De Mille and Griffith.

Kennedy was back in New York during the first stage of production and did not keep an eye on von Stroheim, a temperamental genius who shot scenes of the story, about a poor convent girl and her love for a crown prince, over and over in search of the perfect effect. He was not only accumulating thousands of feet of film but also beginning to highlight the decadence in the story, interpreting scenes in a way that everyone else on the set realized would never get past the Hays Office. (At one point the convent girl was supposed to lose her panties while curtsying to the prince ; von Stroheim had the actor playing that role pick them up and pass them under his nose before putting them inside his tunic.) When Swanson telephoned Kennedy to express her alarm at mounting expenses and new interpretations of the script, he assured her that he could handle von Stroheim.

Kennedy called her from New York so frequently that, according to a Boston paper, he accumulated the largest private telephone bill in the nation during the year 1929. When they met after one long absence, he blurted out that he'd been faithful to her during their affair. When she asked what he meant, he replied that there had been no new Kennedys since Jean's birth the previous year. He begged her to have his child. When she refused, he begged her to at least come meet his family at Hyannis. Although not understanding his need to reconcile the opposites in his life, she reluctantly agreed.

When Kennedy bought the summer home at Hyannis he had chosen a place far from the pretense of Cohasset, a part of Cape Cod where the *nouveaux riches* moved in with no questions asked. He had remodeled the sprawling house so that it had eleven bedrooms and nine baths as well as a sound-equipped basement theater. Swanson's arrival in the summer of 1929 was a major event in the life of the small resort community—something like a Hollywood premiere. She landed at Hyannis Port in a Sikorsky seaplane as crowds gaped, and came in to shore in a launch piloted by Joe Kennedy himself. For the next few days Hyannis followed her every move as if she were visiting royalty. When she visited the garage clubhouse Kathleen Kennedy shared with playmates and scrawled an autograph on the rough wall, the local paper covered it like a major news event.

Rose welcomed her to the family as if she were what Joe claimed—his closest and most important business partner. Later on, when he insisted that Gloria accompany them on a voyage to Europe, Rose again treated her like a sister, never giving evidence that she knew of the relationship with her husband. It was a consummate performance that left Swanson awed and wondering whether Rose was a fool or a saint.* When she returned from Europe, however, Gloria was picked up by a Kennedy aide and taken to a hotel room where she found Boston's Cardinal O'Connell waiting for her. "I am here to ask you to stop seeing Joseph P. Kennedy," he said. "Each time you see him you become an occasion of sin for him." O'Connell told her that Kennedy had petitioned the church hierarchy to be allowed to live with her apart from his family; he added that it was not Joe who had sent him. (Swanson replied that she would consider the advice.)

Back in Hollywood, von Stroheim and his film, now titled *Queen Kelly*, were increasingly out of control. When the director insisted that the actor playing the old lecher who marries the convent girl dribble tobacco juice onto her hand during the wedding ceremony, Swanson called Kennedy and demanded that he come out from New York. When he arrived he found that there were already some thirty hours of film representing only a quarter of the script. After viewing some of the footage in a projection room, Kennedy emerged with his head in his hands, murmuring: "I've never had a failure in my life." He fired von Stroheim (whose brilliant career then began to go to pieces) and tried another director with a rewritten script. But there was no way to salvage the project. *Queen Kelly* was put on the shelf, one of the greatest debacles in film history.

Kennedy tried to recover from *Queen Kelly* by commissioning another script for Swanson, a frothy comedy titled *What a Widow!* But although he spent heavily on the picture—especially for the clever animated credits spelling out "Joseph P. Kennedy Presents"—the film did not jibe with the grim mood of the country at the onset of the Depression and was dismissed as trivial by critics.

The affair with Swanson ended as abruptly as it had begun—so abruptly that it seemed as if Kennedy had been looking for any excuse to escape what was now a financial and emotional quagmire. During the script sessions for *What a Widow!* early in 1929 he had given the writer who thought up the title a new Cadillac. Swanson discovered that the gift had been charged to her account by Kennedy's executives. She asked him about it during one of their late evenings together at his Rodeo Drive house. Kennedy became so agitated that he stood up from the table coughing and red-faced, and finally bolted from the room, leaving one of his aides to drive Swanson home. A few days later the power of attorney she had given him early in their relationship was returned by mail. She never saw him again, although he continued to have an impact on her life. Phil Berg, the agent for Swanson's first husband,

*Rose's ambiguous cordiality continued up through her last meeting with Swanson in a Paris restaurant in the mid-1960s. Swanson was there with her daughter and her daughter's baby girl. Rose saw them and walked over and gave the child a Kennedy half-dollar.

Wallace Beery, got a call from his client at about this time: "Wally tells me that Gloria has made a deal that's pretty much on the rocks. He brings over the contract between her and Joe Kennedy. There's a clause I never got over. It says that if the picture makes a profit, they'll go fifty-fifty. But if there were losses, Gloria got them all!" In all, *Queen Kelly* wound up costing her close to a million dollars.*

If Swanson left Kennedy sadder but wiser, Kennedy left her and Hollywood $5 million richer and thirty pounds lighter, smoking heavily and in such pain from his ulcers that he checked into Boston's Lahey Clinic certain he had stomach cancer. The *fin de siècle* mood of the country in 1929 had seeped into his life. His own mood was caused not only by the breakup of the affair and the end of a possible career as a Hollywood entrepreneur, but also by the death of his father. P. J. had lived with his daughter Margaret and her husband, Charles Burke, off and on since Mary Augusta's death. He had aged into a pink-cheeked old man with white hair and mutton chops, and wire glasses that made him look like Santa Claus. Like Santa he would sometimes show up at his son's house with a bag of toys for the children, although when they visited him in his own home he was so severe that his grandson Jack remembered being reprimanded for winking. P. J. was proud of Joe but never understood the giant step that had allowed him to become an equal of people like Jeremiah Milbank of the Chase Bank and press lord William Randolph Hearst, let alone Gloria Swanson. When P. J. suffered a heart attack and the priests came to his bedside at Deaconess Hospital in Boston to administer the last rites, Joe was in Hollywood, emotionally farther away than the other side of the continent, and couldn't make it back. P. J.'s funeral was attended by ghosts from the vanished world of Boston politics, Honey Fitz, James M. Curley, and other associates and enemies from the old days. P. J. had crossed an even wider sea than the one his father had traveled some eighty years earlier—a sea dividing immigrant from American. Yet he never forgot where they came from. As executor of his father's estate, one of the things Joe Kennedy found and didn't know quite what to do with was a cache of bonds issued in 1920 by the short-lived Republic of Ireland.

Queen Kelly would not be seen by American audiences for twenty years, and then only in the form of a brief film clip—almost a cinematic pun—inserted into *Sunset Boulevard*, which starred Swanson and von Stroheim in an eerie reprise on an episode that significantly affected their lives and careers.

4.

*A*FATHER DEAD, A ROMANCE ended, a road not taken: what happened to Joe Kennedy in a brief space had all the ingredients of what a later time would call a midlife crisis, and it found an objective correlative in the nation's life with the 1929 Crash and the onset of the Depression. If he was sobered by events, particularly when he realized how close he had come to wrecking his family, Kennedy was far from chastened. If anything, he now felt as free from the constraints of conventional morality as from the pettiness of Boston society. When he returned home, it was not as a penitent guilty over his infidelity but as someone who had tasted freedom and would never again submit to what he saw as outmoded ways. He continued to chase women—starlets and showgirls mainly, but friends of the family and wives and daughters of business acquaintances too. Paul Morgan, a neighbor of the Kennedys when he was a teenager, recalls how he and his friends used to stake out the Gramatan Hotel in Bronxville to see if they could catch Joe Kennedy in a tryst. "Rumors would fly about who was in there with him. We never did find out who was with him, but we knew *somebody* was in there."

Kennedy maintained his suite at the Ritz in Boston and an apartment at the Waldorf-Astoria in New York, in addition to his other residences. While always officially denying the liaison with Gloria Swanson, he talked freely (and often quite graphically) of their relationship when he was "with the boys," allowing his rakishness to become a matter of speculation in the way that his prodigious fatherhood already was.

His marriage continued to thrive despite the gossip his style of semibachelorhood engendered. The summer he returned from Hollywood, he and Rose took long walks in Bronxville, holding hands and chatting, while the children remained behind. Just as he had his hotel rooms and apartments, he allowed her to have a suite at the Plaza Hotel. It was understood that when he was at home she was free to leave. The singer Morton Downey, who had become one of Kennedy's closest friends—aside from the Boston Irish operatives who took care of his business—recalls Kennedy's pride when Rose went to Paris each year and came back looking queenly in the new fashions, pride not only in her trim looks but also in his own ability to outfit her so regally.

Joe and Rose had what their time called an ''understanding,'' although it was based on her decision to ignore his infidelities rather than acknowledge they existed. As one family friend comments, ''She knew what was happening, knew about the girls and all, but she basically liked the life she led, the money and prestige. She bought in lock, stock, and barrel.'' Acquiescing in the Irish chauvinism that allowed Joe to discriminate between love and sex, she received in return assurances that there would be no more grand passions threatening everything they had built together. The deal they made was solemnized by the birth of Teddy, named after Eddie Moore, who, with his wife Mary, had helped keep the Kennedys together during the difficult Hollywood years.

Kennedy had reached a point in his career when it was necessary to figure out what he wanted to do with the great fortune he had accumulated. He could have had countless jobs as a corporate head, but he didn't want to tie his fate to any one institution. The exception he made was his family. Even when he was away, he tended this institution with care. When he was in Hollywood, Rose would line the children up every Sunday to await his phone call. He got his daughters autographs from Gary Cooper and other stars and sent the boys cowboy suits. In an uninterrupted stream of letters he gave advice and praise and hectored them about sports and schoolwork. Even at his most self-absorbed, he was a surprisingly thoughtful father. When Joe Junior was sick with the measles, he received a telegram from Hollywood: ''I have had them myself and know how you feel ... Visit me in California and I will give you a good horse and a complete outfit to use. Your pal, Tom Mix.''

When Rose later referred to her husband as ''the architect of our lives,'' it was a well-chosen phrase. Joe shaped the growth of the family with the same intensity he brought to the companies he reorganized and stocks he pooled. When he was at home there were formal dinners, the children standing as Rose entered and each of them reporting on their doings and responding to his queries as if they were junior executives in the employ of Kennedy Inc. And he himself gave his own account of activities, mapping the horizons they would one day attempt: '' He would bring back word of everything that was going on in Washington,'' a frequent dinner guest remembers, ''exciting things that were going on in New York, something terrific that had happened in Boston. Then he would ask questions: 'Do you know who I'm talking about? Do you know who that man is?' And if no one did, he would say 'Well, find out.' " One family friend remembers a map on the dining-room wall, which Joe would roll down and refer to in making some point about the world political situation. When Joe was not there, Rose would attempt to stand in for him, sometimes with unintended humor as the result: "One time, when she was at the head of the table," says Ted Reardon, another family friend, "she asked, 'Now, children, what is tomorrow?' Everybody was trying to figure out, now what the hell is it? Thursday or Friday? The answer she wanted—it was July 14—was Bastille Day."

Joe would continue to be gone a great deal. (Ann Kelley, a Bronxville neighbor, later said: "Pat and Eunice were always saying, 'Dad says this' and 'Dad says that.' But if I hadn't finally met him, I never would have known he existed.") But even when he was absent he was the crucial Kennedy, the one molding the family ethos and making them act as a unit. In a speech delivered in Boston after his return from Hollywood, he noted that the Irish had always "suffered under the handicap of not possessing family traditions adequate to win the respect of their Puritan neighbors." Using his own nine children as research materials, he set up an experiment that would rectify that defect. The playing fields of Hyannis became an American version of Eton's—a locale for character building, for the instillation of principle by which the Irish would triumph once and for all over their origins. "We want winners," was Joe Kennedy's refrain, "we don't want losers around here." His kids would be the ultimate yardstick measuring the worth of his own life.

Rose contributed to the ethos indirectly. Repressing the reality of her husband's infidelities and other bad news, she established an emphasis on *doing* and a distrust of the inner dimension as the characteristic Kennedy response to the world. Yet she was not only remote from the emotional matrix of the family, but increasingly away from home. (In the six years following her husband's return from Hollywood, according to one estimate, she made seventeen trips abroad.) When Joe was home he was really *there*. Rose had punished by occasional spankings which were increasingly laughed off as the children grew older; all Joe had to do was allow the glasses to slip down the bridge of his nose and stare at an offender with his chilly eyes to achieve instant discipline. ("Daddy's look," it was called.) As his daughter Eunice later said, he believed experience was the greatest creator of character, while Rose believed it was religion. He was the scarce resource they all competed for, the variable that made the experiment yield such remarkable results.

When Rose was snubbed by the Irish aristocrats of New York, he growled that he intended to be buried back in Brookline, where he at least knew the grounds for his exclusion. But instead of trying to insinuate the family into society as his wife would have liked, Joe made them all into proud nomads.

Bronxville was little more than a debarkation point—the place from which the children went to their various boarding schools. Palm Beach (where the Kennedys wintered for years, and where they finally bought a rambling Spanish-style house in 1933) and Hyannis were the places of record, as close as the Kennedys came to a home. Family life took place in these two houses facing away from land toward the sea. Almost peninsular in their isolation, they were ideal locales for raising children who would grow up feeling that the only society that really counted was that of the Kennedys themselves.

The children grew up close, with some of them, like Bobby and Pat and Jean and Teddy, forming "best-friend" relationships. Yet there was always a jockeying for position in what one acquaintance called the Kennedys' "rough love." There was constant verbal testing, aggressive probing of motive and result, that extended to non-Kennedys too. (As one of the kids' friends, Robert Downes, said: "The razzing would begin the minute you stepped inside the house. Your clothes, your speech, whatever: nothing was sacred. It was like getting pecked by a flock of chickens.") Joe Kennedy talked about family constantly. So did Rose. Yet they were both absent from home so much that the "Kennedy family" was a concept the children were in charge of refining.

By the time they were teenagers a hierarchy had been confirmed. At the top was Joe Junior, also called "Young Joe," as if he were a pretender to some throne. His face was Fitzgerald, but in body and soul he was like his father—sturdy and pugnacious, with a quick smile, an explosive temper, and a biting tongue. Bravery and daring were the qualities he quickly saw would hold his position as leader of his generation. Even as a youngster he was a battler. At his first school, the Noble and Greenough School in Brookline, he was once cornered by older boys. After holding them off as long as he could, he broke free and dashed down the street to a Catholic church, where he stood under the arched doorway and shouted, "You can't touch me here! This is a shrine!"

Young Joe had seen more of his father than the other children, having been born before Kennedy became the hero of his own picaresque tale. The remembered closeness made his father's absence more poignant for him than for the others. What he recalled about his confirmation was not the five-dollar gold piece P. J. gave him, nor the signet ring he got from Honey, but rather the fact that his father couldn't make it. When his father was in Hollywood, Young Joe spent time with the Fitzgeralds at the Bellevue Hotel, enticing the old Mayor into telling stories about his political heyday that inevitably fell into the cadence of political oratory, which the boy would then interrupt at appropriate points with applause. His friends recall him as seeming oddly lonely at times, and they were touched at the way he slipped away from the chaos of his own home to sit in their kitchens eating and talking with parents who were always around.

Because Joe and Rose were gone so often, Young Joe took on a large role among the other children. "You know I'm the oldest of my family," he explained seriously to a friend, "and I've got to be the example for a lot of brothers and sisters." His father had given this feeling of responsibility an almost tribal quality by also making his eldest son godfather to the youngest Kennedys, Jean and Teddy. Young Joe worked to carry out his father's implied agenda. It was he who coined the term "Kennedy clan." He always defended the family name, getting into fist fights with schoolmates who made comments about his father's morals or Honey Fitz's days in office. ("The nightmare of Boston," they would call Fitzgerald.) Joe Junior combined his mother's activism and his father's passion for victory into an ethic of conspicuous heroism whose evidences were broken bones and bandages. Sensing that his dominant position in the family could be enhanced by the others' achievements, he rooted for his brothers and sisters while also dealing out discipline. "It wasn't the father they were afraid of," said one family friend. "It was Joe Junior. The real reason they didn't sneak a smoke here and there was that they were afraid he would find out and beat the hell out of them." Yet there was love too, the most intense affection the younger Kennedys got within the family. One of Joe Junior's classmates remembers driving with him to the Cape for a weekend: "The minute we got out of the car, Teddy came running up. Joe grabbed him and kissed him like a father would and hoisted him up to his shoulder. They were like father and son."

Young Joe made enemies easily but also had the Kennedy knack for making friends who were bound to him for life. (One of these, Timothy Reardon, whom he met as a freshman at Harvard, remembers Joe inviting him to sleep in his dormitory room after Tim had missed the last bus home; they flipped a coin for the lone bed and Joe slept on the floor when he lost, to wake the next morning with snow from the open window covering his blanket.) Joe Junior established the tradition of bringing schoolmates home for visits, sometimes many of them at once, so that the Kennedy homes always had a summer-camp atmosphere. Like his father, he was confident of his ability to manipulate his world. His brash, premature worldliness was evident in a letter he wrote his mother about an attempt to fix a speeding ticket just after he'd learned to drive. "I got in touch with a policeman up there [in Orange, Connecticut] I know and he went down and talked to the Captain of the Wallingford Police Force who went to Orange and talked to the Judge but he couldn't do a thing, you know judges in small towns."

Young Joe's power in the family came not from primogeniture (an English rather than an Irish folkway), but from the fact that he was simply the strongest and bravest. If any of the others could have challenged him and won they would have led their generation. The only one who tried was Jack, much smaller but resourceful enough so that his brother always sensed the threat. Young Joe would play football patiently with the younger children, teaching them the rules of the game and helping them with techniques; but with Jack he turned bully, often finding an excuse to slam the ball into his stomach and walk away laughing as his younger brother lay doubled up in pain. He initiated competitions he couldn't lose, such as a well-remembered bicycle race in which he and Jack started in front of the Brookline house and rode around the block in opposite directions, meeting at the finish line in a collision that sent Jack to the hospital for twenty-eight stitches while Joe escaped unscathed. There were fearful fights on the living-room floor that left the other children shaking, especially Bobby, who stood crying with his hands over his ears. Outgunned by Joe, Jack was forced to resort to the skills of the weak—speed and cunning. His mother later told about a typical incident at Hyannis in which Jack finished his own dessert and then stole Young Joe's, running off stuffing it into his mouth with the bigger boy in hot pursuit, finally having to jump off the pier to escape, while Joe stood above watching him tread water and knowing he would have to emerge sometime. Jack always lost in these contests; he always kept trying.

The nature of his challenge was shaped by his health more than his spirit. He was born with an unstable back that made him vulnerable to injury and frequent severe pain. Even before his nearly fatal bout with scarlet fever, he was a frail infant, and as he grew he often suffered strange episodes of pain and lethargy which a series of puzzled doctors tried unsuccessfully to diagnose. His parents, especially his father, refused to acknowledge that Jack's condition was as serious as his medical record suggested, and served as cheerleaders in his attempts to cope. (Bobby captured both the seriousness of the condition and the ironic, stiff-upper-lipism of the family with a comment he made while still a little boy: "If a mosquito bit Jack Kennedy, the mosquito would die.") Because he was so frequently bedridden, Jack was the only Kennedy who became a reader, consuming parables like *Pilgrim's Progress* and romances like *King Arthur and His Knights*. (Family friend Kay Halle recalled that the first time she saw him, thirteen-year-old Jack was in the hospital working his way through Winston Churchill's *The World Crisis*.) He was interested in words and meanings—the only one in the family, his sister Eunice pointed out, who "looked things up." In a sense he became a secret agent in the family, one who paid lip service to the bruising activism that organized the rest of them but saw things from a more self-aware and ironic point of view. In 1932, two friends picked him up at the Bronxville railroad station when he came home from boarding school for vacation. He said sarcastically, "I want to stop by the house for a minute and check the nursery and see if there's anybody new in the family." (He came out and said, "By God, there is." It was Teddy.) Even after he was married he once commented to a writer that he himself had no desire for a large family because experience had shown him that it involved "institution-alized living, children in a cellblock."

He followed Joe Junior to the Noble and Greenough School in Brookline (later renamed Dexter), where the two of them played with another pair of brothers, William and McGeorge Bundy, in the backfield of the school football team. After a year at Canterbury, a Catholic prep school, where he spent much of his time in the infirmary, Jack followed Joe Junior to Choate, where he too was called "Rat Face" until visited by Rose's orthodontist. Jack drank heavy cream and ate starchy foods, but still lost weight. In a letter to his father he wrote that while at mass he had gotten "sick and dizzy and weak. I just about fainted and everything began to get black so I went out and Mr. Hume caught me. I am O.K. now. Joe fainted twice in church so I guess I'll live." Yet he was really not sure. At one point he became so sick with his "wasting disease" that he was taken to New Haven Hospital and his Choate classmates were told that he was near death and that they should pray for him in chapel.

Two subjects always on Jack's mind, then, were his health and his older brother. Betty Young, whom Jack met at a Field Club dance in Bronxville and dated on weekends when he came home from Choate, remembers how the conversation would always shift back to Joe whenever they were alone and there wasn't any music or entertainment going. "He talked about him all the time: 'Joe plays football better, Joe dances better, Joe is getting better grades.' Joe just kind of overshadowed him in everything."

Jack was an academic and discipline problem. Although his letters home were filled with resolutions about bringing his grades up and doing better, his friends tended to be practical jokers and troublemakers. One of these was a large, bearish boy with a high forehead and a piercing nasal voice named Kirk LeMoyne Billings, or "Lem," who was to become a lifelong participant in the Kennedy drama. Although a scholarship student at Choate, Lem was descended from a family of *Mayflower* aristocrats, tracing his ancestry on his father's side to Governor Brewster of Plymouth and on his mother's to John J. LeMoyne, a French physician whose son, Dr. Francis LeMoyne, became a noted abolitionist who established LeMoyne colleges and institutions for blacks in Memphis, Tennessee. Lem became valuable to Jack because of his size and strength—six foot two, 175 pounds, at age fourteen—which evened the conflict with his brother Joe in touch-football games and wrestling matches.

They met as sophomores going out for the student yearbook, "The Brief." As part of the "healing" ritual by which prospective candidates were selected, Jack had to sell advertising for "The Brief," which he did by getting accounts from the Oxford Meat Market in Palm Beach and the Hyannis Grocery store, as well as from stockbroker friends of his father's. In June 1933, in a post-term letter from Hyannis to Lem (who was already on the board), he reported his success, closing with "I'll see you next fall, which is a damn sight too near for comfort."

Lem's father, a noted physician, died that year after losing his fortune in the Depression, and Lem eagerly accepted when Jack invited him to visit the Kennedy family in Hyannis. The first day he arrived he went to take a shower in a small glass-enclosed tub and was scalded when he turned on the hot water by mistake and couldn't get the door open. Lem was taken to the hospital, and "got to know all the Kennedy children" when they visited him. From then on he spent more time with them during holidays and summer vacations than all their other friends combined.

Lem was a collector as a boy—stamps, coins, and other possessions that gave a sense of belonging. He noticed that Jack and his brothers and sisters didn't think in these terms. "They really didn't have a real home with their own rooms where they had pictures on the walls or memorabilia on the shelves but would rather come home for holidays from their boarding schools and find whatever room was available." He and Jack would arrive and Jack would say to his mother: "Which room do I have this time?"

Yet there was something about the family—some exuberance and daring that Lem found irresistible: "With them, life speeded up." He became devoted to Jack. Although he was a year ahead of his friend at Choate, he held himself back so they could graduate together. Jack was intrigued and gratified by the intensity of Lem's affection, but he never forgot the inequality that underlay their relationship, and allowed him the role of court jester. Lem, who combined a Victorian sensibility with a reasonable tenor, was constantly being cajoled by Jack at parties to sing a Mae West song called "I'm No Angel," while Jack enjoyed his difficulties with the slightly prurient lyrics:

> Aw, come on, let me cling to you like a vine,
> Make that low-down music trickle up your spine,
> Baby, I can warm you with this love of mine—
> I'm no an-gel!

On Lem's first visit to Palm Beach, Jack pulled out a hundred-dollar bill —a considerable sum for Lem, who had difficulty even raising the bus fare to Florida—and said, "I'll give you a hundred dollars right now if you'll take off all your clothes, walk into my father's Bullpen [an act absolutely forbidden—the Kennedy children themselves had to phone on an inside line for permission to enter this walled sanctuary near the pool], and say 'Hi, Dad—I know you've always wanted me to call you Dad—and these are words I've always wanted to tell you,' and then sing 'I'm No Angel.' "*

*Lem could not bring himself to do it. But when he was visiting the White House twenty-five years later he told Joseph Kennedy, who was also there, the story. "Sing it now," the President's father said. Lem was incredulous. "Here?" "I want to hear it now," Kennedy replied. "Sing it." So Lem sang "I'm No Angel." Kennedy said, "Jack should have offered me a hundred dollars for listening to it."

Although he needled Lem about his vulnerability as a "poor relation," Jack was capable at times of a sense of guilt which he attempted to expiate by an almost brotherly concern. In March of 1936, while commiserating with Lem for having lost his scholarship at Princeton, and at the same time accusing him of being a spendthrift, Jack urged his friend to make up his mind to come to Hyannis for a visit: "If you decide to go on vacation you come here as we have plenty of room. However, you have been a terrific ass and unless you come around now you haven't a chance."

They became "Johnny" and "Billy"—although Jack, with his increasing verbal acuity, would also call his friend "Delemma," "LeMoan," "Pneumoan," and other nicknames. The relationship was punctuated by emotional scrimmages in which Lem would try to neutralize Jack's annoying aloofness and oblique hostility, while Jack fended off his friend's aggressive loyalty with humor and sarcasm. Sometimes Jack's technique involved the punning irony and verbal assault which had come to dominate his private persona. ("Dear Pithecanthropus," he addressed the high-foreheaded Lem in one letter, "Or Sub-Man or Pithecanthropus Erectus, the walking Ape man, 'The skull showing a hair case about halfway in size between that of a chimpanzee and man ...' ") Sometimes there were bawdy allusions to Lem's physical size, which Jack transmogrified into a comic grossness. ("Dear Barney Oldfield," he wrote after Lem's departure from a weekend at Palm Beach, "Your trip must have been a nasty one. The car seat must have had a delectable smell after having you sit on it for thirty four hours ...")

Lem tried to hold his own, although as the more emotionally engaged of the two he was often hurt and on the defensive because of imagined insults. The seasonal invitations to the Kennedy vacation homes provided ideal grounds for his confrontations with Jack, most of them triggered by Lem's easily wounded pride. "Of all the cheap shit I have ever gotten this is about the cheapest," Jack complained from Palm Beach one winter. "You were invited down on Thanksgiving when the family was not coming. But then you were too busy and you and Rip [Horton] were going to St. Lawrence. Then you decide to come as Rip was going to. But by that time the family had decided to come down. Then you get hot in the arse because there may not be room enough, not forgetting that there was room enough at Thanksgiving but you didn't want to come until Rip decided he wanted to come. . . . Then I heard from Dad saying it was okay. That was the situation: as regards the cheap shit you are pulling, you can do what you want. . . . If you will look at this thing you will see you are not so fucking abused."

They undertook their adolescent rites of passage together, Lem usually playing a sort of straight man. Jack was such a reckless driver that he had come to the point where one more ticket would cause him to lose his license. One night he was speeding when a cop appeared behind them, and they changed places while the car was moving so Lem could take the rap. Together they went up to Harlem in full evening dress to find a prostitute, so that they could lose their virginity to the same woman. Jack went into the small room with the woman he selected, while Lem, in a bowler—as he told the story later—waited in discomfort at the door. When Jack came out, however, he had to pressure Lem into going into the room. But Lem's typical role remained that of the escort and tag-along, as when classmate Pete Caesar and Jack went AWOL from Choate's Festivities Weekend with their dates, Pussy Brooks and Olive Cawley, and thence to a nearby farm, where Pete and Pussy smooched in the parked car, and Jack and Olive ensconced themselves in one corner of a vacant barn, while Lem in white tie and tails hid in a pile of hay in another, discreetly waiting for everyone to be done.

Lem's lack of success with women provided an endless source of sarcasm for Jack. "If I hadn't just come from talking to girls who think that the words Billings and whacky are synonyms I would be impressed," Jack wrote Lem on one occasion. "[Olive] Cawley is just piling it to you. You don't think she would say it was sex between you.... You know she and K think your sex appeal is a joke..." On another occasion, after Lem had tried to defend himself by arguing that the only reason for Jack's success with girls was that he was Joseph P. Kennedy's son, Jack insisted that they take out two blind dates, arranged by someone else, and impersonate each other. He even arranged for Lem—"John F. Kennedy" for the evening—to pick up his date in Joe Kennedy's Rolls. "We had one very competitive night trying to see who would do better," Lem recalled, "and I'm afraid he was satisfied with the results."

Because they both had older brothers who outshone them (Fred "Josh" Billings, who also preceded Lem at Choate, was captain of the football team and president of his class), they made their mark at Choate through mischief. The imperious and pedantic headmaster George St. John, who had consciously patterned Choate on Eton, constantly referred in his "chapel talks" to what he called a "mucker" as the worst kind of boy he knew. About five percent of the boys in his school were muckers, he said, and if he knew who they were he would expel them. Immediately Lem and Jack banded together to form a clandestine organization that Jack named the Muckers Club, promoting the *esprit* by having as its insignia pins designed by a local jeweler in the form of a shovel. When St. John found out about it, he expelled all thirteen of its members. (Lem later recalled: "Jack and I were labeled public enemies number one and two of the school in that order.") The headmaster wrote a perplexed letter to Joe and Rose contrasting Young Joe and Jack and asking how two boys from the same family could be so different. Jack received a stiff note from his father, who had to make a personal visit to the headmaster to get Jack reinstated: "Don't let me lose confidence in you again because it will be pretty nearly impossible to restore it.... Get yourself into shape so that a man can't write a halfway report on you."

Badly outclassed by his older brother at the beginning, Jack managed to stay in the competition, winning a niche in the family by his humorous self-deprecation and his doggedness (he told Lem that he would someday be Jack's biographer and that the book should be titled "John F. Kennedy: A Medical History"), which turned his disability into an advantage. Not long after arriving at Choate, he had sent a letter to his father reporting on his older brother: "He was roughhousing in the hall a sixth former caught him he led him in and all the sixth formers had a swat or two. Did the sixth formers lick him. O Man he was all blisters, they almost paddled the life out of him. What I wouldn't have given to be a sixth former." He went on to describe the two of them coming home for vacation: "... to show me how tough he was [Joe Junior got sick] so he could not have any thanksgiving dinner. Manly youth." The last two words captured the irony that would more and more become the second Kennedy son's distinctive signature. Joe Junior had won the Harvard Trophy as the outstanding senior at Choate. Jack was chosen "most likely to succeed" in his senior year, a fact that mystified everyone until they found out that he had rigged the election.

Jack's biggest problem was still his health, a fact which prevented his father from being too severe with him. After he graduated from Choate in 1933 his father sent him to London, but he became seriously ill with a "blood condition" that had plagued him throughout his life and that had been diagnosed as leukemia, then jaundice, and then hepatitis, with doctors finally admitting that they didn't know what the problem was. In 1935 he enrolled at Princeton (where he went with Billings in an attempt to establish his independence from Young Joe, who was at Harvard), but the same illness forced him to leave school before finishing the semester. In Peter Brent Brigham Hospital in Boston for a series of tests, he jauntily described to Lem what had obviously been a grim ordeal: "I have just undergone the most harrowing experience of all my storm tossed career. They came in this morning with a gigantic rubber tube. Old stuff I said and rolled over thinking naturally that it would be stuffed up my arse. Instead they grabbed me and shoved it up my nose. I didn't know whether they thought my face was my ass or what but anyway they shoved it up my nose and down into my stomach. They then poured alcohol down the tube, me meanwhile going crazy as I couldn't taste the stuff, and you know what a good stiff drink does to me. They were doing this to test my acidosis. ... I had this thing up my nose for two hours and they just took it out (don't be dirty, Kirk) and now I have a 'head on' and a 'hard on' as when they had finished a beautiful nurse came in and rubbed my whole body."

A second letter from the hospital showed how his sense of irony had shaped a philosophical attitude: "They haven't found anything yet except that I have leukemia and agianalecucytosis. Took a peek at my chart yesterday and could see that they were mentally measuring me for a coffin. Eat drink and make love as tomorrow or next week we attend my funeral.'' As if to emphasize the conclusion, he added: ''Got the hottest neck ever out of Harson Saturday night. She's pretty good. So am looking forward to bigger and better ones.'' He urged his friend to take action that would ''bring us a good bottle of champagne or a fuck,'' and speculated about whether or not an old schoolmate had previously been sexually involved with one of his current girlfriends. (''Whether or not he screwed her, she got quite a scare when I gave it to her.... However I couldn't feel any maidenhead and she is quite sexy.'')

After his release from the hospital he went with Joe Junior to do summer work at the J Six Ranch in Arizona, a forty-three-thousand-acre spread belonging to a friend of Arthur Krock, the *New York Times* reporter, who had become close to Joe Kennedy. Krock had suggested the plan as a way of toughening Young Joe up for the next Harvard football season and restoring Jack's health. (''If you could see what a thing of beauty my body has become with the open air, riding horses and Mexicans, you would stuff such adjectives as unattractive when you are speaking of my body, right where they belong...'' Jack wrote to Lem.) To test his new tan, and to explore the terrain his father had mapped and which would hold a lifelong fascination for him, he took a side trip to the film capital. (''I met this extra in Hollywood that is the best looking thing I have ever seen,'' he wrote, adding a tag to the letter: ''The Extra's delight, or how I got my tail in Hollywood.'' By the end of the summer he was well enough to enter Harvard that fall, which was where his father had wanted him to go all along.

If Jack won a place in the family by his ability to cope, his sister Rosemary won hers by her inability. By the time she was four or five it had become clear that her problems could not be helped by the series of doctors Rose took her to. Rosemary followed her two older brothers to Dexter for kindergarten but couldn't keep up with the other children and from that time on attended special schools. At home, Rose spent extra time with her. (Paul Morgan remembers her walking the active child up and down Pondfield Road in Bronxville of an afternoon, gratefully stopping at his house to let her burn off energy by chasing his Great Dane around the yard.) The other children made attempts to include her, but friends who came over noticed that there were many games and activities in which she didn't participate, and others in which she was just ''part of the background.'' People were told she was shy. Only the closest family friends knew what the bemused look, the lack of complexity behind the clear hazel eyes, really meant.

As a teenager, Rosemary looked normal. She could repeat what she heard and form sentences on her own. But she had trouble retaining what was said to her. ''You could talk to Rosemary,'' says one of the few acquaintances who knew what was wrong, "but you could never have a conversation. She talked like a ten-year-old—just chattering all the time."

Rose insisted that the two older boys come home from Choate to take her to tea dances, explaining their absences by telling school officials that her daughter had an "inferiority complex." She encouraged the boys to get their friends to fill in her dance card, although she danced in an awkward half-trot, and to cut in on each other as they did for the other girls. She tried to create a pattern of normality around her—out of love and pity, but also to protect all the rest.

Rose's fatalism made it possible for her to deal with what had happened. She treated Rosemary as normally as possible, encouraging her to test herself in the way she did the other children (letting her travel in Europe with only sixteen-year-old Eunice as a companion). Joe was unable to deal with the problem as coolly; his daughter's retardation upset him as no other subject did. Once when they were together at the Rodeo Drive house, Gloria Swanson happened to overhear a snatch of one of his telephone conversations involving hospitals and doctors in which he said something about donating an ambulance if something could be done for his daughter. Afterward, not knowing the magnitude of Rosemary's problems, Swanson innocently suggested that he consult one of the health-food doctors she had discovered in Hollywood. Kennedy turned on her, his face livid: "I don't want to hear about it! Do you understand me? *Do you understand me?*" When some of the doctors suggested that the girl might do well in a mental hospital he responded: "What can they do in an institution that we can't do better here at home—living with the family?"

Writing from her special school at the Sacred Heart Convent in Rhode Island, Rosemary continued to address painstakingly lettered notes (some with grammar and spelling corrected by the nuns) to her father:

Dear Daddy:
I had a lovely time on Saturday. Thank you ever so much for coming down to see me. Sunday I also had a good time. I would do anything to make you so happy. I hate to disappoint you in any way . . .

. . . Thursday, I went to Girl Scouts. I am taking Nature up . . . Jack is taken me to the next dance. He is going to take me in his new car . . . I gave Jack $1 he didn't ask it either. 2 cents paid for his papper . . . Lots of love kisses you darling daughter,

Rosemary

She was denied the privileges she saw her brothers and sisters routinely enjoying—sailing out into Nantucket Sound by themselves in one of the family's boats; going alone to the train station to return to boarding school after weekends at home. Sometimes she ran away from the person sent to put her on the train. As she grew older she had increasingly serious tantrums. Along with the competition between Joe Junior and Jack, her condition became a dominant motif of her generation of Kennedys. Although she herself became the Kennedy apart, her disability was the unacknowledged fact that helped unify the rest of them.

Rosemary's problems vaulted Kathleen into prominence in the family, making her in effect the first daughter, although her own natural gifts probably would have won this position for her in any case. She was blond and petite, with the deep-set agate eyes of her mother's side of the family; full-faced, slightly heavy in the jaw—a "soft Kennedy," an acquaintance once put it, comparing her with her darker, taller, toothier, and more angular sisters. She was perhaps not as pretty as Pat, nor as intelligent as Eunice (who, Kennedy friends and acquaintances said, was the family's most natural politician), but Kathleen was the most lively and vivacious of all the girls, as if she was trying to make up for Rosemary's defects by an excess of normality of her own. Family friend Dinah Bridge later said she was "like sunshine," and that when she came into a room "everything seemed to sort of lighten up."

The nickname her father gave her—"Kick"—fit her perfectly, summarizing her naturalness and lack of affectation. (One of the Kennedy governesses always remembered how when she was on her way out of the house to go shopping with some friends she suddenly said, "Oh my goodness, I forgot to say my morning prayers," and quickly went down on both knees in front of everyone.) Part of her high spirits led to a defiant streak; more than any of the other girls she was outspoken and blunt, challenging the family system in a way her older brothers couldn't or wouldn't do. A powerful reason was her father, who had long acknowledged that he was no impartial judge of his children—"All my ducks are swans," he liked to say—but Kathleen was "especially special."

Like her sisters, she was obliged to go to Sacred Heart convent schools and acquire the trappings of Catholic womanhood, but at home she sat with her two brothers at the "big table," feeding on her father's ambition and his cynical observations about the world, while the younger children and Rosemary ate at the "little table" with the governesses.

Joe argued with his father, challenged his authority, even boldly contradicted him. Kick, like Jack, learned to get her way through charm. She spent her adolescence getting Joe Junior and Jack dates with her friends and going out with her brothers' roommates at Choate and Harvard. Among those who fell in love with her was Jack's friend Lem, who squired her to the World's Fair, and in one famous family incident escorted her with Jack to the celebrated Cotton Club in Harlem. When her father found out the next day, he focused his fury in a smoldering mute anger that expressed maximum displeasure and dominated the silent house.

"These three—Joe Junior, Jack, and Kick—were like a family within the family, a charmed triangle," says one Kennedy friend. "They were the pick of the litter, the ones the old man thought would write the story of the next generation." At times it seemed that they were almost sexually bonded. Kick dated and had crushes on most of their friends at one time or another. In turn she provided friends for them to date, and afterward kidded them about the bobby pins she found in the rumble seat of one of the family cars.

Among the girls Eunice was clearly her father's natural child—competitive, aggressive, athletic (although like Jack she suffered from a mysterious ailment that sapped her strength). Unable to compete with Kick's charm, she drew into a defensive alliance with her mother, announcing her ambition early to be a nun. "Eunice took herself seriously, was very plain, dressed dreadfully, really was a pill," one girlhood friend remembers. Charlotte McDonnell recalls visiting the Cape and sharing a room with Kick: "There would be a bathroom in between, and then Eunice's room, and you couldn't use the bathroom or flush the toilet at night because it would wake Eunice up, even though she had on an eye mask and earplugs."

Kick tended to overshadow the other girls with her vitality, too. In any case they were part of the family's second tier, the children who with Rosemary sat with the governesses at the "little table" while Joe Junior, Jack, Kick, and sometimes Eunice ate at the "big table" with their parents. The children of the little table were unquestioning conscripts in the family ethos. Pat and Jean were anonymous so far. Teddy was the baby of the family, a dangling modifier, the jokester who accepted the duty of saying things that would make everybody laugh, the chubby boy his sisters all wanted to cover during the touch-football games. Because he'd come along at a time when Rosemary was becoming a major worry, his parents had been afraid he'd be born defective. When he wasn't, they were overjoyed, and a situation was established in which he could do no wrong. There were disadvantages to being the last born. Sometimes his father would rail against some politician or diplomat, calling him a "horse's ass" or worse, and then point at Teddy and say, "Hell, the guy knows about as much as that kid over there." But unlike his older brother Bobby, Teddy at least had no trouble finding his place.

Bobby was so much younger than Joe Junior and Jack that no one expected much from him and as a result he had trouble determining what he should expect from himself. He was the runt of the litter—small, uncoordinated, inarticulate. Rose was interested in his religiousness and proud that he wanted to be an altar boy; when she was at home she came into his room each night to hear his Latin and test his catechism, although even she worried that he might grow up "puny and girlish." He always tried to please but always seemed to do things wrong. Wanting to emulate his father's legendary childhood business successes, he got a paper route in Bronxville, but he couldn't make a go of the daily routine and the family chauffeur wound up making the deliveries. He tried to play with his brothers and their friends in the increasingly serious football games at Hyannis, but his earnestness always got him hurt. His sister Pat, the person closest to him in both age and emotion, later recalled the single incident that seemed to typify both his desire to please and his awkwardness. One evening, hearing the call to dinner and determined not to trespass against his father's well-known desire for promptness, Bobby came running; he forgot the glass partition separating the living room and the dining area and crashed into it, and shards of falling glass cut him all over his body. Once when someone was praising the young Kennedys and Bobby's name came up, his sister Eunice blurted out: "Bobby? Forget it. Let's talk about the other boys."

He was the only Kennedy who seemed star-crossed; but there was a strange, almost mystical intensity about him, a tendency to push impatiently at his fate. Worried that it was taking too long for him to learn to swim, for instance, he once threw himself out of a yawl into Nantucket Sound to finally sink or swim. Joe Junior, whom Bobby idolized, characteristically jumped out of the boat to save him from drowning. Equally in character, Jack, who had a more distant relationship with his younger brother, stood on shore speculating whether the act showed courage or foolhardiness.

As the 1920s came to an end, and with it the era in which he had acquired the bulk of his fortune and the beginnings of his myth, Joe Kennedy began to think less like a free-lance and more like the progenitor of a family line. He recognized that the Depression meant a dramatic break with the past and began to shift his view to the larger world, looking for ways to make it through the coming crisis unscathed and also ready to make a serious bid for power for himself and these children whom he had come to see as an extension of himself.

Earlier than most investors he had sensed that the economy was in serious trouble. The Establishment had made a connection between the great bull market of the Jazz Age and the American Way, but Kennedy had always remained an outsider, even after he made his reputation in Hollywood as an architect of high-powered mergers and consolidations. In 1929 he had tried to pay a courtesy call on J. P. Morgan, pillar of the financial community, and been snubbed. He had no reason, therefore, not to join with the infamous "Sell 'Em Ben" Smith and other corsairs who plundered the stock market as it wallowed like an overloaded galleon in the weeks before the Crash. Working from a desk at the Madison Avenue branch of the brokerage firm of Halle and Steiglitz, Kennedy became a leader of the fraternity of bears who rode the market down toward Black Thursday. His reputation spread even to the children. Once when he came home from a day of profiteering his daughter Jean pointed at him and squealed, "Daddy is a bear! Daddy is a bear!'' For a moment he was taken aback, but then he grinned and bent over to give her a bear hug.

In the space of a few weeks he made huge profits short-selling stocks like Anaconda and Paramount. (Some estimates of his profits in the slide of 1929 ranged as high as $15 million, and it has been said that by 1930 he was worth over $100 million.) But he was different from "Sell 'Em Ben" and the others. While he was willing to make money as the bubble burst, he was much more concerned about banks closing and Hoovervilles springing up than the other Wall Street bears; he was especially concerned by the radical rhetoric of those calling for wholesale political and social reorganization. As he later described his fears at this critical juncture in American history: "I felt and said I would be willing to part with half of what I had if I could be sure of keeping, under law and order, the other half.''

Like other businessmen, he believed in a free marketplace. But his was not an abstract, semitheological commitment. He was a pragmatist, with an Irish heritage of commitment to survival, and he was therefore willing to consider alternatives. He had held Young Joe out of his first year at Harvard, for instance, to send him to London to study under the renowned socialist teacher Harold Laski. Kennedy himself found Laski's beliefs reprehensible, but he wanted his son to speak a language that would be understood in the new world being created by the Depression. Not sure about the exact shape of things to come, he foresaw that the center of gravity in America would shift from big business to bigger government, and he wanted his family to be ready.*

When his future rival for Secretary of the Treasury, Henry Morgenthau, Jr., took him to Albany to meet Governor Franklin Roosevelt in 1930, Kennedy realized that he had an opportunity to participate in a mid-course steering correction that might save American capitalism while also establishing himself as a political power. "I wanted him in the White House for my own security and the security of our kids," he later said of FDR, "and I was willing to do anything to help elect him." The socialite Kay Halle, another early Roosevelt supporter, recalled seeing Kennedy going into FDR's hotel suite two years later with Felix Frankfurter for a meeting arranged by Rexford Tugwell, Robert Sherwood, Raymond Moley, and others who would become New Deal stalwarts: "He was unmistakably Irish, with his copper-colored hair and a beaming smile that exposed his shining teeth . . . 'I'm Joe Kennedy,' he said. 'I've never had the thrill of being part of a presidential campaign. So I've put some money into Mr. Roosevelt's campaign, and I'd like to come along with you and take part in the fun.' ''

---

*Morton Downey recalls Kennedy's plans for the boys. "He said—and this was in 1930—that in the next generation the people who ran the government would be the biggest people in America.''

By the time of the convention he was in a position to participate in crucial decisions. Most other Irish Catholics stuck by Al Smith, darling of the old cause, but at the end of three ballots Kennedy was working hard to break the convention deadlock in Roosevelt's favor. The balance of power rested with William Randolph Hearst, whose candidate, John Nance Garner, had no chance but enough delegates to determine the outcome. Kennedy, who had met Hearst during his days in Hollywood, when the press lord was trying to buy a film career for his mistress Marion Davies, called Hearst at the eleventh hour and told him that if he didn't persuade Garner to throw his votes to Roosevelt, he was likely to get Newton Baker, a former member of Woodrow Wilson's cabinet whose internationalist politics Hearst abhorred. The threat worked. Kennedy immediately let it be known that whatever future history books might say, it was he who had gotten the nomination for FDR.

During the campaign Kennedy gave Roosevelt $25,000 and lent the Democratic National Committee another $50,000, efforts that won him a position on the campaign finance committee. Soon he had risen to the status of general adviser to the candidate, touring with him in a private railroad car along with Jim Farley and Brain Truster Raymond Moley. While his conservatism in foreign policy made him an ideal emissary to someone like Hearst, his status as a leading Catholic layman allowed him to keep radio priest Father Charles Coughlin from blasting Roosevelt's candidacy. He became the Democrats' Mr. Fixit. Long-time FDR backer and future Kennedy watcher Eddie Dowling said, "He moved in close to those in power. He knew what he wanted and fought for it because he felt he had as much right to it as anyone else." It was no particular point of view that he wanted to see implemented, no particular program. It was a personal prize—the reward for loyalty which had been coin of the realm in the wards his father and father-in-law had run. As the campaign drew to a close, Kennedy felt certain that he would be given a position in the cabinet. At the lavish victory party he threw at the Waldorf on election night, he moved through the crowd like the winning candidate himself.

He and the President-elect were a study in contrasts. FDR was courtly and indirect, making his way by keeping those around him off balance, seeming to give people exactly what they wanted while actually giving only what he wanted them to have. Kennedy was profane and blunt, impatient with nuance and altruism, willing to admit he acted from self-interest. The later mistrust between the two men was probably unavoidable given their temperaments; but the ultimate causes for it went back to the 1932 election. Kennedy, who had grown up in a political ambience that was cynical about every principle save one—that a supporter must be rewarded for his support —was forced to watch others step forward to claim a share of the spoils of victory, many of them having contributed far less than he.

The post he most coveted, Secretary of the Treasury (which would have given him an opportunity to have the last laugh on Morgan and the other economic royalists who had treated him like an inferior over the years), went to William Woodfin, a little-known industrialist. Roosevelt crony Tommy Corcoran passed the rumor that Kennedy might be picked for Secretary of Commerce, but nothing came of it. Wintering in Palm Beach, Kennedy tried to keep his name in front of the President-elect by sycophantic messages ("The nuns were praying for you," he said in a telegram after a visit to a convent), but the days stretched into weeks and soon all the major posts were filled.

There were demeaning offers of jobs as a member of a commission studying the boundary dispute between the United States and Brazil, and as director of the New York State office of the New Deal's National Recovery Administration. But they only rubbed salt in Kennedy's wounds. Soon his blandishments of Roosevelt turned to envenomed attacks. While visiting Palm Beach, Raymond Moley, one of Kennedy's few friends within the New Deal, was shocked at the abuse of the President and his first hundred days in Kennedy's long-distance telephone conversations with Hearst and others. Only after Kennedy had threatened to call in all his loans to the Democratic Party did Roosevelt invite him to the White House. Kennedy came away from the meeting committed to biding his time and remaining on the edge of the action through his friendships with Moley and the President's eldest son, James, a frequent visitor at Palm Beach and a recipient of Kennedy's help in getting the National Distillers Association to take insurance with James's company in Boston.

Like a son punishing his father with delinquent behavior, Kennedy (who had listed himself simply as "capitalist" in the twentieth-anniversary bulletin of his Harvard class) turned with a vengeance to making money. The impending repeal of Prohibition had made liquor and related stocks attractive once again. Some of the manipulators with whom Kennedy was friendly had begun buying up the stock of plate-glass manufacturer Libbey-Owens-Ford—whose name could be confused by the unwary with the Owens Illinois Glass Co., which made bottles—and circulating rumors that the company was in line for major business from the distillers. Kennedy joined the pool they formed, buying options to purchase the company's stock at $26 a share and then "churning" millions of shares until the price was up to $37, whereupon he sold off at a handsome profit and left Libbey-Owens to fall back down below the original price.

Even while he was pocketing his $60,000 share of the pool's profits, he moved to take advantage of Repeal more directly, officially going back into the business with which his family had been associated since first coming to America. With fierce competition raging for the products of British distillers, Kennedy left for England in September 1933, along with Rose and Jimmy Roosevelt and his wife. Bringing the President's son to important lunches in London allowed him to imply a White House endorsement for his quest, and soon he had been named U. S. agent for Haig and Haig, John Dewars Scotch, and Gordon's Gin. Meanwhile he used his Washington leverage to get "medicinal" licenses issued to his company, Somerset Importers, so that he could begin bringing in liquor and warehousing it in anticipation of Repeal. Jimmy Roosevelt apparently expected to be rewarded with a part of the business, but it didn't work out that way. "Maybe Jimmy thought he and Joe were going to be partners," said a friend of both men. "If so, he soon found out that when Joe Kennedy is starting a business, he doesn't have partners." It was understandable why Kennedy would not want to share the profits: the liquor deals he made at this time would be worth a million dollars a year to him in the future.

Roosevelt became increasingly aware that Kennedy would continue to be a loose cannon on the deck of the New Deal until he received a payoff for his support in 1932. He offered the Ambassadorship to Ireland, but Kennedy treated it as a kind of insult, an attempt to manacle him with the ethnic identity he'd spent his whole life trying to escape. ("I told him that I did not desire a position with the government unless it really meant some prestige to my family," he haughtily wrote Young Joe after rejecting the offer.) Then Roosevelt surprised everyone by offering him the chairmanship of the newly formed Securities and Exchange Commission.

Although the post did not have the prestige of cabinet rank, the SEC was the centerpiece of New Deal efforts to encourage economic recovery and restore confidence in business; it was certain to be very much in the public eye, and was therefore automatically attractive to Kennedy and controversial for those who had followed his recent financial maneuvers. While he tried to line up support for his nomination, they took aim at it. "Mr. Kennedy, former speculator and pool operator, will now curb speculation and prohibit pools," deadpanned *Newsweek*, while the *New Republic* called him "the worst of all parasites, a Wall Street operator." The outcry was loud enough to make Roosevelt think of backtracking. At a White House crisis meeting convened to discuss the adverse publicity, Raymond Moley told Kennedy that he had one final chance to speak up if there was anything in his record to disqualify him from the position. "Kennedy reacted precisely as I thought he would," Moley wrote later. "With a burst of profanity he defied anyone to question his devotion to the public interest or to point to a single shady act in his whole life. The President did not need to worry about that, he said. What was more he would give his critics—and here the profanity flowed freely—an administration of the SEC that would be a credit to the country, the President himself and his family—clear down to the ninth child." After Roosevelt reaffirmed his commitment to making the appointment, Kennedy leaked the story to the papers in a way that made it appear that he had been reluctantly drafted. "Having almost everything else," the

Boston Post wrote the next day, "he wants to leave a name known for public service as well as business success. This is what made him accept a position that he did not want."

Kennedy entered public service on July 2, 1934, at the SEC's temporary headquarters in the Federal Trade Commission offices. To counter the adverse publicity about his appointment, Roosevelt got his friend Bernard Baruch to persuade Arthur Krock, then the *New York Times*'s Washington bureau chief, to do a story on Kennedy. When, after lengthy interviews, Krock filed a story summarizing Kennedy's career exactly as he described it —highlighting the Horatio Alger aspects and defending the recent financial doings—it was the beginning of a unique thirty-year relationship.*

The SEC quickly became one of the glamour spots in the first Roosevelt Administration. The best and brightest of the young attorneys who flocked to Washington wanted to work there. (William O. Douglas was one who took a job; Adlai Stevenson and Alger Hiss were two who almost did.) Moreover, the commission established one of the best records of all the new "alphabet-soup" agencies. The Stock Exchange adopted the trading rules it promulgated. Corporations complied with new guidelines for disclosure and accountability. Kennedy even attacked short selling, making a species he knew quite well, the Wall Street bear, more honest. He became one of the most traveled of FDR's men, logging 65,000 miles by air in his first year on the job. He tried to compel compliance by persuasion, but he was capable of getting tough when that didn't work; he lashed out at business critics of the SEC as "unthinking reactionaries."

He also became a fixture in the Washington whirl. He rented a twenty-five-room Maryland estate overlooking the Potomac. It was called Marwood, but Kennedy, living there alone with Eddie Moore and his Irish cronies except for occasional weekends when Rose and the children came down, called it "the Hindenburg Palace." He rose early enough to go for a ride along the private bridle paths or to swim naked in the pool and still be at his desk by seven-thirty in the morning. In the long summer evenings he sat out

---

*A pair of realists others had doubts about, the two men took to each other immediately. Although superficially quite different—Kennedy cheerfully anti-Semitic and charming, Krock a sepulchral Jew from Kentucky—they saw that their agendas might well intersect. Each had something to give the other in an immediate way: Kennedy could provide Krock with a bounty of good things—vacations in Florida, complimentary cases of scotch, and, most of all, blunt appraisals of and inside information about the new administration—and Krock could provide Kennedy with something like a personal public relations effort which, coming from the chief of the *Times*'s Washington bureau, had undeniable authenticity. Each had longer-range plans in which the other might also prove useful, as the relationship developed. Kennedy would support Krock for the editorship of the *Times*, and Krock would support him for the presidency.

on the veranda listening to Beethoven's Fifth and other favorite symphonies on the phonograph, growling at aides who asked for livelier music-hall jigs: "You dumb bastards don't appreciate culture."

Over the next few months he became one of the most talked-about personalities on the Washington scene, a man whose advertisements for himself reporters found refreshingly real in the gray world of understated bureaucratic aspiration. The Kennedy beat was considered a plum not only because of his outspoken opinions, however, but also because of the buffets and cocktails at Marwood, and other perks. Nor was it just reporters: Kennedy managed to be on good terms with press people ranging from Hearst to Colonel Robert McCormick, isolationist publisher of the *Chicago Tribune*, to muckraker Drew Pearson. Over the next few years, Henry Luce ordered up two cover stories on Kennedy in *Time* and an elegant feature in *Fortune*, allowing him to see the draft and make minor corrections. Kennedy knew exactly the tone to strike in his dealings with such men. When Eugene Meyer, publisher of the *Washington Post*, saw pictures of the Kennedy family in his paper and sent a note saying that Young Joe seemed to look like his father while Jack favored Rose, Kennedy replied with the fey assurance of one who knows he is an attractive commodity and intends to remain one: "Joe Jr. will probably never read the *Washington Post* again. Jack, on the other hand, thinks that any paper who has a publisher so discerning and with such fine judgement should be supported by the entire country."

In Washington, Kennedy had finally found his destiny; politics offered him a sense of belonging and being at the center of things that no amount of wealth could provide and no amount of social snobbery could deny. Even those who disliked Kennedy found something almost touching in his attempt to capture the quicksilver movements of history and his role in them. In 1933, for instance, when the Supreme Court decided to review Congress's decision to take the country off the gold standard, Kennedy—who as SEC chairman had been in the cockpit of the battle because uncertainty about the outcome had made stock prices fluctuate wildly—maintained an open line to the Supreme Court Building to keep abreast of deliberations. When told that the constitutionality of the law had been upheld, he quickly telephoned the White House with the news. Later he dictated a detailed memorandum which concluded: "I am writing this because I feel the occasion is an historical one. I feel that the opportunity of being the person to relay this information to the President would be of value historically to my family." Frequent requests to FDR for autographed pictures and handwritten notes ("about three lines in longhand for my children") dominated Roosevelt secretary Missy LeHand's abiding memories of Kennedy from her White House years.

Roosevelt became a frequent enough visitor at Marwood to warrant the installation of a special elevator. He would watch unreleased movies Kennedy had flown in from Hollywood in the auditorium in the basement, sip scotch provided by Somerset Importers, and eat lobster flown down especially from Boston. Tommy Corcoran would bring his accordion and the President would extemporize faintly ribald songs in his rich baritone. In return for the hospitality, there were weekends at the White House for the Kennedy family and rides with the President at Hyde Park in his blue Ford roadster specially equipped with hand controls.

It became a personal relationship with everything except mutual trust. Kennedy's telephone conversations with Roosevelt might begin with respectfully laconic responses: ''Yes, Mr. President . . . No, Mr. President . . .'' But as the conversation went on he would often become heated, lapsing into a more familiar form of advice: ''Now listen to me, boy, you do that and we'll all wind up in the shithouse.'' (Arthur Krock was present during one of these exchanges and rose to leave, but Kennedy motioned him to sit down and witness how well he handled the President.) For his part, Roosevelt was amused by Kennedy and grateful that someone was willing to argue the no position in a way that most of his yes-men would not. But if the democrat in the President liked Kennedy's spunk, the aristocrat couldn't help scorning someone whose reach seemed chronically doomed to exceed his grasp. Sometimes the badinage between the two men became quite sharp. When FDR kidded him about Gloria Swanson, Kennedy replied with snide references to the President's relationship with Missy LeHand. The competition between them didn't stop at the threshold of the Oval Office. Roosevelt's son Elliot later recalled an occasion in which his sister Anna was the object of Kennedy's attention. ''After lunching with him one afternoon at the Ritz Carleton Hotel . . . my sister discovered that she too was on the list. She eluded his embraces by running around his suite, dodging behind the sofa, scuttling around the piano, with Joe in amorous pursuit until he lost his breath.''

After resigning from the SEC in triumph in the summer of 1935, Kennedy went to Europe on a combined vacation and fact-finding tour, taking Rose, Kathleen, and Jack with him. On the passage over he met General Motors official Lawrence Fisher, one of the famous brothers who had perfected automobile body design. After talking to Fisher for a couple of hours, Kennedy sent someone to find his son, who arrived flushed and disheveled from a game of deck tennis. ''Jack,'' the elder Kennedy said, ''I want you to meet Mr. Lawrence Fisher, a top official of General Motors, because I want you to see what brothers can do who work together.'' When they arrived in Europe Rose tried to enter Kick in the Holy Child Convent School in Neuilly, outside Paris, but she refused to stay there because it was too strict.

One of the European political leaders Kennedy visited was British M.P. Winston Churchill. During dinner at Chartwell, his country estate, Churchill suggested that England and the United States ought to pool their naval resources to quarantine the Nazis; Kennedy replied that it wouldn't work because there were ''too many Irish haters of England'' in America.

As Roosevelt's campaign for reelection began, Kennedy decided to write a book to rally the business community, most of it by now deeply disenchanted with the President. He began by offering Arthur Krock $1000 a week to be his ghost writer: "I am enclosing a copy of a letter I received from the President last week. I gather from it that he is anxious to have [the book] done, and if it is done, I should like to have it done in bang up shape." Titled *I'm for Roosevelt*, the work, which appeared in late summer, was an encomium to the President as a good shepherd who had guided American capitalism through the Valley of the Shadow. Perhaps the most interesting line in the book had nothing to do with Roosevelt at all. In a gratuitous comment in the introduction, Kennedy wrote, "I have no political ambitions for myself or my children ..."

Kennedy put out even more effort for Roosevelt in 1936 than in 1932 and expected more of a reward. Secretary of the Treasury was still his preference, and Krock dutifully boosted him for the job. But with his recovery plans at a critical juncture, FDR was more chary than ever about having Kennedy in this sensitive position. As he said to Postmaster General Jim Farley, "Joe would want to run the Treasury in his own way contrary to my plans and views." In the spring of 1937, the President put Kennedy on hold by giving him the chairmanship of the Maritime Commission, a job from which Kennedy resigned after several fractious months of dealing with radical unions and reactionary shipowners. "This was the toughest thing I ever did in my life," he said.

All the Kennedys' eyes were now on Europe. In March 1936, German troops had entered the Rhineland after Hitler had denounced the Locarno Treaty demilitarizing the region. Four months later a rebellion of right-wing officers, led by General Francisco Franco, launched a civil war in Spain. Germany threw its support to the rebel side, supplying tanks and air power. Italy joined the fray and Mussolini boasted of the formation of a "Rome-Berlin Axis."

On June 30, 1937, Jack and Lem sailed on the *George Washington* for Le Havre. Their plan was to take a two-month tour of the Continent in Jack's convertible Ford sedan, which they had brought along for the occasion. Lem had to scrape his fare together, and Jack agreed to live within Lem's budget while they were in Europe, which often meant eighty-cents-a-night lodgings. Jack, just twenty years old, was intent on taking the political temperature of the European situation and kept a diary in which he noted his impressions. Lem, who had just completed his first architecture course at Princeton, insisted on stopping in the cathedral towns and lecturing Jack on the elements of Gothic design.

Driving south through the Loire Valley, they tried to enter Spain but were turned back by guards at the border and had to content themselves with interviewing Loyalist refugees in St. Jean de Luz. "The refugees of St. Jean

de Luz were upper class and from the non-Franco group," Lem remembers,
"so we heard some pretty blood-curdling tales of what the Francos were
doing in Spain. Jack spent a great deal of time talking to the refugees,
making notes and writing." They attended a bullfight in Biarritz, visited
Lourdes, and gambled in Monte Carlo. In Italy they had a private audience
with papal secretary and Kennedy family friend Cardinal Pacelli, and attended a Mussolini rally. Afterward, Lem did Mussolini interpretations for
Jack all the way to Munich, where they encountered hostility toward Americans: "The whole feeling we got from the Germans was that they were
arrogant, superior to us, and wanting to show it." When the American
travelers attempted handshakes, the Germans saluted them and said, "Heil
Hitler." Jack and Lem quickly developed a response, throwing back their
hands casually and saying "Hi ya, Hitler." They went to Nuremberg, just
missing an appearance by Hitler, a fact they regretted long afterward. Returning via Amsterdam and Brussels with a dachshund they had bought in
Germany, they arrived for a three-day stopover in London, where Jack became so severely asthmatic—running a fever, breaking out in hives, and
swelling up until his eyes closed—that they had to get rid of the dog.

On the voyage back, Jack met a massive Dutch wrestling champion in the
ship's gymnasium, who complained that he had no one to wrestle to keep
himself in shape. Jack proposed Lem, instantaneously inventing half a dozen
interscholastic tournament triumphs for his companion. Typically, Lem
went along with the ruse, even after discovering that the Dutch champion
outweighed him by a hundred pounds. The bouts, which Jack enthusiastically refereed, lasted the duration of the trip, as the hapless Lem was thrown,
twisted, and slammed from one end of the gym mat to the other.

Joe Kennedy too was trying to figure out a way to get into the eye of the
European storm. One evening after his retirement from the Maritime Commission, he turned to Jimmy Roosevelt, who was visiting him at Marwood,
and said that there was one other job besides Treasury that he'd like to have:
"I'd like to be Ambassador to England." Jimmy was taken aback. "Oh,
c'mon, Joe," he replied, unable to picture his friend among the English
upper classes, "you don't want that." But Kennedy was dead earnest: "Oh,
yes, I do. I've been thinking about it and I'm intrigued by the thought of
being the first Irishman to be Ambassador from the United States to the
Court of St. James's."

When FDR heard of the request he threw his head back and laughed so
long and hard that he almost toppled out of his wheelchair. Finally catching
his breath, the President shook his head and said he was sorry but the
ambassadorship was out of the question. Then, before Jimmy had a chance
to relay this message to Kennedy, his father called to say he had been recon-
sidering and ask him to arrange a meeting.

When young Roosevelt ushered Kennedy into the Oval Office, the President asked him to step back by the fireplace so he could "get a good look" at him. Puzzled, Kennedy did as he was told. "Joe," the President continued, "would you mind taking your pants down?" Kennedy stared back in disbelief, then slowly unhooked his suspenders, let his pants fall to the floor, and stood in his shorts looking, Jimmy Roosevelt thought, "silly and embarrassed." FDR broke the silence. "Joe, just look at your legs. You are just about the most bowlegged man I have ever seen. Don't you know that the Ambassador to the Court of St. James's has to go through an induction ceremony in which he wears knee britches and silk stockings? Can you imagine how you'll look? When photos of our new Ambassador appear all over the world, we'll be a laughingstock. You're just not right for the job, Joe."

Kennedy looked straight at Roosevelt: "Mr. President, if I can get the permission of His Majesty's Government to wear a cutaway coat and striped pants to the ceremony, would you agree to appoint me?"

"Well, Joe, you know how the British are about tradition. There's no way you are going to get permission, and I must name a new Ambassador soon."

"Will you give me two weeks?"

FDR nodded and Kennedy pulled up his pants and went out the door, leaving the President chuckling. Not long afterward he returned with the permission he had promised to obtain.

Kennedy wanted the ambassadorship because it was the most prestigious job in the diplomatic service and the one most unexpected for an Irish Catholic to hold. Roosevelt was intrigued with the appointment simply because it was unorthodox; but he also hoped that Kennedy, an outsider through and through, would be exactly the sort of man who could report on the increasingly menacing European situation without falling prey to the Anglophilia that had traditionally colored the views of American ambassadors to the Court of St. James's.

As the appointment was made public on December 9, 1937, Joe became a Boston hero, with the *Post* and the *American* running series on his career, including a genealogy headlined "Kennedy Family Has Royal Blood Antedating the King's." Al Smith called him "Mr. Irish-American," and Honey Fitz was quoted in the *New York Times* to the effect that the ambassadorship was "the most important job the Administration has to give out." Joe called his sister Loretta, the unofficial historian of the family, and asked her to locate all the old Boston Irish friends of his father and urge them to come to Logan Airport to see him off when he left to take ship in New York.

5.

ON FEBRUARY 23, 1938, JOSEPH
Kennedy sailed for England to make his fortune, just as his grandfather had
hoped to do nearly a century earlier when he left for America. Rose stayed
behind in the hospital; she was recuperating from an emergency appendec-
tomy which the children had found out about only when it was reported in
the newspapers. In addition to the ever present Irish handyman and valet
Eddie Moore, Kennedy took along several other aides. One was Harvey
Klemmer, formerly of the Maritime Commission. "We're going to London,"
Kennedy had joked when he informed Klemmer of the job, "but don't go
buying a lot of luggage. We're only going to get the family in the *Social
Register*. When that's done, we come on back and go out to Hollywood to
make some movies and some money."

All during the passage, Kennedy remained ebullient. Klemmer was convinced that war was coming, but the Ambassador—Kennedy had already
taken the title—wouldn't hear of it. "Oh, Christ, Harvey, drop that war
business. You're just a pessimist." But Klemmer held his ground. "No, it's
coming. There'll be war, and before it's over, your sons are going to go out
there and do and die like everyone else." A look of deep apprehension
crossed Kennedy's face and he quickly changed the subject.

Arriving in London, Kennedy quickly installed himself in the palatial
embassy at 9 Prince's Gate which J. P. Morgan had donated as a gift to the
American people, and established himself as boss of nearly two hundred
diplomatic service employees. He liked the patriotic motif of the embassy
landscaping—flower boxes with red geraniums, white daisies, and blue
forget-me-nots. But he was less certain about the decor within. "I have a

beautiful blue silk room,'' he wrote Jimmy Roosevelt soon after arriving, ''and all I need to make it perfect is a Mother Hubbard dress and a wreath to make me Queen of the May. If a fairy didn't design this room, I never saw one in my life.''

Kennedy immediately began cultivating the English press as assiduously as he had American newspapermen back in Washington. He held his first news conference at his embassy office, feet propped up on his desk and hands clasped behind his head, warning journalists that they must not expect him to develop into a statesman overnight. ''Right now,'' he continued with a candor unusual in the international diplomatic community, ''the average American isn't as interested in foreign affairs as in how Casey Stengel's Boston Bees [as the Braves were briefly known] are going to do next season.'' When he played his first round of golf on the Stokes Poges course in Buckinghamshire, he shot a hole-in-one off the second tee. If this stroke of luck was heaven-sent for someone seeking to get off to a good public relations start, so was the quip Kennedy came up with to accompany it: ''I am much happier being the father of nine children and making a hole-in-one than I would be as the father of one child making a hole-in-nine.'' The English press dubbed him ''The U.S.A.'s Nine-Child Envoy'' and ''The Father of His Country.''*

Rose arrived late in March, bringing everyone with her except Joe Junior and Jack, who were both at Harvard; Rosemary, who was in her special school in New York; and Eunice, who was to escort Rosemary to London after the term was over. Rose displaced some of the twenty-six embassy servants from their upstairs bedrooms to make space for the later arrivals and enlisted Kick as an assistant hostess. The younger children played in the upper stories of the cavernous embassy, telephoning each other from various rooms and making appointments to meet in certain corridors. Teddy took control of the elevator, asking housekeepers what floor they wanted as part of a game of ''department store.'' Concerned as always about exercise, Joe and Rose laid in a supply of bicycles for use on the immense marble terrace in the embassy's back yard.

The family had been so well covered by the press back home that after the Lindbergh kidnaping Rose had finally asked Henry Luce to feature them less often. But in London their every move made the front pages—Teddy taking an upside-down picture of the changing of the guard, Bobby's awkward attempts to begin a conversation with Princess Elizabeth at a party— and Rose didn't complain.

Over the next few weeks the entry into London high society continued at

---

*Kennedy's prodigious paternity was so talked about that someone actually did research and found that he was far from holding the record for most children by an employee of the federal government. A man who worked at the Treasury, one Andrew White, had seventeen.

a dizzying pace. Rose found herself taken under the wing of Air Attaché Michael Scanlon and his wife, Gladys, leaders of London's smart set and intimates of the Windsors and Wallis Simpson. She took voice lessons to plane the edges off the grating accent (one Englishman woundingly referred to it as a "Boston whinny"), and went to Paris with Gladys Scanlon to shop for gowns for herself and Kick and Rosemary for their formal presentation at court. Kick, who had gracefully put off a proposal from Lem Billings ("Come on, Lem, you're not the marrying kind") and who now kept up a regular correspondence with him, wrote Lem about the great event. ("Wish you could be here for it. I so often think of you when I meet a guy who thinks he's absolutely the tops and is just a big ham. What laughs you and Jack would get. Very few of them can take any kidding at all.... Anyway you are still the mystery man in my life.") The presentation had become a crucial event for her mother, who selected white net dresses for the girls and one of gold and silver embroidered lace over a white satin foundation for herself. The girls attended "curtsy schools" for days before the presentation. Rose borrowed a tiara of rubies and diamonds from Lady Bessborough. Fully dressed, she looked into the mirror and "felt like Cinderella." When she went to Joe's room to have him look her over, he grinned and said, "You're a knockout." The court ceremony went off beautifully, and no one appeared to notice when Rosemary stumbled slightly as she bowed before the Queen.

Soon life settled down to a normal pace. Teddy and Bobby went off to prep school each morning in gray flannel shorts and maroon blazers. Rose found a Montessori school in Hertfordshire for Rosemary, and the other girls entered the Sacred Heart Convent in Roehampton. One of their fellow students recalls that "they were like birds of paradise, bringing a glamour and worldliness that contrasted with the attitude of the dour daughters and displaced European aristocrats and English girls in tweeds." Pat was tall, with auburn hair and violet eyes; an "Irish beauty," the English called her with only slight condescension. Jean was still a little chubby and less dignified. On the first day of school, when the teacher pointed out a mistake she'd made in her arithmetic, she coolly eyed the figures on the paper and said, "Well, five goes into nine in America; I don't see why it doesn't in England." Eunice chased the ball aggressively in her first field hockey game, yelling, "Hey, hey," as if it were a touch-football scrimmage back home. Afterward one of her teammates informed her that nice girls in England didn't behave that way. Others at the Sacred Heart school were struck by what one called Eunice's "rather alarming" piety—striking St. Theresa poses while praying in chapel, arms outstretched and head bowed in histrionic prayer; insisting on wiring Jack the night before the first Friday of every month to remind him of his first Friday obligation.

Kick, no mere schoolgirl any longer, but launched into society, managed with grace what Eunice did not. "She had an absolutely wonderful sense of humor," remembers Fiona Gore, one of her new acquaintances in London's most exclusive social circle; she was "bright-eyed and constantly teasing like the rest of the Kennedys, but without the abrasiveness of her brothers. She would manage to get us all doing crazy things, strip away our reserve. One time a group of us were eating dinner, and someone tossed a dinner roll to someone else. Suddenly we were all throwing rolls at each other. Kick had started it, of course, and by the end was not only throwing rolls like everyone else, but standing on the table and throwing them. If someone else had done that, it might have been rude or shocking; but she had this way about her that made it seem absolute liberation."

Joseph Kennedy was coarse, rich, and Irish, a completely new experience for the London diplomatic community. In the United States his behavior had made some regard him as a sort of rhinestone in the rough, but in England he was seen as the real thing—a representative American. Some of the nicer people were shocked when he called the Queen a "cute trick"; but Her Majesty herself appeared amused by it, just as she did when he rushed across a ballroom floor to grab the first dance with her in defiance of court protocol, which insisted that her equerry should first invite him to make the request. Some aristocrats smiled at the way he would insist that Kathleen be properly chaperoned at Wimbledon and then disappear into the crowd himself with a buxom blonde. But soon he was on a first-name basis not only with the foreign policy establishment but also with important outsiders like the newspaper magnate Lord Beaverbrook and the Astor family.

Yet from the outset, Kennedy made it clear that, unlike other ambassadors who'd gotten their jobs as political rewards and used them simply for social enhancement, he intended to be involved in the development of American foreign policy. The Roosevelt Administration's view of Europe and the world was just then in flux. Never patient with systematic thought, FDR had no overarching policy, preferring to make it up as he went. Mistrusting the professionals in the State Department, he relied on cables and reports from his ambassadors. It was a situation tailor-made for someone like Kennedy, who had also decided that the careerists in the State Department were "a bunch of cookie pushers." He plunged into the job, resolving to be equal to a situation growing in menace every day.

Just eleven days after Kennedy arrived in London, the Nazis pushed into Austria. First cabling that Hitler was bluffing, he afterward maintained that the *Anschluss* had no long-range significance, citing a dinner he attended with Chamberlain at which the Prime Minister "likened Germany to a boa constrictor that had eaten a good deal and was trying to digest the meal before taking on anything else." Although twenty years older than Kennedy, the Prime Minister was much like the Ambassador: a self-made businessman, a pragmatist. He had met with Hitler and didn't like him—he was "uncouth and certainly not the kind of fellow one would like to go around the world with on a two-wheeled bicycle," Chamberlain said—but felt that the Nazi dictator was guided by self-interest and a desire for an equal economic participation in Europe; that he was "a man who could be relied upon when he had given his word." Kennedy liked this view. He liked the Prime Minister's decency, the dignity and reserve that some who had known the Kennedys found reminiscent of P. J. Kennedy himself. Over the increasingly hectic months ahead, the two men became friends. In a letter to the political commentator Walter Lippmann Kennedy called one of Chamberlain's appeasing speeches about Nazi aggression a "masterpiece": "I sat spellbound in the diplomatic gallery and heard it all. It impressed me as a combination of high morals and politics such as I had never witnessed."

Chamberlain's most clamorous support came from the Astor family, and soon the Kennedys were frequent visitors at the magnificent country estate of Cliveden. The radical British paper the *Week* had coined the term "Cliveden Set" for the group that supported the Astors' philosophy of appeasement. Yet Cliveden was more a salon than a conspiracy, dominated by the American-born and often outrageous Nancy Astor, first woman member of Parliament, who made her home a clearing house for people who shared her views on the world political situation. One was Kennedy. Another was Charles Lindbergh, now unlucky Lindy, in self-imposed exile after the kidnaping and murder of his young son, traveling through Europe giving out accounts of the fearsome power of Goering's *Luftwaffe*. In a diary entry for May 5, 1938, the American aviator wrote: "Anne and I took the train to London for a lunch engagement at Lady Astor's. In addition to Lord and Lady Astor, there were Mr. and Mrs. George Bernard Shaw, Ambassador Kennedy and Ambassador Bullitt . . . Kennedy interested me greatly. He is not the usual type of politician or diplomat. His views on the European situation seem intelligent and interesting. I hope to see more of him."

In appointing him to the Court of St. James's, Roosevelt had counted on Kennedy's remaining what he had always been, an opportunist. The President could not have predicted that the European situation would act as a catalyst on the new Ambassador, causing him to become obdurate in his commitment to stop the war or, that failing, at least isolate America from the conflict. His views had something to do with the background in business which made him feel that peace was a precondition for trade and commerce and thus for prosperity; that war caused social dislocation and made society vulnerable to disastrous creeds such as communism. But ultimately it was instinct rather than philosophy that made him react as he did: an Irish atavism involving fear of that sudden cataclysm which would sweep away a lifetime's patiently accumulated gains. In joining with the Cliveden Set, Lindbergh, Chamberlain, and others who wanted to appease Hitler, Joe Kennedy undertook the one great crusade of his life.

But in the late spring of 1938, Kennedy's two great aims of furthering his career and preventing war did not seem incompatible, or, for that matter, impossible. Impatient with the ponderous machinery of the State Department, he began to act as a free-lance, proposing himself as a sort of super-ambassador for the whole European continent who could resolve problems through personal initiative. He met with Herbert von Dirksen, the German Ambassador to England, and, according to von Dirksen, told him he would like to "improve German–United States relations" and undertake a "tour of study" to Germany. Kennedy took a "dim view" of the Soviet Union and believed Hitler's regime had been economically beneficial for the German people. Noting that he felt Germany should have a free hand in the East and that Chamberlain was probably eager for a settlement, Kennedy also said that the American press and the President himself were strongly influenced by Jews. "It was not so much the fact that we wanted to get rid of the Jews that was harmful to us," von Dirksen reported in a cable to Berlin, "but rather the loud clamour with which we accompanied this purpose. He himself understood our Jewish policy completely; he was from Boston and there, in one golf club and in other clubs, no Jews had been admitted for the past 50 years."

While holding these and other private conversations, Kennedy was also involved in a quite public wooing of opinion makers at home. He'd begun to send back letters filled with his observations about international events and headed "Private and Confidential." These attempts to keep his name in the public eye at home seemed to work (although the honor of getting one of these communiqués was somewhat diminished when the recipient discovered that several other people had gotten the identical bulletin). A major article entitled "Will Joe Kennedy Run for President?" ran in *Liberty* magazine, and when a poll showed him running fifth among Democratic hopefuls if FDR decided against a third term, Kennedy glowed for days.

On June 15, the Ambassador returned to America to fan these political hopes and to attend Joe Junior's Harvard graduation. He was in contact with reporters by ship-to-shore radio, and when the *Queen Mary* docked, the questions he had to field were primarily about his presidential hopes. Krock outdid himself in a column about his good friend: "Here is Kennedy back again, the rage of London, the best copy in the British press, his counsel steadily sought by statesmen of the country to which he is accredited, his influence manifest and powerful in all matters in which the United States has an interest in Great Britain. . . . Here he is back again, undazzled by such a taking up socially and officially as no American perhaps has known abroad since Franklin's day."

All this talk bothered Roosevelt, whose affection for people diminished in exact proportion to their potential for becoming rivals to his throne. When the "Private and Confidential" letters were shown to him he became annoyed enough to accede to those around him who wanted Kennedy's wings clipped, and he allowed press secretary Steve Early to leak copies of the

correspondence to the *Chicago Tribune*, along with a backgrounder that led
to an unattributed story that the President and the Ambassador had met in
a "frigid atmosphere because Mr. Roosevelt had received positive evidence
that Kennedy hopes to use the Court of St. James's as a stepping stone to the
White House in 1940." Kennedy was furious at what he regarded as back
stabbing, although when he brought it up the President artfully disavowed
any part in the story.

He was further frustrated at Harvard, which along with Roosevelt's presidency was one of the few institutions that did not bend to his will. In 1936,
Kennedy had run for a seat on the board of governors, finishing tenth in a
field of twelve and angrily attributing his defeat to anti-Catholic bias. Now,
back from England, Kennedy was angling to get an honorary degree. When
he heard that the degree committee had decided that the ambassadorship was
an insufficient mark of distinction for such an honor, he tried to save face
by refusing the degree in advance, as if it were some kind of political offer.
Roosevelt chuckled. "Can you imagine Joe Kennedy declining an honorary
degree from Harvard?" The Ambassador did not attend Joe Junior's commencement exercises, giving out a public statement that he wanted to stay
near his son Jack, who was ill.

Kennedy returned to Europe with his two sons in late June, traveling on the
French liner *Normandie* because what he had seen during his tenure as
Maritime Commissioner had left him with little faith in American ships. The
idea was that his boys would learn statecraft up close, like the sons of another
famous Ambassador to England from the Bay State, Charles Francis Adams.

Young Joe had grown up to be tall, powerful, quite handsome, able to flash
his father's smile and his steely look as well. He had the Ambassador's taste
in women—showgirls at El Morocco, the Stork Club, and other New York
night spots, rather than the Irish Catholic debs who stalked him in Boston.
He had tried hard to be popular at Harvard, but some of his classmates
found him difficult to take. Afraid of being thought of as "rich" and thus
taken advantage of, he had placed a sign beside his pipe tobacco on his desk
asking anyone who took any to leave a quarter in a jar. It was felt that he
wanted to be friends with the best athletes and always to have the prettiest
girls at the party. He had not gotten into one of the top clubs and it rankled
when he had to settle for the Pi Eta. "It was better than nothing," says
James Rousmaniere, one of his brother Jack's roommates, "but it created a
bad feeling in him." Joe had close friends like Timothy J. Reardon, Jr., all-
American quarterback whom he had met when they both went out for freshman football and Joe asked to throw some extra passes before practice
because he had "stiff hands." But most people, says Rousmaniere, "wanted
to dislike Joe and found ample reason to confirm their feelings. He had a
mean streak. He would kid people until they bled. He couldn't stop." He

was like his father, committed to bulling his way through situations, making up in persistence what he lacked in grace. It showed in the way he played football—"with his face," as his friends kidded him. "Joe would put his head in the way if he had to make a block or a tackle," one friend recalled. "He was fearless although he had no great ability."

The center of Young Joe's life was his family. While he was in London studying with Harold Laski, his roommate there, Aubrey Whitelaw, had been struck by the way he kept photographs of his brothers and sisters on the top of his dresser, occasionally talking about what each would do when they were grown as if he were addressing them personally. He would go to Laski's jammed lectures and then to the more select teas held afterward at Laski's home. Young Joe made no secret of his ambition: to be the first Irish Catholic president of the United States if his father didn't get there before him. ("We used to needle him about it," his close Harvard friend Tom Schriber recalls. "We called him 'the old Prexy.'") Laski would often expound some thorny point of political science and then turn to young Kennedy and ask, "Now, Joe, what will you do about this when you are President?" And Joe would try manfully to answer the question, his sincerity winning the socialist's respect in a way that his intellect alone could not have. During the midterm break the Laskis invited him to accompany them on a visit to the Soviet Union; he enjoyed their company and was impressed by the country until he came to the Anti-Religious Museum.

Young Joe had returned home from his first stay in England ready to demonstrate his new sophistication by arguing against his father's views. "The Communists," he told his brothers and sisters, "are interested in the welfare of the people. They take more interest in them than under the capitalistic system. They share with each other so that nobody is really poor. Dad doesn't know much about it, but I think it's great." There had been ferocious arguments at dinner, with Kennedy finally becoming angry enough to send Young Joe away from the table. ("He had to leave without finishing dinner so often that I thought it was a miracle he ever gained any weight at all," his cousin Mary Lou McCarthy said.) But secretly Joe Kennedy was well pleased with his son, knowing he would always be a family loyalist. And indeed, by the time Young Joe reached his senior year at Harvard, whatever influence Laski may have had was gone, and he was consistently defending his father's positions, notably in his senior thesis, "Intervention in Spain," a study of the anti-interventionist Hands Off Spain Committee in which he echoed the Ambassador's criticism of the Spanish Republicans as "a bunch of Communists and atheists."

However conservative he might have become in politics, however, he was a radical in terms of risk taking, the daring he'd shown as a boy having developed into a pronounced tendency toward heroism and a contempt for consequences his friends found unsettling. Visiting Wyntoon, the Hearst family's country place at the foot of Mount Shasta, Joe had decided he must swim the freezing and swift McCloud River. William Randolph Hearst, Jr., recalls: "I'd always been told never to go near it because the water was so cold; not even to fall into it, because it would numb your muscles and you wouldn't be able to swim. Joe was the first guy I ever saw do it." Later, at St. Moritz, he jumped onto a bobsled for the first time and shot down a run where experienced bobsledders had lost their lives, going so fast that he came close to the world's record time.

Joe Junior and Jack called each other "Brother," a term neither Bobby nor Teddy ever adopted, as if acknowledging that they were the brothers who counted, the near-equals who would struggle for precedence in the future. For the time being, however, Jack pleaded no contest, and resigned himself to living in the large shadow his brother cast. "I want you to know I'm not bright like my brother Joe," he had told the headmaster at Winthrop House when he got to Harvard. And now, accompanying his father back to England, he was still thin, looking younger than his age, possessing an odd combination of vulnerability and high spirits that people found attractive. He had tried to play football but had injured his back, suffering the disc problems on which all his health problems would later be blamed. The year before, he had gotten onto the swimming team, and wrote Lem at Princeton a series of letters showing his excitement.

On January 20, 1937, Jack wrote, "Dear Pneumoan:... Beat the number one man on backs [by] ten yards. Supposed to swim in a meet today but have a fucking cold contracted from you so can't. Still out for boxing due to the coach labelling me "the most natural boxer in the freshman class." I am not very big or fast but I must be natural ..." A few weeks later, he wrote, "Dear LeMoan:... The swimming is going pretty good. Am swimming on the medley relay team and so far have beaten my max every week. Have taken seven seconds off my time, so Billings you ought to be right up my alley and you know which alley," and a few days after that: "Dear Kirk: ... Have been in strict training for a month now and get off tomorrow night as we swim Yale. Have taken eight seconds off my time and am now down to 107 in the 100. Am going to swim in the medley but it looks pretty tough as Yale has pretty good men ..."

He was also boasting about his sex life. "I can now get tail as often and as free as I want which is a step in the right direction," he wrote Lem shortly after New Year's 1938, and a few weeks later, in anticipation of a trysting visit to his friend at Princeton, entreated him, "Get me a room way away from all others and especially from your girl as I don't want you coming in for a chat in the middle as usual and discussing how sore my cock is." But for all the bravado, his health remained poor and much of his time was spent shuttling between his bed in the infirmary and the practice pool, drinking milkshakes to try to build up bulk against the mysterious malady which had been with him since he was a boy. Bouts of sinus trouble frustrated his efforts also, and even a circumcision ("As for your rather unnatural interest in my becoming circumcised," he wrote Lem, using his nickname for his penis, "JJ has never been in better shape or doing better service").

Young Joe had occasionally talked to swimming coach Harold Ulen about Jack's progress and was amused one time to hear that his kid brother had hidden in the shower to escape photographers who were interested in him, he feared, only because he was a Kennedy. As the elder of the two, Joe Junior pressed his advantage on all fronts. Once when he saw Jack with a beautiful girl at the Stork Club, Joe had him paged, and while Jack was at the telephone picked her up and took her home. (In the cab he and Reardon flipped a coin to see who would "make the love pitch." Reardon lost and had to wait outside the girl's apartment for his friend until three in the morning. When they got back to Bronxville Jack was waiting in the bedroom, "skinny as Mahatma Gandhi" and "mad as hell.") On one miserable Cape day, the sea was so rough that a championship race Jack and Young Joe had entered was called off. Reardon, who had walked down to the water with some of the other Kennedy kids "to see the two heroes off," asked Joe what the commotion was about. "Ah, these cream puffs say the sea is too bad for us to race," Joe answered. Then he called out, "Hey, Jack, come here." They climbed in the boat and went out together and then "Jack either jumped or was pushed and Joe came around and picked him up and brought him back in, and said, 'There. What the hell do you mean it's too rough?'" (The race was still canceled.)

More easygoing than Joe Junior, and free from his obsessive need to justify himself, Jack had gotten into Spee, one of the better clubs at Harvard. He had also begun to have "serious" girls. One of these was Frances Ann Cannon, an attractive Sarah Lawrence coed, whom he arranged to see at the 21 Club whenever he visited New York and whom the family thought he might actually ask to marry him. ("Jack is taking out Frances Ann Cannon this weekend," Kick wrote Rose, "so we can all hardly wait.") But a few days later she invited him and his friend Charlie Houghton to her mother's apartment and introduced them to her new fiancé, the writer John Hersey. It was characteristic of his serious relationships that despite what he led his sisters and others to think, they weren't really that serious. "If the subject of marriage came up," remembers Charlotte McDonnell, who was also seen as a possible fiancée, "Jack would never talk about it directly. He would say 'Torb [MacDonald, a Harvard friend] thinks it's a good idea. Of course it would be ideal if you were a rich Italian from Boston.'" Even the dating game received only a part of his attention. "It wouldn't be unusual," Charlotte McDonnell says, "for him to call me and say, 'Do you want to go to the theater? We'll have dinner first,' and then the next thing you'd know there was no dinner. The downstairs phone would ring and Lem would be on the other end, saying with a giggle, 'Well, Jack's tied up. He's having a massage.' Then Lem would come over to get me and bring me to Jack and maybe we'd go to the theater and someplace afterward.''*

Jack had not only accepted his place in the family but had come to see that being a foil to his older brother had certain advantages. As his roommate James Rousmaniere observes, ''I believe that Jack was very glad Joe had taken on the obligation of his father's ambition. He felt that Joe, as the number-one son, had to face a lot, as it worked out, that he would just as soon avoid. The situation gave him a certain independence that he valued.'' Young Joe had to be committed to the Kennedy iconography and was; meanwhile Jack could quietly decide not to be overwhelmed by the family or the father. He was feeling his way toward independence in gestures whose implications weren't always obvious, even to him. When he had gone to Europe with Lem, for instance, he had approached the Spanish embroilment with the Ambassador's pro-Franco prejudices; but the letters he wrote home showed an inquisitive mind impatient with family orthodoxy: ''While I felt that perhaps it would be far better for Spain if Franco should win—as he would strengthen and unite Spain—yet at the beginning the [Republican] government was in the right morally speaking as its program was similar to the New Deal.'' At Harvard a friend once saw Jack going off to church on a holy day. He was normally far from pious and the friend asked him about it. '' He got this odd, hard look on his face. 'This is one of the things I do for my father,' he said. 'The rest I do for myself.' ''

When the Ambassador docked in London with his sons, he was annoyed to find that Honey Fitz, who had been visiting Rose and the smaller children in his absence, had helped himself to the engraved ambassadorial invitation cards, filling them in and sending them to pals back in North Boston. Rose had also taken her father to Cliveden, where he had met the Prime Minister and his wife and spent the evening trying to figure out if he was related to the Irish Mrs. Chamberlain, whose maiden name had been Fitzgerald.

Jack took up his work helping his father at the embassy with enthusiasm: ''Met the King this morning at Court Levee,'' he wrote his friend Lem. ''It takes place in the morning and you wear tails. The King stands and you go up and bow. Met Queen Mary and was at tea with the Princess Elizabeth, with whom I made a great deal of time. Thursday night I'm going to Court in my new silk breeches which are cut to my crotch tightly and in which I look mighty attractive.''

---

*The romance between Charlotte and Jack was broken up by Charlotte's father, James McDonnell, one of the ''First Irish Family'' patriarchs who despised Joe Kennedy as an unscrupulous upstart. ''Charlotte used to weep on my shoulder because old James McDonnell forbade Jack Kennedy ever to see her again,'' Charlotte's Manhattanville College roommate, Ann Kelley, recalls. ''He said he'd disown her and throw her out if she did: 'No child of that man is entering my home!' he said.''

While Jack explored London society, Joe Junior reestablished himself as the leader of the clan. He spent time with Teddy, who, though still fat, resembled him strongly; both had bluer eyes than the others' and a physique and constitution more clearly Fitzgerald. Joe Junior praised Pat and Eunice and his goddaughter Jean, and complimented Rosemary as the ''prettiest of them all.'' But Kick was the sister he was closest to. They got up early in the morning to ride, cantering down Rotten Row together, and in the evenings they made the rounds of the great estates—not only Cliveden but also Chatsworth House, seat of the powerful Cavendish family. Kick, who was as ambitious as her brother, was going out with William Cavendish, Marquess of Hartington, eldest son of the Duke of Devonshire and heir to over 180,000 acres with estates all over England and revenues of over a quarter of a million pounds a year.

Kick was just eighteen and Billy, as everyone called him, was almost twenty. They were a study in contrasts: she upstart Boston Irish; his blood line so refined he had been mentioned as a suitable husband for Princess Elizabeth. She was petite, bright and pretty; he was saturnine and well over six feet tall, stooped, forever clasping his hands behind his back or chafing them together nervously as if uncertain what to do with them. She was all on the surface, like a plant (Billy later provided the simile) whose roots have been pinched to force a luxuriant external growth; he was something of an intellectual, spending hours looking at his family's collection of rare books, one of the best in Europe, including a Gutenberg Bible and a first edition of Milton's *Paradise Lost,* and brooding about whether people liked him for himself or because he would one day be a duke.

Billy's sister Anne felt that he was one of those aristocrats ''you would have thought had been wiped out in the First War,'' and that Kick's teasing irreverence was just what he needed. (''Hello,'' she would say to the butler answering the phone at Chatsworth, ''is the King perchance in his castle today?'') His cousin Fiona Gore thought them a ''wonderful'' couple. ''Here was this lively American girl who through some odd circumstance had become the toast of the town, and she was paying all this attention to Billy. It gave him such confidence. She swept him right off his oh so steady feet.'' They sparkled as a couple, yet it was understood that they would never get too serious because the Cavendishes were not only the leading Protestant peers of the realm but had a virulently anti-Irish and anti-Catholic background. They had been nobles since Henry VIII gave Sir William Cavendish a share of the booty coming from confiscated lands of the Catholic Church; Billy's maternal grandfather, Lord Salisbury, had been a Prime Minister noted for comparing the Irish ability for self-government to that of Hottentots; Billy's grand-uncle on his father's side, Lord Frederick Cavendish, had been a Draconian Governor General of Ireland, and had been murdered at Dublin's Phoenix Park, a site pointed out to Rose by Honey Fitz as a Catholic monument when they visited in 1908. And so the romance

—proscribed by the Cavendishes as well as the Kennedys—took on the overtones of a forbidden love, or, as Billy himself said, "a Romeo and Juliet
thing."

Joe Kennedy was pleased to see how easily the children moved through
English society. Perceiving the limitless future that seemed to lie in front of
them made him even more concerned about the clouds of war lowering over
Europe as Hitler edged toward Czechoslovakia. One speech he gave that
summer had a particularly personal aside: "I should like to ask you if you
know of any dispute or controversy existing in the world which is worth the
life of your son, or anyone else's son?" But Secretary of State Cordell Hull
deleted the sentence of the text, and when FDR heard about it he said of
Kennedy: "This young man needs his wrists slapped rather hard." Despite
his annoyance at these unilateral attempts to make policy, however, the
President still saw his Ambassador as potentially useful in his evolving
third-term plans, especially if Roosevelt's possible rival, Vice President
John Nance Garner, decided to strike a deal with Irish Catholic Jim Farley
and give Farley the second spot on a Garner ticket. "In that event," Interior
Secretary Harold Ickes theorized in his diary, "the President might have to
turn to Joe Kennedy as a candidate for Vice President. That would match a
Roman Catholic against a Roman Catholic. While Farley would be able to
command certain undoubted political advantages, Kennedy would be able to
command the great conservative business support and his campaign would
be well financed since he himself is a very rich man."

Always an adroit puppeteer in domestic politics, the President had begun
to pull more strings in foreign affairs, balancing between isolation and
internationalism, acceding to the strong antiwar mood at home but trying to
take advantage of opportunities to thwart Hitler in Europe. Kennedy's stubborn advocacy of his own ideas made this performance far more difficult.
Kennedy liked Chamberlain while Roosevelt thought him "slippery"; the
President admired the Prime Minister's outspoken critic Winston Churchill
while the Ambassador thought him a drunkard and an imperialist blowhard.
Kennedy had gone to Britain expecting to be an antagonist but had found a
large number of the English believing as he did. Roosevelt was amazed by
the network of ironies: "Who would have thought that the English could
take into camp a red-headed Irishman?"

On September 12 Hitler denounced the Czechs at Nuremberg. Two days
later Chamberlain was in Berchtesgaden for a talk with Hitler. As the Prime
Minister was returning with the Fuehrer's demands, Kennedy was also going
into action to preserve the peace. He sent a summons to Charles Lindbergh,
who was in Paris spreading his gospel of the invincibility of the Nazi war
machine. Lindbergh arrived in London the next day in a drizzling rain and
made his way to the embassy. Wanting his family to be present at the history

he was about to help make, Kennedy arranged for Rose and the older children to join them at lunch. As they ate, he painted the diplomatic picture in harsh dark strokes: if Hitler moved, Chamberlain would be unable to carry England any further toward compromise. Lindbergh then talked of air power and how long it would take the Germans to level Paris or London, insisting that "Germany has such a preponderance of war planes that she can bomb any city in Europe with comparatively little resistance." Kennedy asked Lindbergh to put what he had said in writing and the next day cabled the contents to the State Department.

Kennedy slipped a copy of the Lindbergh report into Chamberlain's hands just before he flew to Bad Godesberg on September 22 for another meeting with Hitler about Czechoslovakia. The Prime Minister was prepared to accept almost all of Hitler's demands, but on arriving found that the Fuehrer had upped the ante. Chamberlain returned with an ultimatum from the Germans which was impossible even for appeasers to accept. London officials ordered trenches dug and gas masks handed out.

Kennedy sent the younger children off to Ireland, where they would be safe in the event of a surprise Nazi attack, and wrote to Krock: "I'm feeling very blue myself today because I am starting to think about sending Rose and the children back to America and stay here *alone* for how long God only knows. Maybe never see them again . . ." Two days later, with Hitler's ultimatum about to expire, Kennedy phoned Rose in Scotland, where she was once again traveling by herself, and told her to get back because war was imminent and they needed to make plans for the family.

Meanwhile, Chamberlain had gone to Munich for a four-power conference on the situation. Germany, Italy, and Great Britain were represented; the Czechs were excluded. On September 30, after thirteen hours of bargaining, Chamberlain returned to England; he emerged from his plane carrying a black umbrella and waving an agreement giving Germany Czechoslovakia's Sudetenland—an area containing almost all of the country's riches and national defenses—and announcing that he had bought "peace in our time."

Kennedy was elated. "I have just gone through the most exciting month of my life," he wrote back to Senator James Byrnes of South Carolina. "Between trying to keep up my contacts so we could know what was really going on before it actually happened so we would not be caught unprepared and contemplating the possibility of the bombing of London with eight children as prospective victims, well, it has just been a great page in my life history." It had all turned out exactly as he had predicted six months earlier, just after he arrived in England, when he wrote in one of his Private and Confidential letters: "Germany will get whatever it wants in Czechoslovakia without sending a single soldier across the border."

In the afterglow of Chamberlain's Munich negotiations, with most Britons hailing the bargain, it seemed that Kennedy had once again gambled big and won. Over the next weeks he plunged into a euphoric defense of Munich, speaking at every forum available. Using his eye for details, he asked Will Hays to censor the views of Englishmen who dissented with the settlement in a newsreel Paramount made during the Czech crisis. He was also back in touch with German Ambassador von Dirksen, amending his earlier proposal of a visit with the caveat that "he would go to Germany only if he were certain of speaking to the Fuehrer," as the Ambassador cabled home.

Kennedy's major post-Munich effort was the Navy League's annual Trafalgar Day dinner. He was the first American ambassador ever chosen to keynote this affair, and his speech not only defended Chamberlain but proposed the Munich settlement as a guideline for future rapprochements, claiming that the resolution of the Czech crisis had shown that it was possible to "get along" with dictatorships.

Reaction to the speech in Britain was cautious. But in America the White House was flooded with telegrams and phone calls asking if American policy had changed. Kennedy was attacked by journalists like Walter Lippmann and old friends like Frankfurter, as well as old enemies in the State Department, although many among the latter were gleeful because, as one of them said, the speech had "defeated any political ambitions which [Kennedy] might have had." Jack, who had returned to Harvard and was the only member of the family in the United States, could manage only a halfhearted endorsement, writing his father that "while it seemed to be unpopular with the Jews, etc., [the speech] was considered to be very good by everyone who wasn't bitterly anti-fascist . . ."

FDR, the sometime idealist who was really supremely pragmatic, saw that public opinion on the United States role in international affairs was finally beginning a seismic shift. Kennedy, the opportunist who was suddenly involved in an inviolable principle, did not. His isolationism became more entrenched and unyielding at exactly the moment that the President was moving toward internationalism in a way that would cut the ground out from under his Ambassador. When, in a radio address delivered a week after the Trafalgar speech, Roosevelt seemed to repudiate Kennedy's views ("There can be no peace if the reign of law is replaced by a recurrent sanctification of force; there can be no peace if national policy adopts as a deliberate instrument the threat of war"), Kennedy felt that he had been betrayed and wrote Jimmy Byrnes: "I'm so goddamned mad I can't see!"

While the controversy over the Trafalgar Day speech was still seething, an event occurred which placed it (and the Munich negotiations) in a different context. Nazi mobs rampaged through Germany's Jewish communities, smashing homes, raping and beating Jews. The shattered glass of Jewish shop windows gave a name to the horror: *Kristallnacht*. By the time it was over, hundreds of synagogues and thousands of Jewish businesses were destroyed. In addition to the many Jews murdered, some thirty thousand had been detained for transshipment to Buchenwald, Dachau, and Sachsenhausen.

Kennedy was at least a casual anti-Semite in his personal life, but in the wake of the German action, he went to work unilaterally to deal with the issue. Soon the *New York Times* was reporting that he had worked out with Chamberlain a program for a total emigration of German Jews to Africa and the Western Hemisphere under the joint administration of Britain and the United States. But the State Department, which had not been consulted, ignored Kennedy; American Jewry wasn't interested because the plan was in conflict with their ideas about a Palestinian homeland; and the President, who saw it as an attempt by Kennedy to recapture the political momentum the Trafalgar Day speech had cost him, didn't even bother to comment.

It was the first time in Kennedy's life that he had been mired in a situation he couldn't affect by some bold stroke, the first time the pendulum which had always come in his direction (this was his own metaphor) was now clearly swinging away. As his credibility and influence in Washington ebbed day by day, one of his few comforts was his family, especially Young Joe, who was back in London after a grand tour on a diplomatic passport that had taken him to Prague, Warsaw, Leningrad, Stockholm, and Berlin. Joe had found Russia grimmer than it seemed when he visited with the Laskis; he was more impressed with Germany. (''They are really a marvelous people,'' he had written home, ''and it is going to be an awful tough thing to keep them from getting what they want.'') He tried to help his father— publicly supporting the plan to get the Jews out of Germany and privately agreeing that U. S. Jews were trying to compromise America's neutrality.

As that fall deepened into winter, father and son took pleasure in each other's company as they hadn't time to do for many years. They rode horses together in the morning. On Saturdays they walked with Teddy to the sailing pool in Hyde Park. Joe Junior put his little brother's boat in the water and then sat back with his father as Teddy ran to retrieve it. The Ambassador, who hadn't sat much in his life, sat and watched his first and last born, brackets of his paternity. The moment was made more poignant by the fact that almost everyone in Europe felt this was the calm before the storm.

While Young Joe took the rest of the family to St. Moritz for a winter vacation, the Ambassador went home on the *Queen Mary* to try to repair his relations with Roosevelt. Flying to Washington from New York, he spent two hours at the White House discussing the Munich Pact and trying once again to bring up his plan for the resettlement of Germany's Jews. When he departed, he left a memorandum his London staff had worked up about what he saw as America's three possible responses in the event of Britain's collapse: trying to overturn Nazism; retreating to Fortress America; or—his own preference—going along with the division of the world into spheres of influence (the United States, Russia, Germany, Japan, France, and England each controlling its own zone). This program, which somewhat resembled the ward system in Boston during his father's day, was never officially commented upon by the White House or the State Department.

From Washington Kennedy went to Palm Beach with Jack, who had decided to stay out of Harvard for the spring semester to return to London with his father. The Ambassador sat naked at the poolside "bullpen," gleaming in the Florida sun from repeated applications of cocoa butter, as he held off-the-record briefings for Damon Runyon, Walter Winchell, Colonel McCormick of the *Chicago Tribune,* and others—a "virtual publicity bureau," as one Boston reporter saw it. Rather than feeling defensive about Munich, Kennedy boasted to Winchell that his decision to bring Lindbergh to London at the height of the Czech crisis had influenced Chamberlain not to challenge the Nazis.

When he got back to London with Jack in mid-February, there was a cable waiting from Joe Junior, who had left to witness the climactic phase of the Spanish Civil War: "Sorry I missed you. Arrived safely in Valencia. Going Madrid tonight." Concerned but proud, Kennedy shook his head after reading the message. "I wish he would stay out of the firing. His mother will die when she hears he is in Madrid." Yet he gave his son's itinerary to the press and was pleased to see him called "a young crisis hunter."

Joe Junior had gone directly to the heart of the Spanish darkness. He was at Barcelona when it fell, and then went on to Madrid while it was under siege by Franco's troops, groping for his own contacts with fifth columnists. Antonio Garrigues, later Spanish Ambassador to the United States, was a member of the Franco underground. "Joseph became deeply enthused in these activities," he recalls, "which, as all decidedly dangerous ones, were really absorbing. He even joined us in some of our 'missions' in Madrid." Putting himself in constant danger more from a sense of adventure than from political commitment (he was once spread-eagled against a wall by a group of soldiers and saved only by his diplomatic passport), he walked the city's streets in his gray flannel trousers and V-neck sweater, an Ivy Leaguer present at the final agony of the Republic. (When he came home he brought a piece of shrapnel in his suitcase, saying to Ted Reardon and others: "See this? It just barely missed. I picked it out of my coat when I was on the roof of the Embassy.") "The entrance of the Nationalist troops into Madrid was not a glamorous one," he wrote in an article his father helped him get published in the *Atlantic.* "The city was taken prematurely by Franco sympathizers within the city. Some daring ones rode through the streets with the Nationalist flag in their cars ... Soon the old city, sick to death of war, had Nationalist flags in nearly every building."

While Madrid was falling, Pope Pius XI died and the Ambassador lobbied successfully to be named U.S. representative at the coronation of the new Pope, the former Cardinal Pacelli, who'd been a house guest of the Kennedys in Bronxville during his American tour in 1936. (Rose had roped off the sofa the Cardinal sat on at their house, keeping it as a relic of the visit.) With everyone in the family except Young Joe present, the commotion when they appeared at the ceremony necessitated a shift in the seating arrangements that caused Count Ciano, Mussolini's son-in-law and Minister of Foreign Affairs, to threaten to leave in protest.

The next day the Kennedy family had a private audience with the Pope, who blessed their suitcase full of rosaries and then reminisced about his trip to America. Teddy afterward told American journalists how he had climbed up on the papal knee and chatted. "I told my sister Patricia I wasn't frightened at all. The Pope patted my head and told me I was a smart little fellow. He gave me the first rosary beads from the table before he gave my sister any."

"Just got back from Rome where we had a great time," Jack wrote Lem when they landed in London. "Pacelli is now riding high, so it's good you bowed and grovelled like you did when you met him. Teddy received his 1st communion from him, the first time that a Pope has ever done this in the last couple of hundred years. He gave Dad and I communion with Eunice at the same time at a private mass and all in all it was very impressive.... They want to give Dad the title of Duke which will be hereditary and go to all of his family which will make me Duke John of Bronxville and perhaps if you suck around sufficiently I might knight you. However, Kirk, he's not going to accept it, so don't say anything about it—be sure, because I realize that this would be a great opening for that sense of humor. Went to Court in my knee breeches and made my gracious bow for the King and Queen, and was really quite a figure.... Enjoyed the issue of the Choate news. My God, they all sound like fairies, both faculty and student body." He added a P.S.: "Everyone thinks war inevitable before the year is out. I personally don't, though Dad does."

After the trip to the Vatican, Jack went to France and stayed with Ambassador Bullitt in Paris, where he had lunch with the Lindberghs. "The most attractive couple I've ever seen" he wrote in May 1939 to Lem, who, back in the States, was selling Coca-Cola dispensers to drugstores and soda fountains to support himself through Princeton. "She takes a rotten picture and is really as pretty as hell and terribly nice." Writing from France a few days later Jack tried to analyze the increasingly dangerous European situation: "Just listened to Hitler's speech which they consider bad, though it's too early to tell. Things were looking better this last two weeks with the formation of the 'Peace Front.' The situation is so damn complicated that it is impossible to estimate the difficulties over there. For example: in trying to get Russia into the Peace Front, they have to be able to have her bring troops in case Germany attacks Poland or Roumania. However, Poland and Roumania have a defense alliance against Russia which they fear almost as much as Germany.'' Coolly noting that the gathering storm of war which was causing his father near-hysteria was ''damn interesting,'' Jack added a postscript showing that he continued to be more interested in the world of Eros than that of Mars: ''The gal . . . has a cigarette case engraved with Snow White lying down with spread legs and the Seven Dwarfs, cocks in hand, waiting to screw her. Very charming.''

When he returned to London, Jack began to prepare for a European tour, retracing the path his brother had taken the previous fall. He went to Poland, then to Latvia, and took a plane ride over the Soviet Union and a steamer to Istanbul, before journeying to Palestine. Along the way he sent back incisive and well-written reports which showed that he had come a long way since his days as head of the Muckers Club. He predicted that the Poles would fight over the question of Danzig and analyzed the depth of the conflict between Zionists and Palestinian Arabs. (''The ironical part,'' he wrote after an evening in which the Jewish underground had set off thirteen bombs in the Jewish quarter of Jerusalem, ''is that the Jewish terrorists bomb their own telephone lines and electrical connections and the next day frantically phone the British to come and fix them up.'')

His father was appreciative and impressed; yet he hungered most for word from his oldest son. When Young Joe's letters from Spain arrived he read them to Lady Astor and her circle at Cliveden. He also read them to Chamberlain and London *Times* editor Geoffrey Dawson. (When he had a collection of them, he called in his aide Harvey Klemmer: ''Make a book out of these,'' he said, tossing the batch to Klemmer, ''and send your kids through college.'' The title the Ambassador had in mind for the thirty-six letters was ''Dear Dad.'')

As the inevitable backlash against the Munich Pact developed, Kennedy became the object of a whispering campaign in England. Behavior which had once been regarded as vaguely endearing—the way he sometimes ducked into his private office in the embassy with some young woman and then reappeared shortly afterward with a smile on his face; his occasional sorties into the British stock market—was now used against him. It was claimed that he was on the payroll of the film industry; that he used his connections with the Maritime Commission to make windfall profits by demanding scarce ship space for his shipments of Haig and Haig. Czech patriot Jan Masaryk, in exile in London, charged that just before the invasion of his homeland Kennedy had sold Czech securities short and wound up with a profit of 20,000 pounds.

Back home there were calls on the floor of Congress for his resignation. Although he still had support, a growing number of people now openly criticized him as being soft on Nazism. From a variety of sources, including the industrious J. Edgar Hoover, Roosevelt was supplied with copies of the left-wing British newspaper the *Week* in which Kennedy was quoted as saying that the President's policy on Spain "was a Jewish production," and also predicting that FDR would fall in 1940.

Kennedy was increasingly cut off, the isolationist who was himself isolated. Backed into a corner, he did not moderate his position but if anything became more adamant about his feelings. United States Ambassador to Ireland John Cuddahy stopped in London and found Kennedy "coarse and vulgar" in his comments about Roosevelt. When he remonstrated with him about talking so tactlessly in front of the servants and anyone else who happened to be near, Kennedy replied that he "didn't give a damn." He lectured congressmen stopping in London on European fact-finding missions about how the Germans would march over Poland with ease. He urged Chamberlain to institute war regulations right away to give the English "a little taste of what was to come. They might not be so anxious for the Poles to refuse to negotiate and so start war." At an embassy evening to which Kick had invited Billy Hartington and other young Englishmen who were talking eagerly about getting into uniform, he showed a film about World War I. Throughout the showing, the Ambassador muttered a sarcastic running commentary, especially during a scene that showed English Tommies being slaughtered in the trenches: "See that? That's what you'll look like if you go to war with Germany." Kick sat red-faced, and afterward apologized to Billy: "You mustn't pay any attention to him. He just doesn't understand the English as I do."

On September 1, German tanks rolled across Polish borders, overwhelming the twelve brigades of mounted cavalry that stood against them. Two days later Kennedy was summoned to No. 10 Downing Street for a preview of the speech Chamberlain would make in the House of Commons in a few hours in front of a packed gallery that would include Rose and Joe Junior, Jack, and Kick, his children who would be, he feared, most affected by the war to come. Halfway through the text, Kennedy felt his eyes brimming with tears.

He returned to the embassy and cabled Hull that Britain would declare war at eleven the next morning. He then phoned the President, who was in bed, and reported the substance of the Prime Minister's speech in a voice shaking so badly that Roosevelt had to soothe him. Kennedy predicted a return of the Dark Ages, saying that chaos would prevail no matter who won the war. "It's the end of the world," he repeated over and over, "the end of everything." Like Stephen Dedalus, another Irishman, he had come to see history as the nightmare from which he was trying to wake himself.

As if to validate Kennedy's vision of the coming war as an apotheosis of random and pointless destruction the United States could not hope to escape, he was aroused in the middle of the night after the Prime Minister's declaration of war with news that the British liner *Athenia,* on its way to the United States carrying three hundred Americans, had been torpedoed west of the Hebrides. After cabling Roosevelt, he woke Jack and sent him to Scotland to help the survivors and find out details of what had happened, and ordered Joe Junior to book space on other ships for survivors. In response to the flood of queries from anxious relatives, Kennedy sent out hundreds of personal telegrams, paying for them out of his own pocket because government funds were unavailable for this purpose. He also made arrangements to send his own family back home.

Just as he and Rose had a compact to fly on separate planes when they traveled, he had the whole family return in stages. Only Rosemary was to be left behind in her small Hertfordshire Montessori school, remote from potential bombing runs. Rose, Kathleen, and Bobby left first. Kathleen begged to stay with her father, pointing out that he was allowing Rosemary to remain in England. But he was adamant, alarmed almost as much by her relationship with Hartington (as the courtship got stronger, Rose had constantly reminded him that the Cavendish family was as Protestant as the Church of England) as by the international situation. In the end Kick sailed with the others on the S.S. *Washington.* Joe Junior was next, making a point of telling reporters about the family's rescue efforts for the *Athenia* passengers when he docked in New York, and also of defending his father's position. Then Pat, Jean, and Teddy, and finally Jack, who flew home on a Pan American Clipper at the end of September.

The pressure and activity temporarily checked the fear and dismay that had almost gotten out of control during his late-night phone conversation with the President. But Kennedy was still desperately casting about for a way to avert the cataclysm. Reacting to the "peace offensive" that Hitler had launched to gain time for consolidating his gains from appeasement and *Blitzkrieg,* Kennedy sent a plea to the Secretary of State on September 11:

> It seems to me that this situation may crystallize to a point where the President can be the savior of the world. The British government as such certainly cannot accept any agreement with Hitler, but there may be a point where the President himself may work out plans for world peace. Now as a fairly practical fellow all my life, I believe that it is entirely conceivable that the President can put himself in a spot where he can save the world.

Calling it "the silliest message that I have ever received," Roosevelt instructed Hull to draft a blunt reply emphasizing that there would be no further appeasement of Hitler. "The President desires me to inform you for your strictly confidential information . . ." the Secretary of State wrote coldly, "that this Government, so long as present European conditions continue, sees no opportunity nor occasion for any peace move to be introduced by the President of the United States."

As German tanks temporarily halted at France's Maginot Line, beginning the long wait known as the "phony war," Kennedy's eclipse was hastened by the rise of Winston Churchill, now in the War Cabinet as First Lord of the Admiralty. Relations between the two men were poor. At dinner with Churchill at the art historian Kenneth Clark's a few months earlier, Walter Lippmann had said that Kennedy was predicting the British would be defeated, whereupon Churchill had stubbed his cigar with one hand and scornfully waved his whiskey and soda with the other while launching into one of his Ciceronian periods: "No, the Ambassador should not have spoken so, Mr. Lippmann; he should not have said that dreadful word. Yet supposing—as I do not for one moment suppose—that Mr. Kennedy were correct in his tragic utterance, then I for one would willingly lay down my life in combat rather than, in fear of defeat, surrender to the menaces of these sinister men." In a gesture rich with symbolism for the future, Roosevelt now sent a note to Churchill inviting him to open a personal channel of communication to the White House on the very day that he rejected Kennedy's proposal to explore German peace terms. Kennedy would be given the task of bearing the sealed messages between Roosevelt and Churchill that arrived in the diplomatic pouch, messages that dramatized his increasing irrelevance.

Taken out of the center of things, Kennedy looked toward home for news to keep him going. There were letters from all of them—Joe Junior in his first year at Harvard Law School asking about the war; Jack in his last year at college asking for a higher allowance; and Rose asking him to take care of his spiritual health. ("I'm praying that I shall see you soon. Do pray, and go to church, as it is very important in my life that you do just that.") She was running things tightly as always—up at 6:00 A.M. posting war news on the bulletin board which the children were to read and be ready to discuss at breakfast; each Sunday lining them all up to speak to their father on the one transatlantic call per week he was allowed.

On November 3, Kennedy wrote his daughter Pat that he still went out to the residence he'd rented near Windsor Park every evening, "and between you and me it's pretty lonesome." He turned his attention to Rosemary, the only other Kennedy still in England, visiting her school and occasionally having her visit on weekends. He was distressed that she was getting fat, and told her that he wouldn't allow her to have her picture taken unless she lost weight. In one of those letters filled with eerie ellipses, she said, "Many, many thanks for coming to see on Friday. You were darling. I hope you liked everything here . . . Mother says I am such a comfort to you. Never to leave you. Well, Daddy, I feel honor because you chose me to stay . . . "

The call came to return home for Christmas, and Kennedy was glad to go. When he arrived in New York on December 6, reporters were there to meet him as usual. Hugging Rose, who had broken through the press lines to kiss him, he told them that this would be his last public job. Kennedy made the terms of his allegiance clear again when he went to Boston to speak three days later. "As you love America," he exhorted his audience, "don't let anything that comes out of any country in the world make you believe you can make a situation one whit better by getting into war. There is no place in this fight for us." Then he went to Palm Beach for Christmas, tired and sick, trying to extract himself from the European centrifuge. He didn't appear in the news again until mid-February, when he gave a series of interviews promoting isolationism. To emphasize that his words were meant as an indirect message to Roosevelt, the statements were accompanied by new rumors of a possible Kennedy dark-horse candidacy that would amount to a plebiscite on foreign policy, and by calls for a Kennedy-for-President drive in Massachusetts which he allowed to percolate for a couple of days before quashing them. He gave this reason for his lack of ambition: "I know I'll die young. Therefore after this job I want to quit public life. I want to establish my older sons firmly enough so they can look after the younger generation."

With great reluctance he returned to England on February 28, 1940. The reception he got upon landing was decidedly chilly. There might still be doubts at Cliveden about the war, but most of the rest of England was ready to fight. Kennedy refused to be muzzled, however. When he heard patriotic rhetoric about protecting democracy, he bristled. "For Christ's sake, stop trying to make this a holy war, because no one will believe you. You're fighting for your life as an empire and that's good enough." He didn't conceal his opinion that England would be "thrashed." He railed against his countrymen who volunteered for the British Army, charging that such rashness might cause American civilians to be shot as collaborators when the Germans occupied England. His journalist friend Joseph Kingsbury Smith, who had been badly hurt in an automobile accident, asked Kennedy's advice about the insurance settlement. "He told me that I'd better settle before the Germans took England over and set up a different system; so I did settle for the very low sum I was being offered and as a result I wound up paying nearly $20,000 worth of medical bills out of my own pocket."

In May, after the Germans invaded Norway, Chamberlain's government fell. On the day Churchill replaced him, the Nazis moved west, easily out-flanking the Maginot Line and beginning to overrun France with a velocity that sent the British Expeditionary Force reeling back toward Dunkirk. The new Prime Minister's special relationship with Roosevelt meant that Kennedy was now a pariah. One of Kennedy's few remaining friends noted that the Ambassador "does not go out to any dinners nowadays; in the old days he wanted as much as a month's notice for a luncheon or dinner appointment." The tenor of material accumulated about him in British Foreign Office files was summarized in a memo initialed by Lord Halifax: "Mr. Kennedy is a very foul specimen of double crosser and defeatist. He thinks of nothing but his own pocket. I hope this war will at least see the elimination of his type."

The State Department view was not much different. On May 1, an aide to Hull was present when the Secretary put down the telephone after talking to Kennedy, shook his head, and said, "His mind is as blank as uninked paper." Roosevelt was not only bypassing him with messages, but with fact finders as well, people like Colonel "Wild Bill" Donovan, future head of the Office of Strategic Services, who arrived in London in mid-July as the President's personal representative and came back with views diametrically opposing Kennedy's: England could and would withstand a German invasion.

The only news Kennedy got that wasn't bad came from home. At Harvard Law, Young Joe had helped found a collegiate version of America First— the Harvard Committee Against Military Intervention. He also grasped the torch of political ambition that now seemed to have passed his father by. After taking speaking lessons, he got involved in Democratic Party politics, campaigning to become a delegate to the 1940 convention at which it had once seemed his father might be a candidate. (Honey Fitz had to lean on some of his old friends to get his grandson's candidacy certified for the Brookline area, since technically he didn't live there.) After running hard to get elected, Joe Junior pledged himself to Massachusetts' Jim Farley, Postmaster General, Democratic Party chairman, and leading candidate in the absence of an official announcement by FDR that he would be the first President in American history to run for a third term.

Young Kennedy got to the convention and found Roosevelt backers booming a "draft," intending to beat the three-term issue by creating a summons from the delegates too compelling to be denied. Whether or not to hold for Farley when most of the rest of the Massachusetts delegation was stampeding toward Roosevelt presented a dilemma. With his father too far away for consultation, Joe sought advice from Arthur Krock, who told him that Farley would release him if he wanted to be released and that his father would want him "to do the honorable thing." The Roosevelt men at the convention telephoned Kennedy in London asking him to straighten his son out. Kennedy's reply was blunt: "No, I wouldn't think of telling him what to do." Joe Junior stood fast and cast one of a handful of Farley votes, a vindication of his conscience and his family.

At the time this closet drama was being played out, Jack too was doing something, although typically it was intellectual rather than activist. He had applied himself industriously at Harvard since returning from his months as a junior diplomat and traveler in London, and had completed a year and a half of work in a year. He had decided to do a senior thesis on Munich. The project had originated with the Ambassador, who'd told a friend: "When I was in the States with Jack and heard some professors talking about Munich, I realized they knew nothing about it. I said to Jack, 'You get down to it and tell them about it.'"

The unwieldy title of the thesis suggested a vindication of his father's position: "Appeasement at Munich: The Inevitable Result of the Slowness

of the British Democracy to Change from a Disarmament Policy.'' But while
the Ambassador arranged interviews and wrote memoranda for the thesis,
some of Jack's views strayed far from the Kennedy party line—especially
when he singled out Winston Churchill as a prophetic figure and a hero.

The thesis got a *cum laude*, and some of the professors thought it might be
publishable. The Ambassador asked Krock to get his agent to handle it. But
when the newspaperman offered to write a foreword, Kennedy said that he
wanted someone better known and persuaded Henry Luce to do it. By August, *Why England Slept* (one Harvard professor maliciously suggested that
''Why Daddy Slept'' might have been a better title) had been rushed to
press and was climbing the best-seller lists. After sending autographed copies to the King and Queen and other English dignitaries, the Ambassador
wrote to Jack: ''You would be surprised how a book that really makes the
grade with high-class people stands you in good stead for years to come.''
Perhaps sensing that his younger brother was finding a way to move out of
the giant shadow he himself had always cast, Joe Junior wrote his father
about Jack's book: ''It seemed to represent a lot of work but didn't prove
anything.''

The Ambassador had written Krock that in London he was nothing more
than ''a $75 a week errand boy'' and tried to get his friend to do something
that would bring him home. Krock sent up a trial balloon suggesting Kennedy as a good candidate for chairman of the Democratic National Committee, but nothing came of it.

Kennedy's mood alternated between febrile bravado and gloomy self-pity.
He scrawled an uncharacteristically sentimental postscript on a little note to
Rose: ''It's hell to be here without all of you. I get news you are more
beautiful than ever. Maybe you do better away from me ...'' He told one of
the few journalists who remained friendly: ''Perhaps when the bombing
begins in earnest there will be a little less of this wishful thinking and they
[the English] will come down to brass tacks. I think I'll have my baptism of
fire here, go through one good raid before I quit and go back.'' But on
September 7, the day the first large-scale German bombing attack hit London, Kennedy cabled a single sentence back to Washington: ''There's hell to
pay here tonight.''

During the Battle of Britain Kennedy had long conversations with Klemmer. ''The British have had it,'' he said. ''They can't stop the Germans and
the best thing for them is to learn to live with them.'' ''What would happen
if they subjugated the whole world except the U.S.?'' Klemmer wondered.
Kennedy swatted at the air: ''Hell, you can't hold people down. Look at
Ireland. The British never did conquer the Irish.''

England's resolution didn't waver during the weeks of day and night
bombing and dramatic aerial warfare, as Kennedy secretly hoped it might.

In fact his own behavior came under closer scrutiny, some higher placed Britons accusing him of lacking grace under fire and noting that whenever an air raid struck he was likely to be hiding out in his "funk hole" near Windsor with some Paris model. Gradually he became known as "Jittery Joe" and "Run, rabbit, run" behind his back. Even Americans were aware that he was regarded as a coward. Klemmer remembers: "Once the Blitz started, he went to the country almost every night. He kept saying he had nine kids to look after, this big family he was responsible for. He took off every night before it got dark." Kennedy himself adopted a sort of gallows humor. In the middle of the Battle of Britain he said to Clare Boothe Luce, who was researching a book about Europe at war: "I may be going back any day now. Tell me, how do you think I'll look best when I land? In pine, mahogany, or copper?"

Circumvented by his government's policy and exposed to the dangers of a war he had struggled against, Kennedy realized that he remained in London only because Roosevelt wanted to keep him from injecting himself into the presidential campaign at home, where Republican challenger Wendell Willkie was proving surprisingly effective in using the Democrats' alleged "secret war plans" as his central issue. Kennedy alternately fumed about the way he was being treated and boasted that he could "put 25 million votes behind Willkie and throw Roosevelt out." Luce and other high-ranking Republicans plotted with him to return and swing the election to their candidate with a last-minute endorsement.

A desire to be in the political fray tugged at him, and family continued to be an even stronger gravity as he received reports of the benign and homey chaos at Hyannis in the early fall of 1940: "Jack was autographing copies of *Why England Slept* while grandfather Fitzgerald was reading to him a political story from a newspaper. Young Joe was telling them something that had happened to him in Russia. Mrs. Kennedy was talking on the phone with Cardinal Spellman. A tall and very attractive girl in a sweatshirt and dungarees turned out to be Pat who was describing how a German Messerschmitt plane had crashed near her father's house outside Windsor. Bobby was trying to get everybody to play charades. The next thing I knew all of us were choosing up sides for touch football and Kathleen was calling the plays in the huddle for the team I was on."

The Ambassador asked to be brought home and got no response from the State Department. On October 16 he sent a cable demanding to be recalled, then telephoned Under Secretary of State Sumner Welles to say that he had deposited a document containing a full expression of his views with his "private secretary" Eddie Moore in New York, with instructions that it was to be released to the press if he was not back by a certain date. Finally word came back from the State Department that he was to return home for consultation.

Kennedy made the rounds saying his goodbyes, knowing he wouldn't return. He shook hands with the staff at the Grosvenor Square embassy for the last time, leaving them in tears, and took Harvey Klemmer to lunch at Claridge's, saying he was going home to tell the American people that "Roosevelt and the kikes were taking us into war." He was photographed for the last time in front of the Chancery, then the crowd of photographers dispersed, leaving him suddenly alone to walk across Grosvenor Square by himself. One of his last acts was to stop and visit Chamberlain, who was in bed dying of throat cancer. The old Prime Minister, with whom so much of Kennedy's fate had been entwined, pulled him down close to his face and whispered, "I can tell you, though I haven't told my wife: I want to die." On October 23, Kennedy climbed aboard a British plane to fly to Lisbon to connect with the Pan Am Clipper. Still defiant, he carried with him an air-raid siren that had done duty in the Blitz which he said he would install at Hyannis to summon his children in from sailing.

As speculation built that Kennedy's return would result in an endorsement that could tip the election to Willkie, FDR sent him messages in Lisbon and again at a refueling stop in Bermuda commanding him to come directly to the White House before making any statements to the press. Rose and his four daughters were waiting when he touched down on October 27. He called Roosevelt and heard the usual amiable voice: "Ah, Joe, old friend, please come to the White House tonight for a little family dinner. I'm dying to talk to you." Kennedy didn't know, of course, that as FDR spoke, he was drawing a finger across his throat.

Their meeting was a vintage Roosevelt performance, beginning with the inclusion of Rose, who had always considered him "the most charming man in the world," in the dinner invitation. All the way down to Washington she counseled prudence. "The President sent you, a Roman Catholic, as Ambassador to London, which probably no other President would have done..." She also reminded him, with a realism befitting someone who had grown up in Boston Irish politics, that their son Joe's political chances could be permanently injured by a rash act that might later be interpreted as treachery.

With Senator and Mrs. Byrnes also present, Roosevelt flattered Kennedy all during dinner. It was Byrnes's job to ask the Ambassador to make a speech endorsing the President. Kennedy refused, launching into a recitation of his grievances. Instead of defending himself against the charges, Roosevelt shook his head sadly and blamed the State Department people, who, he said, had disgraced themselves in making one of his ambassadors suffer such humiliation. After more blandishment, Kennedy was sufficiently placated to agree to make a speech, at which point Missy LeHand quickly sprang to the phone to tell the Democratic National Committee to reserve air time. To save face, Kennedy insisted that he would pay for the broadcast himself and would not submit his speech for advance review.

Kennedy made no comment to newspapermen after the White House visit. Henry Luce and other Willkie supporters tried to reach him, but he refused their calls. Speaking the next day over nationwide radio, he dropped a bombshell—although not the one the Republicans had hoped for—by disputing Willkie's claim of a "secret commitment" to support England, even though he knew all too well about the private correspondence between Roosevelt and Churchill. In what observers called the most effective speech of the entire election campaign, he ended with the point closest to his heart, returning to the figure of speech he had used what seemed like light-years earlier in England: "My wife and I have given nine hostages to fortune. Our children and your children are more important than anything else in the world. The kind of America that they and their children will inherit is of grave concern to us all. In the light of these considerations, I believe that Franklin D. Roosevelt should be elected President of the United States." Kennedy was with Roosevelt on November 4, election eve, at Boston Garden, and must have felt that his influence was not totally used up when the President gave his celebrated pledge: "I have said this before, but I shall say it again and again: your boys are not going to be sent into any foreign wars."

Four days after FDR had won his third term, Kennedy agreed to do an interview with *Boston Globe* reporter Louis Lyons on his views about the future. When Lyons arrived at Kennedy's suite at the Ritz, the Ambassador, just back from another stomach checkup at the Lahey Clinic, was sitting in an easy chair with his suspenders down, eating apple pie covered with slices of American cheese and giving a background briefing on European affairs to two other journalists, Charles Edmundson and Ralph Coghlan, whose *St. Louis Post-Dispatch* was sympathetic to isolationism. As Lyons sat down, Kennedy turned to him and began an impassioned, if rambling, lecture about his fear that war would soon engulf America despite Roosevelt's pledge:

> I'm willing to spend all I've got to keep us out of the war. There's no sense in our getting in. We'd only be holding the bag ... I know more about the European situation than anybody else, and it's up to me to see that the country gets it ... It's a question of how long England can hold out. Hitler has all the ports of Europe. The German *Stukas* are already over Africa. Keep out of the war and keep the hemisphere out of it. If any of the Latin Americas act up, kick them in the teeth ...

Lyons had covered the Ambassador during the 1936 presidential campaign, writing articles favorable both to him and to the administration. On the basis of this past experience, he expected Kennedy to be blunt and opinionated. But there was something extreme in all this, even for Kennedy. For instance, asked an innocuous question about Eleanor Roosevelt (Lyons was only doing a "soft" news feature for the Sunday supplement), Kennedy blurted out one of the anti-Semitic remarks normally reserved for cronies: "She bothered us more on our jobs in Washington to take care of poor little nobodies who hadn't any influence, than all the rest of the people down there together. She was always sending me a note to have some little Susie Glotz to tea at the Embassy.'' But his least diplomatic remarks came at the expense of the country where he'd served the past two years. ''The war would drain us,'' he insisted. ''It would turn our government into national socialism. Democracy is finished in England ...'' At the end of his monologue, Kennedy escorted the stunned Lyons to the door and said, ''Well, I'm afraid you didn't get much of a story.''

The piece appeared two days later. Neville Chamberlain had died the night before but Joe Kennedy made the news. His comments appeared under the headline: ''Kennedy Says Democracy All Done in Britain, Maybe Here.'' Kennedy came home from Sunday mass to find a furor awaiting him. At first he claimed that his comments had been off the record and pressured *Globe* executives to repudiate the Lyons story in an editorial statement, and he asked Krock for advice about damage control. The journalist was frank in his appraisal of the situation in Washington: ''The general impression here seems to be—and this goes for the State Department also—that whatever the facts about the off-the-record restrictions, the sentiments sound very much like yours ...'' Meanwhile, there was no closing this Pandora's box. The press all over Europe denounced Kennedy's comments, the Berlin *Boersen-Zeitung* alone editorializing in his favor. Even the isolationist America First Committee, whose leaders had secretly considered Kennedy as a possible future head of the organization, felt constrained to criticize the statement.

Angry because he felt his comments to Lyons had been misinterpreted (he retaliated by canceling Somerset Imports' lucrative advertising contract with the *Globe*), Kennedy struggled to keep his career from being swamped by the storm currents the story caused. ''The bombers may be tough in London,'' he wrote his friend Beaverbrook, ''but the ill disposed newspapers are tougher in America ... Tell my friends not to pay any attention to anything they read unless I sign or deliver it myself.'' But when Kennedy went to California to talk to Hearst about becoming involved in his media empire, he continued to make injudicious remarks. Word leaked out that in meetings in Hollywood he had urged movie makers to stop producing work offensive to Hitler and not to give him cause to believe that ''Jewish money'' was seeking political influence through films. He was summoned to Hyde Park for a private conference about the *Globe* story. As Eleanor Roosevelt later recalled it, the meeting had been going on for scarcely ten minutes when an aide rushed in to say that her husband wanted her right away. ''This was unheard of. So I *rushed* into the office and there was Franklin white as a sheet. He asked Mr. Kennedy to step outside and then he said, and his voice was *shaking*, 'I never want to see that sonofabitch again as long as I live ... Get him out of here.' ''

Roosevelt's resolve to banish Kennedy proved as impermanent as his continuing protestations of affection; he recognized that the Ambassador—he would relinquish the position but never the title—still had power as a spoiler and must be handled with care. Fearful that Kennedy might become the charismatic leader of the isolationist movement and a direct political threat, the President continued to woo him from afar and kept him a dangling man.

For his part, Kennedy, as always, saw Roosevelt's game and as always was powerless to combat it. Visitors to Palm Beach noted that he had moved the autographed pictures of the President and other one-time New Deal comrades to inconspicuous positions on the walls of his den, subordinating them to mementos from the Pope and the Royal Family. He still wanted to play a role in the intensifying debate on foreign affairs, and at times over the next few weeks convinced himself that he would. Lindbergh, General Robert Wood of America First, and other isolationists approached him as perhaps the one person who might give their crusade authenticity and political direction—no one was better placed to make the case against the administration. The Ambassador told them in private that they could count on him, but he refused to make a public commitment to their cause. His whole life had been an effort to be an American, to be at the center of the national mainstream, and the possible consequences of braving the tide and becoming alien were too daunting. As a result his statements to the press during the next few crucial weeks were equivocal and impotent.

In mid-January, Kennedy purchased radio time to explain his views. Roosevelt heard of it and summoned him to the White House for an hour's "chat." After that, what Kennedy had billed to fellow isolationists as a hellfire-and-brimstone attack on the administration turned out to be little more than a petulant complaint addressed to the press. Without specifically mentioning the *Globe* story, he decried the "growth of intolerance" and the increasing tendency to equate dissent with "defeatism." He said that he favored aid to Britain (using the same argument he would later use to explain why he had favored Munich) because "by helping Britain we will be securing for ourselves the most precious commodity we need—time—time to rearm." On the other hand he insisted that the United States shouldn't "give beyond the absolute minimum requirement for our own protection ... because in addition to wanting to aid Britain the American people want to stay out of war."

After hearing the speech, liberal columnist Dorothy Thompson crowed that Kennedy had "out-Hamleted Hamlet." It was a performance he repeated a few days later when called as the first opposition witness in the congressional hearings on sending material aid to the English war effort. Privately he was against Lend-Lease, recognizing that it would make neutrality a fiction; but he couldn't bring himself to articulate his position forcefully and his five hours of testimony became a theater for his vacillation.

As Joe Kennedy flailed about, Young Joe, identifying himself more and more with the Kennedy family's hope for ultimate political regeneration, argued the Kennedy position with the recklessness that was one of his traits. His stand against Roosevelt at the convention had made him a public figure in his own right. Now he stepped into debates at Harvard as a fiery and outspoken proponent of isolationism. Already working in the Harvard Committee Against Military Intervention, he appeared on the same platform with Senator Robert Taft at Boston's Ford Hall shortly before the Ambassador testified on Lend-Lease and said that trading with the Nazis made more sense than "sending an air force to Britain with pilots, and battleships to convey supplies." In a phrase that drew special criticism from England ("He is a smart-aleck of a boy who . . . will not help his father's standing"), young Kennedy added that the United States would be better off acceding to Nazi domination of the Continent than plunging into a war that would strain the American economy beyond its limits and thus unleash the forces of radicalism.

Yet Joe Junior was always more comfortable in the realm of action than of ideas. When FDR declared a state of national emergency that spring, he decided to skip his final year at law school and enlist as a naval air cadet. Explaining his action in a letter to his father, he wrote, "I think that Jack is not doing anything, and, with your stand on the war, that people will wonder what the devil I am doing back at school when everyone else is working for national defense." He was still stung by the charges of cowardice which had followed the Ambassador home from London, and when he was sworn in, his statement to the press had the defiant ring of someone who sees himself as the champion of a cause: "My father, especially, approves of what I'm doing. He thinks I'm doing what I should be doing, and he's glad for it."

Trying to pick up the gauntlet that his elder brother had thrown down, Jack, who had left Stanford Business School after a few aimless weeks the previous fall, wanted to follow suit, but he failed the physical examination for both the Army Officer Candidate School and the Navy because of his back. He wrote one of Joe Junior's friends who wanted to sell him a life-insurance policy, "I will let your company be the lucky one, although all the other companies are fighting to get me. I'm in a bit of a quandary though, as on the one hand I would be one of the last to go due to my sensational health record and yet I would like to get insured in case I get killed . . ."

Later that spring, in a commencement address at Oglethorpe University, the Ambassador gave one more major speech in behalf of his beliefs. But it was more for the record—an exposition of the philosophical background of isolationism and an attempt to connect it with the American mainstream—

than a call to action. Realistically he knew his dreams of running for national office were dead, knew too that there would probably be no more offers of important appointive positions, no further influence at the center of the great drama now beginning. He had no choice but to admit that his moment in the spotlight was ended, and that if he was to disprove Scott Fitzgerald's contention that there are no second acts in American lives, it would be through Young Joe.

As the summer of 1941 began, he watched the family mobilize along with the nation. Young Joe commuted to Hyannis for weekends from his training base at Squantum, just outside Boston. Jack pursued an ambitious regimen of exercise and conditioning in the hope of getting into some branch of the military. Even sixteen-year-old Bobby was talking about leaving prep school for the service, and the girls, especially Kick and Eunice, discussed joining the Red Cross or even the Women's Army Corps.

Everything Joseph Kennedy had feared was inexorably happening, although it was still possible, in the timelessness of a Hyannis summer, to hope that it would remain a European problem. The family had a typical Kennedy experience—sun-tanned and sea-swept, filled with nonstop touch football on the sloping lawns, sailing races, outdoor movies at night, and hordes of visitors. Young Joe's friend "T. J." Reardon and Jack's friend Torbert MacDonald, both All-Americans at Harvard, played touch football opposite each other in backfields quarterbacked by Kennedys, the girls on the line anchored, as always, by Lem and Bobby. John Hersey glimpsed eight-year-old Teddy at his dancing lessons—foxtrotting with a girl taller than he was, chewing gum, and reading a comic book over her shoulder as he went through the motions. American and innocent was what Charles Spalding, a visitor who became a family friend, thought the Kennedys were: "You watched these people go through their lives and just had a feeling that they existed outside the usual laws of nature; that there was no other group so handsome, so engaged. There was endless action—not just football, but sailboats, tennis, and other things: movement. There was endless talk—the Ambassador at the head of the table laying out the prevailing wisdom, but everyone else weighing in with their opinions and taking part. It was a scene of endless competition, people drawing each other out and pushing each other to greater lengths. It was as simple as this: the Kennedys had a feeling of being heightened and it rubbed off on the people who came in contact with them. They were a unit. I remember thinking to myself that there couldn't be another group quite like this one."

The family: it was the one thing Joe Kennedy built that he thought would never fail him. But that summer of 1941 was the last time they would all be together.

6.

$\mathcal{T}$HE WAR TURNED OUT TO BE
exactly what Joe Kennedy feared—the uncontrollable calamity so deeply
embedded in the collective memory of the Irish; a sudden and destructive
quirk of history that respects neither wealth nor stature, nor the most carefully laid plans. For Kennedy, it was the tragedy that changed his world
and his family as well, penetrating its defenses, shuffling its hierarchy,
causing gaps that could never be filled. For the Kennedy children, it was
tragedy and something more—the grand backdrop for their individual rites
of passage, the perilous bridge over which they had to pass to get from their
father's era to their own. For the whole family, the war was a violent break
with what had gone before; it required that new selves be created and a new
destiny embraced.

Their first casualty of the wartime period, however, did not come in Europe or the Pacific but at home, in the secret struggle they had been waging
for twenty years to establish a place for Rosemary in their future. The year
following her return from England had begun well enough, but then things
had started to fall apart. The basic skills she had labored so hard to master
in her special schools were deteriorating. She gained more weight, coming to
look like a freckle-faced girl prematurely encased in a matron's body. As
always she wanted to please, but it had become increasingly difficult to do
so. In the past, as her older brothers and sisters moved out into the world,
she had joined the circle of the younger children in the family. But now they
too were striking out on their own, and she was left behind as the last and
perpetual child. If her understanding of abstractions had grown more and
more cloudy, her perception of the superiority of the others' lives was sharp

and accurate. Rather than closing, as her parents had hoped, the gap between Rosemary and the rest of them had begun to widen. Charlotte McDonnell had noticed it when she was with the family in St. Moritz. ''Foreigners didn't realize how retarded she was and would ask her out. Rose would have Joe Junior chaperon her, and Rosemary would say, 'Well, why does Joe have to come?' Her mother would answer: 'Oh, they're just foreigners, dear, and Joe is not going to bother you. He'll just be in the room.' ''

If Rose was worried about what might happen as a result of Rosemary's obvious sexual maturity, Joe was concerned about the embarrassment she might cause in political campaigns to come. Relatively speaking, her retardation was mild, and in a more tranquil atmosphere, one less geared to constant and conspicuous achievement, a place might easily have been made for her. But her inability to keep up in the contests of wit and endurance, and especially her inability to share in the social life of Kick and Eunice and go out with young men as her younger sisters did, left her disoriented and angry. She began to have tantrums, and then rages which developed into near-clonic states during which she smashed objects and struck out at the people around her. Rose tried to quarantine these eruptions, but sometimes they escaped the control of nurses and attendants and burst into the family's daily life. In one traumatic incident during the summer of 1941, Rosemary, who was sitting on the porch at Hyannis, suddenly attacked Honey Fitz, hitting and kicking her tiny, white-haired grandfather until she was pulled away.

It was considered a domestic matter, one that affected the women in the family more than the men. John White, a newspaperman who became a close friend of Kathleen's, found himself quizzed rigorously when she discovered that he was researching a series of articles on mental illness. ''Kick would draw me out on the details—not just draw me out but absolutely drain me, although never saying why. This went on for a long time. One day we were walking in the park and she was, as usual, interviewing me to find out what new things I'd discovered. I told her that she had it all: I didn't know anything else. She finally admitted why she was so interested. It was because of Rosemary. She spoke slowly and sadly about it, as though she was confessing something quite embarrassing, almost shameful. I got the feeling that her family viewed Rosemary as a beloved failure, perhaps a disgrace.''

As long as Rosemary had tried to improve, tried to look and be like the rest of them, the family had surrounded her with the same tremendous support they gave Jack as he fought his way through the back injuries and the mysterious wasting illness that had afflicted him on and off since childhood. Winning was important, but the struggle, especially against high odds, was almost equally so. They had presented Rosemary at court, applauded her small steps as major victories. But there had been, as one close family friend says, a ''deep denial'' in the attitude toward the girl. Now that she was no longer able to try, the family was ready to consider options they might otherwise have rejected out of hand.

One of the developments John White had investigated which Kick was especially interested in was experimental neurosurgical techniques, in particular the prefrontal lobotomy, or ice pick operation. In 1941 there was still euphoria about its possibilities, but there was also a literature that indicated the seriousness of its side effects. Nonetheless, there were rationales even by Catholic theologians which legitimated the procedure, and that fall Rosemary had the operation at St. Elizabeth's Hospital in Washington. As she convalesced it became clear that while the surgery had ended her wild moods, it had altered the rest of her personality too, severing all but the most minimal connections with the life of the rest of the family.* (One of those who took care of Rosemary later on said, "The lobotomy wasn't necessary. With medication she would have been just fine.") From this point on, as Rose later said, describing what they all felt as the most terrible disaster to have befallen them, Rosemary would function at a "childlike level."

For a while the family considered institutionalizing her somewhere near home. But it was clear that her closeness not only might prove embarrassing later on, but would be an emotional burden for them all. At the recommendation of Cardinal Cushing, the family's personal spiritual adviser after Cardinal O'Connell's death, they sent her to St. Coletta's, a nursing convent in Wisconsin. There she had her own apartment and attendant, and access to a chauffeured car; Rose and Eunice, but never Joe, regularly flew out to visit. In the future, instead of having to manage Rosemary herself, they would only have to manage information about her. Those who asked were told that she had turned out to be shy and withdrawn, and had chosen to devote her life to a religious order working with retarded children.

Rosemary's departure might have caused a greater sense of loss if it had come at some other time. But there was little respite to consider its implications as the Japanese attack on Pearl Harbor in December 1941 pulled the nation and the family into war. Privately Joe Kennedy believed that FDR had set up the Japanese attack to provide an excuse for intervention in Europe (a thesis later argued by Charles Beard and other revisionist historians), but his still pressing desire to be in the middle of things kept him from making public statements. He hoped that the outbreak of war, even a war he had counseled against, would return him to Washington, where his proven executive skills might restore his reputation. The day after Pearl Harbor, he cabled Roosevelt: "Name the battlefront. I'm yours to command."

---

*Timothy Shriver, Eunice's son, says the operation "made her go from being mildly retarded to very retarded."

But it was a replay of 1932, when Roosevelt had let him cool his heels while others of less ability were given high government jobs. After the telegram had been ignored for several weeks, Kennedy followed it up with an abject letter pleading with the President to use him. There was talk of a low-level position in the shipbuilding industry, but the CIO, which had not forgotten Kennedy's antagonism toward the maritime unions, moved to blackball him. There was more talk about a subordinate position in government transport, unsnarling the railroads. When presidential confidant Jimmy Byrnes suggested a position as mediator between government and small business involved in the war effort, Kennedy described his response in a letter to a friend: "I told him to stick it . . ."

Roosevelt was petitioned by leading national politicians, in addition to the *Boston Post* and the Boston City Council, to put the Ambassador to work. But the London experience had soured him on Kennedy and he continued to placate him without doing anything definite. When it became clear what was happening, Kennedy fulminated against "Jews and radicals and certain elements in the New Deal" for putting him "in the leper colony." Seeing his alienation from Washington, isolationists once again appealed to him to enter their lists, but Kennedy kept his distance. "I am withstanding all efforts to get me to make speeches or to write articles," he confessed to Beaverbrook a few months later, "because I don't want to do anything that won't help us win the war and get out of this mess. They expect criticism from me so I am suffering in silence."

To silence and exile, Kennedy added the third of what James Joyce had seen as typical Irish survival traits—cunning. Increasingly fixed on the Massachusetts governorship as a position for Young Joe to begin his political career after the war, the Ambassador moved to block a potential opponent of his son when Roosevelt hand-picked an attractive young Irish Catholic congressman to run against incumbent Senator Henry Cabot Lodge, Jr., in 1942. Kennedy considered running against Joseph Casey himself in the Democratic primary but didn't meet the residency requirement. Looking around for a proxy, he saw the perfect candidate in Honey Fitz. He scorned his father-in-law, calling him "a drunken old bastard" and getting impatient at the way he told his stories at family gatherings, sometimes laughing so hard at his own jokes that he wet his pants. (Honey called Kennedy "Big Joe" and was afraid of him; in the middle of a story he would say to his grandchildren, "Uh-oh, here comes Big Joe, we got to get out of here.") But the Ambassador knew his seventy-nine-year-old father-in-law had one more campaign in him and got his cousin and political handyman Joe Kane to organize the effort against Casey. ("Honey Fitz has thrown his hat into the ring as candidate for the Senate," Jack wrote to Lem Billings. "He told me confidentially that he would win in a breeze and he does have a good chance. It seems his opponent—Casey by name—had a baby six months after he got married and Mrs. Greene and the Catholic women . . . are busy giving him the black-ball for it.'')

Honey Fitz lost the primary,* after a rousing battle in which he traveled all over the state singing ''Sweet Adeline'' and giving the stinging speeches prepared by the New York writers Kennedy had hired. But he had bloodied Casey badly, and the Ambassador quickly moved in with a *coup de grâce* by secretly throwing his financial support to Lodge. In the general election, Lodge used recordings of Honey Fitz's speeches as radio commercials to great effect, and Casey was swamped so badly that his political career was ended. The message came through loud and clear in Washington: the President might control the destiny of the nation, but Massachusetts was Kennedy turf.

While his father was clearing the way for his political future, Young Joe was in the middle of flight training at the U.S. Naval Air Station in Jacksonville, Florida. He had acquired a pilot's panache—leather jacket, white scarf, and small cigars which he smoked in cocky moods. But being heir apparent was a serious affair. He had gone into the service with a private mission: to prove the Kennedys were not cowards or defeatists. His father had merely shrugged off these charges, but Young Joe could not do that. He was headstrong, impetuous, still almost fanatically devoted to the family. His friend Tom Schriber was with him at the Washington airport when a plane the Ambassador was on touched down. ''Young Joe, about to catch a plane back to the Jacksonville Air Base, decided that he had to see his father before he left and started pushing his way through the crowd. The armed guard at the landing ramp yelled, 'Halt or I'll shoot!' Joe just pushed him aside and ran to see his dad.''

As he followed the progress of Honey Fitz's rejuvenated political career in the campaign against Casey, Joe Junior kept the family up to date on his own efforts. He made a point of writing to all his brothers and sisters, especially his godchild Jean. He was the only one who paid much attention

---

*Tommy O'Hearn, a nephew of Fitzgerald's who chauffeured the old man from one stop to another in the campaign, recalls, ''We started going good toward the end. It was felt by those close to the campaign that with a little more activity, a little more financial support, we might have beat Casey.'' But the Ambassador, as always, was interested only in sure things. A few days before the primary, he met with Joe Kane, who had commissioned a Boston advertising agency to design a campaign that would tip the balance to Fitzgerald.

''But can he lick Lodge?'' Kennedy asked, looking at the expensive advertising layout.

''No,'' Kane answered.

''And the campaign would cost between two and three hundred thousand dollars?''

''Yes.''

Kennedy shrugged and buttoned his overcoat and then headed for the door: ''Isn't that nice. I don't know where you're going, but I'm going back to the Ritz.''

to Bobby. Rose enrolled him in the Catholic Portsmouth Priory, where, as he said in a letter home, "I'm certainly doing a lot of praying," but his father soon switched him to Milton Academy, where his classmates remembered him as painfully shy, constantly tugging at his forelock, standing awkwardly with the toes of one foot over the other. Bobby would occasionally get a girl to let him walk her back from Sunday chapel, an important prep-school rite, but he would trail five feet behind her, head down, self-defeated. As an arch-Catholic in a WASP setting "he must have felt like an immigrant," thought his friend Mary Gimbel, who watched him at school dances get a partner for a few minutes and then retreat to lean against a wall, one foot on the other, mumbling to nobody in particular, "Who could be dippier than me?"

Recognizing that Bobby was especially needy, trying to cope with the fact that he was once again too young—in this case to be part of the great military adventure—Joe Junior was especially solicitous of him and wrote often: "I have gotten out of the primary squadron, having completed precision landings, acrobatics, etc., so now I am in the larger planes. I have just finished soloing in the fastest planes they have around here, which goe [sic] about 180, and it was a lot of fun.... Tomorrow I start formation in the larger planes, first in three plane formation, and then in nine plane formation. I have done three plane formation before, and found it was good fun..." He invited Bobby for a visit and smuggled him into the copilot's seat of his plane, letting him take the controls once they were aloft.

Some of the men at Jacksonville were put off by what they interpreted as Joe's arrogance. He had passed up the opportunity to learn to fly fighter planes in favor of mastering the ponderous PBY Catalina sea planes because, as he said, he felt he should pilot a Navy patrol bomber and command a crew. Yet he made an effort to be one of the boys. His success with women was legendary, and he would come back from leave with pictures of starlets and showgirls he had dated in New York. He was insubordinate enough to get demerits and sometimes spend the weekends marching in punishment. But the men liked his sense of humor except when its cutting edge was pointed at them. While at Jacksonville he became head of the Holy Name Society, a position which entitled him to wake up all the Catholics in the barracks for early mass. The Jews complained to the company priest, Father Maurice Sheehy, that Kennedy was waking them up too. When Sheehy asked him about it, Joe replied, "Don't they have souls? Aren't you interested in saving them?" The priest counseled restraint and Kennedy smiled. "The trouble with you, Father, is you're anti-Semitic."

Joe finished in the bottom tenth of his cadet class. Yet many had washed out of the rigorous training procedures and the final evaluation described him as "good officer material." When he graduated, his father came down to Jacksonville for the ceremony. Kennedy was supposed to address the graduating class, but he became so choked with emotion that he couldn't finish his speech, and pinned Joe Junior's wings on his lapel in proud silence.

Joe Junior was assigned to Banana River, Florida, having volunteered to work as an instructor in hopes of piling up flight hours so that he would be more likely to get his own command. He called home often, continuing to keep tabs on his sisters and brothers, especially the one right behind him.

Jack had taken a brief interlude on the West Coast, enrolling in Stanford University's business school in the fall of 1940. He was far more concerned with the high life than with balance sheets. "Still can't get used to the coeds," he wrote Lem, "but am taking them in my stride. Expect to cut one out of the herd and brand her shortly. But am taking it very slowly, do not want to be known as Beast of the East." A month later, after a visit to Hollywood where he talked to Spencer Tracy and Clark Gable at a party, Jack wrote again, this time concluding on a more serious note: "This draft has caused me a lot of concern. They will never take me in the Army—and yet if I don't [go] it will look quite bad."

He left Stanford after the first of the year and came home, to spend much of his time in a regimen of physical conditioning. By the end of the summer he had badgered his father about getting into the service until the Ambassador finally wrote to Admiral Alan Kirk, whom he'd known as naval attaché at the London embassy. Now head of the Office of Naval Intelligence, Kirk had arranged for the Navy to abide by the results of a physical examination conducted by family doctors. In September Jack was inducted and assigned to ONI in Washington. (The Ambassador also arranged for Lem Billings, who was having a difficult time getting into the service because of poor eyesight, to be assigned to the American Field Service, the civilian-manned ambulance corps.*)

Young Joe had been irritated with his father for not keeping Jack out of the military because of his back, and even more annoyed when his younger brother became an ensign before he did. But for the time being Jack didn't pose a threat to anyone. Rail-thin and sickly, he became a desk jockey at ONI, receiving and transmitting the ignored intelligence data that documented the alarming buildup of Japanese forces in the Pacific on the eve of

---

*Jack wrote Lem—addressing him as "Dear DeLemma"—about his father's recommendation: "You should feel rather complimented as he has not been doing any of that lately. As I imagine that you were sent a copy of the letter may I refer you to paragraph four line six beginning 'to go on and add to this his peculiar qualities would be superfluous.' Now the particular word that interested me is 'peculiar.' What could he possibly be referring to—your habit of picking your chin—your paranoiac desire for sunburn—or perhaps he means that rather 'peculiar' expression that comes over your face when you start inhaling your asthma medicine."

Pearl Harbor. On weekends he would drag Lem, who frequently visited him at his Washington apartment, to the touch-football games held on the Washington Monument Mall every Sunday afternoon. Lem hated these outings because he had to take his glasses off to play and couldn't see to catch the passes which were the main feature of the game. Yet Jack insisted, and Lem's ineptitude in front of strangers was a constant source of embarrassment to him, and friction between him and Jack.

Kick was also in Washington. She had been at odds with herself since coming home from England two years earlier—toying with the idea of attending Sarah Lawrence but instead enrolling at Finch, a junior college where she told everyone she was just "killing time" until she could get back to London. She gave teas for British War Relief, went to polo matches with her old boyfriend Peter Grace, and went out with her brothers' friends, who seemed "dreadfully immature" in comparison with the English noblemen she had dated abroad.

By the spring of 1940 Kick was getting what she called "gloomy letters" from Billy Hartington, who was now serving with the British Expeditionary Force at the Maginot Line. She knitted him a scarf as German forces pushed his unit back. In June she pressed her father almost hysterically to find out whether Billy was among those evacuated from Dunkirk. Relieved to hear he had made it, she tried to get her parents to let her go back to England but they refused. She waited. The next spring she wrote one of her English friends: "We do live in upsetting times. There is so little if anything these days that is a sure thing. I suppose it seems funny for me to say this when we haven't begun to feel the horrors and uncertainties of real war. But sometimes I feel that almost anything is better than an existence that is neither one thing or another."

At the end of the summer of 1941 her father asked Arthur Krock to get her a job on the isolationist *Washington Times-Herald,* so that she could at least feel near the center of things. Kick was hired and left home, as it turned out, for good.

The other employees at the paper expected just another of the ornamental young debs the *Times-Herald* frequently hired as cheap labor. But Kick won them over immediately. Because of her father's connections, she was in constant demand in diplomatic and political circles, the most sought-after "extra girl" in the city. Yet she had that charismatic Kennedy innocence: coworkers remember her averting her glance when she was with them in public for fear some prominent figure she had spotted might recognize her and somehow embarrass them. Sometimes they caught her at the building entrance after lunch, stuffing the mink coat she'd worn to some state function into a paper bag before returning to the office.

After a few weeks as assistant to executive editor Frank Waldrop, she began to work with thirty-one-year old John White, who was in charge of the paper's personality feature, ''Did You Happen to See——?'' It was the beginning of a close friendship—meticulously chronicled in White's diary —with overtones of the wacky romances in the film comedies they often attended together. Kick took the sharp-tongued Jean Arthur role (calling White a ''shrunken, bald-headed, irritable old man), and White bounced her insults right back (she was an ''ignorant, thickheaded mick'').

White lived with his sister Patsy and her children, and Kick visited frequently. She was attracted by the family atmosphere and also by the fact that the Whites were, in her phrase, ''free thinkers.'' White recalls: ''She'd sit and talk about anything. She just loved to talk. She was like Jack in this regard—she had an insatiable curiosity about people. It was like both of them suspected how cloistered their growing up had been and were trying to make up for it by finding out what made people who didn't happen to be Kennedys tick.'' White's diary shows that Kathleen was trying out her parents' world view on him, passing off their opinions as lightly held arguing points while actually trying to find out what he thought. ''KK calls to me all birth control is murder. I say her position is just Catholic Church technique for helping keep membership.'' Their relationship had an innocence about it in other areas too. ''She loved to cuddle,'' White recalls. ''I don't think that there had been much of that sort of thing when they were kids. But it had to take place apart from sex, which she referred to as 'the thing the priest says not to do.' I remember one night when I was rubbing her back and she was getting sort of sleepy. She suddenly looked up at me almost as if she was about to cry and said: 'Listen, the thing about me you ought to know is that I'm like Jack, incapable of deep affection.' It was one of the few times I got the feeling she was revealing something about herself.''

Jack had always been attracted to Kick's honesty and independence. In Washington he was attracted to Inga Arvad, one of her coworkers on the *Times-Herald*, as well. A striking Danish woman with a colorful, faintly dangerous past, Inga was only a little older than Jack but light-years away in experience. As a young woman she had gone to Germany to see the rise of fascism first hand. Claiming to be a correspondent with a Copenhagen newspaper, she had gotten an interview with Goering and moved in high Nazi circles for a time, appearing at the 1936 Olympics with Hitler, who called her ''the perfect example of Nordic beauty.'' Since then there had been many men in her life—including an absent husband, the Hungarian World War I flying ace Paul Fejos, and more recently a mysterious Swedish businessman named Axel Wenner-Gren, whom Allied intelligence suspected of espionage. By the time she was hired at the *Times-Herald* (like Kick with an assist from Krock, whom she'd met in a course at the Columbia Journalism School) Inga herself was under FBI surveillance as a possible German spy.

The Ambassador probably knew as much about her as FBI director J. Edgar Hoover did. ''Mr. Kennedy kept track of everything his kids did,'' Lem Billings said later, ''especially the boys. If he sensed that they were concealing something, if he had some kind of clue but not the entire story, he'd pretend he knew about it and start probing and more often than not he'd worm the whole business out of them.'' Nor did he rely on his psychological powers alone. ''After two or three dates,'' John White recalls, ''Kathleen sat down one evening and told me all about myself, things I'd even forgotten. She said someone had told her father about us and he had put one of his Irish operatives on the case. The verdict was that I was 'aimless but harmless.' She told me he did that with Jack too.'' Jack and Inga doubledated with John White and Kick to relieve Joe Kennedy's fears that the mysterious woman would get his son alone; but they would stop the car soon after leaving so that Jack and Inga could get a cab and go off into Washington high life on their own.

The Ambassador had good reason to be concerned. Inga was Jack's first deeply passionate attachment and it brought him into open conflict with his family. On one weekend visit to Palm Beach that Inga Arvad later described in detail, Joe Kennedy alternated between haranguing Jack about the relationship and trying to seduce her himself. Finally, Jack's superiors in Naval Intelligence became concerned enough to transfer him to Charleston, South Carolina, to lecture workers in defense plants on how to defend the plants and themselves against enemy attack, a post he described to Lem Billings and other friends as ''Siberia.''

His defense work had made him reflect on themes he had explored earlier in *Why England Slept*. In February 1942 he wrote to Billings, ''I wonder what's happening to this country. I never thought on my gloomiest day that there was any possible chance of our being defeated. But ignoring the military defeats we are suffering, which seems to be what everyone else is doing, ignoring that and just looking at the furor caused by a dancer and a movie actor (Melvyn Douglas) being appointed to civilian defense, which doesn't really mean a damn thing, to waste all that public indignation on that small event while all around us are examples of inefficiency that may lick us, Nero had better move over as there are a lot of fiddlers to join him. . . . It seems a rather strange commentary that it will take death in large quantities to wake us up, but I really don't think anything else ever will.'' The letter also expatiated on the larger forces at work in the war: ''I don't think anyone realizes that nothing stands between us and the defeat of our Christian crusade against paganism except a lot of chinks who never heard of God and a lot of Russians who have heard about Him but don't want Him. I suppose we can't afford to be very choosy at a time like this. When you get to Africa make friends with any brown, black or yellow man you happen to meet. In the *Decline of the West*, Mr. Spengler after carefully studying the waves of civilization, prophesized that the next few centuries belonged to the yellow man. After the Japs get through uniting Asia it looks as though Mrs. Lindbergh's 'wave of the future' will certainly have a yellow look.''

In early spring Lem stopped off in Charleston on his way back from

Nashville, where he had attended his brother's wedding, and found Jack frustrated and unhappy, but doing Charles Atlas workouts to build up his body in preparation for an operation on the chronically "unstable" back he had had since childhood, which he was scheduled to undergo in April. When Lem returned home to Baltimore, he found that the American Field Service was ready to send him to Africa. He also found a letter from Jack waiting for him, which began: "Dear Lemmer: I finished the ATLAS courses and believe I'm well on my way to HEALTH, STRENGTH and PERSONAL POWER, whatever Personal Power is. I can see that with time I will be Powerful, Graceful and Magnetic."

Jack added a note: "I haven't seen Inga, but I understand that she is heading for Reno. It would be certainly ironical if I should get married while you were visiting Germany." The possibility of such ironies did not amuse the Ambassador, who knew that Jack and Inga continued to see each other. On one of her visits to Charleston the FBI bugged her hotel room on orders from Attorney General Francis Biddle and ultimately Roosevelt himself, capturing Jack talking unguardedly about his work in between the sounds of their lovemaking.

Finally Joe Kennedy pulled more strings with James Forrestal, an old colleague from Wall Street who was now Secretary of the Navy, and got Jack transferred from intelligence to sea duty. In July 1942, Jack went to Northwestern University to attend Midshipmen's School. Lem, meanwhile, a private in the American Field Service, was bound for Cairo aboard a secret convoy, where he would soon see service in the desert war against General Rommel's forces in Egypt. "As you probably haven't heard," Jack wrote to him, "Inga-Binga got married—and not to me—She evidently wanted to leave Washington and get to N.Y.—so she married some guy she had known for years who loved her but whom she didn't love. I think it would have been much smarter for her to take the train, as they have several a day from Washington to N.Y. Anyway she's gone—and that leaves the situation rather blank."

Jack now began to apply himself in earnest, repeating the pattern that went back to his years at Choate, in which he alternated between troublemaking and achievement. When Admiral John Harlee showed up at the school to recruit volunteers for PT boat crews, he was especially interested in young men from upper-class families with sailing experience. The small, swift PTs —naval equivalent of the cavalry—had a romantic image as a result of their involvement in the rescue of General MacArthur from Corregidor in 1941 and other acts of derring-do in the early days of the war. Those who joined Harlee's elite corps didn't have to work their way up through the hierarchy of a large ship; they got quick command and saw action quickly too. Sensing a way out of the situation with Inga and the Navy brass that had made him more of a mucker than he had been at Choate, Jack volunteered for the PTs.

("The regulations are very strict physically," he wrote Lem. "You have to be young, healthy and unmarried, and as I am young and unmarried, I'm trying to get in. . . . So far in the war the fatalities [in the PTs] are ten men killed for every survivor.") On October 1, he reported to the PT training school in Melville, Rhode Island.

In Narragansett Bay, where he and his brothers and sisters had competed in sailboat races, Jack went on practice torpedo runs. He met Paul "Red" Fay, Jim Reed, and others who would become lifelong friends. To keep him happy there, and away from Inga, his father arranged for Torby MacDonald to be transferred from a desk job to Melville. Jack also became a close friend of a tall intellectual from Yale named Chuck Spalding, who saw a side of Jack the others didn't—a literary and thoughtful side. Both of them were Anglophiles, which Spalding recognized as having Oedipal overtones for Jack given the Ambassador's attitudes. They both read books like Cecil's life of Melbourne and *Pilgrim's Way* by John Buchan. Spalding became a sort of Jack Kennedy specialist, fascinated with him because he was so different from the other Kennedys. "The old man didn't have the ability to let people be neutral. For him there were only two alternatives, lackey or enemy. Jack liked everyone. He had only one requirement, that they be interesting."

Jack did so well that after graduation, when Fay, Torby, and others went on to combat units, he was kept behind as an instructor. He argued with Harlee, who later said, "He insisted that he be sent overseas to one of the squadrons in combat. . . . He yearned with great zeal to get into a war zone . . ." But perhaps because of his questionable physical condition he was kept behind until his father intervened yet again, this time at the son's urging, and Massachusetts Senator David Walsh got him into a combat unit headed for the South Pacific. "I'm now on my way to war . . ." he wrote to Lem on a stopover in San Francisco for equipment. "This job on these boats is really the great spot of the navy."

At a time when Young Joe was stuck in a squadron of gull-winged PMP Mariner reconnaissance planes stationed in Puerto Rico—with oil slicks of merchant vessels torpedoed by German submarines as the only evidence of action in his patrols of the Atlantic—Jack was going off to war, the beneficiary of an odd and fortuitous train of coincidence that could have ended in shame and dishonor but instead gave him a chance to redeem himself. Once again he had jumped ahead of his elder brother in a dramatic coup. Rose, who missed many of the nuances in the family, saw this one. "This was the first time Jack had won such an advantage by such a clear margin," she said later. "I daresay it cheered Jack and must have rankled Joe Jr."

As the nation mobilized, the Kennedys spread out. Rose wrote chatty "Dear Children" letters which summarized everyone's doings and mailed out nine carbon copies. She told about the problems Joe Junior and Jack encountered in the service, the daily brushes with naval discipline more than the dangers, and about Lord Halifax's son and others Kick was seeing in Washington. Eunice was at Stanford, "enjoying her classes and [the] whole new vista of ideas ... opened up to her." Pat was finished with her high-school examinations and thinking of getting an apartment in New York. Bobby had "improved very much in his desire for reading," and Jean had "broadened her outlook and acquaintances." Teddy was getting more adept serving mass and no longer stumbling on the dais. ("His terpsichorean efforts have improved and I did not see him fall down at all the last time.") Rose herself had completed a first-aid course, and, with a sharp eye for the rich and famous, had just seen Gloria Vanderbilt on her honeymoon in Palm Beach: "she looks just like her pictures."

Joe Kennedy was not included in this picture of domesticity. Cut off from public advancement, he no longer felt the need even for the minimal prudence of his days as Ambassador and was once again a shadowy figure with his own agenda, moving between his various residences and doing exactly as he pleased. Usually Rose did not fit into his plans. Tom Schriber, Joe Junior's good friend, was occasionally at the Palm Beach house and often heard Kennedy telephone his wife and tell her not to come down because he was busy with his friends. He bought nylons and other black-market goods and showered them on his daughters. He had bought a substantial interest in the Hialeah race track and was often there in his box, making two-dollar bets and using Joe Timilty or some other Boston crony as a "beard" for the young woman he happened to be seeing at the time. In New York he was seen frequently at the Stork Club, El Morocco, and other watering places of café society, and a writer who tabulated the numerous times he was mentioned in gossip columns found only one time that he was seen in the company of his wife.

Jack's troubles in Washington had gotten Kennedy interested in the FBI, and, unable to join the Roosevelt Administration, he had enlisted with J. Edgar Hoover, becoming a Special Service Contact for the Bureau in Hyannis. The agent who forwarded word of his recruitment to Washington was well aware of his value: "Because of his diplomatic background and his innumerable contacts in the international diplomatic set, he has entree to these circles and he is willing to use his entree on behalf of the Bureau. . . . In the moving picture industry he has many Jewish friends who he believes would furnish him, upon request, with any information . . . pertaining to Communist infiltration into the industry . . . [or] with reference to any individuals who have Communist sympathies."

As always when he had time on his hands, Kennedy thought about making money, the one endeavor that did not lead to controversy. But his objectives were now different from before. The greed of acquisition of his younger days had been replaced by the desire to protect the great fortune he had already accumulated, which he was convinced would be jeopardized in the social upheavals to come as a result of Roosevelt's war. He was acting defensively when he began to speculate in real estate soon after the war began.

Eventually he would hold huge tracts of land in Florida and South America in addition to oil leases in Texas; but the focus of his real estate investment was residential and commercial property in Manhattan. He had gotten involved in real estate early in 1941, when he decided to move his legal residence from New York to Florida, where there was no income or inheritance tax. His friend Cardinal Spellman put him in touch with John Reynolds, realty agent for the New York Archdiocese, to help with the sale of the Bronxville house. Reynolds convinced Kennedy that Manhattan's depressed prices were a prelude to a land boom, and together they began an aggressive strategy of acquisition that would eventually make Kennedy one of the largest landlords in the city.

The Ambassador poured millions into real estate. Determined as always to get the most for his money, he became a pioneer in "leveraging" his investment—making the smallest possible down payments, letting rents more than cover the mortgage debt, reselling for a price higher than the purchase price and several times the sum he was at risk. In 1941 he bought a million-dollar building on Sixth Avenue with $200,000 down; he held on to it for a few years and then sold it for $1.5 million. A $1.9-million building at Fifty-ninth Street and Lexington Avenue was acquired for a down payment of $100,000 and then resold for $5.5 million. When he saw what he had, Kennedy began to raise his rents aggressively, doubling and even trebling them, regardless of whether or not the tenants were involved in war-related work. The culmination of his real estate activity would come in 1945, when he purchased from Marshall Field the Chicago Merchandise Mart, then the largest office building in the country, for $12.5 million; Field had spent $30 million to build it. After renovating the Mart, filling it first with federal and then, as its value and rents rose, corporate tenants, Kennedy ultimately took in each year, in rents alone, more than he had paid for the building. In all, Reynolds estimates that not counting the Mart, Kennedy's profit from his wartime real estate speculations was more than $100 million. Trying initially to protect his fortune, he had almost doubled it.

But the central drama in the family had shifted away from the fifty-five-year-old Ambassador to his children. The younger ones were still safe at home, but the three oldest, about whom he'd always been most concerned, were increasingly in harm's way. Young Joe was patrolling the Atlantic seaboard and impatiently angling for an assignment that would allow him to see action. Kick was casting about for ways to return to England. Jack was going into the Pacific war zone.

It was the time when Jack got away from the family and acquired perspective on his father and his expectations. On the troop ship that carried him from San Francisco to the Solomon Islands, Jack spent a lot of time with another thin lieutenant in the PTs, Jim Reed, talking about his father and describing the knack he had for getting to the heart of the matter by making a chopping motion with his hand. Reed was there when a proper Bostonian on board buttonholed Kennedy and said condescendingly, "I was amazed, Jack, when I heard your father on the radio." Jack asked why. "Well, I thought that cheap Boston-Irish accent would come through, but it didn't. He spoke rather well." Jack was furious. "He almost punched the guy," said Reed. "Joe Junior would have."

While Young Joe was something of a martinet in his plane, demanding "Aye, aye, sir" and all the other perquisites of rank from his crewmen, Jack, who took command of *PT 109* on the island of Tulagi near Guadalcanal in late April of 1943, was looser, aware of himself not only as director but as actor too, and therefore not able to take the role as seriously as his older brother did. Jack did not feel he had to champion the family's honor; getting away from home, in fact, involved self-discovery and not, as with his brother, a quest to vindicate the Kennedy name. His letters home show that his ambition to be a writer was not unrealistic. They were no longer attempts to impress with the power of his analysis and to fashion ideas that fit the Kennedy party line, but descriptions of the realities of the war he was beginning to encounter. On May 6, he wrote Lem Billings about a Japanese air attack the day his troop ship arrived in the Solomons: "During a lull in the battle—a Jap parachuted into the water. We went to pick him up as he floated along—and got within about 20 yards of him. He suddenly threw aside his life jacket and pulled out a revolver and fired two shots at our bridge. I had been praising the Lord and passing the ammunition right alongside—but that slowed me up a bit—the thought of him sitting in water —battling an entire ship. We returned the fire with everything we had—the water boiled around him—but everyone was too surprised to shoot straight. Finally an old soldier standing next to me picked up his rifle, fired once, and blew the top of his head off. He threw his arms up, plunged forward and sank—and we hauled our ass out of there."

Away from the family Jack began to question some of the Kennedy orthodoxies, among them the religion that was so important spiritually to his mother and socially to his father. A fellow Catholic who served with him in the South Pacific later recalled long bull sessions in which Jack expressed his skepticism and then said that he would "work everything out" with one of the family's spiritual counselors, Bishop Fulton Sheen, when he got back from the war.

It was a time of liberation for Kick too. She had heard news from her friend Dinah Bridge that Billy Hartington had become engaged to Sally

Norton, niece of Lord Mountbatten. Kick was convinced that it was only her absence that had made him take this step and that her reappearance in London would change his mind. In late March, she left her job with the *Times-Herald* to join a Red Cross training program, seeing this as the way to get back to England. On June 17, as Jack was going into the front lines of the PT war against Japanese shipping, she boarded the *Queen Mary* wearing a winter uniform and carrying a gas mask, musette bag, first-aid kit, and tin helmet, one of 160 nurses among thousands of troops.

The crossing was precarious; Kick's sleep was interrupted by a sharp swerve every half-hour or so to avoid German submarines. After making it to Greenock, Scotland, Kick and the other Red Cross recruits took the train to London, where she met her English friends David and Sissy Ormsby-Gore and stayed at their Hampstead home while she awaited her assignment. She used the opportunity to renew her acquaintance with old family friends like the Astors, but she had returned to England because of one person, Billy Hartington, who came down to London from his base at Alton and took her to the Four Hundred Club. Kick found Billy "older and more ducal" but otherwise the same as he had always been—"unlike anyone I have ever known." On July 14 she wrote her mother, "Billy and I went out together for the first time last Saturday. It really is funny to see people put their heads together the minute we arrive any place. There's heavy betting on when we are going to announce it. Some people have gotten the idea that I'm going to give in. Little do they know..." Actually it was a far deeper relationship than she let on to her parents. In a letter to Lord Beaverbrook on Red Cross stationery she canceled a scheduled dinner because she had a chance to spend the weekend with "Bill" and his family at one of their country places. To Jack she could be both more personal and more ironic about the dilemma than she could to her mother: "Of course I know he would never give in about the religion, and he knows I never would. It's all rather difficult as he is very, very fond of me and as long as I am about he'll never marry.... It's really too bad because I'm sure I would be a most efficient Duchess of Devonshire in the post-war world, and as I'd have a castle in Ireland, one in Scotland, one in Yorkshire, and one in Sussex I could keep my old nautical brothers in their old age..." She ended the letter: "Well, take care, Johnny. By the time you get this so much will have happened." Indeed, before it arrived, Jack would be missing in action, presumed dead, and, in a sense, reborn.

On August 1, intelligence had reported that four Japanese destroyers were steaming through the Blackett Strait, and fourteen PT boats set out to intercept the armada of war and cargo ships ferrying supplies to the Japanese stronghold on the island of Vila. At two thirty in the morning, after failing to make contact with the Japanese, *PT 109* with Jack at the helm was cruising back toward the base at Rendova when a large shape loomed up suddenly on the starboard side. It was the Japanese destroyer *Amigari,* and seconds later, before Kennedy could change course, it plowed into *PT 109,* cutting the PT in half.

At the moment of impact Jack thought to himself with typical detachment, "This is how it feels to be killed." He wasn't, but two of his men were, and three others were badly injured. He swam to get one of them, "Pappy" McMahon, and towed him back to the wreckage of the boat, where they clung to the hull until daylight with the other survivors. As the remnants of *PT 109* began to sink, they all headed for a tiny island three miles away, Kennedy breast-stroking and pulling McMahon, who was hanging on to a piece of wood, by a tow rope clenched in his teeth. After they were washed up on the beach, Jack and his men rested. That night he stripped naked and swam back out into the Blackett Strait again, carrying a .38 revolver to fire in case a search vessel passed nearby. He turned back at dawn, and, as the story later emerged, was unable to make headway against the strong riptide; he was so exhausted that he gave himself over to the current, thinking it would carry him out to sea, but he was swept up safely on land.

They were afraid there might be Japanese soldiers on the tiny island, but while they found a Japanese cache of candy and crackers, there was no enemy. There was another harrowing swim out to open sea to look for rescue, but no luck. Two islanders came by in a canoe and Jack carved a message on a coconut shell for them to take to an Australian coast watcher several islands away: NATIVE KNOWS POSIT HE CAN PILOT 11 ALIVE NEED SMALL BOAT KENNEDY. On the sixth day after their ordeal began, an island boat arrived to take Kennedy and his men to a rendezvous with a PT rescue boat. As it pulled away the men were singing "Jesus loves me, this I know, for the Bible tells me so . . ."

In Hyannis, as Joey Gargan, Teddy's cousin and playmate, later recalled, there was no inkling that anything was amiss. The Ambassador woke the boys every morning and took them riding at the stables in Oysterville. One morning he went without them and returned looking flushed. Asked what was wrong, he said he had just heard the news that Jack was safe over the radio of his Cadillac and had been so excited that he had driven off the road. Then he admitted that he had known for three days that his son was missing, although he had told no one, not even Rose. The relief and joy which he now shared with the others were amplified by the private knowledge that he had, in effect, sent Jack into battle to get him away from Inga Arvad.

Later on, *PT 109* would become a modern version of Washington crossing the Delaware. At the time it was seen differently. Barney Ross, one of the survivors, thought at first that the whole affair would be considered a "disaster." It was rumored that on first hearing of the fate of *PT 109,* Mac-

Arthur grumbled that Kennedy ought to be court-martialed. In a letter to Lem, Jack himself treated the episode quite casually. ("We have been having a difficult time for the last two months. Lost our boat about a month ago when Jap can cut us in two and lost some of our boys. We had a bad time for a week on a Jap island . . .") But while there was some confusion about how the accident occurred and whether or not better seamanship should have been employed (some doubted that the highly maneuverable PT boat could have been hit at all if the crew had been alert), there was never any doubt about Jack's conduct in the aftermath of the collision. It was exactly the sort of saga of bravery and survival that the wartime press was looking for. The *New York Times* put the story on page one; the Boston papers did too, adding an artist's conception of crucial scenes in the seven-day ordeal.

Jack adopted a manly modesty in his public statements on *PT 109*, saying that the only virtue he saw in the experience was that "everyone stood up to it." He was embarrassed by his father's immediate and unabashed lobbying for a medal.

But making that naked swim into the Blackett Strait was a kind of baptismal rite, and there was a new tone of self-confidence in his letters home. "When I read that we will fight the Japs for years if necessary," he wrote after recovering sufficiently to take command of another PT, "and will sacrifice hundreds of thousands if we must—I always like to check from where he is talking—it's seldom out here. People get so used to talking about billions of dollars and millions of soldiers that thousands of dead sounds like drops in the bucket. But if those thousands want to live as much as the ten I saw—they should measure their words with great, great care . . ."

There was jubilation at Hyannis—not just because Jack was safe but also because of the coup he had scored, a coup that was, in the context, easy to see as a vindication of the family. On September 6, when the Kennedy clan and family friends assembled to celebrate the Ambassador's birthday, Jack's heroism was the topic of the day. At one point in the celebration, one of the Boston politicians proposed a toast: "To Ambassador Joe Kennedy, father of the hero, our own hero, Lieutenant John F. Kennedy, of the United States Navy." Joe Junior, home on leave from relatively mundane duty flying observation missions outside San Juan, lifted his glass manfully with the others and smiled throughout the evening. But that night his father's crony Joe Timilty, with whom Joe was sharing a room over the weekend, heard him weeping. In a moment that showed something of the pressures that underlay the prerogatives of being firstborn, Young Joe suddenly sat up in bed, oblivious of Timilty's presence, and began clenching and unclenching his fists in a rage, muttering, "By God, I'll show them." Three weeks later he was on his way to England to test himself in a battle at last.

The squadron he joined was stationed on the coast of Cornwall, a little piece of the U.S. Navy landlocked into an air force base. Flying the PBY 4 on patrols into the Bay of Biscay was less glamorous work than he had thought it would be. The heavy planes skimmed the waves for eight hours on each patrol, with the crew hoping for the mathematically slim chance of sighting a surfaced submarine. Kennedy saw nothing in his first weeks in action: the closest he came to battle was when his plane was sighted by enemy fighters and lumbered ignominiously up into the clouds to avoid an engagement.

He came to look forward to brief furloughs in London. He saw other famous American sons, Elliott Roosevelt and William Randolph Hearst, Jr., as well as Smart Set Londoners. He saw a great deal of Kick, who had become a favorite in the Red Cross canteens, known as the "girl on the bicycle" as a result of a news photograph showing her pedaling to work in uniform. Just as Kick had introduced Jack to Inga, so now she introduced Joe to Pat Wilson, a raven-haired Australian beauty with Kennedy-blue eyes whose first marriage, to the Earl of Jersey, had ended in divorce (although it had been called the "dream match" of the year). She had married again, a banker named Robin Wilson, twelve years her senior, who was a British Army officer now stationed abroad. Joe fell in love with her; it was the first serious affair of his life. They spent weekends together in the English countryside and he bought a Raleigh bicycle so that he could pedal from his base into the nearest town to telephone her. This love, in fact, made him part of the peculiar ambience of London in early 1944—not quite the determinedly cheerful bravery that had marked the Battle of Britain, but something quieter, with its own sense of foreboding about the fearsome price the expected Nazi invasion attempt would exact. Kick felt that she and her brother were in the eye of the hurricane. "Joe finished up his leave a bit tired," she wrote after one hectic weekend. "But I suppose that is the way with everyone. One feels one must pack all the fun possible into the shortest space of time."

The fact that Joe had begun a serious relationship with a married woman made him more sympathetic to Kick's dilemma than he might otherwise have been. The vise that compressed her and Billy was inexorable: as heir to the leading Protestant peerage in England, Billy couldn't allow his children to be raised as Catholics; as a Catholic, Kick couldn't be married in a Protestant church. Rose was irreconcilable: religion was the only area in her life beyond compromise and she saw this as a matter of a soul's damnation. Joe and everyone else recognized that the marriage was sentimentally appealing and tried to find a way out, but the problem seemed insoluble.

Just after the first of the year, there had been a brief ray of hope when Billy stood for Parliament in a West Derbyshire by-election. If he won a seat in Commons, it would not only remove him from the Army, where he had served since before Dunkirk, but also force him to give up his title, thus partly closing the religious gap that separated him from Kick. She worked in his headquarters mailing out flyers reminding constituents that a vote for Hartington was a vote for Churchill. Billy appeared on the hustings—very tall and a little stoop-shouldered in aristocratic fashion, his thinning hair brushed back with military severity, speaking into a microphone held for him by his butler. While not renouncing the privileges of class, he spoke to crowds, already impatient for changes in the social system, about the need for increased social security, economic reconstruction, and other changes in the postwar world. When the votes were counted, however, his socialist opponent had won by more than five thousand votes. Billy went back to his regiment still the next Duke of Devonshire.

Seeing how important Kick was to their son, the Cavendishes had softened somewhat in their opposition to the match. But the Kennedys had become even more unyielding. In the increasingly agitated letters that passed back and forth between London and Palm Beach that winter and on into the spring, Kick argued the issue against Rose, Eunice, and Bobby, most religious of the Kennedys. Only Young Joe was on her side, calling her two or three times a week to offer support and also writing to the family urging tolerance for her dilemma. Jack, who had been Kick's primary confidant, was far less involved in the family melodrama. ("In regard to Kick becoming a Duchess," he had written to Lem seven months earlier, "I doubt it—but it would be rather nice—as I believe it would give me some title or other.")

At this point the war was over for him. He had given up his command, weeping, and come home on medical leave thin and malarial, suffering again from the back problem which he would later blame alternately on Harvard football and Navy service. After stops in Hollywood to see Inga Arvad—who was now trying to break into the movies and had cooled toward him as much as he had to her—and at the Mayo Clinic, he made the rounds of New York night spots, back in sexual competition with his older brother, who had warned him, "I know you will be disappointed to hear that before leaving [for England] I succeeded in dispersing my first team in such various parts that it will be impossible to cover all the territory." Nonetheless, Jack did all right, adding the allure of a published author and battle veteran to his personal attractiveness. (One of the comments he made to the girls he took out who asked about his heroic ordeal was that while swimming nude in the Blackett Strait he had thought a good deal about sharks and his testicles: "And I swam a lot of backstroke.") It was the combination of Jack's self-deprecating manner and what he had endured that attracted John Hersey to the story of *PT 109*. Hersey, now married to Frances Ann Cannon, began to write a story for *Life* magazine. It turned out to be too long and not topical enough for *Life*, but it was published in the *New Yorker* in early June and drew considerable attention, gaining an even wider audience when the Ambassador got Paul Palmer, editor of *Reader's Digest*, to reprint it there.

At about the time the Hersey article appeared, the Ambassador noted in a letter to Beaverbrook: "Young Joe has just volunteered for an extra month's duty before he's sent home, which will give him 40 missions. Although he's had a large number of casualties in his squadron, I'm still hoping and praying we'll see him around the first of July." Spurred on by the fact that his younger brother was now the subject of admiring feature articles, Young Joe flew during the D-Day invasion of France in June 1944 as part of the immense effort by American and British pilots to blanket the Channel with constant overflights alert for the telltale snorkel of German subs hunting stragglers in the invasion fleet. He did this job, but he still seemed driven. Fellow fliers noted something like desperation in his efforts. At one point he disregarded orders and flew so close to German fortifications on the Isle of Guernsey that the plane was hemstitched with flak and there were murmurings among the crew about his unnecessary recklessness. As if seeking a metaphor for his turmoil, he became an almost fanatical gambler while on leave in London. An English friend, Frank Moore O'Ferrall, recalls: "It didn't matter what it was—cards, horses, cockroaches crawling up the wall, any mortal thing." On one occasion the two of them went to the Salisbury races. Joe had no winners in the first five races; in the sixth he bet a ten-to-one underdog named "Clever Joe" and won.

Kick and Billy were also caught up in an atmosphere dominated by uncertainty about the future. As D-Day approached, they had decided to force events. In an informal compact they agreed that if the English aristocracy was left unchanged by the social upheaval sure to follow the war, and if the dukedom was thus still preeminent, their children would become Protestant; if, however, the class system was modified in a way that made the title less important, their children would be baptized as Catholics. There was a flurry of hysterical telegrams from Rose and doomed last-minute negotiations that ultimately involved Cardinal Spellman ("Archie Spell" in the coded cables passing between Hyannis and London like diplomatic traffic); an English Jesuit who had advised Evelyn Waugh on his conversion (and who told Kathleen that her only hope of salvation would be for Billy to die before her); Archbishop Godfrey, the English papal legate; and through him the Pope himself. When all the religious diplomacy failed, Kathleen and Billy prepared to marry in a civil ceremony.

The marriage, which took place under threat of excommunication, was performed on May 6, 1944, in the small red-brick building of the Chelsea Registry Office. The British press had speculated whether the Kennedy family would attend the wedding, but only Joe Junior, in dress uniform, was there to stand up with her. Lady Astor, whose aversion to Catholicism was legendary, also came in a show of support for Kick, because she thought the disapproval of the Kennedy women unkind. The Cavendishes were there, along with the Marchioness of Salisbury. Billy's best man was his fellow officer the Duke of Rutland. Kick was dressed in pink crepe with a mink jacket and a diamond brooch. Rice being rationed, the guests threw rose petals instead.

Kick never forgot her brother Joe's courage in representing the family at her side. ''When he felt that I had made up my mind he stood by me ...'' she later wrote. ''In every way he was the perfect brother doing, according to his own lights, the best for his sister with the hope that in the end it would be the best for the family.'' After the ceremony the newlyweds cut into a frosting-less cake purchased with the pooled ration stamps of the wedding party and left for a honeymoon at Compton Place, one of the Duke's houses, in Eastbourne.

The marriage created something of a scandal among Irish Catholic friends at home. One acquaintance of the family recalls: ''The reaction of my own mother was one of horror. What a terrible cross for poor Rose to bear! What a valiant woman she was! That sort of thing.'' Rose knew it was coming and two weeks prior to the ceremony checked herself into New England Baptist Hospital for ''minor surgery'' so that she would be unavailable to the press. She told the friend who brought her the bad news, ''I'm glad I heard it from you first. This gives me time to prepare. The press is probably outside my door right now.'' In fact, reporters did position themselves at the hospital door, but all they got was a statement that ''Mrs. Kennedy was too sick to discuss the marriage.''

Although Joe Kennedy presented a united front with his distraught wife, privately he was far less bothered by the union than she was. He set aside extra money for Kick so she would ''not be dependent on the Cavendishes'' and he wired her secret congratulations: ''Remember you still are and always will be tops with me.'' The Irish romanticism which surfaced at odd times was brought out by what he admired as Kick's defiant act of selfhood. After the air had cleared somewhat, he wrote Beaverbrook: ''I see now that I've lost one of my daughters to England. She was the apple of my eye and I feel the loss because I won't have her near me all the time, but I'm sure she's going to be wonderfully happy and I can assure you England is getting a great girl ...''

Jack, writing Lem Billings from Palm Beach, took ironic note of the torch his friend was left carrying for his sister: ''Your plaintive howl in not being let in on Kathleen's nuptial plans reached me this morning. It was certainly evident that you weren't irked so much by her getting married as by her failure to inform you. You might as well take it in stride and as sister Eunice from the depth of her righteous Catholic wrath so truly said: 'It's a horrible thing—but it will be nice visiting her after the war, so we might as well face it.' At family dinners at the Cape when you don't pass Hartington the muffins, we'll know how you feel though.''

After the honeymoon, Billy went back to his unit in France and Kick

sailed for home to patch things up with her parents. Eighteen-year-old
Bobby was in the Naval Reserve at Harvard and "pleading to be permitted
to enlist in Navy Aviation," as his father wrote a friend, but he refused to
have any more Kennedys at risk. Joe Junior's extended tour was over. He
had given up hope that the war would furnish the existential opportunities
he needed to reassert his primacy over Jack, and had in fact packed his gear
for the voyage home, when he heard of a top-secret and extremely dangerous
mission for which experienced pilots were being sought. Without knowing
the details of what was involved, he immediately volunteered.

Code named Aphrodite, the top-secret project was aimed at the V-1 rockets
that had come to represent the thrashing tail of the dying German war effort.
Allied intelligence had identified what it thought were the launch sites of
the flying bombs raining down on England with such devastating effect—
some mysterious and much-photographed bunkers at various sites in Ger-
man-controlled territory across the Channel. Since late 1942, for months
before the first buzz bombs struck London, Allied planes had attacked, dropping 36,000 tons of bombs at a cost of 154 planes and 774 airmen. The
bunkers remained intact. Ignoring the proven success of U.S. dive-bombers
against the Japanese Navy in the Pacific campaign, air strategists came up
with a desperate remedy for a desperate situation. They would make a
guided missile of their own—a bomber loaded with explosives which a pilot
would get into the air and on course, bailing out once a mother ship had
taken remote control and begun to line the plane up on target by means of a
television camera in its nose.

Young Joe pressed his case so fervently that he was chosen to command
the flight. For the next three weeks he trained in secret at a base in Dunkes-
well, in the remote countryside of East Anglia. Making practice runs in a
bomber loaded with ten tons of sand, while the PBY 4 that would fly the
mission was being gutted and modified to carry a load of explosive larger
than anything yet dropped, Kennedy perfected the take-off and switch-over
to remote control, signaled by the code words "Spade Flush." A week before
the mission was scheduled to go, four Air Force B-17s were sent on a separate
Aphrodite mission but none of them made it anywhere near the target. The
Navy program went ahead, the proven danger making it even more attractive
to Kennedy, who cheerfully told his gambling friend Frank Moore O'Ferrall, with whom he went to the races at Ascot, that he was involved in
something where his chances were no better than fifty-fifty.

On August 11, the night before take-off in the plane called "Zootsuit
Black," Kennedy stalked around the barracks nervous and annoyed because
he was not allowed to bicycle to a public telephone and make a goodbye call
to Pat Wilson. He said he was sorry he had ever volunteered for the job, but
when electronics officer Earl Olsen took him aside to say he was uncertain
about the circuits and wanted time to make some changes, Joe wasn't in a

mood to listen: "I appreciate what you're trying to do but I don't have any say about things like that. I just volunteered to fly." Olsen pressed him—all he had to do was ask for a delay until the electrical system was changed. Kennedy repeated that he had already volunteered. "Sure you volunteered," Olsen said, "and you can unvolunteer, too, don't you see? You're risking your neck for nothing." Olsen pleaded with him to see the commanding officer about putting the mission off. "No," Kennedy said finally, "I don't think I will. I think I'm going to fly it." If there was a death instinct at work in his stubbornness, as some of the others in the squadron later speculated, there was also a belief in his invulnerability.

Army brass called in black troops to load the ten tons of TNT—the largest bomb so far assembled, carrying enough of a charge, it was estimated, to devastate an area of many miles. Young Joe phoned William Randolph Hearst, Jr.'s wife, Lorelle, just before taking off. "I'm about to go into my act," he told her, in what was perhaps a cryptic reference to differences with his father over his strong support for Kick's marriage, "and if I don't come back tell my dad—despite our differences—that I love him very much." As he climbed into the cockpit of Zootsuit Black, another pilot asked him if he had his insurance paid up and saw the famous Kennedy grin: "Nobody in my family needs insurance." Shortly before six o'clock in the early evening, he got the heavy plane into the air.

August 13 was a Sunday morning. The Kennedys were together at Hyannis because it was summer and because Kick, now the Marchioness of Hartington, was home for her first visit in a year. It seemed as though the family might actually make it through the war in one piece. Jack was mending, and the Hersey article was making him a national celebrity. Young Joe was scheduled to be back soon. It was after lunch and Rose was reading the paper while the Ambassador took his daily nap; the younger children were talking quietly so as not to disturb him. Two priests appeared at the door and said they had to see Mr. Kennedy. Rose invited them in to wait until he woke; they said it was urgent, that Young Joe was missing. Frightened and confused, Rose ran upstairs and told her husband, who leaped out of bed and came down hoping it would be a reprise of Jack's experience and Kennedy resourcefulness would save Young Joe. But the priests told him the details they had withheld from Rose. Twenty-eight minutes after take-off, and just after the code words "Spade Flush" signaled that the bomber had been given over to the control of the mother ship, there had been a sudden gasp and then a huge fireball and an explosion so great that its concussion damaged aircraft flying support and forced them to land. There was no hope. Young Joe was dead.

After the priests left, the Ambassador went out onto the porch, drawn and white, and told the children. "I want you all to be particularly good to your mother," he said. He urged them to be brave, as their brother would have wanted, and to go on with the sailing race planned for that afternoon. All of them except Jack did carry on. Suddenly the oldest Kennedy of his generation, he walked alone on the beach, frail and crippled, while his father went upstairs and locked himself in his bedroom.

PART 2

THE STAND-IN

A heritage cannot be transmitted; it must be conquered.

—ANDRÉ MALRAUX

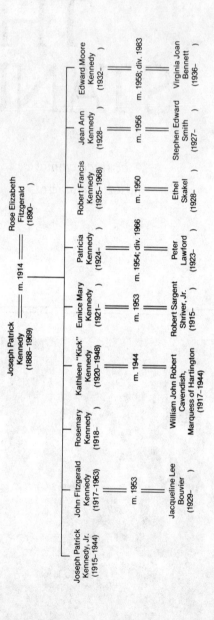

Joseph Patrick
Kennedy
(1888–1969)

≡≡ m. 1914 ≡≡

Rose Elizabeth
Fitzgerald
(1890–   )

Joseph Patrick
Kennedy, Jr.
(1915–1944)

John Fitzgerald
Kennedy
(1917–1963)

m. 1953

Jacqueline Lee
Bouvier
(1929–   )

Rosemary
Kennedy
(1918–   )

Kathleen "Kick"
Kennedy
(1920–1948)

m. 1944

William John Robert
Cavendish,
Marquess of Hartington
(1917–1944)

Eunice Mary
Kennedy
(1921–   )

m. 1953

Robert Sargent
Shriver, Jr.
(1915–   )

Patricia
Kennedy
(1924–   )

m. 1954; div. 1966

Peter
Lawford
(1923–   )

Robert Francis
Kennedy
(1925–1968)

m. 1950

Ethel
Skakel
(1928–   )

Jean Ann
Kennedy
(1928–   )

m. 1956

Stephen Edward
Smith
(1927–   )

Edward Moore
Kennedy
(1932–   )

m. 1958; div. 1983

Virginia Joan
Bennett
(1936–   )

1.

*L*ABOR DAY HAD ALWAYS BEEN special for the Kennedys—a last fling with the long Hyannis summer, a final time to be together before going off to their separate schools. It was a punctuation point in their year, one of those moments that dramatized the passage of time and the changes it had made in them—less a holiday, really, than a transition. This was particularly true in 1944, when they gathered for the first time since the diaspora of the war.

Jack had invited some of his PT friends and their wives—Red Fay, Barney Ross, Jim and Jewel Reed, Lennie and Kate Thom—and the new visitors quickly discovered that when the Kennedys were together they focused intensely on each other. The brothers and sisters joked with Kick about her new title, staging elaborate bows and curtsies and calling her ''Your Ladyship'' as they passed in the hall. During one lunch, Jack, his malarial jaundice hidden under a carefully acquired tan, made a casual comment to Eunice that she should join the WAC, and when she dismissed the idea spent the rest of the afternoon trying to convince her. Bobby, who was trying desperately to get onto active duty, kept asking Jack for war stories. When one of the non-Kennedys present happened to remark on a book Kick was reading by Anne Morrow Lindbergh about her husband's isolationism and consequent fall from grace, Kick interpreted it as an oblique criticism of her father's politics and launched into a spirited defense of his ambassadorship.

To a stranger like Jewel Reed, it was akin to visiting an exotic tribe which had its own folklore and customs and its own world view as well. It required a cryptographer's talents, she decided, to unravel the meanings in their private talk. But there was a paradox: while the family communicated through what amounted to a secret code, it seemed to keep them at arm's length from each other rather than producing intimacy. As one of their spiritual advisers said: "The hardest question you can ask a Kennedy is 'How are you?' They can't deal with the ramifications of that question." The brothers and sisters expressed their affection in barbed jokes that played on well-known failings—Jack's scarecrow physique, Kick's awkward hips, Bobby's shortness—and kept each of them in line. The mother and father seemed almost as distant from the children as from each other. Along with her husband, Jewel had heard about the famous Kennedy mealtimes from Jack and assumed that they would be like public affairs seminars. But the Ambassador, who limited the guests to one cocktail apiece before dinner, sat at the head of the table and, without mentioning the war or other national issues as she expected, quizzed each of his children perfunctorily about their performances in the day's sports. Rose sat at the foot of the table, breaking in at inappropriate times to ask conversation-stopping questions and then lapsing into silence. At the end of the meal she took out a compact, powdered her face and freshened her lipstick, and then waited pointedly until everyone noticed that she was ready to excuse herself and stood while she left the room. It was a ritual that reminded Jewel Reed of the empty courtesies extended to housemothers she'd had at Smith College.

On Sunday evening Jack and his friends stayed up late. Seeing that they had sneaked liquor out of the Ambassador's well-stocked but seldom used cabinet, Bobby rushed up: "Gosh! If Dad finds out about this, he'll be awfully mad!" Kick snapped at him, "Look, you're upsetting our guests. Just get lost, okay?" After Bobby had gone, the friends sat out on the lawn passing an open bottle around. Then Jack started them all singing. *PT 109* veteran Barney Ross was doing a command performance of "Alexander's Ragtime Band," including gymnastic flips punctuated by the others' clapping, when the upstairs window flew up, sash smacking the frame, and the Ambassador stuck his head out. "Jack!" he shouted. "Don't you and your friends have any respect for your dead brother?" Before anyone could respond, he had slammed the window down again. It was then that Jewel and the others realized what nobody had mentioned: that the death of Joe Junior had been the submerged theme of the weekend, a bulky iceberg without a tip to warn them. It was the first Labor Day without him, the experience which gave the holiday even more of a ceremonial quality than it would otherwise have had and made the endless competitions in golf, tennis, and sailing into something like funeral games for a fallen hero.

When his friends asked him about his brother, Jack had tried to dismiss it in the manner of a war-weary veteran. "It was a matter of statistics. His number was up." But there was more to it than that. More than anyone else, Young Joe had established their *Kennedyness*, and his death had caused a metaphysical lurch, raising questions about their ultimate purpose which had previously remained unasked. Jack came close to the mark a few weeks later when he was composing the introduction to *As We Remember Joe*, a memorial volume of reminiscences by family and friends that he was putting together to give his parents for Christmas. He wrote of his brother almost as if Joe had been some Renaissance prince whose premature passing cast doubt on the chain of being and the meaning of life itself: "His worldly success was so assured and inevitable that his death seems to have cut into the natural order of things."

Unable to admit their grief, let alone share it, the family mourned in inarticulate loneliness. For weeks Rose walked on the beach like a tiny black shore bird, going to her study each evening to answer letters of condolence on the black-bordered stationery she would continue to use long after the prescribed mourning period was over. Bobby continued trying to get an opportunity to vindicate his dead brother in battle. Kick still cried whenever the subject of Young Joe came up. "I'm so sorry I broke down tonight," she wrote to a friend who had called from London asking what to do with the record player, typewriter, and other personal items her brother had left behind. "It never makes things easier ... I don't know whether I'll even want to use the much-discussed typewriter, but it will always make me think of that hard talker Joe. I still can't believe it. It's hard to write. I don't feel sorry for Joe—just for you ... and everyone that knew him 'cause no matter how he yelled, argued, etc. he was the best guy in the world ..."

But it was Joseph Kennedy who was hardest hit, spending evenings alone in his room listening to Wagner overtures on the phonograph. "For a long time he had the look on his face of someone who has seen something frightening and can't get it out of his mind," in the words of Lem Billings. He shivered at the drafts that circulated in the Hyannis house, muttering Irish atavisms about banshees. He had always prided himself on his sophistication, and had set out to acquire worldliness in the same premeditated way he set out to acquire his fortune; there had always been a reservoir of innocence about him—the pleasure he took in his own rake's progress, his conviction that he was blessed with the luck of the Irish and could win at the high-stakes game he'd chosen to play without ever putting anything of real value at risk. The political world had been intractable, but otherwise he had taken what he wanted—surprised that it was available, delighted that it yielded to his desires so easily. He was devastated now that his hopes for Young Joe— the least controversial aspect of his ambition and the least tinged with malice or chicanery—were denied; stunned that he should have had to make such a huge and unexpected installment payment on the purchase of his dreams at this late stage in his life.

"He was the oldest boy and I have spent a great deal of time making what I thought were plans for his future," he wrote in a pathetic reply to White House secretary Grace Tully's note of condolence. And when Joe Junior's old friend and roommate, Robert Downes, visited Hyannis after hearing the news, he was shocked at how vulnerable the Ambassador had suddenly become. Almost immediately upon seeing him Kennedy burst into tears. ''I feel bad that I was away so much when the boy was growing up,'' he sobbed. ''I didn't know him like I should have. I cheated him.''

And once involved in tragedy, it was difficult to break free again. A few days after Labor Day, when Jack's friends had left and he had registered at the Chelsea Naval Hospital in Boston as an outpatient, the rest of the Kennedys went to New York. Rose was in her suite at the Plaza and Joe in his at the Waldorf, with the children shuttling between. A call came from England for the Marchioness of Hartington. The voice floating on the overseas line had news of her husband Billy. He had gathered his men for one more rush at German positions and was saying, ''Come on, you fellows...'' when a sniper's bullet smashed into his chest. Once again the Kennedys wanted to believe a mistake had been made, but then a call came from the Cavendishes confirming news of the death and asking Kick to come back to England.

Joe called her old friends John and Patsy White in Washington. ''I still hate you guys,'' he said to Patsy, ''but she needs you. Please come up and help.'' Arriving in New York, Patsy White found Kathleen pale and sick, looking tiny and alone, isolated inside the élan that worked so well in good times but was no help in time of sorrow.

''Have they given you a sleeping pill?'' she asked.

''No,'' Kick replied, shaking her head sadly. ''My mother just keeps taking me to mass and saying that God sends us no cross heavier than we can bear.'' Kick kept saying, as if stunned, ''The amazing thing about Billy was that he loved me so much. I felt needed. I really felt I could make him happy.'' She told Patsy White her main regret was that she hadn't gotten pregnant.

The British Government sent a plane for Kathleen. When she landed in Chatsworth, she threw her arms around Billy's sisters and said she was glad to be ''home.'' She went to Belgium, where Billy had been buried, and then returned to England to stay with her in-laws. She spent her days talking to her dead husband's friends and getting her dead brother's belongings ready for shipment home. Referring bitterly to the worry she and Billy had expended on which religion to choose for the children who now would not be born, she said to a friend, ''Well, I guess God has taken care of the matter in his own way, hasn't He?'' Billy's sister Elizabeth later said of Kathleen, ''I never met anyone so desperately unhappy in my life. I had to sleep in her room night after night. Her mother had tried to convince her that she had committed a sin in this marriage, so that in addition to losing a husband, she worried about losing her soul.''

Back home Joseph Kennedy reeled under the effects of the catastrophe he had always dreaded. "For a fellow who didn't want the war to touch your country or mine," he wrote Lord Beaverbrook, "I have had a rather bad dose—Joe dead, Billy Hartington dead, my son Jack in a naval hospital. I have had brought home to me what I saw for all the mothers and fathers of the world . . . As I sit here and write you this letter with the natural cynicism that you and I share about a great many things, I wonder if this war will do anything for the world . . ." When vice presidential candidate Harry Truman came to Boston on a fund-raising trip, Kennedy maneuvered him into a corner so that they were momentarily alone and then snarled at him, "Harry, what are you doing campaigning for that crippled son of a bitch that killed my son Joe?"

The wounds Joe Kennedy acquired in the last few months before the fighting ended scarred him for life. Years later, when interviewers happened to ask about his first son, Kennedy would break down crying, try to compose himself, and have to wave the question off. "Every night I say a prayer for him," he told one of them, his friend Bob Considine. "Joe is now and always will be another part of my life." He would continue to grieve, almost as if for a lost self. But the next part of his life did not involve reappraisal or diminution of his hopes. Rather, its central drama would be the transformation of what had been a joint venture between him and Young Joe into a drama involving the entire Kennedy family, with Jack as the central character.

It had been obvious to Jack from the moment the news came from England that he would now become executor of his brother's fate. By that Labor Day weekend, with Joe Junior scarcely three weeks dead, he was already feeling the pressure. At one point, watching his father cross the lawn in the distance, Jack nudged his friend Red Fay. "God! There goes the old man! There he goes figuring out the next step. I'm it now, you know. It's my turn. I've got to perform."

Fay and the other Navy buddies with whom Jack had discussed the future in bull sessions in the Pacific felt that he had come to enjoy the ongoing competition with his older brother and the role of the underdog, the one of whom not much was expected and whose accomplishments were therefore all the more dramatic. He had appreciated the maneuverability he got as a result of Joe Junior's willingness to be the lightning rod for their father's expectations. Jack had even implied that he was willing to play an auxiliary role in Joe Junior's political future as a way of continuing to enjoy this freedom. Meanwhile, journalism and teaching were two professions that he had talked about, although it seemed to his friends he would be equally happy as a generalist and dilettante. Now his brother's future was suddenly his. "I can feel Pappy's eyes on the back of my neck," he said to Fay that Christmas. ". . . when the war is over and you are out there in sunny California . . . I'll be back here with Dad trying to parlay a lost PT boat and a bad back into political advantage. I'll tell you, Dad is ready right now and can't understand why Johnny boy isn't 'all engines full ahead.' ''

It was not that he lacked confidence. On the contrary, he felt that he could have outperformed his brother in politics as he had in other areas of life. But there was a difference between winning and being given victory by default. While he had more than held his own in competition with Joe during his life, his brother was now invulnerable, his superiority sealed forever in his father's heart, his unfulfilled promise the core of a developing Kennedy iconography.

Jack knew his father was proud of him and the accomplishments that added luster to the family name, but he also knew that the qualities that animated him—irony, concealment, detachment—were foreign to the Ambassador, who had made no secret of the fact that he thought his second son had a perhaps fatal lack of the ''sociability and dynamism'' that he was convinced would assure Young Joe a successful political career. Jack sensed the double bind: if he succeeded it would be as a stand-in for his brother; if he failed, the failure would be his own.

''I'm shadow boxing in a match the shadow is always going to win,'' he told Lem Billings. That was about as much as he ever said about it. He spent much of the fall of 1944 having his bad back treated at the naval hospital and trying to deal with his brother's demanding ghost. He organized a campaign to fire Harvard football coach Richard Harlow, who had denied Joe Junior a chance to win his letter by not putting him into the Yale game in his senior year; he also worked on *As We Remember Joe*. Yet the anti-Harlow campaign foundered, and his father opened and closed the book of reminiscences (which Jack had had privately printed at a cost of $5,000) without even reading the elegant threnody that comprised the introduction.

It was a family in which survivors' guilt could be exorcised only through action. Choate headmaster George St. John was correct when he said of Jack in a letter to the elder Kennedys, ''I'm sure he never forgets he must live Joe's life as well as his own.''

Looming over everything else was his health. In the fall of 1945 he had another operation on his back, which turned out to be, he told Lem Billings, a ''disaster.'' He was weak and wasted—not only from continuing pain and persistent malaria but from the mysterious illness that had plagued him off and on since he was a child. After Christmas he went to Arizona to recuperate, as he had in 1936 after falling ill in England, and to wait for the Axis surrender.

Pat Lannan, another guest at the dude ranch outside Phoenix, struck up an acquaintance with Jack after being impressed by the way he would charge his horse down hills at breakneck speed when they went riding. A self-made man (he would later head ITT) not unlike the elder Kennedy, Lannan also noted the way Jack's father's presence seemed to hover over him. The Ambassador called frequently to see how Jack was feeling. When he found out that the food was indifferent, he had a box of steaks and chops shipped out from Boston; when he found that Jack had become interested in the postwar labor situation, he put together a crate of books on the subject. "I'm being fattened up in body and mind," Jack wryly observed, leaving the implication that it was for some sort of kill. When Lannan asked him what he planned to do with his life, Jack replied that he was thinking of entering "public service." Lannan tried to get him to be more specific by asking if he meant politics, but Jack refused to use the term, repeating that he saw his future as one of "public service."

Jack left Arizona and had another examination at the Mayo Clinic, meantime casting about for some sort of activity that would broaden his experience and outlook. With his father's help he got an appointment as a correspondent for the Hearst newspapers and went to San Francisco that fall to cover the founding conference of the United Nations. His dispatches, which were syndicated alongside his picture and a biographical note about his heroism in the Pacific, were not particularly insightful. (In one he compared the conference to an "international football game with Molotov carrying the ball while Stettinius, Eden and the delegates tried to tackle him all over the field.") But everybody who counted was in San Francisco, as the conference became a long toast to the end of the war, and he enjoyed himself thoroughly. Arthur Krock preserved a classic image of Jack lying on his hotel bed in full evening dress with a cocktail in one hand and the phone in the other as he left a message with his editor: "Tell him that Kennedy will not be filing tonight."

His friend Chuck Spalding, who was now working in Hollywood as an assistant to Gary Cooper, came up to San Francisco for a visit. Together they arranged to meet the brother of Lord David Cecil, who as author of the famous biography of Melbourne was one of Jack's heroes. Cecil's brother, a diplomat with the British U.N. delegation, had a huge overbite that brought out Jack's sadism. "One of the delicacies of this part of America is a locally grown asparagus," he told the Englishman when they went out for lunch. "It also happens to be a specialty of this restaurant. It would be a very great shame if you came here and failed to have the asparagus." Cecil ordered it and, as Jack had foreseen, had a terrible time eating it because of his overbite, finally having to tilt his head back and slide each individual spear down into his mouth. By this time, Spalding recalls, "Jack was laughing so hard he practically went under the table."

As the conference was ending, Kennedy and Spalding went down to Hollywood on what Jack called a "hunting expedition." Inga Arvad was in Hollywood still trying for a career in the movies; so was his new flame, the actress Gene Tierney. But Hollywood was more than starlets and endless parties. Joe Kennedy had often expressed his opinion that after the New Deal had completed the destruction of the old social hierarchies begun by the Depression, Hollywood, with its ability to manufacture status overnight, would provide the aristocracy of the coming era. Spalding found Jack fascinated not only by the tinsel and glitter but by the way that sex appeal, even more than sex itself, became power; by the way ordinary people came to inhabit the extraordinary celluloid identities created for them.

The two men made the rounds of Hollywood night life, rubbing elbows with Cooper, Clark Gable, and other stars: "Charisma wasn't a catchword yet, but Jack was very interested in that binding magnetism these screen personalities had. What exactly was *it*? How did you go about acquiring it? Did it have an impact on your private life? How did you make it work for you? He couldn't let the subject go."

By summer Jack was in England for a month to cover the British elections, and after that he went on a two-week tour of Germany with Navy Secretary Forrestal that the Ambassador had arranged. Jack was one of only a handful of American journalists to predict—accurately—that Churchill would be defeated by Clement Attlee's Labour Party, but he spent most of his time zooming around London in the little car Kick had acquired to beat the fuel shortage and getting acquainted with the people in her social set. One person he made of point of looking up was Pat Wilson, the beauty his brother had been in love with. She was a widow now; her husband had been killed in battle shortly after Joe. When Jack began squiring her around London night spots, it wasn't clear whether it was a platonic act of loyalty to his brother's memory or a posthumous continuation of the carnal competition they had carried on while Joe was alive.

If Jack seemed to be something like an American Prince Hal having a final spree, his father was at home making sure that the dissipation was a prelude to the serious business that lay ahead—the 1946 elections. Joe Kennedy realized that he himself would be a central issue in the campaigns to come. Privately he was still bitter about the people he felt had killed his own political career (when FDR died in April 1945, he wrote Kick that it was "a great thing for the country"). But with Jack's prospects in mind, the Ambassador took steps to create a public countenance for himself, one not associated with the anger and controversy of the past. In the spring of 1945 he gave $10,000 to the Guild of St. Apollonia, making sure that newspapers reported the gift and told the story of the pledge he'd made years earlier as a struggling Boston businessman to give half his net worth to the same organization if three-year-old Jack recovered from scarlet fever. Other gestures had a lighter touch. He announced with some fanfare that he was putting half a million dollars into Massachusetts' economy, but he didn't say that rather than being a fresh investment the money came from the sale of his remaining stock in Columbia Trust. It was a neat symmetry: the bank that had been his stepping stone would play a role in his son's career as well.

Kennedy got Governor Maurice Tobin to appoint him to a commission looking into the postwar Massachusetts economy, and spent the spring and summer of 1945 touring the state in his midnight-blue Chrysler limousine. (He later claimed, only half jokingly, that the only other thing he ever asked of Tobin was to make sure that Honey Fitz did not get another term as Boston Port Authority Commissioner.) The appointment was of great value, for it gave Kennedy a semiofficial status as he immersed himself in Massachusetts politics. During his travels he talked with local politicians, Chamber of Commerce officials, and labor leaders. He found out who was who in state and local government, and let them know that the Kennedys were back, ready to reestablish the connections severed twenty-five years earlier when he had fled Massachusetts' religious and social bigotry.

Having completed his crash course in state politics, the Ambassador began to speak out on national issues. His posture was no longer that of a pariah fighting the national consensus but of an elder statesman trying to help shape the postwar world. Hearing that his son Joe's old teacher Harold Laski, now chairman of the British Socialist Party, had said that capitalism was dead, Kennedy lashed out at him in late 1945, speaking almost as if he were a stand-in for Uncle Sam: "How dare Laski have the gall to assert that capitalism is dead when the British Empire has been twice saved in 30 years by the capitalistic United States? I know Laski and he is an arrogant apostle of anarchy who has spent his time shuffling between Moscow [and] London..." And a few months later, when he assaulted the new Truman Administration in *Life* for combining "appeasement, uncertainty and doubletalk" in relations with the Russians, he meant it to be music to the ears of conservative Boston Catholics whose worries about the expansion of "godless Russian communism" had increased after Roosevelt's wartime Yalta Conference with Churchill and Stalin.

While his father was making himself seen and heard, Jack adopted an official address at the Bellevue Hotel (pronounced *Bella-View* by the local pols), where Honey Fitz lived, and began accepting speaking engagements. "One is going to be at the Waldorf Astoria on October 4," he wrote at the end of August to Lem Billings, who was still in the Navy, "the other speakers being [Bernard] Baruch, [Thomas] Dewey and [Secretary of State] Byrnes ... Am making other talks and also assistant to the chairman of the Boston Community Fund; as you can see I am getting ready to throw my slightly frayed belt into the political arena anytime now. I am expecting you back to vote early and often." In November there was another stay in the hospital, but in early 1946 the speaking campaign was well under way. Coordinated by a public relations agency his father had retained, Jack's talks were informative recitations of what he had seen during the war and afterward at the U.N. conference and the British elections, delivered in a high-pitched, scratchy voice. In this shakedown cruise, Jack was so gaunt that his shirt collar gaped open and his gray suit hung from him as if it were a size too large. When one Hyannis Rotarian said he looked like "a little boy dressed up in his father's clothes," he was right in a figurative as well as a literal sense.

As father and son began putting the Kennedy name back in public view again, they were aided by Joe Junior's holy ghost. In the last months of the war the Ambassador had redoubled his efforts to secure a Congressional Medal of Honor for the family's martyr, although he finally had to settle for the Navy Cross, which Rose accepted in a well-publicized ceremony in June. Meanwhile, the Ambassador had gotten his friend Forrestal to name a new destroyer after his son, and late in July the U.S.S. *Joseph P. Kennedy, Jr.*, slid into the waters outside the Bethlehem shipyards, christened by Young Joe's sister and goddaughter Jean. Three months later, again with the Ambassador's connivance, an account of the fateful mission over England was finally declassified and released to the public. The day the news bulletin was flashed from Washington, he went to a local radio station and listened alone in one of the studios, eyes closed and face rigidly impassive, then went out alone to take a cab home.

Watching this Kennedy name-dropping, *Time* drew the logical conclusion that the Ambassador was trying to get himself recalled to Washington in some high appointive office. In fact, he had considered and dismissed that possibility shortly after Vice President Truman assumed the presidency. "I'm seriously considering ... whether I might not say to [Truman] that I'd like to help in any way I can," he had written Kathleen, "but if he's going to give me a job, I'd rather have him give it to Jack and maybe make him minister to some country or Assistant Secretary of State or Assistant Secretary of the Navy." Jack's career was what mattered now; the only question was where and how to launch him. The Ambassador, who had been hesitating between lieutenant governor and Congress as the proper first step, had his mind made up for him when his father-in-law's old nemesis James Curley gave up his seat in Congress to run once again for mayor. Incorporating the East Boston wards of P. J. and the North End dearos of Honey Fitz, the Eleventh Congressional District was Kennedy country. At a family meeting in Palm Beach, the Ambassador told everyone that this was the race they had been looking for. "We're all in this together," he said, looking around the room. Stealing a glance at her frail, sickly brother, Eunice asked, "Daddy, do you really think Jack can be a congressman?" The Ambassador smiled. "You must remember—it's not what you are that counts, but what people think you are."

Like Joseph McCarthy, who was fabricating his "Tailgunner Joe" legend in Wisconsin politics, the Ambassador saw that the elections of 1946 would be decided by the men and women who'd experienced the war as a jumping-off point in their lives. Whatever else people thought about his son, Kennedy wanted to make sure they knew he was a war hero. Once he announced his candidacy in late April and was officially campaigning, Jack began every speech by recounting the story of *PT 109*, using it as a parable of the American fighting spirit and as a lead into the problems confronting the nation in the postwar world. Rather than tiring of the story, his audiences came to look forward to it, adopting it as a sort of local legend.

The Ambassador had gotten a Veterans of Foreign Wars post named after Joe Junior, and many of the people who first began to spread the word about Jack were young ex-servicemen who had joined it. In fact, most of the visible campaigners—including Jack's own friends Torby MacDonald, Billings, Fay, Reed, and Spalding, as well as young pols from the Eleventh District like Dave Powers and Billy Sutton—were men who had been in the war. They spilled out into the wards Jack would have to conquer, giving his candidacy a look of battle-tested idealism, but ultimate control always rested with the Ambassador, who with his cronies was working behind the scenes from his suite at the Ritz. Mark Dalton, a Navy veteran just out of law school who was hired first as speech writer and later as campaign manager, recalls always having to go to Kennedy's inner sanctum for his orders: "He'd be sitting in his hotel room, somewhat in shadow. With him would usually be Joe Timilty, former Police Commissioner, and Archbishop Cushing. In this sense he was surrounded by the powers sacred and secular, both of them subordinate to him. I remember once when he got mad at Cushing and yelled, 'Who the hell does he think he is? If he wants that little red cardinal's hat he'd better shape up because I've got a hell of a lot more friends in Rome than he does.' It was strong stuff for a young Catholic man like myself. Going to see Mr. Kennedy in those days was like going to visit God."

What seemed like a campaign by citizen politicians was really the last curtain call of the ward politics that formed part of Jack's Boston-Irish legacy. The Ambassador gave free rein to Joe Kane, his cousin on his mother's side of the family and one of the last of the great practitioners of the old school of politics. Now sixty-six, the short, stumpy Kane had come up as a protégé of Martin Lomasney's and had earned his reputation as "the Connie Mack of Boston politics." (In one celebrated campaign he had all of Curley's signs—"Boston Needs Curley"—painted over to read "Boston Feeds Curley.") It was Kane who had the idea that the visible campaigners should be young veterans, and he who came up with the campaign slogan: "The New Generation Offers a Leader." When popular City Councilman Joseph Russo opposed Jack in the primary, Kane dug up another Joseph Russo and inserted him into the race as a ringer to split the Russo vote.

While Jack was going around town giving his *PT 109* speech, Kane was painstakingly putting together ward-by-ward alliances which stretched from the tenements of the North End to the congeries of intellectuals around Cambridge. Lem Billings, who stayed with Jack at the Bellevue off and on during the campaign, remembered the suite as being a sort of Boston-Irish Grand Central Station: "Jack and I would go to bed and there'd be these Irish politicians smoking cigars and talking strategy in the next room. We'd wake up the next morning and they'd still be there smoking and talking."

Another monument from the past, Honey Fitz himself, also got involved. At the age of eighty-three, Honey had become, as Jack circumspectly put it, "eccentric." He spent his days taking Teddy to the zoo and to Red Sox games, staging his entrances as if he were campaigning. He regularly went to the beach and covered himself up with sand, which he claimed allowed the body to soak up vital iron and bromides. He had taken to calling himself "The Greatest Mayor Boston Ever Had" and made speeches on the slightest occasion, as in his exhortation to the people of Boston to wear long underwear because it was good for the New England textile industry. When he heard that Edwin O'Connor was doing research for *The Last Hurrah*, Honey made a point of seeking him out. "Come with me, young man," he said. "I'll show you the home where I was born." He then led O'Connor to an apartment in a North End building where the current residents, an Italian family, were eating dinner. He let himself in the door and waved. "Good evening, Mrs. Genaro, I'm just showing this young man the home where I was born, pay no attention to me," and took O'Connor through all the rooms, recounting his memories in rapid-fire sentences.

Honey was sometimes conscripted to take Jack to meetings where the Fitzgerald name would be an asset. (On one such occasion he immediately broke into "Sweet Adeline," and then rambled on about the issues in the campaign until Jack finally tugged at his coattail and whispered, "Grandpa, remember, *I'm* the candidate.") He also wandered down to his grandson's suite at the Bellevue to offer advice and wound up talking about the good old days and laughing so hard at his own off-color jokes that he doubled over with a wheezing cough. One evening when Honey walked into a strategy meeting, Joe Kane, who had been a bitter Fitzgerald enemy in the old days, said to Jack, "Get that son of a bitch out of here." Jack began to protest but Kane held firm: "Either he goes or I do." Jack put his arm around Honey's shoulder and guided him out the door, saying, "I'm sorry, Grandpa..."

"With those two names, Kennedy and Fitzgerald, how could he lose?" Jim Curley later asked about Jack. Yet when he entered the race, victory was far from sure. He was attacked constantly as a carpetbagger. Each of his nine opponents in the primary said at one time or another that he was a lightweight running on one incident in a long war; that he was nursing at the breast of a political tradition to which he was connected by name rather than residence; and that he was being supported in more ways than one by his father's money. Jack was equally harsh on himself. He knew his parents felt that Joe would have done it better; he may even have heard the Ambassador's comment to one of his cronies: "With what I'm spending I could elect my chauffeur." But he forged ahead anyhow, setting himself a brutal schedule that would have exhausted the strongest of men. "He was running because it was required," Lem Billings said, "but he was also running because he thought he might be able someday, somehow, to locate *himself* in the middle of this complex mix of duty, expectation and all the rest of it."

Some five hundred speeches were written by the public relations firm; Jack delivered them all in his stiff, wooden manner. Yet occasionally something would shine through, a hint of the persona he was trying to create, the small piece of territory he was trying to claim as distinctively his own in the middle of the wide expanse that had been ready-made for him. Sometimes it was a wry wit. "I guess I'm the only one here who didn't come up the hard way," he noted at one candidates' night after all his opponents had laid out a claim to being common men. Sometimes it was a sense of the moment. In an appearance before the Gold Star Mothers at a local American Legion Hall he paused at the end of his speech and said hesitantly: "I think I know how all you mothers feel because my mother's a gold-star mother too." Sometimes it was a sort of awkward glamour that shone through his sickliness and formality.

There was nothing special about his platform. In domestic affairs he stressed housing, jobs, and other issues appealing to veterans. In foreign relations he repeated his father's warnings about a world about to be convulsed by "the struggle between capitalism and collectivism." If he was not particularly impressive before large audiences, he was extremely effective in small groups, where what Dave Powers (a native of the Charlestown section of the Eleventh whom Jack had recruited himself) called "an aggressive shyness" came into play. Talking with people he would ask about all aspects of their lives with unfeigned curiosity—how they earned their livings, what their families were like, what their ambitions were and how they planned to attain them. It was a genuine version of the sincerity most politicians contrived—an opportunity to encounter the "real world" from which he felt his upbringing had isolated him.

"Jack became easily engrossed in people and ideas," Jim Reed says. "It was something of a paradox given his extreme self-consciousness, but it was probably the most pronounced aspect of his personality and maybe his salvation as a first-time campaigner. He'd come to our house for dinner and get involved in some discussion and totally forget what was happening. Once in the middle of a soup course he pulled a caramel out of his pocket and started chewing on it while he talked. That sort of thing happened a lot in the '46 campaign. He'd go out on a job and start talking to the workers and become so involved in what they did that he'd have to be pried away."

To Lem he gave the impression of someone who would have really enjoyed himself under different circumstances. But he was in constant pain. Sometimes he had trouble getting up out of a chair, stretching his torso experimentally before rising as if trying to locate an alignment that he could momentarily live with; there were dark rings under his eyes. Those around him realized that he was carrying the burden of his dead brother as well as that of his recalcitrant body. When *Look* reporters came for an interview, he told them that he was only trying "to do the job Joe would have done." One day in the middle of a packed schedule he surprised Mark Dalton, who regarded him as a somewhat denatured Catholic, by insisting on ducking into a Catholic church. He came out a little while later looking grim and said, "I just lit a candle for my brother." Billy Sutton, a political operator and Boston-Irish funnyman whom Kane had brought into the campaign, was surprised when Jack handed him a tie while dressing for an appearance one afternoon and said, "Here, this was Joe's. I'd like you to wear it because I think if you'd known Joe you would have been a great friend of his." Cambridge lawyer John Droney, asked to the Bellevue to meet Jack and possibly help in the campaign, was put off by all the old pols smoking cigars and left. But Jack, incredibly skinny and still yellow from malaria, pursued him out into the corridor, saying that he too had doubts about politics and was in the race only because his brother Joe had been killed and his parents thought him best fitted to carry on. When Droney said that he was still not sure, Jack looked at him sadly and said, "Sometimes we all have to do things we don't want to do."

On one level the campaign was Jack's personal drama. But it involved the rest of the family as well. Eunice and Pat went to block parties and campaigned house to house. Bobby also presented himself. Hawk-faced like his mother, with eyes deep in their sockets, he had gone over his father's head to Forrestal to get released from his officers' training program at Harvard so that he could sign on with the U.S.S. *Joseph P. Kennedy, Jr.,* as an ordinary seaman. (His only sea duty was a trip to the U.S. naval base at Guantanamo, Cuba, early in 1946.) Feeling that his brother's death might make an opening in the family for him, he had written his father: "I wish, Dad, that you would write me a letter as you used to to Joe and Jack about what you think about the different political events and the war as I'd like to be able to understand what's going on better than I do."

Bobby's desire to serve presented a problem. "It's damn nice of Bobby wanting to help," Jack told Red Fay, "but I can't see that sober, silent face breathing new vigor into the ranks." Assigned to get Bobby into a more outgoing campaign mood, Fay took him to a movie with a vaudeville show; midway in one of the acts, convulsed with laughter himself, he turned to Bobby and saw that he was staring at the stage without a smile. Eventually Bobby got assigned to three working-class wards in Cambridge, working under Lem Billings, and "campaigned as if his life and Jack's depended on it."

Effective individually, the Kennedys also represented more than the sum of their parts. As the campaign drew to a close, all the women in the district who were registered Democrats received engraved invitations to tea with the family. The city's old-time pols snickered at the innovation until on the appointed night nearly two thousand women lined up outside the Commander Hotel in Cambridge, many of them in rented evening dresses, and waited to pass down the receiving line headed by Jack and his parents. The Kennedys' fabulous rise had taken place recently enough to make it an available middle-class fantasy; yet they had gone so high under such eccentric conditions that they were an aristocracy unto themselves.

By the end of the campaign, Joe Kennedy had pulled out all the stops. When his information suggested that Jack would get more votes than all his opponents combined, he commissioned the *New York Daily News* team to come up to Boston and do one of their famous straw polls to make sure. He used his movie connections to get Pathé newsreel photographers to shoot footage showing Jack campaigning, which was shown in theaters in the Boston area a few nights before the election. And he had reprints of the *Reader's Digest* version of John Hersey's article about *PT 109* sent to every registered voter.

Joe Kennedy knew in advance that the vote on June 18 would be a landslide. Yet no matter how large the mandate, he was made aware the day before of how fragile the victory would be. Jack marched in the traditional Bunker Hill Day Parade as commander of Joseph P. Kennedy Jr. VFW Post 5880, with the other veterans stretched out behind him so that it looked as if the new generation itself was marching on the Eleventh Congressional District. But by the time he completed the five-mile walk, Jack was exhausted. Just past the reviewing stand he collapsed and was taken to the nearby home of Boston politician Robert Lee, who later said, "He turned yellow and blue. He appeared to me as a man who had probably had a heart attack." As Jack was stripped to his underwear and sponged off, Joe Kennedy came in and fumbled in his son's pockets, asking, "Has he got his pills?" but not specifying what the pills were for.

The next night, as early results showed that he would get nearly 50 percent of the ballots, Jack slipped off with Honey Fitz to see the Marx Brothers in *A Night in Casablanca*. As the vote piled up, the Ambassador, forgetting the earlier bravura about electing his chauffeur, savored the unlikeliness of having elected this sickly, inexperienced twenty-nine-year-old. "I would have given you odds of five thousand to one that this couldn't have happened," he said to a friend, shaking his head at the wonder of it.

The victory landed Jack on the front page of the *New York Times* and won him a big story in *Time*. The lopsided Democratic margin in the Eleventh District insured his election in November. Yet it was hard for him not to see it as more of a memorial service for his brother than his own achievement. On August 12, the second anniversary of Joe's death, the Ambassador announced the establishment of the Joseph P. Kennedy Foundation, and Jack, its president, presented its initial gift of $650,000 to Archbishop Cushing for the construction of a hospital for handicapped children. In planning for his office staff in Washington, he hired as his chief aide Ted Reardon, whom Joe Junior had promised such a job when they were roommates at Harvard and planning their lives. On Armistice Day, Jack, who had just won a landslide victory over his Republican opponent, gave a speech to the Veterans of Foreign Wars. When he came to the line, "No greater love has a man than he who gives his life for his brother," he broke down crying and couldn't finish.

2.

*W*HEN THE NEW CONGRESS convened in January, Jack showed up tanned from weeks in the sun at Palm Beach. His name guaranteed him more attention than the usual freshman lawmaker, but his father had put frosting on his celebrity by engineering his selection as one of the Ten Outstanding Men of 1946 by the U.S. Junior Chamber of Commerce. Jack, more interested in other outstanding young men of the Eightieth Congress, spent his first days in Washington scouting the competition, chief among them a young Californian who struck Jack's aide Billy Sutton as "very dapper dressed" and "the star of the show." It was Richard Nixon, and after meeting him at the National Press Club, Jack admiringly noted that Nixon's victory over the well-known liberal congressman Jerry Voorhis was the equivalent of knocking off someone like John McCormack, dean of the Massachusetts congressional delegation. He joined Nixon on the Education and Labor Committee; along with George Smathers of Florida they established a friendly rivalry over who would do the least amount of time in the House before moving on to the Senate.

Jack rented a three-story row house in Georgetown, where he installed Margaret Ambrose, the giant Irish cook who had been with the Kennedys for years, and aide-de-camp Sutton, whom he maliciously introduced to strangers as "one of the Suttons of Boston." Like Dave Powers later on, Sutton was one of those Boston-Irish utility men who functioned as a sort of Sancho Panza for Jack, as their predecessors had for the Ambassador. One of Dave Powers's abilities that Jack found intriguing was his almost total recall for sports statistics; with Sutton it was his talent for mimicry. During his first days in office, Jack sometimes put Sutton on the phone to colleagues and told him to imitate the ranting of radical Congressman Vito Marcantonio, and doubled up with laughter as the ruse took hold.

When another congressman said that Jack looked like a college freshman, he was not just referring to his youth. He dressed in the first clothes he found, often showing up on the House floor in crumpled khakis, old seersucker jacket, food-spotted tie. His house was a chaos, with rugs wadded up, clothes draped over the chairs, and women's underthings stuffed into the crevices of the sofa. (The columnist Joseph Alsop, enemy of the Ambassador but surreptitious friend of Jack, once found a moldy half-eaten hamburger hidden behind books on the mantel.) One girlfriend of the time, Jane Blodgett, remembers, "Jack was very casual. He'd go to the 21 Club or he'd go to a Howard Johnson's. It didn't seem to make any difference to him. He'd go to a Howard Johnson's and be just as happy with milkshakes and hamburgers as going to 21."

Some of Jack's friends found this scorn for appearances appealingly ingenuous. Others felt there was something adolescent about it, the life style of someone stuck in the role of son long after time for a transition. Jack's secretary at the time, Mary Davis, was irked by the way he spent his days tossing a football back and forth in his inner office with Ted Reardon and then loaded her down with work on the weekend. Almost everyone was annoyed by his refusal to carry money and by the constant demands for small, on-the-spot loans that were never paid back. Some tolerated it as a sort of toll they paid to get invitations to Hyannis and Palm Beach. Others, including Smathers, finally began submitting expense vouchers to the Kennedy office in New York for reimbursement for the lunches, cab fares, and even church offerings made in Jack's behalf. Drawing something like a Hegelian synthesis out of his own family history, the Ambassador had made it clear that he didn't want his children to enter business any more than his own mother had wanted him to enter Boston politics. But he was bothered by their naïveté in financial matters, and finally begged Smathers to sit Jack down and explain "the facts of life," the way people normally dealt with finances. But this was, as another friend said, "like trying to tell a nun all about sex." The Ambassador happened to be present when Jack lectured an aide about how the $5000 a year he was earning was "more than enough" to support his family and put himself through law school. After sitting silently for a few minutes he finally exploded, "Good God, Jack, how can you say a thing like that? Don't you realize that you're spending $50,000 on incidentals?"

Partly as a result of the Ambassador's concern about Jack's health and habits, Eunice came to live in the Georgetown house too, working at a job her father had gotten her as executive secretary of a Justice Department commission on juvenile delinquency. Unlike her younger sisters, Pat and Jean, whose interests were clothes and movie stars, Eunice had always envied the web of expectation and achievement that seemed to link Joe Junior, Jack, and Kick, and had tried to gain membership in their club. After going to Stanford she did social work in Harlem, and later worked in the State Department dealing with the problems of American prisoners of war returning from Germany. Wide-mouthed and freckled, she, like Jack, was definitely a Kennedy rather than a Fitzgerald. She too was subject to debilitating illnesses which she also bulled her way through. Like Jack she tended to ignore appearances, and her father probably had her most in mind when he asked Gene Tierney, with whom Jack was still having an affair, although now at long-distance, if she would please teach his daughters how to walk properly. But the Ambassador admired Eunice's drive and paid her the supreme compliment: "If that girl had been born with balls she would have been a hell of a politician."

Eunice brought another dimension to the Georgetown house. The family cheerleader, she also had an unpredictable and volatile sense of humor (she once appeared at a party Jack gave dressed as a pregnant nun) and brought a variety of people into the Kennedy orbit. One was Joseph McCarthy, whom she dated a few times. McCarthy later claimed to have met Jack during the war in the Solomon Islands, to have ridden in *PT 109* and even been allowed to fire its machine guns. Jack remembered none of this; but he liked the Wisconsin Senator's crude humor and irreverent attitudes toward authority, and enjoyed barbecues in the back yard of McCarthy's house. Jack was less taken with Sargent Shriver. He remembered him vaguely from Canterbury, the Catholic prep school he had attended briefly, and he knew that Shriver, whose Maryland family was socially prominent but financially threadbare after the Depression, had gone on to Yale as a scholarship boy. Someone who could declare, as Shriver had when he became editor of the Yale paper, that he was "Christian, Aristotelean, Optimistic, and American," could not appeal to Jack, although he could to Eunice.

Shriver was working as an assistant to the editor at *Newsweek* when she met him at dinner at the St. Regis with Peter Hoguet, a friend of both, to whom Shriver had previously confided his ambition to work as the "right-hand man" to some top business leader. Hoguet introduced Shriver to Eunice as "a fellow who would like to work for your father," and Eunice followed through. Kennedy first sought his advice about whether the letters Joe Junior had written from Europe might be published. When Shriver reported back that he thought they were not publishable, Kennedy hired him to help oversee his real estate holdings and also assist Eunice in her work with juvenile delinquents. Aware that he ran the risk of being seen as a fortune hunter, the handsome, earnest Shriver nonetheless began what a friend called a "ferociously dogged courtship" of Eunice, although she tried his affection sorely by picking up the phone at three or four in the morning and calling him for a chat during one of her frequent bouts of insomnia.

As part of her job at the juvenile delinquency commission, Eunice sometimes brought young truants and troublemakers home for meals of Margaret

Ambrose's fried chicken, occasions on which Jack tried to have pressing business elsewhere. "We want you to be happy children," she would tell them as they ate. "Happy children become happy men and women." Sometimes she also brought retarded children home. It was clear to Billy Sutton that this was a personal act of contrition having to do with Rosemary, whom Eunice remained closer to than anyone else in the family. She never mentioned her sister, however, and neither did Jack, except once when he said enigmatically out of the blue: "I guess there'll always be a Rosemary."

Once Jack took office, he and his father had to deal with each other's eccentricities in a way that hadn't been necessary when Joe Junior was alive and serving as the primary medium of exchange between them. They were more similar than either acknowledged, and as likes they often repelled. Yet there was instinctive understanding too. Both realized, for instance, without ever having to discuss it, that a strategy of mutual denial would be necessary if Jack's career was to take off.

For Jack it had to do with his health. Denying the seriousness of his illness was, by the time he took office, almost second nature. Since his childhood he had been engaged in an elaborate pretense that he was as vigorous as the rest of the family. Approaching his thirties he was accustomed to holding his mysterious infirmity at bay, examining and criticizing it and distancing it with irony, as he did with other curious facts in his environment. Even his closest friends heard no complaint. They had learned to avoid the subject of his health, even when he was obviously suffering. Phyllis MacDonald stumbled over this code when she and her husband went to a football game with Jack during his first term in Congress. Seeing Kennedy painfully pulling himself up the inside stairs toward the grandstand, Phyllis hissed at her husband, "For Godsakes, grab his elbow and help him." Torby cut her off, "No! Don't even mention it!"

For Joe Kennedy the denial had to do with his own ambitions; working hard to rehabilitate himself, he found that limelight still had an almost irresistible attraction. In 1948, Truman appointed him to the Presidential Commission on Government Reorganization headed by Herbert Hoover, and he probably could have had other administrative jobs in Washington. But he realized that however hard he had worked to create a new persona in the aftermath of the war, the other one would always be in the background— associated with appeasement, isolationism, and anti-Semitism;* the Ken-

---

*In 1949 the State Department published a 1280-page collection of previously secret German diplomatic messages, among them von Dirksen's cables about his conversations with Kennedy in London. The headline in the *Boston Globe*, "Kennedy Pro-German, Anti-Jewish, Said Nazi," captured the public impact of the documents. Kennedy's disclaimer, "It is complete poppycock as far as I'm concerned," did little to dispel the impression.

nedy of his youth who had made his money mysteriously and gratified his appetites without regard for appearances. He realized that, aside from Jack's uncertain health, he himself would always be the primary obstacle his son would have to overcome. And so he made the choice, more difficult for him than most men, of obscurity. He had hired James Landis, former dean of Harvard Law and his own one-time opponent in the New Deal, to help him write his autobiography. But when he showed a draft of the manuscript to Arthur Krock, his old friend had said that while "a small part was readable, interesting and new, for the most part it was a tedious repetition of the public record." Krock advised Kennedy to do a "frank" apologia for his life. If he had, it could have been a fascinating work—picaresque tales of an immigrant family's rise—but Jack's career made it impossible to tell the true story. The Ambassador realized that his only alternative was to settle back into the shadows and derive his satisfaction from helping manufacture Jack in much the same way he had manufactured himself.

The Ambassador had begun to get his affairs in order as soon as Jack was elected, almost as if he were the one who was going to Washington. He sold the liquor business, which had generated tremendous income along with ominous rumors about underworld connections. He transferred a quarter of the ownership of the Merchandise Mart to Rose and a quarter to his surviving children, which would take care of their needs for life. He transferred another quarter to the Joseph P. Kennedy Jr. Foundation, whose charitable gifts to the archdioceses of New York and Washington would help to leaven Jack's political progress, and kept a quarter for himself. In New York he made what had always been a one-man show into a formal headquarters, hiring half a dozen employees and installing them in a suite in the old Marguery Hotel on Park Avenue. Joseph P. Kennedy Enterprises took care of the household expenses of the Kennedy children and acted as a central switchboard. (Rose peppered the staff with memos such as one which read: "Please inform Pat that red is in this year.") But its primary responsibility was handling the family money. The Ambassador had investments in oil and gas for tax advantages, but he turned down an invitation from Tex Thornton to be an initial investor in what became the fabulously successful Litton Industries because he saw that defense work might embroil Jack in conflicts of interest. He also passed up chances to buy controlling interests in Eastern and National airlines, the Brooklyn Dodgers, and other businesses foundering in difficult postwar economic conditions.

A fortune the size of his couldn't help but increase just by its own momentum: not long after Kennedy Enterprises moved to a new headquarters at 235 Park Avenue in 1950, *Fortune* estimated its value at up to $400 million. The Ambassador summed up his position by saying, "A certain amount of shopkeeping remains to be done, but no more acquiring is necessary." Uniquely liquid (James Landis once observed that Kennedy was one of the few wealthy men he knew who could write a check for $10 million without first having to sell something), the fortune had become a political treasury as the office became a political headquarters.

The Ambassador bombarded Jack constantly with opinions, position papers, unsolicited advice. He told him what people to call on as advisers, what issues to emphasize, what alliances to make. Nor was he content to rely on his influence as father, treasurer, and most important constituent. Shortly after going to work as Jack's administrative representative, Ted Reardon got a call from Palm Beach. "It was Mr. Kennedy. We exchanged some pleasantries and then he got down to business. He wanted me to be his ear in the office and report to him exactly what Jack was up to. He made it clear to me that he could and would make it worth my while financially. He was pretty insistent. It was hard to find a graceful way to say no."

Early in Jack's career, Kay Halle happened onto a private moment during a Washington garden party in which the Ambassador was badgering Jack about how to vote on some bill in the House. Finally Jack snapped at him, "Now look here, Dad, you have your political views and I have mine. I'm going to vote exactly the way I feel I must on this." The scene was memorable because it was so unusual. For the most part Jack's mode with his father was resignation rather than defiance. "I guess Dad has decided that he's going to be the ventriloquist," Jack told Lem, "so I guess that leaves me the role of dummy."

On some issues he tried to live up to the ideal of his campaign rhetoric and show the qualities the new generation could bring to politics. He kept his promises on the pressing question of housing by adopting as a special project the Wagner-Ellender-Taft Bill, which was designed to construct fifteen million low-cost homes during the coming decade. Banking and realtors' groups, both more interested in the booming market for homes for the middle class and affluent, opposed the measure. Jack took the role of advocate for the returned servicemen living with their families in Quonset huts: "Any veteran who watched the American supplies pouring on shore at the Normandy beaches; who saw Pacific islands cleared and air strips rolled in four or five days; who saw the endless waste of war and the seemingly never ending productivity that replaced the waste ... Is it any wonder that the veteran cannot understand why he is not housed?" And when the American Legion, for its own complex reasons, lined up against the bill, Jack didn't hesitate to take on this venerable institution in an escalating war of words which ended when he snapped: "The leadership of the American Legion has not had a constructive thought for the benefit of this country since 1918!"

He also separated himself from the old guard on the issue of James Curley's imprisonment. The aging Purple Shamrock had been elected Mayor of Boston again in 1946, but since then he had been convicted of mail fraud in connection with wartime contracts and sent to federal prison at Danbury.

Curley was old and sick, and Massachusetts congressional leader John Mc-
Cormack was passing around a petition calling for a commutation of the
sentence. Jack alone in the state's delegation refused to sign. Authority
figures ranging from his father to Archbishop Cushing urged him to do so,
but Mark Dalton and other younger supporters pointed out that this was an
opportunity for him to show that he was indeed the leader offered up by the
new generation.

There was also distance between the Ambassador and Jack on foreign
policy. Joe Kennedy was suspicious of Truman's proposal to finance the
governments of Greece and Turkey in their struggle against communism.
Kennedy phrased his displeasure in fiscal terms—the United States was
already struggling with a postwar recovery of its own and couldn't afford
the obligation—but it was clearly an updated version of his prewar isolationism. His idea, to keep America strong and not worry about the ideological affiliations of the rest of the world, was expressed most fully in an
appearance before the University of Virginia Law School arranged by
Bobby, who had enrolled there after graduation from Harvard. "If portions
of Europe or Asia wish to go Communistic or even to have communism thrust
upon them," Kennedy said, "we cannot stop it. Instead we must make sure
of our strength and be certain not to fritter it away in battles that could not
be won. . . . We can do well to mind our own business and interfere only
where somebody threatens our business and our homes."

Jack, on the other hand, joined the internationalists and supported the
Truman Doctrine, as the administration's proposals became known. In his
first speech on foreign policy, on April 1, 1947, he took direct issue with his
father's position: "We should still fight to prevent Europe and Asia from
becoming dominated by one great military power and we will oppose bitterly,
I believe, the suffering people of Europe and Asia from succumbing to the
soporific ideology of Red totalitarianism." He supported the reconstruction
of Europe through the Marshall Plan with fervor equal to that the Ambassador was using in condemning it as "an overwhelming tax on our resources
that will seriously affect the well-being of this country."

Yet in spite of his flashes of independence, Jack's world view was still
congruent with his father's. Like the Ambassador he was a fiscal conservative, someone who might well have called himself a "Taft Democrat"* because of the similarity of his views to those of the Ohio Republican. He was
sympathetic to the antilabor provisions of the Taft-Hartley Bill, and, according to UPI reporter (and later White House press secretary) George Reedy,

---

*Years later he would tell David Ormsby-Gore, then British Ambassador to Washing-
ton, "I used to take my economic views from my father, because I thought he knew a
lot about it. But when I read back the speeches I made about the economy in the late
forties, I'm absolutely horrified. Nothing that I said then would I ever agree with
now!"

actually considered voting for it—suicide for any northern Democrat—until John McCormack dissuaded him. Eventually Jack issued a one-man minority report that was a plague-on-both-your-houses castigation of management and labor.

As to the domestic "Communist menace," he was, if anything, even more of a hardliner than his father. In its hearings on revising the labor laws, the House Labor and Education Committee got off into the issue of Communist infiltration of the union movement. Jack made his first headlines during this set of hearings, questioning witnesses with a sharpness that made colleagues assume he was a lawyer, and eruditely quoting Lenin's views on the imperative for Communists to resort to any stratagem to get into a union and carry out the party's work. Jack seized the anti-Communist banner forcefully in his questioning of Harold Christoffel, from Local 248 of the United Auto Workers. At issue was a 1941 strike against Allis-Chalmers, which Jack alleged had been carried out in response to orders from Moscow to cripple United States war preparations. After boxing the witness into a corner with his knowledge of the Hitler-Stalin Pact, Jack got former Communist Louis Budenz, one of the first to become a professional witness against his former faith, to affirm that the Allis-Chalmers strike had indeed been meant as a blow to America's national defense. Jack then offered a motion to charge Christoffel with perjury. During the hearings he went to the Pittsburgh suburb of McKeesport for a debate with Richard Nixon on the merits of the Taft-Hartley Act. Afterward the two congressmen rode back to Washington together on the train affably discussing the Communist threat.

As the summer recess neared, Jack went home to celebrate his thirtieth birthday. Mark Dalton remembers an eerie moment when everyone at the table proposed toasts, each trying to outdo the other with the right combination of abrasiveness and affection in the Kennedy tradition. As an afterthought, the Ambassador asked Teddy if he had anything to say. The fourteen-year-old placed things squarely in the odd perspective which for Jack had become reality when he held up his water glass and said : "I would like to offer a toast to our brother who is not with us."

Not long afterward, Jack left for Europe as part of a congressional fact-finding tour, beginning with a stopover in Ireland to visit Kick. She had "gone completely English," as he remarked to Lem Billings. Upon her return to London in 1944, she had taken up her Red Cross work again, trying to distance the shock of the deaths of Joe and Billy Hartington by filling up her days. She had written melancholy letters home such as the one dated April 1, 1945, to Frank Waldrop of the *Times-Herald:* "At present I am directing and entertaining at nurses' club in London. Very nice job and plan to stay on here until summer anyway. It seems hard to believe that the war is really going to be over soon. I'm glad, thankful, but I don't think anyone feels terribly joyful. Do you?"

After the European war ended, in May of 1945, she had gone on a succession of religious retreats to a nunnery at Kendal, in the North of England, not only to cope with her guilt but to reenter the Church after the excommunication for her marriage. Gradually she became more like her old self. Her friend Jane Kenyon-Slaney was with her on a rare sunny day when her sorrow finally seemed to thaw: "She smiled sort of sadly and said, 'It's such a wonderful day. You don't think that Billy would mind if I wore a really flowery dress, do you?'"

When V-J Day brought World War II to an end in August, she had resigned her Red Cross job, bought a house in Smith Square, and made plans to visit her family. The reunion early in 1946 had at first been joyful, but then she had felt a distance, particularly in her mother's manner. She had come in time for Jack's congressional campaign, but she was the one family member besides Rosemary kept out of view, lest reminders of her marriage cause a Catholic backlash. She moved to a room in the Chatham Hotel in New York and began going out with a café society lawyer and gentleman jockey named Winston Frost, whom she had known before the war. But when her father found out through his network of informants, he intervened to stop it before it caused additional political embarrassment to Jack. The Ambassador told Kathleen that Frost was a playboy and hired columnist Walter Winchell to provide specifics; then he inundated her with a series of irritated phone calls discrediting Frost's character, including the claim that he was being kept by another woman. Her father's relentless assault make Kick realize that she too had changed. Behavior she had found amusing before her marriage now seemed intolerably intrusive. She booked a voyage back.

Back in England she embarked on a period of personal exploration, a time in her life something like her father's earlier breakout from Boston into the wider world. Just as Joe Kennedy had felt confined by the idea that being born Boston Irish meant sharing in a group fate, so Kathleen chafed at the assumption that she had to participate in the collective effort of the Kennedys to establish the family in American politics. Jack had shouldered the burden; she decided to go her own way. She used her title of Marchioness of Hartington not only because it indicated her social achievement but also because, as she remarked lightly to a friend, "It's rather nice not having to be a Kennedy. Lord knows there are enough of them as it is."

Her prewar social life in England had revolved around a self-contained set of people, most of them at least distantly related, Astors, Ormsby-Gores, Ogilvies, Cavendishes. But now social protocol was disappearing, along with the rest of the old ways. Living alone with a housekeeper in Smith Square, she did as she liked—went out with eligible men her age and launched herself into society. She lunched with Churchill and Beaverbrook and made her place into something of a salon for such celebrated people as Anthony Eden, George Bernard Shaw, and Evelyn Waugh. The men she was dating also reflected her sense of independence—Richard Wood, son of Lord Halifax, a Protestant, and Seymour Berry, a wealthy seventy-year-old aristocrat with a raffish reputation, who showered her with diamonds. But the only serious one, Kick confided to Jack after his arrival, was the eighth Earl of Fitzwilliam, whom she had met at the Commandos Ball, held in honor of the special unit Churchill himself had set up in 1940.

Peter Fitzwilliam, whose family traced its ancestry to William the Conqueror, was one of the heroes of the war, having won the Distinguished Service Cross for secret missions in the North Sea. "No one I have ever met has made me completely forget myself," Kick had written in a wartime letter to her friend Jane Kenyon-Slaney. Fitzwilliam did. He was a horse fancier, elegantly aristocratic, long-faced, handsome, Protestant—and married. At the Commandos Ball he lavished attention on Kick—who was wearing a pale pink gown with aquamarine and diamond clips—despite the presence of his wife Olive, who was much in evidence as president of the fund for the evening's affair. "Peter and Kathleen sort of eyed each other awhile," one friend commented, "and then they were together." Another says, "It was overnight and it was the real thing—illicit, passionate, encompassing. One got the impression that she'd discovered something she didn't really plan to experience in life."

The Fitzwilliams didn't have the status of the Cavendishes, but they were nearly as wealthy. Their ancestral estate was Milton, near Peterborough; they had also acquired through marriage the famous Wentworth Woodhouse in Yorkshire. Set on twenty-two thousand acres, including some of the richest coalfields in the kingdom, it was thought to be the largest private home in Europe, with 365 bedrooms, one for each day of the year. There was also a beautiful Irish estate, Coollatin, in County Wicklow, which had once included lands so vast that it was said one could ride all the way to Dublin without leaving the property.

A horseman and gambler (he was president of the Racehorse Owners' Association and possessed one of the finest stud farms in England), Fitzwilliam was something of a rake, in contact with both the aristocratic circles of London and the gamy elements of the city's night life. Harry Sporborg, his close friend and financial adviser, commented, "Peter had all the charm in the world—to a rather dangerous extent, really." Kick's friend Jane Kenyon-Slaney found him "like Joseph Kennedy himself—older, sophisticated, quite the rogue male. Perhaps in the last analysis those were the qualities required to make her fall deeply in love."

On his arrival in Ireland, Jack met Kick at Lismore, the Duke of Devonshire's magnificent estate in County Waterford, once the home of Sir Walter Raleigh. It had been acquired by the Cavendishes as part of the spoils of the Irish conquest. Jack came equipped with a letter of introduction from Aunt Loretta, who'd visited Ireland with P. J. Kennedy in the twenties, and he drove out to New Ross to find "the original Kennedys," as he called them. The little village and the ancestral home, with whitewashed walls and thatched roof and barnyard animals clustered around the front door, seized his imagination. When he got back to Lismore and told Kathleen about it she laughed, asking a question that showed exactly how well she'd assimilated to the English: "Did they have a bathroom?"

Jack went on to London to catch a plane and meet the congressional delegation on the Continent. Before he could leave London, however, he collapsed with acute nausea and low blood pressure, and was rushed to the London Clinic. The diagnosis was Addison's disease, a malfunction of the adrenal glands that causes weakness and an inability to fight infection. It had apparently been developing for years and was responsible for the life-threatening sicknesses of his youth. The "Addisonian crisis" had been long in coming; now there was no denying the possible ramifications. Jack's friend Pamela Churchill, who had been at Lismore and had traveled with him to London, recalled later that the examining doctor at the London Clinic said to her: "That American friend of yours, he hasn't got a year to live."

Typically, the Kennedys regarded it as a crisis of explanation as much as a crisis of fact. "Congressman John F. Kennedy announced today that he was 'much better' after a month's bout with malaria and planned to sail home this week," read the press release handed out by his office. When he did sail, however, it was in the *Queen Mary*'s hospital cabin, and according to family friend Frank Waldrop, he was so sick when the *Queen* docked in New York that a priest came aboard to give him extreme unction as he was taken off on a stretcher. Over the next few months, while Jack was admitting the seriousness of the illness to close friends (although not by name—he told one that it was "something like walking leukemia"), his office insisted that it was nothing more than a recurrence of the malaria he had contracted in the Pacific, making it somehow unpatriotic to probe further. Jack recuperated by spending hours on the beach and under sun lamps, disguising the brownish pigmentation of the Addison patient as a healthy tan. His diagnosed affliction now joined the other skeletons dancing in the Kennedys' closet—his father's private life, Rosemary's retardation, and soon, Kick's love affair with a married man.

Jack kept Kick's secret until she herself came home early in 1948, accompanied by her sister-in-law Elizabeth Cavendish, to tell her family about Peter Fitzwilliam and her intention of marrying him. (The fact that his wife Olive was a serious alcoholic helped relieve Kick of some burden of guilt, but Fitzwilliam's family legal advisers still told him a divorce was out of the question.) Kick spent the first weeks of her visit in Palm Beach, but was unable to bring herself to raise the issue. When she went to Washington to visit her brother, he affected skepticism on the issue of love and marriage but was unusually solicitous toward her. One day when she was supposed to fly with him in a light plane for a weekend in Virginia, he told Ted Reardon, "The weather looks a little iffy. It's okay for someone with my life expectancy, but you should persuade her to go with you by train."

From Washington Kick went on to New York, where she confided her dilemma to some of her friends. Charlotte McDonnell (now Charlotte Harris) remembers, "My reaction to it was: having done just about the worst thing she could have by marrying Billy, holy good night, now look what she's done!" But Charlotte was even more struck by the difference in Kick's attitude toward the two romances. "Billy I think was a very conscious decision. But not Fitzwilliam. It was passion. It was hysterical. It was all 'I gotta do, I gotta go.' If she couldn't marry him, she was ready to run off with him. She just wasn't concerned about consequences."

It was not until a week before her scheduled departure, when she had been in America more than two months, that Kick finally revealed her secret. The family had gathered in White Sulphur Springs, West Virginia, for the reopening of the Greenbrier Hotel, which was owned by a family friend. While tea was served to the two hundred guests in the ballroom of the antebellum-style mansion, Kick fended off society writers who asked her about the rumors that she had been seen with the wealthiest man in Ireland. Then, in a quiet moment on the last evening of the weekend, she told her parents. It was Rose who took the offensive, reminding her that to marry a divorced man would deny her the sacraments forever. In a move Kick had feared but still not expected, her mother threatened to disown her, saying that if she went ahead with her plans, Rose would never see her again. As Kathleen wept, her mother added, in one of those characteristically inappropriate gestures that showed how she saw woman's role, that she would also have her father cut off her allowance.

Kick was profoundly shaken. Her mother's strictures about money didn't bother her (as Billy's widow she was independently wealthy), nor was she upset about the religious issue. But she did worry about being forced out of what Lem Billings called the "true mother church"—the family itself. Returning to Washington, she went to spend a weekend with her old confidants from the *Times-Herald* days, John and Patsy White. Unable to sleep, she came into Patsy's bedroom and lay down beside her. "I don't know what to do. Eunice made me a date with Bishop Sheen and I don't want to go. What good can it do? I'm not going to change my mind about Peter. It's just more pressure." They talked about it for a couple of hours, Kathleen agitated by the family pressure and annoyed with herself for being, at twenty-eight, still so vulnerable to it. "What would you do?" she finally asked.

Patsy White hesitated a moment: "I'd call Bishop Sheen and cancel the appointment."

"You're right, really, it's my life. There's no point going through catechism all over again. I'm going back to England and do whatever I have to do so I can be with Peter."

The day before she left, Kick had lunch with Tom Schriber at the 21 Club. "She looked radiant," Joe Junior's old friend later remembered, "really alive. She was revved up, ready to go. She had written off her mother, but not the old man. She said, 'I'd like to get Dad's consent. He matters. But I'm getting married whether he consents or not.'"

The Ambassador, meanwhile, was searching for some compromise. While Kick was returning to London, he was making plans to travel to the Vatican as a side trip from a congressional fact-finding tour about the Marshall Plan; he hoped to obtain some sort of dispensation that would allow the marriage to take place without imperiling his daughter's standing as a Catholic.*

Shortly after Kick had returned to her house in Smith Square, Rose appeared; in a scene that, according to an eyewitness, left her daughter cowering and in tears, she invoked the Church's condemnation of divorce and demanded that she call off any marriage plans and return home, or be cut off from the family forever. The vehemence of her mother's stance made Kick determined to seek the support of her father, who was going to be in Paris the weekend of May 15. She and Fitzwilliam had already planned a getaway in Cannes on the Whitsuntide holiday weekend. Now they decided to stop in Paris on the way back for lunch with the Ambassador at the Ritz, and have him meet Fitzwilliam. Kathleen asked Jane Kenyon-Slaney and her new husband, Max Aiken, Lord Beaverbrook's son, to join them at the lunch in Paris for "moral support."

On Wednesday, May 12, Kick and Fitzwilliam stopped at Milton to visit his cousin. They talked about moving to Fitzwilliam's estate in Ireland and about seeing the Ambassador. "I'm going to do all I can to try to bring the old boy around," Fitzwilliam said. "If religion is the problem, I'll build him a bloody church if he wants." The next morning they climbed into a DeHavilland Dove eight-seater and flew to Le Bourget airport, near Paris, and went into town to meet with friends while the plane was being serviced. By the time they got back to the airport, the weather had turned bad. Their pilot urged them to wait until the storm was over, but Fitzwilliam, looking forward to the two days they would have alone together in Cannes, was adamant.

By late afternoon, as they were passing through the Rhone Valley, the plane was struggling against treacherous winds and rain squalls. A southeasterly wind had blown them off course, so that by the time they passed Valence they were heading straight into the storm. Suddenly the Dove, whipped by cross-currents, was gyrating wildly. A few minutes later it slammed into the side of a mountain near the tiny town of Privas, causing such a loud explosion that villagers below awoke. By morning they had reached the wreck. Peter Fitzwilliam's body was battered, crushed beneath

*On March 23, Kennedy cabled Beaverbrook that he was planning to see the Pope on his trip abroad but hoped to be able to see his old friend later on. On March 31, he cabled to say that the plan to get together depended on "what happens in Italy."

his seat. Kick, who had been sitting in the rear to balance the plane, was still fastened in her seat, her body askew, her legs broken, a gash on the right side of her face, her shoes knocked off by the force of the impact. The bodies were placed in a farm cart and pulled down to the village.

Word came to the Kennedy office at the Capitol, and then to the Georgetown house where Jack was lounging on a couch listening to a recording of the musical comedy *Finian's Rainbow*. Billy Sutton took the call. "Is it for sure?" Jack asked, when Sutton relayed news of his sister's death. The government employee on the other end of the line said that the report hadn't been confirmed. "Tell them to call back when they know one way or the other," Jack said, and went on listening to the record. When another call came a few minutes later saying that Kathleen's body had been definitely identified, "How Are Things in Glockamora" was playing. He looked at Sutton and said, "That Ellen Lagin sure has a sweet voice," and then he turned his head and began to cry.

The Ambassador identified Kick's body. He also managed to get through to the Boston papers, and the story that appeared on the front pages said that the couple had been the most casual of acquaintances and Kathleen had accepted the invitation of a ride only because she had had a pressing appointment in France. Appearances preserved, he then accompanied Kick's body to England, acceding to the Cavendish family's suggestion that she be buried in their family plot at Chatsworth. Billy's parents took care of all the funeral arrangements, including payment of the priest, which the Ambassador in his distraction over the loss of his favorite daughter neglected. The Duchess provided Kick's epitaph: "JOY SHE GAVE / JOY SHE HAS FOUND." Alastair Forbes, among others, was moved by the drama of the scene—"The stricken face of old Joe Kennedy as he stood alone, unloved and despised, behind the coffin of his eldest daughter and the hundreds of British friends who had adored her and now mourned her." Unbending to the last, Rose refused to attend, and had Jean send out a memorial mass card which shocked those of Kick's English friends who recognized the prayer as a plea for a plenary indulgence, applicable to souls in Purgatory.

Back home, John White, Kick's first and most innocent love, wrote the black-bordered obituary for the newspaper where they'd met. "It seems a strange, hard thing to sit at this desk, to tap at this typewriter (your old desk; your old typewriter), to tap out the cold and final word—goodbye... It seems like such a short time ago that you came to the *Times-Herald*. Bright, pretty, quick, vivid, filled with ever bubbling enthusiasm, eager, eager to learn everything.... Kathleen. Little Kathleen. Where have you gone?"

A few weeks after returning home, Joe Kennedy wrote Beaverbrook, who had become his confidant in tragedy: "The sudden death of Young Joe and Kathleen, within a period of three years, has left a mark with me that I find very difficult to erase . . ." For the women in the family, it was not a secular tragedy but rather a morality play, or, as Kick herself had said after Billy Hartington's death, a case of God settling things in His own way. When she happened to run into John White at a party some months later, Eunice lashed out at him savagely, implying that he and his sister had been somehow responsible for her sister's estrangement from her faith and thus for her death. Lem Billings, who had never stopped loving Kathleen, was shocked at Rose's attitude: "For her that airplane crash was God pointing his finger at Kick and saying *no!*"

Although he didn't show it, Jack was perhaps most affected of all the family by Kick's death. When he was growing up, she and Joe Junior had been the stars, the ones blessed with looks, health, and personality, the ones most likely to succeed. Joe's death might be attributed to "statistics." But Kick had lost her life to love, and the repressed romantic in Jack, always impressed by his sister's willingness to take risks in behalf of her feelings, was devastated. The weakest leg of the charmed triangle that had joined him with his brother and sister, he was now the only one left. This fact gave rise to daunting conclusions about the nature of things. "Kathleen and Joe [had] everything moving in their direction," Jack said later, in words that seemed to comment obliquely on his own situation. "That's what made it unfortunate. If something happens to you or somebody in your family who is miserable anyway, whose health is bad, or who has a chronic disease or something, that's one thing. But for someone who is living at the peak, then to get cut off—that's a shock."

Over the next few years, Jack thought and talked constantly—almost compulsively, it seemed to many of his friends—about death. He told Joe Alsop flatly that he doubted if he would live past the age of forty-five. Ted Reardon remembers walking home to Georgetown with Jack one bright spring afternoon after a House session. Jack suddenly stopped: "Tell me, Teddy boy, what's the best way to die?" Standing under the blossoming cherry trees around the Tidal Basin, Reardon replied that it did not seem to be an appropriate day for pressing such a question. But Jack persisted until Reardon finally tried to get the conversation over by saying the best death was from old age. "You're wrong as hell." Jack gave him a triumphant look and started walking again. "In war—that's the best way to die. The very best way. In war."

George Smathers, who saw Jack as "deeply preoccupied by death" throughout the late 1940s and early 1950s, remembers a fishing trip when the subject came up. "He wanted to know which I thought was better—freezing to death, drowning, or getting shot. I wasn't responsive enough, I guess, because he started answering the question himself with the care one usually devotes to philosophical issues. Because of his experience in the PT boat, he felt that drowning was out. He was against freezing because it took so long. And he didn't much relish getting shot. He talked about poison rather hopefully; that seemed to be the preferred solution. After he'd finished this lengthy inquiry into the best ways to die, he leaned over to me and said: 'The point is that you've got to live every day like it's your last day on earth. That's what I'm doing.' ''

That was the remarkable thing: he had identified himself as a terminal case, but he never became doomy, morbid, or self-pitying. If anything, his obsession with death made him even more lucid and companionable. In Chuck Spalding's opinion, this conviction that he had to live each day as though it was his last gave his days a special intensity and weight: ''There was something about time—special for him, obviously, because he always heard the footsteps, but also special for you when you were with him. Death was there. It had taken Joe and Kick and it was waiting for him. So whenever he was in a situation, he tried to burn bright; he tried to wring as much out of things as he could. After a while he didn't have to try. He had something nobody else did. It was just a heightened sense of being; there's no other way to describe it.''

But if this quality made Jack an interesting companion, it also made him more ambivalent about keeping a congressional seat warm for his brother's ghost. Eugene McCarthy of Minnesota, a congressional colleague in Jack's second term, recalls him striking what became a typical pose as he sauntered onto the House floor with his hands in his pockets and said to no one in particular, ''Well, I guess if you don't want to work for a living, this is as good a job as any.'' After the excitement of the first term wore off, his days there became a form of serving time, part of his indeterminate sentence. He seemed ''lost,'' according to his first secretary, Mary Davis: ''I don't think he really knew if he wanted politics, if he was going to remain with it, or what politics was going to do with him.''

His congressional profile was pretty much what might have been expected of Joe Kennedy's son, despite his liberalism on housing and his support of the Truman Doctrine in Europe. He was for the constitutional amendment limiting a President to two terms; he took the conservative view that a sick and incompetent Roosevelt had ''sold out'' U.S. interests at Yalta. He launched a blistering attack on the Truman Administration for the ''loss'' of China. (''Our policy in China has reaped the whirlwind. . . . What our young men had saved, our diplomats and our President have frittered away.'') And he appeared at Harvard's Graduate School of Public Affairs in November 1950 to support the McCarran Act (passed over Truman's veto, the act included a provision that Communists register with the federal government) ; say he thought Joseph McCarthy, who was beginning to win headlines with his charges about Communist infiltration into high places ''may have something''; and admit that he was happy when Richard Nixon defeated Democrat Helen Gahagan Douglas in the California Senate election because she would have been "hard to work with."

What struck Kennedy watchers as much as the opinions themselves was the fact that they were tossed off so casually, without passion or conviction. They were the opinions of someone going through the motions. Supreme Court Justice William O. Douglas, a family friend, said, "I think time was heavy on his hands . . . I'd see him at Palm Beach or Hyannis or Washington and he never seemed to get into the mainstream of any political thought, or political action, or any idea of promoting this or reforming that—nothing . . . He was sort of drifting."

Perhaps because of his sense of how much had been repressed in the family and how dangerous the examined life might be for a Kennedy, Jack always inveighed against what he called "psychologizing." But it didn't require clinical insights for his friends to understand the source of his malaise now. The cumulative weight of his brother's and sister's deaths bore down on him; he was also terribly ill a good deal of the time.* But the real problem continued to be his father.

Although well into his sixties, a time when most men step back a little, Joe Kennedy had continued to occupy most of the family's psychic space—creating obligations without relinquishing power, giving so much that nothing could be personally achieved, defining what the game was and how it must be played. Although he had devoted his life to escaping his origins, he was like the figure Conrad Arensberg described in his classic study of rural life in Ireland: "The father and husband is normally owner and director of the enterprise. The farm and its income are vested in him . . . The sons, even though fully adult, work under their father's eye, and refer necessary decisions to him. . . . The subordination of the sons does not gradually come to an end," wrote Arensberg. "It is a constant . . . For 'boyhood' in this instance is a social status rather than a physiological state . . . 'You can be a boy forever, [one Irishman] said, 'as long as the old fellow is alive.' "

But if he was a throwback to the Irish patriarch, Joe Kennedy was also very much the primal father of Freudian myth, blocking his children's entry to adulthood by the sheer force of his own appetite. His sexual exploits had always been a subject of intense interest for Jack and boyhood friends like Lem, who had been allowed to peer through the keyholes of the family's private life. As they all grew older Jack continued to tell locker-room stories

*The chief problem was still his back, which pained him so badly that he often found it difficult to walk. The Addison's disease made further surgery hazardous. It had been brought under tenuous control by a new drug called DOCA—desoxycorticosterone acetate—which, when implanted in pellet form in the flesh behind the thigh, leaked hormones into the system. The Kennedys cached emergency supplies of the pellets in safe-deposit boxes around the country. DOCA improved daily life but did not make infections or illnesses less life-threatening.

about his father's conquests, although trying now to make them seem like the comic lechery of an aging Molière character. (He told a close friend about the time one of his sisters' friends woke up in the middle of the night at Hyannis and saw the Ambassador standing next to her bed, beginning to take his robe off as he whispered, "This is going to be something you'll always remember.") Women visitors were struck by the way Jack would come by with an impish smile as they were about to retire and say to them, "Be sure to lock the bedroom door. The Ambassador has a tendency to prowl late at night."

But at another level they all realized that it wasn't funny. The wife of Jack's friend Ed McLaughlin, future lieutenant governor of Massachusetts, told of being summoned to Joe Kennedy's suite at the Waldorf on some trivial pretext and, after having to fight him off physically, hearing him yell as she went out the door, "Your husband is just a two-bit politician and I can kill his career!" Sometimes the Ambassador used Joe Timilty or some other crony as a "beard" when he was with a woman in public, but more often he disregarded appearances altogether, at least within his own house. For several months in the late 1940s he had a young woman named Edie living at the Palm Beach house with him, bringing her to meals and integrating her into other aspects of the family routine and telling people who came there that she was a friend of his daughters.

Rose continued to pretend that it wasn't happening, going through her days as if she had a conventionally happy marriage and ignoring all the infidelities and insults. (Sometimes it was almost too much, though. Jewel Reed was present at a surprise birthday party for Rose at which everyone gave thoughtful gifts except her husband, who wrapped up a box of golf balls at the last minute: "For an instant a look of hurt passed over her face.") If there was a touch of the heroic in her determination to forge ahead, the pretense also trivialized her. "Jack loved his mother," Lem Billings said later, "and he tried to stand up for her against the old man. But on the other hand he recognized that she'd been beaten down so long that she'd become sort of empty. I think it colored his idea of what women were, and what relationships between the sexes were all about." Indeed, one friend who enthusiastically told Jack about her engagement was surprised by his response. "Do you really want to get married?" he asked glumly. "There are so many unhappy marriages." Once he sadly said to another woman in a discussion about his family, "My mother is a nothing."

Jack's affairs were less a self-assertion than a search for self—an existential pinch on the arm to prove that he was there. But for him, as for the Ambassador, it was a game of numbers, and he scored with impressive frequency. With Joe Kennedy it was starlets and chorines; with Jack it was airline stewardesses and secretaries. They appeared almost nightly at the Georgetown house (especially after Eunice left in 1948), in such numbers that Jack often didn't bother to learn their names, calling them "sweetie" or "kiddo" the next morning. They came late at night and left early in the morning, driven off unceremoniously by Billy Sutton to their office or air terminal. (One woman who knew him at the time says, "He was as compulsive as Mussolini. Up against the wall, Signora, if you have five minutes, that sort of thing. He was not a cozy, touching sort of man. In fact, he'd been so sick so long that he was a sort of touch-me-not.") For those who managed to become something more than one-night stands, there was an occasional trip to Hyannis when the family was away at Palm Beach. One such date, just nineteen when she met Jack, was surprised to see him go through the empty house like an intruder, peeking into his father's room and looking in his dresser drawers and picking up objects on all the surfaces as if he hadn't seen them before. He went out into the garage and sat in the driver's seat of his father's Cadillac convertible, putting the top up and down like a kid without a license, not daring to drive it out onto the highway. "Jack really wasn't comfortable unless Torby MacDonald or some other male friend was around to make macho jokes with," this woman says. "He was nice—considerate in his own way, witty and fun. But he gave off light instead of heat. Sex was something to *have done*, not to *be doing*. He wasn't in it for the cuddling."

Like his father he was capable of treating women callously. Bobby Baker, Senator Lyndon Johnson's aide, once ran into Jack in the congressional dining room where he was sitting with a friend named Bill Thompson and a stunning woman. Thompson waved Baker over, obviously put up to it by Jack, and said, "Bobby, look at this fine chick. She gives the best head in the United States." Baker glanced nervously at the woman, who was smiling obliviously while Kennedy was convulsed with laughter. "Relax, Bobby," Jack finally said. "She's German and she doesn't understand a word of English. But what Bill's saying is absolutely right."

Yet there was always a hint of uncertainty, as if here, as in politics, he was speaking in lip synch with his father's voice. Jewel Reed was struck by the way he would come by and pick up her husband Jim and take him to a cast party after a play or ask him to go along on a trip to Bermuda, completely ignoring Jewel herself: "He had absolutely no idea how middle-class married life worked." "He knew he was using women to prove his masculinity," said Lem Billings, "and sometimes it depressed him. I think he wanted to believe in love and faithfulness and all that but what he'd seen at home didn't give him much hope. So he sort of bumped along." Chuck Spalding felt it was instructive that Jack was fascinated by Byron: "He'd read everything about him and read most of the poetry too. There were a lot of similarities. Byron too had that conflict between irony and romanticism; he too wanted the world to be better than it was; he also had the disability—the club foot—and the conviction of an early death; and most of all he had the women. In that regard most of all Jack was Byronic. He had the hunger for women and the realization that the hunger was displaced, which led to a fed-upness with women too. The whole thing was more philosophical than physical."*

One of the women Jack courted but never captured, a woman who later became a well-known writer, says: "The whole thing with him was pursuit. I think he was secretly disappointed when a woman gave in. It meant that the low esteem in which he held women was once again validated. It meant also that he'd have to start chasing someone else. I was one of the few he could really talk to. Like Freud, he wanted to know what women really wanted, that sort of thing; but he also wanted to know the more mundane details—what gave a woman pleasure, what women hoped for in marriage, how they liked to be courted. During one of these conversations I once asked him why he was doing it—why he was acting like his father, why he was avoiding real relationships, why he was taking a chance on getting caught in a scandal at the same time that he was trying to make his career take off. He took a while trying to formulate an answer. Finally he shrugged and said, 'I don't know, really. I guess I just can't help it.' He had this sad expression on his face. He looked like a little boy about to cry."

*Years later Jack Kennedy invited Lady Diana Cooper, an acquaintance from his London days, to the White House. Speaking of Eunice, Lady Diana said that she thought her beautiful. "In what way?" Jack wanted to know. "She has a wild originality of countenance," Lady Diana said, quoting Byron on his lover Caroline Lamb. "And is she mad, bad, and dangerous to know?" Jack replied, using Lady Caroline's description of Byron.

3.

*I*N OCTOBER 1950, HONEY FITZ
died. Except for Curley, himself a sick and dying man, he was the last of the
great bosses of Boston politics. His end marked not only the passing of a
colorful age but of a political style as well. (One of Fitzgerald's few remaining enemies from the old days, asked why he bothered to come to the funeral,
said, "Because I wanted to look at the son of a bitch and make sure he was
dead.") For Jack, his grandfather's passing raised the questions surrounding the heritage which hung over him like a huge charge of static electricity
in yet another way: If the old world of Honey Fitz was dead, when would
the new world, his world, finally be born?

He had run unopposed in 1948 and faced only token opposition two years
later. He could have gone on being reelected to Congress indefinitely, but he
had been chafing at the regimen of the House since he arrived in Washington.
The old-boy networks and the seniority system oppressed him; even worse
was the relative anonymity of the members. "We're just worms," he complained. "Nobody pays much attention to us nationally." He had toyed with
the idea of seeking another, higher office from the moment he was first
elected. Now he decided that 1952 had to be his year. He wasn't sure what
position he was running for; he was just running—away from the early
death that seemed to be gaining on him, and toward the apotheosis that would
allow him to step out of the viscous matrix of family obligation. His desperation was implicit in a comment he made to Lem: "I've decided to go up or
go out."

Ignoring the handicaps of youth and inexperience, not to speak of a relatively undistinguished record in Congress, he began coming home to Massa-

chusetts on weekends after his 1950 victory, crisscrossing the state in his father's limousine, snatching a few hours of sleep crumpled in the back seat, and snacking on greasy take-out food between speaking engagements before civic groups. After the first few weeks the toll it was taking was clear to friends. George Smathers, who knew as well as anyone how precarious Jack's health was, tried to persuade him to hold off. ''I said, 'For Chrissakes, Jack, wait until you're better. You can't do this now. You won't survive it. What in God's name is the rush?' He looked at me and said, 'I can't wait. I don't have time. I've got to do it *now!'* ''

The first task was to augment his reputation. For his dead grandfather the political world had been the city of Boston; for Jack it was the world itself. Foreign relations was the subject in which he felt strongest, and the ground, as he saw it, where the Kennedys had chosen to make their stand. And so early in 1951, while Congress was in session, he left for Europe on a six-week fact-finding trip. With his father making sure his tour received maximum coverage in Massachusetts newspapers, Jack visited all the hot spots on the Continent—West Germany, Spain, and Yugoslavia, where he had a well-publicized interview with Marshal Tito, who downplayed rumors of an imminent Soviet invasion. Jack toured installations of the recently formed North Atlantic Treaty Organization, and had an audience with the Pope which was timed for the Boston Sunday papers.

Returning home, he made a radio report on the trip, affirming the necessity of making Western Europe a first line of defense but saying the U.S. commitment to NATO ought to be based on a ratio of American to European troops that would force allied countries to share the burden of rearmament. Appearing before the Senate Foreign Relations Committee a few days later, he sideswiped the Truman Administration's talk about the possibility of war in Europe by testifying that his trip had convinced him the Russians were unlikely to risk a confrontation: ''Why should they take risks they don't have to? . . . Stalin is an old man, and old men are traditionally cautious.''

Next, Jack planned a trip to Israel and the Far East. This time Pat and, at his father's insistence, Bobby would go with him. Up to now, as Jack later acknowledged, he hadn't really known his younger brother very well. Having been away during most of the war, he hadn't witnessed the personal drama that had transformed Bobby into the most intense member of the family and the most loyal to its household gods. He wrote off Bobby's most salient feature—an iron-willed determination—as masochistic gung ho, missing the insight of his perceptive friend Chuck Spalding: ''Bobby felt he was weak. He felt he had to toughen himself up and get rid of that vulnerability everyone had remarked on since he was a boy. This was the way for him to get someplace in the family. The drive was incessant, just fierce. He simply remade himself. He got so he could just go through a wall.''

When he returned to Harvard after serving on the destroyer named for his dead brother, Bobby had a football career that was a triumph of the will; he played with fractured leg bones, dislocated shoulders, and other ailments, and so impressed the coaches that they awarded him a letter despite his mediocre ability. Because of poor grades at Harvard he had gone to the University of Virginia Law School, where he received his degree as a result of what one of his professors called "sheer persistence." (The high point of his academic career was a research paper on Yalta which mirrored Joseph Kennedy's postwar views.) The ongoing nature of his struggle finally became clear to his father. "He is just starting out and has the difficulty of trying to follow two brilliant boys," Kennedy wrote Beaverbrook. "This in itself is quite a hardship and he is making a good battle against it."

Sometimes the hardship led to explosions that showed how far the battle was from being won. John Magnuson, who was at Harvard with Bobby, remembers going to Cronin's, a local beer hall, to celebrate his birthday. At the other end of the long bar was Bobby, with his classmate Kenny O'Donnell and other friends. Unbeknownst to Magnuson, Bobby was picking up the tab for beers for everybody in celebrating *his* birthday. Magnuson recalls: "My friends soon burst into 'Happy Birthday' and got to the point of 'Happy birthday, dear John . . .' when suddenly a guy comes from behind with a beer bottle and hits me in the head. It was Bobby Kennedy." Magnuson was taken to the hospital for a couple of stitches; a few days later O'Donnell came around and apologized for Bobby, saying "it just wasn't his nature to apologize."

The Harvard swimming coach who had both Kennedys on his team remembered Jack for his "floatability," while what struck him about Bobby was that he was "heavy in the water . . . He would sink, sink quite easily." It was a good metaphor for the difference between the brothers. Jack's sensibility was buoyantly literary; Bobby's was heavily moral, however inchoate. Bobby sought responsibility as compulsively as Jack tried to evade it. And while Jack was distinguishing himself by the number and brevity of his sexual liaisons, Bobby was carrying on a serious courtship of Ethel Skakel, a friend of his sister Jean's at Manhattanville College.

There were symmetries between the Kennedys and the Skakels: both were large, active, and wealthy Catholic families. George Skakel, Sr., was even more a self-made man than Joe Kennedy, having started as an eight-dollar-a-week railroad clerk and gone on to build the Great Lakes Carbon Corporation, one of the largest privately held businesses in the country, before settling in Greenwich, Connecticut. Ethel's mother, Ann Brannack Skakel, a massive woman who weighed two hundred pounds and was several inches taller than her husband, was as devout as Rose, going to seven o'clock mass at St. Mary's Roman Catholic Church on Greenwich Avenue every morning. But all of Ann Skakel's children accompanied her, from the time they were four, including in their devotions a prayer for their father, who stubbornly held to his Dutch Protestant faith. Also different was the discipline in the Skakel household, which was lax enough to allow Ethel's brothers to become the terrors of the neighborhood, perching in upper-story windows of the family mansion with air rifles to snipe at the boys who came to see their sisters.*

Ethel was the sixth of the seven Skakel children, so hyperkinetic that a French teacher described her as *"un paquet de nerfs."* Her Manhattanville yearbook, "The Tower," captured what had become her two most character-istic traits—madcap energy and compulsive pranks: "An excited hoarse voice, a shriek, a peal of screaming laughter, the flash of shirttails, a tousled brown head—Ethel! Her face is at one moment a picture of utter guileless-ness and at the next alive with mischief . . ."

From their first contact on a ski trip to Mont Tremblant in Canada, ar-ranged by Jean, Ethel's eye was set on Bobby. At first Bobby preferred Ethel's older and more serious sister Patricia, but eventually he saw Ethel's virtues and started coming up on weekends from Charlottesville to see her. The chemistry became apparent. She too had considered the Church as a vocation as a teenager; like him she was fiercely competitive and loyal, dividing the world into "goodies" and "baddies." In other key ways she was different—as certain of her opinions as he was tenuous ("I like films such as *South Pacific*," she said, "shows such as *My Fair Lady*, books such as *The King Must Die*. I do not feel easy in the company of highbrows . . ."), as effervescent as he was moody. She complemented and, in a sense, com-pleted him. People were touched by how understanding she was of his shy-ness although not the least shy herself, and how she would begin a story and then realize he was standing there and say, "Bobby, *you* tell it," just to get him involved.

On June 17, 1950, before the assembled families and some of Bobby's Harvard football buddies who served as ushers, they were married at St. Mary's Church. Rose came from Hyannis for the wedding; the Ambassador drove up from New York with his sister Loretta. Starting late, the services were momentarily enlivened when George Skakel, Jr., sitting in a pew behind Lem, threw some pennies in the aisle and asked Lem to retrieve them. When Lem bent over to do so, George gave him a solid kick that sent the six-foot-two Billings rolling toward the altar. Afterward, there was a lavish reception at the Skakel estate. At twenty-five Bobby had become the first male of his generation to marry; he would soon be the first to have children, naming the

---

*In another legendary family ritual, they invited youthful guests to pile into an old wooden-sided station wagon they had picked up at the 1939 New York World's Fair and take a tour of the estate. Then they started the car, drove down the hill behind the house, and swerved sharply, dumping all and sundry into the pond at the bottom. Afterward they would winch out the car and drag it back to the top to wait for the next load of victims.

first girl, who was born in 1951, after Kathleen, and the first boy, born the following year, after Joe Junior, and only then allowing himself the luxury of a namesake.

Jack had begun the October 1951 trip that would take them from Israel to Japan wondering, as he put it to Lem, if Bobby would be "a pain in the ass." But as they went from country to country, talking with military and political leaders ranging from Israeli Prime Minister David Ben-Gurion to American General Matthew Ridgway, he saw his brother as if for the first time and came to appreciate his dogged effort to evaluate the issues. The diary Bobby kept and the letters he wrote home show how profoundly affected by the discovery of the underdeveloped world both Kennedys were. In Europe the cold war was a stalemate, but the Far East seemed a volatile battlefield in the contest between communism and the Free World, with new countries emerging every day from the chains of colonialism and facing fateful choices about their future. What struck Bobby at a dinner the Kennedys had with Nehru, aside from the intense attention he paid to Pat, was the Indian Prime Minister's statement that communism was appealing to emerging countries because it had associated itself with ideas that were "worth dying for." Recording this in his diary, Bobby added, "Must give the same aura to democracy . . . We only have status quo to offer these people. Commies can offer a change."

Jack might have phrased it in less Manichean terms, but he had the same view. (The trip made a "very, very major impression" on his brother, Bobby said later on, while future Kennedy foreign policy adviser Walt Rostow called it "the formative experience.") Saigon was the most memorable stop. They stayed at the U. S. Embassy residence, watching the nights flash with the guns of the Viet Minh forces ringing the city. Jack had long conversations with U. S. consular officer Edmund Gullion about the war the French seemed incapable of winning and about colonialism itself. Gullion cautioned him against drawing false parallels between Indochina and Korea, and emphasized that the real opponent the French were fighting was nationalism, not Communist subversion, and that this was what doomed the French effort. As Jack listened intently, tapping his front teeth with his index finger, as he did when trying to concentrate, Gullion felt that he was instinctively (if not ideologically) sympathetic with the situation in the developing world—with struggles that seemed so analogous to an Oedipal revolt against unyielding paternal authority. As Jack was leaving Saigon, he asked what lesson was to be learned from Indochina and Gullion's response was succinct : in twenty years there won't be any more colonies.

While Bobby was writing letters to his father criticizing American support for the French and saying he believed that in an honest plebiscite 70 percent of the people in the country would vote for Ho Chi Minh ("Because of the great U.S. war aid to the French, we are being closely identified with the French, the result being that we have also become quite unpopular. Our mistake has been not to insist on definite political reforms by the French toward the natives as prerequisite to any aid. As it stands now we are becoming more and more involved to a point where we can't back out''), Jack arranged what turned out to be an abrasive interview with General Jean Marie de Lattre, after which the commander of the French forces complained to the State Department that the Kennedys were attempting to undermine French policy.

The Far East trip ended in Japan, where Jack became ill with an infection that caused his fever to shoot up to 106 and once again made the family fear for his life. But he seemed to take strength from Bobby's presence, and was on his feet when they arrived home. Again he made a radio talk to report on the insights acquired during the trip: that "the fires of nationalism so long dormant have been kindled and are now ablaze"; and that "communism cannot be met effectively merely by force of arms." Although it wasn't apparent at the time, the brothers had not only found each other but had located one of the issues that would later become an obsessive concern for both of them.

The question of what higher office Jack would run for was still open. To a large degree the answer was dependent on Governor Paul Dever, the current boy wonder of Massachusetts politics. As head of the state Democratic organization, Dever had the right of way in deciding whether to stand for reelection or to go after the Senate seat held by Republican Henry Cabot Lodge, Jr. When Dever continued to procrastinate into the beginning of 1952, Jack became increasingly irritated and after fuming for several days finally called him. "Now, Paul," he said, "you'll have to make up your mind. It doesn't make any difference to me. If you want to run for the Senate, I'll run for governor. If you want to run for governor, I'll run for the Senate. Will you please make up your mind and let me know?"

Actually Jack regarded the Statehouse as a place where someone "sat in an office handing out sewer contracts," while the Senate was where foreign policy was made. He counted on Dever not being willing, as he was, to gamble everything on a risky challenge to Lodge, one of the luminaries of the Republican Party, in what promised to be a Republican year. When Dever finally called him on April 6 and said that he had decided to go for reelection, Jack put down the phone and smiled at an aide. "We've got the race we wanted."

Even so, at the beginning he may have underestimated just how formidable an undertaking it would be. Fitzgerald and Kennedy might be names to conjure with in Boston, but Lodge was a trademark throughout the state and all over New England. Lodge represented an older and far more distinguished political dynasty than Kennedy, and despite Curley's proletarian contempt for him as "Little Boy Blue," Lodge had significant snob appeal even for upwardly mobile Irish who had celebrated their escape from the ghetto of their grandfathers by flirting with the Republican Party. Republicans, especially a Brahmin like Lodge, were respectable; Democrats, especially Irish jailbirds like Curley, were not.

Lodge was not unfriendly to the Kennedys. Joe Kennedy had contributed to his campaign against Roosevelt's candidate Joseph Casey in 1942, and when rumors began to circulate that Jack might possibly run in 1952, Lodge advised the Ambassador through an intermediary to save his money. Coupled with the historical overtones (Honey Fitz had run unsuccessfully for the same Senate seat against Lodge's grandfather in 1916), this well-meaning gesture only made the challenge more irresistible. Joe Kennedy growled to a reporter friend, "All I ever heard when I was growing up was how Lodge's grandfather had helped put the stained-glass window into the Gate of Heaven Church in South Boston."

The 1952 campaign organization was wholly different from the one that had first sent Jack to Congress. Veterans' issues had faded away and so had the friends who had provided the façade of amateurism for the 1946 campaign. Lem Billings was working as an advertising executive with the Emerson Drug Company in Baltimore (where he invented and helped market "Fizzies"); Chuck Spalding was back in Hollywood trying to turn books into movies; Red Fay was in the family construction business in San Francisco; and Jim Reed was building a law practice. Joe Kane and the other old pols of Boston who had survived Honey Fitz were increasingly obsolete, especially in a statewide race. With Paul Dever monopolizing the state Democratic Party for his own reelection plans, it was necessary to build an alternative structure.

It was in 1952, therefore, that the nucleus of the famous "Kennedy machine" was put together by loyalists who saw the family as a political party unto itself; who saw that politics in the postwar era would be less an art than a science. One was Kenny O'Donnell, Bobby's hard-bitten, mercurial friend from Harvard (where he had been captain of the football team). Bobby persuaded him to quit his job with a paper company and go to work with Mark Dalton even before Jack made up his mind what office to run for. Another was Larry O'Brien, just Jack's age, a youthful version of the Irish political operative of the vanishing era who had connections all over the state. Together the two men became a sort of Alphonse and Gaston routine, the one always looking on the bright side and the other on the gloomy side. In addition, there was Sargent Shriver, on leave from Kennedy Enterprises, and James Landis, who had left Washington after twenty years of service in Democratic administrations so impoverished that he had become virtually a pensioner of the Ambassador. His impressive New Deal and academic credentials made Landis an ideal person to carry the message about Jack to the Cambridge intellectuals, who had so far remained underwhelmed. Landis completed a survey of the state's economic condition and noted that the key textile industry was gradually moving South toward cheaper labor, which led to early attacks on Lodge and also to Jack's campaign slogan: "He'll do more for Massachusetts."

Most of all there was Joe Kennedy himself, who, as Eunice said, "had thought and questioned and planned for two years," and who was one of the few people in state politics who believed his son would "knock Lodge's block off." There was a campaign committee, but the Ambassador made it clear that he was in charge. He took an apartment at 84 Beacon Street so that he could be at the heart of things, and insisted that he okay expenditures, pass on advertising layouts, and ratify decisions involving campaign policy and philosophy. He also caused such turmoil that the early stages of the campaign were marked by chaos that threatened to paralyze the whole effort, something Jack understood but was powerless to change. When the Ambassador attacked Mark Dalton, who had served as unpaid campaign manager since 1946, humiliating him during a meeting, Dalton came to Jack for a vote of confidence and Jack shrugged impotently as if to say: You don't think I'm the boss, do you? Dalton left. Later on, the Ambassador discovered that some of the workers in the Boston office had prepared an ad which read "McCarthy and Communism—Both Wrong" and began to scream at them for being anti-American, a drama Jack happened to walk in on and just as quickly turned around and walked out.

As morale dropped and workers threatened to mutiny, Kenny O'Donnell, sensing that only another Kennedy could intervene, called Bobby in New York and told him that the campaign was heading for "absolute catastrophic disaster" unless he took it over. "I'll just screw it up," Bobby responded, pointing out that he was making good headway in the job with the Justice Department's Internal Affairs Division that his father had arranged for him, and that he knew nothing about electoral politics. O'Donnell persisted, drawing out a scenario of humiliating family defeat if matters were allowed to drift. Finally Bobby relented and agreed to leave for Boston.

Almost immediately the potentially disastrous situation began to change. As Ted Reardon said, "It was Bobby's first front and forward opportunity in the family and he just broke his butt." His motives, unlike his father's, seemed so selfless and his energy was so contagious that within days after his arrival campaign workers were referring to what had happened as "before the revolution" and what was now happening as "after the revolution." Working with Larry O'Brien, Bobby designed a structure in which Kennedy "secretaries" would function in each precinct as a shadow organization to the regular Democratic Party machinery. He went up and down the state, making the campaign seem like a quest, avoiding publicity himself whenever possible, but when it was necessary conquering his stage fright to make brief, stuttering speeches in behalf of his brother. (''My brother Jack couldn't be here,'' he mumbled to the first crowd he had to face. ''My mother couldn't be here. My sister Eunice couldn't be here. My sister Pat couldn't be here. My sister Jean couldn't be here. But if my brother Jack were here, he'd tell you Lodge has a very bad voting record. Thank you.'')

O'Donnell's hunch had been right. Not long after Bobby arrived, the Ambassador moved back into the penumbra which had become his preferred milieu. Occasional glimpses would be caught of him, as when he sat high in the balcony of an auditorium where Jack was debating Lodge, furiously scribbling notes and giving them to a pair of runners who carried them to the stage. But for the most part his presence would be inferred by otherwise unexplained political phenomena, as when John Fox, publisher of the conservative *Boston Post,* began attacking Lodge in a series of editorials that culminated in a front-page endorsement of Jack. The financially strapped *Post,* it would later come out, had received a substantial loan from Kennedy Enterprises.

The Ambassador would continue to provide the money. Tip O'Neill, who served several terms as a state assemblyman before taking Jack's old seat in the Eleventh Congressional District, says: ''From 1952 on, whenever the Democrats nominated a man for governor the nominee went to New York and met Joe Kennedy and expected to take home maybe $50,000 or $60,000 in his valise.'' At the beginning of every campaign, everyone in the family would receive a letter from Kennedy's office, where their trust funds were administered: ''Greetings, you have just made a political contribution ...'' But if the Ambassador remained the financier, from now on Bobby was the political ramrod. Joe Kennedy had been forced to be his own heavy during his abortive political career—the would-be candidate and also the would-be candidate's hatchet man. When Bobby came into the campaign against Lodge, he took the political dirty work on himself, allowing Jack to remain (in Jack's words) ''a virgin.'' Bobby saw that the problem Jack faced as a pragmatist was not to be perceived as an opportunist. He took that identity upon himself, fighting the daily battles of territory and resources, earning as campaign ribbons the adjectives that would follow him from now on— abrasive; mean; ruthless. State legislator John Powers recalls one instance when Bobby jumped up from the table in the middle of a meeting and began jabbing his finger at a candidate for local office who he felt was using Jack and shouting, ''I don't want my brother to get mixed up with politicians!'' The other man yelled back, ''Listen, he put his name on the ballot the same as the rest of us. Who the hell do you think you guys are?'' and lunged across the table. The two men had to be pried apart. Something similar happened later on when Governor Dever, who had watched his own campaign begin to falter, asked for a meeting to discuss merging the regular party machinery with the supercharged Kennedy organization. "Don't give in to them," Jack told Bobby, "but don't get me involved." The meeting was so abrasive that Dever cut it short and when Bobby had left telephoned the Ambassador: "I know you're an important man around here and all that, but I'm telling you this and I mean it. Keep that fresh kid of yours out of sight from here on in."

Bobby's willingness to accept the role of the family's political id made Jack appreciate him as his other qualities hadn't. Tommy O'Hearn, a distant Kennedy cousin in charge of outdoor advertising in 1952, remembers an afternoon when Jack, with all the cold anger he concealed in public, attacked him because he had been embarrassed by Lodge's charge that Kennedy bill-boards were printed out of state by nonunion labor. "Look at what a Christly mess you've made of things," Jack stormed. "That's the sort of carelessness that's going to cost us." O'Hearn replied, "Blame that sonofabitch brother of yours; he's the one that ordered me to do it so he could save a dime of your father's money." Jack chopped at the air with his hand: "Oh, bullshit, everybody bitches about Bobby, and I'm getting sick and goddamn tired of it. He's the only one who doesn't stick knives in my back, the only one I can count on when it comes down to it."

Before the campaign got under way, Ted Reardon had spent weeks working on what became known as the "Black Book," or "Lodge Missal," which focused the Kennedy attack by targeting Lodge as a "me too" politician who came down on both sides of all key issues.* Much of the campaign rhetoric would be spent on what Lodge had or hadn't done about the fugitive textile industry, the St. Lawrence Seaway, and other state and regional issues. But another thrust was to suggest that Lodge was insufficiently zeal-ous in his anticommunism, particularly in regard to the Far East. This was calculated to appeal to Republicans still smarting over Lodge's support for General Dwight Eisenhower as the Republican presidential nominee rather than Senator Robert Taft. ("He has been much closer to the position of Taft than has Lodge," Reardon wrote of Jack. "Indeed the latter has been at the head of the so-called bipartisan foreign policy parade since 1947.") The Kennedys' adroit use of the issue that had brought Senator Joseph McCarthy to the front pages showed how well thought out the plan was.

The Ambassador himself had no doubts about McCarthy. Since Eunice

---

*Reardon began his "Black Book" catalogue of "Lodge's Dodges," as the list became known, with: "While he terms himself a liberal his record is replete with examples of sniping attempts to cripple progressive social legislation. His pre-war isolationism in regard to foreign affairs has given way to his present internationalism. And while he has, since the war, been riding at the head of the Administration's foreign policy parade, he has been unwilling to accept responsibility for errors, although willing to accept plaudits for success..."

had introduced them a few years earlier, he had wired McCarthy into the circuit by which he kept himself informed, consulting him frequently and, on occasion, advising him. (Roy Cohn, a McCarthy aide, was present when one of these calls came through and watched McCarthy listen long enough to determine that it was the Ambassador, then put his hand over the receiver and ask that someone check the size of the Kennedy contribution to make sure it was worth the effort.) Jack was less enthusiastic, but at a reunion of the Spee Club early in 1952, when one of the speakers congratulated Harvard College for never having produced either an Alger Hiss (although the Law School had) or a Joseph McCarthy, Jack had jumped up angrily: "How dare you couple the name of a great American patriot with that of a traitor!" Out of the public eye, however, he had told friends that McCarthy was "just another shanty Irish" whose act was going to make it tough on all politicians. Understanding that McCarthy would become the tar baby who entangled everyone who took a punch at him, Jack kept his distance.

When Adlai Stevenson was about to bring his presidential campaign into Massachusetts, Sargent Shriver sent him a memo recommending that the Democratic candidate point out Kennedy's support for the minimum wage, decent housing, and other verities of Truman's "Fair Deal," but that he refrain from attacks on McCarthy while mentioning with approval that Jack had gotten the first successful perjury conviction of a subversive in the Christoffel affair. ("Up here this anti-communist business is a good thing to emphasize ...") Late in the fall, as the impact McCarthy was having on Democratic candidates across the country became clear, the Party National Committee asked Jack to take part in a political broadcast condemning McCarthyism, and he refused. McCarthy repaid him in kind: he agreed late in the campaign to make appearances for Lodge, but stipulated that he would not attack the Kennedys directly. Lodge rejected the condition with patrician distaste: "I certainly didn't want him coming in just on the basis of defending me."

The Massachusetts Senate race ignited the imagination of the country, becoming a dynastic feud between two famous names. Lodge campaigned with his wife in fluent French among the state's French-Canadian population; his aristocratic sister-in-law appealed for the votes of "Italian-Americans" in Italian. The Kennedys, meanwhile, descended en masse, the women making appearances in flared skirts embroidered with "Vote for John F. Kennedy." Ethel Kennedy gave birth to her second child just after making a campaign speech in Fall River, and not long before voters went to the polls, Archbishop Cushing baptized the newborn son Joseph Kennedy III in a well-publicized ceremony.

Because the Ambassador was suspect, especially in the Jewish community, for the views he had expressed before the war, Rose was made into the parent of record. Personally she might be frosty and remote. (Once Larry O'Brien's wife was to drive her to a plane that would take her to a campaign appearance. After Elva O'Brien had waited for a long time in front of the hotel, Rose finally appeared, got into the back seat, and cut off attempts at conversation curtly: "Would you forgive me? I'm very tired and don't feel like talking.") But she had an unerring instinct for politics. On "Coffee with the Kennedys," a morning television spot with her daughters, she chatted engagingly about Jack's youth, reading from her famous index cards and answering viewers' calls on the toll-free line about the vicissitudes of raising a large and boisterous family. As Kenny O'Donnell said, "She had a perfect knack for saying the right thing at the right time and always striking the right note." But there was no shift of real power in the family. An ad man in charge of television commercials was rehearsing one in the Kennedy living room in which Rose chattered on about how Jack had picked blueberries in Maine during family trips there when he was a boy. The Ambassador sat in the corner, apparently engrossed in a book—but when the ad man met him leaving Kennedy headquarters the next day, the elder Kennedy muttered quietly but distinctly: "The blueberries are *out*."

In the past an Irish candidate would display his family to demonstrate piety and stability. But the Kennedys were there as a time-lapse photograph of the workings of the American dream. If the Lodges showed how history could select a family, the Kennedys showed how a family could seize history. When they appeared at the teas that had been started in 1946 and were now a major weapon in Jack's campaign arsenal, thousands showed up to meet and gawk at them. Lodge said condescendingly, "I'm sure they are quite pleasant little affairs and I'm sure they are nonfattening," but the Kennedys' appearances had something he couldn't match.

Another virtue of the teas was that they gathered people in one place, so that Jack could come, stand propped up against a wall for a couple of hours, and have meetings with state politicians afterward, thus avoiding the strain of many campaign stops. He was in constant pain throughout the fall of 1952, having exacerbated his back problems by sliding down a fire pole as a campaign stunt in Springfield. He often had to use crutches, which he would hand to aides before an appearance so he could walk in looking jaunty and youthful.

The ghost of his brother was still present. On election eve, millions of copies of an eight-page tabloid were circulated throughout the state. Alongside drawings of Lieutenant Kennedy rescuing his *PT 109* shipmates was a page featuring a picture of Young Joe under the headline "John Fulfills Dream of Brother Joe Who Met Death Over the English Channel." Joe Junior's old friend Ted Reardon thought Jack's accomplishment in 1952 outweighed anything his brother was capable of: "Joe was smooth, but he didn't have Jack's finesse or anything like it. If Joe felt somebody was trying to use him, he'd say 'Drop dead, Charlie' and that would be that. Jack was the politician, the one who wouldn't turn anyone away, who would find an advantage in every situation. Joe probably wouldn't have stood up to Lodge. He certainly wouldn't have handled the situation the way Jack did." But Jack didn't see that yet. He would drag himself back from campaigning and soak in a hot tub, sometimes sobbing from fatigue and frustration. His father tried to keep him going, telling him that if he could manage to beat Lodge, the sky was the limit. "I will work out plans to elect you President," a family friend overheard him tell his son. "It will not be any more difficult for you to be elected President than it will be to win the Lodge fight. While it will require a tremendous amount of work on your part, you will need about twenty key men in the country to get the nomination, for it is these men who will control the convention..."

Stevenson was inundated by Eisenhower in Massachusetts, as he was nationally, and Paul Dever was ousted from the Statehouse by Christian Herter. Jack managed to survive, beating Lodge with 51 percent of the vote. Late on election night, as the returns made it clear that he had won (Rose immediately said, "At last the Fitzgeralds have evened the score with the Lodges"), Jack stationed a lookout to keep an eye on Lodge headquarters up the street from his own. When Lodge was seen getting into his limousine, Jack assumed that he was coming to concede and ordered everyone to be polite and sportsmanlike and applaud graciously when his opponent entered. The limousine approached and then sped by without slowing. "Sonofabitch," Jack muttered as he watched it disappear. "Can you believe that?"

He had promised to sing "Sweet Adeline" if he won, and he did, although he took a long time to work himself up to it. In part it was an acknowledgment of his roots and a signal that he had now vindicated his grandfather's loss to another Lodge in a bygone age. But it was also a pun, for the class competition and ethnic pressures of the past were dead now. In losing to a prior Lodge, Honey Fitz had flailed out at him: "The robber baron is still his highest ideal and his dearest friend." But Jack had met and beaten his opponent on his own ground. The Cabots and the Lodges, used to talking only to each other and to God, couldn't talk to the voters in the way the Kennedys could. Paul Dever recognized that Jack had stepped onto new ground when he said with grudging admiration: "He is the first Irish Brahmin."

4.

*J*ACK SHOWED UP AT EISENHOWER'S inaugural ball with Jacqueline Bouvier. The journalist Charles Bartlett took credit for introducing the couple in 1952, but Dinah Bridge, a family friend who was staying with Bobby and Ethel shortly after the birth of their first child in 1951, saw what was probably the first meeting: "We were all sitting around having breakfast, and Jack was there and Jean. Around the corner of the front door came this beautiful girl in riding clothes ready to pick up Jean to go riding . . . And soon after that, I think one night later, she was invited to supper . . . and she was sort of put through her paces." They played Categories and the other word games at which Jack had always excelled. He was annoyed and intrigued when Jackie outperformed him. Lem Billings, who would become something of a connoisseur of their relationship, felt it was appropriate that it should have begun with games: "From the beginning there was a playful element between them. Jackie gave him a good match: that's one of the things Jack liked. But there was a serious element too. Who was going to win?"

Jackie was far different from the others with whom Jack had been involved—intelligent, socially more substantial, and, in Lem's words, "classier." There was something in her manner—a sense of portent and aloofness —that elicited cattiness in other women. Like members of some eighteenth-century salon, they gossiped about how she was forced to straighten her "kinky" hair and shop carefully for shoes to minimize her large feet. "Her eyes are so far apart," said a woman who considered herself a friend, "that you wonder how they see the same image." Men had quite a different reaction. It was not so much her looks, although she made the most of her physical assets, but her manner that was striking: breathless and apparently naïve, yet capable of ruthless insights; circumspect and ladylike, yet often strongly sexual in its overtones. There was a dangerous sense of irony which she usually kept sheathed but which Jack found especially appealing. "He saw her as a kindred spirit," said Lem. "I think he understood that the two of them were alike. They had both taken circumstances that weren't the best in the world when they were younger and learned to *make themselves up* as they went along."

The Bouviers were immigrants too, although by an earlier and less traveled route than that of the Kennedys. The first Bouvier in America, a friend and supporter of Napoleon's brother Joseph, King of Spain, had arrived in Philadelphia thirty years before the Great Hunger. He was Michel, a cabinetmaker who made a fortune by speculating in land, and, after encountering anti-Catholic prejudice not unlike that awaiting County Wexford's Pat Kennedy, moved his family to the more tolerant and cosmopolitan atmosphere of New York. The family became allied with the Drexels by marriage and thus with the House of Morgan. Striving upward, they made the *Social Register* in 1880, just as P. J. Kennedy was beginning to diversify from saloonkeeping to politics. By the time Jackie was born, in 1929, the Bouviers were a sprawling family like the Du Ponts, with feuding collateral lines and generations linked by the endless drama of the squandering and consolidation of wealth.

What Jack and Jackie had in common had less to do with families per se, however, than with fathers who had been the crucial influences on their lives. The similarity between the two men was not in business skills: John V. Bouvier III had turned a $750,000 inheritance into a $100,000 estate at the end of a lifetime of investing. Nor was it in tough-mindedness: Bouvier was not driven by anything as powerful as Joe Kennedy's seemingly paradoxical desire to vindicate and divest himself of his ethnicity. The similarity was in the way they integrated their children into their personal dramas and the *aperçu* they shared about human nature: you are what you make people think you are.

Hair parted as if by calipers, dark face ripely handsome, flying a silk handkerchief in his pocket like the Jolly Roger, Bouvier had made a reputation as a sexual corsair sailing through society parties from Manhattan to the Hamptons. Because of his swarthy skin and Gable-like looks and manners, he acquired nicknames alluding to his amorous play—the Black Sheik, the Black Orchid, and, less exotically, Black Jack. Before and during his marriage to Janet Lee, daughter of a self-made millionaire, he made his mark as a womanizer. What women found attractive was not just the matinee-idol looks but also his company. "Bouvier was unusual among philanderers of that day," one of his conquests said. "Women were not just collectibles for him. He actually liked their company, liked the feminine perspective and the *social* quality of women's lives."

His daughters, Jacqueline and Lee, whom Bouvier continued to dominate after being divorced from their mother, grew up with a similar view, though with the gender reversed. The company of men was preferable to that of women; the relationship between the sexes was the only social drama worth devoting a life to. Even after his former wife had found a new husband— Hugh Auchincloss, who was so wealthy from family holdings in Standard Oil that he owned two estates (in McLean, Virginia, and in Newport)— Bouvier remained the major force in the girls' lives, grooming and educating them, supporting them beyond his shrinking means, shaping their sensibilities and future prospects.

Later on Jackie said of her younger sister: "Lee was the pretty one. So I guess I was supposed to be the intelligent one." Her father had sent her to Miss Porter's and then Miss Chapin's, where she listed her ambition in the yearbook as "not to be a housewife." She told her schoolmates stories about her father's sexual prowess, making a lusty tale out of her mother's tearfully self-pitying account of how he had engaged in his first extramarital affair on their honeymoon, forty-eight hours after they were married; the other girls lined up to see Black Jack when he came to pick Jackie up for the weekend.

Under his guidance she went from a pouting young girl in jodhpurs on her favorite horse, Danseuse, to the young woman Cholly Knickerbocker called "Queen Deb of the Year." During two years at Vassar, however, she considered herself unfinished, "a chubby little thing eating pastries and studying with inky fingers half the night." She spent her junior year in Paris discovering her Bouvier roots and then returned to take a degree at Washington's George Washington University in 1951. She won *Vogue*'s coveted Prix de Paris, but turned down the opportunity to return to France for fear, as she said at the time, she "would never come home."

"Uncle Hugh-die," as she called her stepfather, was a friend of the ubiquitous Arthur Krock, who helped get Jackie her first job on the Washington *Times-Herald* as the paper's inquiring photographer, the same position Inga Arvad and Kathleen Kennedy had once held. She started in 1952 at $42.50 a week, carrying a bulky Speed Graphic to snap people's pictures and ask fey questions that bore her distinctive mark. To children: Why don't Santa's reindeer come down the chimney? To pets in the veterinarian's waiting room: What's wrong with you? Many of the questions had to do with what Black Jack Bouvier had described to her as "the gentle war"—the war between the sexes. "Noël Coward once said, 'Some women should be struck regularly like gongs.' Do you agree?" And: "Winston Churchill once observed that marriages have a better chance of survival when the spouses don't breakfast together. Do you agree?"

"Jackie's great talent," one woman friend said at the time, was "the ability to give a sense of portent even to the trivial." Her sister Lee's fiancé, Michael Canfield, was once rowing the two of them around a lake, watching them whisper intently in the bow of the boat. He assumed that the subject was of the greatest importance, perhaps a family crisis involving their infamous father. A few days later he found out that they had been discussing gloves. A male acquaintance defined Jackie as the sort of woman who, when she meets you at the airport, automatically gives you her car, saying in effect that men are born to drive, women to be driven.

In 1952 Jackie became engaged to stockbroker John Husted, despite the violent opposition of her mother, who felt that he was neither socially nor financially distinguished enough. Husted got a sense of the brittle independence that lay beneath his fiancée's apparent vulnerability when he took her home and his own mother offered her a picture of him as a keepsake. "No, thank you," Jackie replied, "if I want any photos I can take my own." Husted, working in New York, began to get a sense that his days were numbered when the letters from Washington became less frequent and more perfunctory, and especially when one of them concluded with the admonition: "Don't pay any attention to any of the drivel you hear about me and Jack Kennedy. It doesn't mean a thing."

Jackie did one of her *Times-Herald* interviews with Jack, asking him how senators worked with the Senate pages. She translated reports on Indochina from the French for him. She was disturbed by the "spasmodic" nature of his courtship and rumors of his involvement with other women, but rakish behavior like her own father's had its attractions too. More difficult for her than Jack himself was the Kennedy family. The first weekend she spent at Hyannis was the social equivalent of foreign travel. In addition to Rose's self-absorbed hauteur and the Ambassador's energetic lapses of taste, there was the inbredness and in-jokyness of the Kennedy sisters, whose treatment of her she later compared to a sorority hazing. When Jackie showed up for dinner dressed more formally than all the rest, they began to rag her the way they did each other. When she said that her name was pronounced "Jaclean," Eunice noted under her breath, "Rhymes with queen." They called her "The Debutante" and ridiculed her "Babykins" voice. The charge was led by Ethel, who had always prided herself, as a family friend put it, on being "more Kennedy than thou." When Jackie noted ingenuously that she had once hoped to be a ballet dancer, Ethel looked down at her shoes: "With those feet of yours? You'd be better off going into soccer, kid." Jackie bit her tongue, but after the weekend was over gave her sister Lee a savage account of life at Hyannis, including a description of the way the Kennedys compulsively played games in which they "fell all over each other like gorillas."

At the Eisenhower inaugural, Lem Billings, seeing how different she was from the other women Jack had taken out over the years, took her into a corner and tried to tell her the "facts of life." In general terms, he described Jack's sickness and his amours, emphasizing the dangers of getting involved with a man who was twelve years older and "set in his ways." Later on, Jackie would tell Lem ruefully that she wished he'd made his friend seem a little less of a challenge during their tête-à-tête. But it probably wouldn't have mattered. "She wasn't sexually attracted to men unless they were dangerous like old Black Jack," Chuck Spalding observed. "It was one of those terribly obvious Freudian situations. We all talked about it—even Jack, who didn't particularly go for Freud but said that Jackie had a 'father crush.' What was surprising was that Jackie, who was so intelligent in other things, didn't seem to have a clue about this one."

She commented to a woman friend: "All I want to do is get married to Jack." Her sister Lee had gotten her marriage to Michael Canfield annulled and had married Prince Stanislaus Radziwill, thus entering London high society as a princess. But Jack was, if anything, a better catch, considered the most eligible bachelor in America. By the spring of 1953, it was obvious that the romance had progressed further than any of the others Jack had carried on since the war. Lem Billings expected a proposal, although it was hard for him to imagine Jack actually asking the question: "I couldn't visualize him actually saying 'I love you' to somebody and asking her to marry him. It was the sort of thing he would have liked to happen without having to talk about it." Jack solved the problem by waiting until the *Times-Herald* had sent Jackie to London to cover the coronation of Queen Elizabeth and then proposing by telegram.

Black Jack Bouvier sized Kennedy up as a kindred soul in their first meeting. ("They talked about sports, politics, and women," Jackie later reported, "what all red-blooded men like to talk about.") Janet Auchincloss was a different matter. "She has a tendency to think I'm not good enough for her daughter," Jack wrote to Red Fay, noting that he would have to make her a "special project." With his mother he traveled to Hammersmith Farm, the Auchincloss estate at Newport, and went for a walk with Jackie while Rose and Janet began hard bargaining over the terms of the September wedding. When negotiations became strained, the Ambassador flew down from Hyannis to take over the diplomatic war with Mrs. Auchincloss. "I remember standing behind her in the airport as he got off the plane," Jackie recalled later on, "his hand in his pocket, his smile on, and I thought as he came down the steps, even though I was on her side, 'Oh, Mummy, you don't have a chance.'" The Ambassador knew a social climber as well as he knew himself. The ceremony he negotiated with Jackie's mother would take place at Hammersmith Farm but it would be a Kennedy affair.

Jack delayed the announcement of the engagement until the *Saturday Evening Post* had completed and published a feature story about him and his charismatic eligibility called "The Senate's Gay Young Bachelor." Then the Kennedys set out to make the wedding the social event of the year. At a bachelor party attended by all of Jack's old friends, Bobby, the best man, earnestly sweated out a toast; then Jack mischievously got even with his pretentious in-laws-to-be by having everyone throw the expensive crystal glasses into the fireplace "according to an old Auchincloss custom." The Bouviers complained about the "clannishness" of the ceremony Joe Kennedy had planned—Archbishop Cushing presiding like some Irish country priest, despite the fact that Janet Auchincloss was an Episcopalian now married to a Presbyterian; an organ soloist from Boston named Mrs. Maloney; and a wedding cake baked by an Irish bakery in Quincy. Yet it was Jackie's father who provided the low melodrama for the affair, becoming so drunk in his Newport hotel suite that he was unable to get to the church on time to give the bride away.

During their honeymoon in Acapulco, Jackie wrote a poem imitating Stephen Vincent Benét:

> *He would build empires*
> *And he would have sons*
> *Others would fall*
> *Where the current runs*
> *He would find love*
> *He would never find peace*
> *For he must go seeking*
> *The Golden Fleece*
> *All of the things he was going to be*
> *All of the things in the wind and the sea.*

Yet if she was a romantic about Jack, he was a realist about her. When a paper she had written for his brother Teddy's art history class at Harvard came back with an "A" and the comment "keen perceptions," Jack told a friend, "No perceptions: it's all sensibility." When she gave him a very private manuscript about love and marriage that she had written for her younger half-sister, Jack, in a gesture reminiscent of his father, scanned it quickly and then offered to get it published. She had a further glimpse of what was in store for her during their first Christmas at Palm Beach, when she gave him an elaborate oil painting set in the hope that they would spend wind-swept moments together on the beaches painting and reading poetry. But almost immediately *all* the Kennedys began using the set, squeezing paint out of the tubes onto makeshift palettes, flattening the brushes, competing with each other to see who would come up with the best picture. "It was a nine in the morning to nine at night thing," Lem remembered. "They started outside, and then, when it got dark, they all trooped inside dripping paint all over. Rose got frantic and made them go into the bathrooms to paint. So there they were—everyone madly painting away while sitting on the toilets and the edge of the tubs. Jackie stood there with *this look* on her face."

After an initial suspiciousness, Jackie became close to the Ambassador, in whom she saw some of the charm of her own father. The two of them would often sit on the lawn at Hyannis gossiping about the high and the mighty while the rest of the Kennedys played touch football. But her relations with Rose, whom she icily referred to as *Belle Mère,* deteriorated rapidly. On one occasion at Palm Beach, Rose, irked by Jackie's penchant for sleeping late, inquired of Mary Gallagher, who was Rose's secretary, if Jackie was coming down soon. ''You might remind her that we are having some important guests for lunch and it would be nice if she would join us.'' When the message was transmitted, Jackie responded by doing a malicious imitation of Rose's puritanical manner and high-pitched voice and made a point of staying in her room until the important guests had come and gone.

She also defended herself as best she could with Jack, studying his vulnerabilities and picking at them daintily. ''Jack went crazy when someone sulked,'' said Lem, who himself had played on this frailty since they were boys. ''He couldn't stand the tension and he'd go absolutely crazy trying to contrive ways to restore a friendly atmosphere. Jackie saw this almost immediately, and used her sulks masterfully.'' She also enjoyed pricking his ego with her wit, as on the occasion early in the marriage when the two of them were vacationing in the South of France and were invited aboard the yacht of Aristotle Onassis, where Jack's idol, Winston Churchill, was guest of honor. Jack dressed in his best formal attire and was very attentive, hoping to make an impression, but the former Prime Minister was in his cups and, in the words of a friend, ''not recognizing people.'' As they left the yacht, Jackie looked at her husband's dinner jacket and said, ''Maybe he thought you were a waiter, Jack.''

There were other petty irritations. Jackie spent money rapidly, and Jack, who tried to compensate for his financial naïveté by being niggardly, became upset when the bills came in. There was constant environmental as well as emotional manipulation. They bought Hickory Hill, a three-story Georgian estate in Virginia once owned by Supreme Court Justice Robert Jackson, and Jackie dealt with it as she had with their first apartment in Georgetown, redecorating, changing the kitchen wallpaper three times in a three-month period, and making Jack feel, he complained, ''like a transient.''

Yet it was a good match. ''They were so much alike,'' Lem observed. ''Even the names—Jack and Jackie: two halves of a single whole. They were both *actors* and I think they appreciated each other's performances. It was unbelievable to watch them work a party. Jackie would be sitting with some old guy who'd almost have nodded off and suddenly ask a question so filled with implied indiscretion that this old guy's eyes would almost pop out of his head. And for the remainder of the conversation he'd practically be married to her in intimacy. Jack was exactly the same way. Both of them had the ability to make you feel that there was no place on earth you'd rather

be than sitting there in intimate conversation with them.'' Anita Fay says
that women felt uncomfortable around her not only because of these qualities
—which Truman Capote later compared to those of a geisha—but also because of a profound self-absorption: ''In the pictures of all of us you'd
always find yourself getting snapped with a scarf flapping over your face or
with a silly look or something. But there would be Jackie—her hair and
everything else just perfect. From the first time I met her I felt I was in the
presence of a very great actress.''

She could play the perfect consort, standing demurely behind Jack on
Edward R. Murrow's ''Person to Person'' as he read from the poem ''I Have
a Rendezvous with Death'' and talked about Joe Junior. Like his brothers
and sisters, Jack was a noble savage in social matters, and Jackie tried to
domesticate him, making him dress better, broadening his appreciation for
art, and improving his manners. She also kept him from such solecisms as
leaving the room when the conversation of guests ceased to interest him and
going upstairs to bed without even bothering to say good night. ''Jack appreciated her,'' says Chuck Spalding. ''He really brightened when she appeared. You could see it in his eyes; he'd follow her around the room
watching to see what she'd do next. Jackie *interested* him, which was not
true of many women. Unfortunately, however, this wasn't enough. There
were many ways to treat a woman, but as he saw it only one way to treat a
wife—and that was the way his father had treated his mother.''

Jackie thought she had known what she was getting into. Shortly after the
marriage she had talked of Jack's ''violent'' independence and had said, ''I
don't think there are any men who are faithful to their wives. Men are such
a combination of good and evil.'' She wasn't prepared for how flagrant his
womanizing would be. She found herself stranded at parties while he sneaked
out with someone who'd caught his eye; she found herself the object of the
barbed pity of other women in her circle. Being elected to the Senate had
made him a much more public personality than he had been, and created a
situation in which he no longer had to work to meet women. He ''hunted''
with fellow philanderer and Senate colleague George Smathers, arranging
to meet young women at the Carroll Arms, an apartment ''hideout'' on the
Potomac. (''Jack liked to go over there and meet a couple of young secretaries,'' Smathers says. ''He liked groups.'') Jackie heard about it all.

''Jack kept assuring us that she didn't suspect, when it was obvious that
she knew exactly what was happening,'' says Jim Reed. ''He was so disciplined in so many ways. Discipline was, after all, the secret of his success.
But when it came to women he was a different person. It was Jekyll and
Hyde.'' Another friend says: ''After the first year they were together,
Jackie was wandering around looking like the survivor of an airplane
crash.''

Marriage was so out of character for Jack that some cynics who saw ulterior motives in everything having to do with the Kennedys assumed it was an attempt to pull a cloak of respectability around his philandering and provide the paraphernalia of family life necessary for higher office. There was some truth in this, but becoming a husband and (he hoped) father had other meanings. It was an acknowledgment that he was stuck between passages in his life, an attempt to make a commitment that would get him to the next stage. Joe Junior was still a nagging specter in the background of everything he did. (Shortly after moving to the Senate Jack met Werner von Braun and surprised the German rocket expert by describing his brother's death in detail and insisting that it had come as part of what he called an early experiment in guided-missile technology.) But he sensed that the victory over Henry Cabot Lodge, unlike the election to Congress, was his own achievement. Never having had an explosive period of conflict with his father that could be annealed into a more equitable relationship, he had to try to declare his independence by stealth, a continuing guerrilla war.

A gesture with symbolic overtones as well as real consequences for the future came when he hired Theodore Sorensen as his aide. Square-faced and crew-cut, his skin pocked with childhood acne scars and his eyes narrowed by the reflection from thick glasses, the twenty-four-year-old Sorensen was an ambitious young attorney who had come to Washington to work in government. He was as different from someone like Ted Reardon in origins and philosophy as could be imagined. His father had been a crusading attorney general in Nebraska, an advocate of woman's suffrage, a sojourner on the Henry Ford Peace Ship and a close friend and backer of the Progressive Nebraska Senator George Norris. Sorensen himself was a pragmatic liberal looking for a place to have an impact on the federal government.

His first interview with Kennedy was somewhat strained. He challenged Jack over his fecklessness on McCarthyism, his red-baiting of Owen Lattimore and other old China hands, and other positions, making it plain that he was applying for a job less because he agreed with his politics than because he thought he was going places. Jack replied almost apologetically that he was more liberal than his record might indicate: "You've got to remember that I entered Congress just out of my father's house." Sorensen thought it unlikely that he'd be offered a job. In addition to philosophical differences there was the issue of the Ambassador. "Jack Kennedy wouldn't hire anyone Joe Kennedy wouldn't tell him to hire," a friend had said, "and with the exception of Jim Landis, Joe Kennedy hasn't hired a non-Catholic in fifteen years." But Jack hired Sorensen nonetheless, the first important aide not to come from the claustral world of family politics.

Sorensen was not the sort of person to toss a football around with in the office, but he had unlimited energy and virtually no private life. He soon began submitting articles under Jack's by-line to such magazines as the

Atlantic, the *New Republic,* and *Saturday Review.* He was willing to comment about almost anything in Kennedy's name, and a query letter he wrote to one editor suggested a wide range of titles for future contributions: "Must You Retire at 65?"; "A City Senator Looks at the Farm Problem"; "What Is Happening to Our Fishing Industry?"

Sorensen "assimilated" to Jack in somewhat the way Boswell did to Dr. Johnson. Adept with *Bartlett's,* he located exactly the historical allusions that Jack regarded as Kennedyesque; his fluent prose fell naturally into the florid, almost Churchillian patterns which embodied exactly Jack's conception of public rhetoric. Sorensen even did a creditable enough imitation so that he could impersonate Jack on the phone when he was too busy to take a call. Staff members who liked the easygoing Ted Reardon worried that he was being eclipsed by the newcomer, who was soon writing the crucial memos, taking the important calls, relaying orders from the inner office. But if Sorensen was taking over it was with Jack's backing. The Ambassador had seen that immediately. When he met Sorensen for the first time, at Hyannis in the fall of 1953, he looked him over and then said, "You couldn't write speeches for me. You're too much of a liberal. But writing for Jack is different."

Shortly after they had begun to work together, Jack asked Sorensen what cabinet posts he would choose if he could have his pick. "Justice, Labor, and HEW," said Sorensen, who was interested primarily in the domestic concerns of traditional liberalism. "I wouldn't have any interest in any of those," Kennedy replied, "only Secretary of State or Defense." The shape of things to come in the world, especially the Third World, had continued to interest him since his 1951 trip to the Far East. Indochina, in fact, had become something like a personal issue. Justice William O. Douglas had gone to Vietnam in 1952 on his own fact-finding trip and had met the Saigon political figure Ngo Dinh Diem. When Diem visited the United States in the spring of 1953, Douglas arranged for him to have lunch with Jack, who came away from the conversation impressed with the idea of an indigenous alternative to both the colonialism of the French and the communism of the Viet Minh. By that summer, Kennedy was opposing the Eisenhower Administration's request for a $400 million military assistance grant to France unless the funds were used "to encourage through all means available the freedom and independence" desired by the people of Vietnam. Instead of going directly to French military operations, he wanted U.S. money to help train native groups that, after independence, would fight communism in their own behalf.

Three months before Eisenhower articulated Secretary of State John Foster Dulles's "domino principle," Jack was saying that a Communist takeover in Indochina would imperil Burma, Thailand, and other independent states. But he differed with the means by which the adminstration sought to achieve security in the area. The prospect of massive nuclear retaliation might deter the Soviets from marching into Western Europe but it couldn't control a guerrilla war of local uprisings and political subversion. Uncritical support for the French could not deal with what seemed the tides of history. "The war," Jack said on June 30, 1953, "can never be successful unless large numbers of the people of Vietnam are won over from their sullen neutrality and open hostility to it... [and] are assured beyond doubt that complete independence will be theirs at the conclusion of the war."

As the French garrison at Dien Bien Phu came under heavy siege in the spring of 1954, and pressures mounted to involve American forces in the climactic battle, Jack delivered a major speech on Indochina. Addressing the Senate on April 6, he reviewed two years of unrealistically optimistic predictions about the war which had concealed the truth from the American public. In part because of his Anglophilia and his belief that the British had liquidated their position in India with "civility," he was against preserving French colonial rule: "To pour money, matériel and men into the jungles of Indochina without at least a remote prospect of victory would be dangerously futile and self-destructive.... I am frankly of the belief that no amount of American military assistance in Indochina can conquer an enemy that is everywhere and at the same time nowhere..." He went on to say that what was needed to fight Communist aggression was "an effective native army to meet their native armies."

At the same time that he was spearheading a debate about French colonialism, he was also criticizing Eisenhower's talk about cutting defense expenditures, and insisting that the United States maintain "a clear margin of superiority" in military strength. Using Sorensen's ready eloquence as a speech writer, he discussed the conflict between East and West in terms that rivaled the apocalyptic vision of Secretary of State John Foster Dulles. "We are in truth the last hope on earth. If we do not stand up now—if we do not stand from among the conflicting ideas of neutralism, resignation, isolation and indifference, then all will be lost, and one by one free countries of the earth will fall until finally the direct assault will begin on the great citadel —the United States."

In some sense such rhetoric was a concession to the temper of the times. Yet it also reflected Jack's own repressed romanticism, the hitherto mute vision of derring-do that Sorensen was now giving voice to, and the conception of the entire world, not just Europe, as a global arena for the contest against communism, which had been percolating at least since the 1951 Far Eastern trip. The primary personal consequence of such militant internationalism at this point in his life was to sharpen the conflict with his father. Some friends felt that when Jack said that there were "issues which he and I don't even discuss any more," it was a tactical maneuver to put public distance between himself and the Ambassador. But his friend Chuck Spalding says, "It's true—they really did disagree. The old man wasn't at all happy about some of the positions Jack was taking on foreign affairs when he got to the Senate. They went for about a year without talking about these matters at all. There was a real strain there."

In these crucial areas Joe Kennedy changed from mentor to tormentor, a symptom of the multiplicity of ties that continued to bind Jack. Red Fay was present at a meeting with Hearst newspaper editors not long after the Senate victory. The Ambassador was also present, monopolizing the conversation, fulsomely airing his own conservative and isolationist views. Jack listened for a while, a look of annoyance settling on his face, until he suddenly got up and walked out. "Jesus, Jack, what's happening?" Fay asked, catching up with him in another room. "Why did you do that?" Jack shrugged. "Listen, I've only got three choices. I can sit there and keep my mouth shut, which will be taken as a sign that I agree with him. I can have a fight with him in front of the press. Or I can get up and leave."

His health also seemed to suggest that there was no escape from his predicament. By mid-1954 his back was so painful that he often simply remained in the Senate chambers listening to tedious speeches rather than going back to his office, as other senators did, between quorum calls. He had trouble walking even with crutches. His weight dropped from 180 to 140. ("Don't worry," Eunice said to concerned friends, "it's nothing serious, just a result of Jackie's cooking.") It was becoming a question of how long he could continue to hide the gravity of his condition. Reporters were beginning to get queries from their editors about the Kennedy health problem. Was it a malignancy? Was he going to have to drop out of politics? Boston reporter Ernest Warren came to Ted Reardon and asked him to quiet the rumors by making public an authentic medical history. "No"—Reardon shook his head despondently—"old Joe doesn't want that to be done. We can't do it now."

Jack wanted to have an operation to fuse the degenerating discs in his back, but none of his doctors would agree because of the Addison's disease, which made surgery a life-threatening procedure. Finally Jack made a plea to Dr. Philip Wilson of the New York Hospital for Special Surgery: "I'd rather be dead than spend the rest of my life on these goddamned crutches." Wilson told him that because of the adrenal insufficiency his chances were no better than fifty-fifty. Jack decided to take the risk, although he understood the possible consequences. As he told Larry O'Brien upon preparing to enter the hospital: "This is the one that kills you or cures you."

Some Kennedy watchers suggested Jack was having the operation to avoid taking a position on the Senate's move to censure Joe McCarthy for his excesses, which was then about to come to a vote. It was a difficult situation, another one of those times when he felt particularly immobilized by family ties. After the victory over Lodge, Joe Kennedy had called on the Wisconsin

Senator for yet another favor, asking him to appoint Bobby chief counsel of the Subcommittee on Investigations.*

Jack had been furious when he heard the news, launching into a tirade in front of Ted Reardon which he finally terminated by shaking his head and saying, "Oh, hell, you can't fight the old man."

Bobby was disappointed when he found out that he would not be chief counsel but would be subordinate to McCarthy's new wunderkind Roy Cohn, who as assistant U.S. attorney had helped to convict Julius and Ethel Rosenberg as atomic spies, and who at twenty-five was eighteen months Bobby's junior. Kennedy's first chore was to investigate an alleged influx of homosexuals into the State Department, after which he turned to a study of trade between Great Britain and other Western allies and Communist China, whose troops were engaged against American forces in Korea. Jack had called it a "trade in blood," and Bobby pursued his study as if it were a family vendetta, finally composing a letter of protest to Eisenhower which he hand delivered to the White House. When Vice President Nixon persuaded McCarthy that the charges would backfire on the administration and become a windfall for the Democrats, the letter was "retrieved" before it was officially accepted. The incident was both frustrating and embarrassing to Bobby, who seemed flustered when reporters queried him about it and said worriedly, "Did somebody see me go in there?"

Meanwhile, his resentment of Cohn was developing into a relationship almost like that of warring siblings, and led him to resign from the committee in July 1953, shortly after the subcommittee's Democratic minority had "walked out" in protest when McCarthy was given sole control over the hiring and firing of staff. For the next few months he served in a minor capacity his father arranged for him on the Hoover Commission, a period of intense frustration and unhappiness. "He felt he was getting nowhere," Lem Billings remembered. "He was angry and got mad at people all the time. A lot of people thought he was an asshole." In one celebrated episode, while playing touch football on the Georgetown campus he got into a scrap with a student thirty pounds heavier than he was, which ended up in a "bloody brawl." To get his mind off his troubles, he traveled with William O. Douglas to the Soviet Union, where he paranoiacally refused to eat most Russian food and refused to consult a "Communist doctor" when he became ill.

In January 1954, when the Democratic senators returned to their seats on McCarthy's subcommittee and offered Bobby a job as their minority counsel,

*Bobby was hired by Francis D. "Frip" Flanagan, general counsel for the McCarthy subcommittee. A week later Flanagan got a call. "Hey, Frip, Joe Kennedy here. I understand Bobby's gonna work for you, and I just want you to know that by God you won't have any trouble with him. But if you do, I'll give you my private number, and just give me a call."

he accepted. As McCarthy began what was to be his last crusade, picking the United States Army as his target, Bobby quickly resumed his feud with Roy Cohn, which culminated in an ugly confrontation outside the Army hearings when Cohn threatened to "get" Democratic Senator Henry Jackson, and then threatened Bobby when he came to Jackson's defense. "Don't you 'warn' me, Cohn," Bobby exploded. "Don't try to get away with it. You tried it with the Army. You tried it with the Democratic senators. Now you're trying it with me ..." The two men had to be separated by onlookers. Adverse public reaction to the Army hearings pushed the Senate toward censure of McCarthy, which created a dilemma for Jack. ("How could I demand that McCarthy be censured for things that he did when my own brother was on the staff?" he later asked Kenny O'Donnell during a recapitulation of the episode.) His father, moreover, continued to be one of the Wisconsin Senator's staunchest boosters. Writing Jack from Paris, where he'd gone to accept a posthumous *Croix de guerre* for Joe Junior, the Ambassador denied that McCarthy had damaged United States prestige abroad, as critics charged: "The public isn't the slightest bit interested and the agitation against him is caused by the same kind of group here as in America. As far as the strained relations you have heard so much about, this is a lot of bunk." Returning home, the elder Kennedy repeated the message for reporters in one of the impromptu press conferences Jack and his advisers had come to dread: "I have run across people who were critical of him because he called General Marshall a traitor. I found, however, that those who resented his remarks were willing to agree that Marshall was responsible to a considerable degree for the loss of China, and certainly was not one of our best Secretaries of State."

The Ambassador felt sympathy for the McCarthy conservatives (lineally descended from the prewar isolationists) in their attacks on Democratic "appeasement" of Communists. In the spring of 1954, their clamor focused on the proposed "Bricker Amendment" to the Constitution, which would limit the President's treaty-making powers, a symbolic way of assaulting Roosevelt's alleged sellout of Eastern Europe at Yalta. Jack opposed the amendment, but Bobby, whose senior seminar paper in law school had concluded that Roosevelt had "lost the peace" at Yalta, sent a letter to the *New York Times* condemning Roosevelt's role. (The letter was answered by future biographer Arthur Schlesinger, Jr., who called it "an astonishing mixture of distortion and error.")

McCarthyism, therefore, had become a sticky familial issue rather than a strictly political one for Jack. If he did not exhibit courage, as Eleanor Roosevelt and other liberals charged, it was because he feared to confront his father, not his Senate colleague. Jack had anxiously watched the parliamentary maneuvers around the censure movement, trying to find a way to avoid taking a position that would bring him into conflict with the Ambassador. When it looked as though it might be impossible to continue finessing the issue, he had Sorensen draft a speech, but even in this undelivered statement he struck only a glancing blow at McCarthy, concentrating his fire instead on Bobby's enemy Roy Cohn and Cohn's associate David Schine. Jack had come to regard the Wisconsin Senator almost as a perverse talisman. Kenneth Birkhead, who was doing research on McCarthy for the Democratic National Committee, found Jack an almost compulsive consumer of the information he dug up: "He used to get in touch and ask me about various things. He asked me to come up and talk about McCarthy, and if there was a new McCarthy charge, he would ask if this fit anything I knew ...I don't think there was another member of the Senate who spent as much time asking me about McCarthy..."

It was no doubt something of a relief, therefore, when he entered the hospital on October 10, as Senate controversy over the censure motion was about to enter its most fervid phase. One friend recalls the scene in his hospital room as almost regressively like that of a college dorm. A poster of Marilyn Monroe in blue shorts standing with legs spread well apart had been placed on the wall upside down so that her feet stuck up in the air; a Howdy Doody doll lay on the bed next to him and there was a tank of tropical fish near his pillow. Young women he called his "cousins" visited him. Every few hours Jackie would come. in and sit with him on his bed, giving him tidbits of gossip acquired since her last visit, nibbling at the uneaten food on his tray, and evaluating the nurses she could tell had already caught his eye.

Priscilla Johnson, a Harvard researcher who sometimes visited him in the hospital, was struck by the strength of his denial of illness. "He'd be on his stomach and the doctors would be doing all this horrid stuff to him and he'd be on the phone to someone getting the latest gossip. The hospital staff couldn't believe it." She brought him Isaiah Berlin's *The Hedgehog and the Fox* and other books, and he would call her at 3:00 A.M. to kiddingly complain about how hard they were. "Jack had a voracious curiosity," she concluded, "but it really didn't have much to do with abstract ideas. He had a very precise sense of what was useful and what wasn't, and that determined how far he pursued things."

The spinal surgery that took place on October 21 was exactly the climactic event doctors had feared. Jack insisted that the two-part operation be accomplished in one step, willing to take the risks with his life that he wasn't with his politics. The Addison's disease affected his resistance, as doctors had feared; he contracted a staph infection and lapsed into a coma. His father was inconsolable. "Jack's dying," he said as he wandered into Arthur Krock's office, dropped onto the sofa, and began to cry, the first such strong emotion his friend had seen since Joe Junior's death. Once again the last rites were administered. Secretary Evelyn Lincoln and others on the Kennedy Senate staff got contradictory bulletins from the hospital every hour or so, some claiming that Jack had rallied and others suggesting that he had suffered another reverse and was sinking closer to death. Finally he began to hold his own and then inch his way toward recovery.

While he recuperated, the McCarthy issue finally came to a vote. Jack was the only Democrat failing to vote or "pair" on the question of censure, which passed by a large margin on December 12. The loyal Sorensen tried to take the blame, saying that he should have acted in Jack's behalf.* But it was clear to everyone close to the Kennedys that a political virtue had been made out of a physical necessity. During his recuperation Jack told Chuck Spalding he knew that when he finally left the hospital reporters would besiege him about McCarthy. "Do you know what I'm going to do? I'm going to reach for my back and I'm just going to yell, 'Ow-w,' and then I'm going to pull the sheet over my head and hope we can get out of there."

It was not until just before Christmas, however, that Jack was finally released. He was weak and depleted; he had a raw, suppurating wound in his back with pieces of bone oozing out. One wing of the Palm Beach house was converted into something like a hospital suite. Jack, lying in the sun, would ask Lem Billings to check on the wound: "Is it still open? Is stuff still running out of it? Does it smell bad?" The weeks passed and he didn't see the benefits he had hoped for. It was not certain that he'd ever walk again, let alone walk without crutches or a cane. He was alive, but it seemed he had lost the gamble. The stoicism that had carried him along since he was a boy began to slip. Only those closest to him saw the despair into which he was sinking. Lem said, "It was a terrible time. He was bitter and low. We came close to losing him. I don't just mean losing his life. I mean losing him *as a person.*"

In February of the new year there was another infection, then another operation to remove a steel plate inserted earlier and to graft floating bones. (Jackie asked Grace Kelly to dress up as a nurse and feed Jack, but he hardly noticed and didn't recognize her. The beautiful movie star came out of his room saying, "I must be losing it.")

Gradually, after that operation, Jack began to mend. He still had shooting pains in his back; his range of motion was so restricted that he had to turn his entire body to look at or speak to someone beside him; and for every step forward there seemed to be two steps back. When he finally returned to his Senate office in May, he tried to show a visitor how vigorous he was by

---

*In *Kennedy,* published in 1965, Sorensen wrote: "The responsibility for recording or not recording him on the censure vote . . . fell on me. I knew, had he been present, that he would have voted for censure along with every other Democrat." But in 1977, talking to the historian Herbert Parmet for his book *Jack,* Sorensen said that Kennedy "was sufficiently conscious in that hospital to get a message to me on how he wanted to be paired. I think he deliberately did not contact me . . ."

rocking energetically in a rocking chair Jackie had bought him, and he rocked backward so hard that he turned the chair over and landed on his back.

But with the operations behind him, the shadow that had clouded his future for so many years began to lift. For the first time, he felt that there might be a cure for the long disease that had been his life. He met Dr. Janet Travell, a New York pharmacologist, who put him on novocaine injections that made his back pain bearable. She also prescribed the cortisone pills which were becoming available as a better way of controlling his Addison's disease than the steroids he'd been implanting in his body for years.

The biggest gamble he had ever taken seemed to have paid off in a symbolic death and rebirth. Although his public mask rarely slipped, close friends saw the difference. "There wasn't so much talk about death any more," said Lem Billings. "Jack had grown up thinking he was doomed. Now he had a different view. Instead of thinking he was doomed, he thought he was lucky."

During his long convalescence in Palm Beach, Jack had occupied himself with a project begun months earlier. Perhaps to prepare himself to take a more forthcoming position on McCarthy, he had started to compile a list of senators who had taken principled positions on controversial issues; the list had become a book. The indefatigable Sorensen, who had canvassed friendly academics including the historian James MacGregor Burns for senators to be included, had suggested Senator Norris as one of those to be profiled; Arthur Krock had lobbied for Robert Taft. Soon the list included John Quincy Adams, who was forced to resign his Senate seat for supporting the policies of Thomas Jefferson; Daniel Webster, whose presidential hopes were dashed when he tried to preserve the Union by supporting the Compromise of 1850; Thomas Hart Benton; Sam Houston; and others. They were men very much like Jack's own father in the passion of their beliefs if not the nature of their ideas; mostly conservative men whose careers had foundered on the rocks of some great cause.

Profiles in Courage was completed by the time Jack resumed his Senate duties, and was published later that year. It was a book that squarely addressed the nation's growing sense of spiritual indirection, affirming the vitality of democracy and the individuals who made it function at a time when the Communist threat abroad was creating fears about the durability of the American political system. *Profiles* found an enthusiastic audience which ranged from those interested in history to those looking for social uplift. Jack found himself hailed by reviewers as an American version of Lord Cecil, the English writer and statesman he so admired, and *Profiles* headed for the best-seller list. He shrewdly poured the money the book earned—over 125,000 hardcover copies were sold in the next two years—

into advertisements which bought name recognition as well as selling more copies of the book. It was the third time that literature had played an important role in his life. *Why England Slept* had established him in the family; the Hersey article had established him as a war hero; and now *Profiles* had established him as something more than just another politician.*

The reception of the book and his performance on television shows, such as "Person to Person," made Jack a Democratic celebrity, and he was invited to narrate *The Pursuit of Happiness*, a film produced by Dore Schary that would open the 1956 Democratic convention. He began to regard the convention as a major opportunity and positioned himself to take full advantage of it. After announcing his support for Adlai Stevenson, he initiated a messy fight in Massachusetts to wrest control of the delegation from anti-Stevenson party regulars. It was the sort of bitter internecine struggle characteristic of Boston politics that he had always avoided—meetings that came close to being gang fights; plans to block rival delegations from entering meeting halls; endless intrigue in rooms that actually were smoke-filled. His father had urged him "not to get down in the gutter with the Curleyites," but taming the party machine was a way of asserting his independence, of claiming his heritage by showing that he could play the game of hardball his grandfathers had mastered.

Understanding that his religion might keep him from even being considered for Vice President—the long-shot prize he was aiming for—he dispatched Sorensen on a national tour to show party leaders statistical data demonstrating that a Catholic on the ticket could actually help by stopping the hemorrhage of ethnic votes to the Republicans which had begun in 1952. On his way to his annual summer vacation on the French Riviera, Joe Kennedy, who foresaw the debacle if Stevenson was rematched with Ike, again counseled caution: "If you are chosen, it will be because you are a Catholic and not because you are big enough to do the job." Jack had Sargent Shriver write to his father and tell him Stevenson had been assured that "you were 100% behind Jack, that you gave him and his campaign everything you had even if perchance you might disagree with the basic wisdom of the decision Jack might make."

---

*There was a whispering campaign by Drew Pearson and others concerning the true authorship of the book. Joe Kennedy asked his friend J. Edgar Hoover to go after the "group of New York people" involved in the charges that Sorensen had done almost all the work and eventually did get a retraction by ABC, which had aired the Pearson charges. Jack pressed his handwritten notes on critics and asked his colleague Richard Neuberger of Oregon, the most literary of the senators, to review the manuscript materials with an eye toward determining authorship. James MacGregor Burns says that Jack felt Sorensen was not forthcoming enough in denying his authorship and that their relationship was temporarily strained. Jack's old friend Blair Clark was surprised by his particularly angry reaction when he jokingly threatened to tell people that he was the "real author" of *Why England Slept*.

With Jackie, who was eight months pregnant, Jack arrived in Chicago for the August 13 opening of the convention feeling that at last he had a hand in his own political career. His narration of the Schary film was enough of a success that he was invited to make Stevenson's nominating speech, and he immediately sat down with Sorensen to write something closer to his own purposes than the draft written by Arthur Schlesinger, Jr., which the Stevenson forces had supplied. With this speech Jack solidly established himself as a leading contender for the second spot on the ticket, along with Senators Hubert Humphrey and Estes Kefauver. It presented Stevenson with a dilemma: he preferred Humphrey, but didn't feel he could alienate the others. In a decision that earned him Jack's contempt, he threw the nomination for Vice President to the convention floor at eleven o'clock on the evening of his own nomination.

The ability to pressure Stevenson behind the scenes had been the Kennedys' most potent weapon. Now they had just over twelve hours to put together an organization for a public contest. Bobby rushed to get started, beginning by calling the Ambassador in France. The old man's sharp words slashed through the room as Bobby held the receiver away from his ear and rolled his eyes. When the transatlantic connection was broken before his father had finished enumerating the ways in which they were idiots for jeopardizing Jack's future, Bobby quickly hung up and made no effort to get his father back on the line. "Whew! Is he mad!"

His annoyance typically overcome by family loyalty, Joe Kennedy tried to pull strings from abroad by lining up support from old party stalwarts like Jimmy Byrnes. Jack scrambled for support in a series of all-night meetings, becoming so intense that on a cab ride from the convention hall to his hotel room a friend saw him whispering, "Go! go! go!" to himself and hitting his thigh with a fist to the cadence of the words. Bobby cajoled and browbeat to line up support from states he knew almost nothing about. When Jackie wandered into Kennedy headquarters the next morning he gave her a dazed look and asked, "Do you know anyone in Nevada?"

When the voting began the next day, the brothers were well enough organized to hold their own with the powerful Kefauver organization, battle-tested in the spring primaries. On the second ballot some states began to change to Kennedy. At the conclusion he had 618 votes, most of them from the South, and when Kentucky changed its 30 votes, he was only 38 shy of the nomination. He had begun to dress for his victory appearance before the convention when Tennessee Senator Albert Gore, one of the also-rans in the contest, gained recognition and shouted into the microphone that he was withdrawing in favor of Kefauver. This began a move away from Jack. As it gained momentum, Bobby went from delegation to delegation, begging them with tears in his eyes to hold fast. But it was no use. By the time the stampede had ended, Kefauver had been chosen.

After a graceful appeal for unity, Jack flew back to New York with Jackie, leaving her to rest at Hammersmith Farm while he went on to Europe for a vacation. He was still depressed at the loss and completely exhausted when he stopped to see his father on the Riviera. The British writer William Douglas Home was with him when he arrived at the rented mansion, took one look at the opulence and bowing servants, and said, "Well, I see Dad's roughing it again this year." A few days later, in the midst of a sunbath, Jackie's former brother-in-law Michael Canfield asked Jack why he wanted to be President. Without opening his eyes Jack replied, "I guess it's the only thing I can do."

Leaving the Riviera with his father's benediction—"God is still with you and you can still be President if you want to and if you work hard"—Jack went off to meet George Smathers for a yachting trip on the Mediterranean which turned out to be a bacchanale, with several young women getting on and off the boat at its ports of call. "Unique among them," says one member of the Kennedy party, "was a stunning but not particularly intelligent blonde who didn't seem to have a name but referred to herself in the third person as 'Pooh.' She fascinated Jack, who was wound very tight when he arrived in Europe and almost completely unwound a few days later." He was so much at sea, in fact, that after word reached the yacht that Jackie had given birth to a stillborn child, a girl, he was in no hurry to return home. But finally, three days after receiving word of the tragedy, with Smathers insisting that he must patch up the tattered marriage if he expected to have any career at all in national politics, Jack caught a plane home. When Jackie left the hospital it was for Hammersmith Farm, the Auchincloss estate in Newport, not their own place. During the next few weeks they saw little of each other; word of their estrangement built until Drew Pearson finally made it public and Joseph Kennedy took it upon himself to broker a treaty saving the marriage.

Both Jack and Bobby traveled around the country campaigning for Stevenson. Jack made some hundred and fifty appearances in more than a dozen key states, following his own schedule and leading the Stevenson people to complain that if he wanted to help the candidate instead of himself he would be at home in Massachusetts mobilizing the working-class Catholic vote. But the contempt the Kennedys had acquired for Stevenson as feckless and indecisive grew even more pronounced during the listless campaign. Bobby, who had boarded the Stevenson train at his father's urging for a first-hand look at how a national campaign was run, filled a notebook with dour observations about the candidate's woolly-headedness and the tendency to waste precious time on hours-long discussions of such matters as the difference between fusion and fission. Finally, with a flourish of disgust, he jotted down the most damning thing a Kennedy could say about someone—"he was just not a man of action at all"—and cast his own vote for Eisenhower.

The year 1956 was pivotal for Jack. Still far from declaring his independence, he was nonetheless increasingly guided by his own ambition rather than his father's. He was doing things because he wanted to rather than because he was obligated. The extent to which he was shedding the spiritual burdens he had carried since entering public life was suggested by a comment he made after the Stevenson-Kefauver ticket was mauled in November. Voluntarily bringing up the subject of his dead brother, which he usually tried to avoid, Jack said: "If he had lived, he would have gone on in politics and he would have been elected to the House and Senate as I was. And like me he would have gone for the vice presidential nomination. But unlike me, he wouldn't have been beaten. Joe would have won the nomination . . ." In the past he might have left it at that; but now he saw a different moral, one which acknowledged that he knew he was different from and perhaps even better than the ghost-candidate who had haunted him all these years: ". . . and then he and Stevenson would have been beaten by Eisenhower and today Joe's political career would be in shambles and he would be trying to pick up the pieces."

5.

*J*OE KENNEDY SEEMED REMARK-
ably unchanged as he approached his seventieth birthday. The rusty hair
had silvered and he was bald on top, but he was still freckled and open-
faced, looking, in the words of a friend, like a "prematurely aged twenty-
year-old." Yet the young man's brashness he had carried with him well into
middle age had finally been subdued, becoming the autocratic reserve of the
patriarch. He was feeling intimations of the mortality that had stalked his
children but so far exempted him. In 1955 he had written to Beaverbrook
complaining about a "stomach condition of rather suspicious origins," and
the following fall went to France for a series of operations he managed to
keep out of the news. There was no malignancy, as he had apparently feared,
but he continued to grouse about the rebellion of the body. Fatigue, neuritis,
dyspepsia, and occasional cardiac arrythmia were the symptoms; old age, he
had to admit, was the cause.

More tightly controlled and stoical, Rose seemed to slip through her passages with less strain. Her husband was constantly agitated by the question
of how the torch would be passed to the next generation; for her, the key to
survival had involved the willful narrowing of her field of vision, learning
to ignore much that went on around her and concentrating on small things.
She still organized her itinerary by pinning notes to the front of her dress
and, using this detailed agenda, walked through her days at home with hair
in curlers and Scotch tape applied to her forehead to smooth out frown lines,
demanding that the rapidly turning over staff address her as "Madame."
Tenaciously serene, she sometimes communicated wisps of memory or advice
to her children in the laconic notes which had become a family joke. In the

middle of a crucial investigation of Teamster boss Jimmy Hoffa, Bobby got one that read: "I suddenly thought of your slippers the other night. Will you please ask your secretary . . . to have them resoled. Unless you do this they will become so worn that they cannot be repaired like the others and they are very expensive." She demanded and got a certain deference from the children, especially her daughters, who made up skits and rhymes to honor her at Mother's Day:

> *Other mothers have this and that*
> *But ours is one you can whistle at . . .*
>
> *Grandma Moses sure can paint*
> *But we prefer our traveling saint . . .*

She was still an indomitable traveler and made a point of going to Paris each year, often alone, for the spring collections. Arriving in May, she would take a small hotel room and spend her mornings looking at new fashions. She devoted the afternoons to visiting places such as the Ile de St. Honoré monastery, where she was able to sign the guest book "Countess Rose Kennedy" because Pope Pius XII had made her a papal countess.

Joe joined her in France for a few weeks each summer at Cap d'Antibes, where he swam at Eden Roc and golfed at the Biot course. But he was still a "homebody," in Rose's word, most comfortable in habitat. Sensing that his own time was in limited supply, he was more insistent than ever on promptness and regularity, and installed electric clocks all over the Palm Beach and Hyannis houses so that no one would have an excuse for being late to a meal. He fretted over his weight and would alternate between eating specially ordered ice cream from Sherry's in New York and the chocolates he kept in desk drawers and other hideaways, and diet binges with Metrecal. His own schedule was unvarying: rise at seven and (when on the Cape) ride until eight; breakfast and business until lunch; a nap and a swim; dinner and a movie; in bed by ten. It was a life which created a new synthesis between business and leisure. When friends saw him sunbathing in the "bullpen" of the Palm Beach house—naked except for a wide-brimmed planter's hat, his body gleaming with cocoa butter—there was always a phone in his hand. As Morton Downey commented, "The phone was his instrument. He used it like a Stradivarius."

He placed two-dollar bets from his box at Hialeah. He golfed with Palm Beach cronies for up to $10,000 a match, making sure that none of them lost big but keeping an eye out for the wealthy out-of-towner and then, as George Smathers says, "cleaning his crock real good." On the Cape he went out in his powerful motor launch the *Marlin* to watch family sailing competitions. He would hire several cars to make up a caravan to the Harvard-Yale football game, getting a police escort to precede them with blaring siren—not to arrive sooner, but because he knew that Jack, riding in the car behind, would duck down and shield his face in embarrassment at all the commotion. When he was in New York he ate at the exclusive Pavillon, where a table was reserved for him until half an hour before service began. He and the other Kennedys would scan the menu to see what new delicacies famed owner and chef Henri Soulé had created but usually wind up ordering some boiled or creamed atavism of Cape Cod cuisine; glance over the pastry tray but ask for vanilla ice cream with chocolate sauce. Even in such innocuous scenes as these, however, there were flashes of the essential Kennedy. Once Soulé made the error of not having a chocolate cake ready for a family birthday celebration. ''You failed me,'' Kennedy said to him afterward, glowering. ''I don't have to come here.'' And for a time he dramatized his threat by dining at La Caravelle, Pavillon's chief rival.

His hopes for Jack (only after 1960 would he imply that it had been a ''plan'') were being fulfilled sooner than even he had expected. In January 1957, the Gallup Poll showed that if Stevenson's name was excluded, 41 percent of all Democrats preferred Kefauver as the party's next nominee and 33 percent favored Jack. In March, after *Profiles in Courage* had been awarded the Pulitzer Prize, the order was reversed: 45 percent for Jack and 33 percent for Kefauver. Later in the spring, when Jack was invited to join the Harvard Board of Overseers, it was an even more forceful augury of a phenomenon that seemed to be acquiring a momentum of its own. ''If an Irish Catholic can get elected an Overseer at Harvard,'' the Ambassador said, ''he can get elected to anything.''

But as if by some Newtonian principle of politics, to the degree that Jack became more prominent Joe Kennedy faded further from view. After working indefatigably for thirty years to make himself an eminent American, Kennedy seemed to have vanished overnight. Close friends realized that his disappearing act had begun long before, when he began working behind the scenes for Jack. When Morton Downey once asked him why he didn't tell his sons what he was doing for them, he answered: ''I don't want them to inherit my enemies. It's tough enough they inherit my friends.'' He worked his own shadowy route, getting to know the political bosses and the people who counted; people who, like himself, had decided for one reason or another to do their life's work in anonymity. To the degree that he was involved in public affairs, it was in keeping with this undercover identity. Eisenhower had appointed him to the President's Board of Consultants on Foreign Intelligence Activities in 1954. Kennedy went to the meetings and later, knowing of J. Edgar Hoover's almost pathological fear that the Central Intelligence Agency would intrude onto territory he considered his own, arranged to lunch with the FBI chief and fill him in on what had been discussed. He was ''the Ambassador,'' although many of those who called him this had forgotten or never known where he had been posted. It was as if he were chief diplomat from a small, powerful country within the country —a place whose only citizens were Kennedys.

This country had grown over the years, becoming populous with in-laws and grandchildren, although the original family, the "clan," as Young Joe had called them, remained at the core, never really leaving home, no matter how far they traveled.

Eunice had continued her "social work" over the years, at one point investigating at first hand conditions in a women's reformatory in West Virginia. But she had held a part of herself aloof, and so these activities had remained volunteerism rather than a career. In 1953 she had gotten married. There had been many boyfriends over the years, but Sargent Shriver was the one who endured. After working with her in postwar Washington, he had been sent by the Ambassador to Chicago to oversee the Merchandise Mart, which had become the family's chief source of revenue. Shriver lived in the hotel suite Joe Kennedy kept there, but had to move out temporarily whenever a family member was passing through town. When it seemed that his seven-year courtship of Eunice would never come to anything, he began dating other women. Hearing that he was thinking of marrying one of them, Eunice had hurried home from a European trip, telling a friend, "He's not marrying anybody but me." The wedding was referred to by society page editors as "a shopgirl's dream," the reception as a "Kennedy brawl." Eunice's own toast to her new husband said it all: "I searched all my life for someone like my father and Sarge came closest."

She was "Eunie"—good-humored, active to the point of hyperkinesis, attractive except for a large mouth which heavy lipsticks extended to minstrel size. He was "Sarge"—a Kennedy non-com, the utility man capable of politics as well as business. He became close to Chicago Mayor Richard Daley and won election as chairman of the city's Board of Education. She did rehabilitation work for the House of the Good Shepherd, bringing wayward children home. She also kept in touch with Rosemary, grown plump and increasingly disoriented in her Wisconsin nursing home. In 1954 she and Sarge had a child of their own, Bobby, and the following year their first daughter, Maria.

If Eunice had inherited Rose's religious commitments, Pat was more like her mother in personality. Auburn-haired, vivacious, with a model's striking face and interest in clothes, she'd been star-struck since the days when her father had brought home autographed pictures of movie stars. After graduating from Manhattanville College of the Sacred Heart, she'd worked for a time with NBC radio in New York, resigning in 1951 to become a production assistant for the "Kate Smith Hour."

Pat first met Peter Lawford at Gary Cooper's house during a trip to Hollywood in 1949. He took her to visit M-G-M, where he'd been a contract

actor since first being discovered and had made a career playing male in-
genue roles. ("Wait until you get a few lines in your face," Cary Grant had
told him. "Your career will be made.") They ran into each other again at
the 1952 Republican convention, which Pat attended because of her father's
interest in Robert Taft and where Lawford was a guest of Henry Ford. They
began to date when Pat came to Hollywood to do television production.
Religion was one bar to the romance, Lawford being Protestant. Another
was the Ambassador, who liked to tell of his response, only half-jesting, when
Lawford, who finally agreed to convert to Catholicism, asked his permission
to marry Pat: "If there's anything I'd hate as a son-in-law, it's an actor;
and if there's anything I think I'd hate worse than an actor as a son-in-law,
it's an English actor."

Pat had gone on a trip around the world to get Lawford out of her system.
In Tokyo she realized that it was no use to try and flew home. The wedding
took place in June 1954, an event with stars and stargazers, politicians and
royalty. The newlyweds moved into a Malibu house once owned by Louis B.
Mayer. There was a pool, a projection room whose aperture was hidden by a
painting, and a huge movie screen that rose up automatically out of the
living room; marble for the house alone had cost $75,000. The two formed
the Kenlaw Production Company and, after Joe Kennedy had smoothed the
way by talking to Arthur Krim at United Artists, began work on Lawford's
series, "Dear Phoebe" and "The Thin Man." Their first child, Christopher,
born in 1955, was followed by two girls, Sydney and Victoria.

Jean had been even less clear in her objectives than Pat. After graduating from Manhattanville, she went to Chicago to work in the public relations department of the Mart, then returned to New York as an aide to
Father James Keller, founder of the Christophers, an organization dedicated to the fight against communism and corruption. She met Stephen
Smith, who was an executive for the New York transportation firm
founded by his grandfather William Cleary, an Irish immigrant who'd
worked as a laborer on the Erie Canal and saved enough money to buy the
first of what eventually became a small fleet of tugboats and barges moving
rock and sand up the Hudson for construction. The family was political as
well as wealthy; another grandfather had been a three-term New York congressman.

An excellent athlete despite his diminutive size, Smith had majored in
philosophy at Georgetown but was the complete pragmatist: "a hard-boiled
Freddie Bartholomew," one friend had called him, alluding to the odd combination of boyish good looks and toughness. The Ambassador might have
doubts about Lawford and privately regarded Shriver as "soft," but he
recognized Smith as a kindred spirit and was happy when he and Jean
married in 1956. It was an intimate ceremony presided over by Cardinal
Spellman. Afterward Jean said: "Daddy gave me the choice of a big wed-

ding and a small present or a small wedding and a big present.'' She picked the latter: a huge diamond pin.

Teddy trailed his brothers and sisters in every way. Following Bobby to Milton, he'd been known as ''Smilin' Ed.'' But if he was friendly to everyone, there was no central friend in his life the way Ted Reardon, Lem Billings, and Dave Hackett had been for Joe Junior, Jack, and Bobby. He was the afterthought in the family, as he had been in his parents' marriage. But being the last born had its advantages: he didn't have to jockey for position and attention was guaranteed, especially by his father, whom he continued to remind of Young Joe. ''Teddy was the shining light,'' Peter Lawford says. ''He came of age at a time when the old man often wasn't feeling very well. Everyone else would be treading softly. But Teddy would come home after being somewhere and his father's face would light up and his spirits would rise.''

Teddy was high-spirited, with a gift for good fellowship and mimicry, but somehow unable to escape the role of kid brother. When he was a freshman at Harvard a friend took his Spanish final for him. The clumsy deception was uncovered and both Teddy and the friend, a scholarship student, were expelled. As if to strike out on his own in a gesture combining self-assertion and contrition, he impulsively enlisted in the Army, signing up for a four-year hitch that he thought was a two-year one. His father, furious that he would put himself in a position where he could be sent to Korea, yelled at him, ''Don't you even look at what you're signing?'' He then made phone calls to the draft board that cut the four-year hitch in half and got Teddy a safe European assignment. Back home in 1955, he reentered Harvard, made passing grades and caught passes on the football field, including the winning touchdown in the Yale game. It could have been a vindication for himself and his family, given the lingering irritation over the way Joe Junior's football career had gone; but the Ambassador was no longer interested in such symbolism. Before one crucial game he told a friend, ''I'd like to see Teddy play well and I'd like Harvard to win, but I'm more interested in seeing him out of the game without a serious injury ... Too many of them have been hurt.''

After graduation, Teddy went to the University of Virginia Law School, which Bobby had made a respectable Kennedy alternative to Harvard Law. It was difficult for him. ''He just wanted to get through,'' his classmate (and future California Senator) John Tunney said later. ''It required a lot of discipline, which did not come easy to Ted at that time.'' He lived up to his new nickname—''Cadillac Eddie''—showing up at every party, drinking like a true Irishman, and driving so recklessly that Charlottesville policemen were on the lookout for him. He began dating Joan Bennett, an attractive blonde his sister Jean had known at Manhattanville. When the relationship appeared to be heading toward marriage, Rose called her friend

Mother O'Byrne at Manhattanville and asked about Joan's behavior, grades, and moral character.

With Ted's marriage to Joan in 1958, the family was complete. Formal portraits showed an extraordinarily handsome group, spouses always separate from each other, sitting or standing next to some other Kennedy or Kennedy in-law as if to emphasize that they were all linked by something more profound than marriage. These photographs had sharp nostalgic power, asserting a unity and purpose, as well as a joy in relatedness, that was presumed to be the way things had once been in American family life, but in the postwar era was no longer.

Within this idealized image, of course, there was a constant jockeying for position. With the brothers' wives it was a question of who would produce the most children and adapt most readily to the Kennedy family ethos of competition. Ethel was dominant in both respects. After losing her baby in 1956, Jackie pushed Jack to sell Hickory House to Bobby, as if admitting that she would never be able to fill the bedrooms as well as Ethel, who by her eighth year of marriage in 1957 had seven children and was not stopping at that. Jackie could hold her own emotionally with her sister-in-law, however: she once described Ethel as "someone who would put a slipcover on a Louis Quinze sofa and then spell it Louie Cans." Joan had no such armor. Shortly after her marriage to Ted she came to a sailing party wearing a leopard-print bathing suit. Ethel, in cutoffs like everyone else, eyed her and drawled, "Really, Joan, did you expect the photographers?"

With the male in-laws it was a question of filling the available roles. Lawford was geographically separate, doing his part on the Hollywood frontier, and so the contest was between Shriver and Smith. Shriver had been part of the Kennedy plans for a longer time, but he had always been regarded as a "Boy Scout," in Jack's phrase, because of his fondness for Catholic theology, and a tendency to profess too much. There was also an element of personal ambition regarded as suspect. Doing well as chairman of the Chicago Board of Education, Shriver had been prominently mentioned as a possible Democratic candidate for governor, although that possibility would vanish when he was ordered to relocate in Washington to help prepare for Jack's presidential bid. Steve Smith, on the other hand, was "cool," to use one of Jack's favorite words, a study in hard surfaces. Unlike Shriver, he also came from a moneyed background and could afford to behave more independently. He thus became the "inside brother-in-law," leaving the "outside" role to Sarge.

But to a remarkable degree they were what they seemed—*the family.* Bobby bought a house next door to his father and mother's at Hyannis. Jack bought one next door to Bobby's. The Smiths had a place a stone's throw away, across a public lane. The Shrivers were a ten-minute walk up the beach, Teddy and Joan another ten minutes away on Squaw Island. They vacationed together, spent holidays with each other. At one of these get-togethers Joe Kennedy looked at them all—children, in-laws, and a growing brood of grandchildren—and said: "This is the most exclusive club in the world."

Jack was the one they all worked for. But the central internal drama of the family was the way in which Bobby, once the least relevant member of the club, had emerged as its crucial figure—the one who, in his father's words, would "keep the Kennedys together in the future." Bobby lacked Teddy's instinctive warmth, but he didn't have Jack's need to escape the tribal quality of Kennedy life, either. And he was the one Kennedy brother who could be reached at deep emotional levels. Brooding, passionate, intense, he was more Irish than the others. After meeting him, the poet Robert Lowell remarked, "My, he is unassimilated, isn't he?"

After the 1956 elections, Bobby had gone back to the Senate Government Investigations Subcommittee, where he had been since the 1954 midterm elections brought the Democrats back to power and the senators on the subcommittee had offered him the job of majority counsel. The job had put him increasingly in conflict with McCarthy, their animosity coming to a head when Kennedy appointed journalist Bob Greene to an investigative task force and McCarthy attempted to block the appointment by claiming that Greene was "anti-Catholic" and had once been "indicted," charges he repeated on the floor of the Senate. Clark Mollenhoff, Washington editor of the *Des Moines Register,* was in Kennedy's office when the Wisconsin Senator called. After defending Greene's record and making a futile effort to try to get McCarthy to desist, Kennedy slammed down the receiver and said, "Joe McCarthy, you're a shit."

Yet he never turned his back on this family friend, even when McCarthy's power was broken and he had become mired in alcoholism. (In 1955 Bobby stalked out of a ceremony honoring his selection by the U.S. Chamber of Commerce as one of the Ten Outstanding Young Men of the Year because one of the speakers was Edward R. Murrow, who had just broadcast his famous attack on McCarthy.) Explaining his affection later on, Bobby said, "I liked him and yet at times he was terribly heavy-handed. He was a very complicated character . . . He was sensitive and yet insensitive . . . he would get a guilty feeling and get hurt after he had blasted somebody. He wanted so desperately to be liked." Bobby might have been describing himself.

The Investigations Subcommittee had examined such things as waste and fraud in government procurements of Army uniforms. But Bobby was now looking for something "big" and had begun an investigation of Vice President Richard Nixon's relationship with political fixit man Murray Chotiner, which Investigations Subcommittee Chairman John McClellan had quashed as too dangerously partisan in the preelection period.* Clark Mollenhoff had been after Bobby for more than a year to take on the subject of labor racketeering, showing him his own data on mob infiltration into the Brotherhood of Teamsters and promising to put him in touch with other investigative journalists around the country who were pursuing the subject. Bobby tried to dodge the issue, saying the subcommittee didn't have jurisdiction. But Mollenhoff persisted, ribbing Kennedy about being afraid, telling him that he was evading his duty, and reminding him that the 1951 Senate investigation of organized crime had made national reputations for Estes Kefauver and others.

Mollenhoff had brought the issue up again before the 1956 convention. "Who the hell ever heard of Dave Beck and Jimmy Hoffa?" Bobby replied in exasperation. Mollenhoff shot back: "If you do your job right, everybody will have heard about them and you too." After the convention was over, Mollenhoff cornered him: "Well, goddamn it. Do you believe me now? Kefauver did his investigations five years ago and it got him enough clout to beat your brother's butt." This time Bobby's response was different: "Well, why don't you come down and let's talk about it."

While taking time out from his committee work to document the way Adlai Stevenson's campaign sank into disaster, Kennedy asked Mollenhoff to put him in touch with Ed Guthman of the *Seattle Times*, who was investigating Dave Beck. Bobby arranged to go west and join Guthman in looking into the doings of the Teamsters. It was an eye-opening experience. When he returned to Washington he brought with him harrowing tales of union intimidation and violence. One case which had particularly strong impact had to do with a rival union organizer who disregarded Teamster threats to stay out of the San Diego area, was beaten unconscious one day, woke in terrible abdominal pain, and later discovered at the hospital that a cucumber had been forced into his rectum. While recovering he got a message that if he persisted, next time it would be a watermelon. Equally horrifying to Bobby was the betrayal of the trust of the rank and file through embezzlement by Teamster officials, especially Beck himself.

After listening to Bobby's stories, McClellan agreed to form the bipartisan Select Committee on Improper Activities in the Labor or Management Field, and begin an investigation. Bobby's most serious opposition came not from

---

*Before that it had been the conflict-of-interest cases which had plagued the Eisenhower Administration since its inception. One of these involved Air Force Secretary Harold Talbott, who had compared his own financial activities to Joseph Kennedy in the thirties, when he maintained his liquor business while working in the Roosevelt Administration. This brought an outraged note to Bobby from his father, then vacationing on the Riviera: "First of all, I bought Haig and Haig before I went in government. ... Most important, we never did any business with the government or with anybody who ever did any business with the government. That's about as different from his activities as I can imagine."

the Senate bureaucracy, or from Jack, who got himself named to the committee, but from his own father. ("The old man saw this as dangerous," Lem Billings said later on, "not the sort of thing or the sort of people to mess around with. He felt Bobby was being awfully naïve.") The argument at Hyannis that Christmas was bitter—"the worst we ever witnessed," Jean said. Bobby refused to give in. Afterward Joe Kennedy turned for help to William O. Douglas, who had been a mentor to Bobby since their trip to Russia. But after talking to him Douglas realized that Bobby wouldn't yield and reported back to the Ambassador: "He feels it is too great an opportunity."

The McClellan Committee opened for business in January 1957. Joe McCarthy, an increasingly pathetic and impotent figure, was one of the Republicans chosen from the old Investigations Subcommittee. Four senators were picked from the Labor Committee, Jack among them. Bobby began assembling a staff, among whose key members were friends like Kenny O'Donnell, investigators like Carmine Bellino and former FBI man Walter Sheridan, and journalists like Guthman, Pierre Salinger of the *San Francisco Chronicle*, and John Seigenthaler of the Nashville *Tennessean*, who had also been covering the Teamsters. Eventually the staff would number more than a hundred, the largest ever assembled on Capitol Hill.

The first target was Beck himself. Arrogant and histrionic, the moon-faced president of the Teamsters had grown up with the organization during the two decades it had taken for the union to make the transition from a small collection of inner-city drivers to a huge, powerful organization crucial to interstate commerce. Beck tried to bargain by declaring himself against abuses and promising to clear them up "in time." When Bobby refused to let up, he left the country on a "vacation." During his absence Bobby and his staff combed through Teamster records, reconstructing the omissions well enough to show that "His Majesty the Wheel," as sycophants called Beck, had used union funds to build a $185,000 house and swimming pool for his son and another $85,000 for personal purchases—in all defrauding the Teamsters of some $320,000.

Beck returned in March and took the stand to testify, appearing close to hyperventilation as he waved his hands and grew sweat rings under his arms. Bobby admitted that at first he almost felt sorry for him. But by Beck's second appearance, in mid-May, after he had taken the Fifth Amendment 140 times, Bobby agreed with Jack that his earlier sympathy had been misplaced and went after Beck, commenting later on: "He was dead, although still standing. All that was needed was someone to push him over and make him lie down as dead men should." Beck's fall, however, was not the main act but merely the prologue.

The beneficiary of this part of the investigation had been Teamster vice president Jimmy Hoffa. Supporting and to some extent controlling Beck,

Hoffa played a role analogous to the one Bobby played with Jack—working behind the scenes doing the dirty work and keeping his own counsel, which had allowed Beck to stay aloof from the Teamsters' relationship with organized crime (while tacitly agreeing to it). Hoffa had decided to use the McClellan Committee to get rid of Beck and assume power himself, but Bobby had known of his plans almost since the beginning. On February 13, an attorney named John Cye Cheasty had requested a meeting and told Bobby that Hoffa had given him $1,000 as a down payment against $2,000 a month if he could get a job on the committee and act as an informer. After checking with J. Edgar Hoover, Bobby hired Cheasty as a double agent. On the afternoon of February 19, Cheasty met Hoffa in Washington and gave him some names of witnesses to be called by the committee, with FBI agents following and recording the meeting on hidden cameras. That night, at the home of Teamster attorney Eddie Cheyfitz, Bobby had his first face-to-face meeting with the man whose nemesis he would become.

Squat and powerful, Hoffa exuded a physicality and authenticity which, in another context, Bobby might have admired. At fourteen, Hoffa had quit school to go to work as a warehouseman; at seventeen he had been in his first strike and been badly beaten by strikebreakers. As a young man he had become a protégé of Farrell Dobbs, the Trotskyist organizer who was pivotal in changing the Teamsters' emphasis from city deliveries to "over-the-road" trucking. But the only aspect of Dobbs's Marxism that had made a permanent impression on Hoffa was the view of the capitalist system as a Darwinian struggle in which the outcome was determined by power rather than morality. Hoffa's underworld connections had intensified in the 1940s, when he was a Detroit Teamster leader sending his goon squads to battle those of the CIO for the right to organize into haulaway drivers and had to call on local syndicate figures to help him hold his own. This led to a Faustian pact in which the mob helped him rise to power in return for access to Teamster pension funds, which were soon larger than those of any other union in the country. Kefauver had first focused national attention on Hoffa in his investigations of 1951. Later, Hoffa had been highlighted in the report of a Senate subcommittee investigating rackets in Detroit which found "a wicked conspiracy [working] through the use of force, threat of force, and economic pressures [to] extort and collect millions of dollars not only from members of unions who are in good standing, but from independent businessmen, and, on occasion, from the federal government itself."

Hoffa regarded Bobby as simply a "damn spoiled jerk," the rich kid who had tasted life only from the silver spoon which had been in his mouth since birth. Bobby regarded Hoffa as a representative of pure evil, the greed and rapaciousness within all human nature. Some observers pointed out that, appearances notwithstanding, Hoffa might be said to resemble the Ambassador: someone who had always known what he wanted and had taken the necessary steps to get it. There was similarity also in an insistence on paying lip service to the pieties. (As one Teamster crony said, "There were times when it became nauseating to hear about Hoffa's 'close family life,' and he bragged about it as well, which made it even more sickening.") Coming to know Hoffa in a sense better than he knew himself, Bobby collected all the tales about his enemy's private affairs, his hopes and hypocrisies. He knew, for instance, that the mother of the Teamster leader's "foster son" Charles O'Brien was Sylvia Pagano, the mistress with mob ties with whom Hoffa continued to be connected after his marriage.

During this first meeting, in fact, the subject of fathers and sons was in the air. Talk at the dinner table turned to Dave Beck. Cheyfitz and Hoffa, who had driven over from the Teamsters' Washington headquarters, were discussing how the elder Beck had "mothered" his son, overprotecting and ultimately destroying him. Bobby agreed. By this time he knew something about Dave Beck's crimes, but had come to feel, as he later wrote, that "his attitude toward his son was his worst sin." The other, perhaps related issue that surfaced in this first meeting had to do with toughness. "I do to others what they do to me, only worse," Hoffa told Bobby when they were alone. "Maybe I should have worn my bulletproof vest," Bobby replied. He used the same ironic tone later in the evening, when Ethel called him at Cheyfitz's to tell about an automobile accident she had witnessed in front of Hickory Hill: "I'm still alive, dear. If you hear a big explosion I probably won't be."

Hoffa later claimed that Bobby had wanted to arm wrestle after dinner. While this is questionable, there is no doubt that a sense of physical challenge was present. Bobby later wrote, "When a grown man sat for an evening and talked continuously about his toughness, I could only conclude he was a bully hiding behind a façade." Hoffa described the meeting in similar language, saying that Bobby was "a man who always made a big thing out of how strong and tough he was, how he had been a football player or something at Harvard." What particularly irked Kennedy was double agent Cheasty's report of Hoffa's reaction to the meeting. He said that they'd only have to hang tough for four or five weeks because Bobby would "want to spend the summer at Cape Cod with his family." Hoffa also began to pass the word that Bobby had dressed like a girl when he was young and that he had been a homosexual.

Three weeks after the dinner with Cheyfitz, Hoover called Bobby at home late in the evening to say that Hoffa had just been arrested in Washington for bribery in connection with the Select Committee documents transmitted by Cheasty. Bobby arrived for the booking. After an awkward silence he and Hoffa launched into small talk about physical conditioning and who could do the most pushups. Hoffa was confident about the outcome of the case, but so was Bobby. He told reporters a few days later that the government's bribery case was airtight. Asked what he would do if Hoffa wasn't convicted, he said, ''I'll jump off the Capitol.''

Ethel attended the trial throughout July and reported to Bobby, who was conducting hearings on the Textile Workers' Union. From the beginning government prosecutors were outflanked by Hoffa's attorney, Edward Bennett Williams. Williams used all his jury challenges to disqualify whites, finally seating a jury of eight blacks and four whites. Then he attacked Cheasty for racism, picturing Hoffa as a friend of blacks, and he topped the performance by producing Joe Louis to embrace Hoffa as the trial came to an end.* Bobby was in the middle of an interrogation in the Senate chambers when a note was passed to him that Hoffa had been acquitted. Williams commented that he was sending Kennedy a parachute for his jump.

But Bobby had just begun his pursuit. On August 20, Hoffa made his first appearance before the Select Committee, having raged at Salinger when he delivered the subpoena: ''You can tell Bobby Kennedy for me that he's not going to make his brother President over Hoffa's dead body.'' Bobby had Hoffa on the stand for four days. He began defiant, calling Kennedy ''Bob'' and jocularly scolding when he saw him with his feet on a chair, ''Get your feet off. Don't you know you're dirtying government property?''

Bobby bored in on his connections with underworld figures. Hoffa, mindful that the AFL-CIO had recently passed a resolution against labor leaders taking the Fifth Amendment, fended off the questions by claiming a bad memory. He gave answers which were marvels of illogic, such as this response to a question about the relations between the Teamsters and organized crime: ''To the best of my recollection, I must recall on my memory, I cannot remember.''

As Bobby's questions went on without letup, Hoffa's cockiness disappeared. Instead of smiling he began to fix Bobby with a baleful stare. Bobby approached him as the hearings concluded and warned him about his treatment of committee employees. ''Told him I did not want him to talk to our investigators as he had been doing,'' Bobby wrote in his journal. ''Told him if he wanted to hate anyone to hate me. He agreed.'' When someone asked him how he felt to have deposed Beck only to have made Hoffa the union president, Bobby replied, ''I feel I have a debt to society.''

McClellan read into the record forty-eight counts involving racketeering, fixing elections, and other abuses. George Meany, president of the AFL-CIO, said he would oust the Brotherhood of Teamsters if Hoffa was elected president at the Teamster convention. In addition, Hoffa had been indicted by a

---

*A few weeks later, Select Committee staff member Walter Sheridan, a former FBI man, interviewed Louis, who refused to give the autograph Bobby wanted although he did give one for Bobby's son, Joe III. Sheridan learned that the former world champion boxer was on the payroll of a Chicago trucking firm and had gotten a loan from the Teamsters' pension fund.

grand jury in New York for wiretapping and perjury. As round one of their *mano a mano* ended, Bobby had found an area where he could make his own solid achievement. He was the subject of articles in the national press and his picture was on the cover of magazines. When the Russians shocked the nation by sending Sputnik into space, Lyndon Johnson made a speech suggesting that someone like Bobby Kennedy investigate the problems of closing the space gap. Bobby wrote in his journal: "Am very pleased with myself."

Republicans on the McClellan Committee had felt that Bobby's assault on the Teamsters, a union with ties to their own party, had been a partisan maneuver. In seeking a counterbalance, their attention naturally fell on the United Auto Workers, *bête noire* for conservatives because of the socialist background of President Walter Reuther and his brother Victor. Before his death in May 1957, McCarthy had charged that a hard look at Reuther would leave Dave Beck and Jimmy Hoffa "smelling like roses." Hoffa himself had tried to inflame the issue by calling the UAW president "the leader of Soviet America." Jack and the other Democrats on the McClellan Committee had finally agreed to expand the mandate of the probe to include the Auto Workers and, while Bobby was preparing his case against the Teamsters, an investigator acceptable to the Republicans was appointed to visit Sheboygan, Wisconsin, where the UAW had been engaged in a long and violence-ridden strike against the Kohler Company, manufacturers of plumbing fixtures.

By the end of 1957, the investigation into the UAW-Kohler affair had yielded little more than what was already on file at the National Labor Relations Board—the history of a strike that had lasted four years and had brought out the worst in both sides. Senator Barry Goldwater, who had picked up McCarthy's cudgel against the UAW, raised the question of the Reuther brothers' visit to Russia in 1934 when they were young socialists and called them enemies of capitalism. Unlike the Teamsters, however, the UAW was demanding to be allowed to testify before the committee. Bobby went to Sheboygan to see the situation at Kohler first hand. Though he noted the bitterness on both sides—he said it reminded him of the implacable attitudes of Arabs and Jews he had met on his trip to the Middle East—his sympathies were with the union. He was disgusted by the primitive working conditions at the Kohler plant and by the unreasoning hatred of management. On his return to Washington he summoned the parties to appear before the Select Committee to present their cases.

During the hearings that followed, Goldwater attacked a UAW official who had been an admitted Trotskyist in 1944, saying that this implied the violent methods of communism were part of the union's repertory. Jack broke in: "My brother's name was Joe and Stalin's name was Joe but this should scarcely support an argument that they had anything in common." In his performance as chief counsel, Bobby was as unrelenting with Lyman Conger, the Kohler Company's attorney, as he had been with Hoffa, getting him to admit that workers at the plant were forced to take their lunch hour in two-minute segments while loading pieces of the plumbing fixtures into blast ovens. After UAW officials took the stand and acquitted themselves with dignity, McClellan summarily ended this phase of the hearings.

In Bobby's Manichean scheme of things, Reuther was the reverse of Jimmy Hoffa, the UAW a good union in the sense that the Teamsters had become a bad one. He was also struck by the symmetry of two pairs of brothers, the Reuthers and the Kennedys, working their respective ways for the common weal. There was truth in his perception, but there was also a dimension he chose not to see. "Although Reuther was an honest trade unionist," says Clark Mollenhoff, "there was real corruption in the Toledo local, which Reuther tolerated, and they should have investigated it, but didn't."

Having protected Reuther, Bobby seized the opportunity to do political business. UAW officials were struck by his interest in their activities in behalf of candidates and by how he asked questions with an accountant's eye about the size of their contributions and the number of precinct workers they mobilized. Bobby solicited the union's views for legislation concerning union reform which Jack was preparing as a "positive" outgrowth of the McClellan Committee hearings. And finally, in a dinner meeting with Reuther's executive assistant Jack Conway, he put his cards on the table, saying that he hoped that the UAW, behind Kefauver in 1956, would back his brother in 1960: "We don't want you on the opposite side from us this time."

The McClellan Committee offered many such opportunities for Bobby to act as his brother's keeper, but it was important for other reasons as well. Lem Billings, who watched Bobby's development over the more than two years he worked on the committee's investigations, concluded, "For the first time in his life he was happy. He'd been a very frustrated young man, awfully mad most of the time, having to hold everything in and work on Jack's career instead of his own. I think he found himself during the Hoffa investigation." There was some untouched reservoir of innocence in him. When he went to Nashville to investigate a Teamster local and an acquaintance who didn't know the Kennedy saga asked where Joe Junior was, Bobby's reply was unhesitating: "In heaven." But for the first time he had a sense that he was claiming a portion of the world as his own. His pursuit of Hoffa was not unlike Nixon's pursuit of Hiss—a deflected search for self, an exorcism of personal demons, a way of translating metaphysics into a practical agenda capable of paying real dividends. It was not clear how ironic Bobby was being when he commented to John Bartlow Martin, interviewing him for a *Saturday Evening Post* article, "My first love is Hoffa."

In July 1958 there was a new round of hearings involving the Teamster boss. Since his last appearance Hoffa had become president of the union, which had indeed been expelled from the AFL-CIO; and he had managed to get a hung jury on the wiretapping and perjury charges in New York. But the gravity of his relationship with the mob had been dramatized by the revelations that followed a police raid on the notorious Apalachin crime conference, the underworld summit attended by Joe Bonanno, Vito Genovese, Carlo Gambino, and other mobsters who were linked to the Teamsters through Anthony Provenzano and other intermediaries close to Hoffa.

When Hoffa appeared this time, it was, as the newspapers put it, a "slugging match." Sometimes it would seem that he was about to go under, wilt under the pressure Bobby applied. But then he would be back the next day so defiant and confident that Bobby would feel defeated. He saw how different Hoffa's malfeasance was from Dave Beck's self-enrichment. Hoffa's was like original sin: corruption pervading everything, a catalogue of evil ranging from extortion and embezzlement to physical violence. As he studied the rogues' gallery of witnesses that paraded before the committee, Bobby reacted like the young man who had considered devoting his life to a religious calling: "They are sleek, often bilious and fat, or lean and cold and hard. They have the smooth faces and cold eyes of gangsters. They wore the same rich clothes, the diamong ring, the jeweled watch, the strong, sickly-sweet smelling perfume."

Among them were Antonio ("Tony Ducks") Corrallo, nicknamed for ducking convictions for arrests for robbery and narcotics before Hoffa put him in charge of five New York locals; Johnny Dioguardi, three-times-convicted labor racketeer who had ordered acid splashed in the eyes of the labor columnist Victor Riesel; Joey Glimco of Local 777 in Chicago, arrested thirty-six times, twice in connection with murder; Momo Salvatore (Sam) Giancana, Chicago mobster and friend of Hoffa's, whose path would cross Bobby's later on; Anthony (Tony Pro) Provenzano of the Genovese family, who controlled Local 560 in New Jersey for Hoffa and many years later would become a prime suspect in his murder.

As each one approached the witness stand, Hoffa held up five fingers, reminding him of the amendment he should cite. The plan led to exchanges like this one:

Kennedy: Did you ever do anything to help the union membership? One thing?

Glimco: I respectfully decline to answer . . .

Kennedy: You were one of the major supporters of Mr. Hoffa, and he is one of your major supporters. Is it because of this background that you have?

Glimco: I respectfully decline to answer . . .

Kennedy: You can have a lot of tough people call up witnesses, poor businessmen, poor members of the union, who can't afford to protect themselves, and have them intimidate these people, but you can't come before this committee and answer any questions, can you, Mr. Glimco?

Coming in conflict with men such as these brought up questions of power and potency that had always been in the background of Bobby's life. When he interrogated Giancana, a former hit man who had inherited the mantle of

Al Capone as boss of the Chicago syndicate, the mobster smirked while taking the Fifth and Bobby shot him a withering look: "I thought only little girls giggle, Mr. Giancana." On another occasion, Joe Gallo, alleged trigger man in the notorious gangland murder of Albert Anastasia, walked into Bobby's office and, true to his nickname—Crazy Joey—began frisking someone in the waiting room, saying that if anybody happened to kill Kennedy while he, Gallo, was nearby he would have to take the blame. Bobby came out of his inner office and gave him a hard look: "So you're Joey Gallo, the jukebox king. You don't look so tough. I'd like to fight you myself."

His brother Ted sometimes cut classes at the University of Virginia Law School to come up and watch the hearings. Rose, Eunice, and Jean also came, and even Jackie was there occasionally. Ethel went every day. Driving through Washington with the children, she would sometimes pass Teamster headquarters. "What is that?" she'd ask. "The Teamsters Union," one of the kids would reply. "What do they do there?" the catechism would continue. "Work overtime to keep Jimmy Hoffa out of jail," someone would say. "And?" They would pick up the cue: "Which is where he belongs!"

But in the end, despite 1500 witnesses and 20,000 pages of testimony, Bobby's bout with Hoffa ended in a draw. There was little cooperation from the FBI, which Bobby saw as so fixated on communism that it was paralyzed in the fight against crime. There was little cooperation from the Republican senators on the committee, who made what Bobby had increasingly come to see as a moral problem into a political one. He also ran into opposition from William G. Hundley, chief of the Justice Department's Organized Crime Section, who refused to file indictments on many of the cases Bobby sent over, echoing the charges of civil libertarians that he had lost sight of due process in the heat of his crusade. "I felt that he and his people didn't know what a criminal case was," Hundley recalls. (When he refused to indict, Bobby flared, "You admit to me that there's wrongdoing here and you tell me on top of that you can't make a case. It makes me sick to my stomach." Hundley replied, "Well, I can't be responsible for your gastric juices.") Finally there was Hoffa himself, snarling and defiant to the end, pointing out that the investigations would end with nothing changed: he would be more firmly in control of the union than ever, and Bobby would be "running off to try to elect his brother President."

As the McClellan Committee's mandate expired in the spring of 1959, Bobby sat down to write a personal account of its work. He was determined that nobody would say, as they had of *Profiles,* that someone else had done the writing. ("He'd be up in the morning, pen in hand, with his yellow pad ..." says John Seigenthaler, who helped him edit the project. "He was determined he was going to write this book himself.") In the end, *The Enemy Within* had a laconic, gang-busters tone that captured the author very well. The country that had produced Jimmy Hoffa, Bobby concluded, needed "the will to fight what is evil and a desire to serve."

6.

*L*EM BILLINGS ALWAYS REMEM-
bered the moment he realized exactly what kind of transformation was happening with his oldest and best friend. It was in 1957, and he was visiting
the Kennedys at Palm Beach. Jack was holding his position in the Gallup
Poll as the leading Democratic candidate; his performance in Los Angeles
in 1956 and his winning the Pulitzer Prize had made him the party's most
sought-after speaker and personality. But for Lem and for Jack himself, all
that was something external, something which was happening outside the
confines of their friendship. On this particular evening they were sitting at
the dinner table skirmishing with insults as they had from the time they
were kids. Lem finally said something about one of Jack's more ignoble
sexual conquests, and as they began to laugh, the Ambassador, who had been
listening to the conversation with rising annoyance, slammed his fork down
on the table.

"You're not to speak like that any more." He fixed Lem with the look that
had never lost its penetrating power. "There are things that you just can't
bring up any more, private things. You've got to forget them. Forget the
'Jack' you once knew. Forget all the things you know about his private life.
Forget he ever existed. From now on you've got to watch everything you
say. The day is coming, and it's coming soon, when he won't be 'Jack' any
more at all—not to you and not to the rest of us either. He'll be 'Mr.
President.' And you can't say or do anything that will jeopardize that."

Lem sat there stunned for a moment. Then he glanced at Jack. At first he
had the same look of sly triumph on his face that he used to get when they
were kids and he managed to get one of them in trouble while getting off

scot-free himself. Then he sort of shrugged as if to say: "Look, this whole thing is as much of a mystery to me as it is to everyone else."

His rise had indeed been swift and his transformation dramatic—from a young, cynical, death-obsessed congressman to a presidential contender almost overnight. Many simply took it to be proof of his father's machinations and the ponderous weight of the Kennedy fortune. Jack himself, given something like a normal life expectancy for the first time since he was a boy, believed he had been graced by a sudden accession of the luck of the Irish. In fact, money and luck had both played a role in his emergence, but more important was his decision finally to seize his fate. Those who talked about how he had become his father's son in his single-minded pursuit of power often missed the deeper truth that he had succeeded only because he had also become his grandfathers' grandson: the consummate politician.

His adeptness was shown in the way he handled the issue of labor reform —a highly charged and potentially dangerous issue that had burned liberals and conservatives equally. When Bobby first broached the idea of an investigation into labor racketeering, Jack, naturally cautious, had been cool to it. Meeting Clark Mollenhoff in a Capitol elevator shortly after his brother had begun assembling a staff, he said, "Frankly, I've got some apprehensions about this from the standpoint of what it does to me with organized labor. But Bobby wants to do it so badly." Soon after the investigation began, however, the potential advantages became clear. Jack got much of the benefit from Bobby's crusade and none of the adverse reaction from civil libertarians worried about his brother's methods in pursuing Hoffa. Jack also saw the possibilities of an alchemy that would turn the base materials Bobby was dredging into a more concrete form of political gold. The alliance with the UAW was one part of the formula; the other was a major piece of legislation bearing the Kennedy name.*

In the fall of 1957, while sitting on the McClellan Committee, Jack began related hearings in the Labor Subcommittee, of which he was chair, on ways to remedy the situation his brother was exposing. He called business owners and corporate attorneys for testimony, pointing out that corruption such as that which infected the Brotherhood of Teamsters was possible, in part,

---

*A less obvious but no less crucial advantage he got from it was noted by Clark Mollenhoff: "Before the hearings, the father had the main contacts with the press. But those hearings gave the Kennedy brothers entree into every newsroom in this country that had an investigative reporting group. Bobby became well acquainted not only with the reporters but with the editors too, in Seattle, Portland, Scranton, Des Moines, Los Angeles, Nashville, New York, Chicago, and other cities. The *Chicago Tribune*, for example, couldn't have had much good to say about Jack until then. But because the Kennedys were deeply involved in investigations dealing with the Teamsters Union—the very thing they had wanted done for years—they had to write nice editorials about their investigations. Jack's career really took off with the work of this committee."

because of management connivance and, even worse, because some companies had used mobsters like Hoffa's friend Johnny Dioguardi to break up legitimate union drives. He also called labor leaders, among them George Meany. The AFL-CIO chief was hostile to all laws regulating union activity and personally suspicious of Kennedy. But he came to have a grudging respect for his efforts on the Labor Subcommittee, and donated union counsel Arthur Goldberg to help Archibald Cox, whom Jack had drafted from Harvard, to help draw up a comprehensive labor reform law.

When the Kennedy-Ives bill was introduced in June 1958, it was backed by virtually every union leader in the country (with the notable exception of Jimmy Hoffa). It safeguarded union finances and curbed the subversion of democratic processes, while also modifying provisions of the Taft-Hartley Act that labor leaders found onerous, and it passed the Senate eighty-eight to one. But the Eisenhower Administration, not wishing to have to deal with labor reform in the midterm elections that fall, ensnarled the bill in parliamentary maneuver and delaying tactics so that when Congress adjourned it was still languishing in the House. "Jimmy Hoffa can rejoice at his continued good luck," Jack said angrily. "Honest union members and the general public can only regard it as a tragedy that politics prevented the recommendations of the McClellan committee from being carried out this year." But if he hadn't gotten the piece of landmark legislation bearing his name (a mutant form of Kennedy-Ives would later pass as the Landrum-Griffith Act), he had achieved something more important by convincing labor that he was neither a political lightweight nor antiunion.

While taking a leading position on the most pressing domestic issue of the day, Jack was continuing to speak out on foreign affairs. Using the prized seat on the Senate Foreign Relations Committee which Majority Leader Lyndon Johnson had somewhat unaccountably given him in 1957, Kennedy expanded his earlier views on nationalism.* A subject of continuing, at times seemingly almost obsessive interest was Vietnam. He had become a founding member of the American Friends of Vietnam, a group including Max Lerner, Arthur Schlesinger, Jr., and other liberals supporting the de facto state of South Vietnam, whose government had indicated that it would not accept the provision for nationwide, unifying elections called for in the Geneva

---

*Unaccountably in the sense that Johnson's gift seemed to boost the stature of a rival for the 1960 nomination. But Joe Kennedy had, in Johnson's word, "pestered" him about the seat since Jack arrived in the Senate. Former FDR aide and later LBJ adviser Jim Rowe was at the Johnson ranch in 1957 when a call came from Hyannis that sheds some light on the relations between the two men. "The Kennedys have met, Lyndon," the Ambassador said, "and we've decided that if you run in '60 we'll support you." When Johnson demurred, the Ambassador went on: "Okay, if you don't run, maybe Jack will." Kennedy used the seat strategically, but was not an active member of the committee. The chairman, Senator J. William Fulbright, could hardly remember his being present: "He was always campaigning."

Accords of 1954. ("What we must offer [South Vietnam]," Jack told the Friends, "is a revolution—a political and social revolution far superior to anything the Communists can offer.") As a member of the Foreign Relations Committee, he took on Algeria as well. In a well-covered Senate speech, he called on Eisenhower to acknowledge that despite French insistence that it was an internal problem, the Algerian war of independence actually posed a threat for all Western nations. The United States, Kennedy said, should use its influence to achieve a settlement that would "shape a course of political independence for Algeria."

These views inspired debate not only on the editorial pages of American newspapers but in Europe as well. The French minister for Algeria angrily invited Jack to come to the colony to inspect the prisons and internment camps he had attacked as inhumane. Hervé Alphand, French Ambassador to the United States, called on Secretary of State Dulles to repudiate Kennedy's views. And Adlai Stevenson, traveling in Paris, said the speech had jeopardized the unity of NATO itself. Jack admitted that he didn't want to be known as "the Senator from Algeria," but he didn't backtrack under the barrage of criticism. Invited to contribute an article to the influential *Foreign Affairs,* he returned to the subject of "the struggle against imperialism" once again, charging the Eisenhower Administration with having failed to appreciate "the forces of nationalism [that] are rewriting the geopolitical map of the world."

His formula for dealing with nationalism in the Third World—by presenting an activist alternative to communism—had momentarily disturbed the political equilibrium of the Western alliance, but it was part of the broader vision that was rapidly becoming his theme. To a degree unmatched by any of his potential presidential rivals, he had understood the extent of American perplexity over what seemed a precipitous decline from the nation's preeminence after World War II; the sense of uncertainty about how to handle the challenge of revolutionary communism; the post-Sputnik fear that America had been left behind technologically; and the anxiety that perhaps the nation had exhausted its physical and spiritual resources. He had responded to this mood in one way in *Profiles in Courage*—by asserting the vitality of the nation's character and political institutions. He responded to it in quite another way in his charge that the United States was being victimized by a dangerous "missile gap."

This subject was in the political air. Joseph Alsop, General James Gavin, and others Kennedy admired had been talking about it since 1956. Nelson Rockefeller had made military preparedness a central and polemical emphasis of the influential Rockefeller Brothers Panel Studies. The Gaither Report of the Ford Foundation had reached the alarming conclusion that North America was vulnerable to Soviet long-range missiles.

At the beginning Jack saw the "missile gap" in wholly parochial terms—

as a lever to pry loose more defense spending for New England industrial areas hard hit by unemployment. Almost like Joe McCarthy, who at first didn't realize what he had stumbled onto when he gave his speech about Communists in high places at Wheeling, Jack quickly saw that the issue had great symbolic power. It was a shorthand way of touching a whole range of fears about American potency; it was also a way of confronting Republicans without directly attacking the almost totemic figure of Eisenhower himself. At a 1957 Jefferson-Jackson Day luncheon, Jack charged that the administration was concealing the fact that "we may be as much as several years behind in rocket motors, new fuels, jet engines, radar and nuclear powered plants." In a December article in the *New York Times*—part of the literary cottage industry Sorensen was now operating under the Kennedy by-line— he criticized the Dulles doctrine of massive retaliation as too inflexible, a "Fortress America" approach which abetted "further Soviet advances through 'Sputnik diplomacy' of intimidation and peripheral wars." He began to see the erosion of Western influence in the Third World, and the apparent loss of U.S. military supremacy vis-à-vis the Russians in terms analogous to the great international drama of his youth, when Europe faced the moral and political tensions that led to World War II, and when he had charged in his senior thesis that appeasement was "the inevitable result" of "slowness in rearming."

In a Senate address on the missile gap on August 14, 1958, he compared the reported loss of America's "superiority in nuclear striking power" to England's sixteenth-century loss of Calais, the last foothold of British power on the Continent. "Why cannot we realize," he said, "that the coming years of the gap present us with a peril more deadly than any wartime danger we have ever known?" He quoted Churchill's remarks, "Come then—let us to the task, to the battle and the toil—each to our part, each to our station . . ." When the speech was over, Senator Stuart Symington, noticing his allusions, asked if he meant that the situation facing the United States could be compared with "the situation faced by the British in the late 1930s?" Jack replied: "The Senator is completely correct."

But while the United States should try to take the momentum away from the Soviets in weaponry, it should also "export the revolutionary ideas of the Declaration of Independence, and thus lead, not frustrate, the nationalistic movement against imperialism of any variety, East or West."

It was a cluster of ideas he was making into the distinctive Kennedy vision: in domestic affairs, a sense of "competence," a word of self-definition he pressed on his biographer James MacGregor Burns; and in foreign relations a vigorous entry into the lists against communism. In contrast to the radicalism of the left and the right, his was a radicalism of the status quo, one that did not contemplate great changes, but contained a vision of power wielded with forceful aplomb that caused liberal intellectuals who had previously held themselves aloof to begin to move closer to the Kennedy camp. By 1958 Sorensen was having success as a recruiter, forming an Academic Advisory Committee that included Schlesinger, John Kenneth Galbraith, Walt Rostow, Archibald Cox, Paul Samuelson, and others who were regarded as a "beachhead" on a grand front. The lacunae in his record on the subject of McCarthyism might be bothersome, and so was the fact that he had been less than forthcoming on the Civil Rights Act of 1957; but his position on issues having to do with America's place in the world—and the sense that he was an idealist but not a bleeding heart—made him seem attractive as well as inevitable. Although Joseph Alsop was not one of them, liberals tended to agree with his formulation: "Jack Kennedy is a Stevenson with balls."

"By 1958 all those men who had once been quite snotty about the Kennedys were coming around," said Lem Billings. "We considered it quite a coup to have taken them into camp. But they changed things: weekends at the Cape were no longer as much fun as they'd been before." This comment captures the family attitude exactly. The liberal intellectuals were like the Brahmins of Boston, who had once rejected the family and then, after Joe Kennedy's ambassadorship, come toadying to them—or, as Lem put it, "sucking up." (Arthur Schlesinger, Jr., had, in fact, bitterly attacked the Ambassador in 1947 for his cold war ideas—calling them "cowardice rationalized in terms of high morality"—just as five years later he had dismissed Bobby's criticism of Yalta in the *New York Times* as "an astonishing mixture of distortion and error.") The fact that these liberals had defected from Adlai Stevenson made their possession all the sweeter. Stevenson's reputation as a deep thinker had always annoyed Jack, who pointed out to friends with some asperity that he read more books in a week than Stevenson did in a year. (He was also irritated by the fact that Stevenson, whom he considered slightly effeminate, should have such great appeal for women, and in bull sessions with friends he wondered aloud if he was a "switcher.") Yet he did not want to be considered an "egghead," a term made popular by Stevenson's ovoid dome. He was willing to play Fortinbras to his rival's Hamlet and would have been gratified by the comparison Schlesinger elaborated in his private journal as 1960 approached: "S is a much richer, more thoughtful, more creative person; but he has been away from power too long; he gives me an odd sense of unreality . . . I found it hard to define this feeling —a certain frivolity, distractedness, overinterest in words and phrases? I don't know; but in contrast K gives a sense of cool, measured, intelligent concern with action and power. I feel that his administration would be less encumbered than S's with commitments to past ideals or sentimentalities . . ."

As Jack was preparing to make the big push for the nomination, Pennsylvania Senator Joseph Clark, curious abut how he would deal with issues having religious implications, asked if he would be able to take a contemporary position on international birth control. Jack replied: "I intend to be as brave as I dare." This was close to a political motto. He was pragmatic, testing the limits, but not getting caught on any limb of commitment that might be sawed off from behind. In the same way that he hated to wear hats, which, although part of a time-honored political uniform, he felt didn't "fit" him, he was wary of stepping into any programmatic political philosophy that might not become him. While he had gotten free from the conservative identity his father tried to force on him, he was not much changed from the newly elected senator who told an interviewer of having gotten letters from Massachusetts constituents chiding him for not being a "true liberal" and said, "I'd be very happy to tell them that I'm not a liberal at all." The identity he embraced had less to do with political ideas than with political sensibility. "I'm a realist," he said to the reporter when pressed for a label.

In some sense, no definition fit. He was protean, reacting to everything ad hoc. He had watched with fascination as he became an item of consumer culture—lavishly illustrated feature stories about him and Jackie, him and the new baby, Caroline, appearing not in political journals but in women's magazines and other parts of the popular press. It was a case, as the writer Norman Mailer said later, of superman coming to supermarket. The whole Jack was coming to represent more than the sum of his parts. More than any other political figure of the day he understood that this was a necessary part of the political process. Distinguishing between the private and public selves had been part of his upbringing. In his brief career he had made his father's credo his own: It is not what a person is that counts, but what people think he is.

Jack might once have had doubts about his forced flowering as a war hero after the ambiguous events of *PT 109*, but now the coconut shell on which he'd carved his message of distress sat on his Senate desk. He also kept a portion of the handwritten manuscript of *Profiles* and still showed it to people as proof that he and not Sorensen had written the book. James MacGregor Burns, one of the intellectuals who had been wooed most sedulously, experienced this mythomania first hand when he agreed to do the first Kennedy biography.* Having unlimited access to Jack's files and to Jack himself, the prize-winning historian submitted his manuscript for what he thought would be a cursory review and was startled when Sorensen and

---

*Late in 1958, Sorensen had tried to persuade Burns to come to work in Jack's office. Burns wrote back, "There is no person I would rather work for or whose political prospects I am so interested in." But because of academic commitments he had to have "a more flexible arrangement." The biography turned out to be his contribution. It was an excellent solution for Kennedy. He got what was in effect a campaign biography written by a leading academic historian, a man whose own book on Roosevelt had been nosed out for the Pulitzer Prize by *Profiles*.

Kennedy pronounced it a "catastrophe." They wanted changes made not just on "family matters" (a comment Jack made during an interview about Joe Junior having been "pugnacious . . . a bully"; a reference to Peter Fitzwilliam and the affair with Kick), but on other questions as well. They were bothered by Burns's comment that Jack was "detached," and concerned about his treatment of Jack's attitude toward McCarthy. After a series of letters that failed to satisfy Jack, Burns was summoned to a climactic five-hour meeting in the lobby of the Waldorf in which Sorensen jawboned him about the manuscript, occasionally threatening to call Jack down from his room upstairs. The historian also received a "lovely but unhappy letter" from Jackie and even a call from the Ambassador—"pleasant but steadily coming around to a criticism of the manuscript." In the end the portrait of Jack—a seminal one followed by other writers as *the* source for years to come—bore exactly the coloring Kennedy wanted.

Lem was right when he said that Jack moved into his role "like a method actor." Hollywood stars fascinated him the same way that mobsters did Bobby: they embodied what he was and what he wanted to become; they had qualities he wanted to acquire. It was something his father understood better than anyone else. "Charisma" was not yet a cult term; the vocabulary that distinguished between hot imagery and cold, and defined the relationship between media and message, had not yet been invented. But Joe Kennedy saw that his son had somehow acquired a "universal appeal" that no other politician came close to. "Jack is the greatest attraction in the country," he said to an interviewer on the eve of Jack's announcement of his candidacy. "I'll tell you how to sell more copies of a book. Put his picture on the cover. Why is it that when his picture is on the cover of *Life* or *Redbook* they sell a record number of copies? You advertise the fact that he will be at dinner and you will break all records for attendance. He can draw more people to a fund-raising dinner than Cary Grant or Jimmy Stewart."

Adlai Stevenson, worried about the increasing role of image makers in politics, had attributed his 1956 defeat in part to the fact that he had refused to be sold like a box of Wheaties. Having no such concerns, the Kennedys might have replied that the problem with the Stevenson campaign could have been that it was hawking an inferior product. The Ambassador embraced the intrusion of Madison Avenue and Hollywood into the political process with gusto. Referring to the commodity Jack had made himself into, he said: "We'll sell him like soap flakes."

Bobby joined the presidential effort late in 1959, after finishing *The Enemy Within*. He was disturbed that more progress hadn't been made, and at a December meeting at Palm Beach asked impatiently, "All right, Jack, what has been done about the campaign, what planning has been done?" When his brother didn't answer immediately, he began again: "Jack, how do you expect to run a successful campaign if you don't get started? A day lost now can't be picked up at the other end. It's ridiculous that more work hasn't been done already.'' In a gesture that told much about the brothers' relationship, Jack looked over at his friend Red Fay and, mimicking Bobby's staccato delivery, said, ''How would you like looking forward to that voice blasting in your ear for the next six months?'' Then to his brother: ''All right, Bobby, we've been able to do a few things in your absence, but we're very appreciative of your support and intend to call on it extensively.''

Actually the candidacy had been going on since 1958, when Jack won a smashing victory for reelection to the Senate. The campaign had never really stopped. Steve Smith, who along with Teddy had gotten his electoral baptism in 1958, had moved into a small office in the Esso Building, in New York, and begun accumulating a file with the names of some 40,000 people who'd indicated an interest in the candidacy as well as learning to coordinate Jack's schedule using the *Caroline*, the Convair passenger plane the Ambassador had bought for the months of travel that lay ahead.

By the time Jack announced his candidacy, on January 2, 1960, Hubert Humphrey had stepped forward as a challenger, but he was widely regarded as a stalking horse for Lyndon Johnson, who was hoping that such candidates as Stuart Symington and other favorite sons with strong regional ties would deadlock the nomination, and that Jack would trip over his two main liabilities, his youth and his Catholicism, as he carried his cause to the voters. Such a strategy felt to the Kennedys like another case of the Establishment trying to keep the Boston Irish down, and thus the primary season looming up seemed less a trial by ordeal than a holy war.

Wisconsin was the first test. Humphrey worked the state as intensively as Jack did. Bobby was the spectral presence behind the campaign, as intense in his prosecution of his brother's case as he had been in his prosecution of Jimmy Hoffa, losing a pound a week as he slogged through the freezing midwestern spring. Chuck Spalding, who was organizing the Eau Claire district, was with Bobby on a train that was stopped by snowdrifts nine miles away from a scheduled appearance, whereupon Bobby got out and walked into foul weather to keep the engagement. Jack matched Bobby's effort, catching a few hours' sleep at night before showing up at factory gates, traveling several miles to appear at a coffee shop with a dozen or so voters. His confidence never flagged. Spalding was walking down a street with him shaking hands with passersby when an elderly woman stopped him and said, ''You're too soon, my boy, too soon.'' Jack smiled back at her and shook his head: ''No, this is my time. My time is now.''

As Wisconsin's neighbor and its ''third Senator,'' Humphrey should have won, and when he didn't his candidacy was dead. But Jack did not win the convincing victory he needed to demonstrate his appeal outside New England; he had lost the Protestant districts while winning in conservative Catholic ones. Humphrey raised the religious issue elliptically by charging that Kennedy was an impostor Democrat, the candidate of crossover Republicans. When Walter Cronkite, interviewing Jack for CBS on the night of the primary, asked if being a Catholic had hurt him, Bobby exploded, accusing CBS of violating an agreement not to talk about religion and telling Cronkite that he'd never get another chance to talk to his brother.

If Humphrey had quit after Wisconsin, he might have crippled the Kennedy campaign, which depended on opposition to dramatize its themes. Instead he desperately pushed into West Virginia, giving Jack the dramatic showdown there that he needed. Jack was built up through an adroit television campaign based on a collage of images: the war hero whose exploits were announced over the phosphorescent wake of a PT boat; the intellectual holding his prize-winning book; the father holding two-year-old Caroline on his knees. Humphrey posed as a populist being outbought by Kennedy money. But being rich was not as much in Jack's disfavor as Humphrey assumed. Justice Douglas later told of watching Jack standing by a mine shaft shaking hands. One miner came up and asked, "Is it true you're the son of one of our wealthiest men?" Jack said he guessed so. "Is it true that you've never wanted for anything and had everything you wanted?" Jack reluctantly said it was probably true. "Is it true you've never done a day's work with your hands all your life?" Jack nodded his head. Then the miner said, "Well, let me tell you this. You haven't missed a thing."

Religion was another matter. The sleeping issue of the campaign, it burst into the open when Humphrey adopted a campaign theme song with a subliminal message: "Give Me That Old-Time Religion." It was ironic that Jack, with his casual attitude toward the sacraments, should have had to deal with the question, as Jackie recognized when she said, "I think it's so unjust of people to be against Jack because he's a Catholic. He's such a poor Catholic. Now if it was Bobby, I could understand it."* But in a way West Virginia was the perfect forum: if he was beaten it would be moonshiners' bigotry; if he won, it would mean that Catholicism had overcome its strictest test.

Once the issue had come up, Jack addressed it aggressively. "Nobody

---

*Washington Post writer Peter Lisagor, who was on the panel of "Face the Nation" that dealt with Humphrey's charges about Kennedy wealth and religion, remembers Jackie's peculiar reaction. "I was simply lobbing [the charges] up to [Jack] and he was batting them out of the park one by one . . ." Jackie, meanwhile, was in the studio looking daggers at Lisagor. After the telecast he went up to her and remarked that she seemed offended. "Well, I was," she replied, "because I thought that the questions you asked Jack were absolutely horrible, but Jack says you're a nice person and I'm getting very tense because I'm so involved in the campaign." Lisagor and other journalists following the campaign were amused by this, since her lack of involvement was often commented upon. Yet she was useful. Kennedy aides had wooed the theologian Reinhold Niebuhr without success until Jackie sat next to him at a New York Liberal Party dinner. They were in intense conversation all evening. Afterward Niebuhr said, "She's read every book I ever wrote," and from then on was a Kennedy supporter.

asked me if I was a Catholic when I joined the United States Navy,'' he said at one campaign stop. ''Nobody asked my brother if he was a Catholic or Protestant before he climbed into an American bomber plane to fly his last mission.'' Perhaps because it was a matter of politics rather than belief, the issue of religion brought out the best in Jack, including a response during a telecast on the eve of the primary in which, after being asked for the hundredth time about the separation of church and state, Jack stared into the camera and gave what Theodore White later called the finest impromptu speech he had ever heard by any political candidate. It concluded: ''If a President breaks his oath he is not only committing a crime against the Constitution, for which the Congress can impeach and should impeach him, but he is committing a sin against his God.''

After it became obvious that Catholicism was not going to be the issue on which Jack's campaign foundered, Humphrey began to feel, as he later put it, like an independent merchant fighting against a chain store. He was outspent, but even more he was out-Kennedyed. Teddy had been given the Rocky Mountain states to organize, but Rose and the girls invaded West Virginia and multiplied the Kennedy presence in appearances everywhere. Jack's father was nowhere to be seen, but he remained the crucial Kennedy. Humphrey railed at him as ''Papa Joe'' who was willing to buy his ''little pet anything he wanted, even an election.''

The Ambassador was active in his own fashion. Teddy later told the story of how Jack, shortly after announcing his candidacy, had looked over the schedule, specifying the primaries where he'd have to campaign, and then turned to Joe Kennedy and said, ''And the states *you* have are Illinois, New Jersey, Pennsylvania, and New York.'' This turned out to be accurate. Long before West Virginia, the old man had been doing everything he could—not only writing checks but also trying to pull rabbits out of hats. Former Senator Burton K. Wheeler, who had run for Vice President with La Follette on the Progressive Party ticket back in 1924, was surprised to get a call shortly before the Wisconsin primary in which the Ambassador asked him to attest to a Kennedy contribution to that campaign, so that old Progressives in the state might have a reason to vote for Jack. But the Ambassador's primary job was to go to the bosses in the big industrial states and deal with them in his role as Kennedy boss. He got close to Eugene Keogh, a powerful New York congressman, who later recalled, ''He knew instinctively who the important people were, who the bosses behind the scenes were. From 1958 on he was in contact with them constantly by phone, presenting Jack's case, explaining and interpreting his son, working these bosses.'' Tip O'Neill says that at one point Kennedy heard that the way to Philadelphia boss Billy Green was through a Pennsylvania state official named Joe Clark (not related to the senator of the same name): ''Mr. Kennedy had flown this man Clark to his suite at the Waldorf within forty-eight hours of hearing this information and was entertaining him there.'' Joe Kennedy also worked perhaps the most important boss of all—J. Edgar Hoover, who still had wartime recordings of Jack's trysts with Inga Arvad. Flattering letters arrived regularly at FBI headquarters from Hyannis, where Kennedy was still a semiundercover "Special Agent" for the Bureau, including one late in 1959 that praised Hoover's *Reader's Digest* article, "Communist Illusion and Democratic Reality," which the Ambassador said he was recommending to Sorensen's attention: "There are many thoughts in this article Jack ought to be using as he goes around the country talking to audiences who are completely sympathetic to your ideas but lack imagination to put them into effect."

In the West Virginia primary the Ambassador's main contribution was the suggestion that they recruit Franklin D. Roosevelt, Jr., bearer of the famous name and visage from a bygone era. Roosevelt campaigned through the state with Jack, associating the Kennedy and Roosevelt names in forgotten hills and hollows where the New Deal was still holy writ. (With his precise eye for detail, Joe Kennedy suggested that Roosevelt's endorsement letters be postmarked at Hyde Park, to make it seem as though the former President had returned from the grave to urge a vote for Jack.) The West Virginia journalist Charles Peters points out what a master stroke the use of Roosevelt was: "In a certain sense . . . [he] was almost God's son coming down and saying it was all right to vote for this Catholic, it was permissible, it wasn't something terrible to do. FDR Junior made it possible for many people to vote for Kennedy that couldn't have conceived of it as a possibility before." When the campaign got tough, Bobby pressed Roosevelt into service as more than a symbol, getting him to release to the press material smearing Humphrey (who had been rejected for military service in World War II because of disabilities) as a "draft dodger."

Finally Kennedy resources and resourcefulness led to an irresistible victory in West Virginia. It was not only an indication of the potency of Jack's candidacy, but also the high point of the collaboration between the Kennedy generations. Recuperating at Palm Beach after it was all over, Chuck Spalding found himself lounging next to the Ambassador beside the pool. "Just look at him," the old man said as Jack came into view, speaking with a respect he rarely accorded anyone. "How does he do it? I couldn't have done it. Not a chance." Later on the situation was exactly reversed: Spalding was talking to Jack when the Ambassador did something that caught their eye. "It's amazing," Jack said, watching his father. "People knock the hell out of him every time they get a chance. They forget that he has accomplished as much in his lifetime as three or four men."

7.

$\mathcal{H}$UMPHREY HAD CEASED TO
be a viable candidate; nobody stepped forward to replace him. In late June
Jack was in Eugene Keogh's office in Washington talking to Pennsylvania's
Billy Green, whom Joe Kennedy had been working for months. After their
conference Jack called his father, who was vacationing at Lake Tahoe, to tell
him that Green had swung the uncommitted Pennsylvania delegation solidly
behind his candidacy. "Well, that's it," the old man said. "We've got a
majority." Several days later, Bobby, who along with Kenny O'Donnell was
still romancing Pennsylvania delegates, found out about Green's decision
and called his brother to break what he thought was big news. Jack said he
already knew. "Why didn't you tell me?" Bobby asked. "Because you and
Kenny talk too much," Jack replied.

Bobby continued to worry. He was concerned about Senator Lyndon Johnson's semiofficial candidacy and about the wild-card role Adlai Stevenson
might play at the convention. Stevenson was not a Kennedy enthusiast.
("That young man never says please," he grumbled. "He never says thank
you, he never asks for things, he demands them.") And there was tremendous sentimental support for the former candidate, especially from the circle
of liberals whose dominant figure was Eleanor Roosevelt. She had been feuding with Jack for years, saying that he had shown "too much profile and not
enough courage" on issues such as McCarthyism and civil rights, that he was
merely the creature of his father's deferred ambition, and that he had never
satisfactorily dealt with questions posed by his Catholicism. After another
acerbic preconvention meeting with her that failed to result in an endorsement, Jack made a caustic comment which seemed ironic in light of the

crucial role her son had played in his West Virginia victory: "She hated my father and she can't stand it that his children turned out so much better than hers."

Bobby felt that Stevenson enthusiasts were pawns in Lyndon Johnson's plans. Their man couldn't win, but he could take the convention to a second ballot on which Jack's strength could begin to erode, thus allowing the Texan to make his move. And the relationship with Johnson himself was becoming more and more bitter. Hugh Sidey, who profiled all the major candidates for *Life,* had found that while Humphrey and Symington were scrupulously fair in their comments about Jack, Johnson was vicious. The Texas Senator had told at great length how the Ambassador had begged him to put his son on the Foreign Relations Committee; how Jack had missed roll calls; how he was suffering from unacknowledged and probably terminal illnesses. Johnson had taken up the same themes in background discussions with Peter Lisagor. On one plane ride he had called Jack "a scrawny little fellow with rickets," making a puny circle with thumb and forefinger to indicate the circumference of his ankles. He had claimed, moreover, that if Jack was elected, Joe Kennedy would run the country and make Bobby Secretary of Labor. Bobby heard rumors of the conversation and wouldn't let Lisagor rest until he'd extracted all the details. Then he turned away, a solemn look on his face: "I knew he hated Jack. But I didn't know he hated him that much."

The conflict between Kennedy and Johnson forces had become the dominant motif of the Los Angeles convention by the time it opened on July 11. While Johnson lieutenant John Connally was starting a whispering campaign about Jack's health, the Senator himself was denouncing the Ambassador to state delegations as the man "who held Chamberlain's umbrella." For the Majority Leader it might all be part of the game of politics, but not for Bobby. When Johnson aide Bobby Baker ran into Bobby Kennedy at the Biltmore and mentioned somewhat jocularly that Teddy had been getting rough in statements to the effect that Johnson hadn't yet recovered from his heart attack, Bobby exploded: "You've got your nerve. Lyndon Johnson has compared my father to the Nazis and John Connally . . . lied by saying my brother was dying of Addison's disease. You Johnson people are running a stinking damned campaign and you'll get yours when the time comes."

His eyes ringed with dark circles, a bone-weary Bobby met with campaign coordinators at eight o'clock every morning of the convention to summarize the situation and lay out the day's work. "I remember the second day we were there," one of them says. "Bob stood up on a footstool and said in very curt language . . . that he understood the previous day some of the coordinators had gone to Disneyland. He said, 'If any of you think it's more important to go to Disneyland than nominate the next President of the United States you ought to quit right now!' "

While his brother remained wound tight, Jack was at ease. He debated Johnson before the Texas delegation despite Bobby's doubts and his father's conviction that it was an unwise maneuver. (Reporter John Seigenthaler was with the Ambassador when Jean Kennedy Smith passed by and asked her father his opinion about the debate, and when he said he thought it was foolish replied, "But, Daddy, how can Jack say no? That man challenged us.") Two days later Jack was in the middle of lunch with his father at the plush Hearst estate in Los Angeles, which the Ambassador had rented from Marion Davies as a family center for the convention, when Minnesota Senator Eugene McCarthy's fervent nomination of Stevenson set off the convention's most emotional outburst. "Don't worry, Dad," he said. "Stevenson has everything but the votes."

As the roll call began things went even better than Jack had expected. By the time Wyoming was called, Teddy, who had been working the western states throughout the primary season, could jostle through the crowd and shout to the chairman of the delegation: "You have in your grasp the opportunity to nominate the next President of the United States. Such support can never be forgotten by a President." Wyoming gave all fifteen of its votes to Jack, putting him over the top on the first ballot. Not long afterward, a journalist following the campaign saw a rare moment of intimacy between Jack and Bobby in a private area just outside the convention hall. "It was the first time they'd met since they won it ... [They] walked off into the corner, Bob with his head bowed as he usually did. And I remember ... the only show of emotion was [Bobby] hitting the open palm of his left hand with the fist of his right hand repeatedly and a kind of smile on John Kennedy's face: the ultimate satisfaction." Jack called Jackie, who was watching the convention at Hyannis. Then he made his first appearance before the delegates, and the band began to play "Toora-Loora-Loora."

The day before the presidential balloting, Jack had asked O'Neill to approach the Johnson forces with a peace feeler, urging them not to struggle further because the battle would divide the party. Johnson's closest adviser, Speaker of the House Sam Rayburn, told O'Neill that he'd be open to further discussion, a message O'Neill passed on to Jack at a United Steelworkers' benefit at Chasen's Restaurant that night. Jack said he'd love to have Johnson as his running mate, but he did not want to make the offer and get turned down. He told O'Neill he'd call Rayburn back that night, but apparently told nobody else, not even Bobby, that he was doing so. After Kennedy won the nomination, Senator Stuart Symington seemed such a likely choice (he was strongly backed by labor and had been more or less offered the job in earlier conversations between Jack and Clark Clifford) that two newspapermen close to the Kennedy camp, Charles Bartlett and John Seigenthaler, reported he would get the vice presidential nomination. Joe Alsop,

Washington Post publisher Philip Graham, and the Ambassador, however, had all kept up the lobbying effort for Johnson, and Jack had listened.

The night of his nomination he decided to choose Johnson, and he told Bobby the next morning, not long before the meeting he had scheduled with the Texan. Bobby was shocked and others were livid. Kenny O'Donnell burst into Jack's suite ranting about what he regarded as a sellout. Jack turned pale and maneuvered him into a bathroom, the one place where he could have privacy. "I'm forty-three years old and I'm the healthiest candidate for President in the United States," he said. " ... I'm not going to die in office. So the vice presidency doesn't mean anything." He went on to point out that if he was elected it would be by a small majority and he wouldn't be able to live with Johnson as a hostile Senate Majority Leader. It was an implausible explanation for the offer he'd made, but the emotional O'Donnell allowed himself to be convinced.

As consternation mounted among his supporters at the prospect of having Johnson on the ticket, Jack began to back off, implying that he had hoped to make the offer in the interests of party unity and had assumed that Johnson would turn it down. Bobby went down to Johnson's suite to tell him that there might be a floor fight over the nomination by elements of labor and liberals hostile to him. Operating on what he apparently thought was carte blanche from his brother, Bobby offered Johnson the chairmanship of the Democratic National Committee instead, which brought a one-word response from Rayburn, "Shit!" and caused John Connally to remark caustically, "Who's the candidate, you or your brother?" At this point Phil Graham called Jack to say that Bobby was pressing Johnson to withdraw. Jack responded coolly, "Bobby's been out of touch and doesn't know what's happening," and said that Johnson was still his choice.*

Bobby got all the blame for the snafu. After he had left the suite, Johnson called him "that little shitass." That night, when the Texas oil man H. L. Hunt and his wife visited the suite, Lady Bird ran to them sobbing at the humiliation—"I didn't want him to take it"—while her husband stood in the bedroom screaming at an adviser who wanted him to deny a newspaper account claiming that the offer had been made only because of Johnson pressure. "I'll be goddamned if I'll deny it. Let the sonofabitch deny it." He was referring to Bobby.

---

*Graham's phone call was noted in a memo he prepared about the confused events. Bobby's account was different. He said, for instance, that when he suggested that Johnson clear up the snafu by withdrawing, the Senator had broken into tears. But Bobby's major interest seemed to be dispelling the idea that he and his brother could have been at loggerheads over such an important matter or that Jack would have used him. It was a theme he returned to over and over again. Years after the event, when Jack and Phil Graham were both dead, Bobby came up to Graham's widow and said of her husband (who had given his memo of that day to T. H. White): "He didn't know us; we, my brother and I, never would have been apart."

There was as much dismay at the Marion Davies house as at the Johnson suite. Jack's friend Charles Bartlett later said, "Jack was in a low state of mind; Bobby was in near despair." Bobby's children were splashing in the courtyard fountain, the only signs of happiness on the scene. Lying across the seat of a car, Bobby was disconsolately dictating the steps necessary to get Johnson nominated. Jack was skimming the *New York Times* spread across the car trunk. Bobby was saying gloomily, "Yesterday was the best day of my life; today is the worst day." Then the Ambassador showed up, indomitably optimistic as he strolled around the yard in a velvet dressing gown. "Don't worry, Jack," he said to his son. "In two weeks they'll be saying it was the smartest thing you ever did."

Shortly after Johnson's first-ballot nomination, Joe Kennedy departed for New York, leaving Rose to represent the family at Jack's acceptance speech. Joe watched it on television at Henry Luce's house. As Stevenson, Minnesota Governor Orville Freeman, Humphrey, and others preceded his son to the rostrum to make the customary pleas for unity, Kennedy made a mordant crack about each of them. "There was no respect for any of these liberals," says Henry Luce III. "He just thought they were all fools on whom he had played this giant trick."

Jack began the campaign trailing Nixon because of the exposure his rival received in the Republican convention a month after the Democrats had left Los Angeles. The Gallup Poll had it 53 percent to 47 percent when Jack got his campaign into high gear after Labor Day. The friendship from their days in the House together was gone. Jack now told friends that he owed it to the country to see that Nixon did not become President. He hammered hard on the themes he had appropriated as his own, telling audiences—which were beginning to react to him enthusiastically—that they had "to get the country moving again," a phrase conceived by adviser Walt Rostow that became his campaign slogan, and proclaiming that the world could not exist "half slave, half free," part of a self-conscious effort to appropriate the imagery of the Lincoln presidency, which had become his model of achievement. Understanding that Nixon had to defend the record of the past eight years but was not surrounded by Eisenhower's reassuring and unassailable persona, Kennedy based his campaign on an aggressive call to emerge from the gray uncertainties of the late 1950s into the bright possibilities of the new decade. He was helped by the aura of stardom provided by Peter Lawford's Hollywood connections. Chief among them was Frank Sinatra, who called Peter "Brother in Lawford" and made him part of his Rat Pack coterie. Asked what the singer had in common with his in-laws politically, Lawford replied, "Let's just say that the Kennedys are interested in the lively arts and that Sinatra is the liveliest art of all."

The pivotal moment in the campaign came when the rivals met face to face in the first of four tv debates late in September. Nixon went in as the more experienced performer, having used the medium to save his vice presidency, and indeed his political career, in the notorious Checkers speech of 1956. But television and its audience had changed since then, becoming more sophisticated, less forgiving of such unalloyed sentiment. Still ahead in the polls, Nixon planned to present himself as the survivor of the famous "kitchen debate" with Khrushchev, the veteran who had been reviled by Communists in Caracas, the statesman whose experience would make his opponent seem all the more immature. As the debate progressed, he seemed to be the forensic champion he had been in his senior year at Whittier High, and some who didn't have a television set and heard only the audio portion thought his deeper voice was more convincing than Kennedy's nasal twang and he had won the contest. Viewers had exactly the opposite reaction. Jack was nervous, his hands quivering when not gripping the rostrum. But his face was impassive, except for a slight ironic smile as Nixon struggled with some of his responses. Jack came off as clipped and precise—"cool," to use one of his favorite words. If FDR had been the perfect figure for the age of radio because of his lively and sonorous voice, then Jack, with his imperturbable good looks, was perfect for the television age. His stage personality was in perfect control, while Nixon's private self—nervous, sweating, edgy—kept poking through the political persona in a way that might have seemed reassuringly natural in person but on television was disturbing. It was a triumph for Jack—the first time that seventy million Americans had *experienced* him up close. This exposure established the star quality that the Ambassador had prophesied for him. From this point on, he was mobbed at campaign stops and even had his cuff links ripped off, returning home with his hands and forearms bleeding.* Yet if he had become almost the ideal candidate, there were still flashes of reality. One journalist never forgot the oversized teamster who trailed Jack in his own car for several days, screaming at him at every stop about union busting and other sins. Finally one day he got close enough to be within speaking distance. Jack shot him a withering look and said, "Drop dead, Fatso."

When Charles Levin, editor of the small New England newspaper the *New Bedford Times,* turned off the tv set after the debate, the phone rang. It was Joe Kennedy, taking his own private poll to check reactions of people he regarded as opinion makers. Galvanized by the campaign, he was barely able

---

*Jack was acutely aware of his image throughout the campaign, feeling that he must avoid Nixon's penchant for being captured in ludicrous candid photographs. *Look* photographer Stanley Tretick recalled later on how Jack refused to be captured wearing a funny hat or eating, especially after he saw a picture of Nixon eating a big finger of poi on a campaign swing through Hawaii. After this Jack would grab a couple of hot dogs and slide down in the seat of his car to eat them out of the photographers' range.

to keep to his background role. In October, when he thought Jack wasn't catching Nixon quickly enough, he stepped forward and called a meeting of the campaign steering committee, which Jack immediately canceled; when he sat in on a strategy session and insisted that inflation be emphasized more prominently as an issue, Jack reminded him that the torch had passed: "Listen, you worry about financing and I'll worry about the issues." The Ambassador was one of the sleeping issues of the election himself, as some Republican wit acknowledged by composing this piece of doggerel:

> *Jack and Bob will run the show*
> *While Ted's in charge of hiding Joe.*

Jack knew it too. Red Fay happened to be present during one of the interviews Hugh Sidey conducted with the Democratic candidate. The subject of Joe Kennedy's impact on his children came up at one point and Sidey turned to Fay and asked him his opinion. Fay began to give what he felt was an honest evaluation of the old man's crucial importance until he saw Jack surreptitiously run a finger across his throat and cut his discourse short. Later on Jack chided him, "God, if I hadn't cut you off Sidey would have headed his article 'A Vote for Jack Is a Vote for Father Joe.' This is just the material *Time* magazine would like to have—that I'm a pawn in Dad's hands. That it's really not Jack himself who is seeking the presidency but his father. That Joe Kennedy now has the vehicle to capture the only segment of power that has eluded him . . ."

Although shunted somewhat to the periphery of things, however, the old man continued to take care of oddments of business he felt to be important. Worried about the toes Bobby had stepped on, he arranged a meeting with FDR Junior and others at a ranch in California to discuss ways to heal the open wound caused by Bobby's investigation of labor racketeering. It was decided to ask Frank Sinatra to set up a meeting with Harold Gibbons, a Teamster official. When Gibbons came to Palm Beach for their meeting, the Ambassador was sitting by the pool in his bathing suit. "Well, Mr. Gibbons," he said. "I don't think there's much of a war going on between the Kennedys and Hoffa. I hardly hear the name Hoffa in our house any more." Trying to smooth things over without seeming weak, he went on as if thinking aloud, saying that his children, with the possible exception of Bobby, never learned how to hate. Then he gave Gibbons his gelid stare, as if to show that he was asking for reconciliation from a position of strength: "But me, when I hate some son of a bitch, I hate him till I die."

When leading Protestant clergyman Norman Vincent Peale questioned a Catholic's ability to separate his obligations as President from his obligations to Rome, Jack responded with a measured, dignified speech that observers considered his finest statement of the campaign, but his father had already made his feelings known. "All I can say is that they have a hell of a nerve talking about freedom for the world," he wrote his favorite correspondent, Beaverbrook, "when we have this condition right here in our own country. It seems to me more important than ever to fight this thing with everything we have and that's what we are going to do." Yet at about the same time he wrote this letter he was complaining to Cardinal Cushing that many bishops were not endorsing Jack as they must to insure a large Catholic turnout. (When a Harris Poll showed Irish Catholics lagging behind Jews in support of JFK, the Ambassador fumed: "I think I'd better become a Jew.") He was especially angry with Cardinal Spellman, to whom he had contributed large sums of money for the New York Archdiocese. When Spellman met Nixon at the airport shortly before the election and rode with him in a Fifth Avenue parade, Joe Kennedy refused ever to speak to him again.

Another casualty was his long friendship with Arthur Krock. On October 20, the Ambassador called Krock, who had been expressing his distress at the Democrats' platform ever since the convention, and asked him to "quit the dull line" he was taking in the campaign—notably in criticisms of what he regarded as the party's too liberal positions on civil rights and insufficient resolve to fight inflation. If the candidate had been anyone but Jack, the Ambassador would have shared these doubts; but he expected loyalty to override political considerations. Krock defended himself and his journalistic obligation in a letter which brought a written response from Kennedy that summarily ended a relationship of some thirty years: "What I asked you to do was stop writing these fuzzy columns . . . and try to see such favorable sides of Jack as you are able to see in your other personal friends . . . I judge from reading your letter that you have made a federal case out of it. I haven't the slightest idea what you are talking about."

As the Ambassador moved around New York and other big states running what amounted to a one-man campaign office, some of Jack's friends worried that he would do harm. But Jack replied to one of those who brought the subject up: "Look, I can't control my father. He's an old man and he's having the time of his life going around helping me. Do you think that I can do anything about that, or that I'd want to?"

It was hard to find space between the candidates on the issues. (Schlesinger finally had to publish a pamphlet titled "Kennedy or Nixon—Does It Make Any Difference?") Communist China's sporadic firing on the offshore islands Quemoy and Matsu caused a furor during the second television debate and then returned to obscurity. Cuba threatened to surface when speech writer and strategist Richard Goodwin, acting on research which indicated that Castro was perceived as a bigger threat than Khrushchev, released a statement in mid-October charging that Cuban "fighters for freedom" were receiving "no support" from the Eisenhower Administration. Goodwin did not know that CIA chief Allen Dulles had briefed Kennedy after the convention, filling him in on the plan to invade Cuba that was already in the works. Jack was discomfited by the press release and told Stevenson, who was now campaigning for him, to "get back on high ground and say that Cuba [is] a problem for the [Organization of American States] ..." Nixon was even more discomfited; he was fully aware of the plot to destabilize the Castro regime and had in fact pressed for it to be carried out before the election so he could profit from it, but he now had to attack the Kennedy position as irresponsible, giving arguments against an invasion he actually supported.

All the Kennedys were mobilized. One old pol who invited them to a big gathering was stunned: "They pounced on the meeting like a squad of Marines in a commando operation." Eunice and Ethel campaigned in Texas (but resolutely refused Lady Bird Johnson's request that they wear ten-gallon hats). Teddy continued to work the western states and continued the daredevil stunts that had led him to go off ski jumps and ride wild broncos during the primary season. Rose, Pat, and Jean toured the women's clubs of America. Behind them all was Bobby, driving them and himself so remorselessly that even Kennedy loyalists were mumbling, "Little Brother Is Watching You."*

If Nixon looked more and more like some desperate shanty Irish, Jack looked more and more like the aristocratic politician, the first Irish Catholic Brahmin. He was wholly in his element. Chuck Spalding was with him at a point when the speeches were going well and the crowds were reacting not just politely but with near-hysteria. Jack looked over at him and whispered, "Is it possible that anything can equal this? Could there be anything, anywhere that would be better? It's got to be downhill from here."

Ultimately the election may have turned on a gesture. In late October, civil rights leader Martin Luther King, Jr., was arrested for a sit-in in Atlanta, summarily sentenced to four months' hard labor, and whisked off to the state penitentiary, where supporters feared he would be killed. Nixon's advisers urged him to speak out but he didn't. Jack was also publicly silent, but he called King's wife, Coretta, to offer support, and Bobby followed with a call to the judge. King was released, and his father switched his endorsement from Nixon to Kennedy, saying he would vote for the Devil himself if he wiped the tears off his daughter-in-law's face. (Jack commented that that was a "hell of a bigoted statement," but added, "Well, we all have fathers, don't we?") The Kennedys' gesture was not wholly the result of conscience. The Sunday before the election, pamphlets describing

---

*Bobby was the Kennedy ramrod, but he tolerated no criticism of other family members. *Time* correspondent Robert Ajemian recalls Bobby asking him for his reaction to his sisters' campaigning abilities. "Eunice was a little stodgy ..." Ajemian began, "and Pat was a little too flippant ..." Before he got any further, Bobby snapped at him: "If you say anything more I'm leaving the table!"

their support of King were distributed outside black churches all over the country. And as it worked out the black vote was crucial in such pivotal states as Illinois and Texas.

Jack voted in Boston from 122 Bowdoin Street, the address he had maintained since he first ran for Congress. Then he flew to Hyannis to join the rest of the family. He napped and took walks, talking with Cornelius Ryan, author of *The Longest Day,* comparing his wait for results with the wait of Allied soldiers about to land on Normandy beaches. At 7:15 P.M. the primitive IBM computer used as part of CBS's coverage projected a Nixon victory, giving odds of a hundred to one. Lighting one of the panatellas he smoked in moments of supreme confidence, Jack pronounced the machine crazy. Less than an hour later the network agreed, revising its estimate to predict a Kennedy victory with 51 percent of the vote. As the night wore on, Bobby manned the phones, repeatedly calling the crucial states—Michigan, Ohio, California, Illinois, Texas. When Jack went to bed at 4:00 A.M. Bobby stayed at the controls, waiting for the one state that would put them over the top. It finally came from Michigan at 5:45.

Jack was up at 9:00 the next morning and out for a stroll on the beach, now followed by guards from the Secret Service, which was not as laggard as Nixon in declaring the outcome of the election. He stopped at Bobby's house at 11:00 and was told that Eisenhower was sending a telegram. Finally word came that Nixon press aide Herb Klein was going to concede. Jack sat down and leaned into the tv set. Then, when Klein was finished, he slapped his knees and said: "All right, let's go."

There was a caravan of cars outside waiting to go to the Hyannis Armory, where the President-elect would meet the press. The whole crowd of family and friends piled in and were about to pull off when Pat noticed that Joe Kennedy was not with them. He was standing alone on the front porch, back in the shadows, a contented look on his face. Jack got out of the car and went back to get him, insisting that he come and hear the speech. It was the moment each of them in his own way had dreamed of.

8.

$\mathcal{T}$WO DAYS AFTER THE ELECTION, Jack met with aides at Bobby's house to begin the assumption of power. Sorensen, O'Donnell, and Salinger were named to the White House staff and given roles in the transition; Sargent Shriver was put in charge of compiling lists of candidates for major positions in the administration, while Larry O'Brien looked for people to fill secondary roles. Then Jack headed to Palm Beach to vacation with his father, dropping Jackie and Caroline off in Washington on the way.

It was hard for him to get used to the Secret Service men. Security had a value, as he recognized when agents arrested a Palm Beach man—disturbed by what he regarded as a "bought" election—who had loaded his car with dynamite and planned to ram the Kennedy limousine when Jack and the Ambassador left for mass; but security was surveillance as well as protection, and he knew it would now be more difficult for him to maintain the division between his public and private identities. During those first days at Palm Beach, he tried to get Secret Service agents lurking around his father's property to exchange their uniform of dark suits and mirrored sunglasses for something less conspicuous; the best he could get was a uniform of sport shirts and mirrored sunglasses. Once he impulsively ran down to the beach, dove into the ocean, and swam off to escape them. The next morning a Coast Guard cutter was on patrol not far from shore. Jack squinted at the ship and muttered, "Are they expecting Castro to invade Palm Beach?"

Concerned that the closeness of the popular vote and rumors about irregularities at the polls in Chicago might undermine the legitimacy of the new administration, the Ambassador arranged a meeting for Jack with his old friend, the GOP symbol Herbert Hoover. Hoover, in turn, called Richard Nixon and got him to agree to accept a courtesy call. Jack helicoptered to Key Biscayne for a brief meeting in which Nixon did most of the talking. After it was over, Kennedy shook his head and remarked to Kenny O'Donnell, ''It was just as well for all of us that he didn't make it.''

Later in the first week he flew to Texas for an overnight meeting at Johnson's ranch. Johnson insisted that Jack, O'Donnell, Torbert MacDonald, and others in the retinue get up at 5:00 A.M. to shoot deer. Reluctantly complying with this Pedernales manhood ritual, Jack took three shots to down his buck, which his Vice President-elect insisted on sending to a taxidermist and later presented to Jack as a memento for the Oval Office.

After a week back in Palm Beach talking about cabinet appointments, Jack flew to Washington to spend Thanksgiving Day with Jackie and Caroline in Georgetown. He was returning to Florida aboard the *Caroline* that night when word was radioed that Jackie had gone into labor and been rushed to the hospital. Recalling his absence during her miscarriage in 1956, which had nearly wrecked their marriage, he murmured, ''I'm never there when she needs me.'' When the *Caroline* set down in Palm Beach, he boarded a faster DC-6 and headed back to Washington. Word arrived en route that Jackie had given birth to a baby boy by Caesarian section. As the vital statistics were relayed over the intercom, the press corps—which now traveled with him everywhere—applauded. Smoking one of his panatellas, Jack bowed elaborately and then sat back down to resume discussions about the men who would make up his administration.

Over the next few weeks he flew thousands of miles on the corridor connecting Hyannis, Washington, and Palm Beach. While in Florida he was constantly with his father, playing golf with him, taking walks. It was as if the long exile which had pushed Joe Kennedy into the background during the campaign had ended and Jack had come home to him. When one newspaperman asked the Ambassador if it was accidental that he was now so visible when he had been virtually in hiding for over a year, Joe Kennedy eyed him disparagingly: ''There are no accidents in politics. I can appear any time I want to with my son now.''

The old man didn't try to insinuate himself into the planning that went on at all hours in Palm Beach. But he was frequently present at the meetings, perhaps putting in a word or two, more often in the background, keenly watching the groups of visitors, evaluating their advice and observing Jack as if he were a critic at a performance. Chuck Spalding was with him when he watched television coverage of Jack's December 9 courtesy call on President Eisenhower. The Ambassador watched the set, speaking to Spalding but also his son, talking to the image on the screen as if it was that of an athlete in a sporting event. ''There! Now he's doing it! He's getting to look more and more like a President every day!''

The look and feel of his presidency to come was much on Jack's mind too —what to make of the office, how to seize and subordinate it. Although Schlesinger and some of the other intellectuals around him were already applying the chic term "existentialist" to him, he was typically pragmatic in his approach, concerned less with developing a compelling personal vision about what he should do than with developing in an almost literary sense how, whatever he did, he should look.

The most persuasive vision of the role awaiting him had come from the Columbia historian Richard Neustadt, a student of the presidency, whom he had asked, along with Clark Clifford, to advise on the transition. Neustadt submitted memos with specific advice (the National Security Council should be reorganized, for instance, into a policy-making prosthetic capable of reaching around State Department inertia rather than simply a filter for ideas, which it had been under Eisenhower), but it was through his recently published book, *Presidential Power*, that he was most influential. On the *Caroline* one day shortly after the election, Neustadt handed Jack a copy and recommended that he read two chapters. Proud of his speed reading, which he insisted allowed him to absorb twelve hundred words a minute, Jack said he would read the whole book.* What he found was something like a contemporary equivalent of Machiavelli's advice in *The Prince*—a rationale for circumventing bureaucratic routine and using heroic imagery to enhance his position with the electorate. Great presidents, Neustadt noted, are those who constantly calculate effects and design situations that will result in domestic political advantage. They are artists whose medium is power; actors who learn to use the dramaturgy of high office; and most of all politicians who continue to campaign using the presidency as a platform. Contrasting Roosevelt and Eisenhower in the use of the presidency—to the latter's disadvantage—Neustadt implied that the quest for power is not "dangerous" but natural, indicative of emotional balance. FDR was an enthusiastic student of power who "wanted mastery, projected that desire on the office and fulfilled it there with every sign of feeling that he had come into his own." Ike was ambivalent about power and therefore "his confidence was highest when he could assure himself that personal advantage had no place among his aims." Roosevelt kept his options open and thus enlarged his opportunities for personal influence; Eisenhower had surrounded himself with protective structures which limited his personal initiatives.

"Fascinating stuff," Jack said to Neustadt on finishing his book, thus insuring that the political scientist would become something of a cult figure in the early days of the Kennedy presidency. In fact Jack became a little

---

*He had taken a four-week speed-reading course in Baltimore, arranged for the top executives of Emerson Drug, which Lem Billings invited him and Bobby (who was then chief counsel of the McClellan Committee) to attend.

annoyed at how well *Presidential Power* was doing. When somebody remarked on its sales, he said, "Yeah, we're pushing it." Yet he remained taken by the message that a President was not just an executor but also a politician who could use the office as part of a shrewd effort at image building.

Jack asked Neustadt to prepare two more memos—on how FDR had used the Budget Bureau and how he had used his staff. The legacy of Roosevelt and the comparison to Eisenhower were already very much on his mind and on the minds of advisers close to him. James MacGregor Burns, a student of FDR, had postulated Roosevelt as the ultimate leader, a President able to reshape the national consensus by his use of the office. Arthur Schlesinger, Jr., another student of the New Deal, who had developed his historian father's theory that American politics alternated between periods of great creative energy (as in FDR's administration) and periods of calm and retrenchment, suggested to Jack in a postelection memorandum that "vigorous public leadership would be the essence of the next phase."

"From the very beginning Jack was attracted to a mythic persona," says one friend close to the transition process. "He liked the idea of being a streamlined version of FDR. The only problem was that with Roosevelt the reputation had been the result of some fairly bold acts. Jack would have liked to be seen in those heroic terms, but he was basically very cautious in his approach to the presidency." He told Sorensen specifically to place a line in the Inaugural Address he was drafting that would disclaim any intention to repeat Roosevelt's dramatic first hundred days; the theory he was working on presumed a gradual accretion of power that would culminate in an overwhelming 1964 reelection. His first appointments, to the dismay of O'Donnell and other aides, were to reconfirm J. Edgar Hoover as FBI director and Allen Dulles at the CIA.

He told O'Donnell that he would ignore the advice of Schlesinger, Galbraith, and other Harvard liberals who, he felt, wanted to fill Washington with "wild-eyed ADA people."* Similarly, he intended to ignore people such as O'Brien and O'Donnell himself, who would have brought so many Irish Catholics to town, he said, that they would have had to start a Knights of Columbus chapter in the White House. Instead of the Americans for Democratic Action and other liberal lobbyists and his own "Irish Mafia," Jack listened to the kinds of people whose advice had always counted with him—Joe Alsop, Philip Graham, and of course his father. He listened to banker John J. McCloy, even former Secretary of State Dean Acheson, with whom he had always had a cool relationship—men who strongly represented

---

*Jack had appointed Schlesinger to the White House staff, he told O'Donnell, to hold Adlai Stevenson's hand and field complaints of liberals likely to become disgruntled over the next few years. He also noted that since Schlesinger obviously intended to write a history of the administration, he might as well do it as a coconspirator.

Establishment thinking. "In many ways," Lem Billings said, "Jack still felt something of an upstart, an Irish Catholic who looked to the Brahmins for a model of how to act.

Most influential of all the Brahmins was Robert Lovett. A Republican banker who had been a key figure in the Roosevelt years and Secretary of Defense under Truman, Lovett was often called "Mr. National Security," and Jack tried to get him to become Secretary of Defense or State, but he refused because of failing health. Lovett suggested Harvard dean McGeorge Bundy for the State Department. Jack was impressed by Bundy, but decided that he was too young for State, and instead brought him into the National Security Council. After ruling out Stevenson because he had a constituency of his own, Jack finally picked Dean Rusk, head of the Rockefeller Foundation and another of Lovett's candidates, as Secretary of State.

Lovett had also mentioned Robert McNamara, head of the Ford Motor Company, as a possible cabinet choice. McNamara had been a bright young man working under Lovett during World War II to bring efficiency and precision to the Air Force survey of the effectiveness of its bombing offensives. In checking McNamara out, Sargent Shriver too had been impressed. The former "whiz kid" was not just another corporation executive. He chose to live in the intellectually stimulating ambience of Ann Arbor rather than in some posh Detroit suburb. He was involved in the life of the community and in the ideas of the day. (He had, in fact, been reading *The Phenomenon of Man* when he was first approached, causing Shriver, himself interested in popular theology, to ask enthusiastically, "How many other automobile executives or cabinet ministers read Teilhard de Chardin?") In their first meeting, Jack interrogated McNamara closely, interested as always in understanding someone whose life had been so different from his own. McNamara took Kennedy aback by asking, in turn, if *Profiles* had been written without a coauthor. Having settled that matter, Jack sounded him out on the Treasury post, which McNamara wasn't interested in, and then chose him as Secretary of Defense, which he saw as one of the storm centers of his administration.

Of the remaining posts, the one that drew the most attention was Treasury. Kennedy was interested in C. Douglas Dillon, prominent Republican Under Secretary of State for Eisenhower and scion of the famous investment banking firm Dillon Read. Galbraith and other liberal economists were not enthusiastic, nor was the Ambassador, as ever suspicious of Wall Street. But someone who would reassure the financial community was exactly what Jack wanted, and so Dillon was in.

While filling the major cabinet posts, Jack was also creating opportunities that would bring his friends to Washington. Chuck Spalding refused a post in the Defense Department, telling Jack he thought it would adversely affect their relationship if he was part of the administration. But Red Fay accepted the job of Under Secretary of the Navy and Jim Reed took a job in the Treasury Department. Jack considered Lem Billings for jobs in the Commerce Department, the Post Office, and the Peace Corps, but was unable to come up with anything that suited Lem's unique talent as best friend.

By mid-December the only major position left unfilled was the Attorney Generalship, and the only important person left unplaced was Bobby. He had been the family's candidate for the job at Justice at least since the previous Christmas when Jack was getting ready to announce for the presidency, and everyone was already joking about the rewards and punishments to be dispensed once they got to the White House. "Bobby we'll make Attorney General, so he can throw all the people Dad doesn't like into jail," Eunice had joked. "They'll have to build more jails."

Jack had offered Bobby the position right after the election, but, in conflict between wanting to be in the thick of things in Washington and wanting to create his own career instead of continuing as Jack's appendage, Bobby had refused. He was worried about charges of nepotism, he said, also pointing out that he had been "chasing bad men for three years" and didn't want to spend the rest of his life doing that. Another possibility for Bobby had been the Defense Department. One of the options Jack had offered Lovett was becoming Secretary there for just one year, making Bobby his Under Secretary and eventual replacement. There had also been talk of a job on the White House staff, where the Sorensen and O'Donnell factions were already feuding. But Bobby felt that such a role would put him squarely under Jack's thumb. "I had to do something on my own," he said later, "have my own area of responsibility.... I had to be apart from [Jack] so I wasn't working directly for him and getting orders from him about what I should do that day." Jack had offered to have him appointed to the Senate seat he was vacating, but Bobby indignantly said that the only way he'd go to the Senate would be by election on his own, and so Jack had his old Harvard roommate Ben Smith appointed with the understanding that he would keep the seat warm for Teddy.*

As the rest of the cabinet was being assembled, Bobby had talked about being on his own, traveling and writing and perhaps running for the Massachusetts governorship some day. Justice Douglas, with whom he'd discussed his future shortly after the election, had agreed that this would probably be the best course for him. But Joe Kennedy had remained ada-

---

*Jack had originally intended the Senate seat to go to his old friend from Harvard days, Torbert MacDonald. "Jack had said to Torb, 'When I'm President, what is it that you want me to do?'" his widow remembers. MacDonald, the second-most charismatic politician in Massachusetts, who had already declined opportunities to run for governor, told Jack that he wanted the Senate seat. Jack agreed, "but Mr. Kennedy put his foot down." At the inaugural, Mrs. MacDonald saw Jack at one of the dinner parties. "When he came into the room, the first thing he said was, 'I'm sorry about the Senate seat.' It was painful."

mant that Bobby must go to Washington with Jack.* "He felt that the President should have somebody that was close to him and had been close to him for a long period of time and he wanted me for the job," Bobby said later. "We had some rather strong arguments out here, all the family—a couple of my sisters, Jack, Teddy, and my father."

At 7:00 A.M. on December 14, Bobby pushed his way through the press watch already gathered in front of Jack's Georgetown house for a final summit conference with his brother. The previous night Jack had called and again offered the Attorney General's job. Again Bobby had demurred, only to have his brother cut him off by saying, "Don't tell me now. I want to have breakfast with you in the morning." But as far as Bobby was concerned, the matter was settled. After hanging up the phone, he had shaken his head and said to Ethel: "This is going to kill my father."

He brought his friend John Seigenthaler with him to the meeting, as if to have someone to bolster his resolve. With Jack's black maid Provi making bustling sounds in the kitchen, the three men sat down in the living room and chatted about recent events, Jack expressing special amusement over the way Rusk, whom they had already identified as something of a square, had called Stevenson the previous day and convinced him that it was his patriotic duty to take the job of U.N. Ambassador although he was still fuming over having been bypassed for State.

Finally Bobby looked at Jack and said, "Well, Johnny, what about me?" Jack began to go over the arguments, looking at Seigenthaler but obviously appealing to his brother in words that evoked the Irish insularity they still shared: "I need someone I can completely and totally and absolutely rely on, somebody who's going to tell me what the best judgment is, my best interest. There's not a member of the cabinet I can trust in that way." Then he turned and faced Bobby to describe the delicacy of the problems facing the new administration and enumerate the qualities of toughness and loyalty the new Attorney General would have to possess, qualities which Bobby alone had: "Sure I can call you on the telephone, but what I really need is someone who's there, available to meet with me. I have nobody. There is nobody." Having made this appeal, as close to an avowal of love as any outsider would ever witness between the two brothers, Jack stood up, asked Seigenthaler if he wanted more eggs, and disappeared into the kitchen.

Realizing that the issue had been decided by Jack's frank admission of need, Seigenthaler toyed with his coffee cup for a few moments and then said, "Well, I guess we'd better go." Bobby replied, "No, wait," a note of desperation in his voice: "I've got some arguments." Just then Jack came

---

*Clark Clifford, one of the transition advisers, had been against Bobby's appointment and JFK had sent him to try to convince the Ambassador. Joe Kennedy listened politely as Clifford presented his case and then said, "Thank you very much. I appreciate that. Now we'll turn to some other subject because Bobby is going to be Attorney General."

back into the room, smiling triumphantly, knowing that he had won: "So
that's it, gentlemen. Let's grab our balls and go."* As they were getting
ready to face reporters with a decision that was sure to draw fire (less against
him for making the offer than against Bobby for accepting), Jack lightly
ridiculed his brother about his unruly hair, closing the emotional opening
which he had momentarily created.

Bobby later said that the appointment showed his brother had "the guts
of a burglar." Jack had indeed snatched an important position for a member
of his family. But it was also true that he had stolen into Bobby's life, taken
his independence, and hooked him forever to the older brother's fate. It was
somehow embodied in the Christmas present he and Jackie gave Bobby, a
calf-bound copy of *The Enemy Within* which Jackie had inscribed with her
usual grace: "To Bobby who made the impossible possible." Jack, disdain-
ing that sentimentality, summoned instead the tone of sharp teasing which
was part of their *lingua familia:* "For Bobby—the Brother Within—who
made the easy difficult."

Jack looked to the Inaugural as the event that would dramatize the break
with the past he had promised his administration would accomplish. He had
asked Robert Frost, whose "miles to go before I sleep" had functioned as a
getaway line during his hundreds of campaign appearances, to write a poem
for what they both hoped would begin "a golden age of poetry and power."
Marian Anderson would sing the national anthem. Frank Sinatra and his
retinue of stars would add a sheen to the galas planned for before and after
Kennedy was sworn in.

The centerpiece would be the Inaugural Address itself—not just the usual
collection of platitudes and pieties, but a summation of everything Jack
hoped to stand for: a call to arms; an invitation to the new era. Jack had
told Sorensen to study the Gettysburg Address before beginning to draft the
speech and to try to extract its "secret." (Sorensen concluded, with a tech-
nician's eye, that Lincoln had "never used two or three words where one
word would do.") As the address progressed through endless drafts, it became a sort of anthology of the things Jack had been saying for the past
year, a distillation of the rhetoric that had gotten him elected. Domestic
issues were omitted because he saw them as too complex and "divisive."
Pains were taken to advise Moscow that the torch was being passed from old,
infirm hands to the hands of young, capable men not uncomfortable with the
implications of power; and to inform Americans that in the coming era no
sacrifice would be too great.

Three days before the Inaugural, Jack flew up from Palm Beach with the

---

*The association of Bobby's appointment with "balls" antedates this particular meet-
ing. Two days earlier, when he was being pressed to take the job, Bobby said to Jack,
"If you announce me as Attorney General they'll kick our balls off . . . " Jack replied, "You hold on to your balls and I'll make the announcement."

final draft of his speech; he went over it one final time and then put the original into the drawer of a desk in the *Caroline*. "An early draft of Roosevelt's Inaugural was discovered the other day," he observed with a fey smile, "and brought $200,000 at an auction."

On the day before his swearing in, Jack went to the White House to see Eisenhower again. The first time had been a courtesy call. This time real power was being surrendered and embraced. The President said that only the recognition of China would move him to attack the new administration and lead a popular movement against it. He passed lightly over Cuba and concentrated on Laos, which he forecast would be his successor's primary trouble spot, eventually requiring the commitment of American ground troops. Jack was prepared to be scornful of Eisenhower. His whole posture during the last year had been to imply that the administration's inaction had allowed problems to fester and grow. And when he returned from this briefing he said to an aide, "How can he stare disaster in the face with such equanimity?" Eisenhower, like his own father, was also a monumental figure, a man who had made history; but Eisenhower was oddly innocent of his heroic stature, something Jack found fascinating. (The next day, riding with him in the bubbletop Lincoln, Jack would bring up the subject of D-Day and find to his surprise that Eisenhower hadn't read *The Longest Day,* and that instead of talking about the grand design of this epic event, the man who commanded the invasion said that the Allies had probably prevailed because they had superior meteorologists.)

As Jack was concluding his White House visit a violent storm was dropping eight inches of snow on Washington, blotting out the green dye that Forest Service workers had sprayed onto the lawns around the Washington Monument to give the next day's ceremonies a touch of spring. Some three thousand men worked feverishly through the night with plows to clear the most traveled thoroughfares. The next day was cold and clear. As workers used Army flamethrowers to melt the remaining ice on the streets and sidewalks, Joseph Kennedy was putting on the cutaway he had worn when he presented his credentials to the King twenty-two years earlier (just as Rose was completing minor alterations on the dress in which she had been presented at Court to wear at that evening's inaugural ball). A few days earlier the Ambassador had talked with Hugh Sidey about what would happen to the Kennedys. He saw correctly that his son, who had always covered his tracks so expertly and prided himself on being hard to know, was now about to disappear forever into the national mythology. "Jack doesn't belong any more to a family," he had said. "He belongs to the country." Kennedy talked about how it was America's last opportunity to grasp "the brass ring"; it was do or die. Then he concluded somberly: "Jack is the fellow who will give his life to his country."

He and Rose were seated near Jack when he took the oath of office on the

Fitzgerald family Bible, Douay Version. He was strikingly different from the scrawny, malarial, death-obsessed young man who had entered politics fifteen years before, dwarfed by the giant shadow of his older brother. He was full-faced, partly from the medicine he took and partly from a heaviness that had settled on him as he came into his own. When he exhorted his countrymen to be equal to the ''long twilight struggle'' in their ''hour of maximum danger,'' in a speech that contrasted starkly with Eisenhower's farewell address earlier, with its emphasis not on external threats but on concentrations of economic and military power at home, the elder Kennedys alone could fully appreciate Jack's own struggles and the dangers he had so improbably overcome.

After the torch had been passed, Joe Kennedy went to the luncheon he'd ordered up for the family at the Mayflower Hotel. He found a table the size of a squash court set up in the hotel's buffet room, and hundreds of people, most of whom he'd never seen, milling about. ''Who are these people?'' he demanded of future White House social secretary Tish Baldridge, whom he'd put in charge of the luncheon. ''Your family, Mr. Ambassador,'' she replied. ''They are not,'' Kennedy said. ''Just who are these freeloaders? I want to know exactly why you asked them.'' Baldridge said that they were indeed family—not just Kennedys and Kennedy in-laws, but Fitzgeralds, Bouviers, and Auchinclosses. The Ambassador approached five or six and asked their names. Then he returned to Baldridge and muttered a gruff apology: ''They *are* all family and it's the last time we get them all together, too, if I have anything to say about it.''

As he passed through the crowd looking for real family members, Kennedys, people asked him if he felt different on this day. He insisted that he did not. Yet what had come about was his triumph almost as much as Jack's— the result of a peculiar collaboration working at levels below the consciousness of either man. It hadn't turned out the way he had planned: it was the seemingly ill-suited second son, a stand-in for his brother, who'd made it to the top. Yet it was a result, however unexpected, of forces this son had inherited and dramatically enlarged. As Jack told the world that a new generation was taking power in America, bonfires were being lighted in Ireland at the same stone quayside in New Ross from which the first Kennedy, Patrick Joseph—Joe Kennedy's grandfather—had begun his journey to America a hundred and eleven years earlier. As its ultimate destination was reinterpreted by the Ambassador, it was a journey that had taken almost three lifetimes to complete, the final step having been taken by one who was both the least and most Kennedy of them all.

Attaining the presidency was like arriving on the shores of America yet again—a discovery. After the luncheon filled with strangers who were part of his family, the Ambassador went back to his room to rest. Jack finished reviewing the seemingly endless inaugural parade and began getting ready to step into the swirl of inaugural galas planned for that evening—one last taste of the subtle riches of society before going to work. If he was the first Irish Catholic Brahmin, he was still part of a clan of immigrants. And the rest of the family didn't wait for his arrival to swarm to the White House on a chartered tour bus. They prowled through the corridors, talking about the place in hushed tones, pointing things out to each other, touching the surfaces. Lem Billings and Eunice got away from the rest and made their way upstairs. They were the first ones to find the Lincoln bedroom and took turns bouncing on the bed, giggling like children and photographing each other stretched out on the counterpane. Then Jack's favorite sister looked at his best friend. "You know what this reminds me of?" she asked. "That scene in *Gone with the Wind* where Scarlett's colored servants move into Tara with her after the war. I feel like the old mammy who takes a look around and then says, 'Man, we's rich now.'"

BROTHERS WITHIN

There are two kinds of tragedy. One is not getting what you want. The other is getting it.

—OSCAR WILDE

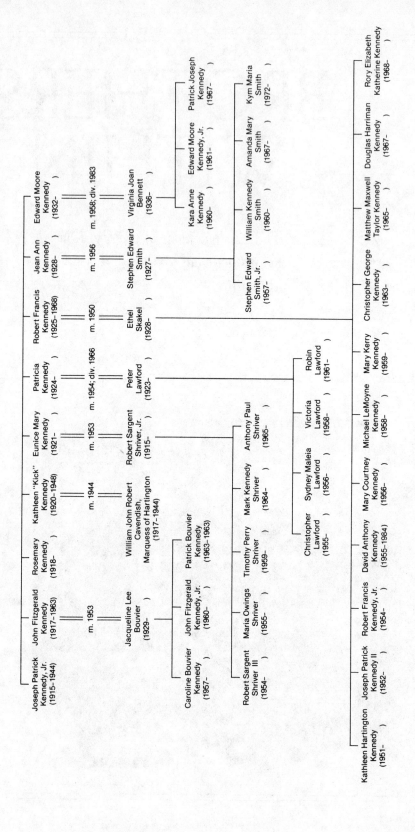

1.

ON THE FIRST DAY OF HIS presidency, Jack Kennedy called John Kenneth Galbraith and asked him to come to the White House for a breakfast conference on the balance of payments. When the economist arrived, Jack decided they should take a tour before getting down to business. "I've never seen anything but the state rooms. I want to see everything—the closets, the pantries, everything." He led Galbraith through the White House rooms, making acid comments about the former occupants and using his recently acquired knowledge of antiques —the result of tutorials by Jackie and Lem Billings—to assay the furnishings. Once he got down on his hands and knees to inspect the underside of a dresser. "Ken, look at this," he said to Galbraith incredulously. "It's not even authentic. It's not even a good reproduction!"

From the outset Jack was determined to furnish his presidency with acts that were original and authentic. In his desire to "keep all options open"— one of the phrases from Richard Neustadt's book which was often quoted in the weeks after the inauguration—he avoided committing himself to a specific political program. But his psychological agenda was always clear: to put a thumbprint on history, and, as he frankly (if somewhat ironically) admitted to Lem and others, to achieve "greatness." His approach was not so much to be equal to the problems he inherited—an inchoate mix ranging from economic stagnation to a growing civil rights movement—as it was to locate crises equal to the historical self he wanted to acquire. His intention to enlarge the stakes facing the country and his presidency was apparent in the State of the Union message he delivered a week after taking office: "Before my term has ended we shall have to test whether a nation organized as our own can endure ... Each day the crises multiply. Each day the solution becomes more difficult. Each day we draw nearer to the hour of maximum danger ...''

He had arrived in Washington as one who had ignored the political rules. And while he wanted to be acknowledged as chief player of the game ("his immigrant side still seeking acceptance," Jackie called it), he was not interested in patiently building congressional coalitions or becoming a spokesman for consensus. He and the men he had brought into government—"the junior officers of the Second World War finally come to power," Walt Rostow's wife nicely defined them—regarded bureaucracy with the same suspicion they had regarded the top brass billeted far from the front. They wanted to create a style that was crisp and efficient, yet flexible and informal. Trying to find an analogy for the distinctive ambience of the new administration, Rostow had said that it was like an extended family. Lem Billings refined the concept even more by claiming that the new administration reminded him strongly of the Kennedy family into which he had been introduced thirty years earlier: a swirl of creative chaos, with everyone ignoring channels and competing for Jack's attention as he and his brothers and sisters had once competed for the Ambassador's.

An institutional symbol of what Jack and the new guard he'd brought to Washington were struggling against was the State Department, that giant beast squatting in a Foggy Bottom lair of procedure and inaction. Talking with his friend Senator George Smathers shortly after the inauguration, Jack grumbled, "You know how many people they employ there? Thousands! You know how many I get to appoint? Hundreds! Hell, they've got their own damned government over there. I'm not going to be able to change their thinking." A congressman who came to the Oval Office for a meeting got a similar message. "I know how they are at the State Department," the President said when the subject came up. "They're not queer, but, well, they're sort of like Adlai."

The institution which seemed an antidote for this torpor and stodginess was the CIA. Joseph Kennedy, who had seen the Agency up close as a member of Eisenhower's Foreign Intelligence Advisory Board, had a bearish view of it: "I know this outfit and I wouldn't pay them a hundred bucks a week." But Jack, always something of a secret agent himself, working for his own clandestine desires under cover of respectability, found the organization's lack of protocol, rhetoric, or moral posture attractive. He liked the élan and the efficiency, and told Bundy in his first days in office, "I don't care what it is, but if I need something fast, the CIA is the place I go ...''

Jack scorned the religious fervor with which John Foster Dulles had prosecuted the cold war, the moralistic framework which he believed had ossified diplomacy and ceded international initiative to the Soviets. Yet he was no less committed to the contest than Dulles had been. The United States was still far ahead of the Soviet Union in economic performance. It was also comfortably superior in military power, as Robert McNamara had determined in his first weeks at the Defense Department, when research showed that the missile gap was in fact a fiction. (General Maxwell Taylor, soon to be a central figure in the administration, always remembered Jack interrupting a meeting to look around the room with his fey smile and ask, "Who ever believed in the missile gap anyway?") Nonetheless going ahead with the military buildup he had promised in his campaign, Jack also moved to confront the Soviets in two areas where they did have a lead. One was space.* The other and more crucial area was Third World countries like Laos, the Congo, and Cuba, where the Soviets had made significant inroads.

Shortly after taking office, Jack had distributed to the National Security Council and Joint Chiefs of Staff a speech in which Soviet Premier Khrushchev claimed that communism would overcome not through conventional war but by "wars of national liberation" launched in the Third World. Since his days as senator, Jack had believed that the grand international drama of the postwar period would revolve around decolonization. Rostow, whom Jack was billing as his "Marx," had provided a rationale for a new globalism: "If over the coming decades the United States should turn its back on the great revolutionary transformation going forward in the underdeveloped countries, devoting itself [instead] to domestic chores and obligations, American society will progressively lose some of the basic spiritual qualities which have historically been linked to the nation's sense of world mission." Yet figures like Ho Chi Minh, Castro, Sukarno, and the others Rostow called Romantic Revolutionaries fascinated Jack for reasons that went beyond cold war politics and the conflict with the Soviet Union. He saw that they had seized the imagination of the world, upstaging the leaders of the European nations. They were the ones making history. "He seemed to regard these people as if they were Boston Brahmins who had some exclusive club they were trying to prevent the Irish from joining," Adlai Stevenson told one acquaintance. "He wanted the dignity of Harold Macmillan, but he also wanted to ignite the passions that Castro did."

Two of the early foreign policy initiatives of the new administration, the Peace Corps and the attempt to help Latin American development through the Alliance for Progress, were attempts to join this ideological battle on equal terms, so that the United States was not merely fighting a defensive rear-guard action as in the Eisenhower era. ("Let us once again transform the [Western hemisphere] into a vast crucible of revolutionary ideas and efforts," Jack had said in announcing the Alliance.) Yet the revolutionary

---

*Jack wrote Werner von Braun in April to see if there was some dramatic way of leapfrogging ahead of the Soviets: "Do we have a chance of beating [them] by putting a laboratory in space, or by a trip around the moon and back with a man? Is there any space program which promises dramatic results which we could win?"

situation of the Third World remained a threat far more than an opportunity. In February, Jack placed an item on the NSC agenda: "We need to develop a doctrine and a policy for the deterrence of guerrilla warfare and begin to apply it soon in concrete cases." And when an interviewer sat down with him to get an impression of his first few weeks in office, Jack mentioned that he had been reading Mao Tse-tung, Che Guevara, and other revolutionary strategists for hints about the guerrilla mentality, sheepishly admitting that one of the books on his shelf was *Guerrilla Warfare: The Irish Republican Army.* "How do you control guerrillas?" he asked the interviewer out of the blue.

One possible answer presented itself when Rostow brought Jack a copy of a report by the mysterious General Edward Lansdale. Architect of the anti-guerrilla campaign against Huk insurgents in the Philippines and also a military observer in Saigon (where his shadowy activities recommended him to Graham Greene as a prototype for *The Quiet American*), Lansdale, whose romantic legend had brought him little official recognition in military circles, painted a gloomy picture of things in Vietnam, where he had watched Eisenhower's six hundred advisers try to use traditional methods for training Ngo Dinh Diem's army. Something more than merely "killing guerrillas" was needed, Lansdale contended in his report. It was necessary to have a counterguerrilla force that would stand by the local peasantry under assault, learning the language, living off the land, promoting democratic alternatives. The people could not be bludgeoned into acquiescence; their hearts and minds had to be won.

After reading Lansdale's report, Jack asked Rostow to look into what was being done in counterinsurgency. When the Army's Special Forces at Fort Bragg were brought to his attention, Jack ordered the thousand-man operation enlarged immediately, ignoring the well-known resistance to elite forces among the Pentagon top brass. He also ordered that special warfare centers be set up, personally selected the new force's equipment and weapons, and even modified the soldiers' gear, suggesting for instance that infantry boots be replaced by sneakers fitted with steel insoles capable of repelling sharpened bamboo stakes.

From the moment of his election, Jack had denied the relevance of comparisons measuring his administration by FDR's first hundred days. That outburst of legislative achievement had been possible, he pointed out repeatedly, because the Depression was a time of crisis, evoking a sacrifice and commitment he felt people were not willing to make in 1960. Yet at the end of his own first ten weeks in office, at least in his attitude toward the rest of the world, there was a sense of latency; a feeling that everything was ready and waiting for the first shoe to drop. In the April 3 edition of the *New Republic*, McGeorge Bundy was quoted as saying, "At this point we are like the Harlem Globetrotters, passing forward, behind, sideways and underneath. But nobody has made a basket yet.'' In fact, the game that would contain all these elements in Jack's world view—the clandestine mobility of the CIA, the shadowboxing with the Russians in the Third World, and the romance of guerrilla warfare—was about to get under way. It was not in Laos, where Eisenhower and the rest of the smart money believed the first engagement would be, but in Cuba.

Point man for the action that culminated in the Bay of Pigs was CIA Deputy Director Richard Bissell. Before World War II, Bissell had been a teacher at Yale, numbering Bundy and Rostow among his bright young men. Since then he had become something of a legend in the Agency as head of covert operations, masterminding the coup which overthrew the Arbenz government in Guatemala in 1954 and overseeing the secret development of the U-2 spy plane. Understanding the administration's closet romanticism exactly, Bissell had struck just the right tone of sang-froid when he first introduced himself to the New Frontiersmen : ''I'm your man-eating shark.'' Jack had been so impressed that he decided after a few weeks that Bissell would be an ideal replacement for aging CIA chief Allen Dulles.

The nucleus of Bissell's Cuba plan—infiltrating anti-Castro guerrillas onto the island so that they could link up with opponents of the regime— had been approved by Eisenhower in mid-1960. Under a flexible mandate from Eisenhower, Bissell had expanded the original concept so that by November 27, when he first told Jack about it in a post-election briefing at Palm Beach, the force had grown to some fifteen hundred men who would be backed by a rebel air force of war-surplus B-26s and escorted to its invasion point by a naval task force.

During the first few months of the Kennedy Administration, the plan continued to develop. Worrying about possible failure, but also anticipating the sweetness of success, Jack was profoundly ambivalent. He insisted that the military be allowed to review the plan, but didn't intervene when the CIA gave only a verbal briefing instead of providing the Joint Chiefs with detailed plans. He vetoed one landing site at Trinidad Bay because he felt it would require the equivalent of a World War II invasion, but he did not apply the same criterion when Bissell came up with a substitute site at the Bay of Pigs. Clandestine, romantic, audacious, the plan had all the elements that appealed to him. It seemed, moreover, to have all the advantages of a sure bet : large rewards for a relatively small risk. Yet he kept postponing the target date and arguing over details. When confronted by Arthur Schlesinger with a memorandum opposing the plan, he hedged : ''You know, I've reserved the right to stop this thing up to twenty-four hours before the landing. In the meantime I'm trying to make some sense out of it. We'll just have to see.''

The vacillation finally exasperated Bissell. ''He kept telling Kennedy,

'You can't *mañana* this thing,' " CIA Deputy Director Robert Amory later recalled. " 'You can cancel it, in which case you've got a disposal problem. What will we do with the fifteen hundred people? They'll run amok in Central Park or something.' "

But if he was cautious himself, Jack was impatient with the caution of others, which he saw, typically, as effeminacy. When Sorensen tried to find out more about the plan, Jack cut him short with the curt observation: "Everyone's trying to grab their nuts on this." Yet as late as mid-March, long after he had officially "signed on," he continued to convey irresolution. Meeting Dean Rusk at the White House on other matters, Jack steered him into the Rose Garden for a private talk. "Do you know anything about the Cuba proposal?" he asked. "I didn't even know there was one," Rusk replied. After Kennedy had outlined Bissell's proposal, the Secretary of State, taken aback by the amateurishness, asked Jack if he was serious. "I don't know if I'm serious or not," he answered, "but this is the proposal and I've been thinking about it and *it* is serious..." Rusk came away from the meeting with the impression that the "proposal," if carried out, would probably not be a major event. When Chester Bowles, his Under Secretary, caught wind of the plan on the Washington grapevine and tried to caution against it, Rusk downplayed its significance. Trying to get a specific idea of its scope, Bowles asked the Secretary if it was large enough to make the front page of the *New York Times*. "I wouldn't think so," Rusk replied.

Bobby wasn't told about the plan until four or five days before the invasion, when Bissell came to the Justice Department to brief him. However, some of Jack's close friends found out earlier. Chuck Spalding was at Glen Ora, the Virginia estate Jackie had taken as a family retreat from White House pressure, a week before the invasion's D-Day. Perhaps because Spalding, more than any of his other friends, shared his literary interest in history, Jack told him what was about to happen so that he could appreciate history in the making.

A week later, on Sunday, April 17, Jack was again at Glen Ora with Jackie and Lem when the first air strikes were launched from one of the rebel staging areas in Nicaragua. In his desire to keep the plan at a "low profile," he ordered Bissell by phone to reduce the planes involved from sixteen to six. The result was that when the B-26s went back to their base, only six of the fifty-five planes of the Cuban air force had been destroyed. Other aspects of the plan were also beginning to fray at the edges. American reporters had seen through the clumsy fiction of the Cuban "defector" who had landed a plane in Florida that was doctored to look Cuban, quickly identifying the pilot as a member of the Miami exile community and thus embarrassing Adlai Stevenson, who had been using the event to deny charges of United States involvement with eloquent innocence at the U.N. To complete the shambles, the provisional government in exile, which the CIA had planned to fly into Cuba for a takeover after the invasion succeeded, had become so difficult when kept from any operational involvement that its members had to be carted off to a remote part of Florida and held incommunicado.

Despite these auguries, Jack phoned Bissell and gave him the final go-ahead to send in the landing craft carrying the exile army to its destination. However, when Rusk called Glen Ora not long afterward and said he was worried about repercussions at the U.N., Jack, in another fateful ad hoc decision, canceled the second air strike which was intended to give the invasion force cover.

By Monday morning, as the exiles' Brigade 2506 began landing at the Bay of Pigs, Castro's Russian-built jet trainers swooped down and sank two of the ships containing ammunition reserves and most of the communications equipment. The men who landed were soon pinned down by Cuban militia. With the plan coming unraveled, Jack returned to the White House. He called his father, the first of several telephone contacts with Palm Beach that day as the news from the landing zone worsened. (After one of these conversations, Rose asked her husband how he was and he said he felt like he was "dying.") Jack also put in a call to Williamsburg, Virginia, where Bobby had a speaking engagement. "I don't think it's going as well as it should," Jack said. Bobby knew from the sound of his voice exactly how badly it was going and immediately took a plane back to Washington.

Until this time, Bobby had been somewhat on the periphery of events in Washington, spending most of his time as Attorney General putting together what even his long-time critic Alexander Bickel of the Yale Law School had to admit was "the most brilliantly staffed department in a long time," and once again picking up his old occupation, as he sardonically described it, of "chasing bad men." He had already made the Organized Crime Section an elite group within the Justice Department. He put pressure on a recalcitrant J. Edgar Hoover to shift the FBI's emphasis from domestic communism to the mob, and insisted that the Bureau drop its long-standing refusal to share intelligence information with the Internal Revenue Service, the Bureau of Narcotics, and other agencies also conscripted into the fight against crime.

While the rest of the administration was still drawing up agendas and making grand designs, Bobby had already plunged into what he saw as one of his main priorities—putting together a target list of organized crime figures and preparing to launch a series of investigations of unparalleled scope. He began with forty names from his days with the McClellan Committee—Johnny Roselli, Johnny Dioguardi, Sam Giancana, and others he had scorned from across the witness table as heavily cologned and well-manicured cowards. Jimmy Hoffa, of course, was at the top of the list, an obsession unto himself. Not far behind was Carlos Marcello, the Sicilian mobster who headed the syndicate in the southern part of the United States and took in more than a billion dollars a year from gambling, prostitution, and other rackets. Along with Santos Trafficante and Meyer Lansky, Marcello had shared in the mob revenues from pre-Castro Cuba, and he was rumored to have given Hoffa a satchel containing a $500,000 contribution for the Nixon presidential campaign.

Finding an old deportation order against Marcello that had never been acted on, Bobby began his pursuit—a sort of allegory warning organized crime figures what they could expect from him in the months ahead. On April 4, federal agents arrested Marcello and hustled him, handcuffed, to New Orleans' Moisant International Airport, where a U.S. Border Patrol plane, its engines already revved, was waiting. He was put aboard without luggage and flown to Guatemala, where he had once bribed officials to give him citizenship. The Guatemalan government expelled him to El Salvador, where he was briefly jailed and then driven thirty miles into the jungle and left stranded in his silk suit and alligator shoes.

Now that Jack was in trouble, however, the vendetta against the mob had to wait. Back at the capital, and seeing his brother's panic, Bobby's first impulse was to *do* something about the Bay of Pigs, to cut through to the heart of the problem and, in a favorite term, "turn things around." But it was too late. Castro was counterattacking and the exile landing force, already short of ammunition, was pinned down on the beach. As advisers considered what appeared the only two alternatives—going in with full U.S. force or trying to maintain the fiction of noninvolvement—Bobby spoke up in anguished tones about how they'd be seen as "paper tigers" by Moscow if they didn't do something. He finally became so upset that Rostow had to take him outside the meeting room and reassure him that there would be ample opportunity to prove themselves in "Berlin, Southeast Asia and elsewhere."

At the annual Congressional Reception that evening, Jack nonchalantly avoided the appearance of concern, although Bobby was deeply upset. ("The shit has hit the fan," he told George Smathers, who had been dancing with Jackie. "This thing has turned sour in a way you wouldn't believe!") At midnight, when the party ended, he went directly back to the nonstop meeting that had been going on for the past twenty-four hours. The reports from the Bay of Pigs were increasingly desperate, as Brigade 2506 was about to be pushed back into the sea. Twisting his hands and peering down nervously through thick glasses, Bissell asked Jack to salvage the mission by authorizing jets from the carrier *Essex* to shoot down Castro's planes and strafe his tanks. Kennedy refused. Admiral Arleigh Burke said they should allow one of the destroyers in the task force lying just offshore to shell the Cuban positions, to give the besieged invasion force some relief. Jack answered sharply, "Burke, I don't want the United States involved in this!" Raising his own voice, the Admiral replied: "Hell, Mr. President, but we *are* involved!'' General Lyman Lemnitzer suggested that it was time for what Bissell had always referred to in prior discussions of the plan as ''the guerrilla option''—the moment when the invaders might give up the large-scale assault and ''melt into the mountains,'' where they would link up with other opponents of the Castro regime. The crestfallen Bissell then pointed out to those who hadn't paid attention to the geography of the Bay of Pigs that the mountains were more than fifty miles away through nearly impenetrable swamps.

Bobby sat miserably off to the side, murmuring over and over, ''We've got to do something, we've got to do something.'' But it was clear to him and everyone else that Brigade 2506 was doomed. After the meeting was over and he and his brother were alone, he came up to Jack with tears in his eyes, put both hands on his shoulders, and said, ''They can't do this to you!''

Publicly the President was statesmanlike in accepting responsibility for the Bay of Pigs. Privately he was devastated. At Glen Ora the weekend after the debacle, Lem watched him throw a copy of *Time* into the fire to avoid having to read about it. His old friend listened as Jack said the presidency was the most unpleasant job in the world and LBJ could have it in 1964. Lem, who had quit his job so that he could devote himself to being Jack's companion, tried to cheer him by changing the subject to his proposed presidential library. Jack shrugged and said he doubted if anyone would want to erect a monument to a tragic administration. The Bay of Pigs had already etched itself into his mind as a metaphor. A few months later, when Robert Donovan was interviewing him for a book about *PT 109*, Jack thought about those earlier events for a moment and then said, ''That was even more fucked up than Cuba.''

One of the conclusions he drew from the experience had to do with how vulnerable the presidency was. In the aftermath of the disaster he summoned Schlesinger, one of the few to have spoken up against the Bay of Pigs, and said he hoped a full account had been kept. The President was reminded that he himself had admonished the historian at the outset of the administration not to record daily affairs at the White House. ''No, go ahead,'' Kennedy now said. ''You can be damn sure that the CIA has its record and the Joint Chiefs theirs. We'd better make sure we have a record over here.'' A more profound lesson had to do with Bobby. ''I should have had him involved from the very beginning,'' Jack told Lem, indicating that he intended to make his brother into a personal ambassador to the dark places in government that he felt had betrayed him in the Cuban fiasco. It was, Lem Billings felt, a crucial moment: ''Up until that time, Jack more or less dismissed the reasons his father had given for wanting Bobby in the cabinet as more of that tribal Irish thing. But now he realized how right the old man had been. When the crunch came, family members *were* the only ones you could count on. Bobby *was* the only person he could rely on to be absolutely dedicated.

Jack would never have admitted it, but from that moment on the Kennedy presidency became a sort of collaboration between them.''

The role of his brother's paladin was perfect for Bobby. ''He would have taken a bolt of lightning for Jack,'' his friend Seigenthaler said later. ''He really didn't care if he was regarded as a great Attorney General. All he cared about was his brother's presidency.'' In the first weeks of the administration, he had tried to shield his brother from many controversial Justice Department proposals such as the bill to permit wiretapping under judicial supervision, telling Assistant Attorney General Ramsey Clark that it was a ''political loser'' and that he personally wanted to take the blame for it because he didn't want the civil libertarians attacking his brother. But the new and broadened mandate he acquired in the aftermath of the Bay of Pigs focused these inchoate yearnings and allowed him to become his brother's avenging angel. His wrath fell first on those closest, notably Chester Bowles, whose memo opposing the Cuban enterprise had been leaked to columnist James Reston. In one confrontation Bobby walked up to the older man, one of the venerable liberals in the party and first of the Stevensonians to come out publicly for Jack, and jammed a finger into his chest: ''As far as this administration is concerned, you should keep your mouth shut and remember you were *for* the Bay of Pigs.'' It was almost as if Bowles gave him an opportunity to attack Jack's own weakness and vacillation when, during one of the National Security meetings held in the aftermath of the Bay of Pigs, Bowles presented a paper arguing that a hasty reaction could compound the disaster. Bobby spoke up angrily from the corner of the room where he'd stationed himself: ''This is worthless. What can we do about Cuba? This doesn't tell us.'' For several minutes he continued to tear apart Bowles's ''soft line,'' finally pronouncing it a ''disgrace''; the word fell on the discussion like a flatiron.

Jack asked his brother to take over the CIA, which looked considerably less appealing to him than it had before the Bay of Pigs. Arguing that such an appointment would inflame the nepotism issue, Bobby said it would be better for him to become the President's personal representative at the Agency. He also agreed to play a role on the committee conducting an exhaustive post-mortem on the Bay of Pigs. Throughout the spring he seemed everywhere: arriving at CIA headquarters at Langley Field early in the morning, then driving into town a few hours later to spend the rest of the day in a windowless room at the Pentagon reviewing the Cuban fiasco, and finally, at four or five in the afternoon, going over to the Justice Department to begin his working day as Attorney General.

The Cuba Study Group, as it became known, was the focus of his activity. Other members were Dulles and Admiral Arleigh Burke from the Joint Chiefs. The chairman was Maxwell Taylor, whose book *The Uncertain Trumpet* had impressed Jack during the campaign and put him on the lookout for the right job with which to lure the retired general back into public life. Like his brother, Bobby was taken by Taylor's knowledge of obscure languages, his ability to recite military history going back to the Greeks and to give an extemporaneous lecture on the foreign affairs of most European countries. But he was struck even more by Taylor's exploits as a commando who'd parachuted behind enemy lines in World War II as commander of the famous "Battered Bastards of Bastogne." Ultimately Bobby named one of his children after him. Not long after they met, Taylor paid him what seemed the supreme compliment: "You're the kind of guy we wanted around to take a hill or hold a trench."

Taylor later recalled that when he arrived in Washington, he found a "shocked administration which was not only reeling from military and political disaster [but also] in complete uncertainty about what had really happened." Throughout April and May, the Cuba Study Group sifted through evidence of the debacle, tracing the decision-making process and interviewing participants and survivors. Taylor was there to hold the military establishment in check and put events into an intellectual framework, but Bobby was the driving force of the group, personalizing the proceedings and putting an emotional charge into everything that transpired. Among those who appeared before him were Armando Lopez-Estrada and Roberto San Román (brother of Brigade 2506 leader Pepe San Román), both of whom had been among the handful of exile soldiers evacuated from the beach. Both were struck by Bobby's intensity and empathy. "He asked me if I wanted to work against Fidel Castro's regime again," Lopez-Estrada later recalled. "Of course I said yes, immediately." The day after their appearance, Bobby arranged for both men to be taken to the White House for a meeting with the President and later to a party at Hickory Hill. The "family atmosphere" at Bobby's house helped heal their wounds. "We really needed [this]," San Román said about the Attorney General's support, "because we were morally destroyed at the time."

The group's criticism was directed at the mechanics of Bissell's plan—its stubborn disregard of the realities of the terrain and inability to keep it secret; its almost paranoid insistence on total CIA control. It did not question the wisdom of trying to overthrow the Castro regime. That was a given. "There can be no long-term living with Castro as a neighbor . . ." the group's final report stated. The group made it clear that the Bay of Pigs was only the first round of a long fight.

But the Cuban fiasco was like a stone dropped into a pond; the waves lapped at distant shores. Bobby later said, "I think we would have sent large numbers of troops into Laos if it hadn't been for Cuba . . ." Jack himself looked at the logistics of involvement there—airfields needed, the terrain to be dealt with, and so on—in a way that he wouldn't have before the Bay of Pigs. Although as late as an NSC meeting of April 27 his military advisers favored going into Laos, he favored transforming it from a big-power confrontation to a lower-keyed antiguerrilla campaign directed at the Pathet Lao insurgents rather than their Soviet sponsors. Yet he didn't want the lesson of the Cuban misadventure to be that there should be a pullback in Southeast Asia. Working to obtain a cease-fire as a prelude to negotiations that would neutralize Laos and give it a coalition government, he told Dean Rusk, "If we have to fight in Southeast Asia, let's fight in Vietnam. The Vietnamese, at least, are committed and will fight. There are a million refugees from communism in South Vietnam. Vietnam is the place."

Apprehensive that Diem would be frightened by diplomatic efforts at disengagement in Laos, Kennedy ordered a hundred more trainers for the South Vietnamese Army and sent more than four hundred Special Forces troops. He also asked Lyndon Johnson to go there in May to show the flag. Johnson balked so often that Jack finally had to corner him: "Lyndon, you've just got to go out there." The Vice President grimaced and replied, "Mr. President, I don't want to embarrass you by getting my head blown off in Saigon." Jack finally persuaded him to take the trip by including his sister Jean and Steve Smith in the diplomatic party as Kennedy hostages.

While the signal was being given that irresolution at the Bay of Pigs did not mean a diminished commitment elsewhere (in a second State of the Union address given May 24 Jack had asked for funding for twelve thousand new Marines, expanded capabilities to counter guerrilla war, and a civil defense appropriation three times larger than Eisenhower's), Soviet Premier Khrushchev unexpectedly accepted the invitation to meet at the summit which had been extended shortly after the inauguration. Most Kennedy advisers were against such a meeting so soon after the Bay of Pigs, but Jack regarded it as an opportunity to reverse his losses in Cuba in one stroke. Moreover, personal diplomacy was for him the essence of governance—a contest of individual wills, a clash of character, the drama of two men settling the shape of things to come in terms reminiscent of the biographies of great statesmen which had always ignited his imagination.

With the meeting set for June in Vienna, he cut his appointments to a minimum so that he could spend time with George Kennan, Charles Bohlen, Averell Harriman, and other Soviet experts. Everything else was secondary. In a brief post-mortem of the Bay of Pigs with Nixon (one of many meetings with Republican leaders he astutely arranged to emphasize the bipartisan responsibility for the defeat) he said, "It really is true that foreign affairs is the only important issue for a President to handle, isn't it? I mean who gives a shit if the minimum wage is $1.15 or $1.35 in comparison to something like this?" As the summit drew nearer, the civil rights movement's Freedom Rides began to disrupt the white South. Jack called Harris Wofford, the administration's point man on civil rights, and barked angrily, "Stop them! Get your friends off those buses!" explaining that he didn't want to be embarrassed in front of the Russians.

On May 28, Jack stopped at Hyannis, bent over with pain after having reinjured his back planting a red oak seedling in Ottawa as a symbol of U.S.-Canadian friendship. He was accompanied by the ubiquitous Lem Billings. (When Bernard West, the White House butler, commented on the fact that Billings was a frequent enough house guest to keep his belongings in one of the six guest bedrooms, Jackie shrugged and said, "He's been my house guest since I was married.") Lem represented continuity for Jack, one constant in the rapid change that had comprised his life. The two of them played backgammon at ten dollars a game, arguing violently over points. They watched "Meet the Press" and "Face the Nation" every Sunday. Jack introduced Lem to the captain of the presidential yacht as "Lt. Jr. Grade Billings"; to Germany's Chancellor Adenauer as "Congressman Billings"; to astronaut Alan Shepard as "General Billings of the Pentagon." Lem was once nearly shot by Secret Service men while climbing over the fence at Hyannis during a prank he was playing on Jack.

Arriving at the Kennedy compound, Jack and Lem found that Rose had already left for France, which would be the first stop on the European schedule. ("Jack was against her going," Billings said later, "but there wasn't anything he could do about it because Mrs. Kennedy was determined to be in on everything.") Alone with a skeletal housekeeping staff, the Ambassador had cut out pictures of voluptuous women and spread them all over Jack's bedroom—laying them on pillows, dressers, and sinks. He had waited up past his normal bedtime for the presidential party, but when no call came to tell him how late it would be, he'd gone to bed in annoyance.

The next morning Jack left early to celebrate his birthday by giving a speech to state Democrats at the Boston Armory, which he concluded by alluding to his trip: "I go as the leader of the most revolutionary country on earth." The following afternoon he was sailing on the Cape with his father and his friend. During a lull he asked Lem, who had started him collecting scrimshaw and other items, what he thought he should give Khrushchev as part of the ceremonial exchange of gifts. Lem shrugged. Then Jack asked: "How about that model of the U.S.S. *Constitution?*" He had seen the beautifully crafted scale model of Old Ironsides several weeks earlier and thought of buying it, but been put off by the price of $500. "Maybe Dad will buy it for my birthday," he had remarked wistfully to Lem with full knowledge that his friend would report back to the Ambassador. He had prized the ship when his father sent it to the White House. Now he decided to take it to Vienna, as he told Lem, because it "represented the U.S. as a young republic—strong, youthful, in love with freedom—exactly the kind of message I want to send Russia."

That afternoon, on his way down the front stairs to the helicopter that would take him to Idlewild, he felt in his pockets and then looked sheepishly at his father: "Oh, Dad, I don't have a cent of money." The Ambassador sent his secretary upstairs for a packet of big bills, which Jack took, grinning, as he went to the door. "I'll get this back to you, Dad." The old man watched him go down the steps and muttered, "That'll be the day."

When they arrived at Orly Airport, French President Charles De Gaulle was there, towering and formidable. Rose was there too, looking Jackie up and down critically before saying "You look very nice, dear." Actually she was stunning, dressed in a green suit designed by Oleg Cassini, whom she had designated her official costumier. ("I want all mine to be originals," she had written him about her clothes shortly before the inaugural, "and no fat little women hopping about in the same dress.") The motorcade to the Quai D'Orsay passed by huge crowds eager to catch a glimpse of the American President and his French-descended wife.

At their meeting that afternoon, De Gaulle immediately told Kennedy that France would not be part of any military action in Laos. It was part of a stern warning against what he saw as a potentially dangerous involvement in Southeast Asia. "For you, intervention in this region will be an entanglement without end ... I predict to you that you will, step by step, become sucked into a bottomless military and political quagmire, despite the losses and expenditures you may squander."

While Jack was in Paris, the issue of intervention came up in a dramatic way when the Dominican Republic fell into crisis in the aftermath of dictator Rafael Trujillo's assassination. Backed by people in the CIA whom he was now getting to know, Bobby thought a U.S. military presence should be sent in. Chester Bowles, who was Acting Secretary of State in Rusk's absence, was adamantly opposed. ("We had just had a fiasco at the Bay of Pigs," he commented later, "and I didn't want another one.") Bobby pressured him to such an extent that Bowles finally had to call Jack in Paris. "Am I Acting Secretary or is your brother?" he asked. When Jack reassured him that he was, Bowles shot back: "Well, will you call your brother and let him know?"*

The Paris leg of the trip had been a stunning success, especially the final evening, when Jack and Jackie were guests of honor at a grand ball in the Versailles Hall of Mirrors that culminated in a fireworks display worthy of Louis XIV. The atmosphere was different in Vienna, where tension had been mounting since Khrushchev's arrival the day before. After a brief introduction, the Russian Premier and the American President went almost directly

---

*This clash, combined with the residual animosity over Cuba, made Bowles a marked man. Bobby and Jack tried to fire him during the summer, but liberals in the administration—the "Chet Set"—protested so much that it was not possible. Bobby did not get his revenge until late that fall, during what became known as the "Thanksgiving Day Massacre," when Bowles was replaced by George Ball and given the largely ceremonial job of Roving Ambassador. "The President snuck up one day and got him fired before he knew it," Bobby later said with evident satisfaction.

to eleven hours of meeting, talking through two meals and a walk in the woods with their interpreters. The discussions ranged from China and Southeast Asia to the Mideast. Eventually the talk turned to war, and Khrushchev repeated the theory Jack had already geared much of his foreign policy to disprove: there were three kinds of war—conventional, nuclear, and wars of liberation; while the first two might be obsolete or senseless, the third kind, which the Soviet Premier called "holy wars," had all the inevitability of history itself.

Charles "Chip" Bohlen, veteran diplomat and Soviet expert, who was present as presidential adviser, later noted: "I would say that there was only one mistake that [Kennedy] made ... [T]hat he got drawn into an ideological discussion with Khrushchev ..." When the Soviet Premier said that Russia, as a revolutionary country, could not help aiding wars of national liberation, Jack tried to answer him on a theoretical level, attempting to cite Lenin and other Soviet theoreticians and foundering. "It seemed to me," Bohlen said, "... that he got a little bit out of his depth."

The acrimonious mood persisted the next day. Kennedy and Khrushchev agreed about Laos (National Security Council member Michael Forrestal and others felt that liquidation of that potential conflict was the only good to come out of the summit). Cuba was discussed only casually but loomed large in the background. Because Jack had not sent troops in without worrying about world opinion—as Khrushchev himself had done in Hungary—the Russian leader concluded that the President was an indecisive young man who could be pushed around. When the subject of Berlin came up, the Soviet Premier announced that he was setting a deadline for a settlement on the divided city and was ready to sign a separate peace treaty with East Germany, leaving the United States and the other Western powers to deal with its regime (which they did not recognize) on the issue of access rights. Jack responded that the United States was ready to defend Berlin "at any risk." At this point, according to one report, "the meeting began to go very badly in terms of table banging and talk about missiles flying."

As the discussions ended, Jack gave Khrushchev the model of the *Constitution* which Lem himself had brought over. He was glad he had sacrificed his birthday present when the Soviet Premier's gift to him turned out to be a silver coffee service from Czechoslovakia. "He regarded this as plunder from a captive people," according to Lem, "and felt that while he'd taken it on the chin in other respects he had at least gotten the best of the exchange of gifts."

Dealing with Khrushchev, Jack later told Lem, was like "dealing with Dad—all give and no take." Stopping off in London to brief Macmillan on the talks, he felt the relationship with his father and the analogy with Munich—the event which had played so powerful a role in the Kennedy family's fortunes—hanging over him. At a gathering at the home of Jackie's sister Lee and her husband, Prince Stanislaus Radziwill, he went up to Joe Alsop and in "an agonizing way" told his hardline journalist friend, "Joe, I want you to know I won't give in to the Russians no matter what happens. I won't give in." Later, talking to James Reston of the *Times* and still trying to avoid the appearance of having been weak, Jack said he would increase the military budget and send another division to Germany to show his resolve on Berlin. He also said that even though the summit had put Laos on the back burner the real challenge would come not in Germany but in Southeast Asia: "We have a problem in trying to make our power credible and Vietnam looks like the place."

Back home, Jack addressed the nation, posing the issue of relations with the Soviets in terms of humiliation or holocaust. He asked for a doubled draft call, a $3 billion increase in defense spending, and a crash program on civil defense emphasizing public and private shelters. Maxwell Taylor suggested an insert for the speech: "I hear it said that West Berlin is militarily untenable. And so was Bastogne. And so in fact was Stalingrad. Any dangerous spot is tenable if men—brave men—will make it so."

In early August, with some six thousand refugees a day fleeing into West Berlin, the East Germans began constructing a wall across the city in the middle of the night. Upon hearing about it, Jack's first words were, "Go get my brother!" He and Bobby talked through the night about the proper response. The next day he ordered a convoy of armored trucks to be sent into the city along the Autobahn. It was not the massive show of force that Dean Acheson and others had called for, but it was risky enough. Bobby later said, "The President felt strongly, and I did, that we were close to war at that time." But the Wall solved the administration's Berlin problem: once its population was securely imprisoned within its borders, East Germany was less anxious about the issue of recognition and the Soviet deadline for signing a treaty was withdrawn.

Jack and Bobby both felt they were trapped in a cycle of international difficulty that had begun with Cuba and would not really be over until Cuba had finally been dealt with. As the fallout from the Bay of Pigs and Vienna at last began to settle, Bobby was working, in Chester Bowles's phrase, to "get Castro." Finished with his stint on the Cuba Study Group, he used his position as the President's personal representative to the CIA to demand action on Cuba. Agency Deputy Director Robert Amory later recalled Bobby as an intense presence in the summer of 1961, "trying to get them to do more and to get them to build up more capability and be more aggressive . . ." By early fall, with the Berlin crisis beginning to fade, Bissell was told in a meeting with the Kennedy brothers, "Get off your ass about Cuba." The harassment which the Agency had sporadically conducted since the Bay of Pigs was not enough.

Bobby heard that Edward Lansdale was back from another trip to Vietnam and conscripted him into the effort. After a preliminary review of the situation, Lansdale, who saw that Bobby regarded the Bay of Pigs "as an insult which needed to be redressed rather quickly," suggested that the correct way to depose the Cuban leadership was to work from within rather than from without. After conferring with Bobby, Jack agreed, putting out a top-secret order "to use our available assets . . . to help Cuba overthrow the Communist regime." It was as if the Kennedy brothers had decided to do the Bay of Pigs over again but do it right this time, by themselves and without outsiders' intervention. Lansdale was appointed chief of operations for a secret war against Havana, code-named Operation Mongoose, which would be controlled by a review committee called the Special Group (Augmented) headed by Maxwell Taylor and Bobby. In a meeting of the principals in his office, the Attorney General, for whom Castro had become a personal issue in the same way Jimmy Hoffa was, made it clear that "a solution to the Cuban problem today carries top priority in the U.S. government," and ordered that "no time, money, effort or manpower . . . be spared."

2.

B Y THE FALL OF 1961, WITH THE
diplomatic reversals of the Bay of Pigs and Vienna behind him, and Bobby
playing his old role as the Kennedy id, Jack Kennedy was able to concentrate
on the symbolism of the presidency, making the office his own through his
unequaled ability to manipulate political imagery. He was the first President
to see the full possibilities of television as a medium of self-promotion and
to understand that it could be used as an adjunct to and even a substitute
for policy. He made his press conferences into witty and urbane entertainments, with some of the elements of a well-wrought television series. But his
effort ultimately stretched to all aspects of the press and the way the Kennedys were portrayed.

One of Jack's qualities which editors and writers soon became aware of
was his all-seeing eye in matters relating to the press. Gilbert Harrison,
editor of the *New Republic,* who had killed a story about the Bay of Pigs not
long before the invasion at a request by Kennedy via Schlesinger, was
amazed to discover how carefully the President scrutinized the contents of
his magazine, even going so far as to call book reviewers to congratulate them
on some favorable piece. He used anger in the same way. Ben Bradlee, one
of his close social friends in addition to being *Newsweek*'s White House
correspondent, found himself banished from the presidential circle for several weeks as a result of a relatively innocuous comment he made about the
Kennedys while being interviewed for an article about power in Washington.

Jack was almost obsessed with *Time,* which he regarded as the quintessen-
tially American publication and was determined to conquer. Each week he
got the first copy of the magazine, delivered by the printer Sunday evening.

By Monday morning he was often on the phone to the Washington bureau, criticizing some offending article. Sometimes he went directly to Henry Luce himself, whom he regarded with a mixture of awe and annoyance as equaling his own father—a headstrong, self-made man.*

He badgered *Time* White House correspondent Hugh Sidey endlessly about the magazine's treatment of his administration. One well-remembered incident occurred the day the astronaut John Glenn was launched into space. Sidey was there, reporting on the jubilation of the Rose Garden ceremony. In the midst of this epic moment, however, Jack was concerned only about a small feature *Time* had just done about photographic spreads on the Kennedys that were appearing in an increasing number of magazines; this article erroneously claimed that he had once posed for the cover of *Gentleman's Quarterly* and he was furious. After reading derisively from the magazine in front of Sorensen and Pierre Salinger, the President told Sidey, "I'm getting goddamn sick and tired of it. This is a lie ... Any President who would pose for *Gentleman's Quarterly* would be out of his mind." Ignoring Sidey's profuse apology, Kennedy continued to rant: "People remember people for one thing. I remember Arthur Godfrey for buzzing the tower. People are going to remember me because I posed for the cover of *Gentleman's Quarterly*." When his secretary rang him to say that Glenn had splashed down and was on the line, Jack picked up the phone, glaring at Sidey: "All right, stand there and see if you can get *this* right ..." Then, after greeting the astronaut with an eloquent speech, he set the receiver down and began berating *Time* once again.

Jacqueline Kennedy had a parallel obsession, a desire to give the presidential experience style and elegance. She had been unhappy in her first days in the White House, comparing herself to a moth hanging on the windowpane of the presidency and telling a Kennedy family employee that she felt as though she lived in a fishbowl with all the fish on the outside. The power was enjoyable: once she sent Air Force One back to Palm Beach to get a Chubby Checker record left there during a weekend vacation. But the role of presidential wife was bothersome, with its built-in expectations about decorum and protocol. "The one thing I do not want to be called," she informed her secretary after the inauguration, "is First Lady. It sounds like a saddle horse. Would you notify the telephone operators and everyone else that I'm to be known simply as Mrs. Kennedy and not as First Lady?"

*In one of their encounters Jack complained about *Time*'s coverage of him. When Luce resisted, Jack pointed at Hugh Sidey: "Now there's an impartial man. Let him tell you ... Does the average man in the street think that *Time* magazine has been fair to me?" Sidey blurted, "No," but then, looking at Luce, quickly added, "But Washington is a Democratic city and thus the average man in the street is probably prejudiced." Luce brightened: "Ah yes, Phoenix now, where I go—Phoenix and New York, they think we've been very kind to you."

Much to Jack's irritation, Jackie had been reclusive, refusing to appear at political events and fund-raisers. Aside from intrusions into her privacy, she also resented the Kennedy in-groupiness in the White House, the possessiveness and provinciality with which they had claimed the place. When Jackie brought together literary people for a special evening there was likely to be an occurrence such as the one John Hersey recalls. He happened to be seated next to Pat Lawford, who kept staring at his name card and saying, "There's something bad about you. Were you for Nixon?" Hersey assured her that, on the contrary, he had been a lifelong Democrat. He hadn't been for Nixon in 1960? No, in fact he had supported Stevenson all the way to the convention. Hearing this, she gave him a cold look: "Oh yes, I knew there was something bad about you." And there was Eunice, the sister most in evidence in the first days of the New Frontier, walking up to Nehru at a cocktail party during a time when the Indian Prime Minister was being particularly difficult, looking him up and down and then saying jocularly, "So that's what you look like, you old rascal you."

But after the visit to Paris, Jackie had been galvanized by the prospect of bringing a new style and grandeur to "the dreary Maison Blanche," giving it a Bouvier rather than a Kennedy touch. Some of her changes were minor : she insisted that the Marine band play constantly at White House soirées instead of sitting silently between numbers like "mournful bellhops"; she noted that the harsh overhead lights in the dining room deepened the lines on women's faces and had them replaced with sconces whose candles cast a diffused pastel glow. There were also longer-range restoration plans to make the White House the ideal locale for the golden age of poetry and power Robert Frost had forecast in his inaugural appearance. She got wealthy friends to donate some 160 paintings as well as pledges of funds for a general restoration. No detail was overlooked : $12,500 went to steam antique wallpaper off the walls of a historic Maryland house and place it on the walls of the Diplomatic Room.

In part it was an attempt, paralleling Jack's own in politics, to gain distance from the previous era. ("Mamie Eisenhower pink" was for Jackie the color that summarized all bad taste.) But Jackie was as sensitive as Jack to the romance of history, and her efforts at restoration were also an attempt to give resonance to the Kennedy era, to integrate it into a long American tradition. "When the Eisenhowers were here they liked modern things—clean, bright colors and things like that," one of the interior decorators involved in Jackie's projects said later. "But Mrs. Kennedy never liked anything new. She wanted everything to look like it had been used ... lived with. If she ever bought anything new in furniture, we would [have to] antique it, age it so that it would look like it had been used ... The paint [on the walls] was put on real heavy ... like it was old. In the State Dining Room it was to simulate cracked paneling like in the old castles in France. We had to paint them on and then . . . put distress marks in with crayon."

Blair Clark, Jack's old college friend who was now a producer at CBS television, had the idea of Jackie taking America on a White House tour. Norman Mailer might compare her performance with that of some breathy-voiced and tightly sweatered weather girl on the local news, but the program made her a media star in her own right. It allowed her to make culture a political event, filling the White House with Nobel laureates and opera stars like Roberta Peters and Grace Bumbry. After Jackie persuaded Pablo Casals to drop his vow not to perform in a country that had supported Franco, the *New York Times* commented about his concert, "It was an indication that the White House was rising to its responsibility and . . . coming of age."

Despite the new sheen on the White House surfaces, however, the first family's life ran according to long-established rhythms. Jackie often escaped to Glen Ora with the children. While she was gone, Jack was free to pursue his secret life, with the Secret Service providing cover for assignations that took place behind the closed doors of the family quarters. Jack was well supplied with stars and starlets through Sinatra and the Hollywood connection. There were longer-term relationships with women like Judith Campbell, a dark-haired beauty whom he and Teddy had met during the 1960 campaign, and Mary Meyer, Ben Bradlee's sister-in-law, who introduced Jack to marijuana and joked with him in the White House bedroom about being high when it was time to push the nuclear button. For more casual sex, there were hangers-on such as the pair of blondes from the secretarial pool whom Jack and his friends called "Fiddle and Faddle" and Jackie referred to contemptuously as "the White House dogs." She knew more about these goings-on than he ever suspected and dealt with them through hauteur, as when she disdainfully handed him some panties she'd found in her pillow slip, saying, "Here, would you find who these belong to. They're not my size."

Given Jack's private life and his unusual relationship with Jackie, the White House could not function as a center of family life for the Kennedy clan. And so Hickory Hill became the home of the New Frontier. With its sloping lawns and three-hundred-year-old stands of hickory trees and its swirl of children and animals, it had taken on some of the qualities of the Kennedy compound at Hyannis thirty years earlier. A visitor might be accosted by Bobby's five-year-old daughter, Kerry, standing on top of a shed and saying, "Do you dare me to jump off the roof?" or eight-year-old David coming down one of the Tarzan swings and screaming "I'm Bat Ma-a-n!" Bobby encouraged the competition and reckless activity which he thought of as a uniquely Kennedy trait. Ethel, whose family was equally kinetic, was a willing collaborator. She was in a school car pool with other women in the suburbs and when it was her turn to drive would conduct—and grade—

current-events quizzes. "If you had a current event involving the President or the Attorney General, you always got an A-plus," one of the girls remembered later on. "But if you had one involving someone else, you always got a B no matter how good it was."

The kids—Bobby's own and their cousins, for whom Hickory Hill was a second home—gave charades and recited poems on family birthdays and other occasions. Once when Jack visited he found the children dressed up in patriotic costumes performing a sort of masque about events from the past. One of them was about *PT 109:*

> *In '43 they went to sea*
> *Thirteen men and Kennedy*
> *To seek the blazin' enemy . . .*

Hickory Hill was also a place where the loyalties of the New Frontiersmen were cemented. Bobby had Schlesinger set up seminars that brought such figures as the celebrated historian Isaiah Berlin to place events of the Kennedy presidency in a larger context. (Jack, who saw this as a "self-improvement scheme" Bobby had inherited from their mother, loved to get gossip about the affairs, especially when they involved intellectual clashes between his parochial sisters and Schlesinger's "heavy thinkers.") Ethel was a madcap mistress of ceremonies, the practical joking of the Skakels (who did such things as giving live "Christmas Seals" to all their friends one year) coming out in her entertainments. She imported the Lester Lanin orchestra for dances and brought in Harry Belafonte to teach them all the twist. She used live bullfrogs as a centerpiece for a St. Patrick's Day dinner; she put distinguished cabinet members in closets with attractive secretaries during impassioned games of hide-and-seek; invited Robert Frost to dinner and gave out paper and pencils to guests for a poetry-writing contest. She and Bobby together pushed officials and dignitaries into the pool. (Salinger went in in tuxedo and cigar which he tried to keep lit; Schlesinger went in with his heavy glasses and professorial dignity; McNamara with the hair that was just as slicked back before he hit the water as after.) It was like a baptismal ritual making them Kennedy followers.

The elder Kennedys were isolated from all this. Rose had managed to create a role for herself as a sort of Queen Mother, working hard to make the Best Dressed List, constructing homilies for women's magazines on the vicissitudes of raising a large family, and taking almost childish pleasure in substituting for Jackie as hostess when Jackie decided to skip some state function. There was even a vein of drollery in her, as Jack found out after Vienna. Learning that she had sent a photograph of himself and Khrushchev to the Soviet Premier for an autograph, he warned her that dealing with heads of state on her own could lead to international complications. She replied in a letter showing that she too could wield the Kennedy needle: "Dear Jack, I am so glad you warned me about contacting the heads of State as I was just about to write Castro. Love, Mother."

For Joe Kennedy, the transition had been more difficult. His negative charge was still strong enough to prohibit public appearances with his son. (Even his rare social visits to the White House were not announced.) He took pleasure in the symbolism of the presidency—the White House communications trailer at Hyannis, the presidential flag flying over the compound when Jack arrived, the presidential helicopter attracting attention when it landed—but he wasn't sure about his role. In the first weeks of the administration he had asked son-in-law Steve Smith to find out if his sons "wanted him." Jack called frequently but rarely asked for advice on policy. ("The old man saw that the calls were perfunctory," White House aide Fred Dutton later observed. "It hurt him that Jack and Bobby weren't asking for his counsel a lot.") And so he lurked in the background of the New Frontier, operating on his own. Television anchorman Chet Huntley got accustomed to the Ambassador calling "every night or so after the show and saying, 'That was beautiful,' or just giving us hell about something." Joe used his remaining Hollywood connections to negotiate a contract with Warners for a movie version of Robert Donovan's *PT 109* and also for *The Enemy Within*.

Yet he was feeling his age—experiencing headaches and pain running down his left arm. He insisted his problems were nothing more than the chronic neuralgia which had afflicted him for years, but there was a new wistfulness in his correspondence with old friends. He concluded one letter to Beaverbrook: "Take care of yourself. There are only a few of us good ones left."

He had one final item on his agenda, and that was a career for Teddy. His last son was his "sunshine," he often said, smiling proudly at the way Teddy would come into the room and pick up his mother from behind and twirl her, saying, "How's my girl?" and then look over and say, "Hi, Dad, you having any fun?" Jack and Bobby had concluded that it was not prudent to be photographed with their father any more than absolutely necessary. Joe Kennedy understood that these precautions were necessary; but he loved Teddy for thumbing his nose at such political wisdom.

After coordinating the western states for Jack during the 1960 campaign, he had thought about making a career for himself in the Rocky Mountains, perhaps as the publisher of a small newspaper. But this hint of independence only provoked a strong summons to the family destiny. Teddy's friend Claude Hooten later said, "He thought his place in the world might be somewhere else, but then his father said, 'Ted, you've got a base here [in Massachusetts]—family, friends. Why go off someplace and prove yourself for nothing?" And so Ted had come home and taken a job as Assistant

District Attorney of Suffolk County. It was clear that this was meant to be a stepping stone, although to what office was uncertain. Hearing all the rumors about his famous employee—some said he was running for attorney general, others for lieutenant governor, and still others for senator—Ted's boss Garret Byrne decided to call the Ambassador. When Byrne asked exactly what his aide was doing, the raspy voice at the other end of the line said, "Lookit—get this straight, will you. He's running for the United States Senate. Now put him on the phone." After the old man had done most of the talking and Ted had hung up, Byrne looked at him and said, "Now you know what you're running for."

Bobby later said that his father felt Teddy "had worked all this time during the campaign and sacrificed himself for his older brother and we had our positions and so he should have the right to run." Jack was less politic. Speaking to the Massachusetts politician John Powers about his father's decision, he said, "I don't want him to run and Bobby doesn't want him to run either. But if he's going to do it, we don't want him to lose..." Steve Smith was dispatched to Boston to set up the campaign as on-the-job training for a larger role he was expected to play during Jack's 1964 reelection drive. Yet it was hard going, especially after the *Boston Globe* uncovered the story of Teddy's expulsion from Harvard years earlier for cheating. Bob Healy, author of the exposé, was summoned to Washington for a meeting with Jack in the Oval Office in the presence of O'Donnell, Sorensen, Bundy, and others who hoped to get the *Globe* to suppress the piece. Unable after lengthy argument to move Healy, Jack looked at Bundy in disgust: "We're having more fucking trouble with this than we did with the Bay of Pigs." His National Security Adviser nodded. "Yes, and with about the same results."*

Joe Kennedy was adamant, letting his two older sons know that he considered this Senate seat—which Jack had gotten his friend Ben Smith to warm after he left it to become President—something he had personally bought and paid for. As Teddy began his campaign, the Ambassador was looking over every detail and expected the rest of the family, even his eldest son, to do their share. On December 4, 1961, his aide James Fayne wrote Jack about a rural Massachusetts publisher named Richard Steele who was annoyed at having written the White House several times about some matter and gotten no reply: "[Mr. Kennedy] wants to be sure everybody understands how important Steele is to Teddy."

Then, in the middle of December, the Ambassador was playing golf one morning with his niece Ann Gargan. Feeling faint, he sat down and then dragged himself to a bench. When he finally rose to walk to the car, he

---

*Talking to Ben Bradlee about the cheating episode, Jack showed himself to be his father's son. "It won't go over with the WASPs," he said. "They take a dim view of looking over your shoulder at someone else's exam paper. They go in more for stealing from stockholders and banks."

staggered drunkenly. Back at the Palm Beach house he went directly to bed. Hearing what had happened, Rose looked in and found him ashen-faced and having trouble moving but said she was sure he would be all right. "There's nothing I can do but pray," she told servants, and went off to a scheduled golf game. Hours later an ambulance was finally called. Having suffered a massive stroke, Joseph Kennedy was taken to a room at St. Mary's Hospital. The room next to his had a plaque reading: "Dedicated to the Memory of Joseph P. Kennedy, Jr."

He was "one breath away," according to Lem, by the time Jack and Bobby arrived on Air Force One. "The doctors came to the family and said, 'Look, this strong, virile man is going to be imprisoned in a body that won't work even if he recovers.' It was an opportunity to pull the plug. But Bobby said no, let him fight for his life." Over the next few weeks, his condition gradually stabilized. But he was almost completely paralyzed on his right side and unable to speak intelligibly. Aphasic, he would talk in nonsense sounds thinking he was making sense. His only real word was "no," run together into a long moan as he tried to give it nuances that would express a full range of thought and emotion.

When he returned home from the hospital, Eunice instructed his long-time aide Leo Racine to call him periodically and give him an update on business operations. "It was awful to have these one-way conversations," Racine said later. "I never knew how much he understood. But then one day I was sitting with him and gave him the local paper and there happened to be an obituary for his old friend Eddie Moore's wife. He looked up and began crying and I knew he could understand."

Immobilized as he was, the Ambassador tried to reassume a role in the Senate campaign. When Eddie McCormack, Ted's primary opponent, launched a personal attack to which Ted wanted to reply, Jack, who had become involved, told him to stick to the issues, and the Ambassador, sitting in a wheelchair, nodded vigorously. But, unable to talk, he was no longer consulted.

He drooled out of the right side of his mouth. The tensor muscles in his right hand contracted, drawing his fingers into a claw. His grandchildren looked at him and were frightened; they would run away crying. He went into rehabilitation at the Rusk Institute and, in a dramatic moment, managed to drag himself a few feet to Jack, who stood applauding with tears in his eyes. But no one in the family was willing to dare his wrath by trying to force him to stay with the difficult and painful physical and speech therapy. Left to himself he slid into permanent invalidism. ("Face it," says one family friend. "He was a hell of a lot easier to deal with that way.") Rose bought a black mourning dress for his funeral which she would in the future pack and take with them when they traveled between Hyannis and Palm Beach. In an act of self-assertion that seemed calculated to pay her husband back for what she had suffered over the years, she told even old and intimate friends like Beaverbrook that a third party was reading the letters they sent her husband and censoring whatever it was felt might agitate him. One of his male attendants later said that when Rose came into his room to visit he became extremely agitated. ''Before he had been the Supreme Being in the Kennedy house, but after the stroke it was like a little smile came over her face as if to say, 'Gotcha now.' ''

Seeing the man who had been like a father to him struck down, Lem remembered once being at Le Pavillon with him when the aged Bernard Baruch came in with a nurse, shuffling along pathetically and mumbling to himself. Shaken by the sight, Kennedy said, ''I don't want to be like that— not ever!'' Now he was much worse: incapacitated and unable to take care of himself, let alone affect what lay in store for his sons. What happened to him caused all the Kennedys to experience a collective shudder in the middle of their triumph. ''Uncle Joe's stroke gave us all a feeling of being suddenly vulnerable,'' in the words of one of his nieces. ''He wasn't really there to protect us any more.''

With the Ambassador disabled, Jack leaned on Bobby even more heavily than before. Douglas Dillon was not alone in noting they had reversed the normal fraternal situation, so that Jack looked up to Bobby almost as if he were an older brother. (''He's got high moral standards,'' Jack replied almost enviously when asked why he thought Bobby was special, ''strict personal ethics...'') There was a new sort of closeness, almost a special language between them. It went beyond the staccato sentences and broad vowels of their Massachusetts upbringing: it was a private talk of ellipsis and intuition. ''It was strange to hear them have a conversation,'' Lem Billings said later on. ''Neither of them ever got out a complete sentence. They were on the same wave length to such a degree that they interrupted to finish each other's thoughts. It was quite a difference from those uncomfortable silences of their earlier days.''

The odd thing about this closeness was that it did not extend to the social realm. The exuberant and fecund Ethel made Jackie uncomfortable. ''She drops kids like rabbits,'' Jackie told a friend. ''It's disgraceful.'' A comic drawing she once made for Ethel showed her idea of the déclassé chaos at Hickory Hill: children hanging out of the windows, on the roof, everywhere underfoot; the old cook packing her bags and leaving by the back door as the new cook arrived on the front porch; Ethel herself looking quizzical and frazzled. Nor was Bobby's intensity what Jack needed for relaxation. Red Fay, who with his wife Anita saw considerably more of Jack and Jackie than Bobby and Ethel did, recalls, ''Whenever we came back from being with the President, they always had this almost pathetic desire to know what had happened during the weekend. Who had been there? What was said? How were people dressed?''

To keep his brother in his place, Jack continued the abrasive kidding which had always been the Kennedy *lingua familia*. At a time when Bobby's reputation in the administration was on the rise, for instance, Jack would sometimes answer calls from the Attorney General's office by holding the receiver away from his mouth and noting with mock portent to whatever friend happened to be present in the Oval Office: "I think it is the Second Most Important Man in the capital calling." Chuck Spalding was with the brothers one day when Bobby seemed moody and preoccupied. "Don't worry about Bobby," Jack said loudly, as he gestured at his brother. "He's probably all choked up over Martin Luther King and his Negroes today." Yet everyone near the White House knew how central Bobby had become. "Every time they have a conference don't kid anybody about who is the top adviser," Lyndon Johnson noted with some asperity. "It's not McNamara, the Chiefs of Staff, or anyone else like that. Bobby is first in, last out. And Bobby is the boy he listens to."

Always the protean figure, Jack quickly disappeared into the iconography of office, treating the presidency as sort of a hideout. For his predecessors, compartmentalizing the public from the private was a psychic strain; for him, it came naturally, and in this sense the presidency was truly the summation of his life's work. In the future, the real self would be seen only in flashes:

—Greeting a tour of wheelchair children not able to tour the White House during normal visiting hours. They had not expected to see him, but he went patiently from one child to another, bending over to chat with each for a few seconds and listen to their observations despite some fearsome speech defects. After talking to one boy he darted off into his office and returned with his old skipper's hat from his days on *PT 109*, put it on the child's head and left, explaining to a bystander, "His father was in the PT boats too. His father is dead."

—Sitting in on one of the Hickory Hill seminars, tapping his front teeth intensely during Princeton historian David Donald's talk about Reconstruction and then, during the question period, bringing up the issue of presidential greatness. What separated a great President from a mediocre one? How did a President acquire greatness? And what about Lincoln? Would he have been regarded as a great President if he hadn't been assassinated? Because of the delicacy of this question, Donald equivocated. But Jack continued to press him earnestly about Lincoln and assassination and where and why he would rank the Presidents.

—Weekending with his old friend Jim Reed and watching a newsreel of a speech he had given abroad; then beginning to cheer, hoot derisively, and comment on the misformed words and choppy gestures as if, Reed felt, "he were watching someone not himself."

—Swimming with his friend Red Fay in the White House pool and becoming angry when Fay mentioned Arthur Schlesinger's self-promotion as the only member of the administration's inner circle who had opposed the Bay of Pigs: "Artie thinks he's going to write a history of this administration, but if he doesn't watch it he'll wind up writing a history of the White House furniture and nothing more than that!"

But while Jack became more elusive in office, disappearing into the mythic status of the presidency, Bobby was just the opposite, becoming daily more real. Jack's face had changed dramatically over the years, filling out even to the point of jowliness, partly as a result of the steroids he took. He would finger his cheek while looking in the mirror and say, "That's not my face." Bobby's face hadn't changed much over the years except perhaps to become more distinctively his own. The eyes were capable, as one woman said, of boring through someone; his nose like a raptor's beak, his jaw set aggressively: he was the Kennedy soldier, perpetually on duty.

"Bobby stories," little epiphanies of ruthlessness, were common fare on the Washington cocktail circuit. How, at a Hickory Hill dinner, he asked Averell Harriman if he had seen a directive he had issued restricting the travel of Eastern European diplomats, and when Harriman said he had seen it and was planning to get to it soon, Bobby had slammed his hand down on the table and told the august diplomat in tones appropriate to reprimand a twenty-five-year-old foreign service officer: "You get on that first thing in the morning!" How he had begun legal proceedings against his father's companion in philandering, Igor Cassini, for not registering as an agent for the Dominican Republic, and against Jim Landis, his father's one-time aide who had written speeches for Jack and had been a family loyalist for years but had neglected to file income tax returns. "Little Brother Is Watching You" became a sort of password among people who ran afoul of the Attorney General.

But Bobby didn't care what was said about him. He had taken upon himself responsibility for the success or failure of the New Frontier. And by the spring of 1962, he seemed to be trying to cover the whole of its vast geography. In addition to ongoing crises such as civil rights, there were daily problems such as the steel crisis, during which he sent FBI agents out in the middle of the night to subpoena the steel company executives who seemed to be defying his brother on the issue of price rises. And there was still his unofficial but increasingly obsessive role as general of the secret war against Castro.

Roswell Gilpatric, another member of the Special Group (Augmented), later said that Bobby was the "moving spirit" behind Operation Mongoose. Time and again he would come to meetings complaining that plans were inadequate: "We should get in there and do more." He put in calls to Richard Helms, who had replaced the hapless Bissell, to check progress on the planned acts of sabotage and subversion. ("My God, these Kennedys keep the pressure on about Castro," the taciturn Helms finally complained to CIA attorney Lawrence Houston.) One of Lansdale's plans which particularly seized Bobby's imagination called for sabotage of the Matahambre copper mines. He was on the phone constantly about it: "Had the agents landed? Had they reached the mines? Had they destroyed them?"

In Lansdale's original plan, Mongoose was to have been a modest program one of whose benefits would be to keep the CIA's appetite for power in check. But by the spring Mongoose was growing apace. Soon the Miami headquarters of Task Force W, the Agency's arm for implementing plans conceived by the Special Group (Augmented), was on its way to becoming the largest CIA installation in the world, one that would ultimately involve five hundred case workers handling some three thousand Cubans at an expense of more than $100 million per year. Bobby was often there to spur them on. More than once he came into conflict with William Harvey, the corpulent, paranoid CIA operative in charge of Task Force W who had become something of a legend in the Agency. (One of these confrontations took place in the Miami headquarters during one of Bobby's visits. After reading the classified messages on the teletype, he tore a strip off and was taking it with him to the door when Harvey yelled: "Hey, where are you going with that?" When Bobby kept on walking, Harvey rushed over to block his way and grabbed the message out of his hand.)

But claustral though it came to seem to those involved in planning, the clandestine assaults on Cuba did not take place in a vacuum. Early in 1962, Jack set up a Special Group for counterinsurgency which was supposed to confront the problem of guerrillas in Southeast Asia and other regions where the U.S. had interests that were challenged, and prevent them from coming to power as they had with Castro. Again Taylor was in charge; again Bobby was the most enthusiastic member.*

Some members of the administration felt that the talk about counterinsurgency always remained an intellectual dalliance for Jack. With Bobby it had clearly become a sort of mania, an elaboration on a global scale of his earlier "chasing bad men." He kept a green beret on his desk. He imported Special Forces troops for weekend exercises at Hyannis, efforts which Sargent Shriver, far less enthusiastic about the clandestine world of derring-do, referred to as "swinging from trees and hanging from fences" and refused to let his children watch.

Early in 1962, Bobby, in Saigon on a stopover during a Far Eastern trip, said: "This is a new kind of war, but war it is in a very real sense of the

*Sometimes his enthusiasm for some particular cause brought him into conflict with Taylor. When the Special Group (CI) was getting established, Bobby wanted Arthur Goldberg to be one of the committee members. Taylor resolutely refused. Bobby got other members to vote Goldberg in; Taylor ignored the results of the vote. Bobby said: "Well, shit, the second most important man in the world just lost another one!" and slammed the door so hard as he left the room that the windows rattled.

word. It is a war fought not by massive divisions but secretly by terror, assassination, ambush and infiltration.... I think the United States will do what is necessary to help a country that is trying to repel aggression with its own blood, tears and sweat ...'' Some of those in the administration who were amused by his enthusiasm began to refer to him as ''Mister CI.'' Suddenly he was talking about the problems Khrushchev would have with the ''Chicoms.'' He referred to men like Taylor and Roger Hilsman, the Director of Intelligence at State who had fought behind enemy lines in Burma, as ''guerrillas,'' oblivious to the distinction between guerrillas and commandos. The mania for counterinsurgency that the Special Group helped to create in Washington soon became ridiculous to someone like the CIA's Robert Amory, a veteran of World War II : ''The extreme kind of reaction to Bobby Kennedy's insistence that everybody get gung ho was that word went out from the Chief of Staff that every school in the Army would devote a minimum of 20 percent of its time to counterinsurgency. Well, this reached the Finance School and the Cooks and Bakers School. So they were talking about how to wire typewriters to explode or how to make apple pies with grenades inside of them.''

The way Bobby moved between committees and agencies—partly as Jack's ombudsman to make sure there were no more disasters, but also as a goad making sure that the darker purposes of the administration were accomplished—was wholly extraordinary. The blood tie was crucial to this unique role. Only the President's brother could have dogged the intelligence bureaucracy the way he did; only a brother could have overridden the checks and balances present even in the secret reaches of government to accomplish the ends he and Jack had in mind. But if brotherhood was his great advantage, it was also the cross Bobby bore, for the more deeply he involved himself in Jack's behalf the more he saw how flawed his brother was. The fullest realization came on February 27, 1962, when he received a memo from J. Edgar Hoover stating that information developed in connection with an FBI investigation showed that Judith Campbell, one of Jack's mistresses since 1960, was also the mistress of Chicago Mafia capo Sam Giancana.*

It could not help but aggravate Bobby's puritanical streak. During the years of his youth he had been his mother's partisan, seeing his father's sexual failings through her eyes, and afterward he had known he was different from the other men in his family. Aggressively faithful to his own marriage vows, he had been the Kennedy who tried to keep others from

---

*Campbell had been introduced to Jack by Frank Sinatra in Las Vegas in February 1960, and made a date to have lunch with him the next day. Teddy, also part of the party, danced with her that night and tried to persuade her to fly with him to Denver the next day, pressing her in a manner she regarded as ''childishly temperamental,'' an assessment Jack agreed with when he told her that his younger brother was unlikely to fulfill the Kennedy destiny.

straying. It was he who was designated to talk to Steve Smith when rumors of philandering threatened to break up the marriage with Jean; he who tried to keep Peter Lawford in line when the same kinds of rumors surfaced. It was Bobby who had been so offended by the writer Gore Vidal's avowed bisexuality that he peeled the writer's hands off Jackie while the two were dancing at a White House function. It had been taboo to bring up the subject of Jack's women directly, but when Bobby heard that his brother had asked for an introduction to a young German woman named Ellen Romesch, he did an investigation, found that she had once had an affair with a Soviet attaché, and deported her in a rush. Family friend Mary Gimbel recalls a scene in which the three Kennedy brothers were getting ready to be photographed. "Jack and Teddy put their arms around Bobby and said sort of kiddingly, 'We three!' Bobby slipped out of the embrace and said in a way that was lighthearted but still made it clear how different he felt from them in certain ways: 'No. *You two!*' "

The revelation of the Giancana-Campbell part of the triangle was more than a moral disaster; it was a political one as well. It was bad enough to be under Hoover's thumb once again. (Bobby later said that the FBI Director had been sending a memo every month or so "about someone I knew or a member of my family or allegations in connection with myself so that it would be clear . . . he was on top of all these things . . .") But even worse, the people he hated most—the chieftains of organized crime—now had a hold on his brother and on the presidency itself.

There was, moreover, an obvious thread leading from the relationship with Campbell to the potentially devastating subject of murder plots against Castro in the works since August 1960, about the same time Bissell was beginning to plan the Bay of Pigs and running on a parallel line. Some of these plots seemed almost to have been designed by a gag writer: using depilatories to make the Cuban leader lose his beard and therefore his machismo; killing him by contaminating one of his favorite cigars with botulism. But there was a more serious dimension and it centered on the CIA's decision to use the mob, another party aggrieved by the Castro revolution, to stage a hit. As its middleman for the plot, the CIA had recruited Robert Maheu, a former FBI agent working for Howard Hughes. Maheu brought in Las Vegas hoodlum John Roselli, who in turn brought in Giancana, an associate of former Havana Cosa Nostra boss Santos Trafficante. Not long before the Bay of Pigs, an attempt was made to slip poison pills into Castro's food; afterward efforts were suspended. The whole matter of mob involvement in assassination plots had come up only because Giancana asked Maheu as a favor to bug the Las Vegas hotel room of comedian Dan Rowan, who he suspected was sleeping with another Giancana girlfriend, singer Phyllis McGuire, and the FBI discovered the bug.

In May, Bobby was briefed about the whole situation. CIA men Lawrence

Houston and Colonel Sheffield Edwards later recalled that he heatedly responded that if the Agency was going to become involved with gangsters
again, he wanted to be informed first, although he did not comment on the
operation itself. If Bobby gave the impression of anger rather than surprise
—"If you have seen [his] eyes get steely and his jaw set and his voice get
low and precise," Houston said, "you get a definite feeling of unhappiness"
—it was because he already knew that Giancana had been used by the CIA
against Castro, having been informed by Hoover a year earlier, in a memo
dated May 22, 1961. And on April 8, scarcely a month before his briefing,
another CIA contact had been made with Johnny Roselli at which the mobster was given more poison pills to use on Castro. According to William
Harvey, Colonel Edwards had made the April contact with Roselli.

In the tangled dramaturgy of events, it was not clear who had been directly responsible for the assassination plans. No one ever specified that Jack
or Bobby had officially ordered them. Yet Richard Helms later noted that
no official order would have been required. An intimation would have been
enough, as when Henry I asked about his antagonist Beckett: Will nobody
rid me of this troublesome priest?

In any case, assassination was certainly in the air. In January 1961, Bissell
had created "Executive Action," telling Harvey—in words he would later
confirm in official testimony but disclaim after a talk with Rostow and
Bundy—that the White House had twice urged him to build such an assassination capacity. As early as November 1961, the President had brought
New York Times Latin American expert Tad Szulc into the Oval Office,
allegedly to look him over for a job in the administration but actually to
hold a peculiar conversation. "What would you think if I ordered Castro to
be assassinated?" the President asked out of the blue. Szulc said he was
against it and Jack said he was too. "He said he was testing me, that he felt
the same way...," Szulc said later, "because indeed the U.S. morally must
not be a party to assassinations." Szulc always wondered if this conversation
had anything to do with the fact that he had caught wind of an abortive
scheme by which U.S. military intelligence would have infiltrated a band of
Cuban exile marksmen into Cuba from the U.S. base at Guantanamo to stage
a hit on Fidel and his brother Raúl.

As late as August 10, 1962, when the Special Group (Augmented) met in
Rusk's office to discuss Mongoose, McNamara brought up anew the question
of killing Castro, and Ed Murrow, then head of the United States Information Agency, and others took sharp exception. "It was the obvious consensus...," the irascible Harvey wrote in a memo about the meeting, "in
answer to a comment by Mr. Ed. Murrow, that this is not a subject which has
been made a matter of official record." Three days later, Lansdale drafted a
new plan of operation for Mongoose and asked Harvey to prepare papers on
several subjects: "Intelligence, Political (including liquidation of leaders),

Economic (sabotage, limited deception), and Paramilitary.'' Harvey exploded at the indiscretion, calling Lansdale to point out ''the inadmissibility and stupidity of putting this type of comment in writing in such a document'' and asserting that the CIA would ''write no document pertaining to this and would participate in no open meeting discussing it.''

The fact that the Giancana-Campbell-JFK triangle threatened to make such plots public now made it all the more vital that Bobby do something. Since he could not really prosecute Giancana, he ordered around-the-clock harassment of him. FBI men parked outside the mobster's house; they followed him so closely on the golf course that he later claimed he lost twenty strokes off his game. When he finally petitioned a court for relief, the Justice Department ordered the federal attorney assigned to the case to decline to cross-examine him. It was also at this time that Bobby cut ties with Giancana's friend and business partner, Frank Sinatra. (''Johnny, you just can't associate with this guy,'' Red Fay recalls hearing him say to Jack.) The break came during a presidential visit to California in June. Anticipating a triumphant role as Jack's host, the payoff for his efforts during the 1960 campaign and afterward, Sinatra had built a helicopter launching pad at his Palm Springs retreat, installed a huge phone bank for communications, and constructed accommodations for the Secret Service and other members of the presidential party. Peter Lawford got the job of telling him not only that Jack would not be staying there but that he would be staying at the home of a rival singer, Republican Bing Crosby.

The Campbell-Giancana affair had temporarily slowed down Mongoose planning. At a meeting on February 20, the Special Group (Augmented) had approved a six-phase schedule by Lansdale (encompassing ''attacks on cadre of the regime, including key leaders'') designed to culminate in ''open revolt and overthrow'' of Castro. But then came the Hoover memo, and a few days after that there was another meeting at which Lansdale's ambitious plan was tabled in favor of an ''intelligence gathering'' operation only. By midsummer, however, with JFK having broken with Campbell and Bobby forcing Giancana on the defensive, Mongoose came back on line in a flurry of activity.

At the August 10 Special Group (Augmented) meeting in which McNamara committed his indiscretion regarding assassination, the indefatigable Lansdale suggested what he called a ''stepped-up Course B'' plan involving the exertion of all possible pressures to overthrow the Castro regime. Ten days later, after some internal discussion—John McCone, who had replaced Allen Dulles as CIA chief, favored a plan whose object was ''splitting Castro off from the old-line Communists''—Taylor told the President that the group favored a more aggressive Mongoose program. On August 23, the National Security Council issued memo 181 stating that ''the line of activity projected for Operation Mongoose Plan B plus should be developed with all possible speed." On August 30, the group directed the CIA to submit a list of possible sabotage targets. Rather than simply turning saboteurs loose, the group retained tight control: one executive on Task Force W was struck by the requirement to submit "detailed plans for every activity . . . in nauseating detail . . . down to such things as the gradients on the beach, and the composition of the sand on the beach in many cases. Every single solitary thing was in these plans, full details, times, events, weaponry . . . the full details of every single thing we did."

But this activity—like so many other initiatives of the New Frontier— had an outcome almost exactly opposite from what Bobby and others involved in the group intended. Concerned at the renewed effort to bring Castro down, a secret war which was a secret only in the United States, the Russians began a dramatic increase of their commitment to Cuba. By early October there were 20,000 troops, along with 150 jets, 350 tanks, 1300 pieces of field artillery, and 700 antiaircraft guns on the island. Republican Senator Kenneth Keating of New York, apparently acting on inside information from the intelligence community, began to blast the administration about the buildup in conventional weaponry but even more about suspiciously large crates being off-loaded in Havana harbor which he claimed contained Russian missiles, forcing the administration to deny that any such thing was happening.*

The picture of Russian aggression that Keating painted seemed alarmingly unprovoked to a public unaware of the secret war being waged against Castro. It also forced Bobby, as the general of this war, into the diplomatic arena. Throughout the administration he had been meeting periodically with a colorful KGB agent named Georgi Bolshakov, who provided a direct line to Khrushchev. But what had been social occasions now took on a new urgency, as Bobby gave Bolshakov hints about the missiles to be relayed to Moscow.

On September 4, in an upstaging of the State Department that showed his

---

*Joseph Alsop had invited Jack to dinner the day he received information about the missiles. Alsop noticed that the President was in a "brown study" throughout the evening. Before dinner, Alsop says, Jack took Charles E. Bohlen, the newly appointed Ambassador to France and a long-time Soviet watcher, into Alsop's garden to try to persuade him to stay in Washington a little longer, to be part of the special group named to advise him as he dealt with the missiles in the days ahead. They got into the sort of discussion Jack loved—about the role of chance in history, the odds of something important happening at any given moment. Defense Secretary Robert McNamara had earlier worked out a mathematical formula for the change in odds of nuclear war if nuclear proliferation were permitted to occur. Ignoring Cuba and the USSR, Jack began to talk about China, where such proliferation was beginning to occur: "Of course the odds are that we will have a nuclear war with China within ten years. But you can't pay attention to the odds. A great power can't surrender if it wishes to remain a great power."

growing influence, the Attorney General met with Soviet Ambassador Anatoly Dobrynin, allegedly to discuss a test-ban treaty. After that subject had been disposed of, Bobby raised the question of the kinds of military equipment being sent to Cuba. Dobrynin replied that Khrushchev had asked him to assure the President that the missiles that had been sent were for the defense of Cuba and that there would be no "offensive" or surface-to-surface missiles. Bobby carried this assurance to Jack and suggested a presidential statement "making it unequivocally clear that the U.S. would not tolerate the introduction of offensive surface-to-surface missiles, or offensive weapons of any kind, into Cuba." He then helped prepare the warning, which Jack delivered in an attempt both to signal the Russians and to take off the heat that Keating was applying with increasing intensity.

The administration couldn't admit that Mongoose had partly provoked the Russian buildup. And it was reluctant to use any means other than Mongoose to deal with it. On September 9, the Special Group (Augmented), meeting more regularly now, discussed whether or not "the matter of attacking and harassing Soviet personnel in Cuba should be considered." Three days later, in another meeting, the subject came up again: "Consideration will be given to provoking and conducting physical attacks on [Soviet] Bloc personnel." A month later Bobby, who now replaced Maxwell Taylor as chairman of the group, told it that Jack was "concerned about the progress of the Mongoose program" and urged that "massive activity" be undertaken within the Lansdale framework. On October 14, four days after Keating charged that half a dozen sites for intermediate-range missiles were under construction, the group decided that "all efforts should be made to develop new and imaginative approaches [to] the possibility of getting rid of the Castro regime."

But when U-2 planes confirmed that launch sites for surface-to-surface and therefore "offensive" missiles were under construction (Khrushchev having apparently gambled that the "secret war" would provide a rationale for shifting the nuclear balance), the problem had clearly outgrown Mongoose and the Special Group (Augmented). A new nucleus of senior officials and presidential advisers, including Bundy, Dillon, Sorensen, and others and calling itself Ex-Com, began meeting on a crisis footing. The inclusion of political operative Kenny O'Donnell in this group suggested that Bobby and Jack were aware of the impact the missiles could have on the November elections. When the early consensus of Ex-Com was for an air strike to take out the missile sites, Bobby passed a note to Jack: "I now know how Tojo felt when he was planning Pearl Harbor." That same afternoon he met with the CIA's Richard Helms to note "the general dissatisfaction of the President" with Mongoose.

The word passed about why the Attorney General and not the President was the focal figure in Ex-Com—that Jack had to keep to his regular schedules for fear of tipping the administration's hand—was convincing only for those who didn't know the extent to which Cuba had become Bobby's game. In his unique position as brother and policy maker, Bobby carried messages back and forth from Jack with an informality that Dean Acheson, one of the "wise men" brought in from outside, found a distressing violation of traditional policy-making procedure. Although Taylor, McCone, Dillon, and others were arrayed with Acheson against him, Bobby, aware that his own efforts against Castro had been centrally responsible for creating a situation that jeopardized Jack's presidency, argued strenuously to change the consensus recommendation from an air strike that would take out the missiles to a blockade. The arguments he made were emotional rather than strategic. The distinction between "offensive" and "defensive" missiles could make sense only to someone who knew that Castro was justified in seeking self-protection. (During the crisis week, the CIA's Harvey bluntly told Bobby and Jack that the crisis was their own fault for telling the Russians they would tolerate "defensive" missiles, an outburst which caused him to be removed from Task Force W.) Bobby's analogy to Pearl Harbor, brought up again in Ex-Com meetings, made no sense at all to Acheson, who quickly demolished it: Cuba was ninety miles away, not thousands; the Russians had lied repeatedly about the missile sites; and rather than being the perpetrator of a surprise attack, the United States would merely be carrying out the response it had warned about in public speeches and private conversations with Moscow diplomats.

But the fact that he obviously had Jack's proxy allowed Bobby to carry the day. Ex-Com became committed to a blockade, or "quarantine," as it would be called in an allusion to Roosevelt's hemispheric policy during World War II. This policy avoided any initial confrontation, but it also assured that if conflict eventually came it would be at a high level. Nonetheless, the Kennedy brothers were aware that the blockade might seem a compromise and looked for candidates to scapegoat for being "soft." Adlai Stevenson fit the requirements. Still bitter about being used in the Bay of Pigs (Michael Forrestal was struck by how he now referred acidly to the President only as "Kennedy"), the U.N. Ambassador had initially been unwilling to use U-2 photos of the missile sites in Security Council debate, fearing that they had been doctored like the aircraft of the "Cuban defector" in the Bay of Pigs crisis. Jack derided Stevenson's suggestion that instead of a blockade there be a trade of American missiles in Turkey for Russian missiles in Cuba. ("Adlai wanted a Munich," Jack later said to Charles Bartlett, who was writing a *Saturday Evening Post* article on the crisis with Stewart Alsop, an article which would include the damning remark.) "He's not strong or tough enough to be representing us at the U.N. at a time like this," Bobby said to Jack. When Stevenson went back to the U.N. and dramatically attacked Soviet representative Zorin for lying about the missiles, the President watched the performance on tv and remarked laconically, "I never knew Adlai had it in him. Too bad he didn't show some of that steam in the 1956 campaign."

On October 22, Jack went on television with a brilliant speech in which he referred back to the era which continued to serve as a central historical metaphor for the Kennedy family: "The 1930s taught us a clear lesson: aggressive conduct, if allowed to go unchecked, ultimately leads to war.... Our objective, therefore, must be to prevent the use of these missiles against this or any other country..." Two days later, after McNamara had ordered nuclear units to load their weapons and Polaris subs to begin their deep runs toward the USSR and Russian ships were approaching the quarantine line, Bobby was with Jack, watching the tension on his brother's face and experiencing the passage of time as a reprise on some crises of the past. ("Inexplicably I thought of when he was ill and almost died; when he lost his child; when we learned that our oldest brother had been killed... ") When the United States naval task force stopped and boarded the Russian trawlers approaching the blockade, the first destroyer to make contact was the *Joseph P. Kennedy, Jr.* It was as if the whole nation was acting out a Kennedy drama of redemption.

Over the next few days, as prospects for war diminished—Acheson was not alone in believing that it had been "a very near thing"—Jack acknowledged that it was his brother's victory. Sitting alone in the White House one evening with Dave Powers, eating warmed-over chicken, the President went over the critical moments—holding out against Taylor, Dillon, Acheson, and the other strong figures in Ex-Com; talking tough to Dobrynin; choosing to answer Khrushchev's first letter agreeing to pull the missiles out and ignoring the second, more truculent letter—and finally he simply said, "Thank God for Bobby."

Bobby was at a horse show with his daughter Kathleen when he got the call from Rusk that the Russians had formally agreed to terms. That evening he was back at the White House for another meeting with Jack, this time a celebration rather than a possible death watch. With Bobby sitting there to share the credit, Jack called Truman and Eisenhower to tell them about the triumph. Later, as Bobby was getting ready to go home to Hickory Hill, Jack said, in a reference to Lincoln and to the peak they had just climbed, "This is the night I should go to the theater." Bobby laughed and replied, "If you go, I want to go with you."

3.

*T*HE MISSILE CRISIS MAY NOT HAVE been, as Walt Rostow grandly called it, the Gettysburg of the cold war. But it was a climactic moment for the Kennedy presidency: a reversal of the humiliations suffered at the Bay of Pigs and at Vienna; a psychological as well as a diplomatic victory in that it allowed Jack, in the columnist Joseph Kraft's words, "to finally win his manhood from the Russians." Yet it was also the moment in which intent and outcome were closer than they were ever to be again, the triumph by which the future would inevitably be judged. In retrospect, the missile crisis would look like the denouement of a carefully plotted play: the moment when fate and character join at the turning point to make the rest of the action inevitable.

Positioned as he was on the front lines of the Kennedy Administration, Bobby seemed to sense the looming problems more than Jack. As the administration began its third year, he was working hard to solve the outstanding crises, yet always fearful, as he complained to John Seigenthaler, that he was "losing ground." Especially after the clarity of the missile crisis, it seemed as though every act was tangled and complex, engendering an equal and often opposite reaction.

As 1962 ended, Bobby was trying feverishly to tie up the loose ends of the Cuban involvement. Working with Cardinal Cushing and others, he put together the package of medical and agricultural aid that would serve as a ransom for members of the exile army still in Castro's jails and bring them back to the United States for the holidays. When Jack decided to go to the Orange Bowl to address the veterans of Brigade 2506, O'Donnell and others objected to the appearance as politically risky, but Bobby, probably speaking for himself as much as his brother, insisted that a trip to Miami would help assuage the "guilt" that remained from the Bay of Pigs. Jackie highlighted this emotional meeting by giving a speech in Spanish in which she alluded to John Junior: "He's still too young to realize what has happened here but I will make it my business to tell him the story of your courage as he grows up. It is my wish and hope that someday he may be a man at least half as brave as the members of Brigade 2506." When members of the exile army presented their flag to Jack, he said, "I can assure you that this flag will be returned to the Brigade in a free Havana!" The Cubans began their chant: *"Guerra! Guerra! Guerra!"*

Yet at the same time hope was extended, the means for achieving it had to be withdrawn. Mongoose was halted; Task Force W and the CIA monolith in Miami were cut back; the Special Group (Augmented) was terminated. There was a crackdown on exile activity and an end to funds for the Cuban Revolutionary Council. Exile leader Miro Cardona went to Washington to plead with Bobby not to turn his back on the anti-Castro forces; he left town bitter at what he called a sellout, accusing the Kennedy brothers of "breaking promises and agreements" for a second invasion. The specter Bissell had used to help coerce Jack into going ahead with the Bay of Pigs in the first place—the "disposal problem" involving a group of angry exiles feeling that they had been betrayed—had become a reality two years later.*

The Cuban communities of Miami and New Orleans, once centers of strong support for the Kennedys, were now centers of opposition. The same was true of the South itself. In 1960, Bobby had used his connections with McClellan and other Senate figures to work the region politically for his brother. Now, three years later, the whole region was a land apart in its hatred for the administration. And in a sense the enmity was undeserved. If the Kennedy brothers were activists in foreign affairs, they were far more passive when it came to civil rights; they were trying to practice a containment policy on black aspiration. Father Theodore Hesburgh, head of the

---

*The vacillation continued in secret intelligence and diplomatic efforts. On May 28, Bobby told members of the Standing Group on Cuba Policy (which, in the organizational musical chairs of the administration, had replaced the Special Group) that "the U.S. must do something even though we do not believe our actions would bring [Castro] down..." Two weeks later, another program of sabotage was initiated, different in scope from Mongoose in that it aimed only "to nourish a spirit of resistance" in Cuba rather than overthrow the government. By mid-October some twenty-five sabotage operations had been approved and the CIA's Desmond Fitzgerald, who had replaced William Harvey, had recruited a Cuban agent who would make one last effort to assassinate Castro. In October, saying he was a personal representative of Bobby, Fitzgerald met with the agent, code-named AM/LASH, to talk about the plot. At almost the same moment, Jack was urging the diplomat William Attwood and the French journalist Jean Daniel, who both had unofficial links to the Havana government, to try to open channels which might lead to a dialogue and eventual détente with Cuba.

Civil Rights Commission, later said of them, "Their attitude was 'don't do anything until you absolutely have to.' " It was hard for them not to regard civil rights as a subject which always manifested itself at an inopportune moment: the Freedom Rides during the Vienna summit; James Meredith's enrollment at the University of Mississippi (an event that left twenty-eight shot, two killed, and white mobs shouting "Two-Four-One-Three, We Hate Kennedy!") during the first stages of the missile crisis.

After the November 1962 elections Jack signed an order desegregating federal housing, using the "stroke of a pen" he had been promising since the 1960 campaign. In February 1963 he signed more comprehensive civil rights legislation. But black leaders had seen that they had to force the issue. In April Martin Luther King, Jr., began demonstrations in Birmingham despite Bobby's attempt to get him to postpone them, and the world saw pictures of nonviolent protestors being attacked by police dogs and fire hoses. King's brother's house was dynamited, and so was the motel where he made his headquarters; the bombing of a black church in Birmingham killed four little girls. Because of the Kennedys' cautious approach to the Meredith case at the University of Mississippi, George Wallace, the new Governor of Alabama, had concluded that he could defy the Attorney General in the enrollment of two young black women at the University of Alabama. The two were enrolled, but Wallace became a rallying point for white southern resistance, and NAACP leader Medgar Evers was assassinated outside his home in Jackson, Mississippi. Hatred attached itself to Bobby, despite his temporizing. "I hope that every drop of blood that's spilled he tastes in his throat," the outgoing mayor of Birmingham said, "and I hope he chokes."

Civil rights was one of those moral dilemmas foreign to Jack's pragmatic cast of mind, as Theodore Hesburgh discovered when he went to the White House to press one of the Civil Rights Commission's demands—integration of the Alabama National Guard—and was told by the President that he might have to call up the guard because of tensions in Berlin and therefore couldn't consider such a move. The Princeton historian David Donald came away from talks with the President surprised that he subscribed to the antiquated view of Reconstruction as a time of black excess which justified current southern fears regarding integration. And when told that African diplomats driving down Maryland Route 40 faced segregated dining facilities, Jack summoned White House protocol chief Angier Biddle Duke and said, "Can't you ask them to fly?"

Bobby had tried to keep the South's congressional power structure happy by appointing federal judges with conservative opinions on civil rights. (Successfully pushing the nomination of Harold Cox, a Mississippi jurist who had once referred to blacks as "chimpanzees," Mississippi Senator James Eastland said to Bobby in reference to the appointment of Thurgood Marshall to the Court of Appeals: "Tell your brother that if he will give me

Harold Cox I will give him the nigger.'') Yet while Bobby frankly admitted that he didn't "lay awake nights worrying about civil rights," he was emotionally receptive in a way that Jack was not. On June 7, 1963, at his father's Park Avenue apartment, he met with Lena Horne, Harry Belafonte, James Baldwin, and other black celebrities and activists. It was an encounter that the black sociologist Kenneth Clark would remember as "one of the most violent, emotional verbal assaults" he'd ever witnessed. One of those present was Jerome Smith, a Congress of Racial Equality worker who'd been beaten and jailed in the South and now showed Bobby the face of black rage by saying it made him nauseated to be in the same room with Kennedy and that not only would he not consider fighting for the United States but he might consider picking up the gun against it. Bobby was profoundly shaken, although later he tried to dismiss Smith, and especially the black celebrities who had supported him, by comparing them—somewhat revealingly, those close to the Kennedy family drama felt—to the "children of wealthy [white] parents...who've got some personal problem [about] where they stand in life...and therefore become extreme and difficult emotionally." When Jack went on television four days later to announce a civil rights bill, Bobby was the only major figure in the administration to back it. He found himself the hated representative of something he had only begun to be involved in. "It is brother Bobby in the Attorney General's Office, rather than President Jack, who has been blamed," wrote one journalist who observed southern reaction.

In the middle of his vicissitudes with civil rights, Cuba, and other items on the agenda of the New Frontier, there was still the question of the mob. In December 1962, after news came that the Cuban prisoners would be freed, Bobby had turned to an aide and said, "Now let's get Hoffa." His hatred of organized crime was like a metaphysical constant, the one concern free from the ambiguity that affected everything else. Driving by the Teamsters' headquarters with his children, he said of the Christmas tree visible in the lobby, "See that? It's a bad Christmas tree. It was bought with money stolen from working people. It's a bad tree." Once, when talking with Assistant Attorney General William Orrick about how to get Hoffa on a deposition, Bobby agreed to a mock proceeding in which he would take Hoffa's part. Orrick began by asking him to state his name and was struck by the fact that he could hardly gag out the words: "James R. Hoffa."

The "Get Hoffa Squad," headed by Walter Sheridan with sixteen lawyers and nearly twice that many investigators, was technically within the Organized Crime Section of the Justice Department but was actually an elite special force answerable to Bobby himself. (The head of the Organized Crime Section, Edward Silberling, said later: "It burned my ass...Half the jobs [of the section] were Hoffa Squad jobs...I didn't have any control over them...") Unlike other Justice Department divisions, the focus of the

Get Hoffa Squad was a person, not a subject area. Bobby said that he was aiming for an institutional response that was flexible and "creative"; the squad was an instrument of personal will in the same way that Mongoose had been.

By the fall of 1962, there were three cases that Bobby was considering bringing against Hoffa. One involved the Test Fleet Corporation, a truck-leasing firm which had been started in 1948 with Hoffa's wife as one of the incorporators and used afterward, the Justice Department alleged, to allow Hoffa to receive payments directly from an employer, in violation of the Taft-Hartley Act. Bobby had maintained intimate daily contact with the progress of the case, even during the thirteen days of the missile crisis, prosecuting it vigorously despite a lack of enthusiasm on the part of Archibald Cox and others in his office, especially Ramsey Clark, who felt the case was "flimsy as hell" and argued with Bobby over the implications of going forward with it. ("Questions of procedure and due process didn't interest him," Clark said. "He had no feel for them—not generally and certainly not where Hoffa was concerned.")

In the middle of the Test Fleet case, which would ultimately result in a mistrial, New Orleans Teamster leader E. G. Partin got in touch with Kennedy investigator Walter Sheridan and said that an attempt would be made to fix the case by buying off the jurors. Partin passed a lie detector test. He allowed federal investigators to listen in on a telephone conversation with Hoffa about plastic explosives apparently intended for Bobby. In one plan the bomb would be thrown into Hickory Hill, and if Bobby "and all his damn kids" survived the explosion they would be burned up in the fire to follow. A second possibility Partin said Hoffa mentioned involved a lone gunman without traceable connections to the Teamsters who would shoot Bobby with a high-powered, telescoped rifle, preferably somewhere in the South where "segregation people" would be blamed. Partin told investigators that Hoffa actually had a .270-caliber rifle in his office to which he would occasionally point when the subject of the Attorney General came up: "I've got to do something about that son of a bitch Bobby Kennedy. He's got to go."

This subject was discussed in places other than the office of the Teamster president. Bobby's unprecedented campaign against organized crime had resulted in indictments against dozens of top mob figures (many associated with Hoffa)—Anthony Giacalone, Carlos Marcello, Anthony Provenzano, Joey Glimco, and others. Aided by the breakthrough of Joe Valachi's prison revelations concerning the existence of a "Mafia," the Justice Department had moved swiftly against organized crime. The year before Jack took office only thirty-five mobsters had been indicted. In 1963, 288 were brought to trial, a figure that would double within the year.

Talk among crime figures became increasingly violent. Johnny Roselli, centrally involved in the CIA assassination plots, said about Bobby, "Here I am helping the government, helping the country, and that little sonofabitch is breaking my balls. Let the little bastard do what he wants. There isn't anything he can do to me . . . I got important friends in important places in Washington that'll cut his water off."

An FBI tap captured a conversation between Angelo Bruno, head of a Philadelphia crime family, and his associate William Weisberg in which Weisberg said, "With Kennedy, a guy should take a knife . . . and stab and kill the fucker. . . . Somebody should kill the fucker." Santos Trafficante, involved with Meyer Lansky in Cuban casinos before Castro and a broker of loans to mob figures from the Teamster pension fund, talked to Cuban exile José Aleman about how the Attorney General was "hitting Hoffa, a man who is a worker . . . a friend of the blue collars . . . Mark my word, this man Kennedy is in trouble and he will get what is coming to him." At about the same time, Carlos Marcello, still smarting over his "kidnapping" in the first weeks of the Kennedy Administration and still fighting deportation proceedings, met with three associates in New Orleans, where he had illegally returned from El Salvador. He talked about his personal hardships and then said, "Don't worry about that little Bobby sonofabitch. He's going to be taken care of." He went on to propose an analogy comparing the President to a dog and the Attorney General to the dog's tail: "The dog will keep biting you if you only cut off its tail, but if you cut off the dog's head it will die."

If the demons Bobby pursued were more malign than he reckoned, the expectations Jack had aroused were more difficult to satisfy—and in some ways more dangerous—than he acknowledged. By making the theme of his first days in office the idea that America could not only compete with the Soviets for the Third World but also achieve victory, Jack had seized the ground of the radical right, exciting its passions with his eloquence. But policy was determined less by the boldness reflected in his rhetoric than by the hesitancy which was closer to his personality. It had happened with Cuba, when he gave hope to the right with the Bay of Pigs but withdrew it by canceling the air strikes and not going all the way with the invasion; cheered Brigade 2506 on but undercut their operation; forced the missiles out of Cuba but allowed the Russians to remain; continued sabotage operations against Castro but tried to open private channels of diplomatic communication. The same syndrome appeared elsewhere. On June 10, 1963, on the eve of signing a nuclear test ban with the Russians, Jack gave a major address at American University, in Washington, proposing détente and coexistence on the basis of the status quo—which meant legitimizing Soviet domination in Eastern Europe. ("Let us reexamine our attitude toward the Soviet Union. . . . We must deal with the world as it is, not as it might have been if the history of the last eighteen years had been different.'') Yet two weeks later, visiting the Berlin Wall, he gave his truculent *"Ich Bin Ein Berliner"* speech, which some advisers feared would undo everything the previous one had accomplished. (''There are some who say communism is the wave of the future. Let them come to Berlin. There are some who say we can work with the Communists. Let them come to Berlin.'')

These actions suggested basic confusion rather than mere indecision, opportunism rather than pragmatism. Nowhere was the syndrome more obvious than in the final drama of the Kennedy Administration, its policy on Vietnam.

Although distrustful of the military mentality, and aware of the tendency in the Pentagon to falsify facts in order to escalate activity, Jack had given the military control over Vietnam. Some sixteen thousand troops had been sent into the battle zone. The military had asked for jets, napalm, defoliants, free-fire zones; Jack had opposed each in turn but given in when he was pressed. His effort was to try to control the conflict, to moderate it without having to challenge the assumptions on which it was based, assumptions about which he may have been privately suspicious but which he publicly endorsed.*

By the spring of 1963, Lansdale's hearts-and-minds thesis had in effect resulted in the incarceration of several million peasants in ''strategic hamlets.'' It had also propped up a regime increasingly repressive, especially as Diem's brother-in-law Ngo Dinh Nhu turned loose his American-trained secret police on non-Communist political opponents. As Buddhist leaders began massive protests against the Catholic regime, a shudder of doubt passed through the administration. Jack privately told his friend Charles Bartlett: ''We've got to face the fact that the odds are about a hundred to one that we're going to get our asses thrown out of Vietnam.'' But he moved to keep information about the deteriorating situation hidden from public view by pressuring the press. (In one incident he tried to get David Halberstam, the *New York Times* reporter in Saigon, transferred out of Vietnam for sending home dispatches that painted a gloomy picture.) And although in a May press conference he claimed to be ready to withdraw the American presence any time South Vietnam requested it, he let policy drift in the direction of replacing the Diem government with one which would commit

---

*While working on defense analyses for the administration, Daniel Ellsberg (who would later leak the Pentagon Papers to the *New York Times*) once lunched with Jackie and asked her if she was familiar with the work of Paul Mus, the French writer who had done sophisticated analyses of why the French were defeated in Vietnam. Jackie replied that she had in fact translated lengthy excerpts of Mus's work for Jack when he was a senator. Ellsberg asked why, if he had read what in effect was a cautionary tale, Jack hadn't resisted pressures to become more deeply involved in Vietnam. Jackie shrugged. ''You have to understand, my husband is a weak man.''

the United States more profoundly, especially after Nhu said that perhaps the Americans should begin bringing troops home, and implied that the conflict might best be resolved by direct diplomacy between Saigon and Hanoi.

The slide began on May 28, when Buddhist monks protested Diem's order forbidding them to fly ceremonial flags on the Buddha's birthday. Nhu's secret police fired on the pagodas in Hue, killing several people. By June, monks were setting themselves on fire in protest, as Madame Nhu remarked that she'd be willing to furnish mustard for the "barbecues." The rapidly deteriorating situation caused a split in the administration. On one side were Harriman, Roger Hilsman, and other liberals who had decided that if the war were to be won, it was time to drop Diem, if necessary by supporting a coup. They were opposed by Taylor, Rusk, and others, who, in Taylor's words, felt that talk of a coup was "complete irresponsibility," that a coup would weaken the war effort and that any government which might succeed Diem would be less effective against the Communists and require a greater United States involvement. Jack tried to steer a middle course between the factions. Seeing the dilemma as having domestic political consequences, he brought in Henry Cabot Lodge as Ambassador to make sure the Republicans shared in the responsibility for whatever happened.

As criticism mounted Jack tried obliquely to reassure Diem, saying in a press conference, "For us to withdraw from this effort would begin a collapse not only of South Vietnam but of Southeast Asia. So we are going to stay there." Diem promised that there would be a new spirit of harmony. But on August 21, Nhu's secret police again smashed into pagodas and made mass arrests. Hearing from Vietnamese generals who wanted to know what the American attitude would be toward a coup, the Harriman group drafted a cable to Lodge on August 24 informing him that the United States could no longer tolerate Nhu's power, that Diem had to be given a chance "to rid himself of Nhu" but if Diem refused "then we must face the possibility that Diem himself cannot be preserved." This was tantamount to support for a coup. With opponents of such a course out of Washington for the weekend, the telegram was sent to Jack in Hyannis and, after what some regarded as an overhasty clearance, forwarded to Saigon.

When Taylor and the others returned, they were furious at the lack of consultation in making a decision that would mean a quantum leap in the hitherto limited involvement in Vietnam. There were arguments of a kind that had not previously taken place in the administration. "My God," Jack remarked to his friend Charles Bartlett, "my government's coming apart." Bobby, who was unable to shape a consensus on this issue as he had during the missile crisis, recalled the infighting later on as "the only time the government was broken in two in a very disturbing way."

It was another moment of decision. Jack could have backed Diem against the Buddhists or the generals against Diem. What he did was similar to what he had done in the Bay of Pigs—give tepid support to the idea of a coup in an August 29 telegram, which emphasized that he retained the right to change his mind. Lodge, who'd become a key supporter of the Harriman group, cabled back a cautionary note: "To be successful, this operation must be essentially a Vietnamese affair with momentum of its own. Should this happen you may not be able to control it, i.e., the 'go signal' may be given by the generals."

Time passed and the "go signal" was not given. Lacking sufficient troops and mistrusting the indecision in Washington, the Vietnamese generals postponed their move, giving Jack and his advisers an opportunity to reassess the decision. With Nhu stepping up his suggestions that the Diem government might seek a separate peace with Ho Chi Minh, thus taking the United States out of the game in Vietnam, a coup still had its attraction. But Jack remained irresolute, while the division in his government deepened. On September 6 he called in Bobby, who, throwing his weight behind those who wanted to turn the screws on Diem, urged drastic sanctions: "If we have concluded that we are going to lose with Diem, why do we not grasp the nettle now?"

On September 9, interviewed on tv, Jack affirmed his belief in the "domino theory" that the fall of Vietnam would mean the fall of all Southeast Asia: "What I am concerned about is that Americans will get impatient and say, because they don't like events in Southeast Asia and they don't like the Government in Saigon, that we should withdraw. That only makes it easy for the Communists. I think we should stay." He sent Taylor and McNamara on a fact-finding mission that he hoped would produce a policy consensus. When they came back on October 2, they recommended a series of sanctions against Diem that would include the withdrawal of a thousand "advisers" and cuts in economic aid, which McNamara said "will push us toward a reconciliation with Diem or a coup to overthrow Diem." The recommendation was accepted and the policy was put into action, although Jack still tried to hedge his commitment by cabling Lodge on October 6 that "while we do not wish to stimulate a coup, we also do not wish to leave the impression that U.S. would thwart a change of government"—an inscrutable distinction in practice.

By early October Saigon was in ferment, bubbling with rumors about the coup to come. The CIA station there cabled Agency director McCone about contacts with Vietnamese generals, noting that some were for assassinating Diem's younger brothers, his brother-in-law Nhu, and even Diem himself. McCone replied, "We certainly cannot be in the position of stimulating, approving, or supporting assassination, but on the other hand, we are in no way responsible for stopping every such threat of which we might receive even partial knowledge." Bobby later claimed that he had wanted to tell Diem what was about to happen but felt that his "hands were tied."

On November 2, the coup took place. Diem and Nhu were murdered. Taylor was present when Jack received the cable informing him of their deaths: "[The President] leaped to his feet and rushed from the room, with a look of shock and dismay on his face which I had never seen before." He was in total despair. Lem hadn't seen him so depressed since the Bay of Pigs. Another friend who saw him in the White House not long afterward, pale and nervous, tried to console Jack by saying that the murdered brothers had been tyrants. He shook his head grimly: "No, they were in a difficult position. They did the best they could for their country."

By the fall of 1963 the administration's stock was still high in foreign affairs as a result of the missile crisis and the test ban, yet there was a feeling that it was increasingly painting itself into corners—especially in Vietnam—from which there seemed to be no exit. Jack's personal popularity remained strong, but suspicions about the Kennedys as a force in American life were growing and, among certain sectors of the population, amounted almost to a phobia. No President ever had a more cordial, more protected relationship with the national press corps, yet even here there were beginnings of disenchantment. Three times in four days CBS newsman George Herman heard Jack lecture journalists who were covering him about how he was not getting the groundswell of public support that Roosevelt got because "the issues were clear in FDR's day and so complicated in his own that people couldn't understand them." *Chicago Daily News* reporter Peter Lisagor concluded after traveling with the President that Jack believed the press had a "narrow and constricted view of his own broader, more conceptual and grander vision of the world and the United States." His father's old friend Arthur Krock launched a widely applauded attack on the administration's news management, which he charged took "the form of *direct* and *deliberate* actions . . . enforced more cynically and more boldly than by any other previous administration." Another *Times* heavyweight, Hanson Baldwin, complained about "astonishing examples of news repression and distortion, management and control, pressures and propaganda."

Bobby was so affected by the escalating hostility and his role in provoking it that he thought of quitting. He later said, "I thought that I had become such a liability and the campaign [against the Kennedys] was getting so bitter and mean . . . People were saying so many things and it was getting more and more of the family . . ." On November 20, his thirty-eighth birthday, there was a little party at the Justice Department. Bobby stood up on a desk and made a corrosively ironic speech outlining the ways in which he had helped his brother by what he'd done in regard to Hoffa, civil rights, wiretapping, and other lightning-rod issues of the administration. Seigenthaler and others who heard the speech thought that even though he had been the key figure of the administration, it was possible that Bobby would no longer be around after the first of the year.

Jack, however, was oddly buoyant. Always able to amuse people close to him, he now moved them too. Those who knew the troubles he had surmounted in his life, and the fragility of his triumph, found tears in their eyes when he would sometimes decide to speak the lyrics of "September Song" during the late hours of some gathering. He had been terribly affected by the death of his infant son Patrick Bouvier in August, having been the last to leave the funeral mass presided over by Cardinal Cushing, weeping and more stricken than anybody could remember ever having seen him. He grabbed at the tiny casket in such a disoriented manner that Cushing had to restrain him, whispering, "Come on, Jack, let's go. God is good." He still thought about and spoke of his own death, as on an occasion after Patrick's burial when he was sailing with Bartlett and Billings one afternoon. The wind vanished, leaving the boat drifting listlessly in the water, and after looking over the side for a long time, he asked suddenly, "How do you think Lyndon would be if I got killed?" He returned to the subject a few weeks later while swimming with Torby MacDonald in the pool at Palm Beach. They were talking about how both their fathers had been incapacitated by strokes and how neither of them wanted such a fate. Torby asked Jack what way he'd choose to die. After thinking for a moment, Jack said: "Oh, a gun. You never know what's hit you. A gunshot is the perfect way."

Yet he was in better shape than ever before. The steroids he had been taking had filled out his face so much that he fretted about having a weight problem, but the medication seemed to have controlled his Addison's disease for good. His back too had improved after his former doctor, Janet Travell, was replaced by White House physician George Bulkey. Bulkey had brought in a team of orthopedists who substituted a demanding regimen of exercise for the procaine injections. By the fall these exercises had succeeded so well, according to Bulkey, that Jack was able to go through "a series of exercises which would do credit to a gymnast and was very pleased with his progress."

He was also coming into his own as a family man. He was tender with his father, who would wait in his wheelchair on the porch at Hyannis on Friday afternoon for the presidential helicopter to come. The Ambassador's decline made him no longer threatening—someone who could finally be loved. Jack would sit with him for a long time, describing presidential problems, sharing the office they had collaborated in procuring. His relationship with Jackie also seemed to have reached an angle of repose. One close friend who knew all about his philandering recalls how Jack phoned him and said, "There are two naked girls in the room but I'm sitting here reading the *Wall Street Journal*. Does that mean I'm getting old?" The friend felt that the marriage had gotten past its most threatening moments and was beginning to mature: "It was more than an 'understanding.' Jack was getting to the point where he really appreciated her—as a political asset and as a person."

Jack enjoyed his children. He was shrewdly aware of their public relations value, photographers discovered. Stanley Tretick of *Life*, for instance, engaged in byzantine conspiracies with Jack to evade Jackie's well-known fanaticism about invasions of privacy and get photographs of the Kennedy children. ("We better get out of the way pretty quick," Jack said nervously during one shooting session. "Things get pretty sticky when Jackie's around.") But there was a personal involvement too. J. B. West, the White House butler, recalled Jack coming down from the private quarters with John-John in the elevator. The boy was yelling, "Don't leave me!" and Jack finally shrugged and said, "Okay, let's go to work," and took the child to the Oval Office to play on the floor. The same was true with Caroline, whom he liked to exhibit. On sailing expeditions on the presidential yacht he would tell about the adventures of the White Whale to keep her and himself amused. The White Whale, which followed unseen in the yacht's wake, was, as Jack described him, especially fond of men's socks. Lem Billings recalled how Franklin D. Roosevelt, Jr., was once on board when the next chapter of the White Whale began to unfold. The White Whale was hungry, Jack said with Caroline looking on, and asked the guest to take off his socks and throw them overboard. FDR Jr. did it, an oblique pun on that day twenty-five years earlier when his father had asked Joseph Kennedy to drop his pants. "We all learned that when Jack began telling Caroline about the White Whale it was time to move to another part of the yacht," Lem said.

And however frustrated he was by the pressures of governance, Jack still loved the politics of the presidency. He speculated constantly about his possible opponents in 1964: Michigan Governor George Romney, whose apparent lack of vices intrigued him, and Barry Goldwater, who he felt would be easier to beat. He woolgathered over possible changes in his cabinet: Rusk to be eased into the U.N. and replaced at State by McNamara; Bobby to be enticed back into government after running the reelection campaign by being offered the job of Assistant Secretary of State with control over the Alliance for Progress. He even looked past 1964, questioning Charles Bartlett during a stay at the Camp David presidential retreat about whether he thought the 1968 nominee would be Lyndon Johnson or Bobby. He gave Bartlett the impression that even though he recognized how much he owed his brother he was "not particularly thrilled" at the prospect of eventually being succeeded by another Kennedy to whom he would be compared. Bartlett concluded: "It seemed to worry him."

He knew that Bobby and his friends were against Johnson and were talking about dumping him. In an effort to close the breech between them the Vice President had gone to Bobby and said, "I know why you're against me. It's because of what they say I said about your daddy at the convention. I didn't really say that." Bobby had Seigenthaler dig out clippings and talk to the newsmen involved to prove that Johnson had indeed made the charges about Joseph Kennedy's appeasement. Frequently exasperated by the Vice

President, Jack was nonetheless amused by Johnson's roguish eccentricities and self-madeness, and told stories about him as if they were vignettes of a vanishing Americana. (One that he particularly liked concerned the time John Glenn was about to take off on his historic space flight and Johnson muttered to himself from a corner of the Oval Office during the countdown: "If only he were a Negro.") Jack regarded Johnson as, like himself, a man of the world, and was avid for gossip about the Vice President's sexual exploits.* He went out of his way to allay Johnson's fears about being removed from the ticket, telling one of the Vice President's aides: "I really feel sorry for Lyndon. I know he's unhappy in the vice presidency. It's a horseshit job, the worst fucking job I can imagine . . . What I want you to do is tell Lyndon how much I appreciate him as Vice President. I know he's got a tough role and I'm sympathetic. Get across to him that he has nothing to fear but fear itself."

Feeling that his likely opponent in the next election would be Barry Goldwater, he wanted Johnson with him. In fact he decided to make a trip to Dallas to mend the feud between Governor John Connally, a Johnson protégé, and Senator Ralph Yarborough. Adlai Stevenson and Senator Fulbright, who had both recently been confronted by unpleasant crowds in Dallas and seen the intensity of anti-administration sentiment there, both warned him about the city. But as Jack told Bobby in one of their last conversations, the friction was making the trip more exciting and more interesting.

Bobby was at home at Hickory Hill on November 22 when the call came from J. Edgar Hoover. New York federal attorney Robert Morgenthau, asked to lunch to discuss the campaign against organized crime, watched him put a hand to his mouth in horror and then say, "Jack's been shot. It may be fatal." He went upstairs to try to get through to Dallas on another line, getting details about the wounds Connally had suffered and confirming that Jackie was unhurt. Thirty minutes later he came down, pale with shock, and said: "He's dead." Afterward he walked outside with Ed Guthman. "I thought they'd get one of us," he said, "but Jack, after all he'd been through, never worried about it . . . I thought it would be me."

Bobby stayed in Washington to begin taking care of the details of the funeral and dispatched Teddy to Hyannis. Rose already knew what had happened. As images flashed through the country of Jackie in her bloody dress and Lyndon Johnson taking the oath of office aboard Air Force One, Rose paced the grounds inside the compound. When she saw her nephew Joey

---

*Johnson reciprocated the feeling. Bobby Baker later recalled that on his return from an errand to the Oval Office he found several messages from Johnson requesting a meeting. "As soon as he spotted me LBJ leaned forward and whispered, 'Tell me, is ol' Jack gettin' much pussy?'"

Gargan she stopped to say to him, "Joey, you should read more. Read Marlborough, Fox, and Burke, like Jack." The Ambassador did not know. Household employees had told him his television set was out of order so he wouldn't see the news. Ted repeated this, but the old man mutely gestured toward the plug. Ted plugged it into the socket but then ripped the other end out of the set and left the room. Eunice finally came in with Ted and tried to tell him what had happened: "Daddy. Daddy, there's been an accident. But Jack's okay. Jack was in an accident, Daddy. Oh Daddy, Jack's dead. He's dead, but he's in heaven. Oh God, Daddy, Jack's okay, isn't he?"

When Rose and the others departed for the funeral, leaving him behind, Joe Kennedy thrashed his way into his clothes and let his niece Ann Gargan know he wanted to be taken to the airport. But the *Caroline* had already left. He was driven home and put back in bed, where he sank down under the covers. Over the next few days he watched the drama of the national mourning and the state funeral on television. Not long afterward Jackie came to visit, bringing the flag that had been draped over Jack's casket while his body lay in the Capitol. After he was asleep Ann Gargan came in and, thinking the flag was a blanket, spread it over the Ambassador. In the middle of the night he awakened and for a moment thought he was dead and lying in state. He screamed so loudly that it roused everyone in the house.

4.

*J*OE KENNEDY HAD A WETNESS AT
the corners of his eyes all through the winter of 1963–64, a condition Rose
insisted on attributing to a lack of muscular control but everyone else realized was caused by sorrow. He sat in the pale sun at Palm Beach slumped
down into his wheelchair, a blanket tucked around his atrophying legs. As
one of his attendants said, "He didn't really bother after the assassination.
He sort of gave up. He was never the same."

Rose spent long hours alone rustling through the attic at Hyannis and the
house at Palm Beach in an effort to sort out Jack's things in case a museum
should ask for some piece of memorabilia. She was like a ghost haunting the
upper reaches of the house late into the night, unable to sleep but afraid to
ask the nurses attending her husband for a sedative lest it keep her from
waking up for early mass.

"The whole family was like a bunch of shipwreck survivors," Lem Billings said later. "I don't think they could have made it at all without Bobby."
Bobby was the rock they clung to. He was the one who insisted that everything would be all right, the one who urged them to set a term to their
mourning and get on with their lives. "He seemed to be everywhere. He
always had an arm around a friend or family member and was telling them
it was okay, that it was time to move ahead."

But what he did for others he was unable to do for himself. He remained
buried in sorrow that wouldn't end, seemingly frozen at that moment of
grief when he had put his *PT 109* tie clip, a silver rosary, and a lock of his
own hair into his brother's coffin. "How do I look?" he asked John Seigenthaler a few weeks after the funeral. Glancing at Bobby's face—the eyes

recessed into their sockets, the jaw elongated into a Modigliani vision of suffering—Seigenthaler replied, "You look like hell." Bobby didn't respond directly but stared off in the middle distance mumbling, "I can't sleep, I can't sleep." Seigenthaler wondered if he would ever come out of it. "He was just inconsolable. He was in perpetual pain, like someone with a terrible toothache that wouldn't go away. It was awful to watch."

Bobby wouldn't say the word "assassination" or "death" or even "Dallas," but spoke only of "the events of November 22." His sisters and especially Teddy took relief in iconography, placing pictures of Jack throughout their homes; but Bobby couldn't bear the visual reminders, and when visiting friends he would go through rooms turning news magazines with Jack's picture on them face down. It was as if a connection even more intimate than brotherhood had been ruptured by the assassin's bullet. "Sure, I've lost a brother," he said to Richard Goodwin during one of those times he was trying to be brave. "Other men lose wives." While the rest of the family bravely emphasized the good times and tried to rid themselves of grief by a week-long wake, he seemed haunted by his memories. Secret Service men posted at Hickory Hill grew accustomed to seeing the lights go on in the master bedroom in the middle of the night and knew that Bobby would come out at three or four o'clock, get into his convertible, and drive off into the freezing winter night with the top down, returning at sunup to shower, change clothes, and go off to the Justice Department as if in a trance.

As the weeks wore on he remained encapsulated within a suffering that surpassed anything those who had regarded him as one-dimensional thought him capable of. Before he had been a small man who looked larger; now he seemed frail, smaller than he was, the victim of a sudden somatic contraction. The columnist Mary McGrory, close to the Kennedys for years, saw Bobby on St. Patrick's Day, four months after the death. Startled by his looks, she tried to soothe him about the future. "It was something like, 'Well, you're young and you're going to be productive and successful...' But before I could finish he just let out a yelp of pain and buried his head in my shoulder." Not long after Jack's death, Bobby and his old schoolmate David Hackett attended yet another funeral, for a friend of theirs who had been killed in a plane crash. Afterward he said bitterly: "Hackett and I have so much experience at this thing that we're offering a regular service for funerals. We select readings and songs of utmost simplicity, and then we pick out a cheap casket to save the widow money. You know they always cheat you on a casket. We pick passages from the Bible and do all that's necessary to ensure an interesting and inexpensive funeral. This is a new service we can provide all our friends."

More even than the others in the family, Bobby had always solved his problems by action, moving on to the next challenge, rushing to confront the next obstacle in his path. His life had been a kind of assault—forcing his way past inhibitions, constructing action out of his obsessions. He was impatient with theories or phrase making, always asking his characteristic question: So what are we going to *do?* Now for the first time he had encountered a situation in which he was faced with a problem of being, in which doing was irrelevant. Incapable of physically affecting the environment of grief in which he now lived, he turned almost desperately to literature in an attempt to make contact with the realm of ideas and feelings—the examined life which the Kennedy ethos had always regarded as something of a hindrance, even a weakness. Friends accustomed to listening only to his staccato insights about tactics now heard him talk philosophy: first causes and last things. He read Camus. Jackie, who had returned from Dallas and told him exactly what had happened on November 22 in every excruciating detail, a ritual that helped cement the increasingly close bond between them, gave him a copy of Edith Hamilton's *The Greek Way,* which he read with tortured avidness, scrawling marginalia and underlining significant phrases on the dog-eared pages. He was especially struck by these lines from Aeschylus: ''God, whose law it is that he who learns must suffer / And even in our sleep pain that cannot forget / Falls drop by drop around the heart.'' And these from Herodotus: ''All arrogance will reap a harvest rich in tears. God calls men to a heavy reckoning for overweening pride.''

This activity may have had some of the ingenuousness of a college freshman's first encounter with great ideas, as friends noted, yet for Bobby it was a real and ferocious search for insight, at times almost a distracted one. Aides at the Justice Department who at first thought he was staring down into his lap during meetings discovered that he was actually reading. Once he appeared at an old friend's house with a book of readings of world literature under his arm. He made her listen while he opened the book and read from a selection about the poet Gérard de Nerval, who often walked around town with a lobster on a leash. When asked why, Nerval replied: ''Because he knows the secrets of the deep.''

He seized on Jack's old garments as if they were talismanic: a cashmere sweater; a tweed overcoat which he was forever asking aides to retrieve from wherever he had left it; a Navy sea jacket from his PT days which he once rescued by diving into a sea whipped by fifty-mile-an-hour winds when it fell overboard during a sailing expedition. If it seemed to friends that he was attempting to grow into his brother's clothes, they understood that these garments were also hair shirts reminding him of his own unworthiness.

Some of those close to Bobby saw it all as a classic case of survivor's guilt. If so, there was a deeper level of responsibility than with most survivors, one which came from the fact that Bobby, like Nerval's lobster, knew the secrets of the deep. He knew what had happened beneath the surfaces of the administration; he knew the role he himself had played. If the fixation on Greek tragedy had something to do with universalizing the implications of Jack's death, it also resonated with his own situation during the previous three years, a situation filled with moral blindness and tragic knowledge which, especially given the family context of pride and ambition, was Oedipal as much in a Sophoclean as a Freudian sense. It was Bobby who had led the administration into dangerous places, daring the gods of the underworld and seizing the fire that finally erupted into anti-Kennedy hatred. He had done it in the service of his brother's presidency, yet he had gone past duty or necessity, using his special status as the brother within to justify what had become at times an almost perverse exploration of self.

While Jack was alive, everything was justified; now that he was dead, it was all called into question. Had his acts created an environment for assassination? Had his zeal helped create the concatenation of forces that wanted Jack dead? "Did the CIA kill my brother?" he asked John McCone in a choked voice soon after the assassination. McCone's answer was no, but Bobby knew as much and in some cases more than the CIA director about "executive action" plots, the secret war against Castro, and the nightmare marriage between the intelligence services and the mob. Bobby's studied neglect of the Warren Commission, which Johnson had set up to investigate the assassination and to quell doubts that Lee Harvey Oswald was solely responsible, suggested to some that the subject was too painful for him to contemplate and to others that he did not want the questions pressed too hard for fear of the answers he might get.*

And always within his grief and irritating it was the nagging question of self. Ramsey Clark, who watched Bobby painfully groping his way through the aftermath of the assassination, felt that part of the sorrow came from finding himself suddenly, almost absurdly free: "He had been so involved with Jack's destiny that the death was like the death of a self; the prospect of carrying on was terrifying because it was like starting from scratch."

Once again in the strange symmetry that organized the Kennedy family destiny, the death of one brother offered the survivor an unexpected and daunting opportunity for self-assertion, an opportunity he had never expected to have and, in a sense, didn't want. As in the case of Joe Junior twenty years earlier, the price of selfhood was agreeing to shoulder the burden of a dead Kennedy's unrealized promise. In Bobby's interpretation this was the "unfinished work" of Jack's presidency, a "Legacy" of programs initiated but not realized. It would probably have been a foreign conception for Jack, whose sense of the presidency as a personal destiny had

---

*While he claimed never to have read the Warren Commission Report, however, Bobby continued to agitate the question of the assassination furtively. When New Orleans District Attorney Jim Garrison was uncovering what he claimed was the master plot, Bobby sent Walter Sheridan to see him. He once asked press secretary Frank Mankiewicz if he thought Garrison "had anything." Mankiewicz replied, "No, but I think there is something." Bobby nodded. "So do I. You stay on it."

(in an irony Bobby could not see) actually been achieved in the national apotheosis following Dallas which had made him the figure of historical romance he had secretly longed to be. In a way it was Bobby, rather than Jack, who had been cut off in mid-flight as the policeman of the New Frontier, blocked in his career as his brother's keeper, and who was now cruelly confronted with the problem he had never really faced: how to define an individual life. Characteristically he began to look for a solution by proposing himself as guardian of the Kennedy flame, the one who would achieve the unfulfilled promise of the Kennedy presidency.

Its origin determined that his pursuit of the Legacy would involve a powerful revisionism. Within weeks after the assassination, on a tour of the Far East whose planning he felt was too far advanced to cancel, he told leftist students at Japan's Wajeda University: "President Kennedy was more than just President of a country. He was the leader of young people everywhere. What he was trying to do was fight against hunger, disease and poverty around the world. You and I as young people have a special responsibility to carry on the fight." These themes—of youth, idealism, and service —would swell in the future, as he spoke about Jack and quoted from his speeches with the apostolic zeal of someone propagating a new faith. The ideal he created was purged of the compromises which had been so great an element in Jack's success; it was possessed of a crusading liberalism which Jack had mistrusted. It was Jack as he should have been, Jack in Bobby's own image as the family moralist. In creating the ideal, he also created his life's work: pushing the Legacy to the top of the hill; trying to be equal to the myth he was creating.

Jackie, too, was drawn by her concern for the Legacy, which for her had to do with monuments and buildings, the memorialization of a moment in time—the New Frontier—when the international spotlight had been on all of them. It was important, she told reporter Theodore White, that people remember that there had been such a time: "It was Camelot." Bobby was impatient with this image. He knew that Jackie had in mind the wistful grace of the Lerner and Lowe musical, but perhaps he also realized that the analogy might just as easily invite comparison to Thomas Malory's vision of an ideal which had been betrayed from within by lust and greed for power, and finally culminated in death and desolation. The irony was that he himself was the perfect Lancelot—ascetic and intense, trying to keep his demons at bay, anxious to quest for the Grail but fearful that he was not pure enough to attain it.

Lem Billings and other friends who quickly transferred their loyalties from Jack to Bobby—where they became just as deeply anchored—recognized that in some sense Bobby was "saved" from his grief by LBJ. He had always needed to externalize and objectify the evils in his world. Hoffa, Castro, and others had filled that function in the past. Now, in his dark night of the soul, Bobby saw the new President as one fixed object in a shifting world. Johnson had always been an enemy; now he was more—the opposite of everything Bobby felt his brother had represented, the anti-Legacy. He was the usurper of the dream, the symbol of things that had suddenly and tragically gone awry, the satyr who made the lost Hyperion shine all the more brightly.

Beginning with the events of November 22, Bobby found much to be upset about. There was LBJ's insistence on being sworn in on Air Force One, a calculated effort, Bobby felt, to keep his dead brother from returning to Washington still technically President. He was upset by what he regarded as Johnson's unseemly haste in moving into the symbolism of office. He collected and stored grievances, such as what he interpreted as a brusque ultimatum to Jack's secretary Evelyn Lincoln to clean out her desk and be gone the day after the swearing in. Encountering LBJ in the Oval Office, where he had gone to get Jack's things, Bobby said, "Can't you wait?"

The columnist Rowland Evans remembers being at Hickory Hill with Bobby in the evenings: "He'd just deluge me with stories about what a sonofabitch Lyndon was. How he was using Army personnel to spruce up his ranch, and things like that. The feeling was one of frustration and bitterness: they had built up this marvelous edifice and just as they were completing it, they had to give it up." When Bobby saw Joseph Alsop he attacked him bitterly for "making Johnson President," referring to the role the columnist had played in the vice presidential selection process in 1960.

If Bobby's reaction to Johnson had some of the smoldering, irrational qualities of sibling hatred, as some connoisseurs of the feud between the two men concluded, LBJ shared some of these emotions. He was aware that he had been a subject of continuing ridicule to what he called "the Bobby crowd," that they had joked over his irrelevance in the vice presidency and referred to him and Lady Bird (in Jackie's acid phrase) as "Uncle Cornpone and his Little Porkchop." It was common knowledge that two weeks before the assassination Bobby's friends had presented him with an LBJ voodoo doll which had been the source of endless merriment as everyone poked it with needles.

Yet Jackie, at least, felt that the new President behaved with an exemplary "generosity of spirit" in the aftermath of the assassination. The brittle survivor behind the grieving symbol of widowhood commented to Charles Bartlett a few weeks after Johnson had taken office, "Bobby gets me to put on my widow's weeds and go down to his [LBJ's] office and ask for tremendous things . . . and he has come through on everything." One request involved continuing her Committee on the Preservation of the White House. Another involved renaming Cape Canaveral after Jack. Jackie had approached this subject with trepidation, expecting LBJ to say, "Look, my dear, that's impossible." Instead he called Florida Governor LeRoy Collins while she was sitting in the Oval Office and badgered him into not only accepting the name change but also becoming its sponsor with the state legislature.

At the same time that LBJ was urging, even begging Kennedy appointees to stay on, Bobby was cementing their loyalty to him and consolidating them into his political family. Two weeks after the funeral, in a conversation with Schlesinger and Richard Goodwin* in his office, Bobby was already beginning to formulate the basis of what would become Jack's legacy: "There are a hundred men scattered through government who were devoted to the purposes for which we came to Washington. We must all stay in close touch and not let them pick us off one by one ... My brother barely had a chance to get started—and there is so much now to be done—for the Negroes and the unemployed and the school kids and everyone else who is not getting a decent break in our society. This is what counts. The new fellow doesn't get this. He knows all about politics and nothing about human beings ..." Bundy and McNamara and other senior officials of the prior administration who stayed on in Washington out of a sense of national duty were regarded almost as traitors; Bobby bitterly accused them of being time servers, feeling that "the King is dead, long live the King."

When Bobby came to his first cabinet meeting after the assassination, he seemed so sullen that even long-time Kennedy supporter Orville Freeman was shocked. The Agriculture Secretary later said: "His general demeanor as he came into the room and sat down was—well, it was quite clear that he could hardly countenance Lyndon Johnson sitting in his brother's seat." Driven and insecure, Johnson tried to bring Bobby around, feeling that despite an initial distance, he had finally begun to make emotional contact with Jack before his death. Bobby not only rejected the overtures but was offended by them. Talking about this period later on he said, "Johnson used to tell Kenny [O'Donnell] and Larry [O'Brien] that he thought I hated him and what could he do to get me to like him ... I didn't have any interest really in becoming involved with him and I thought an awful lot of things were going on that President Kennedy did he was getting credit for and wasn't saying enough about the fact that President Kennedy was responsible."

Nourished by sycophants on both sides, the conflict between the two men

---

*Schlesinger, according to Kennedy associate Ralph Dungan, "declared war on Johnson the day Kennedy went into the ground." Goodwin, on the other hand, had his career rescued by the new President. After losing out in a power struggle with Sorensen, he had been forced out of the White House and into the State Department. There he clashed with Rusk, who felt he was trying to take over Latin American affairs. According to Joseph Alsop, Jack regarded him as ambitious and said to his aides: "Find something for him—but not much." Goodwin wound up at the Peace Corps writing speeches for Sargent Shriver and was brought out of this obscurity by LBJ's assistant Jack Valenti.

escalated into obdurate paranoia. Within weeks, Hickory Hill and the Oval Office were watching each other like hostile opposing governments. The flashpoint came when LBJ heard that fanatical Kennedy loyalist Paul Corbin had taken it upon himself to go to New Hampshire and begin to boom Bobby as a write-in candidate for Vice President on the 1964 ticket. In February LBJ called Bobby to the White House to talk about it, in what Bobby remembered as "a bitter, mean conversation. The meanest tone I heard anybody talk." After a few minutes he stalked angrily out of the Oval Office.

Bobby tried to dig in at the Justice Department, as far as possible ignoring the White House. In January Jimmy Hoffa (who had gloated over the report of Jack's death, saying, "Bobby Kennedy's just another lawyer now") had gone to trial for conspiring to fix the jury in the Test Fleet case. In March he was convicted and sentenced to eight years in prison, and he received another five years in a Chicago trial for diverting union pension funds. At a Justice Department champagne party, Bobby, aware now of the forces his pursuit of Hoffa had unleashed, said grimly, "There's nothing to celebrate." It was impossible to return to business as usual, because being Attorney General had been only an instrument of his larger purpose, which was to advance his brother's presidency.

Late in the spring of 1964, Bobby complained to an interviewer: "I have influence because I have contacts with Averell Harriman and I'm on the counterintelligence committee ... but the influence is just infinitesimal compared to the influence I had before." Examples of how his power had diminished were everywhere, and nowhere more dramatically than in what was happening in Cuba. In the spring of 1964, doing an oral history for what would become his brother's Presidential Library, Bobby complained about how the momentum of harassing Castro built up just before Jack's death had been allowed to diminish as a result of LBJ's caution and inefficiency. "We were making more of an effort in August, September, October. It was better organized than it had been and it was having quite an effect ... But every time [Desmond Fitzgerald] would get a project ready ... nobody [would] want to have a go—got scared of it ..."

Late in June, hearing that Henry Cabot Lodge intended to resign as Ambassador to South Vietnam, Bobby wrote LBJ a note his followers found perplexing, offering to go to Saigon as his replacement. At almost the same time he was considering a direct assault on the executive branch. General MacArthur, one of his heroes, had urged Bobby to go for the vice presidency in 1964. Old and infirm and obsessed with his own sickness, MacArthur predicted that LBJ's bad heart would keep him from serving out a full term, and that by positioning himself as successor, Bobby, in a satisfying twist of fate, could win back what had been snatched away. Bobby argued that even if he managed to pressure LBJ into accepting him as a running mate he wouldn't have "any big influence" as Vice President. He favored the idea of resigning as Attorney General and moving to New York to run for the Senate. Thinking of the prospect he said, "I'm not just a senator. I'm Senator from New York. I'm head of the Kennedy wing of the Party." His brother Ted, Steve Smith, and his sisters agreed. But Sorensen, Schlesinger, and other advisers urged him to stay and fight to make sure that the vice presidential nomination at least went to a liberal. "I can't hang around here," Bobby said to friends. "I've got to get down there and get elected." But Kenny O'Donnell especially cited his duty to Jack's memory. "All right, goddamn it, I'll stay," Bobby grumbled.

But the question of destiny—his own, the Kennedy family's—was never far from his mind. On June 19, while Bobby and his supporters were still pursuing the vice presidency for him, or failing that, for someone like Hubert Humphrey, an event occurred which dramatized the issue of Kennedy fate once again. Teddy had been on his way from Washington (where the Senate, still riding the crest of nostalgia for JFK, had passed the historic Civil Rights Bill) to Springfield, Massachusetts, to receive the state party's nomination to run for reelection in November. The weather was so bad that the captain of the *Caroline* had refused to fly. Determined to go anyway, Kennedy chartered a light plane, which crashed into an orchard while trying to land in zero visibility. The pilot and Teddy's friend Ed Moss were killed; Teddy's lung was punctured and several vertebrae were smashed.

Bobby visited his brother at the hospital and determined that there was no permanent spinal injury, then he went for a walk in the warm night with Walter Sheridan. After a while he lay down on the grass and looked up bleakly into the darkness. "Somebody up there doesn't like us," he mumbled, adding in a constricted voice: "It's been a great year for the giggles, hasn't it?" Yet even here the political issue intruded, and in the next breath he was asking Sheridan if he should go for the Senate or the vice presidency. The next morning, while fielding questions from the press, Bobby was asked whether, given its apparent propensity for tragedy, the family shouldn't step out of the limelight. "The Kennedys intend to stay in public life," he answered sternly, adding the characteristic afterthought: "Good luck is something you make and bad luck is something you endure."

LBJ, meanwhile, continued to dangle the vice presidency in front of everyone. For a time he focused on Sargent Shriver, causing a calculated widening of the schism that had begun when the Kennedy brother-in-law took the post of head of the Office of Economic Opportunity, which Bobby considered part of Jack's poverty program for which the Johnson Administration was, as usual, taking credit. Then, on the eve of the convention, the President, in a blow obviously aimed specifically at Bobby, announced that he would select no cabinet member as his vice presidential nominee. He himself told Bobby beforehand, and took sadistic pleasure later on in imitating what he claimed was the Attorney General's reaction—a convulsive gulp

of the Adam's apple which, according to Stewart Alsop, made Bobby look
"like a kind of stunned semi-idiot." Two days after the meeting, Bobby
announced his candidacy for the Senate. Taking no chances, LBJ made sure
that Bobby's appearance before the Democratic convention that August
came after the balloting for President and Vice President was completed. It
was a wise decision : the emotional moment caused a great rippling of applause which built to near pandemonium, in a spontaneous demonstration
that showed the power of the Kennedy name.

Adlai Stevenson and other potential competitors for the New York Senate
nomination received what the U.N. Ambassador dyspeptically called "unctuous calls" from Steve Smith meant to get them out of the race and put
them behind Bobby. ("The avarice of the Kennedys really makes me sick,"
Stevenson noted, referring to politics rather than money.) But no one of
stature stepped forward to challenge Bobby and he won the Democratic
nomination easily, moving forward to face Republican Kenneth Keating, his
old antagonist from the missile crisis days, in the general election.

He began with a large lead, what one newspaperman called "the guilt and
sympathy vote." Yet from the outset his campaign was listless and unsure
of itself. Bobby tried to adopt the choppy hand movements of his brother
and the rising cadences that had made Jack an effective speaker, despite the
Massachusetts twang, but he spoke hesitantly, and his hands shook so badly
as he read his speeches in a monotone that he had to hide them below the
lectern. It was as if, having accepted the background role for so many years,
he felt unbearably exposed in the limelight. But his stagefright had metaphysical overtones : the political decisions he had made in the past, no matter
how hard or cruel, had been justified by his fealty to Jack's career ; similar
acts now seemed selfish instead of selfless. Traveling with him in the early
stages of the campaign, Ramsey Clark got a strong sense that Bobby felt "he
was being pushed forward by a momentum outside him, carrying on less
because he really wanted to than because people had told him he had to."

At the same time, the identity he'd willingly accepted in the past—the
one who did his brother's dirty work—now came back to haunt him. The
nostalgia surrounding his candidacy at the beginning was soon counter-
poised by attacks against the "Bad Bobby" who had harassed, wiretapped,
prosecuted, and threatened all those years ; the Bobby whose middle name, it
sometimes seemed, was Ruthless. Declaring him an unprincipled carpetbagger, Gore Vidal and other liberals formed Democrats for Keating. Meanwhile, right-wingers were circulating a pamphlet entitled "The Strange
Death of Marilyn Monroe," charging that Bobby had been having an affair
with the film actress and, when she threatened to expose some of his dealings
in appeasing the Castro regime, had her killed by Communist agents under
his control.

He was burdened also by Jack's ghost itself—witty and vivacious and so magnified in memory that it dwarfed Bobby when he appeared beside it. ("They're for *him*," he said sadly to Ed Guthman after a speech in which the crowd had cheered wildly each time he alluded to his brother or quoted from one of his speeches.) And he lacked a Bobby to prosecute his interests. At one point, slipping in the polls, he called Steve Smith, who'd been given control of the campaign, and said softly, "Steve, I just want to tell you one thing. It wasn't like this when I ran my brother's campaign."

Cherubic and avuncular, with a solid liberal voting record, Keating was a difficult target. Fearful of inflaming his reputation for ruthlessness, Bobby was forced to handle his opponent gingerly. Throughout September he watched his huge lead dwindle to the point where he was behind and forced to grasp at the electoral coattails of Lyndon Johnson, the man he loathed, an act so desperate that it prompted Richard Nixon to predict that Bobby would lose and that he would lose big. Then Keating made the mistake of attacking Bobby in front of a Jewish audience for having made a deal with a "Nazi cartel," because the Justice Department had just settled claims involving the assets of General Aniline, a chemical company with ties to the Third Reich which the United States had seized during the war as enemy property. It was a thinly veiled attempt to link Bobby, who had been called his father's son, to the Ambassador's anti-Semitic reputation. Bobby was finally able to strike back, pointing out that the idea that someone who had lost a brother and a brother-in-law to the Nazis would make a settlement favorable to former Nazis was "outrageous." The General Aniline controversy soon disappeared, but it had put Bobby on the offensive for the first time in the campaign.

For Lem Billings, the exact moment that Bobby "found himself" did not involve a speech or a position but a decision about self-presentation. Then working in a New York advertising firm, Lem was consulting with Bobby on his last-minute television blitz. At first they tried to stage man-in-the-street interviews showing Bobby responding to state issues. "He was terrible because he knew he was talking to someone who didn't give a damn about what he said," Lem recalled. "We changed from these preplanned things to films of Bobby in action at places like Columbia University, where he was responding to student questions, many of them pretty antagonistic. He was terrific. He just jumped out of the screen at you." Jack had been comfortable in repose; Bobby was most natural in conflict, finding his center in kinesis. It was the first step toward a discovery of a political persona wholly his own.

Yet when he won—beating Keating by some 700,000 votes although LBJ defeated Goldwater in New York by nearly 3,000,000—it did not lighten his burden. "If my brother was alive," he noted in a muted victory statement to the press, "I wouldn't be here. I'd rather have it that way." Two weeks later, on the first anniversary of Jack's assassination, John Seigenthaler was at Hickory Hill. Somber and preoccupied, Bobby finally put on Jack's aviator jacket with the presidential seal and said, "Let's go for a ride. I want to go to confession." On the drive to church he stared morosely out of the window. Suddenly he said to Seigenthaler, "Let's stop at Arlington and look at Johnny's grave." When they got there, they found the gate locked and climbed over. A military guard saw them and advanced menacingly. "I'm Mr. Kennedy!" Bobby yelled. They went to the grave, where he knelt and prayed. As they were walking back to the car, a puzzled look came over Bobby's face. "You know, I had a conversation with him a couple of days before it happened. He had called to wish me a happy birthday. The thing is I can't remember what he said. I've tried and tried and I can't remember. I've searched my mind over and over. I should have had somebody on the line taking down what he said."

Jack's death remained with him. For all his mordant reading and thinking he was still a Kennedy who reflexively looked for his salvation in externals. In March 1965, not long after he'd taken his seat as senator, an opportunity presented itself when the Canadian government located a 14,000-foot unnamed and unexplored mountain in the St. Elias Range in the Yukon and decided to call it Mount Kennedy as a tribute to Jack. Bobby decided to join the first party to scale it.

He flew into a base camp on a Canadian Air Force helicopter on March 22, joining a party headed by Jim Whittaker, veteran of the American Mount Everest climb of 1963 for which Jack had awarded him a medal. Bobby carried a forty-five-pound pack out of which the rolled-up Kennedy family flag—three gold helmets on a black background, designed for the Ambassador by Irish heraldry experts—poked like an aerial. He had been fearful of the sharp glacial mountain flanked by staggering precipices of granite and ice, and had wondered, only half in jest, if it would claim him. At one point during the slow ascent, he slipped into a crevass and was saved from a fall only by the rope anchoring him to the others. Near the top, his face was drawn in pain and he was gulping the thin air. As Whittaker and the others stood apart, he struggled toward the summit, straddled it and crossed himself, then planted the flag. He pulled out one of the *PT 109* tie clips he had brought on the expedition so that he could later give them to his children ("after they'd been blessed," in Lem's words), dug a deep hole with his pick, and dropped it in. As the others were beginning the descent, he was the last to leave, turning a few steps down and waving a last farewell. It was a moment in which he said goodbye to his brother as a source of guilt and anguish; yet Mount Kennedy as a metaphor was something he would have to climb again and again.

5.

*B*OBBY WAS SWORN IN WITH TEDDY, WHO had won his first complete Senate term, and—as he frequently reminded his older brother—by a margin several times larger than Bobby's. Taking the Senate oath, the two men hardly looked as though they came from the same family. Teddy was large, almost ursine, at ease with himself and wholly clubbable, while Bobby was small and coiled, despite all his efforts to be a public man. What they had in common was that from their youth they had seemed the Kennedy males of their generation least likely to succeed.

Teddy was still in pain from his airplane crash and long convalescence, corseted with a back brace and leaning heavily on a gold-headed cane. At thirty-three he was already an old Senate hand, finding the ritualized pace and articulated structure of Congress congenial. For the past two years he had done an apprenticeship, learning to work his way through Senate protocols and take care of his own political business and that of his home state —notably legislation favorable to New England fisheries and airlines. While Jack and Bobby worried about history, he had seen the Senate as his new frontier—a place spacious enough to allow him to grow into his future— which he warned staff members would necessarily take decades to develop, not just years. His good nature and hard work had won him a grudging respect from colleagues who had been ready to agree with the Massachusetts wit who, during Teddy's first run, proposed the creation of an Edward M. Kennedy Foundation to benefit wealthy and undeserving young men who wanted to start right at the top.

But Bobby's arrival changed Teddy's prospects. He found himself confronted by his old problem, which his mother had once described in these terms : " When you have older brothers and sisters, they 're the ones who seem most important in the family, and always get the best rooms and the first choice of boats, and all those things . . . " Now his brother got first choice in everything having to do with the Kennedy political destiny. "I've got to take second spot to Bobby for now," Ted told his staff during a talk about the altered situation.

They were "Eddie" and "Robbie," affectionate and bound by thick family loyalties that no outsider could penetrate. But there was never any doubt about who was in charge. When *Newsweek* decided to do a cover of the first brother team in the Senate in a hundred years, Teddy agreed to pose for the picture while Bobby said he didn't have time, insisting, however, that the stock photo the magazine used must show him taller than his brother. When the two took weekend trips to the Cape aboard the *Caroline,* it was Bobby who automatically took "the President's chair," as the seat Jack had always occupied was called ; only when his brother was not aboard did Ted sit there. When Robert Docking, one of the family's political allies, was having a testimonial dinner to mark his years as Kansas governor, Bobby sent Teddy in his place along with a telegram containing the sharp needle that enforced family discipline : he was sorry not to be there himself, Bobby stated, and he wanted to be sure his "little brother" was "sent right home" after the ceremony.

The brothers staked out their respective territories in the Senate which their respective staffs jealously guarded, each of them critically eying the *other* Kennedy. Teddy's chief aide at the time, Dave Burke, remembers Bobby as jumping right into the Senate's business and being "very good in committee arguments . . . especially during public hearings [and in an] adversary situation. But on the Senate floor he never gave the same bow to procedures and formality that Edward Kennedy did." Bobby was often rushed and ill prepared, Burke noted, while Teddy, who had spent his long recuperation from the plane accident in tutorials with Harvard scholars, always knew what was happening. The discrepancy became a standing joke between the brothers. Burke recalls how "the chairman or some other senator [on a committee] would ask [Bobby] what exactly he was trying to do and he'd say something like, 'I haven't the slightest idea, but I know it's a good idea so let's do it anyway.' He'd bumble and fumble and his staff guys would be having a nervous breakdown. Edward Kennedy would hand him a note saying, 'I don't care about the òther fellows, I understand it, Bobby,' which would just break him up in the middle of his presentation."

Yet despite the Kennedy élan which joined them, Bobby was a problem for Teddy. On one well-remembered (and from the point of view of Teddy's staff, all too representative) occasion, Bobby became impatient during committee testimony ; he stood up, threw a sheaf of papers in the air, and stalked out of the hearing room before they hit the floor, leaving Teddy red-faced and embarrassed. "Being who he was," a one-time colleague says, "Bobby got away with a lot, but sometimes you had the feeling that in some subtle way it all went onto Teddy's tab."

After his election there had been a brief moment of reshuffling, as loyalists from his brother's administration went their own ways—some, like Salinger and O'Donnell, to pursue their own visions of the Legacy by running for elective office (and losing). In the future they would have the status of a citizens' militia—able to show up fully armed and capable of battle for the Kennedy cause at a moment's notice. Bobby had to find his own staff at a personal cost of over $100,000 a year above Senate allowances. The two key figures who joined him were Peter Edelman and Adam Walinsky. Both were graduates of Yale Law School and of the Justice Department; both were sympathetic to the New Politics emerging out of the coalition between civil rights workers and student activists, and wanted to push Bobby toward its rhetoric and objectives. (Acting respectively as his speech-writing voice and tactician, Kennedy aide Fred Dutton later observed, the two of them functioned as Bobby's Sorensen.) Reacting to the crossfire of ideas and commitments, he came to see the Senate seat as a sort of bully pulpit. His technique would be to attach the polemical amendment rather than patiently draft the legislation, to do the people's business through splashy committee hearings rather than through behind-the-scenes maneuvering, to enhance rather than diminish his status as a senator *sui generis*.

Soon after his election Bobby began a series of foreign trips designed to remind LBJ of his unique status as the Prince Across the Water. They had the aura of presidential visits but also combined elements of anthropological field work and moral witness. In a November 1965 tour of Latin America he avoided the State Department's suggestions of appropriate diplomatic functions in favor of an itinerary that gave him an opportunity to argue with dissident Peruvian intellectuals about whether or not the Rockefellers controlled U.S. foreign policy, to challenge egg-throwing Chilean students to debate about the shape of things to come in hemispheric affairs, and to defend America against Argentine Marxists. He carried his brother's memory with him wherever he went—accompanying Chilean miners into their hazardous shafts and visiting the poor wherever he stopped. On the second anniversary of the assassination, he found himself in Brazil at a lonely community center named for Jack. As the children shyly gathered around he gave them a little speech : "The President was most fond of school. Can I ask you to do a favor for him ? Stay in school, study as long as you can, and then work for your city and Brazil."

A few months later he was in South Africa. When Prime Minister Verwoerd declined to see him, he instead visited with Alan Paton, controversial author of *Cry the Beloved Country*. He journeyed into the bush to see Zulu chief Albert Luthuli, the banished Nobel Peace Prize winner. He dropped in on Ian Robertson, the banned liberal politician. (Bobby asked if the house was bugged and, when the surprised Robertson said he supposed so, jumped up in the air and came down as hard on the floorboards as he could, saying that the vibrations should disturb the bugging devices for at least fifteen minutes. "How do you know that?" Robertson asked. "I used to be Attorney General," Bobby replied.) He lectured white South African students about injustice, touching on the forbidden subject of race. "My brother believed that each of us can work to change a small portion of events," he said in Johannesburg, "and in the total of all those acts will be written the history of this generation."

Back home he continued his explorations, slowly beginning to transform the Kennedy Legacy from a sentimental ideal to a specific set of concerns. In February 1966, after the Watts riot in Los Angeles the previous summer had shocked the nation into an awareness of the agonies of the urban ghetto, Bobby took a well-publicized walk through the Bedford-Stuyvesant area of Brooklyn. He subscribed to the liberal orthodoxy about poverty which was the backbone of Great Society programs just then getting under way, although his moralistic strain made him emphasize jobs over welfare. But the sight of rusted-out cars littering the streets like urban skeletons, buildings decaying amidst rubble and filth, and people living in the stench of failure struck him as "incomprehensible" and "equaling the worst that is found in Latin America." When he spoke out, community activists accused him of being another fact-finding politician who would never be seen there again, once the television cameras had recorded his outrage. As in his 1963 meeting with James Baldwin and other blacks, Bobby was annoyed, muttering on the drive back to Manhattan, "I could be smoking a cigar down in Palm Beach." But over the next few months he worked to put together a coalition of concerned white businessmen, including former Kennedy Administration officials Douglas Dillon and Roswell Gilpatric, IBM's Thomas Watson, and New Dealer David Lilienthal, and formed a pair of corporations to bring foundation money and business capital into Bedford-Stuyvesant, to create jobs and begin the renovation of the community. The model for this effort was his old Milton roommate David Hackett's Committee on Juvenile Delinquency in his own Justice Department, which had originated the idea of fighting poverty through community action, using funds coming from but not controlled by government. As the Bedford-Stuyvesant Development and Services Corporation began to grow and prosper, one young black involved in it spoke for others when he said, "Kennedy puts money where his mouth is."

Not long after Bobby discovered Bedford-Stuyvesant, Walter Reuther suggested that he take his Migratory Labor Subcommittee, already investigating the conditions of the seasonal workers of Appalachia, to look into the circumstances surrounding the farm workers' strike in the grape fields of California's Central Valley. Knowing very little about the situation in California, Bobby reluctantly agreed, although he irritably snapped at Edelman on the plane, "Ah, why am I going on this trip?" When he finally met United Farm Workers leader Cesar Chavez—as willful, devoutly Catholic, and politically savvy as he himself was—Bobby agreed that the trip was worth it. He felt that the stubbornly nonviolent Chavez was a Mexican-American version of Martin Luther King, but without the sexual activities which he knew about from wiretaps and which had always made it hard for him to relate to the black leader. The situation of the migratory workers, moreover, was morally clear-cut in a way that the situation in the ghetto was not. "This is a basic American struggle," he told the farm workers. When Kern County law enforcement officials admitted during his subcommittee hearings that they had jailed strikers without due process, Bobby shot them the frozen stare he had inherited from his father and coldly admonished them to take advantage of the lunch break to read the Constitution.

After that trip, he took the subcommittee to upstate New York to look into migratory labor camps, tangling with labor contractors whom he accused of being "right out of Steinbeck." Next he became aware of the plight of New York Indians and Indians generally. He formed an Indian Education Subcommittee and went to the Blackfoot reservation at Fort Hall, Idaho, where he discovered shocking rates of teenage alcoholism, delinquency, and suicide. Touring the reservation and seeing hovels and old railroad boxcars where Indian families lived, he called it a "crime" that the "First Americans" should live in such circumstances.

In 1967, he went South with the Subcommittee on Poverty of the Senate Labor Committee. What he saw during field hearings in the Mississippi Delta cut beneath all the rhetoric and legislative maneuvering over civil rights: tar-paper shacks emanating a nauseating stench; children with bloated stomachs and listless eyes who looked more like the victims of African famine than Americans. Bobby not only looked inside the dreadful shacks but went inside; he sat down on dirty beds as rats scurried away, and talked to mothers as their pathetic children climbed up on his lap.

It was a remarkable journey of discovery into that other America he had first become aware of during Jack's 1960 campaign. But then it had been purely political, one of those self-dramatizing "issues" designed to catch the eye of an electorate. Now it was something different. If there were political considerations, they had nothing to do with the electoral power of this underclass. Rather, by showing he could talk to these people, Bobby was suggesting to a larger constituency—all those who worried about cities erupting and traditional centers of authority losing their legitimacy—that the Kennedy Legacy had adhesive qualities and he was the politician who could hold things together. Whatever the level of calculation in his adventures into this

American netherworld, however, there was also a personal dimension for which there was no sufficient political explanation. The suffering he saw touched Bobby just as he touched it. A black journalist who accompanied him to Mississippi and watched him sit in a fetid room caressing a child with open sores on its body said, "What shocked me was not that he did it, but that I wouldn't have done it, wouldn't have gone in that place or touched that little baby. It made my flesh crawl, but it didn't seem to bother him." An Indian at Fort Hall said, "Lots of white men would come out from Washington and get upset. But their tears were crocodile tears. The tears in Senator Kennedy's eyes were real."

He went from one powerless and oppressed group to another like a detective obsessively following clues to a mystery which he knew was inside himself. What was his responsibility to these people? What was their relationship to the legacy of his dead brother? It was, once again, as if he was trying to placate and dare the gods in one and the same gesture. For his increasingly evangelical message about America irritated as many as it soothed. Every month his Senate office received dozens of threatening calls from deranged people galvanized not only by the tragic grandeur of the Kennedy drama but by the role of savior and scourge Bobby had taken on himself in this apocalyptic hour. Yet despite the threats, he refused to insulate himself with the kind of security that advisers begged him to adopt. There were no bullet-proof tops on the cars in his motorcades, no plain-clothes bodyguards standing between him and the crowds which obsessively surged up to touch and tear at him.

He seemed to be trying to encounter the worst possible case and be done with it. ("Sooner or later," he muttered to himself in one motorcade, after a sudden fusillade of backfiring from a trailing car made him flinch and go pale.) And when it didn't come, he went looking for it. Climbing Mount Kennedy was only the first of several such encounters with danger. While on the Latin American trip, he got into a native dugout canoe and paddled down a piranha-infested river into a thick jungle fog that closed around him; he was gone so long that others in the party were beginning to give up hope when he returned, looking exuberant at having navigated the waters. While on safari with Ethel in Kenya, he got out of the Land Rover and walked toward a rhino standing near the roadway; although the animal watched him with baleful myopia, Bobby advanced on it until he was only fifteen feet away, whereupon the rhino turned and ran and Bobby looked back at his wife with a smile, immensely pleased that he had faced the animal down. On another occasion he was out sailing at the Cape and heard by radio that his daughter Kathleen had been hurt in a fall in a horse show. Told that the weather was too rough to take the boat in, he dove over the side and began swimming to shore.

There were family skiing trips every Christmas and Easter in which

Bobby, less expert than some of his children, challenged the most daunting slope, the most perilous jump, the run encumbered by trees, rocks, and other impediments at its unseen end. And beginning in 1965 there were river trips of escalating difficulty, on which he took the whole family but always managed to reserve some especially difficult solo act for himself—as when he got off the raft and into a kayak for the first time, and ran the last seven miles of the Salmon River's whitewater by himself. There was usually a public relations payoff: the small army of journalists that followed him everywhere were lined up at the end of the whitewater watching as the final rapid spat his kayak out into an eddy. Yet these acts were authentic enough so that Lem Billings, who accompanied him on some of these adventures, found the spectacle disturbing: "It was like he was thumping his chest, like he was saying, 'Okay, Death, you just try it, I dare you!' "

At the same time he was pushing the Legacy to the top of the hill, he thought, as if for the first time, about what it would be like to break out of his Kennedy chrysalis. "If I wasn't a United States Senator, I'd rather be working in Bedford-Stuyvesant than any place I know," he said in a New York poverty meeting. "I wish I'd been born an Indian," he said to his Senate colleague Fred Harris, whose wife is a Comanche. "If I hadn't been born rich, I'd probably be a revolutionary," he told English journalist Margaret Laing during a discussion of Che Guevara. "I'm jealous of the fact that you grew up in a ghetto," he said to writer Jack Newfield. "I wish I'd had that experience."

Moving away from that monochromatic and monomaniacal Bobby of the Kennedy Administration and before, he began to elaborate a new persona out of the old psychological materials: passionate, filled with tough-minded concern, impatient with a political minuet that required the music of injustice. While Jack had attracted Brahmin intellectuals like Schlesinger and Galbraith, Bobby appealed to journalistic street fighters like Newfield, Pete Hamill, and Jimmy Breslin. While Jack had hidden behind cool wit, Bobby's mode was to make himself available through tense self-irony, always punning on his prior reputation for opportunism and ruthlessness and thus distancing and dispelling it. As he acted out his personal drama through his political discoveries, he emerged as the only Kennedy whose secret chambers could be visited. He became a favorite conundrum for writers ranging from Vidal to Mailer to Lowell to explore and explain. The word "existential" was applied to him with increasing frequency.

If this was his advantage over all other figures in public life, however, it was also his dilemma. He might be perceived as a man of literary complexity, but he was still a politician who had to act in an arena where the existential gesture counted for little. Compromises which in another politician would be regarded as part of the profession in him seemed betrayals—not only of the ideals he supported but of the self he was creating.

New York politics was one arena in which he consistently failed the test. He tried to assert control over the state's Democratic Party after his election in 1964, assuming he could subordinate it as Teddy had in Massachusetts. When the party resisted him, he dismissed it as a "zoo" and ignored its political deterioration. Aide Barbara Coleman recalls Bobby as being "bored out of his mind" during obligatory appearances upstate: "He'd be totally preoccupied with something else and go into a speech unprepared and uninterested. Then five minutes before he was supposed to go on, he'd realize where he was and start to sweat and worry." He and his advisers continued to talk of putting together a coalition of liberals and reform Democrats to break the grip of party regulars, but his listless sorties into the civil wars of state politics usually lined him up behind such candidates as Abe Beame, John Lindsay's opponent for mayor in 1965, or Frank O'Connor, who ran against Nelson Rockefeller for governor in 1966, men he privately scorned.

And while he was almost coquettish with writers interested in the spectacle of his grappling with the complex problems of America, he was less pleasant to those who intruded into the family's forbidden zones. When Red Fay, Jack's old friend, told him he was going to finish an anecdotal book he had begun with the President, Bobby tried to get him to concentrate on his tenure as Under Secretary of the Navy during the administration and forget the anecdotes. Since his had been the most blatantly personal of Jack's appointments, Fay could hardly make a book about his official duties, so he went ahead and wrote a book of Jack's table talk, *The Pleasure of His Company*. Jackie chided Fay for his "locker room humor," but Bobby was livid about the portrait of his brother, not because it lacked respect but because it tended to "diminish" Jack. He demanded that Fay cut out two-thirds of the manuscript. When Fay balked after eliminating ninety thousand words, Bobby accused him of trying to make money off the Kennedys. "I'm going to keep your book from being published," he threatened, thus damaging a fifteen-year friendship almost beyond repair.

He didn't sue Fay. But he did sue William Manchester, whom Jackie had selected to write an "official" version of the assassination less than a month after the fact.* When Manchester delivered the manuscript of *The Death of a President*, she became distraught on the basis of others' readings—she never read it in its entirety herself—and called the book and the problems it caused "the worst thing of my life." She accused Manchester of having taken advantage of her when "the floodgates were open." ("I just went on

*She heard that Jim Bishop, whom she regarded as a vulgar popularizer, was going to do a book, and so were others, and she wanted to control what was said. After she had chosen Manchester she tried to dissuade Bishop from continuing with his project in an exchange of letters that became increasingly acerbic, culminating in her warning: "I will not talk to you about the events at Dallas and nobody connected with it will talk to you."

and on about private things. Then the man went away and . . . afterwards there were so many things, private things, which were mostly expressions of grief of mine and Caroline's that I wanted out of the book . . .'')

When Bobby rushed to her defense, filing a lawsuit to restrain Manchester from prepublishing excerpts of the book in *Look*, his representatives made it seem that he was closing ranks with his widowed sister-in-law, trying to protect her sense of taste and propriety. But, as Manchester later documented, ''Bobby and his political advisers . . . decided that some of the passages in the book might be used against Bob if he should run, as they all assumed he eventually would, for national office.'' The passages Jackie worried about had to do with ''taste''—descriptions of Jack wandering around in his shorts before going to bed, of her searching the mirror for signs of wrinkles, of the problem of removing the wedding ring from Jack's corpse. The passages Bobby worried about involved abrasive relations between him and LBJ after the assassination. At his request, Seigenthaler rewrote Manchester's account of the first post-assassination cabinet meeting so that it was entirely amiable. Over several intense days Manchester was assaulted by all the heavy artillery in the Kennedy arsenal—Seigenthaler, Richard Goodwin, Burke Marshall, Ed Guthman—all of them pressing him to make the hundreds of changes Bobby required, or to abandon the book altogether. Finally, there was Bobby himself, pounding on the door of the hotel room where Manchester had gone to escape the presssure, yelling at the author to let him in and come to terms. The episode, which burst onto front pages as a major story, finally burned itself out after Manchester made a few changes and Bobby and Jackie dropped their suit. But it left an aftertaste: of the 69 percent of the public who admitted to pollsters that they had heard of the ''Manchester affair,'' 20 percent said it had diminished their regard for Bobby.

But Bobby was most hurt by his inability to answer the call on Vietnam. He correctly perceived the war as a dire threat to the nation's basic social bonds and also as a malign force that would ultimately bankrupt the Great Society programs so vital to the poor and minority groups he had made his special constituency. But his positions on Vietnam were marked by an opportunistic ebb and flow, as he tried desperately not to make publicly the break with LBJ that he had made privately years earlier.

During his first few months in the Senate, as Vietnam was just beginning to intrude into the national consciousness, he reiterated the views he had inherited from the New Frontier: ''The United States has made a commitment to help Vietnam. I'm in favor of keeping that commitment and taking whatever steps are necessary.'' By July 1965, after the first important demonstrations against the war, Bobby agreed to give a speech Adam Walinsky had written which was mildly critical of United States policy. But when its advance release to the press caused controversy, Bobby had the sensitive passages (for instance, "victory in a revolutionary war is not by escalation but by de-escalation") taken out.

Bobby's aides had little trouble converting him to antiwar views, but his public statements always lagged well behind his private beliefs. In November 1965, as some student groups were coming under fire for wanting to donate blood to North Vietnam, Bobby said in a press conference, "I'd be willing to give blood to anybody who needs it." Daunted by the controversy that ensued, including Barry Goldwater's claim that this statement was "close to treason," Bobby lay low for several weeks, deciding not to join fifteen other Democratic senators in asking the President to extend the Christmas bombing truce.

On February 19, 1966, he tried again, telling reporters that the Vietcong should have "a share of power and responsibility" in South Vietnam, and was attacked by McGeorge Bundy and others in the administration for raising the specter of a coalition government (Vice President Humphrey quipped that it was like allowing the fox into the chicken coop). In the wake of this controversy Bobby lapsed into a silence that lasted the rest of 1966, as the bombing intensified and 150,000 more men were added to the U.S. commitment. To Jack Newfield, who was among those begging him to speak out, to use the prestige of his name against the war, Bobby replied miserably, "The last time I spoke out I didn't have any influence on policy, and I was hurt politically. I'm afraid that by speaking out I just make Lyndon do the opposite, out of spite..."

If there was a personal reluctance to take the final existential step that would bring his smoldering hatred of LBJ into the open, there was also a political reluctance to subject the Kennedy Legacy to a close scrutiny on the subject of Vietnam. Kenny O'Donnell might later claim that Jack was waiting only for reelection before liquidating the commitment in South Vietnam that had grown so rapidly during his administration, but Bobby knew better. In the spring of 1964, interviewing Bobby for one of the oral histories that would become part of the JFK Library, John Bartlow Martin asked him about Jack's intentions regarding Vietnam. Bobby said, "The President felt that there was a strong, overwhelming reason for being in Vietnam and that we should win the war in Vietnam." Martin asked him if consideration was ever given to pulling out and Bobby replied flatly, "No." The Kennedy connection was emphasized by the fact that the people who had presided over Johnson's buildup were alumni of the New Frontier—Bundy, Rostow, McNamara. There was also Bobby's mentor Maxwell Taylor, who'd taken over the Ambassadorship to Saigon in 1964 and, returning to the findings of his 1961 mission with Walt Rostow, immediately began to agitate for air strikes. He twice recommended bombing to LBJ and was twice turned down, succeeding on his third attempt only because Bundy happened to be in Saigon during a terrorist attack and strongly supported Taylor's position.

Thus Bobby was a prisoner of the past almost as much as LBJ. Even though Edelman and Walinsky and other aides were early and vocal critics of the war, and even though his own instincts were perhaps to oppose it, Bobby himself had to wait until enough time had passed for it to be seen as a Johnson rather than a Kennedy war. In the meantime he tried to place himself on the side of the critics through political semiotics. In a technique borrowed from Teddy, who was devoting his attention to the refugee problem in Vietnam rather than frontally attacking the war itself, Bobby focused on the issue of free speech at home and the right of antiwar protestors to dissent. When asked directly about the war itself he was evasive, telling reporters: "These are very complex problems with no easy solutions."

On January 28, 1967, in the middle of a halt in the bombing of North Vietnam, he appeared before the Oxford Union in England and expressed only veiled reservations about the air strikes. Two days later he was in France, where De Gaulle reminded him of the advice he had given Jack five years earlier about involvement in Southeast Asia. Bobby also talked to Etienne Manach of the French Foreign Ministry, who said that the North Vietnamese diplomatic mission had implied that if the bombing were to stop, negotiations could begin. Returning to Washington with this "peace feeler," Bobby arranged a meeting with the President. Meanwhile, a copy of a cable reporting on the meeting from the U.S. Embassy in Paris to the State Department was leaked to *Newsweek*. Assuming incorrectly that Bobby had done it, Johnson brusquely dismissed the news he brought and went on to attack him personally: "I'll destroy you and every one of your dove friends. You'll be politically dead in six months." Once again Bobby stalked out of the Oval Office, *Time* reported, calling the President a son of a bitch. A week later, after LBJ had ordered a resumption of the bombing, Bobby finally decided to make a break.

Walinsky and Edelman were enthusiastic. Others concerned with the future of the Legacy—notably McNamara, Sorensen, and Ted Kennedy—were not, feeling that Bobby would be hurting the country and his own career. But he moved ahead, characteristically arranging talks with a wide range of war critics, including the *Saturday Review*'s Norman Cousins, radical Tom Hayden, John Kenneth Galbraith, and antiwar activist Al Lowenstein. In a speech on March 2, 1967, he admitted his own and his brother's guilt: "Three Presidents have taken action in Vietnam. As one who was involved in those decisions, I can testify that if fault is to be found or responsibility assessed, there is enough to go around for all—including myself." Then, after summoning up the horrors of the war, he went on to the heart of his proposal: the bombing should be halted, and under U.N. supervision "all political elements" in South Vietnam should decide on the leadership and direction of the country.

Within a few days, as administration officials and their supporters in the press denounced his plan (the once liberal *Reporter* went so far as to accuse the Kennedy family of "its own Bonapartism that aims at permanent power"), Bobby sadly acknowledged that his speech had been too little and too late. But if it did not do much to end the war, it finally emancipated him from his ambivalence on the issue. He had laid to rest, symbolically at least, the Kennedy involvement in Vietnam and transferred the burden to LBJ.

By the middle of 1967, Bobby seemed to be stuck in mid-passage, always edging toward psychological precipices but drawing back from the last step; galvanized by the vision of a realm of pure action but unable to escape the gravity of caution and incremental process. In a political equivalent of Newton's Third Law, he brought the disfranchised into the political process and seemed on the verge of establishing a new coalition, while he also worked to sweeten his relationship with Democratic Party bosses; as he broke new ground in his understanding of race and poverty, he also hung back on the intimately related question of Vietnam.

Yet the fact remained that Bobby, more than any other figure in American politics, conveyed a sense of latency and potential, a "capacity for growth" —the key phrase in the lexicon of his supporters. Hollow-eyed and disheveled, his gray-tipped brindle hair curling over his collar and his socks flopping down around his ankles ("he looks like a damned Beatnik," Senate colleague Thruston Morton complained), he seemed to be involved in a ritual dance with the violence and chaos of the sixties, trying to be equal to a world spinning out of control, gambling on his ability to express and somehow contain its dangerous contradictions. He had made himself a representative American, yet he also seemed somehow foreign—the last Irish Puritan in the way his brother had been the first Irish Brahmin. Robert Lowell captured this part of him when he called Bobby a "pure Celt" in one of his poems and asked the crucial question : "Who was worse stranded?"

6.

*A*T THE TIME OF JACK'S election an official family portrait had showed the Kennedys clustered casually around the Ambassador with the new President at his shoulder—in-laws mixed randomly with Kennedys, husbands and wives posed sitting apart from each other, as if they were part of a unit bound by something more durable and more profound than marriage. If such a portrait had been taken again in 1967, it would have shown gaps—not just in faces missing but in relationships altered, a new sense of anxiety about where they stood with each other and what it meant to be a Kennedy.

As the shots which killed Jack had continued to ricochet through the family, the Lawford marriage had been first and hardest hit. Because of the hold Joseph Kennedy had exercised over his daughters, it had always been shaky. ("I always felt that her love for her father took precedence over her love for me," Peter Lawford would say of Pat years later.) When Bobby, as part of his effort to break the triangle between his brother and Giancana and Judith Campbell, had given Lawford the task of telling Sinatra that his relationship with the Kennedys was over, the marriage had in effect ended too. As Red Fay said, "Frank wouldn't even talk to Peter afterwards. Pat tried to make things up, but it didn't happen. Peter's career began to come apart. The relationship with Pat came apart too." The television show "Dear Phoebe," which Peter and Pat had coproduced, went off the air. There was liquor and other women. Jack had made several calls to the Lawfords' Santa Monica home from the White House in the last months of his life, persuading Pat at least to postpone the breakup until after the 1964 election. But on the day of the assassination, she told her children: "We're getting out of here," and began packing their bags. She returned to New York and the Kennedy orbit as ''one of the walking wounded,'' in the words of a family employee, ''without a lot of hope of recovery.''

The other marriages had also gone through turmoil. In the sexual heat of the New Frontier, Steve Smith had nonetheless kept his marriage with Jean together, perhaps because they were closer to the Kennedy center of gravity than the Lawfords. With Sargent Shriver, the issue was career. LBJ offered him the opportunity to pick up the solo career he had been forced to leave in 1959, when he was established as a major Chicago political figure, to help Jack get elected. Backed by Eunice, he had since become head of the poverty program and one of the ornaments of Johnson's Great Society. Bobby felt that Shriver had allowed himself to become a hostage to the President and relations between them were chilly.

Meanwhile, Jackie had withdrawn from close contact with the rest of the family. She still came to Palm Beach for Christmas and to Hyannis for a visit during the summer. She was personally close to Bobby as a result of his support during the Manchester affair; but she had made it clear that she wanted to be out of the glare of publicity that followed the family everywhere, and that she wanted her children to grow up without being in thrall to the Kennedy ethos.

But of all the changes, the most dramatic had to do with the Ambassador. Before the assassination, Jack, who didn't want to shoulder family responsibilities himself, had insisted on maintaining the fiction that the disability caused by the stroke was just temporary and his father was still in charge. But in the intervening years the Ambassador had shrunk into his wheelchair, giving up all efforts to rehabilitate his locomotion and speech. In some ways he was still the formidable patriarch of the past. When his wife's Fitzgerald relatives, whom he hated, came to Palm Beach for a visit, they had to stay in their room until he had been put to bed so he wouldn't know they were there. But in terms of his involvement with the Kennedy family destiny, he had become little more than an heirloom of the Kennedy past.

Bobby had tried to involve him in his career, wanting it to be seen in the context Jack's had been—as a family experience, a step forward in the Kennedy destiny, which had been plotted out in his youth. During the run for the Senate in 1964, he had gotten attendants to bring his father to New York so he could ask his advice and involve him in the campaign. Disoriented, the old man had answered in incomprehensible babble. ''I'll make changes, Dad,'' Bobby had cried out to him. ''You know I'll make changes. Millions of people need help. My God, they need help.'' But his passionate guilt and drive for expiation were lost on his father. The gap between them had only widened with the Mount Kennedy climb. The Ambassador had been furious, screaming ''Naaaaa'' at the television footage of Bobby in his mountaineering clothes, ripping articles about the climb out of the newspaper and throwing them on the floor. ''Bobby didn't know,'' Lem Billings said, ''that his father was trying to stop this thing that had gotten started—this Kennedy thing of daring the gods. The two of them never understood each other on this question.''

Bobby still craved his father's blessing, but he realized that the old man had become a Sphinx who would henceforth answer only in riddles. He took over leadership of the Kennedys, as the Ambassador had once prophesied he would, holding them all together and giving them a sense of uniqueness and calling. He was the one who remembered birthdays, baptisms, confirmations. He was the one who tried to keep Pat away from the liquor and pills she began to consume in dangerous volume. He was the one who took Jackie's children to their first communion. He was the one who came to exemplify what it was to be a Kennedy to the growing number of children—twenty-seven by 1967—of the next Kennedy generation.

But if they all regarded Jack's presidency as an ideal, they all perceived their Kennedyness through Bobby's reality rather than Jack's memory. Bobby integrated his nieces and nephews as well as his own children into his personal rituals, taking them skiing and on the river trips where they could listen to Jim Whittaker tell about climbing Mount Everest, John Glenn talk about the first ride in space, or Lem talk about the President's youth. (At some point in the trip they would tie up the rafts and assault together, as a Kennedy enterprise, some nearby cliff, Bobby leading the charge up the hill while reciting Jack's favorite speech, the ''we happy few'' call to arms from *Henry V*.) He made a place for them in the Hickory Hill football games, which would sometimes involve Sonny Jurgensen or some other Washington Redskin but always had a Bobby touch—ad hoc decisions to push back goal lines when his team was about to be scored on, elongation of the time periods, the younger kids jumping on the sidelines and cheering (''Hear ye, hear ye, read all about it / We got a team and there's no doubt about it. / Clap your hands! Stamp your feet! / 'Cause Daddy's team can't be beat!'') Bobby had once said, ''Except for war, there is nothing in American life—nothing—which trains a boy better for life than football.'' But what the younger Kennedy generation learned from these games was who controlled the family. As Eunice's son Bobby Shriver recalls, ''If you dropped one of his passes —he was always quarterback—you felt like keeping on running. He had this withering look. You'd get back in the middle and he'd say, 'I'm going to throw to you again and you'd better catch it!' ''

He was son, uncle, father and surrogate father, husband and even surrogate husband. (He spent so much time supporting Jackie and her children that there was gossip about him and his sister-in-law.) As he had established himself as the center of the family, so he established his own children as the future Kennedys of record. He had always had them underfoot at the Justice Department. Especially after Jack died and Bobby took over leadership of the family, they were conscious of their select status. When John-John would not come out to play football or join the other games, they called him "Mama's boy" and said he wasn't a "real Kennedy." When they were being driven to some athletic lesson, they would sometimes tell their cousins, "You're not Kennedys, you're only Shrivers [or Smiths or Lawfords]," and make them sit in the back of the station wagon.

For those who had watched the development of the Kennedys over two generations, Hickory Hill bore an uncanny similarity to the house at Bronxville some thirty years earlier. There were the keepsakes on the wall—although not in this case autographs from the King and Queen and FDR, which Joe Kennedy had sought, but quotations from Jack and other memorabilia of the New Frontier—that "brief shining moment"—such as a framed yellow legal page filled with JFK scrawl and titled "Notes made by President Kennedy at his Last Cabinet Meeting, October 29, 1963," which Jackie had given Bobby as a present. There were pictures of the children with less serious but equally meaningful captions. One of his son David on the White House lawn said: "A future President inspects his property," and one of Bobby Junior sitting next to Jack on an airplane: "A President gets his advice from many sources." There were endless games, with Bobby pushing those too little to play on the swings and exhorting them to "go a little higher." It was casual and child oriented, with kids moiling over the furniture and managing to shatter Etruscan vases and other expensive objects Bobby and Ethel gave each other for Christmas.

Once when Bobby was talking with a friend one of his children came in and happily announced that he had just finished fifth in a sailing race and then left the room. Bobby smiled and said, "If any of us had done that we would have been sent to bed without dinner." It was a revisionist concept that allowed him to feel he was improving on the example of the past. He cuddled his children as his father never had.* He was faithful to the family in a way Joe Kennedy had not been. Yet to a surprising degree he had replicated the milieu his father had created. He had ten children. He had a wife who was pietistic and parochial. (William Manchester had been surprised during a tense visit to Hickory Hill at hearing Ethel complain that her younger children in Catholic school were not being taught a literal interpretation of Noah and the Flood. On another occasion Ethel found herself on a plane next to Chief Justice Warren. Noting that the Court was considering the issue of school prayer, she began to harangue him: "You can't keep God out of the classroom. God is everywhere.") Bobby himself was the center

---

*Lem Billings said, "Bobby was much more openly loving with his children than Joseph Kennedy had been. He touched them all the time. It seems like a small thing, but in the Kennedy family it wasn't. Mr. Kennedy had never touched them much when they were young. Jack was the same way—didn't touch and didn't want to be touched."

of moral authority. He even tried to make the Hickory Hill dinner table into the classroom his father's had been. He would lecture occasionally on the art of war, describing Bunker Hill, Waterloo, and other famous battles. He often announced in advance the topic of discussion so that the children could prepare, and sometimes asked them to memorize a poem like "Gunga Din" or "Casey at the Bat."

Even the internal dynamic of the family he had created seemed to echo that of the family into which he'd been born. His oldest son, Joe III, was given the dynastic burden. "You are the oldest of all the male grandchildren," he had written him from the Justice Department on the day of Jack's funeral. "You have a special and particular responsibility now which I know you will fulfill. Remember all the things that Jack started—be kind to others that are less fortunate than we—and love our country."

Large and slow, enforcer of family rules as his namesake, Joe Junior, had been, Joe was the one who helped the younger kids put on their shoes and smoothed their hair for church and also the one who beat them up. "He was the one whom Bobby and Ethel studied for signs of political promise," Lem Billings said later. "He was the one they wanted to carry on the tradition."

Robert Junior was next. Intellectually more agile, tall and nimble, he skewered his older brother with his wit although he lost to him in fights. Joe would sit miserably through the mealtime quizzes, stammering when his father asked questions such as "Who is Ho Chi Minh?" and finally blurting out desperately, "The Emperor of China?" as Bobby Junior laughed and prepared to answer for him. At night, as Joe was drilled by a governess in charge of improving his poor performance in school, Bobby Junior would listen through the wall. Given a word like "where," Joe would try to get it right, spelling w-e-i-r and then w-a-r-e until Bobby Junior yelled w-h-e-r-e through the wall and waited for Joe to come running into his room to beat him up.

Lem Billings was the first to notice the returning symmetry of things. "That boy is just like Jack," he said to Bobby. Everyone remembered the day that Lem, who generally avoided children, spent several hours in Bobby Junior's room listening to him talk about his collection of pets and other things and then came out and said, "I've just met the smartest little boy!" Jack too had been amused by him and the two had engaged in the sort of witty chat the President loved when seven-year-old Bobby Junior arrived at the White House with a salamander he had caught in the Hickory Hill pool. "What should I do with it?" Jack asked. "Put it in the Fish Room," Bobby Junior replied, punning on the White House room named after the nineteenth-century New York diplomat. "It's too good for the Fish Room," Jack said, laughing. "Better put it back in the pool."

Then there was the third son, David, a lot like his father as a young man —shy, fragile, engaging once his inhibitions were conquered. Bobby teased him about his weaknesses—his "sissy" fondness for wildflowers, his lisp ("Say 'My sister Courtney blows her whistle,' " Bobby would command, and grimace in a stage way when David said, "My sisthter Courtneyth blowth her whisthle"), and his tendency to cry. But Bobby had a soft spot for him too, as if remembering how he himself had been the runt of a prior Kennedy litter. When he saw David being picked on he would take him aside: "Don't let anyone buffalo you. Learn how to fight back and learn how to win." He took him to the sports director who helped all the children and asked him to give David boxing lessons. But while Bobby wanted his third son to be hardened, he also hugged the boy and tried to protect him, as if determined to spare him the sense of being lost in the Kennedy shuffle which he had once experienced.

The children intensified the question of his own future. In the patio with Lem at Hickory Hill during the summer of 1967, watching them play, Bobby shook his head and said, "It doesn't seem like much of a world they're going to inherit, does it? I can't help wondering if I'm doing all I should to keep it from going down the drain."

The question became more insistent that fall, when the antiwar strategist Allard Lowenstein began looking for a presidential candidate who would lead a guerrilla crusade against Johnson and the war in Vietnam. Bobby may have felt the obligation of an evangelical calling. (Walinsky said, "He felt we were living in a crazy, poisonous time, and he felt he was the only guy in the country who could turn things around, make a stand, stop the war and the chaos in the cities.") But instead of taking the existential leap, he listened to people like Arthur Schlesinger, who warned him that he was "too precious a commodity to be wasted on a doomed effort." And so he turned Lowenstein down.

When Senator Eugene McCarthy decided to accept the challenge, Bobby reacted scornfully: "I don't believe it. He is not that sort of fellow. And if he does run it will only be to up his lecture fees..." But it gave him a metaphysical lurch to be displaced. As George McGovern, another senator close to Lowenstein's dump-Johnson move, said later, "I don't think Bob in his wildest imagination ever dreamed that McCarthy would announce... I think he thought, 'My God. I should have done this.' " Despite his growing opposition to the war—in November, when students at Marymount College indicated by a show of hands that they supported the war, Bobby asked them in frustration if they didn't realize that United States actions in Vietnam were like those of the Nazis—he did not try to help McCarthy. In a December meeting he advised McCarthy to stay out of Massachusetts, where Bobby's own polls showed that anti-Johnson sentiment was strong, and concentrate instead on New Hampshire, where polls showed it was weak. Among his other grudges against McCarthy was one that went back to 1960: "He felt he should have been the first Catholic President just because he knew more St. Thomas Aquinas than my brother . . . He made that Los Angeles [nominating] speech for Stevenson just to help Johnson.''*

It was the beginning of another period of vacillation, as in his quandary over Vietnam. There were pressures to run from those who believed in Camelot, including the intimations of a Second Coming; from New Politics figures on his staff like Walinsky and Edelman, who realized, as others did not, exactly how vulnerable LBJ was and who believed that 1968 would mark the end of the old ''bossed'' conventions; from Goodwin and eventually a repentant Schlesinger, who feared that by lying low until 1972 Bobby would dissipate the moral force of the Kennedy Legacy. Opposed were some of the ''President Kennedy'' members of his brain trust, notably O'Donnell and Sorensen, returned to legal practice, who both saw it as too great a risk; Steve Smith, who argued that all Bobby could do was throw the election to Nixon; and most of all Teddy. ''I'm not so sure about [Jack],'' Teddy replied to a question about what family wisdom would say. ''But I know what Dad would have advised . . . Don't do it.'' He felt Bobby couldn't win. He also felt that an unsuccessful run would damage his own ultimate hopes.†

At the turn of the year, however, the argument seemed academic, as McCarthy began slogging through the snows of New Hampshire with little following outside of students comprising his ''Children's Crusade'' and little hope of victory. Early in 1968 Bobby and Ethel were at dinner with Benno Schmidt, one of the businessmen involved in the Bedford-Stuyvesant restoration project, when the talk turned to Bobby's possible candidacy. When Schmidt said that challenging Johnson was not a good idea, Bobby replied, ''I agree with you, Benno. I think if I run I will go a long way toward proving everything that everybody who doesn't like me has said about me.'' Ever the cheerleader, Ethel said: ''Now, Bob, you've got to get that idea out of your head. You're always talking as though people don't like you.'' Bobby smiled indulgently. ''I don't know, Ethel, sometimes in moments of depression I get the idea that there are those who don't like me.'' Later in the conversation he returned obsessively to the subject, telling Schmidt, in effect, that running would be seen as a Freudian slip: ''If I run,

---

*Jack had scorned the Minnesota Senator. Joseph Alsop told Jack that he had encountered McCarthy on a plane in 1960 and McCarthy started to tell anti-Kennedy stories, then went off in a ''towering pout'' to read his Missal when Alsop said he was a Kennedy friend and supporter and didn't want to hear them. Jack responded with a story about P. J. Kennedy. ''Well, Joe,'' he said to Alsop, ''my grandfather always used to say, 'Always mistrust a Catholic politician who reads his Missal on a trolley car.' ''

†Bobby's old friend Dave Hackett later commented about Teddy's staff, ''They felt that Bobby running was going to hurt their candidate, and I say 'candidate' because I think they had ambitions for him to be President . . . They thought he [Bobby] was going to upset things, ripple the waters.''

people are going to think that, one, I've been intending to run all the time, that Vietnam has been the issue that I've been building up, that I've never accepted Lyndon Johnson, that I'm just a selfish, ambitious little s.o.b. that can't wait to get his hands on the White House."

But a few weeks later, the Tet offensive brought Vietcong fighters into the center of Saigon and provided dramatic evidence of how badly the war was going. Suddenly businessmen and other conservatives were reevaluating the war. The challenge that had seemed so futile took on a new urgency as McCarthy rose up out of the snows of New Hampshire not as a snappish, eccentric politician but as a figure of glacial integrity, a hero of the resistance Bobby had always wanted to lead. He had ignored Edelman and Walinsky and the other "moralists" among his advisers, but when O'Donnell, O'Brien, and some of the other "pros" began to change their minds, Bobby started to reassess his position.

There were encouraging polls suggesting that if he entered he would win. California Democratic boss Jesse Unruh, who had been urging him to run all along, called him at Palm Beach to tell him about one such poll. Bobby replied, "You sonofabitch. Why did you have to tell me that?" On March 2, Unruh and others attended a climactic meeting at Hickory Hill amidst the normal mélange of kids and animals. The "no" position was argued by Burke Marshall, Steve Smith, and most persuasively by Sorensen, the "yes" position by Ethel and the kids. Ethel looked sharply at Sorensen after one of his perorations in favor of inaction and said, "Why, Ted! And after all those high-flown phrases you wrote for President Kennedy!" The basic question, as one observer recalls, was: Given the chaos tearing the country apart, what was Bobby saving himself for? At a crucial stage in the argument, the kids rolled down a sign reading "Kennedy for President" from the upstairs window and put "The Impossible Dream" from *Man of La Mancha* on the record player full blast. It was clear to everyone that the campaign to come had found its theme song, even if its candidate still hadn't fully committed himself.

Bobby continued to equivocate. A few days before the New Hampshire primary, in California to offer moral support to Cesar Chavez during his hunger strike, he said to a friend, "What have I got to lose besides Dad's money?" Yet the day after McCarthy's stunning performance in rolling up over 40 percent of the vote, Bobby was writing journalist Anthony Lewis in London: "The country is in such difficulty and I believe headed for much more that it almost fills one with despair. But then when I realize all of that I wonder what I should be doing..." He concluded by telling Lewis that late in the spring he would either be in California campaigning or in London for a visit, but he still wasn't sure which.

McCarthy's unexpected showing—he won 42 percent of the vote and twenty of the twenty-four delegates—put Bobby's equivocation into a crisis context. The same day he wrote to Lewis there was another meeting at which even the Kennedy advisers who had opposed his running saw that it would be impossible to wait until 1972. As one of them said, "Bobby's heart for politics and almost for life itself seemed to be going out because of this irresolution." Another meeting, the decision-making one, was scheduled for two days later. But it was clear what the answer would be. Watching Bobby being interviewed by Walter Cronkite at Steve Smith's house, Teddy blurted out: "What the hell's the point of holding the meeting when he's already made up his mind?"

The next day, in one last desperate gambit to buy time, Bobby set up a meeting with Secretary of Defense Clark Clifford, whom he privately referred to as "Attila the Hun." He arrived with Sorensen and immediately said that he felt the United States should conclude its venture in Vietnam, adding that the war was the only reason he'd get into the presidential race. His solution was the appointment of a presidential commission that would study the war and make binding recommendations. He had a list of candidates to sit on this commission, including himself. Interpreting it as an unacceptable "ultimatum" that would allow Bobby to humiliate him without actually running for the nomination himself, Johnson rejected the idea.

On March 15, with this last exit closed, Bobby was ready. He sent political strategist Fred Dutton to tell Teddy of his decision to run, and Dutton, violating what he regarded as a cardinal rule—never get between two Kennedys—went to Teddy and found him reconciled, although still dubious. ("Bobby's therapy is going to cost the family eight million dollars," he muttered.)

Teddy agreed to go to Wisconsin to try to work out a deal with McCarthy in which he and Bobby would form a temporary alliance and divide the remaining primaries to deny the Johnson-Humphrey forces any of their delegates. Meanwhile, Sorensen and Walinsky wrote drafts of an announcement speech. In the atmosphere of chaos which would mark the campaign to come, Bobby tried to force a reconciliation of the drafts, but they were too different in tone and content and neither author would give a sentence. At one in the morning he gave up, told his advisers to work out the differences without him, and went to bed. Schlesinger, who finally wandered into one of the children's bedrooms at Hickory Hill and tried to take a nap, was awakened at dawn when Bobby padded in in pajamas. He said that Teddy's mission to McCarthy had failed and asked what to do. Schlesinger said he could back McCarthy and take over his delegates if and when he burned himself out. Bobby gave him a scornful look: "Kennedys don't act that way." A few hours later he selected Sorensen's draft, those present felt because he had been Jack's speechwriter, although phrases such as the concluding one—"At stake is not simply the leadership of our party or even our country; it is the right to the moral leadership of the planet"—were out of character with the persona he had developed. Bobby announced his candidacy in the same room of the Senate where Jack had announced his, but there were few echoes of the euphoric time when Jack was making his run. A grim sense of necessity had replaced that former buoyant sense of adventure.

Nor was there any euphoria later, when Bobby discussed his decision with his parents. His father was sad, not only because Bobby was challenging the party regulars but also because he was exposing himself to danger. He simply went to bed. Bobby went up and talked to him: "Try to understand, Dad. I think I'm doing it the right way."

On March 31, three days before what polls predicted would be a disaster for LBJ in the Wisconsin primary, the President withdrew from contention for 1968. The crusade Bobby had begun to look forward to—against the usurper and the usurper's war—was suddenly different and more difficult.

The campaign organization that carried him into the primaries bore little resemblance to the well-oiled Kennedy machine he had put together for Jack in 1960. That effort had ripened for better than a year, maturing in an atmosphere of relative social tranquillity, picking its objectives carefully and achieving them by the application of maximum force over a lengthy period of time. In 1968 the Kennedy forces took the field in an atmosphere of confusion and alarm, disadvantaged always by lack of time and coherent planning and by the fact that the only able campaign manager was the candidate himself. Teddy tried to shoulder the responsibility. One reporter recalled him flying into Wisconsin to set up an apparatus there. He asked all the correct questions: how many students were there at the university, how many Kennedy volunteers from the 1960 effort were still available, and so on; but as the answers came back he didn't seem to know what to do with them. Leaving the meeting, Governor Patrick Lucey, a Kennedy supporter, muttered, "Bobby's trouble is that he doesn't have a Bobby." Another participant said, "If he'd been running this campaign he would have fired everybody in there and started all over again."

The family was involved as before, but it was different from the days when Jack was on the rise and they all felt they were making a joint assault on power. "There was something joyless about it," said a reporter who covered Bobby's sisters' appearances. "There was a sort of grim feeling that they were trying to get back what was theirs." Joe Kennedy followed it all by long distance, troubled and confused and only half-comprehending. Rose was on the scene, but occasionally an obtuse and difficult symbol. During the critical Indiana primary, which involved hundreds of paid staff and a cost of $3 million, she agreed to be interviewed by Walter Cronkite along with her two surviving sons. Fred Dutton was with Bobby when he got in the elevator and went down a floor to pick up Ted and then down another floor to wait, as always, for Rose. When she got in and the elevator began to descend, Bobby began to plan the appearance: "Well, I guess I'll start out by saying . . ." Rose cut him off coldly. "Listen, *I'm* the one being interviewed."

The Shrivers were emotionally distant because Sargent had accepted LBJ's offer of the ambassadorship to France. Jackie had come out of her public relations exile to campaign for Bobby, yet even here there was friction. One evening when the campaign was going well she remarked, "Won't it be wonderful when we get back in the White House?" Ethel, who must have remembered the rumors about Bobby and Jackie after the assassination ("Well, what are you going to do about it?" Eunice had said at the time. "He's spending an awful lot of time with the widder"), gave Jackie a chilling look and said, "What do you mean *we?*" and walked off. Bobby shrugged and followed, leaving Jackie alone.

The campaign became an oddly individual effort, a series of Bobby's own ad hoc moments. As "Bad Bobby" he decided to try to get the Massachusetts legislature to make McCarthy's early primary victory there nonbinding, but Teddy vetoed that plan. "Good Bobby" went to a black ghetto in Indianapolis the night after Martin Luther King, Jr., was assassinated and talked about violence and the social bond, in what many listeners felt was one of the finest extemporaneous speeches they had ever heard.

His public appearances developed into what one reporter called "feeding frenzies." The people who rushed his car, snatching at his cuffs and leaving his hands cut and bleeding, were grasping at a complex symbolism, trying to touch the Kennedy myth itself, that power which had become almost totemic. The people around him worried. At times Bobby seemed oddly fatalistic, appearing almost to court the crazed figure who might be lurking in any of the swelling crowds. As the campaign went on, even members of the press urged him to be more careful. "If they want to get me, they'll get me," he responded. "They got Jack." Leonard Duhl, a sociology professor who had joined the campaign, wrote a memo warning that studies had shown that people who make gloomy predictions—as Bobby was about the shattering consequences of racism, the war in Vietnam, and other issues—get blamed when the predictions come true. Bobby came up and grabbed Duhl playfully by the neck. "Don't worry," he said, "everything is going to be all right."

"Bobby felt he was in Jack's shadow," Lem said later. "He wanted to get out, but that made him guilty: he thought of the desire itself as an act of disloyalty." Yet as the campaign sputtered along, he seemed finally to be coming into his own. Indiana was his equivalent of West Virginia in 1960: the place he had to prove himself, the must-win situation. He went from one neighborhood to another, speaking in the halting staccato way that was so different from Jack's tailored coolness and made him seem, by comparison, almost disturbingly real. He talked to suspicious Hoosiers about the needs of the "invisible poor" in one breath and called for law and order in the next. McCarthy might be a philosopher; Bobby was an evangelist. The day after King's assassination he talked about the type of violence that was "slower but just as deadly [and] destructive as the gun or the bomb in the night. This is the violence of institutions: indifference and inaction and slow decay. This is the violence that affects the poor, that poisons relations between men because their skin has different colors . . ." At a moment when he was being mobbed by people grabbing at him enthusiastically he turned to an aide and said, "All this for a ruthless man? Just think of what they'd do for a kind one."

When the *New York Times* called his Indiana victory "inconclusive," Bobby said to Newfield: "If I was really ruthless I'd find a way to get even with the *Times*." He went on to other victories in New York and Nebraska and began to chase McCarthy west. In Oregon, he ran into a wall: no minorities, little unemployment, relative social tranquillity. ("Let's face it," Bobby said in one of his more telling comments, "I appeal best to people who have problems.") Unable to find the sorts of issues that worked for him elsewhere, he lost to McCarthy, the first primary defeat for a Kennedy. He went home for a brief rest at Hyannis before the final showdown with the McCarthy forces in California. He spent long hours with his father— shrunken now, his skin the texture of vellum, his claw hand shaking with palsy. On the day he had to leave, he bent over the wheelchair and said: "Dad, I'm going to California for a few days and I'm going to fight hard. I'm going to win one for you."

He went up and down the state, working it as if it were a magnified version of a Boston ward. With its large black and Mexican-American populations and white liberal enclaves it should have been tailor-made for him. But he was hurt by the loyalty of antiwar activists to McCarthy and he found himself calling for the debate he had ducked in Oregon. With all the experts anticipating that his more articulate opponent could make him look bad, Bobby more than held his own, and, according to pollsters, brought a sizable portion of the undecided vote to his corner.

On the day of the primary he rested at film director John Frankenheimer's Malibu house. They chatted about *Seven Days in May*, one of Frankenheimer's films which Jack had particularly liked. At midday Bobby went for a swim in the ocean with his children. He saw David, his thirteen-year-old, bobbing in the surf, about to be carried away by the undertow, and swam to rescue him. Later on Frankenheimer drove him to his headquarters at the Ambassador Hotel to watch the returns.

As returns came west he found that he had won by a large margin in South Dakota, which also held its primary on June 5. But the vote in California was disturbingly close throughout the early evening. Finally, around midnight, projections showed Kennedy a clear winner. Realizing that McCarthy was through and that Humphrey was the only remaining obstacle, Bobby said to Goodwin: ''My only chance is to chase Hubert's ass all over the country. Maybe he'll fold ...'' Kenny O'Donnell, his old Harvard roommate who knew better than anyone how far he had come, called from Washington. Bobby left a conference with Teddy, Steve Smith, Sorensen, and Goodwin to take the phone. ''You know, Ken,'' he said, ''finally I feel that I'm out from under the shadow of my brother. Now at least I feel that I've made it on my own. All these years I never really believed it was me that did it, but Jack.''

He went downstairs and made his victory statement. Afterward he detoured through the hotel kitchen to a press conference. Among the workers was a man with a gun.

If there had been time for last words, those uttered by Ajax, one of the figures of the Greek myths that had become so important to Bobby in his last swift years, would have served him well: ''Light, light, if only to die in.''

PART 4

THE LOST BOYS

The whole world is our hospital.

—T. S. ELIOT, *Four Quartets*

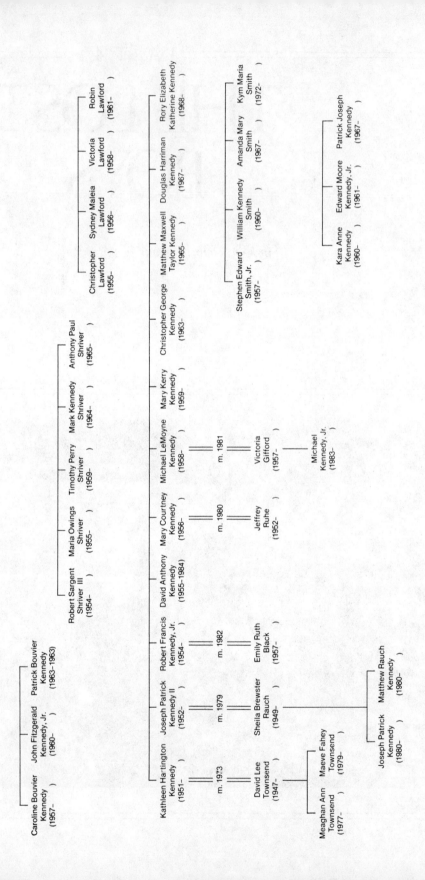

1.

*W*HEN HE THOUGHT ABOUT IT LATER ON, Chris Lawford was struck by how much that Saturday afternoon resembled others he had spent at his Uncle Bobby's house—a swirl of activity, laughter and argument erupting almost volcanically from groups of guests, children and dogs battling against the mainstream of adults in endless serpentining games. A semi-ward of the Robert Kennedy family since his own parents' acrimonious divorce five years earlier, Chris had seen many parties like this one at Hickory Hill. As always, Robert McNamara, John Glenn, Lem Billings, and others of the Kennedys' favorite people were circulating through the crowd. As always there was the guest who suddenly shot out screaming into the pool, emerging soggy and spluttering in formal attire and pointing a finger at whoever had pushed him. And, as always, there was a sense that this was the way things had been and would forever be at the place Chris had come to think of as the center of the universe.

He and his cousins had been on their own all day, as they usually were at such functions, playing catch-as-catch-can, a game his Uncle Bobby said he and his brothers and sisters had played when they were young. Then a pudgy thirteen-year-old who barely managed to hold his own in the nonstop family athletics, Chris had managed to keep from being caught for quite a long time, hiding first in the stable area near the three-hundred-year-old stand of hickory trees for which the estate was named, then inside the tack room. After almost half an hour had passed without anyone looking for him, he came out into the open and noticed that the guests were beginning to leave. He came back cautiously toward the house, trying to find Bobby Junior and David, the cousins who were also his best friends. Unable to locate them, he finally saw Ina, the family's Costa Rican maid, and asked where they were. She gave him a strange look, and when she answered the music in her voice was sharper than usual. "Don't you understand? They bury their father today. They are feeling sad and have gone on up to their beds."

At that moment Chris understood how successful his Aunt Ethel had been in maintaining her illusion since *it* had happened: that nothing had really changed; that Bobby was in heaven, happy to be with Jack and awaiting an eventual reunion with them all. He sat down on the grass, physically sickened by the feelings of loss and abandonment he hadn't had time to feel on first hearing that his uncle had been shot.

Like others in the family, Chris had been galvanized by Bobby's vision. Something like a moment of epiphany had occurred just before the California primary, when he accompanied his mother to the Park Avenue church they always attended. Standing on the front steps and about to go in, he had suddenly stopped, feeling that it was wrong for them to worship with the rich instead of devoting their lives to the poor and helpless as Bobby was urging. His mother had argued with him, her voice straining to a crescendo that caused others to stare, but he had refused to compromise. He would never, he said, set foot inside this church again.

Sitting on the lawn at Hickory Hill, he tried to piece together the events of the past few days, understanding that he could never make a coherent story out of it, and that it would always remain a mosaic of rumors and impressions.

His cousin Bobby Junior had told him during the funeral about how he had gone to bed soon after the announcement that his father had won California and then gotten up eagerly the next morning to read about the details of the victory in the *Washington Post,* only to see headlines about the shooting; he had sat on the living-room hearth for an hour, feeding the newspaper page by page into the fire. Sixteen-year-old Joe, oldest male of the generation, had been at boarding school when his Uncle Teddy called to say there had been a shooting but not to worry because it wasn't as serious as it sounded. When Joe arrived in Los Angeles and saw his father inside the oxygen tent, the familiar face so black and distorted from the bullet that had smashed into the back of his head, he had known immediately that it was more serious than he had been told. And when death finally came, the operating room at the Good Samaritan Hospital had become what Joe, trying to describe the scene to Chris and others who hadn't been there, called a "hellish environment," with doctors and nurses crying and screaming and the adults so incapacitated that he had been the one who had to tell his younger brothers and sisters that their father hadn't made it.

When the body was brought home, those Chris was closest to in the family —his Uncle Bobby's oldest boys, Joe, Bobby Junior, and David—had served at the requiem mass at St. Patrick's. Then the whole family had boarded the funeral train winding slowly down to Arlington. John-John, as they sometimes still called the eight-year-old son of the dead President, had been bewildered by the possible relationship of this new tragedy to the other one he remembered; at one point he asked Christopher Kennedy, Bobby's five-year-old son, if his father would still be going to his office at the Senate. "Oh yes," Christopher Kennedy answered. "He's in heaven in the morning and he goes to his office in the afternoon."

David, thirteen, who had been alone in a Los Angeles hotel room watching his father's victory statement on television when the shooting occurred, had also been in a daze. For much of the trip to Arlington, he had his head out of the window of the train, letting the wind batter his face. Once, as they were entering a tunnel, Phil Kirby, David's close friend from Hyannis whom Ethel had asked along to keep him company, noticed that David didn't see the protruding arm of a steel girder and yanked him back into the compartment to keep him from being decapitated. Both boys had their heads out the window again when a train running on a parallel track to theirs struck a group of bystanders at a crossing; two were killed, one of them cut in half under the wheels. David had been mesmerized by the bloody scene, unable to tear himself away until a Secret Service man got him back down into his seat.

The climax of the train ride, at least for Chris and the others of his generation, had come when Joe, accompanied by Ethel, walked up and down the aisles of some of the passenger cars wearing one of his father's pin-striped suits, shaking hands and saying, "I'm Joe Kennedy, thank you for coming," with such composure that Ethel later said excitedly, "He's got *it!* He's got *it!*" The pronoun needed no antecedent; it meant the touch, the destiny, the political genes all the Kennedy grandchildren were already talking and wondering about.

As the last guests departed from Hickory Hill and shadows began to creep across the grass, Chris Lawford thought about all these events of the past few days, trying to make sense of them; feeling alone and, even worse, unprotected. When Uncle Bobby was alive, he thought to himself, we knew who we were. But now he's gone. What will happen to us? What comes next?

These questions were on the minds of many of the others as well. There were twenty-seven of them, soon to be twenty-eight, as Ethel's swelling pregnancy attested. When they were all together they looked like a remarkable experiment in eugenics—several strains of one particularly attractive species. There were the darkly handsome Shrivers, five children with their father's sensitive eyes and their mother's aggressive jaw; Stevie and Willie Smith, whose round-faced impassivity emulated the masks that had allowed their father to prosper in the family; Peter Lawford's striking good looks in the faces of Chris and his three sisters, as well as a hint of the actor's troubled vulnerability. Among those bearing the family name, Bobby's children had the Skakels' big bones and imposing size, while Teddy's—Kara, Edward Junior, and Patrick—were blond and surprisingly frail. Caroline and John-John had a regal poise all the others lacked.

The country had seen these wind-swept, photogenic faces at different stages of development and watched their growth and change as if by time-lapse photography. They were, as one journalist had remarked, "America's children." Yet while they had been in the spotlight all their lives, they had a curious innocence. The importance outsiders attached to being a Kennedy amused them. They gawked back at the tourists who peeked through the hedges at Hyannis. They scooped up sand from the public beach and sold it as "Kennedy sand" for a dollar a bag. They stood at the fence and answered "Kennedy questions" (What does Jackie eat for breakfast? Where do the Kennedys shop?) for a quarter apiece. Asked what it "meant" to be a Kennedy, Bobby's son David had once replied, "It means that we're exactly the same as everybody else, except better."

But as in their parents' generation, it was the opinion of family members that really mattered to them. They competed with other children in swim meets and sailing contests, succeeding so well that Hyannis Port officials barred them from a certain number of these competitions every season so that other residents could win some ribbons. The competition within their own group was far more intense, far more metaphoric of what they saw as the challenge of their lives. Each of them was always looking for an opening to outperform some rival in the family, always searching for an opportunity to improve his or her standing, always wondering if someone in an age or ability group just above them would slip, always aware above all else that their parents were watching and assessing their performance to see which of them had *it*. If the Beals Street house where some of the prior Kennedy generation were born had been an enigma of latency, the Compound where this generation gathered every summer was a training ground to recapture the achieved greatness that had once belonged to the family. As Chris Law-ford said later, "We were all, every one of us, raised to be President."

Some of the older ones remembered what their parents referred to as "that brief shining moment": trips to the White House; Friday afternoons when the presidential helicopter would swoop down, their Uncle Jack would get out and, after disposing of his aides, drive them all downtown and give them each a dollar to spend at the candy store. Some had the treasured memory of a more intimate contact. For Joe, it was the time he was invited to a special showing of the film version of *PT 109*. ("Thank you for inviting me to the movie," he wrote his uncle the President afterward. "I had lots of fun . . . I think you were very brave. When I grow up, I hope I can be as brave as you are.") For Chris, like all the others a victim of Joe's bullying, it was the time he was being chased through the Compound and came up to the President studying a briefcase full of papers on the porch of his house. "Joe's after me," he'd panted. "Can I hide?" Jack had answered without looking up: "Sure, go hide in the attic." He didn't tell Joe where Chris was; neither did he stop Joe from punching Chris in the stomach when he finally came out of hiding.

But if Jack represented what the family had been—"the President," they all grew up calling him, as if there had been no other—Bobby had represented what they would become. It was he who would come through a room where one of them was lounging on a sofa reading a comic book and say, "Put that junk down right now and get outside and *do* something." It was he who attended christenings and confirmations, graduations and commencements. When their grandmother Rose repeated her favorite saying from St. Luke, "To whom much is given, much will be required," it seemed just another of the religious homilies she left strewn through her conversation. Bobby translated the admonition into terms they could understand: "America has been very good to the Kennedys. We all owe the country a debt of gratitude and of public service." He was the energetic, embracing figure who demanded that they be better than they thought they were; who brought them into the family games and the family destiny as well; who kept them from being nothing more than an exotic collection of celebrities' children. Because of their grandfather's sickness, Bobby was the only head of the family they had ever known. Whether Lawfords, Shrivers, Smiths, or Kennedys, they had thought about their future in terms of him: working at his office, on his campaigns, perhaps even in his administration. He was the one who had defined their Kennedyness, and now that he was dead, the definitions were all called into question.

Sarge Shriver and Steve Smith didn't have the moral authority to fill Bobby's shoes. Teddy was too wrapped up in the political ramifications of the death to be available to them. Rose walked on the beach alone, wearing a tight smile and saying, "God gives us no more than we can bear." Only Joseph Kennedy seemed aware of their dilemma. "Sometimes Grandpa would look at us as if he wanted to say something," Chris Lawford remembers. "His mouth would move sort of convulsively as if some words were trying to get out. Then this cloudy look would come over his eyes and he'd slouch down into his wheelchair and the attendant would wheel him off."

And so 1968 became their first summer of discontent. Before, they had been individuals who drew their respective families closer together by their special relationships (Chris and David, Bobby's son Michael and Stevie Smith, Teddy's Kara and Vicki Lawford). Now they felt as though they were being dealt with as groups, each with demeaning names: The Little Kids, the Girls, the Big Boys. The Girls spent much of that summer going to mass with servants and praying fervently for Bobby's soul. The Little Kids went about the usual summer-camp-style activities with the recreation director Bobby had always hired for them—swimming lessons, then tennis, then horseback riding—but with none of the old spirit. The Big Boys played football games degraded by undercurrents of "Win one for the Gipper" sentimentality. They all had a sense of contraction, of shrinking back inside themselves. "It was so different from Jack's death," Eunice's oldest son, Bobby, said. "Then there had been a coming together. Uncle Bobby had seen to that. In a strange way we'd felt even more like Kennedys than ever—proud at what Jack had been, determined that our time would come again. But once Uncle Bobby died, there was just this sense of splitting apart."

The impact was greatest on Bobby's own children, whom his magnetism had made the center of the clan. By the time of David's birthday on June 15, marked by a spiritless party at Hickory Hill whose high point was Bobby Junior's decision to put a laxative in everybody's milk, the heroic denial Ethel had been practicing since the funeral had begun to crack. Tension was thick in the house. The Little Kids and the Girls were immune from Ethel's dark moods. But the Big Boys were not; on the threshold of manhood themselves, they seemed to pose painful questions about the fate of Kennedy males. Their mother punished them constantly and capriciously, almost as if she blamed them for reminding her of her dead husband. She told Joe he must be the man of the house now and allowed him to sit in his dead father's chair at the dinner table. But when he hit his younger sister Kerry for making noise, she gave him the infantile punishment of having to walk up and down the stairs a hundred times. (Later, Joe went into the yard and, in a moment of tenderness, took the hands of his younger brothers and sisters and began to sing the "Battle Hymn of the Republic," their father's favorite song.) Meanwhile, Ethel kept saying to Bobby Junior and David, "Get out of here!" as if the house itself, with all the pictures of family triumphs, were a sanctuary they defiled by their presence.

A few days after David's birthday, Ethel and the kids flew with Teddy to Connecticut and chartered a boat from Mystic to Hyannis Port. Ethel careened between gloom and febrile gaiety all during the trip. Once she took Bobby Junior and David below and hit them repeatedly with a hairbrush, the first such punishment they could remember, and one that made them cry in spite of their teenager resolutions to be stronger than their mother. "I can't stand it any more," she said when they reached home port. "You guys have got to get away from here." Thus began a diaspora that would continue for years to come, a process of leaving and returning that symbolized the next generation's ambiguous tie to the Kennedy Legacy.

Joe and his friend Chuck McDermott were sent to Spain, where they stayed with the Guardiolas, a large family recommended to Teddy by the American Embassy. For the first few days Joe walked around like a displaced person. He had the Kennedy smile, which had been so striking on his father's funeral train. But it was tenuous and suspicious and usually accompanied by a knot of perplexity at his forehead. Barrel-chested and slow (a lineman, Chuck McDermott felt, in a family that valued quarterbacks and receivers), he had experienced another bad year at Milton Academy. Scholastically behind to begin with, he had lost further ground. Being a Kennedy had also resulted in being constantly tested: girls solicited mash notes not because they wanted a date but because they thought the signature might someday be valuable; boys short-sheeted his bed and even came into his room to vomit on his pillow. Joe had been looking forward to the presidential campaign to release him from his troubles. His father had already been trying to groom him—taking time out from the last raft trip to take him alone to the Navajo reservation, explaining the special plight of Indians in America, introducing him to key aides and letting him sit in on low-level briefings. He had promised Joe that after school was out he could join him full time. "That had been the big thing in his life," says McDermott. "It had allowed him to forget his troubles. Now that future was gone and he was stuck with who he was."

The Guardiolas raised bulls for bull rings throughout Spain. Joe and McDermott watched matadors test the bulls in the practice ring. Joe decided to fight a cow and was slightly gored. They went to see El Cordobes in Seville and were accorded the honor of being invited into his quarters to watch him dress in his "suit of lights" for the ring. As they left, Joe, who was so quiet that he seemed almost to have taken a vow of silence, said to McDermott, "He'll probably get killed out there." El Cordobes fought well and was awarded an ear for his bravery, which he brought to the Guardiolas' box and handed to the Kennedy heir. Joe threw it into a garbage can as they were leaving the stadium. He and McDermott spent the rest of the summer riding motorcycles. Once they found a house which was temporarily uninhabited. Joe ran his motorcycle up the stairs to the second floor, saying that it was something he'd always wanted to do.

Occasionally Joe wrote home, always asking about Bobby Junior. His brother was dark, wiry, and enigmatic, a loner by choice rather than necessity since unlike Joe he had no trouble making friends. The family regarded him as somewhat like the falcons he kept—hooded in intent and conveying a suggestion of danger. Even the practical joking he had inherited from the Skakels had an eccentric and sometimes dangerous bite. When Hyannis neighbor Philip Kirby was invited to join Bobby Junior and his brothers in serving at a memorial mass for their father, for instance, he had told the priest that he was unfamiliar with the liturgy and wasn't sure when to ring the bell. The priest replied that he would signal him by a touch on the shoulder. At the beginning of the service, Philip felt the touch and rang the bell, then immediately realized it was the wrong time. Deeply chagrined and almost in tears at having made a mistake during such a solemn ceremony for his friends' dead father, Kirby had turned to discover who had touched him and seen Bobby Junior smiling triumphantly.

As a youngster Bobby Junior had become interested in animals—first lizards and snakes and later falcons. His father had commissioned naturalists from the Bronx Zoo to make him a walk-in terrarium for his thirteenth birthday. He had encouraged the interest in falconry, although admitting to his son that he was disturbed by the implications of feeding pigeons to the predators. The two of them worked out a compromise with a distinctive Kennedy twist: if a pigeon managed to avoid a hawk on two successive flights, it was "retired" and never forced to face death again.

Struck by the boy's range of interests, Bobby Senior had once remarked that Bobby Junior was "just like the President." Lem Billings had thought so too and had taken him on as a protégé. When Ethel became increasingly difficult in the weeks after the assassination, Lem had volunteered to take Bobby Junior to Africa on an animal-watching expedition, fulfilling a promise his father had made shortly before his death. And so, while Joe was watching bullfights in Spain, Lem and Bobby were touring the Serengeti Plain. Bobby crouched in the veldt grass and stalked animals with a camera, telling Africans that he planned to become a veterinarian. He and Lem kept a journal, which Lem said they would be able to sell to a magazine for a lot of money.

David was very conscious of the coup his brother had scored in having an adult who was fully devoted to him and ready to help him deal with the tragedy. "Lem could have chosen any of us," he said. "I remember the day it happened. Lem appeared and they just sort of walked off together. I thought to myself: Bobby's lucky. I wish I had someone." If his father's death hit David harder than the others, it was because there had been a special bond between them—both were the runts of the litter, sandwiched into the middle of a large family—and because he had always been a sort of golden boy for the family, with his open, freckled face and the wispy blond hair both parents had always tousled when passing by, almost as if fingering some talisman. ("If we ever go broke," Ethel had once told an interviewer, "we'll make a movie star of David and live off his earnings.") He was the only one in the family who hadn't been enthusiastic about the run for the presidency. For weeks after his father's announcement David had been plagued by recurring nightmares about Bobby's death. Distraught over episodes that seemed premonitory, and missing the special attention his father had given him, David had gotten in trouble for throwing rocks at cars passing by Hickory Hill. His father had taken time on the campaign plane to write a note that seemed directed to David as much as the members of the press to whom it was delivered: "He feels very badly about what has happened and has apologized to all concerned. And I want to add that he is a good boy and has always been a source of great joy and pride to the family."

The day of the California primary, he had joined his father in Los Angeles. The two of them had been swimming in the Malibu surf and his feet had been cut from under him by a riptide; he had felt himself being carried out by the undertow when his father grabbed him, scraping his own head on the ocean floor as he reached for David's slippery arm. With a teenager's melodrama, David had decided that he owed his father a life and would look for an opportunity to pay him back in the years ahead. That night as he sat in front of the television set in his room in the Ambassador Hotel and watched the images from the hand-held cameras jostling to get a better view of the new Kennedy martyr bleeding on the floor downstairs in the Ambassador's kitchen, one of the thoughts he had was that the debt would be forever undischarged.

Once Joe and Bobby Junior were taken care of for the summer, Ethel hustled David off to Austria with Chris Lawford as a companion. They went to Meyerhoff, a tennis and ski camp run by the former tennis star Bill Talbert. They skied on a glacier in the morning and practiced volleys in the afternoon. After-hours, David was introduced to The Grateful Dead and to sex: "Some seventeen-year-old girl at the camp realized who I was and picked me up. I was hardly into puberty. Chris told me to take her out and try to feel her tits. I did it. All of a sudden she was unzipping my pants and pulling them down and sort of moaning about how bad she felt that my father had died."

For the rest of their time in Austria, he and Chris sneaked out of their rooms at night with sleeping bags which they took into the girls' dorms, propositioning girls there who they discovered felt guilt and morbid fascination over Bobby's death. They knew it was wrong, but they also knew it was part of a great change in their attitude toward everything having to do with being a Kennedy. "It was like watching a huge balloon lose its air," Chris said later. "Things just didn't have meaning any more." An outstanding tennis player, Chris now found himself not caring whether he won or lost. "I'd be out on the court and I'd just say 'the hell with it' in the middle of the match and walk off. Before Uncle Bobby's death I wouldn't have dared do that. It just wouldn't have been possible: you never gave up, never stopped trying to win. But those kinds of emotions didn't have much meaning any more. David and I sort of decided together that there really wasn't any reason to try to be good any more, so we might as well try to be bad."

When David returned home, things were in a state of ongoing disorder. It had been difficult for Ethel to keep domestic help in the best of times; during the summer there had been several resignations and his ten-year-old brother Michael, most resilient of the children, had taken to answering the phone with the words: "Confusion here." Although the Hyannis Compound was insulated by several acres, Ethel had played music so loudly that the neighbors had been forced to call the police. Seven months pregnant, she bounded around the tennis court every day, even though she was worried about the

baby, which she had come to see as an obscure symbol of Kennedy will. In a
doubles match pitting her and Jim Whittaker against Andy Williams and
Art Buchwald, she had become so furious with frustration that she knelt
down to bang her head on the court surface.

As summer ended with a stream of friends visiting the family—Dave
Hackett, Rosey Grier, Rafer Johnson, and John Glenn were the regulars—
David kept waiting for someone to talk to him about his father's death.
During a rare lull in his mother's almost nonstop activity, he cornered her
in the kitchen and asked her about it. "It's not a subject I want to discuss,"
she snapped, elbowing her way by him.

His brothers were back but leading separate lives—Joe driving around
Hyannis with older friends in their cars, and Bobby Junior spending most
of his time by himself in the woods with Morgan Le Fay, a red-tailed hawk
he had captured and tamed a few years earlier. They all met on the football
field, but the games had turned into desperate Freudian struggles, with Joe
looking for opportunities to smash them into the ground while they waited
for the inevitable moment when his trick knee went out. When this happened,
Joe would writhe on the ground as Bobby stood above him sneering, "Oh,
has our sister hurt his knee?" These were such ugly scenes that Mary Schreiner, one of their sister Kathleen's friends, once yelled at Bobby: "How can
you ever expect to be President if you talk like that to your brother?"

David spent time with his friend Philip Kirby, while Bobby hung out with
some older boys, notably another neighbor, John Kelley. One afternoon when
they were all together, Kelley happened to ask Bobby what he'd done with
the LSD he'd sold him. Bobby tried to change the subject; when Kelley
persisted he said that he'd fed the drug to his parakeet. Later, in the Kelleys'
garage, a favorite meeting place, after David had chided Bobby for keeping
secrets from him, Bobby laid out some mescaline on a piece of wood and
dared him to take it. Kirby, who had watched David try to prove himself
time and again by taking dares, begged him not to take the drug: "Don't do
that, David. Please don't do it." But Bobby egged him on, and after hesitating a moment, David swallowed the mescaline. Later on, when he was hallu-
cinating, it seemed to him that the hedge Bobby was leaning against had
sharp leaves. He asked Bobby to move away so he wouldn't get hurt. But
Bobby laughed and backed deeper into the hedge, whose spines seemed to
David to penetrate his brother's body. "You're dying," he cried out, "just
like Daddy." Bobby smiled and sagged to the ground with his eyes staring
and his tongue lolling out of his mouth in a mime of death.

Although they were not able to articulate it, the boys were aware that they
were stepping over lines they had never expected to cross, lines between good
and evil that Robert Kennedy himself had drawn. Now they found themselves standing on an opposite shore from the one he had occupied, as if to
better see his memory. No matter how old they became, he would always be

"Daddy," as if his meaning had been set in amber at the time of his death, a time which would come to represent antique virtue and morality for them. Not long after the death, when the family was out sailing, the dog Freckles slipped overboard, and each of the four oldest boys dove into the water to save him. "Daddy would have done it," they told an aunt who asked them why they had jeopardized their lives for an animal. "Daddy believed that competition brought out the best in us," Joe would often reply when asked about the ferocious gamesmanship in the family. And years later, when Bobby Junior was nearly thirty, he described his father's code in these terms: "Daddy got in fights, but he would never hit anybody smaller. He was absolutely moral. He was never with another woman before he was married or afterward. He was completely moral."

Daddy: the personification of a love they would never again feel and of a moral order they would never again experience.

As the worst year of their young lives came to a close, they decided to surprise their mother at Christmas with a book comprised of letters about their father. David's said: "Daddy was very funny in church because he would embarrass all of us by singing very loud. Daddy did not have a very good voice. There will be no more football with Daddy, no more swimming with him, no more riding and no more camping with him. But he was the best father their [sic] ever was and I would rather have him for a father for the length of time I did than any other father for a million years."

2.

*T*EDDY HAD GOTTEN A TASTE OF WHAT WAS IN store for him when he was riding the elevator down to the Good Samaritan Hospital's autopsy room with his brother's corpse strapped to a gurney beside him. At a stop along the way, an agitated Al Lowenstein got in and quickly blurted out, ''Now that Bobby's gone, you're all we've got. You've got to take the leadership.'' Summoning the formidable control he would often exercise in the days to come, Teddy assured Lowenstein that he would ''carry on.'' But not long afterward, in a conversation with his aide Dun Gifford, he admitted how tenuous his hold was: ''I can't let go. If I let go, Ethel will let go, and my mother will let go, and all my sisters will let go ...'' That was his problem: in one fateful moment he had become the foundation of a house of cards; he had gone from baby of the family to its head, from last child to last Kennedy. ''The moment Bobby died was like being at a tennis match,'' his friend the journalist Jim Weighart thought. ''All of a sudden all the heads swung toward Teddy. He wasn't ready for that.''

His initial response was withdrawal. At first it seemed natural that he should retreat to the Cape, scene, of the family's good times, and grapple with this new sorrow by walking alone on the beach or taking the yawl *Mira* or sometimes Jack's *Victura* out for the day. But as the days passed he seemed increasingly unable to locate himself in the aftermath of the tragedy. Living in a family of comparisons, he flailed himself for not feeling as much grief over Bobby's death as Bobby had felt over Jack's. Knowing that his office was getting some twenty-five hundred letters a day, ten of them filled with hate and two of those venomous enough to warrant attention by the

FBI, he was afraid, and he flailed himself for that too. Among friends he tried to deal with this fear through bravado—"All I want if someone's going to blow my head off is just one swing at him first"—but the ambivalence of his feelings was better captured in the comment he blurted out to an AP reporter waiting where his boat had tied up: "I'm not afraid to die. I'm too young to die."

The fear was not just physical but metaphysical. The crushing weight of the Kennedy Legacy had suddenly descended on him, not only swollen out of political proportion as a result of Bobby's death, but out of all human scale as well. Rose had given a sense of its apocalyptic size the first weekend after the funeral, when Teddy joined her and his father in the bleak sunshine of Palm Beach to thank the nation for the outpouring of sympathy: "We shall honor him not with useless mourning and vain regrets for the past but with firm and indomitable resolution for the future: attempting to relieve the starvation of people in this society, working to aid the disadvantaged and those helpless inarticulate masses for whom he felt so deeply . . ."

No longer was it enough to be personally ambitious, as Joseph Kennedy and Jack had been; now a Kennedy must prove his right to lead by accepting responsibility for a whole liberal philosophy and social tradition. Nor was there.any longer a sense that the Legacy could be a work in progress, which an inheritor could shape, as Bobby had, to his own contours. It was a completed artifact, Bobby's masterwork; as such, it could not be augmented, only diminished.

Teddy responded to the pressures as he had on other occasions when his private self collided with the Kennedy image: by asserting his right to be the youngest, beyond obligation and responsibility. Leaving Joan and the children behind, he sailed almost every day, stopping at Gene Tunney's island, or at the Dillons' or at Thomas Watson's summer home. As he moved restlessly from one anchorage to another, people were struck by the pouches under his eyes and the derelict stubble on his cheeks, telling each other that he resembled an ancient mariner trying to escape some curse. He was also drinking heavily, and his behavior careened between the jolliness which was his natural disposition and a dangerous recklessness. One day he took his father's power boat the *Marlin* out, cutting through Martha's Vineyard Harbor at full tilt, nearly swamping smaller boats with the wake and leaving bystanders amazed that he had managed to avoid cutting some other craft in two and perhaps killing someone. Not long afterward he invited a small contingent of Green Berets to Hyannis, and after watching them rope up and scale his father's house and then rappel their way back down again, he ushered them to a local tavern where they all drank until they reached a point where they were tossing off jiggers of bourbon in one gulp and then smashing the glasses against a wall while calling out histrionically, "No one shall drink from this glass again." Always he returned to his boat. As one close friend said, "The nautical metaphors certainly fit. He was cut from his moorings, adrift, lost at sea."

He could run but he couldn't hide; 1968 was still an election year and a midsummer Harris Poll showed that a Kennedy on the Democratic ticket might add five million votes to the badly divided party, enough to guarantee victory. In August, Teddy was anchored along the Maine coast when a signal came that there was an important phone call. He rowed a dinghy ashore and took it in a telephone booth perched on a rocky promontory. It was Chicago Mayor Richard Daley. Faced with the prospects of a possibly chaotic convention and a lackluster ticket, Daley talked of a draft. Teddy reiterated what his office had already announced—that he wouldn't take the second spot. Daley said he was still interested. Back aboard the boat, Teddy seemed almost bemused, saying to himself more than anyone else, "What is it all about?"

Shortly before the convention opened, he made his first major political speech since Bobby's death, including the enticing statement, "Like my brothers before me I pick up a fallen standard." He sent Steve Smith to Chicago to canvass delegates and found that some 1200 of the 1312 needed for the nomination were there for the asking. The troops were mobilized, ready to shift their allegiance from Bobby and from McCarthy, who could not seriously challenge Humphrey, to him. But he couldn't bring himself to fight for the nomination. He told aides that it was "Bobby's year," and he didn't want to horn in on his brother's memory. The truth, Dun Gifford felt, was that "he recognized that he had always been pushed forward too soon and knew that he just wasn't prepared to be the leader of the family in any respect." But he did have a sense of the opportunity he was passing up. Watching as Hubert Humphrey was nominated in the middle of the police riot taking place in metropolitan Chicago, an inauspicious beginning for a campaign that would have to face Richard Nixon, Teddy told an aide who'd recommended waiting because he could have the nomination four years later or any time in the future he chose to take it, "You know, someday I'm going to be in Coos Bay, Oregon, or someplace like that and I'll just have blown my last chance at the nomination and I'm going to call you and remind you of what we decided here."

One of the boats Teddy visited during his summer of wandering was Aristotle Onassis's yacht the *Christina*. Like others who came aboard, he was struck by the exotic opulence of the craft: El Grecos on the walls, gold fixtures in the bathrooms, even bar stools covered in leather made from the tanned skin of whale testicles. He admitted the attractions of the dark-eyed Greek girls who seemed to have no well-defined function on the yacht. But he was there less for pleasure than to negotiate with Onassis, who had come to America to get acquainted with Caroline and John and prepare them for his marriage to their mother.

The match had been talked about in the family since the previous spring, when Jackie had called Bobby from Greece to tell him that Onassis had proposed. Joking weakly after recovering from the initial shock, Bobby had said: "For God's sake, Jackie, this could cost me five states." Onassis was different, Bobby realized, from the other men who had squired Jackie around New York during a widowhood that had been at least publicly chaste, men whom one acquaintance described as "all very married, or very old, or very queer." He was different also from real suitors like David Ormsby-Gore, Lord Harlech, who had accompanied Jackie to Angkor Wat in 1967: Harlech was a patrician, an old friend of the Kennedys—someone who, if they married, would be a consort rather than a husband. Onassis was too rich, too Mediterranean, and too involved in right-wing politics. Ethel and Joan, whose husbands would be most hurt by the marriage, had pleaded with Jackie to reconsider. So had Cardinal Cushing, her spiritual adviser. And so she had agreed to wait at least until after the presidential election.

Bobby's death had changed things. "I hate this country," Jackie lashed out in front of a friend. "I despise America and I don't want my children to live here any more. If they're killing Kennedys, my kids are number one targets ... I want to get out of this country." She also saw marriage to Onassis as a release from what she called the "oppressive obsession" with her and her children, and as a rebuke to the Kennedys and others who had tried to use her image as holy widow. ("I like seeing all these politicians deal with Ari's squiggly name," she told another friend.) Above all, it was a way of humbling the in-laws, who, especially in the early days, had been so difficult to live with. As Jack's old friend George Smathers put it, "The Kennedy women had always flaunted their money and power. This was Jackie's opportunity to say to them: Okay, what are you going to say now that I can buy and sell you?"

As news of the engagement became public, reaction ranged from that of the weeping housewife in Kansas City who told a television reporter, "I feel almost as bad as when Jack was assassinated," to the Swedish newspaper that headlined the story "Jackie, How Could You?" When sources in the Vatican suggested that she would be "knowingly violating the law of the church" and was therefore ineligible to receive the sacraments, Cardinal Cushing, now practicing damage control for the Kennedys, had threatened to resign to keep the Church from pressing the issue.

Despite the outcry, on October 10 on the island of Skorpios, Jack's plain gold band was replaced with a ring crowned by a huge ruby surrounded by one-carat diamonds worth $1.2 million. The world reacted as if the Queen of the Flame had sold herself to a Greek satyr. Rose refused to attend the ceremonies and sent Pat and Jean in her place. Teddy remarked bitterly to Lem Billings that on top of everything else he now had to carry what should have been Jackie's load as well.

By the fall he was back in the Senate taking an active role again. He seemed embedded in the symbolism of family: he sat behind his father's old desk in his Senate office, with one of Jack's White House flags beside him, and a framed letter from Jack to Rose on the occasion of Teddy's birth in 1932 ("Dear Mother," it said. "It is the night before exams, so I will write you Wednesday. Lots of love, Jack. P.S. Can I be godfather to the baby?") It was the moment when aides expected Teddy to step out and define himself as the next Kennedy. But he was tentative, as if awed by the prospect. When one reporter asked him to define his political philosophy he paused a moment, then listed a few of the more obvious planks in the platform of liberal orthodoxy and said lamely, "These are many of the programs Robert Kennedy was interested in . . ." It was a curiously flat performance, and a thoroughly passive one; and it was repeated frequently in the weeks ahead. As one Kennedy watcher noted: "Bobby was killed in mid-flight and the Legacy went onto automatic pilot. Teddy inherited the vector."

As the nation seethed in racial unrest and turmoil over the Vietnam War —exactly the wounds Bobby had tried to heal in the last months of his life —Teddy appeared to be trying to find a political hiding place. In part he was reacting to growing cynicism in the country and to the conclusion many Americans were drawing about his brother's death: that it would never again be possible, as it had been for the decade Jack and Bobby had dominated national life, to believe that good government came from good style, that good rhetoric made for a good society, or even that a good man could make a difference. But he was also uncertain about his own qualifications. As one long-time observer said, "He'd always been the spoiled kid brother to whom everything was handed and from whom nobody expected much. He wouldn't be able to play that comic role any more and he knew it."

During Christmas at Palm Beach, he caught wind of growing dissatisfaction among his liberal Democratic colleagues with Senate Majority Whip Russell Long. He got on the phone and immediately began to campaign for the post himself. What intrigued political pundits was not his victory, which was virtually assured, but why someone with his national stature should want a post whose duties were primarily clerical (counting noses on votes, making sure Democrats showed up for roll calls, and generally doing whatever Majority Leader Mike Mansfield needed). Yet as one Kennedy aide pointed out, "It was the perfect solution, really. He looked for and found the one Senate post that would allow him to reproduce the younger-brother role he was in danger of losing."

Yet the pressures he felt could not be released by minor corrections in his external situation, and as 1969 began his behavior was more and more erratic. Returning to the "Cadillac Eddie" image of his youth, he was drinking more and moving faster than he had done in years. His marriage was suffering and so was his reputation among his colleagues. Edward Muskie, a rival for the leadership of the party, acknowledged that Teddy could have the 1972 nomination for the asking, but then wondered, in an off-the-record comment, about his growing penchant for alcohol and fast cars. Joan, who had been left behind during Teddy's disoriented wanderlust of the previous summer, now began showing up at political functions looking dazed and disoriented.

As spring approached, Teddy moved toward a symbolic adoption of Bobby's constituency by scheduling trips to see Cesar Chavez and the farm workers and agreeing to fulfill his brother's promise to take the Subcommittee on Indian Education to Alaska for field hearings. After three exhausting days of travel and hearings all around the state, he was ready to leave; in the airport lounge in Anchorage he began to unwind with frightening velocity. Even before boarding the commercial jet that would take his party to Seattle to change planes, he was drinking with TV reporter Cassie Mackin. There were more drinks on the flight, and, after the stopover, he began to nip from the silver hip flask that had belonged to RFK. Many of the other passengers had gone to sleep, but Teddy was talking loudly and weaving up and down the aisles of the plane shouting "Es-ki-mo Power!" He talked semicoherently about his father, about his dead brothers Joe and Jack, as if the family were the dark mirror which he was searching for his own indistinct features. Most of all he talked about Bobby, saying over and over, "They're going to shoot my ass off the way they shot Bobby." Someone would cajole him back into his seat, but just as it seemed that he had become subdued he would suddenly throw a pillow at a stewardess or shout, "Hey, Cassie!" and toss a dinner roll at the reporter. Members of the press watched with drawn breath as he hovered above a terrified woman with a newborn baby in her arms, balancing a cup of scalding coffee against the turbulence of the ride.

When the plane arrived in Washington, many journalists who had witnessed the bizarre episode filed memos with their papers and magazines. *Newsweek*'s John Lindsay wrote that he felt Kennedy was "under terrible stress, an accident waiting to happen." But nothing was printed because of what was virtually a journalistic safe passage still granted by the media to the Kennedys on questions involving their personal life. There was no sequel to the episode, and for a while it seemed that the behavior had been a momentary aberration and that Teddy would be all right after all. But then, on July 18, the accident that had been waiting for more than a year finally happened when he drove his 1967 Olds off Dike Bridge at Chappaquiddick, drowning his passenger, Mary Jo Kopechne.

The facts of Chappaquiddick would never be precisely separated from the sensationalism that followed the event. Even by his own account, however, Teddy's response to the situation came close to criminal irresponsibility. Instead of calling authorities and getting help, he returned to the rented cottage where the party with the "boiler room girls"—secretaries who had had a key support function in the RFK presidential campaign—was still going on, and got his cousin Joey Gargan to return to the scene of the accident with him and join him in several dives to the submerged car. When their efforts proved hopeless, he still delayed notifying the authorities, instead plunging into the water to swim across the inlet to Edgartown, where he changed his clothes and made a 2:30 A.M. appearance in the lobby of his motel as if to establish an alibi, and then returned to his room to make seventeen phone calls, none of them to the police. The next morning he got up and, joining other guests in small talk about the sailing races scheduled for that day, took the ferry back to Chappaquiddick, where he learned that the body had been found. Only then did he make his report.

It was one of the crucial moments of the Kennedy saga. All during the development of the Legacy a sort of shadow legacy of doubt and suspicion had moved along in lock step, waiting for an opening. If the Legacy held that Joseph Kennedy had been an eminent American who proved the vitality of the melting pot and the potential of the American dream, the shadow legacy insisted that he had been a bootlegger and semioutlaw who had risen by illegal leverage. If the Legacy held that Jack's life had been the remarkable triumph of disciplined grace over illness and pain, the shadow legacy said that he had been a libertine whose achievements were bought for him. If the Legacy held that Bobby had developed a moral passion that made him unlike any other politician in the history of the country, the shadow legacy claimed that he had always been a sinister force and that the apparent sea change of his last years had been a façade for the ruthless ambition that had always been his sole cause.

The shadow legacy maintained that the Kennedy climb to the top had involved contempt for all the rules and a flaunting of all the mores, a Kennedy recklessness and a Kennedy arrogance toward the laws that bound everyone else. The occurrence at Dike Bridge and its aftermath seemed to give credence to it all. The family which before had been the victim of conspiracies now stood accused of perpetrating one.

For a week afterward there was no statement from Teddy despite the fact that the world press had gathered in Edgartown to await his explanation. During this hiatus the best lawyers in Massachusetts, including specialists in motor vehicle law, were flown to Hyannis. All the old Kennedy hands came too—the haunted McNamara, greeted with irreverent banter as "the man who handled the Bay of Pigs and Vietnam"; Burke Marshall, who had become something of a *consiglieri* for the family since Bobby discovered him; Richard Goodwin, Ted Sorensen, Lem Billings, and others. It became a question not only of what but of how much to say. Goodwin argued for making a clean breast, including release of the police report. Others said it was necessary to face the fact that the accident had killed any hopes for higher office. (One of the drafts of the statement floating around Hyannis had the sentence, ''I will never follow the path of my brothers, I will never seek the presidency,'' but the Kennedy sisters objected so strenuously that it came out.) The speech finally written by Sorensen, to whom Teddy had turned in a time of crisis just as Bobby had turned to him for the announcement of his presidential candidacy, gave a version of the accident that strained credulity. But the heroic tone of the speech, telecast nationwide, was even more dissonant than the interpretation of the facts. In a passage that seemed almost an allusion to Jack's swim after *PT 109* was rammed, Teddy talked about ''diving into the strong and murky current'' to try to rescue the dead girl. Later he wondered if ''some awful curse did actually hang over the Kennedys.''* If the appearance was intended to remind the nation what the Kennedys had suffered, however, it missed its mark, serving only to underscore how different Teddy was from his brothers, and what a dramatic break with the past Chappaquiddick represented. Watching the telecast of Teddy's speech from his ranch at Johnson City, LBJ snorted: ''Never would have happened if Bobby was there.''

Chris Lawford, who was in California with his mother and sisters at the time of Chappaquiddick, remembers how he got the news: ''Nobody said a word about what had happened. There were all these hushed phone conversations and then my mother packed her bags and said she had to go to the Cape. That was the way we were always informed of crises—someone arriving in a hurry, or someone leaving in a hurry.''

The accident didn't much affect Chris or his cousins, except, of course, for Teddy's children. It was merely a confirmation of something they had already sensed—that the buildup Teddy was getting in the press as someone who had solemnly taken on family responsibility in the Robert Kennedy tradition was not only a sham but a Kennedy-created sham at that. True, he had flown with Joe to Spain; he had also been present in the operating room when Ethel had the new baby, Rory, by Caesarian section. But he hadn't been there for them as an authority. ''We all felt a lot of bitterness toward him,'' Chris said later on. ''It was probably unfair. There was no real reason for it except that he couldn't fill Uncle Bobby's shoes and didn't try.''

The contrast between the two men had become painfully obvious at the beginning of the summer, before Chappaquiddick, when Teddy decided to continue Bobby's tradition of an annual raft trip. He had chosen to float through parts of Utah and Colorado on the Green River, scene of one of the best of the RFK outings. After a devastating year at school, a year of

---

*After writing the speech, Sorensen himself seemed to have second thoughts. He deleted favorable references to Teddy in *The Kennedy Legacy*, then in galley proofs, and relations between the two men cooled.

personal disorientation and experimentation with the drugs that the coun-
terculture was making increasingly available, the older boys were looking to
the trip as a healing ritual, a way of getting back on the Kennedy track. But
Teddy was too preoccupied with his own troubles to pay much attention to
theirs. He made the trip a floating cocktail party centered on himself, Joan,
Ethel, and the Whittakers and other nonfamily guests. In Bobby's time there
had been no such distinction between child and adult; although they had all
been younger then, the children had joined in the conquest of the river as
equals. Now it was different; the adults, in Chris's words, "wanted to float
along with their frozen daiquiris and not be bothered." At one point the kids
drew their raft alongside, as they had in Bobby's day, and began a water
fight, trying to compel engagement and change the terms of the trip. But the
adults weren't interested. They told them angrily to stop, and when they
didn't, pulled alongside to allow the six-foot-four Whittaker, huge and
threatening, to board the boys' raft and throw David and Bobby Junior
forcefully into the white water.

"We were all upset," Chris remembers. "We didn't want to have anything
to do with them after that. For the rest of the trip we took our sleeping bags
and found the hardest place to get to every night, places where they couldn't
find us, and camped there. We'd sit in the darkness talking about what a
drag the family was, what an incredible asshole Teddy was to let it happen,
how it was never like this when Bobby was alive. We had the feeling that
nobody cared enough about us any more to make us part of the family." By
the time Chappaquiddick unfolded, the Kennedy grandchildren had already
provided their own subtext on its themes.

Ethel had been featured on the cover of *Time* during the spring and had
been named by the Gallup Poll as the most admired woman in the country.
But while her public image was of one who was handling tragedy with
dignity and courage, those close to her felt she was increasingly capricious
and remote. Visitors were appalled by the cutting edge of her aggressive
banter with the older boys. She would push them into the pool but become
irrationally angry when they did the same thing to one of the younger
children. When Mary Gimbel visited Hickory Hill, she was taken aback by
Ethel's tone when six-year-old Christopher fell and hurt himself and began
to cry: "On your feet! You know how to behave. Now get out there and show
some class!" One of Bobby Junior's girlfriends who visited the household
periodically said, "I never witnessed a civil conversation between Ethel and
Bobby. I was terrified by her. I never encountered such hostility before."

Joe tried simply to stay out of her way. Now seventeen, he had finished
another disastrous academic year at Milton. His grades dipped even lower
than they'd been before. He gravitated to the group of students who considered themselves outsiders and spent much of their free time hanging out
in the graveyard across the street from the school, smoking marijuana and

complaining about the teachers and administrators. Because of his prior difficulties at the school, he had moved in with headmaster Tom Cleveland, who saw his problem as involving profound ambivalence about his status as a Kennedy: "In one sense he liked all the glory of who he was and flaunted it a little. But on the other hand it drove him crazy." Cleveland's son John, whose room Joe shared that year, found him to be an odd collection of tics— very touchy about personal possessions; so frightened of silence that he kept the radio on loudly all the time, even while sleeping; complaining constantly of feeling suffocated and insisting that a fan be on and the window be open when he went to bed, even though there were winter mornings when the room was so cold that glasses of water beside the beds had frozen. John Cleveland "had a sense that he didn't have anybody he could lean on. He seemed to think that he was supposed to have his father's death under control, but he didn't. He had a violent temper and would get this swollen look, as if he were about to burst at the seams."

That summer Joe came home to Hyannis and lived in a room over the garage annex. He insisted on bringing in girls, even though what she called his "sexual immorality" nearly drove his mother crazy. But even girls gave him little solace. Moping around Rita Dallas, his grandfather's nurse, Joe said sadly, "I can get any girl I want to go out with me because my name is Kennedy. I don't like it at all. But I guess I'd better get used to it because once a Kennedy always a Kennedy."

But Joe was old enough to drive and was thus able to escape his mother. His younger brothers could not. For them that summer at Hyannis became an almost systematic exploration of the dark side of the Kennedy Legacy, an exploration that was childlike in its manifestations but adult in its implications, an unsettling combination Chris Lawford later compared to William Golding's *Lord of the Flies*.

It had begun benignly a couple of years earlier. Bobby Junior and David would sneak out of their beds after lights out, climb out the window and drop to the ground below. They would stop at the Shrivers' house and whistle for Bobby Shriver and Chris (who often stayed there), and then the four of them would go to an abandoned cesspool down the road to meet John Kelley, Phil and Paul Kirby, and other Hyannis boys. Calling themselves the Hyannis Port Terrors—or HPTs—they would set out on their bikes to raise hell, throwing cherry bombs and M-80 firecrackers at cars, untying boats from the docks so that high tide would leave them beached by morning, and playing other pranks that would have telephones ringing at the Compound all the next day.

But in the summer of 1969, the HPTs became a different organization. The dark leader was fifteen-year-old Bobby Junior (now simply called Bobby). Tall and gangly, with hooded features and defiant blue eyes, he dressed in black and usually had a hawk perched on his gloved hand. The previous March, after months spent in studied defiance of the rules and the administrators, he had finally been expelled from Milbrook, the Poughkeepsie prep school he'd attended for two years. He first called his mother, who refused to do anything about it, and then called Lem, who fumed that Ethel was "like an ostrich, always with her head deep in the sand," and then arranged for Bobby to spend a few weeks in Colombia on a 30,000-acre *finca* belonging to an old friend from Princeton. While there he had worked in the fields and lived with the laborers, spending his spare time roaming through the rain forests capturing iguanas and howling monkeys.

Now he was back at the Cape, involved in a torrid relationship with Kim, one of the neighboring Kelley girls, and often meeting her in "the President's house," as Jack's place at the Compound was still known. After he was forbidden to go there, he transferred operations to the Playhouse, a small house furnished with everything, including a bed, in child-sized scale, which his grandfather had built years earlier for his daughters. When Ethel banished Kim and the other Kelley kids from the Compound, Bobby waited until late at night and then climbed a tree beside Kim's house and went into her second-story bedroom through a window. When Ethel found out about it, she became outraged and banished Bobby too. ("If you can't live by the rules of my house, get out.") After that he set up a tent in the back yard of another HPT, and cooked his meals on a Primus stove, sometimes entering neighbors' houses through the back door and taking what he needed out of their refrigerators as if exacting a Kennedy tithe.

Unlike Joe, Bobby had no expectation that, however burdensome and far away, could give logic to his future. Unlike his younger brother David, he had no faith in others that could be shaken. When family friends came up to him and his brothers at cocktail parties to say how good it was to see them, trying to prove intense affection in a five-minute time span, David would be depressed by the hypocrisy, but Bobby would hear them out, then sneer, "Don't pretend to understand me if you haven't taken acid," and walk away.

Before he took over as leader of the HPTs, there had been a lighthearted anarchy in the group's assault on the peace and quiet of the Hyannis townspeople. One or another of them might stop traffic by dragging himself pitifully across the crosswalk on crutches, then suddenly stop to throw the crutches down and begin to walk, shouting, "A miracle! A miracle!" Now there was a more calculating, nihilistic element in the pranks. They would suddenly dart out into slow-moving traffic in a group; one of them would fall histrionically to the pavement at the moment another loudly slapped a car's fender, and Bobby would point at the "body" on the street and begin to scream "You've killed a Kennedy! You've killed a Kennedy!" Then he would grin at the pale and sometimes tearful faces that gathered around, help the "victim" up off the pavement, and walk away. When some friend or family member said that they must try to have better relations with the residents of Hyannis Port, Bobby would reply, "Fuck them. They tried to keep grandpa from buying a place here, and never wanted us in the first place. We never got a vote from them."

He had brought a human skull back from his trip to Africa the previous summer, and he now made it into a sort of totem for the HPTs, after engraving it with the motto: "Thou Shalt Not Squeal." He got an aerial map of the town and planned their campaigns on it. He ordered walkie-talkies so that they could monitor police frequencies, and gave members of the group code names like "Clamshark" and "Leather." As if acting out some Jungian fantasy about guerrillas inherited from the collective unconscious of his father and uncle, he had the HPTs put on dark clothes and blacken their faces before making their sorties into the night.

The HPTs made Molotov cocktails and talked of unleashing a "war of liberation" on the town, but the only target they actually firebombed was the Hyannis breakwater their grandfather had built. While their imagination revolved around riot and rebellion, their acts tended toward mischief. They built "funnilators" out of ten-foot cords of rubber tubing attached to either side of a plastic funnel with surgical tape, using it as a giant slingshot to shoot water balloons at passing cars from the summit of a hill, aiming especially at police cars. They stopped traffic by having Bobby—perennial victor in what Chris Lawford called "a competition of guts"—walk out into the street and pretend to search for a lost contact lens, while one of the others crammed a potato into the tailpipe of a stopped car, causing a huge backfire. On one occasion the police showed up while they were doing this and they all ran; everyone escaped except Bobby Shriver. Seeing that his cousin was in the clutches of a policeman, Bobby defiantly reappeared from his hiding place, and sauntered up to them. "What have you got in there?" the policeman asked, noting that Bobby had his hand inside his coat. "I have a hawk, and he's trained to kill cops," Bobby answered. "You're lying," the policeman said, but Bobby kept advancing toward him, until they were only inches apart, whereupon he pulled the hawk out and shoved the raptor's beak into the face of the cop, who jumped back with a hand on his gun.

Because of the flamboyance of Bobby's example, LSD and "black beauties" (amphetamine capsules) became part of the HPT ritual. With many semihigh one Saturday night, they all decided it was time to claim the town once and for all. They found a king-sized sheet in Ethel's linen closet and made it into a flag by painting "HPT Rules" across it. Then they got grappling hooks and began scaling the steeple at St. Andrew's Presbyterian Church, a venerable landmark overlooking the town from a rise in the middle of the golf course. The first time the hook didn't catch; it fell back down and hit Tom Frick, one of the older HPTs, in the head, momentarily knocking him out. The second time the hook caught hold, and Bobby went up, to fix the flag at the top of the steeple. The next morning the church elders got ladders to take the flag down before services began. When they discovered the RFK monogram on the sheet, they came immediately to the Compound.

Already on the defensive because of Chappaquiddick, the family elders gathered to decide what to do in a meeting memorable for Ethel's stormy anger. After a long discussion, they decided that the Hyannis summers that had always been so important in establishing the Kennedy identity had to end. It had become dangerous for all of them to be together. Starting next year, the elders told the cousins, they would all be together at the Compound only for the Labor Day weekend.

Along with Jackie's marriage and Teddy's accident, it was one more augury that the dynastic enterprise, so painstakingly assembled over three generations, was beginning to fray and unravel. Almost as if to provide a summary of this feeling of decline and disintegration, the Ambassador's precarious health had begun to fail. Even though he had been sick for as long as most of them could remember, he had been a powerful symbol for the grandchildren. The girls would sometimes come to his room late at night and feed him his favorite snacks of Ritz crackers, wiping the crumbs off his lips as if he were an infant, as his eyes smiled at them. The big boys had come to watch Red Sox games with him on television, remaining silent for long stretches, wanting only to be in the presence of his legendary power in hopes that it might somehow help dissolve the ambiguities which surrounded them.

But since Bobby's death he had been fading in and out of confusion. (In the spring of 1969, when former President Eisenhower died, the elder Kennedy watched televised coverage of the funeral with a stricken look on his face, making sounds and gestures indicating that he thought Teddy had now been shot too and was being buried without his having been informed.) The cardiac arrests he had been having all during his years of illness had begun to come more frequently, triggering the siren doctors had installed in his bedroom and bringing everyone in the Compound running. In a way Bobby's death had been the final shock; he had accepted Chappaquiddick with resignation. His private nurse, Rita Dallas, was there the day Teddy told him about it: "Dad, I'm in some trouble. There's been an accident and you're going to hear all sorts of things about me from now on. Terrible things . . ." He had gone on as his father feebly gripped his hand and pressed it to his own chest, unable to respond. Joseph Kennedy hadn't watched his son's televised speech of explanation. He had been smiling sadly when Teddy came to his room afterward and said miserably, "Dad, I've done the best I can. I'm sorry."

The old man had stopped eating that fall. He rubbed at his eyes with his good hand, causing them to blink and tear. A doctor called in for consultation said that he was going blind. Then his vocal cords stopped working and he was unable even to make the few intelligible sounds by which he had communicated. He lay in bed wasting away. He had been so powerful and competent that it was difficult for his family to accept it as an organic process instead of some kind of punishment. As Chris Lawford said, "It made me wonder what my grandfather could have done for God to do this to him."

By November it had become just a matter of time. A few days before the sixth anniversary of Jack's death, doctors said the family should be summoned. Jackie flew in the next day from Greece and went immediately to Joseph Kennedy's room to spend several hours alone with him, speaking a monologue in her soothing voice. Ethel came up from Hickory Hill, so sick with fever that the doctors attending the old man immediately put her to bed. The Shrivers arrived from France. Eunice stood up to the sight of her wasted father, but Sarge did not. He sank to his knees beside the bed and began to cry. "Oh, Grandpa, I want to tell you how much I love you, and I want to thank you for everything you have done for me. Without you none of us would be anything."

The last night Teddy stayed in a sleeping bag in his room; Jackie stayed too, dozing fitfully in a chair with a blanket over her legs. In the morning the alarm rang for the final time. The Smiths, the Shrivers, Joan and Ethel and Pat came in. After one final look, the in-laws drew back and his children surrounded him—Eunice, Pat, Jean, and Teddy, the only ones left, joined in a protective circle aorund his bed. Rose was brought in at the last minute. She knelt beside him with a rosary, put it to his lips and then draped the beads over his fingers. She and the children had almost finished the Our Father when he died.

For the press, the passing of Joseph Kennedy was only a footnote to the saga he had begun as a young man, when he had decided to escape the landlocked ambitions of the Boston Irish and explore all the forbidden zones of American life. For the family, it was as though history itself were dying. His sister Loretta's daughter, Mary Lou, said: "Even though he had been sick, he had been a source of strength to us all. When we heard he had died, it was like the world turned over." Lem Billings thought of the grandchildren: "If he just could have lived as long and been in as good health as Mrs. Kennedy, it would have been so different for the next generation. He would have reached out and reeled them in. God knows they needed it."

3.

*L*EM HIMSELF TRIED TO FILL THE vacuum, taking on the role of father and grandfather for Bobby Junior, and witness to Kennedy grandeur for the other grandchildren. Different from the others who had been close to the family for a long time, people who ranged from sycophants to advisers, Lem was, in Eunice's words, "as close as you could get to being a Kennedy and still not be one." His special status was validated by a framed photograph in his home of Joseph Kennedy along with a note the patriarch had scrawled on it some forty years earlier: "This is a good time to tell you that the Kennedy children, from Young Joe down, should be very proud to be your friends, because year in and year out you have given them what few people ever really enjoy: true friendship. I am glad we *all* know you."

Lem had indeed been around since what were regarded in the family as almost prehistoric times: football opponent of Young Joe, suitor to Kick, chauffeur to Honey Fitz, best friend of Jack. He had become especially close after the late 1950s, when the ad agency he had worked in for several years went bankrupt. He had drifted into an early semiretirement, buying and reselling New York brownstones he renovated; tending the modest investments he had accumulated over the years; and burrowing into his friendship with Jack. He was close to his own family and proud of its genteel past, but he kept the Billingses compartmentalized and separate from this other, more exciting part of his life. Jack had offered him jobs in the Post Office, the Commerce Department, and the Peace Corps, but Lem had preferred to be an unemployed gadfly, weekending so often in Washington that he was able to reply to those who asked why he had never married, "If I had, I never would have had my own bedroom at the White House."

After the President's assassination, he had acquired a more important role than he'd played before: he was a living reminder of Jack and of the vanished past they had all shared. He had become important in the creation of the Kennedy Center; because of his well-known esthetic sensibilities he represented the family's interests in this and all other monuments. (He defeated moves to rename Pennsylvania Avenue after Jack, saying that there should be only one major Washington, D.C., landmark bearing his name.) He played a similar role in hectic infighting over the JFK Library, which he and Jack had frequently discussed during the thousand days of the New Frontier.

He would have liked to transfer the love and loyalty he had felt for Jack to Jackie and her children. He was touched by the two semiorphans—John-John, who would disconcertingly say to people, "Do you want to hear my father?" and then take them in to hear one of the records of JFK's speeches he kept near his record player; and Caroline, who remembered her father better and who obsessively collected stamps and coins and other memorabilia bearing his likeness. She took "Joan" as her confirmation name, after Joan of Arc, who she told her friends "was killed just like my father." Lem did manage to see them sometimes at Jackie's New York apartment, but the relationship was one-sided, shaped by Jackie's mania for privacy and her possessiveness with the children. Lem occasionally sent John-John pieces of scrimshaw. ("He knows more about whales than Bobby knows about hawks," Jackie wrote with true Kennedy competitiveness after one such gift.) He gave Caroline the pin bearing the insignia of the Muckers' Club he and Jack had formed at Choate when she got in minor trouble at school. At Jackie's request he took both children to see the Laurence Olivier film version of *Henry V* when it was shown at New York's Paramount Theater.

But there were fewer and fewer opportunities such as this after the Onassis marriage, and so Lem had gravitated more and more to Hickory Hill, understanding that it was now the center of Kennedy life. Bobby, sensing the degree to which the assassination had left his brother's friend a displaced person, had adopted him. Large and ursine, blinking through thick glasses and barking out high-pitched laughter, Lem had become a regular there, raffish and yet prissy, a sort of court chronicler reporting on the old days which even Bobby and Ethel didn't recall and functioning as the all-purpose cheerleader, godfather, and pallbearer who could always be counted on.

In the chaos following Bobby's death, Lem had seen the need of the children he left behind more clearly than anyone else. But he had decided that instead of trying to extend himself to all of them, he would focus on one, Bobby Junior, in whose imagination and intelligence he had seen so clear a reflection of Jack when he first got to know the boy. The trip to Africa in the summer of 1968 had solidified the relationship. Lem got some of the same pleasure from Bobby's companionship that he had gotten from Jack's when the two of them traveled in Europe over thirty years earlier. But more than nostalgia was involved. He had seen an opportunity to initiate a Kennedy who might otherwise be lost into his heritage and launch him into public life. All during the trip they had talked about politics and public service. Lem had gotten the fourteen-year-old to keep a journal that showed occasional flashes of his mordant wit (after he threw a football at a lioness who punctured it with her teeth he wrote, "It was my cousin Bobby Shriver's ball anyway") and acuity ("Some animals are smarter than others," young Bobby had written in words that might almost have been self-analysis, "and the smartest animals are the most dangerous"). Lem had taken pictures of the boy—shirtless in the high bush, stalking game with an intense but somehow ironic look on his face—and when they got back he showed the photographs and journal text to New York magazines, pitting them against each other until he got $25,000 from *Life*.

The trip had not only given Bobby Junior a link to the adult world his brothers lacked, but also validated him as leader of his generation. Even those cousins with fathers were envious. Lem was continuity. He was also tradition, centrally placed in an apartment that was a collector's paradise (Chagalls and Dufys; early American folk art; and letters from Washington, Lincoln, Jefferson, and other heroes), with the best assemblage of Kennedyana around. There were massive notebooks of snapshots of the previous generation, bundles of letters from Kick and Jack dating back to the early 1930s, and objects able to convey almost a tactile sense of what it had been to be part of this unique family during its formative years. The ambience at Lem's was different from the atmosphere generated by photographs at Hickory Hill: cold, public, almost solemn. At Lem's it was accompanied by Lem himself, a master storyteller who made the people in the myth come alive, as if by verbal holography. ("You listened to him," one of Bobby Junior's friends said, "and these people became so real that you might have expected Kick and Jack to come walking in the front door, arm in arm, talking and laughing.") For the younger Kennedy generation, going to Lem's was like entering Merlin's Cave. For Bobby Junior it had soon become something more—oblique instruction for the day when he would pull the sword from the stone; the day when he would reclaim and extend the Kennedy Legacy.

But for the time being, Lem had to work just to keep Bobby's head above water. He had enrolled at Pomfret, an exclusive prep school in Connecticut, but was soon in trouble again. As in his previous year at Millbrook, he did not go home on his six free weekends and Ethel did not visit him. His only emotional link to the adult world of the Kennedys seemed to be the non-Kennedy, Lem.

Lem visited frequently. The two of them would walk out into the countryside—the large, burly man and the gangly boy beside him pointing up at the trees, decoding bird calls, and talking about animals. Lem tried to shore up Bobby's precarious sense of self by explaining that rebellious uncertainty was a normal stage in Kennedy development. He told about the Muckers'

Club at Choate, the problems Jack had caused there, and how Joseph Kennedy had been summoned by the headmaster to deal with them. ''It was like growing up with the President,'' Bobby remembered. ''Lem told me about my father, too, the first time anybody really had. We'd be walking along and talking about something and he'd say, 'Oh, that reminds me of something Jack and I did with your father when we were seventeen and he was ten...' '' If the talks were liberating because they made the dead Kennedys something more than family icons, they also gave Bobby subtle license to continue on his course.

It was in one way an attempt to complete what writers had called his father's ''unfinished odyssey.'' But since his father had already traveled the paths of light with such authority, Bobby sought out the dark places his father had never been. Not long after enrolling at Pomfret, he had been hitchhiking on the Cape and was given a ride by an unemployed twenty-year-old local named Doug Spooner, who eventually became a close friend and companion on these travels. ''He seemed like such a lonely kid,'' Spooner recalls of the first meeting. ''At first he didn't talk much. But then he sort of loosened up and told me that his mother had thrown him out of the house and he needed a place to stay. I had a shack on the peninsula and I said he could·stay there for a while.'' For Bobby, Spooner was an example of someone living by his wits in a world not dominated by family connection. A scratch golfer, he survived in part by hustling local businessmen and vacationers. ''Gambling runs in our family too,'' Bobby said enigmatically during one of their discussions, ''except that we play a game called Kennedy roulette.''

Over the next few weeks the two went around the Boston area looking for action. On one occasion they were in a rough section of Cambridge to play basketball with some blacks. The talk turned to pool and Spooner, not admitting how well he played, agreed to shoot a few games with one of the blacks at a local bar. With Bobby watching, Spooner and his opponent began playing nine-ball at fifty cents a game. Spooner kept losing until the ante had been upped to ten dollars a game; then he began to play in earnest and quickly won two hundred. ''Naturally the guy said that he didn't have the money on him. He said that Bobby and I should come to his house later on and he'd pay us off with a bag of marijuana. So we waited and when it was time went to the address he'd given us, a real run-down place. There was no answer when we knocked. I was ready to leave even though there was a light on and we knew the guy was in there. But Bob started pounding on the door and screaming insults, telling him that if he was afraid to come out to just slip the money under the door. Suddenly the door flies open and the guy shoots out with a four-foot machete in his hands. I jumped back, but Bob didn't. The guy swung the machete at him as hard as he could. I thought that was it—another Kennedy dead. But at the last minute the guy sort of rolled his wrists so that instead of hitting him with the cutting edge of the blade, he hit him with the flat. We ran like hell."

In July Bobby went home to the Cape. Avoiding his mother, he hung out with Kim Kelley and her brother John. A letter he wrote to Mrs. Kelley captured the personality exactly, especially in the attribution of his own feelings to his friend, and in the veiled allusion to his father's favorite poem of moral uplift, Tennyson's "Ulysses": "John and I are seated in your abandoned automobile contemplating our next move. It is 9:00 (pm) and we take off for our destination presently. We feel rejected because of your apparent blaze [sic] attitude to the news we gave to you last night of our departure. We do not know what to attribute this negative attitude to, but John feels that it is due to a lack of care for him . . . And I am forced to accompany him as a nursemaid. There is adventure in the air and the high seas offer quite an enigma for an unsatisfied mind."

Bobby and Kelley hung out with other ex-members of the proscribed HPTs, among them Bobby Shriver, who had tried to keep pace with his more adventuresome Kennedy cousins by experimenting with marijuana at Exeter the previous year. One of the people in their circle was Andy Moes, a bearded taxi driver in his early twenties who gave them free rides all around the Cape, once even taking them into Boston for a Red Sox game. One day they were all sitting on the Kelleys' fence when Moes drove up and said he was looking for some marijuana. "He was whining that he had this girlfriend," Bobby Shriver recalls, "and that he had to have a joint to get laid and all that. Finally he offered me ten dollars. I said, 'Shit! Ten dollars for one joint? I'll take it.'" Not long after that, Bobby Kennedy's favorite hawk, Morgan Le Fay, got loose and was discovered in a treetop in Cohasset. Moes was once again on the spot, offering to take him the hundred-mile round trip in return for a joint, which they smoked on the way.

A few days later there was a knock on the door of the Shrivers' house, where Ethel and her kids had joined them for dinner. Several policemen and squad cars were outside. The family was informed that Moes was an under-cover narcotics officer and that both Bobbys, Shriver and Kennedy, were accused of possession of *cannabis sativa*. (Bobby Shriver told his parents indignantly, "We never had any *cannabis sativa*. What is *cannabis sativa* anyhow?")

In the chaos that followed, Ethel chased Bobby Junior through the back door, caught up with him outside, and shoved him into the bushes. "You've dragged your family's name through the mud!" At the court appearance, where the boys would receive a year's probation, she was tight-lipped and grim as she and Ted pushed through a crowd of nearly a hundred newsmen and television cameras.

Afterward, Ethel continued to rage. "I have no control over you," she yelled at Bobby. "You don't listen to me! I'm throwing you out of the family!'' In desperation she called in her husband's friend, the Harvard psychiatrist Robert Coles, to deal with her son. Coles tried to use the family's deep-seated fears about ''headshrinkers'' and about the possibly paralyzing effects of self-assessment in urging Bobby not to become mired in the confusion that threatened his generation but rather to project himself onto the outer world as his father had.

In disgrace, Bobby took six hundred dollars out of a savings account and bought a used Ford. Telling nobody where he was going, he headed west. Arriving in Los Angeles, he sold the car for two hundred dollars and began hopping freight trains and sleeping in boxcars with tramps and vagrants. Once he decided to go to San Francisco and sneaked aboard a car carrier, only to discover two days later that the train was headed to San Antonio. ''I had no contact with home,'' he says, ''except that every couple of weeks I'd call Lem. I was riding around with bums. It was good: I could be one of them and not be a Kennedy.'' He stayed for several days in Berkeley, panhandling for a few dollars a day on Telegraph Avenue and using the money to buy drugs.

Back in Hyannis, Ethel's kids were being systematically isolated from the rest of the family. Steve Smith urged his two sons to stay away from them, and began designing a house at Bridgehampton as a summer place. Something like the same process took place with the Shrivers. More contemplative than his in-laws, Sarge had always been uncomfortable with an ethic that he felt sacrificed feeling to action. (Once, when one of his children fell down and received the admonition ''Kennedys don't cry,'' he had scooped the boy up and told him, ''That's okay, you can go ahead and cry. You're a Shriver.'') But now something more was at stake, and he took his oldest son aside and told him that the cousins were all reaching a crossroads and had to choose. ''He made me see that what was going on was different from the HPT stuff,'' Bobby Shriver said later. ''It was drugs, trouble with the police, a record, maybe jail someday. I got a sense of consequences and realized that I'd better figure out a way to move ahead and get on with my life. I also got a sense that the Bobby Kennedy family was dangerous.'' Bobby Shriver was ''yanked'' from the group, in Chris Lawford's term, and never really became part of it again.

While Bobby Junior was the author of much of the angry defiance in Ethel's house, David got blamed for it almost as if by reflex. ''It was almost on general principle that she blamed me,'' he says. ''Her idea was that it didn't really matter whether or not I had actually done anything, I would do it sooner or later so she might as well get heavy with me in advance. I remember it all clearly: this was the point in my life when everything began to turn against me.''

His sole friend in the family was Chris Lawford, even more an orphan than David, since Chris's mother had decided on the spur of the moment to take his younger sisters and live in Paris, leaving him in boarding school. ("I don't want anything to do with this family for a while," Pat had told him when she left. "I'm going to France to get my own life together, away from the Kennedys.") Knowing that Bobby was on the road, David and Chris, both now fifteen, decided to hitchhike to New York. They arrived dirty and ragged, and walked around town with no money for several hours before finally ending up at Grand Central Station, where they began to beg from commuters. "It was great being just ordinary people and not Kennedys," David says. "Also it wasn't bad money. At one point we were making the equivalent of about forty dollars an hour." They took the money to Central Park to buy drugs. Heroin was selling for two dollars a bag on Dope Hill, and they bought some and snorted it for the first time. Then they looked for girls, and invited a few back to Pat Lawford's vacant Fifth Avenue apartment. Word got around that there was a party, and soon the place was filled with black street people and white hippies. David went to sleep and woke up in the middle of the night to find winos and bikers frying eggs in the kitchen. When neighbors threatened to call the police, he and Chris managed to get everyone to leave.

When they got back to Hyannis several days later, Ethel gave no indication of having realized they had been gone. David was so estranged from her for the remainder of the summer that he often slept on a blanket in the soft hedges behind the house. As the school year approached, he transferred to Middlesex, even though it meant repeating the ninth grade, because Chris was there, and Chris now represented his only real link with his family.

David had always been the one in his family who would try anything. (His boyhood friend Phil Kirby remembers how David's older brothers would go out onto the Hyannis breakwater that their grandfather had built, slimy with algae and especially treacherous at a point where the wall had been breached by a hurricane years earlier. They would taunt him with being afraid to follow, and although the ten-foot waves smashing through the opening could easily have swept him out to sea, he would eventually follow, grinning at having passed yet another of their tests.) Now he was trying drugs. He made a small reputation at Middlesex for religiously smoking marijuana with his morning cup of coffee and dropping acid at least once a week. Imitating Bobby Junior, who had been the first to experiment with drugs, he and Chris let their hair grow to their shoulders and became part of the school's rebellious "hippie" faction, building huts in a nearby forested area and fighting off the more authoritarian "neofascists" who staged raids on their tribal life style.

David rarely heard from his mother that school year, although as the spring semester was ending he was informed that she had arranged for him to go to the Blackfoot Reservation in Montana with another Middlesex student for the summer. ("My father had been involved with the Indians. She was obviously hoping that having an experience with the downtrodden would awaken my hereditary social conscience.") David made appearances at tribal functions and was given the name "Yellow Dove" because of his blond hair and his father's remembered message of peace. The high point of that summer of 1971, David's sixteenth year, came when he and his schoolmate discovered a marijuana field during a hike. They harvested the plants and hung them to dry in the attic of the Indian couple they were living with. But they became impatient and crept downstairs one night to boil the leaves in water. The Indian woman awoke and came in to see what was going on. "She was standing there looking at me with this strange expression on her face as if to say, 'What is the son of Robert Kennedy doing making marijuana tea in my kitchen?' "

At Pomfret School, Bobby insisted on living in an all-black dorm and ignored his schoolwork to read Franz Fanon, Eldridge Cleaver, H. Rap Brown, and other authors whose black anger appealed to him. As usual he had trouble with the rules. ("Like all the rest of us, Bobby grew up feeling that being a Kennedy you could do virtually anything you wanted," Chris says. "It was good because you got away with things other people wouldn't dream of; it was bad because it destroyed your sense of what was worth doing.") Bobby had his girlfriend Kim come up to visit, hiding her in his room at night and by day taking her to a basement where he had set up a hot plate to avoid having to dress for meals in the dining commons. Toward the end of the year he was expelled from his third school in four years.

That summer, while David was at the Blackfoot reservation, Bobby ran afoul of the law again. Sitting in a car at Hyannis with Kim, eating an ice-cream cone, he was accosted by one of the summer cops hired by the town because of the large numbers of tourists drawn by the Kennedys. According to Bobby, the cop bent down into the driver's window, gave a sneering look at Kim, and said, "What's that thing you got with you there in the front seat?" Bobby spat his ice cream in the cop's face and was arrested on the spot. Taken to court to face charges of "sauntering and loitering," he sullenly repeated the phrase "The officer is lying" during several points of the cop's testimony. After being convicted and spending the night in jail, he left Hyannis with Kim for Lem's apartment in New York and stayed there the rest of the summer.

When September came, Lem enrolled him for his senior year in Palfrey School in Watertown, Massachusetts. He also arranged for Bobby to live off-campus in the home of the Brode family. "When Bobby came to the door that first time," Mrs. "Joey" Brode recalls, "he looked like a bird with a broken wing. He was terribly thin and there was something not coordinated about him—quite handsome, but at the same time sort of flapping, too tall and skinny. But there was such intensity and depth in his eyes that you forgot about the Ichabod Crane look and thought to yourself: My God, there's a soul in this bird body.'' After talking for a few minutes in the kitchen, she offered him a piece of the coffee cake she'd just made from Damson plums. He ate the whole thing by himself. She realized that the hunger was not only literal but also a metaphor: the desire to be given something homemade; the desire to be emotionally nourished.

As the school year progressed, she was struck by the care Lem took of Bobby, handling all his financial arrangements and calling him from New York almost every day. ''They were on the phone constantly. Lem was the only adult who seemed to care. Ethel never called, and never visited, while Lem came up quite often. It was touching, this relationship. It was like Lem was trying to protect a heritage by protecting this boy. But there was more to it than nostalgia or reliving his past friendship for Jack. There was real love on his part. Bobby was the son he'd never had.''

Lem exhibited a fatherly pride as Bobby slowly began to make some sense out of his life. He never worried about having misplaced his faith in him as the Kennedy grandchild who would ultimately distinguish himself. But he was concerned that something might happen to him before his cocoon opened. Lem's friend Bucky McAdoo says, ''We'd be sitting in his apartment and a call would come that Bobby had been picked up for drugs or something. Lem would go white.'' His brother Fred Billings says, ''Bobby put him through some very tough times. Lem hadn't had much experience dealing with children before he ran into this Kennedy wild bunch. He was often close to tears because of his frustration and despair.''

But under Lem's patient guidance, Bobby began to transmute the nihilistic persona he had embraced after his father's death into a more heroic one, a persona befitting one making a bid to become undisputed leader of his generation. During his year at Palfrey, Bobby met a Brandeis student named Andy Karsch, and immediately made friends with him. ''He was very anxious to impress. The first day I knew him, he put on some climbing spurs and went right up this huge tree. Later on he came over to my house and saw a paperback copy of De Tocqueville's *Democracy in America* and insisted that he could tear it in half. I said he couldn't. We bet and then he started going at it, straining until he was purple in the face. He didn't tear it, but the book looked like it had been mangled by a wild animal.''

One reason Bobby was courting Karsch, it soon became clear, was that he had been an all-state quarterback at boarding school. As soon as he and Karsch were friends, he challenged his brother Joe, then going to a local prep school called Manter Hall, to a football game. With Karsch, the team Bobby put together was victorious over the team Joe quarterbacked. After the victory, as his older brother walked off the field glowering, Bobby was exuberant.

"By the end of that year," Joey Brode recalls, "Bobby was coming into his own. He had developed a sense of charisma that the older brother just didn't have. The younger Kennedys, brothers and cousins, would come up to Cambridge and just wander around forlornly if Bobby wasn't there to lead them." Bobby's chief disciples were David and Chris, whose allegiance to him rather than Joe was now established. Chris emulated him by getting expelled from Middlesex for drugs, David by taking on some of his derring-do. Andy Karsch has never forgotten a time when they were all throwing snowballs near Harvard Square. One struck a passing car, which slid to a halt. A huge man climbed out (they would later learn that he was an offensive tackle for the Boston College football team) and advanced on them. "He was yelling about our irresponsibility, and we were sort of retreating as he walked toward us. All of a sudden David, all 120 pounds of him, steps up and punches this guy right in the face. The rest of us were too petrified to run. David looked over at Bobby with this dumb grin as if to say: There, are you proud of me now? This huge guy stands there for a minute with an absolutely dumfounded look on his face, then just shakes his head in disbelief and gets back in the car and drives off."

Bobby sold David a pound of marijuana, which he took to Middlesex and hid in a suitcase. When it was then stolen from its hiding place, Bobby appeared at the school, dressed gaudily with a bandanna around his head, telling students that he was a "cutthroat dope dealer" there to find who had burned his client. He cornered the thief and so terrified him that he went to school authorities and told them everything. They asked David who the dope dealer was and he said he didn't know him by name. But looking through back issues of *Time*, somebody located a picture of Bobby Junior and identified him as the one. David was suspended.

Trying to keep the two brothers apart, Ethel arranged for David to go to work in the lettuce fields with Cesar Chavez that summer. ("Your father felt he was one of the most moral men he'd ever met," she told David. "Maybe he'll do you some good.") David scarcely saw Chavez or any other uplifting Chicano role models while picking up farm worker garbage for two dollars an hour at La Paz, the farm worker headquarters. After his tour of duty with the UFW was over, he went to see Chris, who was visiting his father. "I knocked on the door and there's Peter Lawford," David recalls. "I hadn't seen him for years. The first thing he does after saying hello was offer me a pipe full of hash."

In the fall of 1972, Bobby entered Harvard, convinced by the hours he had spent with Lem that the only way he could seize his heritage was not by slowly growing into it but by striving for a mythic Kennedy identity right from the start. He began attracting followers in the same way that Jack had as a young man, exercising the magnetism Lem had described to him in such detail. One of those who gravitated to him was Peter Kaplan. In every way his opposite—Jewish, intellectual, cautious, literary—Kaplan represented a world of ideas for Bobby, who in turn represented a sort of noble savagery for him: "He was out for freshman crew and he had really built himself up, getting real strength into that lean body. He had a sort of feral look, like Mowgli in *The Jungle Books*. He was totally at home with nature. During Visit Week he climbed a tree to get into the third-story window of the dorms rather than going up the stairs like everybody else. Later, when we were roommates, I came home one day and found him fooling around with this huge rattlesnake, not defanged. He used to allow the snake to wrap itself around a ski pole and fed it by hand. Word got around and people started coming in to watch. Finally the school officials said he had to get rid of it."

Kaplan felt that Bobby adopted a "swashbuckling Douglas Fairbanks defiance," in part because of stories he had heard of Harvard snottiness toward the Irish during his grandfather's day. It was also because he had accepted what he interpreted as the challenge posed by the martyrs of the previous generation. The high point of his derring-do came in an almost legendary event that became known among his Harvard friends as "the Bhutto leap," so called because it was undertaken as a result of a bet with Mir Bhutto, son of the president of Pakistan, Ali Bhutto. "Bobby's dorm was Hurlbut and next door was a building called Pennypacker, not actually in Harvard Yard, but like Hurlbut six stories high," Kaplan recalls. "The gap between them was ten or twelve feet. Bobby bet Mir, who was in our circle, that he could jump the gap. People heard about it and gathered below, a large crowd shading their eyes and looking up as if waiting for Superman. The distance wasn't that great, but it looked twice as big as it was; if he missed he'd probably die. Suddenly Bobby just soars across. Everybody down on the ground gasped and shook their heads in disbelief."

But if some saw it as heroic, others looked for deeper significance. Another Harvard friend who later studied massage says, "It was like someone who wants a massage but is so desensitized that he has to be 'hurt' to feel anything at all. I think this sort of thing, which Bobby did quite often, was a way of giving himself a sort of existential pinch on the arm and reminding himself that he was alive."

The summer of his freshman year, Bobby went skiing in Chile with Karsch and Kim Kelley, who broke her leg and had to return alone. In Portillo they met Harvey Fleetwood, a young reporter for the *New York Times*. One day they all decided to ski up to the Christ of the Andes, the statue on the border of Chile and Peru. Putting sealskin covers on their skis, they herringboned their way up the mountain. Near the top, shots suddenly rang out—from the guns of the Chilean border guards, as they later discovered. Perhaps two dozen rounds thudded into the snow and ricocheted off boulders. The next thing they knew they were all skiing down through the heavy powder with Bobby yelling in exhilaration.

Lem put the piece Fleetwood wrote about the trip for the *Times* into the scrapbook he had begun for Bobby and worked with him on an article to be published under Bobby's by-line about what he had seen and heard of post-Allende Chile. When the piece was accepted by the *Atlantic Monthly,* Lem clapped Bobby on the shoulder: ''That's how Jack got started—through writing.''

4.

*J*F THE CHILDREN OF THE FAMILY were involved in a disorienting mixed metaphor—a Freudian struggle on the plains of an imagined Camelot—the adult Kennedys were engaged in the more serious but no less figurative task of trying to climb Mount Kennedy. Teddy had started to push his rock back up the hill in his 1970 Senate reelection campaign, winning a large majority in part because he promised Massachusetts constituents that he did not intend to try for the presidency in 1972. Steve Smith, meanwhile, had expressed interest in the nomination for governor of New York, and for a brief period had met with Democratic Party leaders and given speeches around the state. But the elliptical style that made him so effective behind the scenes made it difficult for him to establish a public persona, and he had settled for the familiar role of king-maker, taking a hand in the ill-fated gubernatorial campaign of Arthur Goldberg as part of a state ticket that included Ted Sorensen for senator and Adam Walinsky for state attorney general. All of them were soundly defeated, proving that the Kennedy "magic" Smith had always been presumed to have worked only when a real Kennedy was on stage with him.

A similar realization awaited Sargent Shriver, who, with the irrepressible Eunice, had been thought of as a possible alternative locus of power in the family. In 1968 Hubert Humphrey had put out feelers for the vice presidency to Shriver, which Teddy immediately vetoed. But while he was Ambassador to France, Shriver had struck out more forcefully on his own, trying to make a record which could eventually be parlayed into political capital back home. He had done well with people-to-people diplomacy, gossiping with Alsatian miners and lunching exuberantly with textile workers in Lyons; but he had been less successful in his formal role. (Career foreign service officers cringed during embassy dinner parties when he went up to their French opposite numbers and said in ragged French, "Tell me, what do you *really* think of De Gaulle?") And though he had let Maryland party bosses know he was available as a candidate for governor when he returned to the United States early in 1970, the call never came. Afterward he had set out on a national speaking tour to boost Democratic candidates for Congress, and in 1972 came to the party convention as a Kennedy surrogate, hoping for the vice presidential bid. At first George McGovern, who had won the nomination as an insurgent outside the party machine, was scornful of Shriver, putting him well down on the list of possible candidates. ("*Shriver!* Who wants him? All that Shriver talk is coming from Shriver himself," he had said with uncharacteristic asperity when the name kept coming up.) When the offer finally came it was so tainted by the process which had given and then withdrawn the bid from Missouri Senator Thomas Eagleton that it seemed a sort of booby prize. Shriver tried to summon some of the Kennedy enthusiasm in the campaign against Nixon, but he came across, as one journalist put it, as "awfully happy" in the middle of what quickly became a debacle.

The fact that their elders seemed stalled placed subtle pressures on the next generation. RFK had often told his children and their cousins that politics was "a way of giving to others, a way of keeping from turning in on ourselves." He had meant that it was an ideal of public service—the noblest profession, Jack had liked to say—which would keep them from becoming idle and selfish. But an alternative interpretation of his injunction was that an interest in politics would keep them from having to look within; that it would provide a shorthand way of coming into their own without having to deal with the emotional turmoil at the family's core. This—as well as the fact that politics had become the family business each wanted to inherit—was precisely what made the prospect attractive.

While Bobby Junior was now well established as the leader of the kids themselves, his brother Joe was still the one all the adults except Lem felt would have the political career. He had gotten an initiation working as an advance man for Teddy in Massachusetts in 1970. It had, however, been a costly experience for him: when he asked Milton for a leave of absence, school officials had refused because his grades were so poor, and he had withdrawn, losing an academic year. He was integrated into political life in a way his cousins were not—the firstborn male, the one with the dynastic name, the one who had shaken hands with his father's bereaved supporters on the funeral train. All the others had been able to experiment with anonymity and escape, at least temporarily, the onus of being a Kennedy (Bobby Junior, Chris, and David by begging and panhandling; Bobby Shriver by starting a catering business under the name "Bobby Cotton"; Stevie Smith by capitalizing on his anonymous name). None of this was possible for Joe. He was the one forced to make speeches and appearances; the one called on to dedicate Washington's RFK Stadium and to accompany his mother and younger brothers and sisters to his father's grave on assassination anniversaries. When he finally graduated from prep school in 1971, he was the one who went to work for the recently established RFK Memorial Foundation, interviewing potential grant recipients and visiting Indian reservations, pockets of poverty on the Mississippi Delta, and other areas loyal to his father, almost as if he were an ambassador from the grave.

It was difficult for him to locate something real inside the symbolism which enveloped him. ("I'm like a BB rattling around in a boxcar," he told a friend during a tongue-tied discussion of the difficulties of being crown prince.) There was also the fact that the more flamboyant Bobby Junior, free of the obligations that faced Joe, was surpassing him as a figure of authenticity and daring. And so Joe continued to founder. That quality of psychic explosiveness present even when his father was alive grew more intense. Robert Coles, who had come to have something like a family counseling practice for the third generation, was called in to (in family parlance) "work on" Joe.

To avoid family comparisons, Joe rejected Harvard and enrolled at MIT in the fall of 1972. But the intellectual atmosphere was too rarefied there, and he spent much of his time receiving counseling from one of Coles's colleagues, MIT psychiatrist Joseph Brenner. There was no real therapy; Brenner, like Coles, just tried to adjust the velocity and direction of Joe's pell-mell movement into the world. It was a delicate situation. The boy was used to being treated like a Kennedy, but he became upset when the deference was too obvious. Finding out that the professor of the single course he was taking at MIT had decided to give Joe a "B" for purposes of his "morale," Brenner congratulated him during one of their meetings, only to have Joe begin to scream about the way people were always forcing "special treatment" on him and his family.

Late in 1972, Brenner called his friend Diane Clemens, professor of history at Berkeley and a coordinator in JFK's 1960 campaign, to tell her about the twenty-year-old Kennedy heir and the trouble he was having, and to ask if she could help. Soon afterward, a call came from Robert Coles, who said Joe was in the room with him and wanted to go to Berkeley to study and get some distance on the ongoing family drama. Finally Joe himself came on the phone. "I hate academics," he told Clemens. "I hate universities. There's probably no reason for me to go to school at Berkeley." Sensing that she was being tested, Clemens replied, "Who cares? If you don't want to do it, don't do it." After so much sycophancy, Joe seemed to find this sort of attitude refreshing: Clemens soon heard that he had decided to come to Berkeley after all.

Within days of arriving in town and moving into a room in Clemens's hillside house, Joe was asked to join the Regents' Committee to pick professors for the University of California Law School and attend meetings with influential alumni who obviously wanted to use his name and presence in their fund-raising plans. He ignored them all, spending his time sitting in his room staring at the television and waiting for Clemens to get home from her classes so he could follow her into the kitchen and talk while she prepared dinner. She recalls, "Like all the other Kennedys, I guess, he was always trying to find some limits, not only limits as to what could be done, but also as to what could be said and thought. One day, for instance, he started this quite obnoxious bragging about never having read a book cover to cover in his entire life and saying that he never intended to. I told him that this was dumb. Then he got quite huffy. The next day he brings Teddy's book about health care and says, 'See this? My uncle wrote a book. We're not all illiterate.' I asked him if he'd read it. He gave me that aggressive, toothy smile and shook his head no."

Joe had enrolled in a couple of classes but rarely went on campus. Aside from borrowing Clemens's car occasionally for mysterious visits across the Bay to San Francisco's Chicano community, he spent most of his time in his room, talking on the separate phone line he had gotten installed. The calls were all to Massachusetts ("intelligence-gathering operations," Clemens thought) to his cousins and his friends.

During one of their nightly talks in the kitchen, Joe came in with a desperate look and announced melodramatically, "I'm through! I'm through! It's all over!" Knowing that he wanted her to extract the information from him, Clemens patiently asked what was wrong. Bit by bit he told her. He had heard that his brother Bobby had gone out for freshman crew at Harvard and done quite well, so he had gone to the Cal crew coach and asked to get on the team. He had gotten a private tryout on the estuary next to the Bay and somehow managed to turn the small boat over, dunking himself along with the coach. "I'm through!" he kept moaning, cradling his face in his hands.

Joe talked often about his grandfather and what he had done in the early part of his life when he was, in effect, "becoming" a Kennedy. He was intrigued by the rumors that had always linked Joseph Kennedy to rum-running and organized crime, and in their chats he sometimes speculated to Clemens about how and why the old man would have made such alliances. He made it clear that he too would like to become a romantic figure of evil and make an illicit fortune, not so much for the money as because it would be an achievement that would help establish him as unique within the family. He admitted that he had been making trips across the Bay because he had gotten to know a Chicano hustler named Raúl and the two of them were thinking about buying a boat and smuggling in drugs from Central America.

"This fantasy seemed very important to him," Clemens remembers. "It seemed to represent something that was real. He always said, 'I can get a much better education outside of school. We Kennedys belong in the real world. That's where we function best.' "

On the rare occasions Ethel called, it was always person to person, using the operator, Clemens thought, to avoid having to talk to her. When Joe told his mother that he had in effect dropped out of Cal, she had Teddy get San Francisco Mayor Joseph Alioto to offer him a job paying $750 a month in the city's Public Health Department as "Coordinator for Federally Funded Programs." Joe talked to reporters about the cuts Nixon was making in spending for the poor and claimed that his family associations would bring integrity to the program: "I thought that with the framework my father and uncle set up, I might come in and maybe they could trust someone in my position." But after about three weeks on the job, he resigned. "He knew he was being used," one coworker later said, "and he didn't like it. He thought they'd put him to work on important things. But they just stuck him in a corner to show him off when they needed the glamor."

Clemens was struck by Joe's erratic behavior. It was as if his emotions were somehow pneumatic; when he became upset he seemed to swell up with anger and anxiety. She had placed no restrictions on his coming or going or on his guests, but he insisted on smuggling girls into his basement-level room in the terraced house by squeezing them through the windows. One afternoon Clemens's eleven-year-old daughter, who had established a flirtatious pestering relationship with Joe, locked him into his room and out of the main part of the house. Hearing her giggling on the other side, he began to batter the door with his body, although he could have gone outside through his private entrance and come around to the front. Finally smashing his way out, he screamed "I'm going to kill you!" and chased the girl upstairs, causing her to hide trembling in the attic. By the time Clemens returned home, he had calmed down and was almost tearful: "I've got to talk to you. Something terrible has happened. I did something awful."

Yet even though he was always contrite afterward, it seemed that the slightest thing could cause him to lose control. During their ritual meeting in the kitchen one evening, he and Clemens began talking about the growing Watergate scandal. She said, "God, it's so depressing. It makes you want to go out and get a gun and start shooting." Joe, extremely agitated, jumped up and stepped toward her, shaking a finger menacingly: "Don't you say that! Don't you ever say that again! Do you understand me? No guns! No more shootings!"

Once he disappeared for a couple of days. Clemens didn't think much about it until Raúl and his wife brought over a note that had been mailed to them: "I, Joe Kennedy, leave all my life's possessions to Raúl and Linda. This includes my television set, car and other possessions. These people have been good to me.'' Clemens tried to get in touch with Robert Coles, but he was traveling. Finally she did get through to her friend Joseph Brenner, who said he would get in touch with the Kennedys. ''I'll never forget it,'' Clemens says of the instructions that came back to her. ''They said to keep looking for him, but under no circumstances to call the police.'' She got in her car and spent much of the night driving to all the spots where she thought he might be, even patrolling local freeways to look for the evidence of auto accidents in which he might have been involved. The next morning she got a call from Raúl, who said that when he arrived at his job as a longshoreman, Joe had been stretched out in the sun near the wharf asleep. ''He's already forgotten about the note,'' Raúl said. ''He says it's yesterday's news.''

Early in the spring, after complex negotiations with the family headquarters in New York and complaints that Steve Smith was making it difficult for him to get access to his money, Joe bought a Toyota pickup. Then he told Clemens that he was ''going on a trip'' and left. When he returned a week later, the brand-new vehicle was in shambles—the windshield filigreed, the top crushed and the fenders mashed in. He said that he'd been driving around in Washington and Oregon and at one point had fallen asleep at the wheel and rolled the pickup into a ravine alongside the freeway.

A few days later, driving through Berkeley late at night, he was in a collision with a car driven by a sixteen-year-old and spent the night in the hospital under observation. Two days after being released he decided it was time to get back to Boston. Clemens tried to get him to stay until he was in better physical and psychological shape, but he took the caution as a dare, telling her, ''I'm going and nobody can stop me!'' She helped him load the battered truck, which now looked several years old, and he softened, kissed her cheek, and mumbled an embarrassed thanks as he got in the pickup and started the engine. Watching him drive off, Clemens thought to herself: I hope that boy gets straightened out before he hurts someone.

The other cousins were like Joe—always trying to get distance from the family but always returning as if in response to a gravitational pull whose power could not be overcome. Since Chris Lawford didn't have the magic name, the political career they all talked about would be much harder for him. He thought that perhaps the Lawford part of his identity offered a way out, and so after graduating from high school in January 1973, he went to Southern California to live with his father and work in films.

Tall and slim now, having outgrown his adolescent pudginess, he had his father's lustrous dark hair and fine features. But although he was ''movie-star handsome,'' as gossip columnists pointed out when he arrived in Hollywood, he was more interested in production than acting. He got a job at Universal Studios and went around to some of the more important producers there, reminding them obliquely that his grandfather had been one of the great men of the early days of the cinema and that he had Kennedy power behind him.

Although just eighteen, he became close to Elizabeth Taylor, a long-time friend of his father's, and spent several weeks accompanying her on the social whirl. They went to Disneyland by helicopter, to Hollywood parties by limousine. When Taylor's actor friend Roddy MacDowell decided that she should meet Mae West, and staged a summit meeting of the two great sex goddesses at his apartment, Chris went with Taylor. MacDowell opened the door and showed them into the living room, where West was standing in a skin-tight silver and gold gown, flanked by two athletic young men. After five minutes of chatting, Taylor whispered, "Christopher, let's get the hell out of here," and they left.

The relationship with Taylor ended one evening when Chris escorted her to a party at the home of millionaire automobile salesman Henry Wynberg. Chris felt out of his element because he was so much younger than most of the guests, and when Wynberg suggested that he would take Taylor home if Chris wanted to leave with someone else, Chris asked her if it would be all right. Taylor agreed but had second thoughts and later told him reproachfully, "I ran after your car as you were pulling out, destroying my heels in the process, and yelled at you to stop, but you were apparently too infatuated to hear me."

Chris's major failure in Hollywood occurred not with stars or starlets or at the studio, but with his father. Still traumatized professionally and personally by the aftermath of the Sinatra affair, frozen out of the business by his former friend's continuing anger at the Kennedys for snubbing him and on the outs with his former in-laws, Peter Lawford had been unable to get his life back on track. Chris worked hard to reestablish the relationship which had been severed when his mother walked out on the marriage, his Kennedy half trying to make amends to his Lawford half. "Peter and I would stay up all night doing dope together and talking about family problems," Chris remembers. "We'd have what seemed a breakthrough—saying we loved each other and hugging and all that. But the next morning it would be all gone. He'd snap at me and absolutely cringe if I called him 'Dad' instead of 'Peter.' "

After one of these nights of temporary, drug-induced camaraderie, Chris decided to tell his father about how disoriented he and his cousins were, how lost without adult guidance. "I need you, Dad," he said, and began to cry. "I need you to be my father—at least for a little while. My life is a mess, and if I go back East again it's going to get worse." Lawford looked at him in disgust and said, "You must be high on something. Get the hell out of here."

Chris returned to the East Coast, entered Tufts College, near Boston, and picked up his relationship with David. But Bobby, increasingly confident of himself, sensed Chris's dilemma and began asking him to come with him when he went to New York to stay with Lem. Chris understood that Bobby acted less from a desire to save him than because Bobby had entered a period in his life when he was gathering disciples, but it was still a kind of salvation. Now he too would experience Lem's remarkable ability to bring the Kennedy saga alive, and to make someone of his generation feel like a beneficiary rather than a victim of the Legacy. Lem healed the wounds Chris had suffered in Hollywood by telling him the story of his parents' romantic courtship, describing how much they had loved each other when they first married, and detailing the factors beyond either's control which had led to their breakup. Chris was allowed to stay in "Bobby's room" when he wasn't there. In a gesture that seemed symbolic, Lem began an album for Chris to go along with the several he had already started for Bobby.

The fact that Chris was now part of a triangle with Lem and Bobby also meant that David, more than ever, was odd man out. He had been allowed to reenter Middlesex on condition that he not live on campus. He had taken a room with a family in Concord and, knowing this was his last chance, tried to apply himself. But school and life itself had become difficult for him, especially after Chris returned—something David had looked forward to—and immediately abandoned him. When Joe returned from Berkeley, he sensed David's growing desperation and tried in passing to take a paternal interest in him. But as David said, "Joe had problems of his own and couldn't keep his mind on me for more than a few minutes at a time. It had reached that point in the life of our family where it was every man for himself."

When summer came, Ethel arranged another trip to keep David occupied and out of the house. This time there was no effort to involve him in any socially redeeming activity. He was given a job doing manual labor at a place called Caribou Ranch, near Boulder, Colorado.

Just before he left the Cape, David was talking to Pam Kelley, younger sister of the girl who had been involved with Bobby so long. Spunky, with rimless glasses and long blond hair, Pam confessed that she too was having trouble with her parents. She asked David if she and a girlfriend could go west with him in his car and he said yes.

All during the trip across country David tried to get Pam's friend to sleep with him, but she wouldn't yield and finally flew home. So he slept with Pam. "I told him I'd had a terrible year," she recalls, "and that I'd been feeling nobody loved me. He smiled that wounded, angelic smile of his and said that he'd been going through the same thing. We sort of decided to love each other." Pam had known him all his life and watched what had happened— how hurt he had been by his eerie involvement in his father's death, how he had tried to be like Bobby Junior but didn't have the same talent for self-dramatization, how he had been traumatized by being alone within the family. ''He didn't have the hardness or the physicalness of the rest of them; David was always the soft one.''

Ethel found out that they were together in Colorado and became enraged. (''She went around complaining how the Kelley girls were always seducing her boys,'' Pam says wryly. ''That was a laugh.'') They couldn't stay together any more at the ranch, so Pam slept in the Chevy Impala and sat out on a hill watching David shovel chicken manure all day. After he got off work they would drive into Boulder to drink beer and play pool in a working-class bar.

After several weeks they decided to go back home. As they were driving across the country they picked up a young man who was hitchhiking and took him as far as St. Louis with them; when they parted, the rider suggested they make a detour to visit his parents in New Orleans. They did and it was like a honeymoon. ''This boy had called ahead and when we showed up his mother had everything ready,'' Pam remembers. ''The only thing was that she had arranged to put us in two different bedrooms. David asked if we could sleep together and she said yes. It was a wonderful week we spent there. They had a swimming pool, wine for dinner every evening. She gave us dimes to ride the trolley downtown.''

When they got back to Hyannis all this changed. They went first to the Kelleys', where Pam dropped off her clothes, and then to Ethel's. They stayed together in the Playhouse on the back lawn. ''It was a Saturday night,'' Pam recalls. ''We slept in this tiny miniature bed and the next morning David got up and said, 'Uh-oh, I've got to go to eleven o'clock mass.' I said, 'What am I supposed to do, stay in this two-by-two house and wait? No way. I'll sneak out and meet you someplace for lunch.' David panicked and said for me to sit tight because his mother would go into a rage if she knew I was with him. Then he left. I had started my period that night, the little white room of the Playhouse was half red—the sheets, the mattress, and the rest of the little miniature bed. I just rolled everything into one bloody pile and bolted. I was scared of Ethel, who was always hysterical even when she wasn't mad. I thought that if I was caught she'd hang me from the Compound flagpole.''

Later that day she met David again. He had gotten a call from his brother Joe, who had sat down with Ethel and Teddy for earnest talks after returning from Berkeley and promised to get his life together. Joe had been accepted at the University of Massachusetts for the fall, and was having a last summer fling on Nantucket, staying in a rented house with friends. That day he invited David to come over and spend the day and to bring Pam with him. ''David was ecstatic,'' she says. ''Here, finally, someone in the family was taking notice of him.''

They spent that Sunday at Nantucket sailing with Joe and his friends.

That night they had a cookout on the beach. The next morning they got up and went for a last swim before catching the ferry back. Joe commandeered a friend's jeep to take them to the jetty.

"He was doing his SuperKennedy act," David said later. "There was all this crazy energy. I suppose Teddy was that way before Chappaquiddick." As Pam Kelley remembers the drive: "We were all sort of standing up in the jeep. Joe was cutting through the woods, spinning the jeep in circles. We were yelling and laughing and acting crazy. There was a rest area on the other side of the highway and Joe started to cross over to it. He didn't see this station wagon heading toward us until the last minute. Joe swerved and we hit a ditch with our tires on the right side, breaking the jeep's axle and flipping us. We held on to the roll bar for a couple of flips and then had to let go. Me and David were right together . . . in the air. I remember tumbling and seeing David's face. I hit the ground. When I tried to get up, nothing happened."

For Joe, it meant an appearance in court (before a Nantucket judge who had been a college classmate of his dead uncle Joe Junior) and the suspension of his driver's license. For Pam Kelley, it meant days in and out of a haze of pain killers and then an awakening into the cold realization that she was paralyzed. The first person she saw was Ethel, always before an enemy but now the angel of mercy, twittering sweetly as she bustled around straightening the hospital room, setting flowers in vases, putting iced tea on the bedside table. Ethel brought Rose, who brought chocolate cookies she had baked herself. She brought Teddy, sun-tanned and salty from having just finished sailing. Every night she brought a projectionist and a movie to Pam's room. "Everybody would gather there, even the nurses. While they were watching, I'd ease into the wheelchair I was trying to get used to and go out into the hall and smoke a cigarette while they watched the film. They never missed me."

David was in the same hospital with fractured vertebrae. In a traction device and unable to move, he read Hunter Thompson's *Fear and Loathing: On the Campaign Trail 1972* through prismatic glasses like those Teddy had used when he broke his back. He knew that Pam's injuries were more serious than his. But when one of her friends broke the news to him that Pam would never walk again, he started screaming at her. He managed to get out of bed and walked stiffly to Pam's room. "That fucking bitch friend of yours," he began yelling as he saw her. "You wouldn't believe the shit she's been telling me . . ." Pam looked up at him, amazed that his family, whose lawyers had been talking to her and her parents about a million-dollar settlement, had told him nothing. "It's true," she said.

Even after David had checked out of the hospital he kept coming back to visit Pam, who was then undergoing physical therapy. "He'd come in and see me and then tell the doctors that the pain in his back and neck was intense and that they had to readmit him.'' He sat beside her bed, trying to make her believe that her injuries were not as bad as the doctors had said, that she would recover from her paralysis, and that when she got out they would be able to take up where they had left off. Sometimes he would phone her and bait her into arguments. ''It reached the point where I'd just have to say, 'Look, I'm sorry, David, I know what your needs are but I've just got to hang up now.' A few minutes later the phone would ring and I'd hear this enraged voice scream, 'You're an asshole!' and then he'd slam the receiver down.''

''You finally find someone to love,'' David later said about Pam, ''and you lose her. It's the shits.'' But there were other problems. While in the hospital he had been given morphine, which was better than any drug he had taken before: ''It felt great, just great. I'd drift off to sleep and wake up and figure it was eight hours later and time for my next shot. Then I'd look at my watch and realize that it had only been an hour and a half. I'd start yelling in agony to get them to hurry up.''

Totally bereft of support inside or outside the family, David looked for newer and darker boundaries to cross. Drugs provided the route, the morphine he had taken in the hospital leading him to shoot heroin on the outside, a drug which he had been introduced to with Chris in Central Park, and which Chris and Bobby were already using. ''I was swallowing Percodans and shooting heroin. With heroin you don't feel any pain. You could lose your girlfriend, your father, everything, on the same day—and you wouldn't feel a thing.'' He did heroin alone because Chris and Bobby had shut him out. ''They'd hang out at Lem's place and never invite me. I'd think about what a great time they were having and do heroin by myself.''

He shot the drug all during his senior year at Middlesex, the fall after the jeep accident, although he had convinced himself that he was just a ''chipper,'' able to take heroin or leave it. At the beginning of the spring semester, he decided to go to Nashville for his senior project because that was where his father had triumphed over Hoffa, and because John Seigenthaler, now publisher of the Nashville *Tennessean,* had offered him a job as a part-time reporter. He arrived at the Seigenthaler house thin and wasted looking. As they were talking, his father's old friend got out an album of pictures taken many years earlier, at the time Robert Kennedy brought David with him when he made a speech at a Nashville high school gym. ''David looked at himself in those pictures like they were a strange sort of mirror,'' Seigenthaler says. ''He looked at them a half-dozen times at least, mesmerized by them, and he kept asking me questions. There was a tremendous desire to know his father, to really know him. There was also a tremendous desire to know the person he himself had been in those pictures, and was no longer.''

John Warnecke, son of the San Francisco architect who had designed the

JFK grave at Arlington, was also in Nashville. Seigenthaler had brought him there, ironically, because his life also had involved a tailspin into drugs after the death of RFK, whose campaign he had worked on in 1968. "David was the skinniest, littlest kid, a mass of shirttails hanging out," Warnecke says. "He was shooting smack: that was clear to anyone who knew drugs. I had the only hot tub in Nashville, having had it shipped down from the Bay Area. I invited him over. He came and took off his jacket and these little popper syringes and packets of white stuff would fall out. We'd talk and he'd say how the family treated him so bad. His brothers were doing everything he was doing and he was the one taking the heat from Ethel. It became clear that he thought of himself and in fact was what they call in family therapy 'the designated sick one,' the one whose sickness allows everyone else to feel healthy by comparison."

After David began nodding out at press conferences he'd been assigned to cover, Seigenthaler reassigned him to the *Tennessean*'s Washington bureau. It was midsummer and Ethel and the younger kids had already left for the Cape. Richard Goodwin, then trying to set up a Washington bureau for *Rolling Stone*, was house sitting at Hickory Hill and using it as headquarters for what appeared to be an ongoing party. David got home and found himself in the middle of a scene that involved a huge blowup of JFK on the lawn, pretty girls in bikinis splashing in the pool, and a jukebox blaring acid rock. A young congressman worried that he might soon have to vote on the impeachment of Richard Nixon was walking around in a bathing suit, drawing on a marijuana cigarette and saying, "Should I vote to impeach, or shouldn't I?" while other partygoers chanted in response, "Impeach! Impeach! Impeach!"

After the crowd left, David was alone with Goodwin and *Rolling Stone* writer Hunter Thompson. Thompson said he wanted to take some acid; David asked if he could join him. Later on, Thompson said to Goodwin in his best Gonzo style: "This kid's going to the edge, all right. But I don't know if he'll make it back."

5.

*A*s THE SUMMER OF 1974 AP-
proached, Bobby Junior and Lem began talking about a river trip which
would summarize the joint enterprise he and Bobby were embarked on. The
subject hadn't come up since the debacle with Teddy in 1969. But now Bobby
got the idea of a different kind of trip—one that would be both a reprise on
and an advance over the great trips his father had created in an earlier and
better time; a trip he would dominate as RFK had dominated those of prior
years. Lem mentioned the Apurímac, a wild river at the headwaters of the
Amazon, and Bobby went to Harvard's Widener Library and researched it,
coming back in excitement to say that it was untamed and virtually unexplored. They decided almost on the spot to do it.

The fact that the Apurímac had never been traveled fit it into the metaphor Bobby was flirting with. He told Lem he had decided to "go into the
eye of the storm," go down roads no Kennedy had ever before traveled in an
attempt to attain an identity whose epic dimensions would quickly vault him
to the status of his own father and uncle. "I can't do it the way they did,"
he would say. "The conditions aren't the same. I've got to take short cuts."
When reminded of difficulties and risks, he had a ready answer: "If you see
your limits, you won't even reach them. To strive, to seek new worlds—that's
what my father stressed."

Once the leader of this expedition toward selfhood, Lem had changed
imperceptibly over the years until he had gradually become the follower. He
and Bobby had begun like Falstaff and Hal, with Lem trying to tempt
Bobby away from nihilism and toward an acceptance of the power that was
part of his heritage. He had succeeded so well that Bobby was now ready to

make a serious bid for fame. But Bobby had also tempted Lem with a different kind of power, the power of narcotics, which had come to function as a sort of lost-and-found room for him and others of his Kennedy generation.

At first it was marijuana. Lem had smoked it to prove his authenticity and to show Bobby that he was not like all the other family friends who professed to understand what the kids were going through after RFK's death but didn't really try. Then it was LSD. One Aspen acquaintance recalled a scene there during Ethel's annual Christmas skiing pilgrimage: "Bobby and some of the other kids were milling around this guy Billings, a larger, much older man. All of them were tripping, Billings right there with the rest. He was quiet for a while and then he started babbling about what a mind-expanding experience acid was, how it made you rediscover youth and vice versa. 'We're all one!' he started to say in that high-pitched voice. 'The world is one!' Everybody sort of smiled: it was one of those madcap acid rants you thought had gone out with the sixties."

But it went further than recreational usage. Bobby had become the drug master of his generation, and as he descended step by step into a netherworld of narcotics, Lem followed right behind him. Bobby brought angel dust to his apartment, and Lem tried it. Bobby brought speed and Lem shot it, despite the fact that he was developing a heart condition that sometimes left him gasping for breath. One of Bobby's friends, present at the apartment one of the first times Lem shot cocaine, remembers the scene: "Lem was lying on the bed and complaining that it wasn't having any effect. 'I'm not getting high, Bobby!' he kept saying. 'I'm not getting high! Give me some more!'"

Lem also shot heroin, going with Bobby even into this last forbidden zone. Sometimes they went to Harlem together to score. One friend remembers, "There was one time when Bobby got burned by some rip-off artist. There were dangerous-looking characters all over the place, but Bobby started screaming and beating on the door. Lem pulled him away, and when those black dope dealers came after us, we all ran, Lem and Bobby leading the way, laughing like hell."

The thrill and excitement was part of "scoring." There was also, as the term suggested, the element of competition, almost as if it was a perverse sort of athletic contest. Bobby had to be the best at everything. (At about this time he and Chris were seeing the same girl, and when he found out that she thought his cousin performed cunnilingus more satisfyingly than he did, Bobby wouldn't relent until the girl gave him another chance and admitted that he was actually better at it than Chris.) Being able to "handle" drugs and to "maintain" better than the rest of them was one of the sources of his dark power. Phoebe Sheldon, who knew Bobby in Cambridge, recalls how Joe would sometimes drop in at their drug parties. "Joe would soon get very antsy. He'd want to go out and nobody would want to go with him because they figured he'd do something dumb while he was high, like drive or find a field someplace and decide to play soccer and break an ankle, which he once did. So Joe would keep pacing, getting more and more nervous, until he finally took off by himself. Then Bobby would sort of smile and say, 'Joe ought to stop doing dope. He's too into it.' The English on these words was clear: "He can't *deal with it* like I can.' "

Lem's one-time Princeton roommate Francis McAdoo was struck by the change in his old friend as he moved deeper into Bobby's ethos. Once fastidious and even fussy, insisting on a clean-cut, Brooks Brothers look, Lem started dressing casually, allowing his hair to grow long, and filling his talk with street slang. "You'd pass him somewhere and hardly recognize him," McAdoo says. "He looked like a hippie. He was trying to live like young Bobby, and he was burning the candle at both ends. It was Bobby this and Bobby that. It was strange. It was like I didn't know him any more."

The assault on the Apurímac was meant to be a celebration of this new reality in the Lem-Bobby relationship. The group of adventurers they put together included Bobby's old friend and co-hustler Doug Spooner, the journalist Harvey Fleetwood (whom Bobby invited along to write up the trip, as his Arthur Schlesinger), and David and Chris. Bobby and Fleetwood decided to be the advance party. They flew to Lima, and from there set out for the town of Arequipa, about five hundred miles away. Fleetwood was at the wheel of their rented car as they began to ascend into the high plains. At a point in the badly paved road where visibility was poor, a peasant child dashed out and they hit him. "I was really shaken," Fleetwood later recalled, "but Bobby behaved with perfect poise and calm, obviously working to live up to the Kennedy ideal of grace under pressure in the middle of this crisis. He was just twenty, seven years younger than I was, but he took charge right away. He jumped out and gave the kid first aid, splinted his broken leg and carried him into the car, then drove us back to the nearest town and took the kid to the hospital. When he found out that the hospital didn't have pain-killing drugs, he went to a local pharmacy and bought some himself. We didn't leave town until it was clear that this kid was going to be okay."

They finally rendezvoused with the rest of the group in the mountain town of Ayacucho, where the others had been dropped off by a chartered plane from Lima. From Ayacucho it was a twenty-four-hour ride through the "high jungle" of the Andean foothills to San Francisco, the last village outpost, which sat at the edge of the river. Pigs rooted in the streets, which were covered with six inches of mud, sewage, and human excrement; short-statured Indians transferred coca leaves and barbasco root from canoes onto trucks.

Fleetwood, who watched Bobby closely throughout the trip in fascination with behavior which seemed really larger than life, was struck by his recklessness in all things, but especially in food. "During the time we were in this little town of San Francisco, Bobby ate anything and everything, even though he had a bad case of dysentery. He'd take these pills of paregoric, but he claimed that the only thing that worked was some tincture of opium we'd brought along. But he kept eating strange things—another of his dares. At one point we were at some peasant's house and boiled rat was served for dinner. Bobby ate it. Not only that, he sat there with this weird smile and then pulled one of the eyes out of the rat's head and ate that too. Then he pulled the other one out and handed it to Lem. Lem shook his head, then sort of shrugged and popped it into his mouth.''

Some three hundred Indians a year got caught in the Apurímac's wild current and were smashed to death in its rapids. One couple had tried it for the *National Geographic*. Others had failed with tragic results. When Fleetwood saw the river and realized that it would take them a week to get to a doctor if anything happened, he got cold feet. But the others, led by Bobby, began to needle him about it, and he stifled his doubts. Bobby insisted that they eliminate any technology that would make the trip easier, and that they go down on balsa logs which they would cut themselves and lash together with native vines. After several days' work they were ready. The rafts were loaded with supplies they'd brought with them—canned goods and a few tools, a medicine chest well stocked with morphine prescribed by Fleetwood's mother, who was a doctor, and some items purchased locally—a few chickens and three sticks of dynamite. David stood on the sidelines watching everyone else work and cynically commenting on the expedition: "Here you have it, my big brother's own personal heart of darkness.''

Bobby had met an Indian named Epifenio and got him to act as guide, along with his one-eyed brother-in-law Camilo. Just before they were ready to go, Bobby dared anyone to join him in trying to swim the river. Spooner agreed to try, but he had to turn back after getting about a third of the way across. Bobby continued, getting sucked under twice by the current and then surfacing farther down after the rest of them thought he had drowned; he finally managed to drag himself ashore on the other side. After this ritual proof of Bobby's right to leadership, Lem fell into a ravine and gashed his leg. Bobby was equal to this crisis too—using skills he had somehow acquired in the days when he still believed he would be a vet to sew the wound up with twelve stitches. Then they set out.

Suffering from dysentery and other ailments, they were like sailors on the Raft of the *Medusa*. Harvey Fleetwood made an entry in his diary two days into the trip: "Stopped at Cativirini Franciscan settlement.... Redid Lem's bandages, put antiseptic on my cut, gave Chris painkiller for his ankle which he reinjured. *Campas* [local Indians] don't believe in good spirits, only bad. Show fear and your [sic] dead ... Bobby sick. Lem's wounds infected, David strep throat ...''

They ate the canned food they brought along with them, and the live chickens kept in a cage at the back of the raft. (''Bobby would get one of them.'' Fleetwood recalls, ''and hold it by the neck and crack it like a whip to kill it.'') They beached the rafts at night, trying to find high ground for their camp to guard against the alligator-like caimans, poisonous snakes, and packs of river rats the size of cats. Sometimes they saw Indians; they traded Harvard sweatshirts for bows and arrows which Bobby used to shoot tree monkeys, which they roasted and ate. They also traded for coca leaves, which they chewed as a supplement for the medical morphine which was soon depleted in recreational shooting.

Bobby was very much the leader, always acting in a way to reinforce his status. One day he staged a breathtaking leap between their two rafts, just as they were navigating a stretch of hazardous rapids, and managed somehow to make it. David, on the other hand, was almost willfully counterheroic, having brought *The Making of the President 1968* and half a dozen other hardcover books which he read all during the journey, and hoarding cartons of cigarettes which he doled out one at a time to the others on the expedition in payment for doing his part of the work. (''He was the opposite of Bobby, who did everything,'' Chris Lawford says. ''David refused to do *anything.*'')

Fleetwood's diary recorded the quality of their daily life on the river: ''Caught 180 pound catfish last night. A big mother... The next day we dragged the great fish behind us, pulling him up to see if he was still alive. At times he seemed to be pulling the boat. But that night he tired and in the morning he was dead with a huge gaping hole in his side where the piranhas had gotten to him. As we pulled him out four or five fish were still eating him. Throughout the rest of the day we dragged the half-eaten fish behind us, attracting smaller fish and often going after the smaller fish with a machete. We ate well that night...''

Midway through the trip they hit a series of roller-coaster rapids that broke up both rafts and spilled their canned goods into the river, although they managed to make it to shore and to save the chickens, medicine, and dynamite. While some of them lashed new balsa logs together, Bobby, Lem, and Chris made a smaller raft and went on ahead to reconnoiter. They had tied up along the bank to try to dig the roots of a yucca-like plant they thought might be edible when a band of Indians began shooting arrows at them. One penetrated the canteen near Lem's leg. As Lem began to yell, Bobby rummaged for the bow and arrows he had earlier obtained in a trade. He hadn't brought them. Chris found a stick of dynamite and held it up. ''Lawford was standing there holding it, telling me to hurry,'' Bobby recalled later. ''We could hear the Indians coming at us through the bush. We put a blasting cap and a fuse in the dynamite. As the Indian who'd shot at us stepped out on the bank of the river, I lit the dynamite. Lawford held it until the fuse had almost burned down, then threw it. It landed in the water right next to the Indian. Then it exploded, sending water thirty feet in the air. He and all the rest of them took off.''

The guides Epifenio and Camilo had brought liquor with them and were always drunk. Epifenio delighted in outraging Lem, who was unable to get away from him because of his leg wound. Fleetwood recalls, ''Epifenio would lie on the raft and hold his penis up and then urinate in an arc into his mouth. Lem would yell, 'Make him stop it, Bobby, make him stop it!' '' Near the end of the trip, Bobby told Epifenio that he had decided to give him the tents and the rest of the gear that had survived their various mishaps. Camilo became jealous. In a drunken rage he charged Bobby with a machete, gashing him in the back; he was aiming a *coup de grâce* at his neck when Chris Lawford jumped him from behind and wrestled him to the ground.

Ragged and sick, they finally reached their Atalaya put-out point. They got the owner of a light plane to fly them to San Ramo, and from there made an eleven-hour bus trip to Lima over a sixteen-thousand-foot mountain pass. While the others were suffering from headaches and gasping in the thin air, Bobby decided that he needed his sweater, which was in a duffel bag lashed to the top of the bus. He opened the window and, as the vehicle lurched along the narrow mountain road, climbed out onto the roof to get it.

Back at Harvard that fall, Bobby was reaching the peak of his powers. The semiarticulate Kennedy distrust of words that his roommate Peter Kaplan had noted when they first met as freshmen two years earlier had been replaced by what Kaplan now regarded as ''an almost frightening facility with language.'' The stringy, avian quality Joey Brode had been struck by during Bobby's last year of prep school was also gone. He was now physically imposing—six-two, rangy and strong, with sharp good looks which added to the impression of raw power. He had developed a repertory of eye-catching tricks—drinking half a beer and then slapping the palm of his hand down so hard on the mouth of the bottle that the bottom fell out; holding one foot in his hand and making it a ''rope'' which he jumped over with the other foot. People watched him wondering what would come next. There was a sense of latent magic, as if a kind of manic energy crackled at his fingertips.

More than ever Lem was obsessed with comparisons between Bobby Junior and Jack. After their return from South America, he compared the performance on the Apurímac to Jack's adventures in the Solomons with *PT 109*. In slips of the tongue that happened so often they became a standing joke among their friends, Lem frequently called Bobby ''Jack.'' He once lectured Andy Karsch, who had refused to go with Bobby on some trip: ''I used to do it for Jack and you've got an obligation to do it for him. He'll need a best friend.'' Lem also spent a lot of time talking about Bobby to Chris: ''He had filled several albums with stuff about Bobby—letters, pictures, and so forth. He had one about me with some pictures, clippings about me and Elizabeth Taylor, that sort of thing. He made it pretty clear to me what role I was supposed to play. I was going to be to Bobby Junior what my Uncle Bobby had been to Jack—the family supporter, the one who would sacrifice everything, the one who made sure that his destiny came true."

With clinical detachment, Lem compared Bobby's sexual charisma to Jack's and concluded that he was even more successful with women than his old friend had been. ("Jack had all the charm in the world, of course," he said, "but he didn't have the caring quality that Bobby has.") He allowed Bobby to bring women to his apartment, sometimes two at a time, a situation that allowed him to go from one to another in an Olympian display of virility. Almost asexual himself, Lem took a vicarious interest in sex through Bobby, acceding to an almost conspiratorial involvement in the liaisons that made him an oblique part of the sexual bond. An item which found its way into one of the albums was a letter Bobby fabricated and sent to Lem—a letter whose tone echoed that of the notes Jack had sent Lem when they were young men:

Dear Mr. Billings,
 I realize this may be an inconvenient way of telling you, but I ask you to bear the discomfort of my disgrace with me. Lord knows the weight that I bear. Because of events of this weekend and the particularly delicate situation which has arisen concerning Bobby Kennedy and myself, I will no longer be able to live in this house. Oh! how this pains me to write it! My father made me promise never to smoke pot, and he thought in letting me stay with you he had put me in the hands of a careful guardian. Little did he know that even the best appearances mask the fetidly immoral exterior. So I took of the drug and let Bobby take of me. How I feel about Bobby is of no consequence; he is a good boy but he has asked too much and taken advantage of his great strength with women. There are liberties I cannot allow or live with. You were kind to me, Mr. Billings, but I'm afraid you planned this and I must apprise my father of this fact. Of course to protect Bobby I must tell him it was you who compromised me. I hope you see the sense. If you wish you may reach me at this number tonight. After that I may not be reached because I will be taking refuge in St. Anthony's Church convent. Goodbye forever.

                                                    Anna Marie

But women also involved a potentially serious subject as far as Lem was concerned: the right marriage. The woman he eventually married, Lem counseled Bobby, should be someone like Jackie: wealthy, well born, pretty, cosmopolitan, intelligent. Duff Pacifico, a part-Indian with exotic good looks who had become Bobby's chief girlfriend, recalls sitting at Lem's listening to him and Bobby go over the issue of the future marriage at great length and microscopic detail. She had already been faced with Ethel's aggressive-

ness. (''*South* Pacifico, you say?'' Ethel had replied when Bobby first introduced Duff to her. ''What a unique name.'' Later, when they were standing
outside in the winter chill, Duff's nose had been running slightly and Ethel
had stepped up and daubed at it with a Kleenex.) Now Duff had to listen to
this discussion of the wedding-to-be, so detailed that it even involved making
lists of ushers and guests to be invited; only the bride was unnamed. ''Lem
used to tell Bobby that the main quality he had to look for in a wife was
money and that I wasn't rich. He said it in front of me and when he saw that
it hurt my feelings he got very apologetic and said, 'I didn't mean to make
you feel bad. I just meant that Bobby's got to think about his future. The
Kennedy fortune isn't what it used to be, you know. He'll have to marry
somebody with a lot of money if he's going to be President.' ''

All Lem's talk about the presidency whetted Bobby's appetite. He talked
for hours with Peter Kaplan, who had read widely in American history of
the 1930s, about Joseph P. Kennedy's alleged anti-Semitism and prewar
appeasement. A similar interest in the Kennedy past, a subject rigorously
avoided by adults in the family, led his cousins to undertake academic projects about their elders. (Bobby Shriver wrote a senior thesis at Yale on
''crucial business decisions'' that had helped his grandfather amass his fortune; Maria Shriver wrote hers on Jack's 1960 primary campaign in West
Virginia.) But in conversations with Kaplan and another Harvard friend,
Eric Breindel, about the Kennedys' involvement with Joseph McCarthy,
Bobby's interest in the past was not academic; he was like a political candidate trying to brief himself on harmful facts that might someday be thrown
at him at a news conference. It was at about this time that a friend of his
sister Kathleen's, hearing the growing talk about Bobby and the presidency,
asked him if it was just talk or if it was something he felt he actually should
or could do. He looked at her intently for a moment before replying, ''I feel
that it is my destiny.''

Under Lem's close tutelage, he began making public appearances. On October 24, 1974, he appeared at the Catholic Youth Convention in Texas,
speaking on the question ''Where Is the Idealism of Youth Now?'' Calling
it an antidote to the cynicism created by Watergate, several congressmen
read the speech into the *Congressional Record*. A few weeks later he was in
Africa, in the Amboseli Game Reserve of Kenya narrating an episode of
''The American Sportsman.'' Stripped to the waist, he stalked game with
Masai warriors and speculated on Rousseau's ideas about noble savagery.
(Off camera, he also joined the Masai in their traditional warriors' drink of
milk and cow's blood.) The article in the *New York Daily News* promoting
the television show was headlined ''RFK Jr. Like Father,'' and much of it
was given over to a catalogue of Bobby's growing list of adventures. At
about this time, moreover, Bobby became involved in the State Assembly
campaign of Peter Shapiro, former editor of the Harvard *Crimson*, in a

South Orange, New Jersey, community of blue-collar workers, blacks, and Hispanics. Walking the precincts in a pin-striped suit and suede cowboy boots, Bobby helped tip the balance to Shapiro, who scored an upset victory.

He was developing a distinctive world view to go along with his ambition. In part it was his own reading of the sociobiology of Harvard Professor Edwin O. Wilson. Bobby was attracted to it, friends felt, because of the central role genes and the will to succeed played in Wilson's theories. Another ingredient was a strong bias against introspection. It was that same fear of the interior life that all Kennedys had, the fear that exploring the emotional dimension would reveal something about the family drama which in turn would rob them of the ability to act. In Bobby's case, this predisposition was buttressed by advice he claimed to have received from Robert Coles: Don't worry; go out there and have an impact on the world; work out your difficulties through activism. Knowing how important Coles had been to his father's discovery of issues such as race and poverty, Bobby allowed himself to be influenced by the psychiatrist's personal as well as professional ideas. Largely because of Coles's deep involvement with the South and southern literature, Bobby decided to go to Alabama to look for a subject for his senior thesis.

The first person he saw was George Wallace, then beginning to gear up for the 1976 campaign, the last and least successful of his presidential efforts. Peter Kaplan, who accompanied Bobby to Alabama, was struck by the historical ironies of the scene: the tall, muscular son of the Attorney General who, twelve years earlier, had been the nemesis of the feisty segregationist Governor, who was now sickly-looking and paralyzed by a would-be assassin's bullet. "Wallace received us in his office. He looked pretty awful, sitting behind his desk in his wheelchair. But it was obvious that he felt a tremendous bond with Bobby. When he'd been shot, Ethel had gone to see him and invited him to stay at Hickory Hill. He hadn't done it, but he hadn't forgotten the offer either. He felt compelled to explain himself politically to Bobby, trying to reconcile himself to the Kennedys." Even though he was ecumenical in his hunger for experience, Bobby himself felt the "weird resonance" of having his father's former adversary now trying to justify his political philosophy to him.

Bobby and Kaplan took a house in Montgomery. When word got around that a Kennedy was in town, there were death threats and cars full of yelling people roaring by in the middle of the night. Veterans from the civil rights movement immediately formed a protective shield. But it was clear that times had changed. Part of Bobby's itinerary involved a visit to the state legislature. Kaplan recalls, "There was an air of business being carried on with slight boredom. But when Bobby entered, there was a sudden electricity. A couple of the more liberal members came over and then suddenly everyone was mobbing him, grabbing his hands and slapping him on the back. It was like something had clicked. I'd seen him in political situations before and he'd always acted intelligently but a little stiffly. This time he started flashing the Kennedy smile and pumping hands in a way I'd never seen him do before. He was a candidate.''

Bobby gravitated to Frank Johnson, a liberal federal judge who'd been constantly at odds with Wallace and the segregationists in the sixties. There was a sudden and powerful chemistry between the two of them. Bobby knew his father had been an admirer of Johnson (although he had not recommended southern judges of Johnson's caliber for federal appointment during his tenure at the Justice Department). Johnson's own son had just committed suicide. Bobby began to interview Johnson extensively, fleshing out a story of how he had used his influence and power to achieve reforms of the judicial, prison, and mental health systems of Alabama, and how he had waged virtually a one-man war against Wallace and the segregationists. Bobby had intended to be in Alabama only a few weeks but wound up staying much of the semester, talking to Johnson and those around him.

Back in New York for periodic visits, Bobby talked about the senior thesis. Lem told him that if he played his cards right it could be published as a book, just as Jack's senior work on Munich had been. But even as they were talking about how this work could help launch his political career, they were scoring and shooting dope. One of their friends told Lem it sounded like madness to be talking about drugs and the presidency in almost the same breath. ''No,'' Lem replied. ''You don't know Bobby. He's got that incredible Kennedy ability to bring off the impossible. He'll do it. Wait and see. He can handle it.''

6.

NOT JUST FOR BOBBY AND Lem, but for all the rest of them too, the presidency continued to shimmer like a glorious mirage. There had been other great political dynasties, but none had quite the same reverence for this office. In the Adams's generational saga, the presidency had always been surrounded by a forbidding anxiety and self-doubt. For the Roosevelts it had been a counterpoint between individual ambition and a patrician ideal of noblesse oblige. For the Kennedys, however, politics and more specifically the politics of the presidency—a symbol of both personal achievement and group arrival—was part of the family folkways, written into the genetic code of each individual, as obsessive a trope as that of the crown in Shakespearean history plays.

Nothing, it seemed, could dim its luster. Friends of the family were amazed to hear even the second tier of children, some of them no more than ten or eleven years old, talking about the presidency. But it also seemed that nothing they did could bring it within their grasp again. In the aftermath of Watergate, for instance, a time which should have been ripe for a renaissance of Kennedy nostalgia, questions raised by the scandal about abuses of power led the Church Committee back to Mongoose and the secret war against Castro, and to a constellation of other issues ranging from mob involvement in assassination plots to Jack's private life which made the family vulnerable to a new and damaging revisionism. Sam Giancana was dead, the victim of a gangland hit at his Oak Park, Illinois, home before he could testify. But Judith Campbell, now Judith Campbell Exner, was alive. She was originally identified in the Church Committee hearings only as ''a close friend'' of Jack's, but her name was leaked to the press by Republicans who feared a "whitewash" of this episode. The *Washington Post* printed Exner's name. The *Chicago Tribune* got Jack's former secretary Evelyn Lincoln to admit that she'd called the White House frequently.

When she finally talked, Exner did not shed much light on Jack's sexual escapades, saying in her December 1975 news conference: "To me he was Jack Kennedy, not the President." But she did bring the American public into his bedroom for the first time. Her admissions initiated a flood of press reports about Jack and his women, a subject which had been taboo in his own lifetime. Jayne Mansfield, Angie Dickinson, Kim Novak were among the stars now linked to him. Marilyn Monroe was posthumously quoted by columnist Earl Wilson as having said after being with Jack, "Well, I think I made his back feel better." There were detailed lists of the places where he had carried out his liaisons: the Carlyle Hotel, the White House swimming pool, Peter Lawford's house, the private compartment of Air Force One.

Some Kennedy loyalists stonewalled. Dave Powers, for example, told reporters, "The only Campbell I know is chunky vegetable soup." Inside the family there was perplexity. One of Sargent Shriver's close friends happened to be out sailing with him when the damage caused by Exner was spreading, and asked him about family reaction to the charges. Shriver answered with the obtuseness that always made him so hard for the Kennedys to deal with: "Well, Eunice recently asked if any of this could be true. She was upset, as you can imagine, and I said to her: 'Well, we were around Jack a good deal in Georgetown when he was first elected to Congress and we know he wasn't pure before marriage. Whether or not he was pure after marriage is something we don't know. Maybe you should ask Teddy.' A few days later she came to me and said that she was feeling better because she had asked Teddy about the rumors and he had assured her they were false."

While the family refused to comment about information concerning Jack's personal life, they tried to counter what was said about his administration. When David Eisenhower wrote an article in the *Wall Street Journal* criticizing the Democrat-dominated Church Committee for making too much of the involvement of his grandfather's administration in the death of Congo insurgent leader Patrice Lumumba and too little of the Kennedys' pursuit of Castro, Teddy's office urged Bobby to reply. He did, stepping forth as the family's paladin, creating a point-counterpoint debate which was ultimately reprinted in several publications, including the *Saturday Evening Post:* "I would say to young Mr. Eisenhower that it is the duty of our generation to search backward for the footsteps left by great men like his grandfather— not to uncover their sins but rather to find the source of their greatness.... We must find out where we lost the trail.... Only then can we face the task, as my father was fond of quoting Aeschylus, 'to tame the savageness of man and make gentle the life of the world.' "

All this turmoil was occurring just as Teddy was considering making his long-delayed move. Some Kennedy apologists had outdone themselves in testifying about how Chappaquiddick itself had made him a better senator. (Notable among them was Arthur Schlesinger, who suggested that as a result of the accident "iron had gone into Edward Kennedy's soul.") What Chappaquiddick had done was buy him a respite from the demands of the Legacy, and he had used the time to put together a political identity he had never before had to create. It was basically the liberal identity RFK had made into Kennedy orthodoxy, but with Teddy it involved less a moral imperative than a legislative one. He had been a whirlwind of activity in the early seventies, sponsoring close to two hundred bills and amendments of his own and co-sponsoring twice that number with colleagues. He had taken important stands on handgun control, tax reform, and campaign financing reform. He had begun his long advocacy for national health insurance. He had taken on the responsibilities of the Judiciary Committee.

Yet the slide in his private life—which Chappaquiddick and the Church Committee had made fair game for the press—had continued. A month after Chappaquiddick, Joan had miscarried a third time, the last attempt the couple would make to have more children. ("After that," she said later, "I just thought we'd tried enough.") The marriage had gradually become a shambles. Some blamed Teddy's womanizing; some blamed Joan's alcoholism. One journalist friend, visiting Hyannis, was about to leave when Teddy asked with a bitter undertone if he would like to see Joan. The journalist said yes and Kennedy took him out the back door and gestured at one of the family cars where she was passed out drunk in the back seat, obviously the victim of a two- or three-day binge rather than a single afternoon of drinking.

Late in 1973, twelve-year-old Teddy Junior had been found to have bone cancer and in December his leg had been amputated. (Rose had paced outside his room during the operation saying to herself over and over, "One must not be defeated, one must not be defeated," a mantra that gradually changed to "I must never be vanquished.") Afterward there was a harrowing regimen of chemotherapy, with Teddy standing beside his son, chatting with him or showing him movies as he suffered the pain and nausea of a different kind of needle from the one which had become so central a part of his cousins' lives. But extra attention to "TK," as the boy was known, meant less for the other two. Patrick, Teddy's youngest, was so sick with asthma that he took steroids and often had to have oxygen administered. Fourteen-year-old Kara, chubby and insecure, had fretted about "catching" her brother's cancer. Experimenting with marijuana and hashish, she began running away from home and showing up at halfway houses where her father would be called to come and pick her up.

Because of all these problems and because of uncertainty about how far the new mood of revisionism concerning the Kennedy Legacy would go, Ted took himself out of the running in advance for the presidential nomination in 1976. Sargent Shriver almost immediately stepped in, announcing his candidacy in a speech extolling the glories of Jack's administration and concluding, ''And I intend to claim that Legacy . . .''

In a certain way the Shrivers came closest to providing the family with a moral center of gravity. Sometimes Eunice's views were dictated by the narrowly religious precepts that had always been so much a part of her life. Yet there was also a generosity in her attitudes. Hers was the one house where the drugged and disoriented Kennedy kids found safe haven. She continued to bring her sister Rosemary to Maryland from the Wisconsin nursing home for visits. (Rosemary would swim there, still freckled and smiling, her hair cut in bangs, looking, as Eunice's son Timmy observed, like a sixty-five-year-old girl.) Eunice had played a central role in the creation of the Special Olympics, perhaps in an unconscious rebuke of the winner-take-all philosophy which her father had infused into the family and which had claimed Rosemary as a victim. Every year she would bring fifty or sixty retarded children to Timber Lawn, the rambling summer place she rented. They called it Camp Shriver, and every morning she and whichever of her own children were present came out to lead the flag-raising ceremony and the playing of the ''Star-Spangled Banner.''

But none of this helped her husband much. He had miscalculated the new mood concerning the Kennedys. Audiences in New Hampshire, where he manfully slogged through early snows on cross-country skis, groaned when he tried to summon Camelot and one party leader in Massachusetts referred to him twice as ''Eunice'' during an introductory speech. He also miscalculated how much support he could count on from the family. Before his appearances on ''Face the Nation'' or ''Meet the Press,'' Eunice would urge him to listen to her brother: ''You've got to spend some time with Ted because he knows how to handle these things.'' After Sarge had finished a lackluster performance, Eunice would say, ''See, if you'd just spent some time with Ted he would have shown you how to do it.''

In fact, Ted was not the least interested in a successful Shriver candidacy. He had assured Eunice that while he had to remain publicly neutral he would help Sarge privately. But Paul Tsongas, then a young Massachusetts congressman who had decided to support Shriver because he had served under him in the Peace Corps, changed his mind when he was on a plane with Teddy and Tip O'Neill and heard Kennedy ridicule his brother-in-law: ''Poor Sarge, I hope he doesn't stay in it too long because it's going to be hard on Eunice's health.'' Later on, Bobby Shriver remarked bitterly, ''Teddy didn't do shit for my father in 1976.''

Teddy concentrated on his own Massachusetts reelection. As if to try to bind the next generation to his political fate, he brought in Joe as campaign manager for what was a sure thing and encouraged the cousins to campaign for him. Yet the sense that there was still a common family political destiny was evaporating. Pat Lawford continued to spend much of her time in Paris, often wearing the clothes of French designer Jean Louis Sherrer. The Smiths had more or less withdrawn from Hyannis in favor of their Bridgehampton estate. Rose had become a sort of specter, whose only function in the family seemed to be that of protocol officer. "The fact that you write to me," she said in a typical note to Bobby Junior after he had sent her a thank-you note for some present, "pleases me because it is a very good habit to establish. . . . Grandpa felt that way all his life and we were always careful about these courtesies . . ."

Jackie had returned to America, her marriage to Onassis having ended long before the billionaire's death, when he was critically ill with myasthenia gravis and had retained long-time Kennedy foe Roy Cohn as his lawyer in projected divorce proceedings that his death made moot. But she was no longer in the Kennedy orbit except on ceremonial occasions. Her children, unlike their cousins, were cerebral, interior, subdued. Caroline had not only her mother's fear of notoriety (she would bolt from theaters just before intermission lest someone recognize her when the lights went on) but also the Bouvier archness. (She said to a friend about Jackie, "Can you believe that voice?") John had gotten along better with Onassis than his sister; he had been delighted when his stepfather took him fishing and gave him hundred-dollar bills to buy bait. But he too seemed more Bouvier than Kennedy, having that sense of irony so much a part of his mother's character. (Once during a Christmas stroll he asked Jackie to buy him some street artist's trinket and when she said it was too expensive yelled at her, "You're the richest woman in the world and you say it costs too much!")

Only Ethel was left as a regular at Hyannis, a merry widow but also an eccentric one, who spent a good deal of time in such endeavors as sending personalized valentines to friends. (One that came to Lem had a photograph of her on the lap of a black woman she'd somehow persuaded to dress as Santa Claus. It bore this inscription: "Roses are red and violets are blue and if it weren't for Kunte Kinte, I'd be you.") Someone asked her if she planned to marry the singer Andy Williams or one of the other men with whom she was occasionally linked. "Oh no," she replied seriously. "How could I possibly do that? With Bobby looking down from heaven that would be adultery."

For Christmas 1976, Ted put together one of those privately printed keepsake books that had circulated within the family since Jack designed *As We Remember Joe* some thirty years earlier. It was called *Words Jack Loved* and was filled with anecdotes about the President's love of reading and excerpts from his favorite books. Ted ended it with words of his own: "There are cherished memories here. Some may bring a tear to the eye. . . . The last thirteen years have passed so quickly. So many things are different now. Yet the value of these words remains—to keep us going when times are rough; to remind us of what he meant to us as a son and a brother, a husband and father; to carry us back to those great days when his energy, spirit and brilliance came together in that glorious adventure we shall never realize and never forget." It was clear to all who read the volume that the last Kennedy was attempting to hold up the beau ideal of the presidency one last time. Yet what stood out in the passage were the words "never realize." The phrase seemed almost a Freudian slip, telling the family that while Ted wanted them to rally around for one last roll of the presidential dice sometime in the future, they should not hope for too much.

Chris Lawford was one who was increasingly coming to see the presidency as containing a sharp and dangerous paradox. It had made them what they were as a group; it also alienated each of them from what he or she might have been as an individual. "The presidency is in our system and we can't get it out," he said later. "We can't get free enough of it to consider doing something else with our lives." In his view it was an ideal that ultimately infantilized them rather than encouraging maturity; it gave a millenarian cast to their lives as they killed time awaiting the second coming; it made him and his cousins into lost boys living in a political never-never land whose inhabitants never grew up.

Half a Kennedy, with no certain place in the family system (except in Lem's conception of him as Bobby's "Bobby" when the metamorphosis into "Jack" was complete), Chris had been so affected by the Church Committee revelations and by the inability of the family elders to achieve the much-discussed Kennedy restoration that he had begun to wonder whether the Kennedys were in fact an elect with a manifest destiny in American life. The dilemma, as he saw it, was that nobody in his generation could make a move until Teddy made a move, and Teddy, for various reasons, was immobilized. So it was a matter of waiting and toying with heroic fantasies that seemed to have no pertinence to the real world. In his own mind, he compared the situation faced by the grandchildren to that of characters in some absurdist drama whose theme had to do with waiting and boredom.

Moreover, although he couldn't really admit it to himself, Chris was sick of the family's brand of politics. Partly to avoid working on Teddy's 1976 reelection campaign, he had taken a leave from Tufts and gone to Washington to enroll at Georgetown. While there, he fell under the influence of Philip Berrigan and other radical Jesuits whose belief in principled political action seemed an antidote to what he was beginning to see as his family's mania for pure power. He became involved in the New York Senate campaign of Ramsey Clark, who seemed to embody his Uncle Bobby's belief that "one man can make a difference." Chris remembers, "Before, everything I did had been Kennedy-related. I did it out of family obligation, because it was part of the joint Kennedy undertaking. Ramsey's campaign was a cause rather than a family responsibility. It was much more satisfying to me than anything else I'd done because it was not just expected, but philosophically worthwhile." The only problem was that Clark managed to get only 10 percent of the vote.

For RFK the idea that "one man could make a difference" had implied an ideal of individual commitment for the common good. For Chris and his cousins, this principle had become ensnared in the narcissism which was part of the Legacy. Chris thought about working with poor people in the Baltimore ghetto, and about other undertakings in keeping with the themes of his Uncle Bobby's last few years of life. But he realized he couldn't tolerate some anonymous enterprise lacking instant gratification and apocalyptic "Kennedyesque" overtones. So he returned to New York and his relationship with Lem and Bobby, the only thing in his life with any emotional charge at all. Even here his marginality was always clear. An almost-Kennedy, he was also almost Lem's best friend: "At times, when it was just the two of us, we'd draw incredibly close. He'd say to me, 'If only I'd met you before I met Bobby.' But then Bobby would blow into town from his latest adventure, and I would be second fiddle again, and I'd see that Lem would always mean more to me than I'd ever mean to him."

Early in 1978, Chris went to a New York night club where a rock singer named Jennifer Jacobson was entertaining. Although he had been living with another woman for several years, Chris was stunned by Jennifer. He went home with her that night and they were together for the next six months, a period when he was trying to keep up with Bobby and Lem in their descent into a netherworld of hard drugs. Jennifer was attractive to Chris in part because her vision was unclouded by guilt or romanticism about the Kennedys, and she saw him in a light in which he'd never been seen before. "Like all the Kennedy kids," she said, "Christopher is both tremendously savvy and tremendously naïve. It was the oddest combination of innocence and experience I'd ever encountered."

Jennifer saw immediately that Chris and Bobby were addicts—not mainlining heroin addicts, perhaps, although heroin was the summa drug for them —but addicted to narcotics in general: "Christopher and Bobby liked heroin. But they'd settle for a cupful of Valium, some Percodans, or whatever else was there. Drugs were obsessive. There was a desperate need to escape. Most of us who do dope just want to leave our lives behind. You got the feeling that whatever they said, they wanted to leave their whole ancestry behind. Chris was fearless when it came to the ghetto. He'd march into Harlem with a tennis racket over his shoulder and demand what he wanted. I'd done drugs before, but what he did was to make it dangerous and exciting. We started challenging fate in every way possible."

Always there were Bobby and Lem and what was becoming an increasingly surreal scene at Lem's apartment. Jennifer felt that Lem was strongly antifemale but recognized that the Kennedys were dependent on women and even more dependent on women being dependent on them. "What he'd do was interpose himself between Bobby and Chris and their girls. He'd get close to the girls when they were hurt by the infidelities and say, 'Don't worry, I'll talk to him. I'll work it out for you.' Then he'd go to Bobby or Chris and say, 'That girl sucks. You've got to get rid of her. She's no good for you.'"

Once the best place to make an emotional connection, Lem's apartment was now the best place to make a drug connection. "Chris would take me," Jennifer says, "and Bobby would take whoever he was with. There was always the period of sitting around making small talk. It was really a period of waiting for somebody to decide when and how we were going to score. Then there would be the fighting over who got to do it first. Bloody needles. Doors slamming. Lem in his bathrobe and shorts yelling, 'Bobby, get in here quick!' and then going into the bathroom to get his shot. The women were supposed to sit there waiting for the drug leftovers. It was always a macho scene, a shootout: which of them could do the most drugs, which of them could do the most women."

Chris tried to keep up with Bobby but he couldn't. He became more and more dependent on heroin, less and less able to "handle it." He was sick and despondent for long periods. Worried about him, Jennifer helped him enroll in a methadone program under an assumed name. But methadone turned out to be a "nightmare high," as well as physically debilitating. Chris's weight ballooned some forty pounds, to two hundred twenty. He contracted pneumonia. Jennifer thought he was dying. Desperate, she called Robert Coles, who told her that Chris had to decide to seek help on his own. Not knowing what else to do, she called Pat Lawford, who came in a cab and took Chris to a hospital. From there he was transferred to McLean's, a Massachusetts clinic specializing in the mentally and emotionally disturbed whose distinguished alumni included such figures as Robert Lowell and Sylvia Plath. Jennifer went up to see him and found that he was in a room with another drug addict and an apparently hopeless schizophrenic. "He came to the door and we talked awhile and the first thing he asked me was if there was any way I could get him some dope."

Although no longer close to Chris, David was on a parallel journey that would also lead to a brush with death. After his stint at the Nashville *Tennessean*, he had managed to get admitted to Harvard. Other students grew used to his disheveled appearance—an unvarying uniform of rumpled shirt and dirty Levis. "I never saw him without a Colt 45 Malt Liquor in one hand and a cigarette in the other, no matter what time of day it was," says a woman who lived on the floor above him at Winthrop House. "He looked fragile, kind of skeletal, with this terrible pallor. It was so at odds with that healthy Kennedy persona—touch football, sailing, beaches."

He spent time with *Boston Globe* reporter Tom Oliphant, whom he'd met the previous summer while working as a journalist. "He'd bring papers over to my apartment in Cambridge," Oliphant recalls, "and we would generally talk about school and school subjects. Sometimes he'd come over and just sit. He was an excellent writer and he was doing work in school that was out-of-this-world good. He wasn't bookish, but he had an original and at times brilliant way of looking at things. But he was clearly in deep psychological trouble."

One of David's problems was how to deal with the afterglow of Bobby's meteoric progress through Harvard. Even more, there was the ongoing issue of his place in the family itself. Being difficult and out of synch—the one whose life called into question the illusions the others insisted on maintaining—had become his role. It was most apparent on ceremonial occasions such as the family's annual Christmas at Aspen. Joe would take an apartment of his own. Bobby would be active with his younger brothers, consolidating his status as leader. (Once a skier accidentally knocked Ethel down, and Bobby, along with brother Michael, flew down the Aspen slopes in pursuit; they finally caught the man, knocked him down, and then punched and kicked him. Ethel, beaming, called them "My Dobermans.") David would spend the holiday on the living-room couch, reminding everyone of his pain and disorientation, having a maid bring him food as he read and rested. The more he proposed himself as a symbol of the fact that something was out of kilter with his generation, a subject nobody wanted to talk about, the angrier Ethel became. "She just tore into David sometimes," a family friend recalls. "I remember once she misplaced two hundred dollars. She came in and immediately began accusing David. He told her it was ridiculous—he had money, what did he need two hundred dollars for? She just kept it up, absolutely vicious, wouldn't let him go."

But for the most part, the problem was not too much attention but too little. The filmmaker Bob Rafelson, another Christmastime acquaintance at Aspen, recalls David forlornly following Hunter Thompson around, and clearly looking like a drowning person on his third trip down. "Bobby came over one night. He was at the top of his game—writing a book about some Alabama judge, and doing these little macho tricks, doped up and talking about falconing and politics. I steered the conversation around to his brother David and said I thought he was awfully sickly looking, on the verge of really going under. Bobby thought about it a minute and said yes, somebody ought to wean David away from Hunter, who he said was a bad influence. But then he was off again, talking about something else. David didn't seem to be a high priority for him or anybody else."

In 1976, while most of his cousins were campaigning for Sarge's abortive presidential try or Teddy's Senate reelection, David was on a forty-day binge shooting drugs. Bobby's friends Peter Kaplan and Eric Breindel went to David's room at Harvard, found him practically comatose and with a spiking fever, and took him to Massachusetts General Hospital. Doctors diagnosed bacterial endocarditis, a potentially fatal inflammation of the lining of the heart caused by dirty needles.

"At first," David recalls, "there was the usual outpouring of concern. We Kennedys aren't much for the day-in, day-out thing, but we sure put out in a crisis. My mother was there, Teddy, Joe, somebody pretty much around the clock." They sat beside his bed in the darkened room. Muhammad Ali was called and sent David one of his robes as a get-well present. Art Buchwald came for a visit to make him laugh. But when it appeared that he would pull through, the concern began to taper off.

He was hospitalized for six weeks. Then, as summer approached, his family designed another trip. "They said I needed activity to keep my mind off things," David says. "Actually they needed me gone so I wouldn't annoy them." Bobby's old Harvard friend Mir Bhutto arranged for David and Doug Spooner to go to Pakistan for a visit. Shortly after arriving, the two of them were taken wild boar hunting with General Zia (who would later overthrow President Bhutto and put him to death). "We were in helicopters with M-16s, honorary members of the Pakistan Rangers," Spooner recalls. "It took us all day and half the night to get a boar, but finally we did. While we were up in Peshawar looking at the Khyber Pass, Khaddafi arrived in Pakistan. Bhutto got the idea that it would be good for a Khaddafi and a Kennedy to meet. So he had Khaddafi fly up and we met him and had this brief conversation. Khaddafi's entourage was extremely nervous, jumping to anticipate his every need. Afterward we flew out of Peshawar in a staff plane behind Khaddafi. A lot of his people were on the plane with us. One of them came up and asked David what he thought of their leader. David gave them his drug grin and said, 'Well, I think the guy's a little unpredictable.' Every Libyan in the plane began to laugh hysterically."

Back home, David sank deeper and deeper into a nightmare world, a world which had come to resemble what was supposed to be the normative Kennedy world turned inside out. He dropped out of Harvard and devoted himself almost exclusively to scoring heroin. He spent a good deal of time in the Roxbury ghetto. ("My father was concerned about blacks in one way," he would say later, "and I was concerned about them in another—as people from whom I could get drugs.") One day a black dealer told him he'd meet him in a public toilet to make a transaction. When David showed up, the man overpowered him, tied him up, and tried to stab him with a knife. David jumped back so that the knife only sliced him along the abdomen, and managed to get away. Later on, after his wound healed, he was disappointed that the scar wasn't more severe. "I was modeling myself on the James Caan character in *The Gambler*. I saw that movie over and over. I loved the last scene, where Caan had finally pushed things so far that the black guy cut his face, and then he goes to the mirror and sees the wound and smiles. I could relate to that.''

When he was released from the hospital after his endocarditis, his family had gotten him a psychiatrist, Lee Macht, a thirty-nine-year-old ''boy wonder'' who'd been commissioner of the Massachusetts Mental Health Department and was chief of psychiatry at Cambridge Hospital. After the knifing in Roxbury, Macht, worried about David's compulsive risk taking, agreed to prescribe Percodans to keep him out of dangerous places. David's reaction was to use more and more drugs. In April 1978, he bought an ounce of cocaine, which he had planned to sell, but instead went to a girlfriend's house and started shooting the cocaine with Dilaudids, a morphine surrogate. When the cocaine wore off, the Dilaudids took over. The girlfriend came into her bedroom, where David was sleeping, and was unable to wake him. She called Spooner, who saw that David had o.d.'d and rushed him to the hospital, where he was revived. Afterward, recuperating at Spooner's, David was called on by the group he had begun to think of as ''The Committee to Keep David Out of the Picture''—Teddy, Steve Smith, Richard Goodwin, Robert Coles, his brother Joe, and his elder sister Kathleen. They all persuaded him to agree to let Kathleen be his guardian and then sent him to McLean's, the same place Chris had gone earlier to deal with his drug problem.

''It looked like the Ritz on the outside and the Snakepit on the inside,'' David recalls. ''The first thing I saw when I went in there was a guy on all fours barking like a dog. Literally. That's when I knew I was in trouble.'' He managed to get a call out to Kathleen. She came to visit and started crying when she saw his surroundings. She promised to have him out that afternoon, but she didn't come back for three days, and then told him, ''The others say not to trust you—that you'll say anything to get out.'' When David asked her how long he'd be there, she replied that she didn't know.

Three weeks later, David was released and sent to Sussex, England, to become a patient of Dr. Margaret Patterson, a Scottish surgeon who had invented what she called ''Neuro Electric Therapy.'' One of her most celebrated patients, Who guitarist Peter Townshend, had endorsed the procedure, which involved wearing a Walkman-like headset emitting signals to the brain that Patterson theorized affected drug dependence. For David, who wore this appliance while living with a family of English evangelicals who spoke in tongues during moments of religious ecstasy, the experience was part of the surrealism which he was coming to accept as his own reality. His family wanted him to stay in England, but after two months there he returned home.

He began hanging out again. He and his brother Bobby met starlet Rachel Ward, whom David regarded (and still does) as ''the most beautiful woman who ever lived.'' The two of them took her dancing. To Bobby's chagrin and David's surprise, she chose to go home with the younger Kennedy brother. It was an intense involvement, the first serious romance for David since Pam Kelley's injury. ''We had good times. She was just really getting into her acting career. I remember once we went to see *The Invasion of the Body Snatchers* and at one point in the movie she let out this blood-curdling scream. 'Practicing?' I asked her. Then at another scary moment I let out my own scream, and some guys in front of us told me to shut up.'' He got intensely jealous when he went to pick Rachel up one night and found Philippe Junot, recently married to Princess Caroline of Monaco, in her apartment. The three of them went to Xenon, a discotheque, although David was in a leg cast as a result of a broken ankle he had suffered while trying to join his younger brothers in a touch-football game. When they sat down at their table, David saw Junot put his arm around Rachel and knocked it off. Junot, who had been trained in martial arts, leaped to his feet and started a brief fight that ended with David on the floor, bleeding from the nose.

''Rachel wanted to get an apartment with me and settle down. But I knew I was too fucked up. I was back on smack. She had no idea of what I was up to. I don't know what she thought of all those little marks on my arms when I was naked. I guess she thought they were some odd Kennedy rash. We never talked about it. I was supplementing the heroin—five times the lethal dose for someone not used to it—with forty Percodans a day. I'd go up to Boston on the shuttle and get five prescriptions from Lee Macht for forty Percodans each. Then I'd go to various drugstores around town and get them filled and come back to New York that evening with two hundred pills. That was the ritual—once a week.''

One Wednesday his temperature began to rise again and he could tell he had been reinfected with endocarditis. He called Macht to arrange to go back to Massachusetts General, but before flying to Boston to be admitted, decided to go to Harlem one last time. He had been a good and regular customer and was well known on certain blocks by his tan BMW. Because he had given his name as ''James'' (after Caan in *The Gambler*) and there were several blacks named James in the drug business, dealers called him ''White James.'' This time he had trouble. As he was making his connection at the seedy, rundown Shelton Plaza Hotel, a huge black man accosted him, demanding his money and then blocking him from leaving the lobby of the shooting gallery while illogically shrieking, ''You get out of here! Don't come in here, you honky!'' As the man hit David in the face repeatedly, a black woman watching the scene slipped out and called the police. ''I should have just said it was no big deal and walked off,'' David now says. ''But I was so out of it that I walked up to the cop in charge and started acting suspicious and said I didn't want to get involved. Naturally I was arrested

and the next day the news was all over the papers. David fucks up again."
The Percodan prescriptions were found in the glove compartment of the car,
leading to proceedings to strip Macht of his license.

As Steve Smith was telling reporters with typical Kennedy euphemism
that David was suffering from "an ailment similar to drug addiction," he
was on his way to Massachusetts General, where he was put on methadone to
ease him off heroin. This time his endocarditis brought no outpouring of
family concern. The only person close to David who visited was Rachel
Ward. When she came, he locked the door of his room and they made love.
In the days that followed he wandered through the corridors of the hospital.
One of the people he met was a young woman terminally ill with cancer.
They talked a few times. He arranged to have a friend bring him a bottle of
champagne, which he took to the girl's room. They drank it and made love.
She died not long afterward.

While David was at Massachusetts General he received another visit from
the Committee to Keep David Out of the Picture. This time they wanted a
lifetime guardianship over him. He refused to sign the papers but, fearing
that they would have him recommitted to McLean's, he did agree to give
them control for six months. A judge oversaw the proceedings at his bedside.
"I was hooked to an IV and I told them to get the hell away from me so I
wouldn't have to hear all the legal garbage. I told them that from an objective point of view I found it rather interesting that the only time anybody
ever gave a damn was when I fucked up."

The decline of Chris and David seemed to make Bobby's equilibrium all the
more remarkable. It appeared that he could indeed "handle" and "maintain" the heaviest drug use of them all, that he could integrate drugs into
his rush of success and never have to admit, even privately, that he was a
"junkie"—a word he used to taunt both of the others. He had finished his
senior thesis and, with Lem's help, turned it into a book. He had also applied
for a Rhodes Scholarship, Lem supporting him with an eloquent letter of
recommendation. ("I have watched him overassert himself with that raw
strength that young men so often [possess] . . . and I have watched him learn
to restrain himself. Since I have known him he has become a man and an
impressive one . . . I am almost sixty years old and I have watched a few
great ones come along. I've fought in a war and I've been active in politics
and business, and I know what qualities are the ones that shape strong men
into strong leaders. Bobby has those qualities . . .") And, following the pattern of his dead uncles Joe Junior and Jack, he had enrolled at the London
School of Economics, in the mind of the family a sort of finishing school for
greatness.

It was the moment when he would make his move, when he would exchange
that sense of latency which had surrounded him like a halo for the past

several years for a start in the real career which he and Lem had talked about. But now that he was finally taking the first steps, nothing worked according to plan. Far from reaching the best-sellerdom of Jack's book, Bobby's, published as *Judge Frank M. Johnson, Jr.: A Biography,* was savaged by reviewers. ("There are oversights that seem inexcusable in a biography," the *New York Times* said, "even allowing for the fact that this is a first book that had its beginning as a senior thesis at Harvard.") The Rhodes Scholarship Committee flatly turned down his application. His experience at the London School of Economics turned out to be only a few weeks in duration—a halfhearted attempt to study at the Strategic Studies Institute while he explored England's political *haut monde* and traveled to County Wexford in Ireland to do drugs in the place where his ancestors had lived.

Compounding Bobby's lack of tangible success was the fact that his brother Joe finally seemed to have found a workable way to be a Kennedy, a way that made their long competition look like a parable of the tortoise and the hare. Joe's stabilization had begun in 1976, when he ran Teddy's reelection campaign, which—however foregone the conclusion of the race itself— gave him a sense of real involvement and success that few of his cousins had experienced. It was part of a general change. As his old friend Chuck McDermott says, "He had just gotten to the point where he wanted to do something with his life and that was more important than getting crazy every night."

He had tried Washington as a next step, taking a job with the Community Services Administration, which aides to Party Chairman Robert Strauss at the Democratic National Committee had pushed because they felt it would give the operation "a lot of credibility." With the aggressive sincerity that marked all his efforts, Joe was soon telling CSA director Grace Olivera how to run her agency, lecturing her in his father's terms about the relationship between poverty and power. ("He bégan to challenge my commitment to the poor. The fact that he was twenty-six and I was forty-eight, that he was white, male, and rich and I was a minority woman who had been poor myself didn't seem to have an effect on him.") After a year in Washington, he resigned and moved back to Boston. People had tried to rush him into running for Congress, especially when Jack's old friend Torby MacDonald died and his seat was available. But the new caution Joe had acquired counseled against it. Instead he began working to set up the Citizens Energy Corporation. Starting with a plan Richard Goodwin helped him formulate, Joe intended to create a business that would show, in a politically exemplary way, how to solve the energy crisis. Citizens Energy would buy crude oil in Venezuela, have it processed in the Caribbean, sell the gas and other by-products at market prices, and use the profits to bring in heating oil which could be sold throughout Massachusetts to the elderly and the poor at a 40 percent discount. The corporation was a way of finally starting a business as the first Joseph Kennedy had done. It was also a way of starting a political career.

Joe was different from Bobby also in the fact that he realized that the price of a political career was an almost antiheroic version of what a Kennedy should be. ''I'm different from Bobby,'' he said to friends. ''I can't parachute down into the name from above. I have to work my way up.'' He understood, too, that he had to renounce any claim to involvement in the dark world that so intrigued his brother. At about the same time he was beginning Citizens Energy, he was getting engaged to Sheila Rauch, a young woman from a Philadelphia Main Line family who had been his girlfriend since high school. Andy Karsch had seen Joe at the wedding of family friend Tim Haydock, where drugs and beautiful unattached women circulated during the reception. ''I'm getting the shuttle back to Boston,'' Joe had said anxiously. ''I've got to get out of here. Everything I see that's worth wanting will only get me in trouble.''

It was exactly this kind of discrimination, this cost-analysis view of the emotionally expensive world they had been born into, that was beyond Bobby. He had all the Kennedy charisma, all the appeal; he had the ability to bind people to his fate. Yet there was an almost willful lack of insight into what he was doing with his life. Increasingly his friends told him that he had to engage in a psychological reckoning that would give him some kind of purchase against the forces that were driving him. He would reply, ''If you've got a problem in this world you've got to deal with it. Bob Coles has always told me that psychiatrists are full of shit. I don't want to be introspective. I just want to deal with the world. It's an unnatural life we Kennedys lead and there's going to be some effects. You just deal with them. If your leg gets cut off, you learn to walk without it—that's what TK did. You don't dwell on the problem. You get up and get moving.''

The trouble was that moving had come to mean moving other people. Bobby had stopped having anything to do with Chris and David, dismissing them as ''junkies.'' He had thrown over his girlfriend Duff Pacifico, to whom he had been closer than any of the others, in favor of Rebecca Fraser, daughter of British politician and old family friend Sir Hugh Fraser. Duff had first read about Rebecca and Bobby in the New York papers, while waiting for the IRT, and had been so upset that she called him in London from a phone in the subway. He had denied the report and had even taken Duff along when he and Lem went to Haiti after he returned. It was a vintage Bobby experience—touring Haitian slums and becoming a sort of Pied Piper to Haitian urchins, who followed him along the beaches imitating his back flips and crammed themselves into his rented car. Lem, flinching from their dirt and smell, would nevertheless drive them to good restaurants where Bobby bought everyone dinner. But when Bobby, Lem, and Duff flew back to New York, Rebecca Fraser was there waiting, and Duff was given her walking papers.

But Lem was hurt most of all. He had trailed Bobby into the drug world and never really found his way out. He spent increasing amounts of his time alone in the elegant apartment whose Americana had once seemed the proper décor for the making of a President, but now seemed irrelevant and merely antique. Unshaven and wearing only a bathrobe, Lem was always waiting for Bobby. He had begun as mentor and had wound up as an abject follower. The drama he had tried to create by sheer force of will—turning Bobby into Jack and thus creating the resurrection which would bring the presidency back to his beloved Kennedys—simply would not happen. At times it seemed almost to have been a drug delusion unfounded in any realistic appraisal of the people involved or the situation in which they existed. "I was right that Bobby is like Jack," Lem said sadly to a friend, trying to salvage some credibility for his dream. "What I didn't see was how much the world has changed. Jack was lucky: he didn't have a lot of Kennedys getting there before him. Everywhere a boy like Bobby looks, there are footprints, all of them deeper than his own."

7.

$\mathcal{T}$HE JOHN F. KENNEDY LIBRARY
was opened on October 21, 1979, one of those crisp fall days which brings
football to the minds of most New Englanders, but which the Kennedys think
of as political weather. When architect I. M. Pei's sweeping, heroic structure
of concrete and glass was unveiled, it was truly Kennedyesque. Facing the
ocean, like the homes Jack had loved, the building had something almost
nautical about it, something yearning to be seaborne.

Like most other things involving the family, the JFK Library had been
born in controversy. Not long before his death Jack had decided that the
papers and records of his administration should reside at a site he and Lem
had picked out near the Harvard Business School. But after the assassination
Jackie decided that the monument should be "more than just another Presidential Library," as she put it to Harvard President Nathan Pusey. And so
it had been moved well away from Cambridge to a spit of land at Columbia
Point, a place more lonely and windward, more epic in scope.

The names of the people who gathered for the dedication ceremonies read
something like a *Who's Who* of Democratic politics—survivors of Jack's
Camelot and Robert's Impossible Dream, those political never-never worlds
which had come to seem almost quaint in the big chill that had followed the
overheated 1960s. The special tang in the air this morning came from the
fact that Teddy, inheritor of the Legacy created in this bygone era, was
finally about to announce his candidacy after so many years of what had
amounted to internal exile, and that the man he would challenge, President
Jimmy Carter, had come to the ceremonies too, passing through the phalanx
of Kennedy old guardsmen and shaking hands with everyone except Jackie,
who looked stricken when he kissed her on the cheek.

428

The Kennedys attending the opening were much changed in the almost twenty years since Jack had won the presidency, all of them older and in some sense sadder. Of the generation that had taken the world by storm in the 1930s, an elegant tribe unto itself, only Teddy and his sisters Eunice, Pat, and Jean were left. The next generation had replaced them. But these grandchildren had grown up in the decade since the RFK assassination, and there was no one at the center of the group portrait, as Joseph Kennedy had always been when their mothers and fathers were first being photographed; no one to give them that almost electrical quality of possibility their elders had possessed at the same age.

Caroline Kennedy stood up first. She was pretty and soft, someone who could have been an American sweetheart if she had been more available in the years of her growing up, but someone who now seemed a little like a foreigner, a visitor to the Kennedy myth. Caroline introduced her brother John, grown up from the orphaned three-year-old in a blue coat saluting his dead father into a handsome young man, but with the same exotic quality as his sister. Those close to the family knew that while Caroline remembered their father—she had continued collecting stamps and other memorabilia during the years of the Onassis marriage—John did not. His college years at Brown had involved a tentative search for his father rather than a defense of him. Taking a seminar on Vietnam, he had researched the JFK role as dispassionately as the other students and gotten his mother to ask her friend Peter Davis to bring his documentary film *Hearts and Minds* into class. After a trip to South Africa, in one of his infrequent meetings with his cousins John had said, "I don't plan to say or write anything until I know which way I want my life to go. But I think whatever I do will probably involve working with blacks." Bobby Junior had heard him out and then smiled narrowly and said, "My father was more concerned with blacks than yours was."

With the sun dodging in and out of the clouds and the wind ripping at the sails of his father's boat *Victura*, soon to be on permanent display inside the library, John F. Kennedy, Jr., read Stephen Spender's poem "I Think Continually of Those Who Were Truly Great." Then Joseph P. Kennedy II, as Joe now called himself, stood up to give a speech he had titled "The Unfinished Business of Robert Kennedy."

Like his brothers and sisters and others of his generation, Joe had been upset by the fact that the film about Jack to be shown at the ceremonies was forty-five minutes long, while the one about his father was only fifteen minutes. When he learned that those in charge of the dedication needed to shorten the program by ten minutes and had decided to trim five minutes from each of the films, Joe had blown up and said he wouldn't take part, relenting only after Teddy pleaded with him. But the speech Joe had prepared was not in synch with the controlled nostalgia and the politics of implication which up to that point had seemed the order of the day. He stood for a moment, wind ruffling his hair, and then began sternly, "As I stand here and think about my father and what his life was all about..." pausing to scowl at the Carter party for a beat before launching into a denunciation of the power of Big Coal, Big Oil, and Big Money. It was a son's version of a Robert Kennedy speech, and at the climax Joe was shouting about the demise of moral courage and jabbing a finger directly at the President. Teddy grimaced and cradled his head in his hands, but the grandchildren leaped to their feet as one, shouting and applauding so loudly that one observer noted later on, "It's Robert, not Jack, who is the once and future Kennedy in this family."

But for the time being it was Teddy who was finally trying to pull the sword from the stone. The confrontation with Carter had become inevitable a few months earlier, when the President tried to raise his plummeting public-approval ratings with an ill-fated speech about the "crisis of confidence" in America which only accelerated the erosion of his support. News surveys taken after the speech seemed to show that Carter could not be reelected. They also showed that Democrats favored Teddy over him by a margin of fifty-three to sixteen. All summer Kennedy had been wooed by Democratic candidates terrified of the bloodbath to come if Carter headed the ticket in 1980. Former Iowa Democratic chairman Tom Whitney, in whose state the first caucus was scheduled, said, "The heart of the Democratic Party in Iowa belongs to Ted Kennedy. It is his for the asking."

Or so it seemed. But euphoria at the idea of a Kennedy revival ignored the persistence of the Chappaquiddick issue. More than a decade had passed, but because it had never been adequately explained, the accident was still a strong factor for voters to deal with. An allied problem was Ted's marriage. Joan had been puffy, gross, old-looking in her appearances during the 1976 senatorial campaign. It had been obvious that she was drinking heavily, and the following year things had come to a head when she left Washington to live alone in an apartment in Boston, seeing a psychiatrist three times a week and attending Leslie Graduate School of Music. "I tried to talk about it," she said in a 1978 tell-all article about her alcoholism for *McCall's*, "but I was embarrassed by it and Ted was embarrassed by it. Everybody was embarrassed by it, but nobody would really talk about it."

Another argument against Ted's candidacy involved splitting the party. In 1968 he had been foremost among those arguing against Bobby's challenging LBJ because he was an incumbent, although the war in Vietnam and the chaos in America's ghettoes had been persuasive moral and political reasons for running. In 1979 there were no such compelling reasons, which opened the candidacy to charges of opportunism and disloyalty; but he decided to run anyhow.

If these negative factors were weighed, it was only, many of those involved in the campaign from the outset thought later, on a loaded scale. When

Teddy announced his candidacy on November 6, two weeks after the JFK Library dedication, the reason for doing so had less to do with objective political factors than with his sense that he had simply waited long enough, waited all the long years after he could have had it in 1968, waited through a decade of penance for Chappaquiddick, waited while the Legacy seemed always to be slipping further away.

It was almost as if he felt that the decision finally to do it—the decision so long discussed and delayed—would in and of itself take care of all the loose ends. But there was an augury of troubles to come in the CBS interview conducted by Roger Mudd a few days before the announcement. An old friend of the Kennedys, Mudd began with amiable banter and then suddenly lunged toward Teddy's weaknesses—Chappaquiddick, Joan, splitting the party. As the candidate became progressively incoherent, Mudd asked how his presidency would differ from Carter's. The answer seemed to summon up all the residual doubts about Teddy in their starkest form: "Well, it's, um, you know you have to come to grips with the different issues that, ah, we're facing—I mean we can, we have to deal with each of the various questions that we're talking about whether it's a question of the economy, whether it's in the area of energy ..."

Yet at first the assumption was that merely being available would be sufficient. In the exuberance with which the campaign began, despite the Mudd setback, Tom Southwick, Kennedy's twenty-seven-year-old press director, told reporters he had researched the question and discovered that he would be the youngest White House press secretary ever appointed. And Stephen Smith, the campaign director, spent a good deal of time in the first weeks wondering how and when to approach Carter to ask him to bow out.

The decision was made to emphasize the image instead of issues. "Leadership" became the buzz word of the first stages of the campaign, as Doris Kearns Goodwin and James MacGregor Burns, both scholars who had done academic work on leadership, traveled with Kennedy and helped with his speeches. The film documentarian Charles Guggenheim, who had done *cinéma vérité* studies of Jack and Bobby shouldering the burden of power, was retained by Smith to do the same for Teddy. Those who had looked forward to the campaign as an opportunity to pick up where RFK had left off and deal with "fundamental issues" were disappointed by the moderate tone with which it began.* They feared that by deciding to stress "leadership" Teddy had created a coin whose opposite side was "character." And

*Ronnie Eldridge, who had been an RFK supporter in New York, was disturbed early in the campaign when Peter Edelman, Teddy's issues director, came to her for a talk about strategy. The name of former Representative Bella Abzug came up and Edelman's reaction left no doubt that he (and the entire Kennedy campaign) considered such a figure too liberal and too controversial. "He said to me, 'Bella! You're kidding! Bella Abzug is the last person we want supporting us!' "

indeed, even if the President hadn't been the most skillful or decisive leader, Carter ads would suggest subliminally, at least no young woman had died in his car, and so far as was known his lust had been confined to his heart.

The real problem of the first days of the campaign remained Teddy himself, curiously disembodied from his ambition, lacking what professional politicians call "fire in the belly." Acknowledged as one of the best stump speakers in national politics, he was unable to raise passions during his first weeks on the road; his swelling voice filled rooms but not the hearts and minds of his audiences. At times he seemed disoriented, off the track, particularly in comparison to the sureness of his brothers, a competence magnified by nostalgia. T. R. Reid of the *Washington Post*, who followed Ted closely, saw a summary of what was wrong in an early swing through California. "The tv reporter asked him what he could do that Carter couldn't or hadn't. This was exactly the kind of question he had to hit out of the park to succeed. And Teddy did a great job of responding by listing sharply and eloquently how Carter didn't understand Congress and was unable to work with it; how he didn't understand the presidency and what it means to the American people; et cetera, et cetera. Suddenly the producer comes in yelling 'cut' and saying that the technicians had screwed up the tape machine. So they take it from the top again. The reporter asks exactly the same question except that this time Teddy gives a totally rambling, incoherent answer it was almost impossible to make any sense out of."

After watching a similar performance back in Boston, the *Globe*'s Ellen Goodman wrote, "I feel embarrassed. I want to change the channel. His voice is strained, his timing is off, his eyes are glazed . . . Everything is wrong. One sentence keeps recurring in my brain: the guy doesn't want it."

By the time of the Iowa caucuses, Teddy had been backed into a corner, not only by his perplexingly uneven performance in the first weeks, but also by the international developments that function as wild cards in every campaign. Three days after his formal announcement, Iranian revolutionaries had taken Americans hostage at the embassy in Teheran. Up to now Teddy had always been lucky: Chappaquiddick had been nudged out of the lead news by the first moon walk; his contretemps with Roger Mudd had been broadcast the same night *Jaws* was shown for the first time on network television. But now, when he wanted to make headlines, he was relegated to the midsection of the evening news; he did not get a lead story until early December, when he made what was widely regarded as a gaffe by saying the deposed Shah of Iran should not have been allowed into the United States for medical treatment. And then, on December 28, the Soviets rolled into Afghanistan, thus making the Carter Administration into a crisis presidency after all, and allowing Carter himself to sidestep the proposed debate with Teddy by stating that he had to remain at the helm in Washington. ("Fuck the fat rich kid,'' a chief aide said.) So while Iowa was originally seen as a short step on a long journey, a caucus state whose outcome would be decided by forty thousand people, it suddenly took on a far larger significance.

When the campaign was still being blueprinted, control of Iowa had been given to Joe. He had done good work in organizing the state, speaking in all the small towns, returning with perceptive and well-digested data on the leaders and situations he'd encountered. As Chuck McDermott, his oldest friend, observed: "Somewhere along the line Joe had acquired the ability to move through a crowd of people and leave a wake of excitement without taking any longer with the individuals than was absolutely necessary. It was that sense of oneself as a commodity, that combination of charisma and economy which natural politicians have."

Yet as Teddy's difficulties mounted and Iowa became more important, Joe's position as director was undermined by the young professionals like organizer Carl Wagner, who had worked for McGovern and Udall and now anchored the Kennedy campaign staff in Washington. McDermott was with Joe driving to a speaking engagement in Iowa when they heard the news that Carter had withdrawn from the debate with Teddy and a local response by Paul Tully, one of Wagner's allies. Telling McDermott that the campaign was being threatened by people who didn't want "an old-style Kennedy campaign in which the family has control," Joe stopped the car and went to a pay phone. He didn't want to bother Teddy with the problem, but he did call Wagner, angrily reminding him that he was supposed to be the sole Kennedy spokesman in Iowa, and then Steve Smith, who was still upset over the library speech and stiff-armed him. Back in the car Joe said angrily to McDermott, "If my father were alive he would have called up Tully and said, 'Look, this is family business and the family does the talking here.' "

A week or so before the caucuses, the situation became grim. The issue arose as to who would give the election night statement—almost certain to be a concession of defeat—to the press. Joe confronted Wagner, with whom he had already nearly come to blows. "Listen, you and your guys have been running the show the last few weeks, so you do it." Wagner insisted that Joe should be the one. "No way, Carl," he replied. "You've done such a hot job handling this thing so you make the statement. You obviously don't need Kennedys to do the talking."

Two days before the caucuses, Joe was working out in a Des Moines gym with McDermott when he was paged over the intercom. He went to the phone and found that it was Teddy calling from the campaign plane. McDermott listened to their cryptic jokes. Then he saw Joe's face take on a set expression. "Okay, listen, pal, I'll do it for you. But those guys have really been jerking me and the rest of the family around." On the night of the defeat, Joe went to the Savoy Hotel and bit the bullet, the last time he would help his uncle out this way.

The loss in Iowa was a crushing blow, not only because it was unexpected or even because it dispelled the notion that Teddy and his people had held for better than ten years—that he could have the nomination for the asking—but also because it caused an identity crisis with profound implications for what was to come. Teddy might propound the tortured metaphor that the nomination was a fifteen-inning game and they had only completed the first round, but he knew he was in deep trouble. He had been assuming all along that he would just glide, never having to adopt a really clear political persona. But now there was a pressure to choose. Steve Smith advised developing the course Teddy had already implicitly selected—taking a liberal line in domestic affairs but acknowledging the conservative trends in the country through a hard-line foreign policy. Bob Shrum, another of those Joe sneeringly referred to as "technicians," said they should embrace the Bobby legacy. That argument won, and on January 25, Teddy appeared at Georgetown University and gave one of the most impressive speeches of the campaign, a programmatic defense of liberalism in an era when it had become unfashionable. No friend of Kennedy politics, the columnist William Safire nonetheless wrote admiringly that it was a pleasure "to see a chastened man shake his head clear, get up off the floor and—by dint of intellectual and emotional effort of a principled speech—give his presidential campaign life and give his political life meaning." In the grim days ahead, as he lost one primary after another, Teddy would cling to the vision he had outlined at Georgetown more and more firmly, almost as if he realized he had ventured out on his own and been defeated, and had come back to shelter under the family identity. To those who admonished him that he was being too liberal he replied, "Regardless of what happens this year, it is my heritage and my family's heritage, and ought to be the Party's heritage."

Part of the heritage, however, was not only what Jack and especially Bobby had said, but what had happened to them. While his brothers had been able to touch and mingle, letting crowds experience the Kennedy charisma firsthand, Teddy could not. He was insulated from the voters by his Kennedyness just as he was insulated from himself. He would go into a place like Newark, which already had the atmosphere of a city under siege, in a bulletproof limousine trailed by a station wagon full of Secret Service men with Uzi machine guns. Security was provided by five concentric rings of sharpshooters and antisniper teams. He had more security than the President: three shifts of Secret Service men with fifty-four on each shift, one hundred sixty-two in all.

In a sense the campaign had begun as a "death watch," in the term of the working press. Would the last Kennedy be killed too? That was the unspoken question which loomed over all others. Over the years the deaths in the family had ceased being the random tragedies of an unlucky group of people and become instead symbols of the Kennedys' right to govern. There was almost the feeling that Teddy had to become an assassin's target in order to join his brothers' demanding ghosts. There were always reporters around in addition to those of the regular "pool," just in case the unthinkable happened. "Teddy was somehow judged adversely by the press as time went by and he didn't get shot," one journalist said later on. It almost seemed to be another indication that he didn't live up to the family ideal, that he was a failure.

There had been a guarded playfulness in the media's treatment of Teddy when the press first climbed aboard the leased Kennedy campaign jet. In an early swing through Iowa, reporters lined up to greet him when he came down from his hotel room for breakfast by playing "Hail to the Chief" on kazoos. But there was also concern among the journalists that they might be victimized by Kennedy charm in the same way their predecessors had been, and a firm commitment to keep this aspect of the family history from repeating itself. In part, Teddy took care of the problem by his own attitude. (*Time*'s Walter Isaacson said, "He ate alone, spent a lot of time alone, wasn't easy to approach. When he did attempt to be gregarious there was a sort of glaze over his eyes that made the heartiness hollow and prevented real intimacy.") But reporters also armed themselves with cynicism. One of the pieces of journalism they read widely and talked about constantly was a *Washington Monthly* article called "Kennedy's Women Problem; Women's Kennedy Problem," a feminist attack based on Teddy's rumored liaisons with socialite Amanda Burden, skier Suzy Chaffee, Canadian Premier Trudeau's wife, Margaret, and others which led the author to conclude that there was a pattern in his life suggesting "a severe case of arrested development, a kind of narcissistic intemperance, a large babyish ego that must be constantly fed." During a swing through Southern California the press heard, via Radio Shack scanners they had bought to monitor Secret Service communications, that Teddy was going to visit his old friend former Senator John Tunney; they all hurried to get there too, hoping to glimpse the women they assumed would be brought in. During the same trip, when Teddy spoke a few words of almost comically disfigured Spanish in an appearance before a Mexican-American political association, one journalist whispered loudly to his smiling colleagues, "Well, what do you expect? It *was* the course he cheated on at Harvard, after all."

By the midpoint of the campaign, the press had adopted a raucously irreverent tone that colored their perception of Teddy's candidacy. Reporters had noted, for instance, that Teddy and Joan could hardly stand each other. There was much speculation on the campaign plane about whether and when they would ever hug or kiss. When Teddy finally did find himself in a situation where it was necessary to give her a brief peck on the cheek, the moment was captured by one of the television cameramen. The press ran it over and over in slow motion on a monitor on the campaign plane, someone providing a sardonic voice-over commentary in the manner of a NASA announcer. ''There he is. He's moving in now. He's putting an arm around her. Here it is, ladies and gentlemen. It's coming. A kiss! We have a kiss. A kiss is confirmed . . .''

They pounced on slips of the tongue like ''fam farmily'' in Iowa and ''I'm an uphill struggle'' later on. They did little broadcasts by ''hot wiring'' the campaign plane intercom. Someone would hum the theme from ''The Twilight Zone'' and then Tom Oliphant would come on in his Rod Serling voice: ''And here we have Cassie Mackin, prolific and well-paid television reporter, already a star and rising ever higher in her profession until . . . she entered *The Bozo Zone.* Then her career was suddenly cut short, and she found herself out of a job . . .'' Rick Burke, Teddy's administrative assistant, would come running from the front of the plane and say that the Senator was furious. The press ignored him. They called Teddy the Fat Rich Kid (after the Carter aide's remark), usually abbreviating it to FRK. They'd say to Burke: ''Where's the FRK taking us today, Ricky?''

FRK—nobody remarked on it but these were Bobby's initials turned inside out, just as Teddy's campaign was a Kennedy campaign upside down.

As Teddy was maimed politically day by day, so was the family. From the time Joe was moved out of control in Iowa by the Washington ''technicians,'' it was never the joyous joint effort that Kennedy campaigns were supposed to be. Because Teddy was her ''special brother,'' closest in age and outlook, Jean Smith had a weight in this campaign that she'd never had before; but it was mainly as an emotionally stabilizing force rather than as a political adviser. Pat Lawford's campaign appearances largely involved appearing with the candidate when Joan wasn't with him, thus implying to audiences that he was being chaperoned by a responsible female adult. Eunice had an annoying ''kid brother'' attitude, and Peter Edelman later recalled the time she pressed her pro-life, anti-ERA views once too often and Teddy snapped at her, ''Eunice, you know I've voted a certain way for ten years and I'm not about to change now.''

Sarge, too, was on the periphery, never certain where he stood. (''Do you Bobby guys still hate him?'' one of his aides had asked Edelman. ''He seems to think you do.'') But the most obvious indication that the family machine of old had become obsolete was the demotion of Steve Smith himself. By the end of the Iowa debacle, Carl Wagner and others were openly discussing Smith's inadequacies—how in the twelve years since his last national campaign things had changed, particularly the use of media and polling, and how his ignorance of these developments was hurting Teddy. And so Smith stood back, allowing Teddy's Washington staff to take over direction of the campaign. He developed ingenious twists on campaign contribution limits—getting Andy Warhol, Jamie Wyeth, and other artists to donate paintings that were then auctioned off—but he ceased to be the mysterious *éminence grise* who had always been associated with Kennedy invincibility.

The grandchildren too were affected. They had entered the campaign with enthusiasm, many of them attending an early meeting at Hickory Hill at which they were briefed by Ethel, Pat, Jean, and members of Teddy's staff. (When confronted with questions about Chappaquiddick or some other aspect of the "character" problem, they were to reply: "The Senator has already answered that in his own way. I'm here to speak about him as a father and uncle.") And at first there was a party atmosphere to their efforts —immediate celebrity status, Secret Service men, frenzied activity. But as things began to go bad, they felt it too. This was particularly true of Teddy's own children, most sheltered and vulnerable of all the cousins. Nineteen-year-old Kara went to a Philadelphia church expecting a warm welcome only to listen as her father was attacked violently by a priest who ended his diatribe with: "He does not deserve to be President." After trying vainly to get in a word of defense, Kara burst into tears and ran from the church. A more typical example of what she would face came on a New York street corner when a man to whom she handed a leaflet came close and said confidentially, "You know your father killed a young woman about your age, don't you?"

The older boys especially had counted on the campaign to banish the ambiguity that had ruled their lives and to take them back home to the presidency. Chris, who had battled back and was eager to prove himself in action, tried to get on board from the moment of Teddy's announcement. He had put off his already long-delayed plan to enter law school so that he would be available for a role in the campaign. He wrote, called, and sent messages to Teddy and Steve Smith, but nothing happened. "It was the old Kennedy runaround. I couldn't figure out what the reason was at first, but then I remembered how I had been visiting David in the hospital during his most recent bout of endocarditis and Teddy had breezed in and, on the way out, said, 'By the way, I hope none of you guys know Barry Landau, that guy who's connecting Hamilton Jordan to cocaine at Studio 54.' As a matter of fact, I did know him. He was a friend of Lorna Luft, Judy Garland's daughter, whom I'd grown up with. Stevie Smith and I and some of the other cousins knew him. After Teddy made this comment, Steve Smith called me down to the campaign headquarters in Washington. He said, 'Listen, Chris, this Landau thing could really blow up and I think that until we find out whether a special prosecutor is going to be appointed we should hold off involving you in the campaign.' I told him that if this was what he was worried about, then he better bring about three quarters of the family in and talk to them too."

Chris had gone to campaign in Massachusetts and New Hampshire on his own initiative in the fall of 1979, demonstrating political savvy as well as star appeal. Recognizing that he was an asset after all, Smith sent him to Iowa. He did well there, even as the operation was falling apart. Yet rather than achieving the oneness that he imagined had characterized Kennedy campaigns of the past, he experienced fierce jockeying from his cousins. He always felt that they were more interested in how well they were performing against each other than in the ultimate goal; always looking over their shoulders; always looking to unhorse each other. The incident, admittedly a small one, that exemplified this problem came early in the spring at a pre-wedding party for his cousin Courtney, who was marrying ABC-TV producer Jeff Ruhe. Groggy from several sleepless days on the campaign trail, Chris showed up for the obligatory toasting, itself a moment of subtle competition. Desperate for something to say, he asked Bobby, who had just given his sister a particularly witty toast, for something he could use when his turn came. Bobby took Chris aside and pointed out that all the waiters employed by the catering service looked vaguely Middle Eastern. He gave him the theme of a toast and told him to conclude by saying: "These waiters are Shiite Muslims and anybody who doesn't give a contribution to the Kennedy campaign is going to be held hostage in this room." Chris gave the toast. When he finished, there was dead silence: the hostage situation was just then being acknowledged as the issue that was helping to kill Teddy's campaign. When the silence was broken, Chris noted it was Bobby who led the jeers.

For Chris, the campaign ended during the holidays in Aspen, when he was busted trying to fill a phony prescription for Darvon, which he was taking as part of his continuing problem with heroin. Smith told him he could go back on the campaign trail after the incident cooled off, but it never happened.

Bobby, meanwhile, had been given control of Alabama. The alleged reason was that he had links there with conservatives around Wallace and liberals around Frank Johnson. Yet since it was next door to Carter's Georgia stronghold and Kennedy strategists had projected a 15 percent showing as a victory, he saw that the post was clearly a means of getting him out of the way.

Nonetheless Alabama was a typically frenzied experience. Bobby adopted the coloration of a good ole boy, wearing his pants low on his hips, sporting dust-covered snakeskin boots, and occasionally spitting his Skoal into an empty Coke bottle. The spring of 1980 became a condensed southern version of the double life he had been leading for the past several years. On the one hand there were evangelical appearances at black churches and other meetings, as he played the Kennedy presence in the state. (At one of them he used the line "Black people are worse off now than they've ever been in the history of this country." A historian traveling with his entourage objected, saying that it would be accurate if he said they were worse off than they'd been in a decade. "You're right," Bobby replied blithely, "but it always gets applause that way, so I think I'll leave it in.'') On the other, there were wild personal scenes. Bobby had taken up with Harris McGough, a Cadillac salesman and Vietnam veteran who claimed to have killed twenty-four Viet Cong single-handedly and kept an arsenal that included bows with razor-tipped arrows, pens that fired bullets, and submachine guns. McGough's house in Montgomery became the appropriate setting for Bobby's excesses. Bragging that he'd had a woman every night for two years, he hunted women obsessively between speeches, even though he was technically still attached to Rebecca Fraser. He and McGough and their friends would let off steam by driving a pair of cars a hundred miles an hour on the highway at night with headlights off, passing a joint of marijuana back and forth from one car to the other.

Bobby was stuck in the heroic persona he had created as a way of surviving the chaos of his teenage years—always having to outdo himself, always having to go one step further than everyone else to validate his status as the Kennedy who would someday ''make it.'' Unlike his brother Joe, he was unwilling and unable to regard politics as a patient process of small steps. Under Lem's guidance, he had in effect been an unannounced candidate for the presidency since he was sixteen, an ambition he held to even as his life style was becoming increasingly wild and unrestrained. At one point in Teddy's campaign, Bobby came to New York for a strategy session and brought with him one of the ''aides'' he had acquired in Alabama. They ran into Bobby's old friend Andy Karsch, who was now working as a media consultant for the campaign. The aide told Karsch he was looking for an appropriate district in which Bobby could run for Congress and had almost settled on one on Staten Island. Karsch, like most of Bobby's friends, knew of the drug problem and thought of him as being ''on his eighth life.'' He was furious. ''It's getting stupid, this manifest destiny plan,'' he said. ''Teddy's showing you that it's all over, but none of you seems to be getting it. You guys play politics the way little girls play house.''

Only David was free from the ambition and delusion. After his Harlem bust, the Committee to Keep David Out of the Picture, which had a six-month temporary guardianship, had given him the choice of going back to McLean's or enrolling in a drug rehabilitation program in Sacramento run by a therapist named Don Juhl. ''Naturally,'' David says, ''I chose the latter. Juhl told me that there were three rules. I had to jog every day. I wasn't allowed to say 'Fuck off and die' any more. And no drugs. If I broke any of these rules it would cost me another month, and every month I was there cost me $20,000 of my own money.''

Nobody in the family came to see him. He lived in a duplex with Juhl and his wife, undergoing what he bitterly called ''therapy by humiliation,'' a Synanon-like use of personal attack and innuendo to elicit ''gut-level response'' and behavioral change. (''What's the matter, David?'' Juhl would say when he happened to show up in a long-sleeved shirt on a warm day. ''Are you afraid to roll up your sleeves and show us your tracks?'') David became increasingly bitter about his family. Always before he had blamed himself; now he began to blame them. ''I feel they should have done something earlier. My mother, although in a sense she wasn't really competent. But even more Teddy, Steve Smith, and the rest of the group who were always figuring out ways to keep Joe, Bobby, and Chris from having to pay the piper, but who just let me go. When they finally did do something, it seemed like it was more to keep me from o.d.'ing in the street and causing a problem for Teddy's campaign, than anything else.''

On April 15, 1980, the guardianship over David ended and he began, in his words, to concentrate ''on having a mental breakdown.'' He locked himself in his Sacramento room with a black-and-white tv avidly watching Teddy's campaign come unraveled just as he had once watched his father being killed. He rarely ate, living for days on nothing more than a couple of pasteurized cheese slices and a bottle of Pepsi. He began to hallucinate. ''I thought I was in the Mafia. I thought I was the Supreme Ultimate Shibumi Assassin. I thought I was Lee Harvey Oswald. I thought I killed my father. Then I thought my father was trying to kill me, trying to drown me in the surf of Malibu.'' When his girlfriend Nancy Narleski visited him, he told her that he felt Teddy had been behind the murder of Al Lowenstein and would kill others if not stopped.

During David's coherent moments he and Narleski staged mock awards ceremonies at which they gave the I'll-never-take-drugs-again award to various members of the Kennedy family who had made that pledge. But there were times when David seemed so sick that Narleski actually feared he would die. On one such occasion she became frightened enough to call Barbara Kirby, one of his childhood friends at Hyannis, who in turn called Joe and told him that she'd heard David was in serious trouble. Joe called Narleski and yelled, ''Don't you call the Kirbys! Everything is under control. There's a lot of things you don't understand. This is the Big Leagues, so butt out. Just forget that David Kennedy exists!'' She asked him if he was threatening her. He answered, ''You can take what I've said any way you want to,'' and slammed the phone down.

David remained in exile. Desperate for some contact with the past, he called his one-time girlfriend Pam Kelley and asked her to come to California to be with him. She agreed to fly out. But then, at the end of the conversation, he said, ''And leave your wheelchair there,'' and she realized how much trouble he was in. ''I can't leave my wheelchair here, David,'' she replied. ''It's part of me and I'm part of it.''

David bummed around Sacramento, staying off drugs only by drinking heavily. The family continued to be an almost nefarious presence on the edges of his life. Applying for a construction job, he was asked by the owner if he was willing to "go all out and bust your butt." He said he wasn't. He got the job anyhow because Frank Gifford, whose daughter Vicki was engaged to David's brother Michael, found out about the conversation, called the man, and asked him to hire David. One day he was on the bank of the Sacramento River, drinking wine with his friends and looking at a copy of *High Times* magazine. There was a picture of his Aunt Rosemary as part of a story on lobotomies. "She had a new pair of white shoes on and she was smiling. The thought crossed my mind that if my grandfather was alive the same thing could have happened to me that happened to her. She was an embarrassment; I am an embarrassment. She was a hindrance; I am a hindrance. As I looked at this picture, I began to hate my grandfather and all of them for having done the thing they had done to her and for doing the thing they were doing to me."

After he got into the news by having his license revoked for drunken driving, the locals discovered who David was. A writer from the *Sacramento Bee* came to do a profile for the paper's "People" section. It concluded: "For the most part Kennedy sits there—nervous, apprehensive, with a perplexed look on his face—and patiently explains over and over again, 'I'm pretty much of a regular guy. My life is pretty much like anyone else's— except that I have a famous last name'... Asked what his mother would like him to be, an amused smile slowly grows on his face and he blithely replies, 'President.' "

As Teddy's ordeal continued, he had begun to have little talks about his future with those members of the press who were not too cynical to listen. The question had long since ceased to be whether or not he would win the nomination; he knew that was impossible now. It was a question about the way to deal with losing. Tom Oliphant remembers, "He kept saying that the presidency was probably not in the cards because of various political and personal reasons, but that didn't mean he couldn't have a satisfying career. He mentioned becoming a maverick senator like George Norris. He was nostalgic, recalling incidents from the family's early days and talking particularly about his father and what an extraordinary man he'd been, and said, 'If nothing else, I can always leave public life and concentrate on writing a book about him.' " He seemed to sense how different his fate would be from his brothers'. They would never age or wrinkle; the passage of years would only make them younger and more vital, their acts more heroic. He, on the other hand, had drawn the more ambiguous lot of the survivor and would have to contend with a normal life span.

The night before the New York primary there was a family conference at the New York Hilton. Joe was there; Bobby had come up from Alabama; Eunice and Jean were there. It was all that was left of the vaunted Kennedy machine. Teddy asked them what he should do. Bobby said it was a question not of when but of how to pull out and find a way to support Carter. Joe said, "The hell with that. Why support Carter? We should keep plugging." After Eunice and Jean weighed in with their advice, Teddy smiled wryly and said, "So. What's the good news?" This broke everyone up.

In the last weeks, Teddy was haggard and pale. Yet a certain calm had settled on him, almost as if he were engaged in some ritual purgation. He doggedly kept at it, taking the punishment and coming back for more. But he could not even take solace in his New York and Connecticut victories, because exit polls showed these were anti-Carter votes and that four out of ten Democrats who supported him in these primaries would not vote for him in the general election if he were nominated. The only successful ads featured attacks on Carter by Carroll O'Connor, tv's Archie Bunker, rather than Teddy himself: his very image had become anathema. By the end he had lost twenty-four of thirty-four primaries, twenty of twenty-five caucuses. Author Garry Wills was correct in calling it "the end of the entire Kennedy time in our national life."

Teddy finally limped into the convention, having endured if not conquered. There he smashed Carter in a speech that became his only triumph, a moment he would preserve on a long-playing record and send out as a keepsake to his remaining supporters after Ronald Reagan's victory in November. Asked what he'd learned after his long travail, Teddy paused a moment and then said, "Well, I learned to lose and for a Kennedy that's hard."

One of those most depressed by the failure of Teddy's campaign was Lem. He had always shared Jack's view of Teddy as the kid brother. At the beginning he had been upset by Teddy's decision to run for President because he knew it would start all the stories about Jack and his women and Bobby and Marilyn Monroe once again. ("My God, why does he have to do it?" Lem groused. "He's just dragging the family through the mud. I don't know about everybody else, but I'm just going to sit this one out.") At the end he had been upset because it had seemed, in his phrase, such a "half-assed effort," one that raised questions about the family's political vitality.

A whole new generation had discovered Lem—Caroline, who was moving through New York's artistic community with various boyfriends; Timothy Shriver, whose godfather Lem had become when Jack was killed; and the middle kids of the RFK family—Courtney, Kerry, and Michael. As Bobby veered more and more onto his own, Lem had encouraged this new wave of Kennedys to use his New York apartment as a gathering spot. He saw it as "rallying the troops from Teddy's defeat." They saw it as their turn to experience the man who had become almost legendary in Kennedy annals.

One of Lem's attractions was that he was a central switchboard, the person who called around to key people in the family every day, getting travel plans and gossip. He was also a fountainhead of information. As Michael said, "He always knew what was proper—everything from what you should get a person as a present on a particular occasion to how to handle yourself in various social situations—the things parents generally teach but ours hadn't."

This new group lacked the emotional charge of Bobby, Joe, Chris Lawford, and David. (Christopher Kennedy, one of the "little kids" in the RFK family, says, "Our lives have not been as extreme. We have not had the adversity or the excitement or some of the problems the older ones have had.") But they had youth and promise. And Lem could have the roaring good times with them that it was no longer possible to have with Bobby and his friends, who were on the edge of their thirties and now trying to mix drugs and careers. Lem would take these twenty-year-olds out drinking at Trader Vic's at the Plaza, where he would have eight or nine Scorpions, his favorite drink. He would regale them with Kennedy stories and they would accompany him back to his apartment and stay there until three or four in the morning looking through scrapbooks and photograph albums. Yet it was different for them. While they were intrigued with Lem, they didn't need him, as Bobby and Chris had. They had gotten parental attention, however haphazard it had been. They had been young enough when Robert Kennedy was shot to have been shielded from the full metaphysical blast of his death. They didn't have the huge needs of their older brothers; they also had a different perspective on Lem, regarding him as a sort of curio. "He was fun to be with," Timmy Shriver says. "But in a way he was sad. Sad because of what had happened to my uncles. We could see that tragedy through the effects on his life. Sad also because he had believed he could make it happen again but couldn't."

He had grown out of touch with his old friends and even with his own family, letting go of the contacts which had once given at least a semblance of independence to his life. Now he was completely dependent on the Kennedys. He telephoned Eunice every day. "We're the only ones left of that early era," he would say, and try to egg her on to join him in lengthy reminiscences about Joe Junior, Kick, and Jack. He became abnormally sensitive to imagined slights. On Sarge and Eunice Shriver's twenty-fifth anniversary, he was seated on Eunice's left instead of her right, which he insisted was the place of honor. He was deeply hurt by this affront and after dinner went around the party drunkenly asking, "Why wasn't I seated on the right?" Another evening Caroline called in a hurry and asked for someone else at his place without identifying herself. Finding out it was she, he got back on the phone and said angrily, "What is this? You call my house and when I answer you can't even take the time to say hello to me." She tried to argue him out of his irritation but he finally hung up on her.

But Lem's greatest anxiety came from Bobby. It was as if his hopes and ambitions for his special protégé had gotten caught up in a prolonged dry labor, as all the charisma and promise of the early years stalled without achieving a payoff. Bobby was about to finish law school but no closer to the political career they had dreamed of than when Lem more or less adopted him twelve years earlier. He and Bobby had terrible fights, like lovers' quarrels, which ended in sulks that lasted for weeks and were followed by melodramatic reconciliations. In between those times, Lem would forlornly call Duff Pacifico, whom he now thought of as the best girlfriend Bobby had ever had, the one who came closest to keeping him focused. "We'd talk for a long time," Duff says. "He'd be close to tears. He'd ask if I thought Bobby loved him. If he was Bobby's best friend."

He was short of breath and had bouts of vertigo, his heart strained by a decade of drugs and liquor and by trying to keep up with people forty years younger than he. He wheezed; he used an asthma inhaler. Before, his talk of death had been something of an in-joke with Bobby, Chris Lawford, and their friends. (In the river trips which had followed the Apurímac, Lem had insisted on bringing a body bag along so that they would have a way of handling his corpse if he died.) Now it took on a more serious, morbid aspect. He went to Pittsburgh with Bobby's old friend Timmy Haydock, whom he had helped get into medical school. While they were there he took Haydock to a cemetery and showed him the spot reserved for him in the family plot. He lay down on the ground to prove that the burial site was large enough for his bulky form. Then he sat on the grass looking down at a pacific pond below filled with waterfowl. "I'll be here all through eternity watching the ducks," he said. Then, after a minute or so of silence, he added: "Being a pallbearer is the worst job. You just sweat and sweat. I've been a pallbearer for so many Kennedys. I know what I'm talking about. God, I'm going to make you guys sweat."

He changed his will every few weeks. He had left everything to Bobby. Then he eliminated him. Then he changed his mind again and added a codicil, leaving him only his apartment and giving the collectibles to his sister.

On May 25, 1981, he was with Michael and his new wife Vicki. Harvey Fleetwood was also at the apartment. Bobby was supposed to come up from Charlottesville, but at the last minute didn't. "Lem was very upset about that," Fleetwood recalls. "He and Bobby had been fighting over the phone about whether or not to go to Haiti that summer. The real subject was the thousand other things they couldn't talk about, things having to do with the death of the Kennedy dream. That night Lem got very drunk. He said to me, 'You've got to take care of Bobby.' I said that he shouldn't worry about Bobby because Bobby had a million friends. 'No, you're one of the only ones who cares.' I said that all this talk didn't mean much because he'd be there to look after Bobby the way he always had. He shook his head and started to cry. 'No. I made a terrible mistake. I took drugs with him. I made a terrible mistake. I let him down.' ''

The next night, in a better mood, he took ten of the younger Kennedys and their dates to see the film *Outlands*. He was enthusiastic, talking of how he was going to help Michael and Vicki design their new house in Virginia, just as he had helped Steve and Jean Smith design theirs at Bridgehampton. He talked loudly throughout the movie. "It was hilarious," Michael remembers. "He pretended that he didn't understand what was going on. He kept saying, 'Why is he doing that?' and 'What is he saying?' and 'What the hell is going on, anyway?' We went back to his apartment and talked. It was a good night."

The next morning, after another conversation with Bobby, he was down again. He called Duff and asked, "Do you think I've wasted my life on the Kennedys? Do you think they appreciate me?" He called Harvey Fleetwood, sobbing on the phone. "I'm taking all my Kennedy pictures off the wall. I don't want to see them any more."

That night he died in his sleep. The autopsy report said that death was caused by a heart attack, although Ethel asked one of Bobby's closest friends later on if he thought that Lem had suffered an o.d. The funeral was at the Episcopal church right around the corner from Lem's apartment. For the Kennedys it was as if the past itself had died; the secret passage they'd used to make contact with their glory days was now forever closed.

In his eulogy, Bobby, whose Prince Hal he had been so long, compared Lem to Falstaff and said: "He felt pain for every one of us—pain that no one else would have the courage to feel . . . I don't know how we'll carry on without him." Eunice had the last words: "I'm sure he's already organizing everything in heaven so it will be completely ready for us—with just the right Early American furniture, the right curtains, the right rugs, the right paintings, and everything ready for a big, big party. Yesterday was Jack's birthday. Jack's best friend was Lem and he would want me to remind everyone of that today. I am sure the good Lord knows that heaven is Jesus and Lem and Jack and Bobby loving one another."

As they were leaving the church someone recalled something Lem had said a few years earlier when he was in one of his jolly moods: "After I go, there'll be no more Kennedys."

EPILOGUE

*T*HANKSGIVING HAD ALWAYS BEEN a festive Kennedy holiday, with children spilling from one room to another of the Ambassador's big house at Hyannis, huge amounts of food, and charades and games afterward. By 1982 it had become a curiously diminished affair, reminding them how thinned their ranks had become, how loosened the ties that bound them, how altered their position in the world. Pat Lawford and Steve Smith were at the Compound with their younger children; Teddy was there with his three. Rose was there too, ninety-three years old, wearing an elegant blue turtle-neck sweater with pearls and gold earrings shaped like scallops.

Teddy's aides had been up from Washington the previous day with charts and poll results. It was time to think about 1984, they had said urgently, time to make sure they set things in motion so that they wouldn't have the shakedown problems that had plagued the 1980 campaign. Their reasons for wanting Teddy to run for President again were persuasive. Reagan support was thinning. Teddy was far and away the leading Democrat. The party needed the moral authority he had acquired by the end of his lonely 1980 run and had just reaffirmed in his Massachusetts reelection campaign.

But politics were banished during the celebration. At dinner Rose, frail and birdlike, pecking at small mouthfuls of food, peered intently through failing eyes in the direction of whoever was talking, while Teddy sat at her shoulder describing who was there, who was saying what. He was defensive about the fact that on most days she was "not herself." Because his children were there and it was a ceremonial moment he knew they would always remember, he tried to encourage his mother to be "all there" during the meal.

The adults talked in their staccato Kennedy way, finishing each other's sentences, imitating other voices, gossiping about relatives not present, avoiding politics. Near the end of the meal they transferred their attention to their children, who had all listened respectfully, and for the next half hour questioned them on their views of what had been discussed, a ritual way of relating between the generations which had been in effect longer than most of them could remember.

Signaling that the meal was over, Teddy leaned back, lighting one of the small cigars he had adopted in imitation of his brothers. Rose asked in her brittle voice, "Has everyone had enough to eat? Would anyone like more?" Teddy said everyone was fine. "Would anyone like more ice cream?" she asked, as if not having heard. "No thank you, mother," Pat Lawford answered, raising her voice. "We're all stuffed." Then Teddy stood up with a glass of champagne, asked for quiet, and, looking down at Rose, told her in the formal terms of his toast how much they all loved her, how generous she was, how she had always put on the best Thanksgiving feast in Massachusetts. Afterward, as she sat smiling in the afterglow of the sentiments, he suggested that perhaps she would like to make her own toast.

Standing with his help, Rose began to speak, and the halting, bemused quality of her dinnertime behavior disappeared as she talked about her family, her background, her life. "I want you all to remember that you are not just Kennedys, you are Fitzgeralds too. The Fitzgeralds are a very famous family in Ireland. There is a public park named for them outside Dublin. The Fitzgeralds came to this country seeking freedom before the Kennedys did. They made money before the Kennedys. When the Irish Catholics had no one to speak for them, the Fitzgeralds did . . ."

She went on to talk about her growing up—the schools she had attended in Europe, and the importance of everyone in the family learning a language such as French so that they could still pray in case there was a religious persecution. She talked about how her mother, a naturally shy person, had forced herself to stay at her husband the Mayor's side during his career. Then, skipping a beat, she asked in a cheerleader's voice, "And who was the greatest mayor Boston ever had?" Taken aback for a moment, Teddy and the rest roared back: "Honey Fitz!" Rose smiled and nodded, and went on talking about how the Fitzgeralds had exemplified duty and public service, about how she had been courted by Sir Thomas Lipton once upon a time, and how she had met her husband-to-be, Mr. Kennedy. Turning to her son she said, "And did your father ever make any money, Teddy?" As soon as the laughter subsided, she had them going again by asking, "And who was the prettiest girl in Boston?" They cheered: "You were!"

"At first I liked Mr. Kennedy, but I didn't love him," Rose went on. "In time, I came to love him very much. Very much." She paused, as if searching for what came next. The others applauded. She seemed ready to go on, to tell the rest of the incredible story of the Kennedys, a story at whose creation she had been present; but it had somehow gotten away from her, and she stood there smiling until the look on her face became confused. After a moment she looked down at Teddy: "I'm so happy when you're here, dear." Teddy gestured toward his children and their cousins: "And all the children too, Mother." Rose nodded: "Yes, and all the children. You all can come to my house any time you want. I'm so happy when you're here." Then she turned and went to the piano and began to play in precise chords and sing in a quavering tremolo. First it was "Tura-Lura," then "My Wild Irish Rose," and finally "Sweet Adeline."

The next day it was back to political business. At a summit lunch Teddy was joined by his three children, Steve Smith, assorted other Joe Kennedy grandchildren, and the writer Dotson Rader, who had been traveling across the country doing a story on the family for *Parade*. Teddy asked Rader for his views. Citing the people he had interviewed in his travels, the writer gave the case for Teddy's running, focusing on what he called the compact between the Kennedys and American history. Teddy thanked him and began to advance a series of reasons why he could win, as Steve Smith took the role of devil's advocate and tried to destroy the arguments in turn. None of the young people spoke, although everyone there knew that TK, Kara, and especially sixteen-year-old Patrick had already told their father in private why they were deeply opposed to another campaign. While making his case, Teddy sometimes looked around the table as if trying to find someone who supported him with whom he could make eye contact. They all averted their faces, staring down at the tablecloth. Finally, after the arguments were exhausted, Smith said, "Why don't we take a vote? Who's for it?" Of all those present, only the outsider Rader raised a hand. Smith shrugged. "So, I guess that settles it." A few moments later, as if to make a transition into less painful matters, he raised his wine glass and made a toast to his brother-in-law that centered on how much they all admired him and valued his career, as Teddy looked off into the middle distance.

Over the next two hours everyone cleared out, going off in cabs and limousines to catch the planes that would take them back to their homes. Finally only Teddy and Rader were left. Teddy chatted awhile about the *Parade* article, then poured two drinks and asked Rader to stay a bit longer. As the late-afternoon darkness began to filter into the room, Teddy began to talk— precisely and with what Rader regarded as unusual clarity. He ranged over all the crucial issues—foreign policy, disarmament, unions and union management, health care, and the need to revive decrepit business and retool the nation for the postindustrial era. As he sat there listening, Rader suddenly realized that what he was hearing was a private performance of a State of the Union message that would never be delivered.

Some of the grandchildren who had never before stood in the family limelight now began to talk about possible political careers. For instance, Kathleen who had spent almost a decade raising two small children with the care and thoroughness she sometimes said she and her cousins hadn't received in their childhood, had run Teddy's 1982 senate reelection campaign and afterward tried to interest her brothers in the possibility of moving her family to Maryland and running for congress there. Her brother David, playing his chosen role as archcynic of the family, told her she was crazy to think she could carpetbag so easily. ''Well,'' she replied defensively, ''Daddy did it.'' David said, ''Are you comparing yourself to Robert F. Kennedy?''

A similar attitude greeted Stevie Smith when he let it be known that he would like to play a role similar to his father's in the future generation, running campaigns and being the quarterback for the family business. Chris Lawford snorted: ''A political boss for the next generation. Great idea, except that there's nobody left to boss.''

Bobby Shriver, who had disappointed his mother by saying that he wanted to devote his postcollege years to making money rather than public service, summarized the prevailing opinion: ''We have to measure what we are by what our parents were. Grandpa had things completely wired—Massachusetts, the whole of the East Coast. He had it under control. He was a political consultant, a political action committee, and a media consultant all rolled into one. His only client was his family. He was fanatically dedicated to making it happen. Nobody in this family is ever again going to decide that it's a life-or-death matter whether or not a Kennedy gets elected to something. Even if they did, they can't make it happen any more. That's what's changed and we might as well admit it.''

Joe, oldest and most serious, had married Sheila Rauch and they had twin boys early in 1983, naming one of them Matthew and the other Joseph P. Kennedy III. His Citizens Energy Corporation was thriving, yet it was less exciting as a business demanding constant attention than it had been as a symbolic political act when he first established it. Although he was just thirty years old, Joe was a familiar subject of speculation in Massachusetts political circles, having been mentioned since 1976 for posts ranging from treasurer to lieutenant governor, from mayor to congressman. His cousins envied his stability yet considered him as passé as Teddy. ''Joe has accepted the old way,'' Chris Lawford says. ''He'll go plodding on, trying to thaw out the ambition that lies frozen at the heart of the family. He'll probably get elected to something someday, but when he does it won't be what he expected it to be and none of us will care.''

Chris himself, his vision deepened by his own vulnerability and suffering, continued to live on the fringes of the family, a fate he realized would never change. Ironically, in September 1980, right after Teddy's swan song at the Democratic convention, he had been arrested for heroin possession in the Roxbury ghetto while accompanying a friend who was actually making the score. Avoiding the felony conviction and possible jail term that went along with the bust, he had gone into a program combining Neltraxon, a ''narcotic antagonist'' to block the effects of opiates, and psychotherapy. The only adult in the family who supported him was Eunice, who flew up to help him dig his way out of the trouble, saying angrily to him and to herself, ''We're so goddamned good at taking care of everybody else's problems, but absolutely lousy at looking after our own.''

The students at Boston College Law School, where Chris had finally enrolled, pressured the school administration not to take disciplinary action against him. He went back there and began what had come to seem the eternal task of putting the pieces of his life together again. But this time, perhaps because of some unanticipated and intangible liberation flowing from Teddy's loss, he was able to stay straight. By 1983 he had finished law school, an achievement that momentarily silenced some of his family critics, although he found that this was not the end of his dilemma. ''I did it for politics,'' he says. ''Law is the stepping stone, et cetera. But politics seems to be over for us. So I face the same old question: Now what? Sometimes I think to myself that I'll just take off and never call Teddy, Steve Smith, Joe, or any of them again. But I know I can't do that. It's my family. But I'll never think of them/us in the same way. I used to think that what my family did was involved with a desire to serve the country. Now I keep asking myself what was it in my grandfather that made him push the family so hard and cause us all such tragedy?''

David, long since accepted as the most flamboyant of these family tragedies, had come back home from Sacramento on emotional probation within the family early in 1981. In March he had attended his brother Michael's wedding to Vicki Gifford, startling Chris and others by how sick and unbalanced he looked and by making such statements as ''I'm a bad person. God is punishing me.'' That previous Christmas in Aspen he had overdosed on his mother's sleeping pills and the others could hardly rouse him when it was time to open the presents. He finally got up and went to the tree, but standing over his gifts he suddenly became unable to move. Bobby, standing behind him, had said with clinical detachment, ''It's weird, the way you're standing there. You look like Jesus Christ on the Cross.''

Everyone half expected David to kill himself eventually. That would be the next great Kennedy drama. But somehow he kept managing to survive one setback after another, drawing strength from the belief that he alone in the family was living without illusions. He got back into Harvard on probation, telling friends that he was taking one course in archeology (''Mummies for dummies,'' he called it in his self-depreciating way) and another in anthropology (''Monkeys for junkies''). When he managed to pass these probationary efforts, he was allowed to take a full program in 1983. Meanwhile, he was seeing a psychiatrist, and for the first time not using the family's scorn for the examined life to subvert the therapeutic setting. (''At the beginning my shrink would ask me about my father and I'd go on about the pictures on the wall. Finally we talked it out and I began to admit where all the hurt in me was coming from.'')

Trying to finish at Harvard, trying to stay off dope, David used his status as pariah as a vantage point from which to view things steadily. ''My Uncle Jack and my father always used to quote that Englishman—politics is the noblest profession. To me, politics is crap. That's the main thing, maybe the only thing I've learned in my life. America needs a rest from the Kennedys and vice versa.''

When David talked to him in these terms, Bobby would smile and call it ''junkie talk.'' David would say, ''You're a junkie too. You just haven't admitted it yet.''

After Lem's death, Bobby had moved into the apartment which had been willed him, borrowing money against his trust to buy the collectibles which had not. He announced his engagement to Emily Black, a classmate at the University of Virginia Law School, and they were married in March 1982. Graduating that June, he got a job as Assistant District Attorney in New York, where Emily found a position in Legal Aid. They made headlines together when she was mugged and refused to prosecute the assailant although Bobby wanted her to. He made the headlines by himself in the fall of 1982 when he failed his bar exams.

That mastery of the diverse and contradictory elements of his life which had always been his pride was failing him. All the time he was working as an Assistant District Attorney he was making the forays he'd always made into Harlem, putting on a Navy watch cap and pulling it down over his forehead and ears so he wouldn't be recognized, driving up to one of the familiar shooting galleries and quickly making his connection, then speeding back into his respectable world. But with Lem's death he had lost the emotional support that had helped him ''maintain''—that underpinning of fantasy which had been his hope and strength. Now it was rumored in the District Attorney's office that he was ''nodding out'' in court and that his cases were suffering.

On May 16, his old Harvard friend Eric Breindel, now a protégé of Senator Daniel Patrick Moynihan and aide to the Senate Select Intelligence Committee, was arrested while buying heroin in Washington with attorney Winston Proude, a Kennedy acquaintance who had outraged Ethel by being friendly to her middle son Christopher and taking him to see the film *Cruising*. (After the bust, Ethel boasted to one of Bobby's closest friends that she'd tipped officials about Proude, although Proude—who attempted suicide afterward—would insist that it was not her information that had led to the arrest.)

In the investigation that followed, authorities not only wanted to know if Breindel had compromised classified material but also inquired into the extent of drug use among people connected with government. Worried that the net would spread to him, Bobby got a lawyer. His behavior became erratic. He had to be rescued on two occasions while sailing in the summer. On August 3, 1983, he was in a Republic airliner headed to Rapid City, South Dakota. The door of the lavatory swung open and another passenger saw him sitting, in stocking feet, on the lid of the toilet, asking for help. Talking incoherently, he was stretched out on some empty passenger seats and covered with a blanket. He turned white, his pulse was weak, and huge drops of sweat formed at his hairline. The pilot radioed ahead for an ambulance.

He was better when they landed, and tried to get off with his flight bag and get to the car that had come to pick him up. But police who had come with the ambulance asked who he was. At first he said his name was Bobby Francis. Then he gave his real name. For much of the next three hours he sat in an interrogation room reading a book on the Middle Ages as police attempted to question him. They finally let him go but kept his bag. Two days later they got a court order to open it and found a gram of heroin.

After pleading guilty, Bobby was sentenced to two years' probation and ordered to spend time in "community service." But the penalty he faced was more severe than the possible felony conviction. As his brother David had said upon first hearing the news of his arrest, "He was the best and the brightest, no doubt about that. If things had been different, he might have made it. As it was, there was no way. Even so, Bobby was our last illusion." Chris Lawford said, "If you think of it as one movement from Grandfather's early days to what has happened to Bobby right now, you realize that the Kennedy story is really about karma, about people who broke the rules and were ultimately broken by them."

Even in the months after his arrest, Bobby continued to occupy center stage. Everyone talked about his progress at the New Jersey drug rehabilitation center where he was trying to prove his contrition; about his wife Emily's pregnancy; about the irony in his having passed the bar exam in a test taken just before his bust. Monopolizing the attention of his Kennedy generation in his travails as he had in his successes, Bobby obscured everything else, especially the fact that his brother David was losing ground in his attempt to find his way into and around the family.

David's first reaction to Bobby's arrest had been one of elation. It seemed a belated justice: the due bill he himself had been receiving regularly for years were finally being forwarded to his brother. He also hoped that Bobby's misfortune and the sympathy it engendered would create greater understanding for him as well. But the opposite was true. Bobby's penitence was as spectacular as his failure: passing his bar exam as a junkie, going five months without drugs or liquor, settling down into an aggressively conservative life style. Instead of being company for David, Bobby again showed how different he was. David found himself even more isolated in the family than before. Because his failings had been so flamboyant and so public, he was held obliquely responsible for what had happened to Bobby; he was still the albatross around the family's neck. "In the best of times David was like a person keeping himself from falling by holding on to the edge with his fingertips," a friend says. "Now you could see the fingertips begin to slip. He could see that there was no place for him in the family. Someone else would have concluded that he should get away from his family. But David concluded that because there was no place for him there, there was no place for him anywhere." Nervous and unable to sit still, let alone concentrate, he left his part-time job reading unsolicited manuscripts at the *Atlantic* and dropped out of Harvard for the second and, final time. Since his exile in Sacramento for drug rehabilitation he had been drinking heavily. He described it as a trade-off: "off dope and onto booze." But now he was back on drugs too. Asked by friends what he was doing, he would say vacantly, "Who knows?"

The family was embarrassed by his needs and bored by his psychodrama. Despairing of helping him, they concentrated on trying to neutralize him. His access to his trust fund was restricted. He told friends that he was being forced to live on $1,500 a month; and that he was living with Paula Sculley, an attractive New York photographer he had met three years ago at a family Christmas party in Aspen, in part because she was seen by the family as a controlling influence. Since marriage had helped stabilize his older brother Joe and, to a lesser degree, Bobby as well, the family pressured David to marry, too. The fact that his family liked Paula made her attractive to him, but at the same time made him wary of her.

In his search for escape hatches, David had reestablished his relationship with his old girl friend Nancy Narleski, who was still anathema to the Kennedys because of her protest against the way he'd been treated during his stay in Sacramento. He spent hours on the phone with her, often semicoherent, fantasizing about getting away from the Kennedys and going to live in Hawaii. "He was under tremendous pressure from his family," Narleski says. "They were terrorizing him. They blamed him for what had happened to Bobby. They told him he had been a bad example. David didn't even bother to point out that it was Bobby who had led *him* astray; he just accepted their framework and felt guilty. One night his brothers called him a traitor and said that he wasn't worthy to bear the Kennedy name. He was crying when he told me this."

Narleski was about to be awarded money from an insurance claim settlement. She saw David's increasing disorientation and desperation, and it reminded her of the time in Sacramento when she had felt he might die. "Just hang on till I get my money," she told him. "Then we'll get away from all this and go to Maui." David helped her plan a getaway, but she suspected that he would probably never be able to leave. "He really couldn't conceive of being apart from them, cut off, on his own," she says. "The Kennedys were his real addiction."

During the Easter weekend the family gathered at Palm Beach, in part because Teddy and his sisters feared that it might be the last holiday for ninety-three-year-old Rose, who was increasingly frail and enfeebled. Some of his cousins didn't come, but David did, returning from a Minneapolis drug rehabilitation program where he had been enrolled under the name "David Kilroy." Because there were too many Kennedys for the Palm Beach house, he registered in the nearby Brazilian Court Hotel. During his stay there, he drank constantly and also managed to find his way to the heart of the local drug scene.

On the morning of April 25, the hotel receptionist got a call from someone identifying herself as "Mrs. Kennedy from Boston," who said that David had been scheduled to return home the previous day but had not been on his plane. The receptionist agreed to check on him. There was a Do Not Disturb sign on his door, but when nobody answered repeated knocks she poked her head inside. The twin beds were rumpled and clothing was scattered all over the room. David was lying on the floor, his head propped against a nightstand. As soon as she felt his cold and waxy flesh she knew he was dead. The evening news showed David's corpse being wheeled out of the hotel in a body bag; the next day's papers devoted as much space to the story as they might have to the death of a head of state.

The Kennedys brought David back to Hickory Hill for a memorial mass before burying him next to his grandfather in the family plot at Brookline. If he had been alive, David, who had compensated for his painful vulnerability by armoring himself with irony, might have noted that his entire family was paying him the respect in death that they had not when he was alive and needy. He might have smiled at his Uncle Ted's statement to the press—that he had finally found the peace that he had not been able to find in life—and wondered if there was a hint of relief in those words. He would probably have been amused by all the talk about a Kennedy curse, as if consequences had nothing to do with people and their acts.

Those friends who had valued him for the individual he was, rather than for the Kennedy he had tried so hard to become, grieved because of David's effort to become restored to himself, an effort which at times had seemed so close to success. But finally he had not been able to cut himself loose from his sense of family expectation and destiny, or from the victimhood which had come to seem symbiotically related to the others' survival.

Like his family, his friends had all wondered at one time or another if he would kill himself; but when it finally came his death was nonetheless shocking. Nancy Narleski says, "I keep asking myself, 'Why? Why David? Why now?' All I can come up with is that maybe his father was looking down from heaven and saw all the hell these people were putting him through and said, 'Come on. You've suffered enough. It's time you were up here with me.'"

BIBLIOGRAPHIC NOTE

Writers approaching the subject of the Kennedys cannot help being struck by the role books have played in the family drama. One of the memorable images of Jack as a young man is that of a thin Harvard graduate sitting around the Hyannis house insouciantly autographing copies of *Why England Slept*, which miraculously managed to work its way onto the best-seller list and gave him a leg up in his long struggle with his brother Joe. Another dramatic literary moment came a few years later when Joseph P. Kennedy returned home from London with his career in shambles, hoping that the steamer trunks filled with material he had accumulated during his ambassadorship could become the basis of a book that would vindicate him and rehabilitate his political prospects. His quest for selfhood through literature was as doomed as Jack's was guaranteed, however, and despite the years he devoted to the project, despite all the help he solicited and the drafts he composed in spiky longhand, Kennedy finally had to admit that what was interesting about his life was not his politics but his experience, and this experience simply could not be discussed. In the mid-fifties there was Bobby, writing *The Enemy Within* on yellow foolscap, determined to complete the book by himself and avoid the charges of using a ghost writer which had plagued Jack when he published *Profiles in Courage.*

Jack's presidency and assassination addicted the nation to the Kennedys' romance and tragedy, making books and articles about the family into something like a sub-industry in American publishing. Yet the Kennedys themselves have remained profoundly ambivalent about such writings. If books were objects of awe because they were so intimately involved in the search for the appropriate self, they were also objects of scorn because words—like selves—could be so easily manipulated. The *arriviste*'s admiration for the book as artifact, which led Joe Kennedy to tell Jack that there was nothing like getting his name in print to launch a young man in the world, eventually fermented into a near-contempt for the outpourings that soon surrounded and threatened to suffocate the family. Books, like everything else, could be bought. Scholars and writers could be seduced and later bullied by the family's distinctive charisma so that they would want to write affirmation, to ratify a congenial version of reality, and to amplify the now self-propelling Kennedy myths.

As the Kennedy fate sharpened and the stakes grew larger, the family recognized that the only books which could finally be trusted were those created by family members themselves—*As We Remember Joe,* Jack's collection of reminiscences about his dead brother; *The Fruitful Bough,* Teddy's testimonial to his father; and other privately printed and circulated memorial volumes. Truth was not an issue in these works; the sole purpose was to give surviving family members a set of household myths, a substitute text for the authentic Kennedy history jettisoned on the way to the top. As far as books by outsiders were concerned, the self-suppression that had made Joseph Kennedy's autobiography remain one of the greatest stories never told inevitably led to the suppression of others; the family was in the business of managing its own news long before the Kennedy Administration was ever accused of news management. Rosemary's retardation, Jack's near-fatal illnesses, Kick's flamboyant search for romance in the relationship with Peter Fitzwilliam—all these aspects of the past were threats to the future, and dealing with them involved not only erasures but also the penciling in of substitute facts. And so, in the years when Jack was afflicted by life-threatening episodes of Addison's disease, newspapermen would be cozened into reporting that the promising young Congressman had merely suffered relapses of the malaria he had contracted during the war. As the presidency became a real possibility, the books that began to appear about the family with increasing frequency told some version of Rosemary's story which portrayed her as a "shy and retiring girl" who had chosen to spend her life working with retarded children. Kick's life after Billy Hartington's death would be bowdlerized to such an extent that she wound up as just another of the sacred dead, an obscure motif in the swelling anthem of unfulfilled promise that helped justify the growing Kennedy ambition. After Jack's death, when there was a Legacy to protect, it was necessary to try to suppress not only potentially damaging facts, but the books of writers such as Red Fay and William Manchester as well.

As the Kennedys increasingly sponsored a literature of apology and affirmation, there naturally arose a literature of reaction. This polarization creates immense difficulty for the biographer. No group of people have been more authentically stirring or romantic in their self-avowal and their political vision. But none have layered their history so methodically with myth and purposeful misinterpretation. No group has been more protected by literary sycophants—scholars and working journalists who have allowed their own fortunes to become so intimately involved with the Kennedys' that the books they produced have become disguised autobiographies. No group, on the other hand, has been more maligned by literary hacks and space fillers bent on making a calculated appeal to the paranoia and perversity the Kennedys' unique status in America have aroused. Because of its mania for controlling its own image, as much as because of its unique place in the country's history, the Kennedy family has become a sort of Manichean battleground where the first casualty is truth. Writing about the Kennedys easily becomes an exercise in symbolism, an attempt to trap the shadows flickering on the wall of the cave.

The JFK Library should be the logical place to begin to establish an empirical base for constructing a Kennedy biography. The people there are unfailingly gracious and helpful. But after working in the library, it is difficult not to conclude that the contents of its collections are as committed to the heroic image of Jack as the intentionally magnificent structure in which they are housed. With significant omissions for security reasons, the Presidential Papers give a look at the policies of the Kennedy Administration, but there are no personal papers to give a look at Jack himself. The surviving private correspondence with family members is part of the Joseph P. Kennedy Papers, certainly the most significant collection housed at the JFK Library, but one that exists in the limbo of "courtesy storage," not yet deeded by the family to the archives and off limits to researchers. There is what at first glance seems a promising collection of material in the 1200 or so oral histories collected at the library, some 800 of them available to researchers. Many of these documents have insights which we have drawn on in this book. Yet for the most part these oral histories are narrow in scope, delicately skirting the critical issues of Jack's personal life such as his health and his relationship with his father and other members of the family. In addition, most of these interviews were conducted during the six months after the assassination, at a time when, in the words of one of the archivists at the library, "the minds of everyone involved were clearly clouded by guilt and incapable of objectivity." The origin of this oral history project—Arthur Schlesinger's idea that members of the New Frontier should begin interviewing each other during the administration to get a head start on writing its history—also influenced the way it was carried out. One finds Kennedy friends and colleagues interviewing each other about the Kennedys, giving most of the documents a fraternal, almost masonic air.

In writing this book we had to establish, in effect, our own archives, as Berton Hersh, Clay and Joan Blair, Richard Whalen, and other writers have done. We interviewed more than 300 people over the four years it took to complete this project, compiling a set of oral histories of our own. Along the way, we were lucky to meet Mary Lou McCarthy, daughter of Joseph Kennedy's sister Loretta, and Mary Lou's daughter Kerry. Loretta Kennedy Connelly had taken on the role of family historian, preserving a view of her mother, Mary Hickey Kennedy, and her father, P.J., along with many of his papers, a role that Mary Lou and Kerry McCarthy have since assumed. If the Connelly Papers (as we have called them in the notes that follow) presented a privileged insight into the early stages of the Kennedy saga, the private archives of LeMoyne Billings presented a view of the Kennedys during a later period. Until his recent death, Lem Billings functioned as a sort of Ishmael in this saga, the outsider who alone saw it unfold and who alone survived to tell the tale. Among his voluminous files was a unique series of letters written by Jack during his formative years, letters that show his developing sense of irony and of humor as well as his immense inquisitiveness, and that collaborate with other evidence to make one aware of what a piece of work this man was. Because JFK's private papers are under the family's control and, according to some Kennedys we talked to, have been "sanitized," these letters kept by Lem Billings may well be the only unexpurgated examples of Jack's correspondence that will appear for some time.

While we were beginning our historical research and reconstruction, we were also trying to get the Kennedys to talk usefully with us. We believed our project would be appealing. Unlike many writers who took them at the midpoint of their destiny and spent whole books trying to hack a path through the lush controversies that have grown up around the Kennedy myths, we wanted to see the family clearly and see it whole, beginning with its origins in America and tracing its history to the present day. However, we immediately encountered that odd combination of literary savvy and suspicion that has become a Kennedy hallmark in dealing with writers. The family knew about and appreciated our book *The Rockefellers*, but they had their own literary agenda. As we discovered soon after beginning our work, there was another family history in the works—by a historian who was functioning as speech writer and adviser in Teddy's 1980 presidential campaign. As far as we were concerned, this presented no problem: the Kennedys were a spacious subject with room enough for two multigenerational biographies, but the Kennedy elders, existing in a world dominated by the political metaphor, found that the existence of more than one author involved them in a sort of election in which they were required to back a candidate. There was much discussion but no real question about their ultimate choice. Later on, discussing their decision not to cooperate with us, Stevie Smith said to a family friend who had intervened on our behalf, "You've got to understand their reasoning. They think of this historian as one of their pocket-people, whom they feel they can count on." Pocket-people: the term is jarring, yet it perfectly expresses the Kennedy attitude toward writers they feel they can control.

But while Teddy, Steve Smith, and others at the top of the family hierarchy stuck with their candidate, many members of the current Kennedy generation became interested in our book. In one sense they were the tail of a comet whose blinding brightness had passed. Yet they were also a summary of what increasingly came to seem to us a completed process—individuals who were squarely in the Kennedy history but curiously not *of it*. To boost his political fortunes by establishing the durability of the Kennedy tradition as well as his own status as family patriarch, Teddy had urged them to make themselves available for two other books. However, while they had cooperated in a superficial way with these projects, they had seen them as another example of "bought" writing. Because we did not approach them under the banal rubric of "Camelot's heirs" they talked about themselves with surprising candor. It was almost as if they saw our book as a way of understanding themselves and the process that had given them great prospects but robbed them of the ability to attain them. The story they told us—about their dark journey in dangerous pursuit of the Legacy that dominated their lives even as it dominated the country's politics—was not only the logical conclusion to the Kennedy story but also an epitome of it, the part that shows the whole most dramatically. Their pain and disorientation cast a new light on Joseph P. Kennedy's dynastic project. Their revelations offered an opportunity, the first we were aware of, to see the family from the inside out.

As we got to know this generation of Kennedys, listening to their disturbing confessions and in some instances watching their self-destructive behavior, we felt that we should make another attempt to contact the family elders. We repeatedly telephoned Steve Smith's office and asked when we could talk with him or Teddy. During the last of these calls, at the beginning of the race for the 1980 Democratic presidential nomination, Smith asked once again what our "topic" was. We said, as we had before, that the broad subject of the book was the generational linkages and lack thereof in the family, and that we especially wanted to talk about the current generation. "A fine idea," Smith said hurriedly, "and I wish you all the luck, really. But listen, we're in the middle of another election here. There just isn't time for the sort of thing you're concerned about."

That, of course, was exactly the problem. There would always be another election; the human concerns of the individuals whose lives had become ensnared in the Kennedy Legacy would always take a back seat to the political imperative of the moment. Running for office had become a way of running away from the problems holding office had created.

Nowhere was this truer, in our perception, than in the attitude of the family toward David Kennedy. Although he had been regarded as the Kennedys' neediest case when his difficulties first began, his drug abuse and disorientation soon became a public problem far more than a personal one, an issue with a "policy" dimension, a matter requiring the practice of damage control in the media. He was, in other words, regarded as a political liability, a potential indictment of family morality. It was for this reason that his close relatives found it so easy to regard him as odd man out and pariah; to make of him the deviation establishing the rest of them as the norm. Like some of his brothers and cousins, he talked to us at considerable length and with considerable candor during the writing of this book. He was by no means the only one to speak frankly about how growing up Kennedy had led to immense personal difficulties. But he alone was scapegoated for the results. In the fall of 1983, David wryly told us, the family pressured him into seeing a prominent Boston attorney to find out if he could "retract" what he had told us in conversations that had stretched over several months. In the spring of 1984, when excerpts of this book appeared in magazine form, David was bitterly criticized for breaching the family faith. The word used in condemning him was "treason," a word with political even more than personal inplications. David was angry at himself for caring so much about their censure, but, as he said in our last conversation with him a few weeks before his death, "They have their own idea of reality which isn't mine but it has a hold on me."

—P.C. and D.H., Nevada City–Berkeley
April 30, 1984

NOTES

PART 1: ARCHITECT OF THEIR LIVES

15
As their limousine: Details of the visit to Windsor are in Rose Kennedy, *Times to Remember*, New York, 1974, pp. 220ff.
17
"The legends of Joe Kennedy": See "Mr. Kennedy, the Chairman," *Fortune*, September 1937, p. 138.
17
"Nine hostages to fortune": Authors' interview with Joseph Kingsbury Smith, March 27, 1980. Kennedy employed this phrase frequently.
21
"Goddamn it!": Authors' interviews with Lem Billings, January 28, 1980; January 15, March 17, 1981.
21
Goody Glover hanged as a witch: Joseph Dineen, *The Kennedy Family*, New York, 1959, p. 23.
22
"If crosses and tombs": Cecil Woodham-Smith, *The Great Hunger*, New York, 1962, p. 238.
22
No further increase in Boston populaton: Oscar Handlin, *Boston Immigrants 1790–1860*, Cambridge, Mass., 1941, p. 94.
22
Death rate as high as in Ireland: Robert E. Kennedy, *The Irish Experience*, Berkeley, Calif., 1973, p. 51.
23
"A race that will never": Cited by John Henry Cutler, *Honey Fitz*, New York, 1962, p. 23.
23
Patrick Kennedy and Bridget Murphy: Details from the early family life of the Kennedys come from "P. J. The First Senator Kennedy," written by Kerry Mc-

Carthy, great-granddaughter of P. J. Kennedy. The Kerry McCarthy MS. is based on interviews with surviving family members in the United States and Ireland, along with letters and documents in the possession of the McCarthy family. Kerry Mc-Carthy and her mother, Mary Lou, kindly allowed us to see and quote from this work and from other materials in their collection, which was originally assembled by Mary Lou McCarthy's mother (and P. J. Kennedy's daughter), Loretta Kennedy Connelly. This collection will hereafter be referred to as the Connelly Papers.

24
Life expectancy for Irishmen: Handlin, p. 115.

24
Bridget Kennedy's notions shop: Richard Whalen, *The Founding Father*, New York, 1966 (paperback), p. 23.

25
Irish residency requirement: Marjorie Fallows, *Irish Americans*, New Jersey, 1979, p. 38.

25
Irish political organizations: See Francis Russell, *The Great Interlude*, New York, 1964, pp. 165ff.

25
Lomasney's deal: Dineen, p. 27. See also Leslie Ainley, *Boston Mahatma: A Biography of Martin Lomasney*, Boston, 1949.

25
"Is somebody out of a job?": Cutler, *Honey Fitz*, p. 46.

26
"Who do you think you're kidding?" Dineen, p. 28.

26
Details of Kennedy's business: Kerry McCarthy MS.; authors' interviews with Mary Lou McCarthy, March 22, May 22 and 23, 1982; authors' interviews with Helen Barron (goddaughter of Kate Hickey, Mary Augusta's sister), February 20, March 2, 1981. Mrs. Barron says: "My father worked very hard for Mr. Kennedy. He opened the store and closed it for him. He died of a perforated ulcer of the stomach in 1912, and that was from worry."

26
The Hickey family: Details from photographs in Connelly Papers and from Kerry McCarthy MS. ("The Kennedy home was one of the most modest dwellings on the street wherein dwelt some of the city's outstanding celebrities. . . . Hero to all of these families was one of Boston's greatest men, Patrick A. Collins, later to become Mayor of Boston. But the great P. A. was ever honored most by his countrymen for having been chosen by President Cleveland during his second administration as Consul General to London. 'Think of it,' the neighbors said, 'P. A. in London.' One of Joseph Kennedy's earliest recollections is that of the awe and almost saintly esteem in which the Collins name was held in his household." *Boston Post*, December 12, 1937.)

27
P. J.'s two bills: *Journal of Senate*, Commonwealth of Massachusetts, 1892, pp. 10, 90.

27
The battle with Lomasney: Joseph P. McCarthy, *The Remarkable Kennedys*, New York, 1960, p. 37.

28
"Dear Dick": The letter is in P. J.'s ledger, Connelly Papers.

28
"It was with a great deal of pleasure": Ibid.

28
"I shall pass through this world": Kerry McCarthy MS.

29
John F. Fitzgerald's youth: See Cutler, *Honey Fitz*, pp. 39ff.

29

"Honey Fitz can talk you blind": Ibid., p. 57.

30

Fitzgerald vs. Lodge: Ibid., p. 64

30

"It would have been a great delight": Ibid., p. 96.

31

"No 'little P. J.s' ": Kerry McCarthy MS.

31

It sounded "less Irish": Ibid.

31

"I thought he was a god": William J. Duncliffe, *The Life and Times of Joseph P. Kennedy*, New York, 1965, p. 3. Mary Augusta herself became even more protective after another son, Francis, died of diphtheria at the age of two. Authors' interview with Mary Lou McCarthy.

31

Joe saves Christmas for Loretta: Loretta recounted the anecdote in the *Boston Post*, December 12, 1937, p. 1.

31

It was Mary Augusta: Authors' interview with Marnee Devine (daughter of Margaret), March 23, 1982. Also authors' interviews with Mary Lou McCarthy and Helen Barron.

31

"The Hickey look": Authors' interview with Marnee Devine. "They were called the Hickey Eyes. Even in my mother's day, when she'd sit at the end of the table, we'd laugh about it, because she would just look, she would never have to speak; she'd just give us a look for bad table manners. The Hickeys were noted for that look."

32

"He missed me": Duncliffe, p. 25. The bond with his mother remained a strong factor in Joseph Kennedy's emotional life. Many years later, according to the family's intimate friend Arthur Krock, Kennedy got a special dispensation from Cardinal Spellman to use the living room·of his Palm Beach home as the site of a special requiem mass for the "repose of my mother's soul," which Spellman himself agreed to perform. Krock, *Memoirs*, New York, 1968 (paperback), p. 329.

32

A constant flow of supplicants: Authors' interviews with Mary Lou McCarthy and Marnee Devine. Also Kerry McCarthy MS.

32

Voted 128 times: Joseph P. McCarthy, "Jack Kennedy—Here to the Presidency," *Look*, October 27, 1956, p. 91.

32

P. J.'s wealth: Kerry McCarthy MS. Authors' interview with Mary Lou McCarthy.

33

"If you are asked your name": Kerry McCarthy MS.

33

"I think I'll choose the tintype": Duncliffe, p. 25.

34

He directed plays: Kerry McCarthy MS.

34

"If you can't be captain": Duncliffe, p. 34.

34

Catholic schools might stunt their ambitions: Mary Augusta encouraged Loretta to take education courses at Columbia Teachers College in New York "at a time when Irish Catholic girls from Boston stayed pretty close," says Mary Lou McCarthy. McCarthy believes that it was ambition, but also part of a plan Mary Augusta had conceived to make sure Joe did not have the burden of having to support his sisters.

34

Boston Latin School "a shrine": Cited by James M. Burns, *Edward Kennedy and the Camelot Legacy*, New York, 1976, p. 22. Marnee Devine says, "Mary Augusta was really the one who was behind it all, behind Uncle Joe's going to Latin school, and later made the decision that he would go to Harvard."

34n

"The Irish not the Jews": Cited in John Henry Cutler, *Cardinal Cushing of Boston*, New York, 1970.

35

Joe would bring some of his college friends: Authors' interview with Mary Lou McCarthy.

35

"Joe sucked up": Authors' interview with confidential source, December 20, 1981.

35

Harvard-Yale game: *Boston Evening American*, December 13, 1937, p. 1 See also Whalen, p. 36.

36

"I did so poorly": *Fortune*, September 1937.

36

JPK tour bus business: Whalen, p. 39. See also *Boston Globe*, December 12, 1939.

36n

"You have plenty of Irish depositors": Rose Kennedy, p. 65.

37

"I want to be a millionaire": *Fortune*, September 1937.

37

Fitzgerald and "Toodles" Ryan: Russell, p. 183.

37

"John, it does indeed": Cutler, *Honey Fitz*, p. 173.

37

Graft in the Fitzgerald administration: See Russell, p. 176.

37

"Sweet Adeline": "Fitzgerald often gave a supporter ten dollars before a speech, telling him, 'Okay, now when I finish you yell out, "Hey, John F., won't you sing 'Sweet Adeline'?"' " "Patsy" Mulkern Oral History, John F. Kennedy Library.

37

Sacred Heart schools: See Stephen Birmingham, *Real Lace*, New York, 1973 (paperback), p. 222. Also authors' interview with Mary Lou McCarthy.

38

In the summer of 1908: See Rose Kennedy, p. 31.

38

"I am an angel": Ibid. p. 37.

38

"I used to be behind her": Gail Cameron, *Rose*, New York, 1972 (paperback), p. 66.

38

Joe and Rose meet on the sly: See Rose Kennedy, p. 59.

38

JPK entertains Samuel Rea: This anecdote comes from a book of reminiscences about Joseph P. Kennedy, *The Fruitful Bough: A Tribute to Joseph P. Kennedy*, edited by Edward M. Kennedy, privately printed, 1965, p. 36.

39

Curley vs. Fitzgerald: See Cutler, *Honey Fitz*, pp. 190ff.

39

"I don't think he ever *did* ask me": Rose Kennedy, p. 67.

40

JPK as youthful family man: Authors' interview with Dina Romano, July 18, 1980. Mrs. Romano, who immigrated from Italy, was the first domestic servant Rose Kennedy hired.

40

JPK vs. FDR: *New York Times,* July 1, 1934, p. 1. See also Ernest K. Lindley, "Will Kennedy Run for President?," *Liberty,* May 21, 1938.

40

"To form the habit of making God": Dineen, p. 35.

41

Contribution to Guild of St. Apollonia: Rose Kennedy, p. 85.

41

"Good Lord, Joe": Duncliffe, p. 52.

41

"I am extremely sorry in your defeat": Kerry McCarthy MS.

41

Honey Fitz and Peter Tague: "In the long history of New England," read Tague's complaint, "this case stands out as one of the most glaring instances of political fraud, perpetrated against the will of the majority of the people that has ever been known. . . ."—Contestants Brief, Contested Election Case of Peter F. Tague versus John F. Fitzgerald, 66th Congress. Tague had beaten Fitzgerald by almost a 7-5 margin in five of the six wards of the Tenth Congressional District. But in Ward 5, controlled by Lomasney, Fitzgerald won by a 5-1 ratio. Ibid.

41

"Rose, were you lying": Duncliffe, p. 49.

42

Mary Augusta's last illness: Kerry McCarthy MS. Also authors' interview with Mary Lou McCarthy.

42

P. J. visits Ireland: Kerry McCarthy MS. Documents in Connelly Papers.

42

JPK and Galen Stone: See Whalen, pp. 59ff.

42

I think the primary notion": Joseph P. Kennedy, "Shielding the Sheep," *Saturday Evening Post,* January 18, 1936.

42

"It's easy to make money": Whalen, p. 71.

43

JPK and Yellow Cab: Ibid., pp. 72ff.

44

JPK and Meyer Lansky: Dennis Eisenberg et al., *Meyer Lansky: Mogul of the Mob,* New York, 1979, pp. 109ff.

44

JPK and Costello: *New York Times,* July 27, 1973, p. 37.

44

Kennedy move to New York: See Whalen, p. 94.

45

"What is it you really want?": Authors' interview with Timothy Mathews, December 18, 1981.

46

"Kennedy can't use a residence": Cited in Whalen, p. 94.

46

Kennedy arrival in Bronxville: Authors' interviews with Bronxville neighbors of the Kennedys—Paul Morgan, November 22, 1980; Betty Young, November 24, 1980; and Nancy Hill, November 25, 1980.

47

"Take Boston": Gloria Swanson, *Swanson on Swanson,* New York, 1980, p. 339.

47

"We must get into the picture business": Edward M. Kennedy, ed., *Bough,* p. 29.

47

"Look at that bunch": Whalen, p. 80.

47

JPK and Prince of Wales: *Boston Post,* December 26, 1937. The anecdote was related in a slightly different form by Kennedy lawyer Bart Brickley in Whalen, p. 77.

47

"Joe has bitten off": Cited in Whalen, p. 77.

47

"Sorry, fellows": *Boston Sunday American,* December 12, 1937, p. 38.

48

JPK and Film Booking Office: See Whalen, pp. 80ff.

48

Harvard Business School seminar: See Joseph P. Kennedy, ed., *The Story of the Films,* Chicago, 1927. Authors' interview with Arthur Poole, August 23, 1979. Poole, a future Kennedy aide, attended these lectures and approached Kennedy about a job after they were completed.

49

"They copied us": Cited by Birmingham, p. 177. Also authors' interview with Anne Kelley, September 30, 1980.

49

"She and her daughters": John Corry, *The Golden Clan,* New York, 1977, p. 73. Also authors' interviews with Anne Kelley and John Murray Cuddihy, November 20, 1980.

49

"When *will* the nice people": Blair Clark, the friend of John F. Kennedy who is the source for this often quoted remark, claims that what Rose actually said was, "When will the nice people of Boston accept Catholics?" Authors' interview with Blair Clark, March 3, 1981.

49

She was didactic: Details of Rose's motherhood from authors' interview with Mary Lou McCarthy. See also Cameron, pp. 103ff, and Rose Kennedy, pp. 91ff.

50

"I didn't know": Rose's attitude toward money matters was a reflection of Joseph P. Kennedy's own. Much later, when asked how much his business career was a collaborative effort with Rose, he said, "I have never discussed money with my wife and family and never will!" See Eleanor Harris, "The Senator Is in a Big Hurry," *Saturday Evening Post,* August 1957, p. 119.

50

"My father built his financial empire": Authors' interview with General Robert Montague, president, Joseph P. Kennedy Jr. Foundation, November 30, 1981.

50

He brought his own staff: Authors' interview with Arthur Poole.

51

"He would not only tell Joe": Authors' interviews with Harvey Klemmer, April 6, 8, 13, 19, 1980; June 23, November 20, 1980. Klemmer joined Kennedy at the Maritime Commission and worked on his staff as a speechwriter for six years after that.

51

R.C.A. merger: Authors' interview with Arthur Poole. Kennedy made Poole vice president and a director of Pathé, which R.K.O. purchased. See also Whalen, pp. 88ff.

52

Swanson seduction: Swanson, pp. 351–357.

53

"The Swamp"–*Queen Kelly* project: Ibid., pp. 368ff.

53

Largest phone bill in the nation: *Boston Evening American,* December 16, 1937, p. 1.

53

Swanson at Hyannis: Leo Damore, *The Cape Cod Years of John Fitzgerald Kennedy,* New Jersey, 1967, p. 21.

54n
Swanson and Rose in mid–1960s: Rose Kennedy, p. 192.

54
"I am here to ask": Swanson, p. 394.

54
"I've never had a failure": In an attempt to salvage the project, Kennedy had director Eddie Goulding brought in to replace von Stroheim, but to no avail. Goulding's agent, Phil Berg, says, "I went over to the Pathé lot and saw the film. It was just dreadful. Somebody said, 'It won't be hard to cut, mandolin picks are very small. They can cut it and make thousands of mandolin picks." Authors' interview with Phil Berg, July 24, 1979.

54
The affair with Swanson ended: Swanson claimed that they never saw each other again, but Harvey Klemmer and others say that she and Kennedy did meet occasionally. Several people report occasions on which Kennedy would telephone the star to impress others in a room with him.

55
"Wally tells me": Authors' interview with Phil Berg.

55
P. J. in old age: Authors' interview with Helen Barron. See also photographs in Connelly Papers.

56
"Rumors would fly": Authors' interview with Paul Morgan, November 22, 1980.

56
Allowing his rakishness to become: Authors' interview with Harvey Klemmer.

57
Kennedy's pride: Authors' interview with Morton Downey, July 9, 1980. Kennedy and Downey met in 1928 when the tenor was singing with the Paul Whiteman band in Chicago. Calling him "the greatest singer since McCormack," Kennedy backed shows Downey was in and made him a frequent house guest and member of his inner circle. According to a later Kennedy confidant, real-estate man John Reynolds, part of Downey's appeal for Kennedy was that he knew and could provide introductions to attractive showgirls. Authors' interview with John Reynolds, March 13, 1980.

57
"She knew what was happening": Authors' interview with confidential source, February 12, 1981.

57
"I have had them myself": Hank Searls, *The Lost Prince: Young Joe, The Forgotten Kennedy,* New York, 1977 (paperback), p. 49.

57
"Architect of our lives": Rose Kennedy, p. 57.

57
"He would bring back word": Authors' interview with Mary Lou McCarthy. The degree to which he was in touch impressed everyone, especially his children. Bobby later said of his father: "Time after time, while growing up, I remember listening to him talk with an important figure in business, the theater, or politics, and always observing that he was the dominant figure—that he knew more, that he expressed it better." (Edward M. Kennedy, ed., *Bough,* p. 210) However, it was always clear that these dinner table sessions were in the service of practical, not theoretical knowledge, and for the benefit of Kennedys, not outsiders. One of Jack's high school friends, Ralph ("Rip") Horton, later said: "No matter how stupid the questions might seem ... [he] would go to great lengths [to answer them] ... If an outsider, such as myself, asked a question ... he would just answer it rather curtly as if he didn't want to be bothered. He was only concerned about educating his own children." Ralph Horton Oral History, JFK Library.

58

One family friend: Authors' interview with Charlotte McDonnell Harris, March 4, 1983.

58

"One time": Authors' interviews with Timothy J. Reardon, Jr., June 10, 13, 1982.

58

"Pat and Eunice were always saying": Authors' interview with Ann Kelley.

58

"Suffered under the handicap": Cited by Arthur Schlesinger, Jr., *Robert Kennedy and His Times*, Boston, 1978, p. 6.

58

"We want winners": Authors' interview with Lem Billings.

58

She was ... remote: Authors' interview with Sancy Newman, February 28, 1980. "Rose would always make the kids leave her side of the house in the afternoon. Like clockwork she'd say, 'Please, children, I'm having my rest now.'" Sancy Newman was a friend and Cape Cod neighbor of Kathleen's when they were growing up.

58

Rose's trips: Nancy Gager Clinch, *The Kennedy Neurosis*, New York, 1973, p. 77.

58

"Daddy's look": Authors' interview with Mary Lou McCarthy.

58

Experience vs. religion creating character: Edward M. Kennedy, ed., *Bough*, p. 218.

59

Bronxville experience: "The kids were all away at school most of the time." Authors' interview with Paul Morgan. "Sometimes Jack would be late for a date. He'd call for me, and he wouldn't be dressed. So he'd take me back to his house while he got dressed. And nobody was around. And I'd say, 'Where's everybody?' They had either gone to Palm Beach or I don't know where they were. It was creepy. It wasn't homey, and I just never knew where anybody was unless they had a party." Authors' interview with Betty Young, November 24, 1980.

59

"The razzing would begin": Authors' interview with Robert Downes, April 24, 1980.

59

"You can't touch me here!": Searls, p. 40.

59

Young Joe spent time with the Fitzgeralds: "One time he sprained his ankle, and he had a cast around it, but he drove up to the Bellevue to pick up old John F. to see the end of the Boston Marathon. The car had a rumble seat, which I sat in, but you could roll down the window and talk. When we got there, there were all these police horses blocking the streets. Joe is saying, 'Oh we can't go up there, Gramps.' And John F. says, 'Go right up. Go ahead,' and we went right up and almost knock a big Irish cop over. He comes down and says, 'What dya think you're doing?' into Joe's window. And he looks in and John F. in this high-pitched voice says something and he says, 'Pardon me, your Honor.' And then he got everyone out of the way so that we practically saw the winner in our arms." Authors' interview with Ted Reardon.

59

Joe Junior in friends' kitchens: "Sometimes when we didn't have anything to do he'd say, 'Tommy, let's go over to your place. Maybe your dad can fry up some bacon and eggs and we can sit at the table and talk to him awhile." Authors' interview with Tom Bilodeau, May 18, 1980. Bilodeau was one of Joe Junior's Harvard roommates.

60

"You know I'm the oldest": Authors' interview with Ted Reardon.

60

"The nightmare of Boston": Authors' interview with Charles Houghton, April 10, 1980. Houghton was another of Joe's Harvard roommates.

60

"It wasn't the father": Authors' interview with Tom Bilodeau.

60

"The minute we got out of the car": Ibid.

60

They flipped a coin: Authors' interview with Ted Reardon.

60

"I got in touch": Searls, p. 58.

60

Youthful competition between Joe Junior and Jack: See Rose Kennedy, pp. 119ff. Also authors' interviews with Lem Billings.

61

"If a mosquito": Rose Kennedy, p. 202.

61

Family friend Kay Halle: Kay Halle Oral History, JFK Library.

61

"I want to stop by the house": Authors' interview with Paul Morgan.

62

The Bundy brothers: Of the three Bundy brothers, McGeorge was apparently the most precocious. Classmate James Storrow, Jr., remembers him sitting in the back of the room and, when called on by the teacher, saying, "I am a most sagacious young man." Storrow interview with Herbert Parmet, who kindly shared his files with the authors. The Kennedy brothers also played on a touch football team in Brookline called the Spitpots, along with Cyrus Vance and Buzzi Bavasi. Authors' interview with Buzzi Bavasi, November 21, 1980.

62

"Sick and dizzy and weak": JFK to JPK, n.d. JFK Personal Files, JFK Library.

62

Taken to New Haven Hospital: Interview with Lem Billings.

62

"He talked about him": Authors' interview with Betty Young.

62

Lem Billings' background: Authors' interviews with Dr. Frederick Billings, November 2, 1981, and Francis H. McAdoo, Sr., October 22, 1981. Also documents and news clippings in Lem Billings' personal archive, hereafter referred to as Billings Papers.

62

Lem and Jack first meet: Authors' interview with Lem Billings.

62

"I'll see you next fall": JFK to LB, June 23, 1933. Billings Papers.

63

"They really didn't": Authors' interview with Lem Billings.

63

"With them, life speeded up": Ibid.

63

"I'm No Angel": Authors' interviews with Peter Kaplan, January 16, 24, March 1, 18, May 13, September 25, 1981; February 28, April 9, 1983.

63n

"Sing it now": Authors' interview with Peter Kaplan.

64

"If you decide to go on vacation": JFK to LB, March 6, 1936. Billings Papers.

64

"Dear Pithecanthropus": JFK to LB, January 27, 1936. Billings Papers.

64

"Dear Barney Oldfield": JFK to LB, April 13, 1936. Billings Papers.

64

"Of all the cheap shit": JFK to LB, December 15, 1936. Ibid. Over the years Lem did become the most frequent guest at the Kennedys', especially on the holidays. Eunice Kennedy Shriver later recalled: "One Christmas my mother said, 'Now we haven't room for any guests this year. We're just going to have the family. We don't want a lot of people staying.' My brother then sent her a wire just before Christmas and said, 'I have a wonderful Christmas present . . .' Then he arrived on the 24th and the present was Lem. . . . We were always thinking of ways to make sure he came." Authors' interview with Eunice Kennedy Shriver, December 1, 1981.

64
Jack and Lem rites of passage: "Rip" Horton, who made a threesome with Jack and Lem at Choate, told Clay and Joan Blair that all three of them went to Harlem where they got white prostitutes for three dollars each. By the time they got back to the Horton family apartment, they were all certain that they had contracted VD and went to a local hospital for salves and creams. Eventually they woke up a doctor in the middle of the night to treat them. Clay and Joan Blair, *The Search for JFK*, New York, 1977 (paperback), p. 26.

65
"If I hadn't just come": JFK to LB, January 20, 1937. Billings Papers.

65
On another occasion: Authors' interview with Lem Billings.

65
Older brothers: "Joe Junior played football at Choate and was in the Student Council, one of the top guys there. Billings' older brother had been a big hero at Choate— captain of the football team, captain of his class. And I think that both Jack and LeMoyne kind of felt that they were not recognized. They couldn't outdo their brothers, so they tried another way, tried to show who they were. . . . Jack would bait Joe, calling him 'the Great Lover from Bronxville' and that sort of thing. Bait him about his gals. One time Joe had a picture of some gal he was especially fond of, and Jack painted a mustache on her." Authors' interview with Tom Schriber, April 20, 1981. Schriber, a classmate of Joe's at Choate, became a friend of the Kennedy family.

65
St. John and the Muckers: St. John had made Choate cloistered and conservative. The application Rose filled out for Joe Junior and Jack contained questions such as: "Is the boy in any way Hebraic?" Friends of Jack's such as "Rip" Horton felt that his rebelliousness at the school may have been related to undercurrents of anti-Catholicism. St. John had decreed that there would be a chapel meeting once a day, at which Catholics like Jack sat silently listening to the other students respond to prayers and later slipped off "downtown" to attend mass by themselves.

65
"Jack and I were labeled": Authors' interview with Lem Billings.

65
"Don't let me lose confidence": Cited in Schlesinger, *RFK*, p. 15. According to St. John's son, the headmaster once said (paraphrasing Theodore Roosevelt's comment about his daughter Alice and the White House), "I can run Jack Kennedy or I can run the school, but I can't do both." Jack's continuing animosity toward Choate was obvious years later in a letter he wrote Lem Billings: "I got an especially sickening letter from Choate wanting me to recommend a boy 'who will carry on the traditions of the present Sixth.' So far I have not been able to think of a big enough prick, but I'm giving it a lot of thought." JFK to LB, May 3, 1939. Billings Papers.

66
"He was roughhousing": JFK to JPK, December 9, 1931. JFK Personal Files, JFK Library.

66
"Most likely to succeed": "Rip" Horton, who helped Jack rig the election, was chosen "most generous." In return for his efforts, Jack gave him a senior portrait inscribed, "To Boss Tweed from Honest Abe, may we room together at Sing Sing." Horton Oral History, JFK Library.

66

"I have just undergone": JFK to LB, n.d. Billings Papers.

66

"They haven't found anything": JFK to LB, January 27, 1936. Ibid.

67

J Six Ranch: Searls, pp. 80–81.

67

"If you could see": JFK to LB, May 25, 1936. Billings Papers.

67

Rosemary and Great Dane: Authors' interview with Paul Morgan. Also authors' interview with Nancy Hill Morgan, November 25, 1980.

67

"Part of the background": Authors' interview with Ann Kelley, September 30, 1980. Kelley grew up with the Kennedy children.

67

"You could talk to Rosemary": Authors' interview with Tom Schriber. As a close friend of the Kennedy boys, Schriber was occasionally asked to escort Rosemary to dances.

68

The older boys and Rosemary: After one such evening, Joseph Kennedy wrote Jack, "Rosemary had a marvelous time and really does not require many gestures like this to make her life worthwhile." Cited in Rose Kennedy, p. 214.

68

"I don't want to hear": Swanson, p. 379.

68

"Dear Daddy": Cited in Rose Kennedy, p. 157.

69

Kathleen was "like sunshine": Dinah (Brand) Bridge Oral History, JFK Library.

69

"Oh my goodness, I forgot to say my morning prayers": Luella R. Hennessey, "Bringing Up the Kennedys," *Good Housekeeping,* August 1961.

69

The "big table": "Just as there were two tables, there were two menus, one for Eunice, Jack, and Jean, who had to put weight on, and another for Joe Junior, Rosemary, Pat, and Teddy, who had to take it off. Kick didn't have a 'problem.' The service was accompanied by ample anatomical teasing by the two sides." Authors' interview with Mary Lou McCarthy.

69

Joe argued with his father: Ibid.

69

Cotton Club incident: Authors' interview with Lem Billings.

70

"Eunice took herself seriously": Authors' interview with Ann Kelley. Eunice's illness—Addison's disease—is confirmed by her son Timothy Shriver. Authors' interviews with Timothy Shriver, June 9, 1980; October 30, 1981.

70

"There would be a bathroom": Authors' interview with Charlotte McDonnell Harris.

70

Teddy the baby: Edward Kennedy later described his childhood environment as a sort of matriarchy: "It was like having a whole army of mothers around me. While it seemed I could never do anything right with my brothers, I could never do anything wrong as far as my sisters were concerned." Cited in Clinch, p. 325.

70

"Hell, the guy knows": Authors' interview with Lem Billings.

70

"Puny and girlish": Authors' interview with Mary Lou McCarthy.

70
Bobby's paper route : Rose Kennedy, p. 116.

71
Hearing the call to dinner : The incident is reported by Bobby's sister Pat in Edward
M. Kennedy, ed., *Bough*, p. 216.

71
"Bobby? Forget it": Authors' interviews with Mary Gimbel, July 11, 1980; March
15, 17, and 19, 1981.

71
Bobby throws himself off yawl : Schlesinger, *RFK*, p. 23.

71
JPK snubbed by Morgan : Whalen, p. 106.

72
Estimates of Kennedy short-selling profits : See *Fortune*, September 1937.

72
"I felt and said": Joseph P. Kennedy, *I'm for Roosevelt*, New York, 1936, p. 3.

72n
"The people who ran the government": Authors' interview with Morton Downey.

72
"I wanted him in the White House": Cited in Joseph P. McCarthy, *The Remarkable
Kennedys*, p. 58.

72
"He was unmistakably Irish": Kay Halle Oral History, JFK Library.

73
"He moved in close to those in power": Cited in Whalen, p. 130.

74
"The nuns were praying": Elliott Roosevelt and James Brough, *A Rendezvous with
Destiny*, New York, 1975, p. 55.

75
"Maybe Jimmy thought": Joseph P. McCarthy, *The Remarkable Kennedys*, p. 60.
Jimmy Roosevelt himself denies having expected any cut of the business. (Authors'
interview with James Roosevelt, December 11, 1979.) But Michael Beschloss claims
that "sources close to the Roosevelt family" told him that Roosevelt was supposed to
get one quarter of the business and went so far as to contact a prominent Washington
attorney regarding breach of contract when it was not forthcoming. Beschloss, *Kennedy and Roosevelt: The Uneasy Alliance*, New York, 1980, p. 292.

75
A million dollars a year : These estimates of the liquor business's worth come from
FBI files on Joseph Kennedy which the authors obtained under provisions of the
Freedom of Information Act.

75
"I told him that I did not desire": Cited in Schlesinger, *RFK*, p. 9.

75
"Mr. Kennedy, former speculator": *Newsweek*, July 7, 1934.

75
"The worst of all parasites": *New Republic*, July 11, 1934.

75
"Kennedy reacted": Raymond Moley, *After Seven Years*, New York, 1939, p. 288.

75
"Having almost everything else": *Boston Post*, December 12, 1937.

76n
Kennedy-Krock relationship : In 1941, Kennedy wrote Krock outlining a talk he'd
had with C. L. Sulzberger in which he'd told the *Times* publisher that he was "terribly disappointed" that Krock hadn't been appointed the paper's editor in chief.
"Sulzberger seemed quite moved by my statement and hastened to explain that . . .
there was no reflection at all on your ability as a most able newspaperman, but he was

of the opinion that he would be criticized if he appointed a Jew as editor since the ownership was in the hands of Jews." JPK to AK, October 10, 1941. Krock Papers, Princeton University Library.
77
"You dumb bastards": Joseph P. McCarthy, *The Remarkable Kennedys*, p. 66.
77
"Joe Jr. will probably": Cited in Beschloss, p. 110.
77
SEC achievements: Arthur Schlesinger, Jr., writes that the SEC under Kennedy "removed the whole process of capital investment from the realm of guess and gamble and rested it—through detailed and continuous disclosure—on a solid mass of reliable fact . . ." (*The Coming of the New Deal*, Boston, 1959)
77
"I am writing this": Grace Tully, *FDR: My Boss*, New York, 1949, p. 157.
77
FDR at Marwood: Authors' interview with Tommy Corcoran, February 17, 1981.
78
"Yes, Mr. President": Krock, p. 310. (In place of "shithouse" Krock left a decorous blank, but he told others what the omitted word was.)
78
"After lunching": Roosevelt and Brough, p. 55.
78
"Jack, I want you to": Edward M. Kennedy, ed., *Bough*, p. 85.
78
"Too many Irish haters of England": Cited in Schlesinger, *RFK*, p. 10.
79
"I am enclosing a copy": JPK to AK, June 25, 1936. Krock Papers.
79
"Joe would want": Jim Farley, *Jim Farley's Story*, New York, 1948, p. 115.
79
"This was the toughest": *Time*, November 22, 1937. Kennedy had done far better with the mess at Maritime than anyone believed he would. Among his other accomplishments was settlement of some $73 million in claims against the government for less than $750,000. *Boston Globe*, December 12, 1939.
79
Jack and Lem in Europe: Authors' interview with Lem Billings.
80
"I'd like to be Ambassador": The incident is described in James Roosevelt, *My Parents: A Differing View*, Chicago, 1976 (paperback), pp. 208–210.
81
"Joe, would you mind": Jimmy Roosevelt says, "It was just a way to have fun with Joe. Because the whole idea of having a Boston Irishman sent to the Court of St. James's tickled my father." Authors' interview with James Roosevelt.
81
Joe called his sister Loretta: Authors' interview with Mary Lou McCarthy.
82
"We're going to London": Authors' interviews with Harvey Klemmer, April 4, 8, 13, and 19, June 23, and November 20, 1980.
82
"Oh, Christ, Harvey": Ibid.
82
"I have a beautiful blue silk room": JPK to James Roosevelt, March 3, 1938. Cordell Hull Papers, Library of Congress. Cited in David E. Koskoff, *Joseph P. Kennedy, A Life and Times*, New Jersey, 1974, p. 121.
83
"Right now": *Time*, March 14, 1938.

83

"I am much happier": Joseph P. McCarthy, *The Remarkable Kennedys,* p. 71.

84

Rose found herself: Authors' interview with Paige Huidekoper, February 16, 1980. Huidekoper was a Kennedy aide at the embassy.

84

"Come on, Lem": Authors' interview with Lem Billings.

84

"Wish you could be here for it": Cited in David Michaelis, *The Best of Friends,* New York, 1983, p. 160. The presentation is discussed at some length in Rose Kennedy, pp. 226ff.

84

"They were like birds of paradise": Authors' interview with Martine Bunnerby, September 11, 1981. Mrs. Bunnerby was a contemporary of the Kennedy girls at the Sacred Heart convent.

84

"Well, five goes into nine": "Nine Young U.S. Ambassadors," *Parents Magazine,* September 1939.

85

"An absolutely wonderful sense of humor": Authors' interview with Fiona Gore, Countess of Arran, October 30, 1982.

85

JPK calls Queen a "cute trick": E. Wilder Spaulding, *Ambassadors Ordinary and Extraordinary,* Washington, 1961, pp. 218–219.

85

Disappear into the crowd himself: Authors' interview with Jane Kenyon-Slaney Compton, November 3, 1982. Mrs. Compton was a good friend of Kathleen Kennedy during the London years.

85

First-name basis with Beaverbrook: The friendship with the English press lord began when Kennedy called to complain about an article in one of Beaverbrook's newspapers. It proceeded from there despite some differences in point of view and resulted in a sizable correspondence. (The Beaverbrook Papers are in the Library of the House of Lords.) Explaining the somewhat unlikely friendship, A. J. P. Taylor said, "Joseph Kennedy was a millionaire. Millionaires were the only kind of people Beaverbrook felt comfortable with." Authors' interview with A. J. P. Taylor, October 23, 1980.

86

Chamberlain's opinion of Hitler: Charles Callan Tansill, *Back Door to War,* Chicago, 1952, p. 432.

86

"I sat spellbound": JPK to Lippmann, March 28, 1938. Lippmann Papers, Yale University Library.

86

"Anne and I": Charles A. Lindbergh, *The Wartime Journals of Charles Lindbergh,* New York, 1970, p. 26.

87

"It was not so much the fact": *Documents on German Foreign Policy, 1918–1945,* Washington, State Department (various dates), I, p. 368.

87

When a poll showed him: Authors' interview with Harvey Klemmer.

87

"Here is Kennedy": *New York Times,* June 23, 1938.

88

"A frigid atmosphere": *Chicago Tribune,* June 23, 1938.

88

"Can you imagine": Cited by Harold Ickes, *The Secret Diaries of Harold L. Ickes,*

II, New York, 1954, pp. 415–416. The inability to obtain an honorary degree capped a history of frustration in Kennedy's dealings with his alma mater. In 1937, at the twenty-fifth reunion of his class, Kennedy had given a New Deal speech which had been greeted with a good-natured razzing that wounded his *amour propre*. The same year Harvard football coach Dick Harlow had infuriated him by not putting Joe Junior into the Yale game, thus denying him a letter.

88

Afraid of being thought rich: Authors' interview with Tom Bilodeau, April 18, 1980.

88

"It was better than nothing": Authors' interview with James Rousmaniere, November 30, 1979. Rousmaniere was a roommate of Jack's at Harvard.

88

"Stiff hands": Authors' interview with Ted Reardon.

89

"Joe would put his head in the way": Ibid.

89

Joe Junior and Laski: Searls, p. 64.

89

"We used to needle him about it": Authors' interview with Tom Schriber.

89

"Now, Joe, what will you do": Searls, p. 68.

89

"The Communists are interested": Edward M. Kennedy, ed., *Bough*, pp. 217–218.

89

"He had to leave without finishing": Authors' interview with Mary Lou McCarthy.

89

"A bunch of Communists and atheists": Cited by Ickes, p. 415.

90

"I'd always been told": Authors' interview with William Randolph Hearst, Jr., May 7, 1980.

90

Joe Junior and Jack called each other "Brother": Authors' interview with Tom Bilodeau.

90

"I want you to know": Payson Wild Oral History, JFK Library.

90

He had tried to play football: Tom Bilodeau recalls a sidelight on Joe Junior's inability to get into the Harvard-Yale game in 1937: "The previous year the same thing happened to Jack in the Harvard-Yale freshman game. It was the same deal—no matter how well you'd done during the season you had to get into that game to win a letter. The game was almost over and Jack hadn't gotten in yet. He went up to the coach and tapped him on the shoulder: 'Hey, how about putting me in?' The coach looked at him and said, 'Who the hell are you?'" Authors' interview with Tom Bilodeau.

90

"Dear Pneumoan": JFK to LB, January 20, 1937. Billings Papers.

90

"Dear LeMoan": JFK to LB, March 13, 1937. Ibid.

90

"Dear Kirk": JFK to LB, March 13, 1937. Ibid.

90

"I can now get tail": JFK to LB, January 13, 1937. Ibid.

90

"Get me a room": JFK to LB, March 3, 1937. Ibid.

91

"As for your rather": JFK to LB, February 1938. Ibid.

91
Jack and Joe Junior at Stork Club: Authors' interview with Timothy Reardon.

91
On one miserable Cape day: Lem Billings remembered a similar incident: "We were sailing to Nantucket in some sort of race on the *Victura*. Joe was the skipper and he just made us stay on the windward rail. I couldn't believe it, it was so cold and horrible. I was never so cold in my life. I was very fed up with him and he wasn't a bit nice about it in my opinion." Authors' interview with Lem Billings.

91
Jack had gotten into Spee: "He had been nominated for Porcellian, the highest-ranking 'final' club, but hadn't gotten in. He felt lucky to get into Spee. Jack tried to get his friend Torbert MacDonald in, but without success. One Irish Catholic was enough for them." Authors' interview with James Rousmaniere.

91
"Jack is taking out Frances Ann Cannon": Rose Kennedy, p. 257.

91
"If the subject of marriage came up": Authors' interview with Charlotte McDonnell Harris.

92n
The romance was broken up: Authors' interview with Ann Kelley, September 30, 1980.

92
"I believe": Authors' interview with James Rousmaniere.

92
"While I felt that perhaps": Cited by James M. Burns, *John F. Kennedy*, New York, 1961, p. 32.

92
"He got this odd, hard look": Authors' interview with James Rousmaniere.

92
Honey Fitz and Mrs. Chamberlain: Rose Kennedy, p. 233.

92
"Met the King this morning": JFK to LB, August 1938. Billings Papers.

93
Kick and Billy: Authors' interviews with Fiona Gore, Jean Lloyd, October 30, 1982; David Ormsby-Gore, October 27, 1982; Jocelyn Hambro, October 27, 1982. Fiona Gore and Jean Lloyd were Billy's cousins; Ormsby-Gore, later Lord Harlech, was his cousin and best friend; Hambro was a classmate.

93
Billy's sister Anne felt: Authors' interview with Lady Anne Cavendish Tree, October 28, 1982.

93
"Hello," she would say: Authors' interview with Fiona Gore.

93
"Here was this lively American": Ibid.

93
The Cavendishes anti-Catholic: For background, see Barbara Tuchman, *The Proud Tower*, New York, 1966, pp. 3ff.

94
"A Romeo and Juliet thing": Authors' interview with Fiona Gore.

94
"I should like to ask you": Cited in Koskoff, p. 158. Roosevelt, upset by the speech, paraphrased the edited sentences to Treasury Secretary Morgenthau as: "I can't for the life of me understand why anybody would want to go to war to save the Czechs." John Morton Blum, ed., *The Morgenthau Diaries: Years of Crisis, 1928–1938*, Boston, 1959, p. 518.

94
"This young man": Blum, ed., *Morgenthau Diaries*, p. 518.

94
"In that event": Ickes, p. 420.

94
"Who would have thought": Blum, ed., *Morgenthau Diaries*, p. 518.

94
He sent a summons: Lindbergh, p. 71.

95
"Germany has such a preponderance": Cited in Telford Taylor, *Munich*, New York, 1980, p. 849.

95
Contents cabled to State Department: The Lindbergh cable said in part, "Without doubt the German Air Fleet is now stronger than that of any other country in the world.... I feel certain that German air strength is greater than that of all other European countries combined.... For the first time in history a nation has the power either to save or ruin the great cities of Europe." See *Foreign Relations of the United States, 1938*, I, pp. 72–73.

95
"I'm feeling very blue": JPK to AK, September 26, 1938. Krock Papers.

95
"I have just gone through": Cited in Beschloss, p. 179.

95
"Germany will get whatever": JPK to AK, March 28, 1938, Krock Papers.

96
He asked Will Hays: *New York Times*, November 24, 1938. Kennedy also tried to have Frank Capra's movie *Mr. Smith Goes to Washington* suppressed, writing Columbia Pictures' Harry Cohn on November 17, 1939: "In foreign countries this film must inevitably strengthen the mistaken impression that the United States is full of graft, corruption and lawlessness.... The times are precarious, the future is dark at best. We must be careful." Copy in Krock Papers.

96
"He would go to Germany": *German Documents*, I, 635.

96
"Defeated any political ambitions": The comment was made by diplomat George Messersmith. Cited in Koskoff, p. 160.

96
"While it seemed to be unpopular": Burns, *JFK*, p. 37.

96
"There can be no peace": *The Public Papers and Addresses of Franklin D. Roosevelt*, compiled by Samuel I. Rosenman, 1938 vol., New York, 1941, pp. 563–564.

96
"I'm so goddamned mad": Cited in Beschloss, p. 179.

97
A casual anti-Semite: Kennedy's anti-Semitism, which he and his sons would later vigorously deny, was real but reflexive, part of the ideology of the melting pot which he devoted his life to climbing out of. His friend Morton Downey recalls a time when Roosevelt sent Henry Morgenthau to Hyannis to see Kennedy, who invited the future Secretary of the Treasury to lunch at the Wianno Club: "The next day he got a call from someone who told him he had gone a little too far by bringing a Jew into the club. Joe told him off. He said to me, 'Can you imagine, this man is representing the President of the United States and this guy has the gall to call me up?' Joe never set foot in the club again." (Authors' interview with Morton Downey.) Yet a few years later, the English politician Hugh Fraser was visiting Jack in Florida and the two of them joined Joe Kennedy in an automobile sightseeing ride. "The Ambassador said, while pointing to some golf club, 'There are some of them in there.' And I said, 'What do you mean?' And he said, 'Jews, don't be stupid.' " (Authors' interview with Sir Hugh Fraser, November 2, 1982.) Kennedy's long-time aide Harvey Klemmer says:

"Joe never spoke well of Jews. He cursed them, called them 'kikes' and that sort of thing. His cronies liked to entertain him with anti-Semitic stories."
97

"They are really a marvelous people": Searls, p. 110.
97

He left a memorandum: Beschloss, p. 181.
98

The Ambassador sat naked: Whalen, p. 251.
98

"Sorry I missed you": Searls, p. 116.
98

"I wish he would": Ibid.
98

"Joseph became deeply enthused": Antonio Garrigues to Robert F. Kennedy, September 28, 1962. Robert Kennedy Personal Files, JFK Library. See also Garrigues Oral History, JFK Library.
98

"See this?": Authors' interview with Ted Reardon.
98

"The entrance of the Nationalist troops": *Atlantic Monthly,* April 1939.
99

Rose had roped off the sofa: Authors' interview with Tom Schriber.
99

"I told my sister": *New York Times,* March 14, 1939.
99

"Just got back from Rome": JFK to LB, March 23, 1939. Billings Papers.
99

"The most attractive couple": JFK to LB, May 3, 1939. Ibid.
99

"Just listened to Hitler's speech": JFK to LB, n.d., May 1939. Ibid.
100

"The ironical part": JFK to JPK, n.d. (1939). JFK Presidential Files, JFK Library.
100

"Make a book out of these": Cited in Lynn McTaggart, *Kathleen Kennedy, Her Life and Times,* New York, 1983, p. 64.
100

Shipments of Haig and Haig: Authors' interview with Charles Houghton. A former classmate of Joe Junior's, Houghton, who worked at the London embassy one summer, felt that Kennedy's efforts regarding Haig and Haig were "in bad taste" and that "at times the Ambassadorship was just a business offer for him."
100

Czech securities: Masaryk's charge cited in Beschloss, p. 241.
101

He lectured congressmen: Authors' interview with James Rowe, January 16, 1981. Rowe, one of FDR's aides, accompanied one of these delegations to London in July 1939.
101

"A little taste": This comment occurs in an unpublished autobiography which Joseph Kennedy commissioned James Landis to write for him after the war but abandoned because of possible adverse effects on Jack's career. A version of this manuscript is in the Landis Papers at the Library of Congress.
101

An embassy evening: Authors' interview with Fiona Gore.
101

He returned to the embassy: Whalen, p. 263.

101
"It's the end of the world": Cited in Joseph Alsop and Robert Kintner, *American White Paper*, New York, 1940, p. 68.
102
"It seems to me": *Foreign Relations of the United States, 1939*, I, pp. 421–424.
102
"The silliest message": Cited in Beschloss, pp. 191–192.
102
"The President desires me": *Foreign Relations of the United States, 1939*, I, p. 424.
103
"No, the Ambassador should not": Quoted by Harold Nicolson, *Diaries and Letters, 1930–1939*, Nigel Nicolson, ed., London, 1966, p. 403.
103
"I'm praying": Marguerite Higgins, "Rose Fitzgerald Kennedy," *McCall's*, May 1961.
103
"And between you and me": Quoted by Rose Kennedy, p. 258.
103
"Many, many thanks for coming": Rose Kennedy, p. 157.
104
"As you love America": *New York Times*, December 11, 1939.
104
Dark-horse candidacy: Whalen, p. 278.
104
"I know I'll die young": Cited in Searls, p. 138.
104
"For Christ's sake": Jay Pierrepont Moffat, *The Moffat Papers: Selections from the Diplomatic Journals of Jay Pierrepont Moffat*, Cambridge, Mass., 1956, p. 297.
104
"He told me": Authors' interview with Joseph Kingsbury Smith, March 27, 1980.
104
"Does not go out": George Bilainkin, *Diary of a Diplomatic Correspondent*, London, 1942, p. 61.
104
"Mr. Kennedy is a very foul specimen": Cited in Koskoff, p. 239.
105
"His mind is as blank": Adolph Berle, *Navigating the Rapids*, New York, 1973, p. 312
105
Joe Junior and Farley dilemma: Krock, p. 317.
105
"No, I wouldn't think of telling him": Cited in Searls, p. 146.
105
"When I was in the States": Bilainkin, p. 194. Kennedy never changed his view of Munich. As late as 1950 he said, "It bought time. I applauded the purchase then; I would applaud it today." *Vital Speeches*, January 1, 1951, pp. 170ff. (Actually the time that Munich bought served the Germans far better than the English, which Jack Kennedy proved convincingly in *Why England Slept*.)
106
Winston Churchill as a hero: On page 51 of the thesis, Jack wrote, "In light of the present-day war, we are able to wonder at the blindness of Britain's leaders and the country as a whole that would fail to see the correctness of Churchill's arguments."
106
The Ambassador asked Krock: He also got Harvey Klemmer, who had become his primary speech writer in London, to take a look at it. "I worked two weeks on it,

night and day, delivered it at four o'clock in the morning on the day that Eddie Moore was to go to New York and take it to the publisher. When I got it, it was a mishmash, ungrammatical. He had sentences without subjects and verbs. It was a very sloppy job, mostly magazine and newspaper clippings stuck together. I edited it, and put in a little peroration at the end." Authors' interview with Harvey Klemmer.

106

"You would be surprised": Cited in Burns, p. 44.

106

"It seemed to represent": Searls, p. 140.

106

"A $75 a week errand boy": JPK to AK, April 22, 1940. Krock Papers.

106

"Perhaps when the bombing begins": Bilainkin, p. 135.

106

"There's hell to pay": Koskoff, p. 258. A few days later he tried to strike a lighter tone in a wire to Roosevelt, comparing himself to "that colored boy in the last war: ... When shells began dropping around him he wailed: 'Lawd, I'se in terrible trouble. You-all better send down one of your angels to help me.' Whammm bang; a shell came closer and he quavered: 'Things am getting worse, Lawdy. I guess you-all better send down one of your saints.' Then, whee bam-bam-bammm; a flock of shells landed even closer to him and the darky cried out; 'Oh Lawd, please hurry, and don't send your Son. You better come yourself, 'cause this is a man-size job.' '' Cited in Koskoff, p. 259.

106

"The British have had it": Authors' interview with Harvey Klemmer.

107

"Once the Blitz started": Ibid. William Randolph Hearst, Jr., says, "I remember hearing from people that he used to go out of town when the bombing was a little rough." Authors' interview with William Randolph Hearst, Jr.

107

"I may be going back": Clare Boothe, *Europe in the Spring*, New York, 1940, p. 200.

107

"Put 25 million behind Willkie": Beschloss, p. 16.

107

"Jack was autographing copies": Damore, p. 57.

108

"Roosevelt and the kikes": Authors' interview with Harvey Klemmer.

108

"I can tell you": Cited in Beschloss, p. 271.

108

"Ah, Joe, old friend": Lyndon Johnson was with FDR during this conversation and later reported it to Krock. See Krock, p. 339.

108

"The President sent you": Beschloss, p. 216.

108

Missy LeHand quickly sprang to the phone: The scene is described by James Byrnes in *All in One Lifetime*, New York, 1958, p. 126.

109

"Nine hostages to fortune": *New York Times*, October 30, 1940.

109

"I have said this before": Tommy Corcoran, who was in control of the Republicans for Roosevelt organization during the third-term push, says that Kennedy's support was important. "It made a difference, perhaps the crucial difference in New York, for instance, with all its Italians, Germans, and Irish who were worried as hell about war. For them Joe's endorsement of FDR was crucial." Authors' interview with Tommy Corcoran.

109

"I'm willing to spend": The story of the *Globe* interview is told in detail by Lyons in *Newspaper Story: One Hundred Years of the Boston Globe,* Cambridge, Mass., 1971. Kennedy tried to give the impression that these comments had been a misinterpreted "slip" which did not represent his true beliefs. But Joseph Criden, an official with the Nieman Journalistic Fellowship Program, examined the circumstances of the interview and found that Lyons had not acted improperly, an opinion which Krock transmitted to Kennedy. (Criden to Krock, November 11, 1940; Krock to JPK, November 12, 1940. Krock Papers.) Moreover, at about the same time he gave the interview to Lyons, Kennedy had a conversation with the diplomat Breckenridge Long, who summarized the Ambassador's views on the shape of things to come as follows: "He thinks we will have to assume a fascist form of government here or something similar to it if we are to survive in a world of concentrated and centralized power . . ." *The War Diary of Breckenridge Long,* Lincoln, Nebraska, 1966, p. 146.

110

"The bombers may be tough": JPK to Beaverbrook, November 13, 1940. Beaverbrook Papers.

110

"Jewish money": Stopping off at Wyntoon, William Randolph Hearst's place near Mount Shasta, Kennedy had a conversation with FDR's son-in-law John Boettinger, who warned the President: "After our talk with Joe in California both Anna and I were considerably worried about what we thought were fascist leanings." Cited in Beschloss, p. 228.

110

"This was unheard of ": Eleanor Roosevelt's reaction was reported by Gore Vidal in the *New York Review of Books,* November 18, 1971, p. 8. See Beschloss, p. 229, for a more complete account of the incident.

111

Isolationists approached him: Beschloss, p. 216.

111

Kennedy radio speech: Landis MS., Landis Papers.

111

"Out-Hamleted Hamlet": Cited in Koskoff, p. 309.

112

Young Joe's antiwar activities: Searls, p. 155.

112

"Sending an air force": Ibid.

112

"He is a smart-aleck": *The London Journal of General Raymond E. Lee, 1940-41,* J. Leutze, ed., Boston, 1971, p. 208.

112

"I think that Jack": Schlesinger, *RFK,* p. 40.

112

"My father": Gene Schoor, *Young John Kennedy,* New York, 1963, p. 155.

112

"I will let your company": JFK to Tom Schriber, n.d. A copy of the letter was given to the authors by Mr. Schriber.

113

Eight-year-old Teddy: John Hersey, interviewed by Herbert Parmet, December 8, 1976. Mr. Parmet gave the authors access to his materials.

113

"You watched these people": Authors' interview with Charles Spalding.

115

"Foreigners didn't realize": Authors' interview with Charlotte McDonnell Harris.

This portrait of Rosemary's development is also based on authors' interviews with Tom Schriber, Ann Kelley, Lem Billings, and Paige Huidekoper; and with Herbert J. Kramer of the Joseph P. Kennedy Jr. Foundation, June 9, 1982.

115

In one traumatic incident: Authors' interviews with George Taylor, May 12, and 21, 1980. Taylor valeted Joe Junior and Jack, among other wealthy Harvard students, and then worked at Hyannis as a chauffeur for Joseph Kennedy.

115

"Kick would draw me out": Authors' interviews with John White, December 6, 1979: March 9 and 10, 1982.

116

Literature about lobotomy: One of the standard texts of the day was *Psychosurgery*, by Walter Freeman and James Watts (Springfield, Ill., 1942). The authors note: "Partial separation of the frontal lobes from the rest of the brain results in reduction of disagreeable self-consciousness, abolition of obsessive thinking, and satisfaction with performance, even though the performance is inferior in quality.... Even though the fixed ideas persist and the compulsions continue for a while, the fear that disabled the patient is banished. How much the relief means to the patient suffering from doubts and fear, morbid thoughts, hallucinations and delusions, and compulsive activities, may easily be imagined.... Not always does the operation succeed; and sometimes it succeeds too well, in that it abolishes the finer sentiments that have kept the sick individual within bounds of adequate social behavior. What may be satisfactory for the patient may be ruinous for the family." Preface to first edition, p. xiii.

116

Rosemary's operation: Rosemary's lobotomy has never previously been publicly acknowledged by the Kennedy family. The fact of the lobotomy has been confirmed to the authors in interviews with Timothy Shriver, Robert Shriver, Christopher Lawford, and Herbert J. Kramer of the Joseph P. Kennedy Jr. Foundation.

116n

"Made her go from": Authors' interview with Timothy Shriver, November 10, 1981.

116

"The lobotomy wasn't necessary": Authors' interview with a confidential source, February 3, 1980.

116

They sent her to St. Coletta's: Cardinal Cushing Oral History, JFK Library. In this interview (conducted by Edward M. Kennedy), Cushing says: "The reason why your father and mother were interested in placing Rosemary in an institution like St. Coletta's was to have her in a religious environment."

116

Privately Joe Kennedy believed: Whalen, p. 376.

117

"Name the battlefront": *FDR: His Personal Letters*, Vol. IV, Elliott Roosevelt, ed., New York, 1950, p. 1290.

117

"I told him to stick it": Letter to Frank Kent, March 2, 1943. Cited in Koskoff, p. 317.

117

"Jews and radicals": JPK to Beaverbrook, December 31, 1942. Beaverbrook Papers.

117

"I am withstanding": Ibid.

117

"A drunken old bastard": Authors' interview with James A. Reed.

117

"Big Joe": Authors' interview with Paul B. "Red" Fay, March 21, 1980.

117

"Honey Fitz has thrown his hat": JFK to LB, n.d., summer 1942. Billings Papers.

Casey always recalled his first meeting with Fitzgerald. "I met him in the lobby of the Bellevue Hotel during the campaign. He came up to me, shook his finger, and said, 'You have maligned me, you have told the people of Massachusetts that I am an octogenarian and that's false.' And I said, 'Well, how old are you?' He said, 'I'm seventy-nine.' " Joseph Casey Oral History, JFK Library.

118n

"We started going good": Authors' interview with Tommy O'Hearn, April 9, 1980.

118

"Young Joe, about to catch": Authors' interview with Tom Schriber.

119

"I'm certainly doing a lot of praying": Schlesinger, *RFK,* p. 30.

119

"He must have felt like an immigrant": Authors' interview with Mary Gimbel, a long-time friend of the Kennedys. Also interview with Dave Hackett, November 1, 1979. Hackett was Bobby's best friend at Milton.

119

"I have gotten": Joe Junior to RFK, n.d. RFK Personal Files, JFK Library.

119

Joe Junior at Jacksonville: Searls, pp. 164ff.

120

"Still can't get used to the coeds": JFK to LB, October 4, 1940. Billings Papers.

120

"This draft has caused": JFK to LB, November 14, 1940. Ibid.

120

JPK wrote Admiral Kirk: Blairs, pp. 109–110.

120n

"Dear DeLemma": JFK to LB, February 12, 1942. Billings Papers.

121

Lem hated these outings: Authors' interview with Lem Billings.

121

Kick in Washington: For an extended portrait of Kathleen, see the authors' "The Kennedy Kick," in *Vanity Fair,* July 1983.

121

"We do live": Kathleen Kennedy to Jane Kenyon-Slaney Compton, May 28, 1941. Mrs. Compton gave the authors a copy of the letter.

121

She had that charismatic Kennedy innocence: Authors' interviews with Frank Waldrop, November 17, 1979; March 3, 1980. Waldrop was executive editor of the *Times-Herald.*

122

Friendship chronicled in White's diary: John White kindly allowed the authors to read and copy the passages in his diary relating to Kathleen Kennedy.

122

"She'd sit and talk": Authors' interview with John White.

122

"KK calls to me": John White diary.

122

"The perfect example of Nordic beauty": The romance between JFK and Inga Arvad and Arvad's background were first uncovered by Clay and Joan Blair; see pp. 122ff. Also authors' interview with Frank Waldrop, who saw the relationship develop, knew all the principals, and later wrote about it in "JFK and the Nazi Spy," *Washingtonian,* April 1975, p. 90.

122

With an assist from Krock: Authors' interview with Frank Waldrop.

122

"Mr. Kennedy kept track": Authors' interview with Lem Billings.

123
On one weekend visit to Palm Beach: Blairs, p. 143.
123
"I wonder what's happening": JFK to LB, February 12, 1942. Billings Papers.
123
Lem stopped off in Charleston: Authors' interview with Lem Billings.
124
"Dear Lemmer": JFK to LB, March 11, 1942. Billings Papers.
124
The FBI bugged her hotel room: Blairs, p. 173.
124
Finally Joe Kennedy pulled more strings: Ibid., pp. 151–152.
124
"As you probably haven't heard": JFK to LB, n.d., summer 1942. Details of Lem's
Africa service in Billings Papers.
124
PT boats: *They Were Expendable,* by W. L. White (New York, 1942), gave a dramatic account of the PTs in the early stages of the war and was later made into a
successful film.
125
"The regulations are very strict": JFK to LB, n.d., summer 1942. Billings Papers.
125
"The old man": Authors' interview with Charles Spalding.
125
"He insisted": John Harlee Oral History, JFK Library.
125
"I'm now on my way to war": JFK to LB, January 30, 1943. Billings Papers.
125
"This was the first time": Rose Kennedy, p. 285.
125
"Dear Children" letters: The one cited here is dated February 2, 1943. JFK Library.
126
JPK in Palm Beach: Authors' interview with Tom Schriber.
126
JPK and the FBI: Kennedy's services as a Special Service Contact for the FBI and
the considerable value agents placed on his service are shown in the private files on
him maintained by the Bureau for some fifteen years, which the authors obtained
under the provisions of the Freedom of Information Act.
127
Eventually he would hold: Koskoff, p. 326. Also authors' interview with Leo Racine,
February 12, 1980. Racine went to work for Joseph Kennedy in 1948.
127
Reynolds convinced Kennedy: Authors' interview with John Reynolds, March 13,
1980.
127
Merchandise Mart purchase: Ibid. See also Whalen, p. 370.
128
"I was amazed, Jack": Authors' interviews with James Reed, April 4, 1980; March
30, 1981.
128
"During a lull": JFK to LB, May 6, 1943. Billings Papers. Jack wrote a somewhat
less graphic letter about this incident to his parents.
128
A fellow Catholic: Authors' interview with James Reed.
128
News from Dinah (Brand) Bridge: McTaggart, p. 123.

129

The crossing was precarious: Kick described her voyage in a letter to her family, June 27, 1943. Copy in Connelly Papers. See also Rose Kennedy, p. 288.

129

Kick found Billy: She made this assessment in a letter to Jack, part of which is quoted by Rose Kennedy, p. 292.

129

"Billy and I went out": Cited in Rose Kennedy, p. 290.

129

A letter to Beaverbrook: KK to Beaverbrook, September 28, 1943. Beaverbrook Papers.

129

"Of course I know": Rose Kennedy, p. 292.

130

"This is how it feels": John Hersey quoted this statement in his *New Yorker* article. Jack also told Lem Billings that this thought went through his mind at the moment of impact. (Authors' interview with Lem Billings.)

130

Details of *PT 109* sinking: See Blairs, pp. 214ff.

130

"Jesus loves me": See Burns, p. 52. This was one of the details that Hersey originally uncovered.

130

In Hyannis: Joey Gargan recalled the situation in Edward M. Kennedy, ed., *Bough*, p. 173.

130

Barney Ross thought: Blairs, p. 345.

130

MacArthur's rumored reaction: Blairs, p. 342.

131

"We have been having": JFK to LB, September 15, 1943. Billings Papers.

131

Some doubted: E.g., Phil Berg, who skippered a squadron in the Pacific during World War II. "This was not a little stream; it was a big strait. Kennedy had the most maneuverable vessel in the world. All that power and yet this knight in white armor managed to have his PT boat rammed by a destroyer. Everybody in the fleet laughed at that." Authors' interview with Phil Berg.

131

JPK lobbying for a medal: "Jack wasn't thinking about medals. Far from it, in fact. The medals were his father's idea. He was going for the Congressional Medal of Honor and had the Navy Cross in mind as a fallback position." Authors' interview with Paul B. "Red" Fay.

131

"When I read that we will": JFK to JPK, n.d. (received September 12, 1943). JFK Library.

131

September 6 celebration: See Searls, p. 183.

131

"By God, I'll show them": Blairs, p. 296.

132

Joe Junior in England: See Searls, pp. 184ff.

132

Pat Wilson: She is identified only as "the girl" by Searls. Authors' interviews with Mark Soden, November 28, 1981, and Jean Lloyd, and phone conversations with Hank Searls and James Ogilvie confirm that it was Pat Wilson Laycock. Mark Soden was Joe's close friend and military buddy in England; James Ogilvie is Pat Laycock's

son-in-law; Jean Lloyd is James Ogilvie's sister. The authors also talked with Pat Wilson Laycock in Dublin, November 18, 1982.
132
"Joe finished up his leave": Rose Kennedy, p. 297.
133
"In regard to Kick becoming a Duchess": JFK to LB, May 6, 1943. Billings Papers.
133
"I know you will be disappointed": Searls, p. 184.
133
"And I swam a lot of breaststroke": Cited in Blairs, p. 342.
133
Publishing history of Hersey article: Ibid., pp. 331ff.
134
"Young Joe has just volunteered": JPK to Beaverbrook, May 24, 1944. Beaverbrook Papers.
134
Fellow fliers noted: Searls, p. 213.
134
"It didn't matter": Frank Moore O'Ferrall Oral History, JFK Library.
134
Kick and Billy negotiate: Interviews with Fiona Gore, Jane Compton. Searls, pp. 207ff. Also Rose Kennedy, pp. 296ff. The possibility of a compact regarding the religion, of the children of their marriage was explored with David Ormsby-Gore. Authors' interview with David Ormsby-Gore, October 27, 1982.
134
Kick and Billy's wedding: *New York Times,* May 7, 1944.
135
"When he felt": Kathleen wrote this remembrance for *As We Remember Joe,* John F. Kennedy, ed., privately printed, 1945. Reprinted in part by Rose Kennedy, p. 297.
135
"The reaction of my own mother": Authors' interview with Ann Kelley.
135
"I'm glad I heard it": Duncliffe, p. 120.
135
"Mrs. Kennedy was too sick": Joseph P. McCarthy, *The Remarkable Kennedys,* p. 110.
135
"Remember you still are": The telegram is reproduced in Edward M. Kennedy, ed., *Bough,* p. 208.
135
"I see now": JPK to Beaverbrook, May 24, 1944. Beaverbrook Papers.
135
"Your plaintive howl": JFK to LB, May 19, 1944. Billings Papers.
136
Eighteen-year-old Bobby: With an irony that underscored his desire to be in the thick of things, Bobby had written Joe Junior: "We haven't really had too much action here on Harvard Square but we're on the alert at every moment for an attack and I'm sure that when it comes we will conduct ourselves according to Navy standards." Schlesinger, *RFK,* p. 537.
136
Code named Aphrodite: For a history of this ill-fated project see Jack Olsen, *Aphrodite, Desperate Mission,* New York, 1970.
136
Chances no better than fifty-fifty: Searls, p. 215.
137
"I appreciate what you're trying": Olsen, pp. 261–262.
137
"I'm about to go into my act": Searls, p. 242. Mary Lou McCarthy says, "Joe and

Rose were mad at Joe Junior because they felt that if he hadn't supported Kick she never would have married Billy.'' Authors' interview with Mary Lou McCarthy.
137
A huge fireball: Details of Joe's death are in Searls, pp. 249ff. Elliott Roosevelt, flying reconnaissance on the mission, recalls only a blinding flash, no debris. Authors' interview with Elliott Roosevelt, December 13, 1979.

PART 2: THE STAND-IN

141
Jack had invited: Account based on interviews with Paul B. ''Red'' Fay, Jr., March 21, 1980; James A. Reed, March 30, April 4, 1980; Jewel Reed, February 27, March 16, 1980; and Kate Thom, January 28, 1980.
141
Calling her ''Your Ladyship'': Authors' interview with Paul B. ''Red'' Fay, Jr.
141
Eunice should join the WAC: Ibid.
141
Bobby kept asking Jack: Authors' interview with James A. Reed.
141
Kick was reading: Authors' interview with Jewel Reed.
142
''The hardest question'': Harrison Rainie and John Quinn, *Growing Up Kennedy*, New York, 1983, p. 127.
142
But the Ambassador: Authors' interview with Jewel Reed.
142
Rose sat: Ibid. Jim Reed shared this opinion. ''You never got the feeling that she was quite all there. She seemed totally out of it. She'd sit there at the foot of the table and break in in the middle of conversations she hadn't been tuned into in the first place. It had apparently always been that way. She was out of it.'' Authors' interview with James A. Reed.
142
''Gosh! If Dad finds out'': Authors' interview with Kate Thom.
142
Barney Ross's performance: Authors' interview with Jewel Reed.
142
''Jack!'': Authors' interview with Kate Thom.
142
''It was a matter of statistics'': Authors' interview with Red Fay.
143
''His worldly success'': *As We Remember Joe*, edited by John F. Kennedy, Cambridge, Mass., privately printed, 1945.
143
''I'm so sorry I broke down tonight'': Shown to authors by Mark Soden during authors' interview, November 28, 1982.
143
''For a long time'': Authors' interview with Lem Billings.
143
''He was the oldest boy'': JPK to Grace Tully, August 29, 1944. Cited by David Koskoff, *Joseph P. Kennedy*, New York, 1974, p. 374.
144
''I feel bad'': Authors' interview with Robert Downes, April 24, 1980.
144
A few days after Labor Day: Joan and Clay Blair, *The Search for JFK*, New York, 1977 (paperback), pp. 359ff.

144

"Come on, you fellows": "The Marquess of Hartington went into battle on 9 September 1944 wearing a waterproof white riding mackintosh and a black beret, carrying a pistol in one hand and a pair of wire cutters in the other ..." Communication to the authors from Major R. E. R. Alderson, regimental historian, Coldstream Guards, January 28, 1983.

144

"I still hate you guys": Authors' interviews with Patsy White, December 5 and 6, 1979, March 28, 1980, and March 13, 1982.

144

The British Government sent a plane: Authors' interview with Elizabeth Cavendish, November 4, 1982.

144

"Well, I guess God": Cited in Hank Searls, *The Lost Prince: Young Joe, the Forgotten Kennedy,* New York, 1977 (paperback), p. 258.

144

"I never met anyone": Authors' interview with Elizabeth Cavendish.

145

"For a fellow": JPK to Beaverbrook, October 22, 1944. Beaverbrook Papers.

145

"Harry, what are you doing compaigning": Merle Miller, *Plain Speaking,* New York, 1974, p. 80.

145

"Every night I say a prayer for him": Bob Considine, *It's All News to Me,* New York, 1967, p. 375.

145

"God! There goes the old man!": Authors' interview with Red Fay.

145

Journalism and teaching: Jack had discussed these careers with Jim Reed and others during the war.

145

"I can feel Pappy's eyes": Paul B. Fay, Jr., *The Pleasure of His Company,* New York, 1966, p. 152.

146

"I'm shadow boxing": Authors' interview with Lem Billings.

146

He organized a campaign: Authors' interview with Robert Downes.

146

He also worked on: Fay, p. 149.

146

His father opened and closed the book: Authors' interview with Red Fay. Later, Joseph Kennedy said to a journalist about the book: "I've started it twenty times, but still go to pieces every time ..." *Washington Post,* November 19, 1969.

146

"I'm sure he never forgets": Cited by Herbert Parmet, *Jack,* New York, 1980, p. 36.

146

The operation was a "disaster": JFK to LB, n.d., 1945. Billings Papers. Also authors' interview with Lem Billings.

146

Pat Lannan: This episode in Jack's life was covered by the Blairs, pp. 376ff.

147

"I'm being fattened up": Authors' interview with Lem Billings.

147

"Public service": Blairs, p. 380.

147

He compared the conference: Ibid., p. 391.

147
Arthur Krock preserved: Arthur Krock, *Memoirs*, New York, 1968 (paperback), p. 326.
147
Together they arranged: Authors' interviews with Charles Spalding, April 22, 23, 1980.
147
Gene Tierney: Tierney wrote about the affair in *Self-Portrait*, New York, 1974. When she met JFK, she was being divorced from the designer Oleg Cassini, who (with his brother Igor) would continue to be involved with the Kennedys for years to come.
148
"Charisma wasn't a catchword yet": Authors' interview with Charles Spalding.
148
Squiring Pat Wilson: Blairs, p. 379; Lynn McTaggart, *Kathleen Kennedy*, New York, 1983, p. 195; authors' interview with Jean Ogilvie, October 30, 1982.
148
"A great thing for the country": Cited in Schlesinger, *RFK*, p. 59.
148
In the spring of 1945 he gave $10,000: Parmet, *Jack*, p. 145.
148
Putting half a million dollars: *New York Times*, January 8, 1946. Kennedy had come under fire for investing so much money out of state in the Chicago Merchandise Mart. His response had been that "the condition of real estate in Boston is scandalous and that of politics is worse." *Time*, September 24, 1945.
149
Kennedy got Governor Maurice Tobin: *Time*, ibid.
149
He later claimed: Authors' interview with John E. Powers, May 26, 1982.
149
"How dare Laski": *Chicago Tribune*, December 6, 1945.
149
He assaulted the new Truman Administration: Joseph P. Kennedy, "The United States and the World," *Life*, March 18, 1946.
149
Pronounced *Bella-View*: Authors' interviews with Billy Sutton, May 27, 1982, and John E. Powers.
149
"One is going to be at": JFK to LB, August 31, 1945. Billings Papers.
150
"A little boy dressed up in his father's clothes": Leo Damore, *The Cape Cod Years of John Fitzgerald Kennedy*, New York, 1967, p. 87.
150
The Ambassador had redoubled his efforts: Authors' interview with Red Fay.
150
The Ambassador had gotten his friend: Parmet, *Jack*, p. 144.
150
An account of the fateful mission: *New York Times*, October 25, 1945.
150
He went to a local radio station: The incident is recalled by Kennedy aide John Dowd in *The Fruitful Bough: A Tribute to Joseph P. Kennedy*, edited by Edward M. Kennedy, privately printed, 1965, p. 102.
150
Time drew the logical conclusion: *Time*, September 24, 1945.
150
"I'm seriously considering": Cited in Michael Beschloss, *Kennedy and Roosevelt: The Uneasy Alliance*, New York, 1980, p. 261.

150

"We're all in this together": Authors' interview with Peter Hoguet, June 2, 1981.

151

A VFW post named after Joe Junior: Blairs, p. 443.

151

Ultimate control always rested: Authors' interview with Billy Sutton. "In January 1946, Jack said, 'Dad wants to see you at the Ritz.' I got out of my GI clothes and got on my new suit. I called and said, 'Mr. Kennedy, this is Bill Sutton.' He said, 'Come on up.' I went up to the room and there was Joe Timilty, Arthur Krock, Morton Downey, and Mr. Kennedy, and he said, 'Mind if I ask you some questions? Who got the most votes in the last congressional election in Charlestown?' I said, 'Higgins got the most; he got 19,000, Douglas got 11,000, and James Hicks got 8,000.' He said, 'That's pretty good, you're pretty close.' That's how I came into the campaign. Mr. Kennedy wanted to know how well I knew the district, because Joe Kane had recommended me."

151

"He'd be sitting": Authors' interview with Mark Dalton, April 19, 1980.

151

The Ambassador gave free rein to Joe Kane: Authors' interview with Billy Sutton.

151

"The Connie Mack": Ibid.

151

In one celebrated campaign: Ibid.

152

"Jack and I would go to bed": Authors' interview with Lem Billings.

152

As Jack circumspectly put it: Ibid.

152

"Come with me, young man": Joseph P. McCarthy, *The Remarkable Kennedys*, New York, 1959, p. 39.

152

"Grandpa, remember": Authors' interview with Red Fay.

152

"Get that son of a bitch out of here": Authors' interview with Billy Sutton.

153

"With what I'm spending": James M. Burns, *John F. Kennedy*, New York, 1959, p. 65.

153

"He was running": Authors' interview with Lem Billings.

153

"I guess I'm the only one": Kenneth O'Donnell and David Powers, *Johnny, We Hardly Knew Ye*, New York, 1973 (paperback), p. 66.

153

"I think I know how you mothers feel": Ibid., p. 60.

153

He was extremely effective in small groups: Authors' interview with Dave Powers, May 18, 1980.

153

"Jack became easily engrossed in people": Authors' interview with James A. Reed.

153

To Lem he gave the impression: Authors' interview with Lem Billings.

154

"To do the job Joe would have done":

154

"I just lit a candle for my brother": Authors' interview with Mark Dalton.

154
"Here, this was Joe's": Authors' interview with Billy Sutton.

154
Cambridge lawyer John Droney: John Droney Oral History, JFK Library.

154
Bobby on the *Joseph P. Kennedy, Jr.: Newsweek,* April 1, 1957.

154
"I wish, Dad": Cited in Schlesinger, *RFK,* p. 59.

154
"It's damn nice of Bobby": Fay, pp. 156–157.

154
"Campaigned as if his life": Authors' interview with Lem Billings.

155
Nearly two thousand women lined up: Rose Kennedy, *Times to Remember,* New York, 1974, pp. 318–319.

155
"He turned yellow and blue": Robert L. Lee Oral History, JFK Library.

155
Jack slipped off with Honey Fitz: John Henry Cutler, *Honey Fitz,* Indianapolis, 1962, p. 309.

155
"I would have given you": O'Donnell and Powers, p. 53.

155
On August 12: Blairs, pp. 512ff. This did not mean that the Kennedys, like the Rockefellers and other families, had turned to philanthropy. The JPK Jr. Foundation was conceived—initially at least—as an adjunct to Jack's political career. Joseph Kennedy himself remained as tight-fisted as ever. Family friend Tom Schriber says: "At about this time, Kennedy's old friend from Wall Street, 'Sell 'Em Ben' Smith, gave $10,000 to Choate and asked the Ambassador to match it for a gift in Young Joe's name. He never did. Mrs. Kennedy resented the fact that Choate was not Catholic. Mr. Kennedy didn't want to give money whose use he didn't control." Authors' interview with Tom Schriber.

156
He hired as his chief aide: An unidentified source told the Blairs (p. 507), "Ted went to Washington because... he'd been Joe's roommate at Harvard and Joe had promised Ted that they would stick together and he would take Ted wherever he went in life." In interviews with the authors, Reardon disagreed that this was the reason he got the job.

156
"No greater love": Authors' interview with Mark Dalton.

157
Engineering his selection: Blairs, p. 536.

157
A young Californian who struck Jack's aide: Billy Sutton Oral History, JFK Library.

157
"One of the Suttons of Boston": Authors' interview with Billy Sutton.

158
Jack told Sutton to imitate Marcantonio: Ibid.

158
Joseph Alsop found a hamburger: Authors' interview with Joseph Alsop, July 22, 1980.

158
"Jack was very casual": Authors' interview with Jane Blodgett, March 27, 1981.

158
Mary Davis was irked: Mary Davis Oral History, JFK Library.

158

Almost everyone was annoyed: E.g., authors' interview with George Smathers, March 15, 1980: "I had become aware that he was a guy who never carried any cash money with him, and hardly knew anything about money, as a matter of fact. Here I was, a relatively impecunious congressman and senator, and we'd go places together—we went to Europe—and Christ, he'd never pick up the check."

158

George Smathers finally began submitting: Authors' interview with George Smathers.

158

The Ambassador finally begged Smathers: Ibid.

158

"Like trying to tell a nun": Authors' interview with Charles Spalding.

158

"Good God, Jack": Authors' interview with George Smathers.

158

Eunice with commission on juvenile delinquency: Joseph Dineen, *The Kennedy Family*, New York, 1959, pp. 125ff.

159

After going to Stanford: Authors' interview with Arthur Poole, August 23, 1979. Eunice lived with the Pooles in Palo Alto. Interview with Herbert J. Kramer, Director of Communications, Joseph P. Kennedy Jr. Foundation, June 9, 1982.

159

"If that girl had been born": Authors' interview with George Smathers.

159

She once appeared at a party: A photograph of Eunice in this costume is in the Billings Papers.

159

Eunice and McCarthy: Blairs, p. 544.

159

McCarthy claim to have ridden in *PT 109:* Roy Cohn, *McCarthy*, New York, 1968, p. 16.

159

He liked the Wisconsin Senator's crude humor: Authors' interview with Charles Spalding.

159

Jack was less taken with Sargent Shriver: Authors' interview with Lem Billings.

159

"Christian, Aristotelean": Robert Liston, *Sargent Shriver*, New York, 1964, p. 39.

159

She met him at dinner: Authors' interview with Peter Hoguet, June 2, 1981.

159

A "ferociously dogged courtship": Ibid.

159

She tried his affection: Authors' interview with a confidential source, April 24, 1981.

160

"We want you to be happy children": Authors' interview with Billy Sutton.

160

"I guess there'll always be a Rosemary": Ibid.

160

"For Godsakes": Authors' interview with Phyllis MacDonald, July 13, 1980.

160

"Kennedy Pro-German": *Boston Globe*, July 17, 1949.

161

He had hired James Landis: For a detailed look at the Landis-Kennedy relationship, see Donald A. Ritchie, *James M. Landis: Dean of the Regulators*, Cambridge, Mass., 1980.

161
"A small part was readable": AK to JPK, July 6, 1948. Krock Papers.

161
He sold the liquor business: Whalen, p. 371.

161
He transferred a quarter of the ownership: *Boston Globe,* March 22, 1947.

161
He made what had always been: Interview with Leo Racine of Joseph P. Kennedy Enterprises, Inc., December 12, 1980.

161
"Please inform Pat": Ibid.

161
Investments in oil and gas: Ibid.

161
He turned down an invitation: Authors' interview with Bobby Shriver, May 16, 1983. Shriver wrote a Yale senior thesis on his grandfather's business decisions, which was based in part on interviews with employees of JPK Enterprises who had worked for Joseph Kennedy.

161
He also passed up chances: James Landis, a former head of the Civil Aeronautics Board, had recommended the airlines in a memo to the Ambassador: "On the airline situation, obviously Eastern is an excellent property . . . Barring a depression, traffic will continue to grow and can grow very significantly if fare reductions can be made. . . . TWA can be made into something if [Howard] Hughes will step out, but it would take a long time to get back anything that would be put into it." Undated memo, Landis Papers, Library of Congress.

161
Fortune estimated its value: In November 1957, *Fortune* published a list of the richest men in America, estimating Kennedy's wealth at $250–$400 million, ranking him among the top ten in the country. The list was published by the *New York Times,* October 28, 1957.

161
"A certain amount of shopkeeping": Authors' interview with Charles Spalding.

162
The Ambassador bombarded Jack: Authors' interviews with Timothy J. Reardon, June 10, 13, 1982.

162
"It was Mr. Kennedy": Ibid.

162
"Now look here, Dad": Kay Halle Oral History, JFK Library.

162
"I guess Dad has decided": Authors' interview with Lem Billings.

162
"Any veteran": John F. Kennedy Congressional Files, JFK Library.

162
"The leadership of the American Legion": Burns, p. 75.

163
JFK stand on Curley: Billy Sutton says that in taking his stand against Curley, Jack defied his father. Authors' interview with Sutton. However, Herbert Parmet writes that the Ambassador supported Jack's decision not to sign the clemency petition. See Parmet, *Jack,* p. 183.

163
"If portions of Europe": *Vital Speeches,* January 1951, pp. 170ff.

163
"We should still fight": *Congressional Record,* January 4, 1947.

163n
"I used to take my economic views": Authors' interview with David Ormsby-Gore, Lord Harlech, London, October 27, 1982.
163
According to George Reedy: Authors' interview with George Reedy, July 7, 1980.
164
Jack made his first headlines: Ibid.
164
"I would like to offer a toast": Authors' interview with Mark Dalton.
164
She had "gone completely English": Authors' interview with Lem Billings.
164
Upon her return to London: Authors' interview with Lady Anne Cavendish Tree.
164
"At present": KK to Frank Waldrop, April 1, 1945. Shown to the authors by Frank Waldrop.
165
A succession of religious retreats: Authors' interview with Lem Billings. The authors also interviewed the present Mother Superior, who was a nun at the time of Kathleen's visits.
165
"She smiled sort of sadly": Authors' interview with Jane Kenyon-Slaney Compton.
165
She had resigned: The reunion and Kathleen's American stay are described in McTaggart, pp. 198–202.
165'
"It's rather nice not having to be a Kennedy": Authors' interview with a confidential source, October 29, 1982.
165
She did as she liked: Authors' interviews with Sir William Douglas Home, October 29, 1982; Lady Jean Lloyd, October 30, 1982; and David Ormsby-Gore.
165
Kathleen's salon: Authors' interview with Sir Hugh Fraser, November 2, 1982.
166
Fitzwilliam's ancestry: *Burke's Peerage*, pp. 466-468. Authors' interview with Joyce Countess Fitzwilliam, November 4, 1982.
166
"No one I have ever met": KK to Jane Kenyon-Slaney Compton, May 28, 1941.
166
At the Commandos Ball: McTaggart, p. 209.
166
"Peter and Kathleen sort of eyed each other": Authors' interview with Jane Kenyon-Slaney Compton.
166
"It was overnight": Authors' interview with Charlotte McDonnell Harris, March 4, 1983.
166
Fitzwilliam's wealth: Authors' interview with H. N. Sporborg, November 2, 1982.
166
Fitzwilliam something of a rake: Authors' interviews with Michael Tree, October 28, 1982, and Fiona Countess of Arran, October 30, 1982.
166
"Peter had all the charm": Authors' interview with H. N. Sporborg.
166
"Like Joseph Kennedy himself": Authors' interview with Jane Kenyon-Slaney Compton.

166
Jack met Kick at Lismore: Blairs, p. 584.

166
Letter of introduction to "original Kennedys": Authors' interview with Mary Lou McCarthy. See also Connelly Papers.

167
"Did they have a bathroom?": Blairs, p. 586.

167
The diagnosis was Addison's disease: Blairs, pp. 586-589. The Blairs were the first to research the question of Jack's health exhaustively and to establish with certainty that he had suffered from Addison's disease that had been life-threatening in severity.

167
"That American friend of yours": Ibid.

167
"Congressman John F. Kennedy announced today": *Boston Herald,* October 7, 1947.

167
Extreme unction for JFK: Authors' interview with Frank Waldrop, November 17, 1979. Jack's aide at the time, Mark Dalton, confirms the seriousness of this episode: "Jack was desperately sick in London. Nobody was supposed to know how sick but some of us did. There was a big Knights of Columbus meeting in Cambridge he'd been scheduled to address. He couldn't, of course, so I called his father at the last minute. Joe began in the usual way—'Cambridge has special memories for the Kennedys ... I went to Harvard and so did my sons,' et cetera. Then he broke down and couldn't go on for a couple of minutes. He knew how sick Jack was." Authors' interview with Mark Dalton.

167
"Something like walking leukemia" Cited in Arthur Schlesinger, *A Thousand Days,* Boston, 1965, p. 96.

167
His office insisted: Ted Reardon later told the authors that he himself didn't know Jack had Addison's disease and therefore "attributed all his problems to the Pacific." Authors' interview.

167
Jack kept Kick's secret: Authors' interview with Lady Elizabeth Cavendish. See also the authors' article on Kathleen: "The Kennedy Kick," *Vanity Fair,* July 1983.

167
Fitzwilliam's wife an alcoholic: Authors' interview with H. N. Sporborg.

167
Kick spent the first weeks: Authors' interview with Lady Elizabeth Cavendish.

168
"The weather looks": Authors' interview with Ted Reardon.

168
"My reaction to it": Authors' interview with Charlotte McDonnell Harris.

168
"Billy I think": Ibid.

168
The family had gathered: Ibid.

168
"True mother church": Authors' interview with Lem Billings.

168
"I don't know what to do": Authors' interview with Patsy White.

169
"She looked radiant": Authors' interview with Tom Schriber.

169n
On March 23, Kennedy cabled: JPK to Beaverbrook, March 23 and April 30, 1948. Beaverbrook Papers.

169

Rose appeared : McTaggart, p. 228.

169

She and Fitzwilliam had already planned : Authors' interview with H. N. Sporborg.

169

Kathleen asked Jane : Authors' interview with Jane Compton.

169

Kick and Fitzwilliam at Milton : Authors' interview with Joyce Countess Fitzwilliam.

169

"I'm going to do all I can" : Ibid.

169

The next morning : Authors' interview with H. N. Sporborg.

169

By late afternoon : McTaggart, pp. 234ff.

170

"Is it for sure ?" : Authors' interview with Billy Sutton. Family friend Dinah (Brand) Bridge remembers getting the news : "Eunice rang up and said Kick was dead, and would I go around. As far as I remember, Eunice, Pat, and Jack were there, and there was a grim tragic restlessness about the atmosphere, with the gramophone playing, and a closing in the ranks of family and friends, but no emotional collapse." Dinah Bridge Oral History, JFK Library.

170

The Ambassador identified : "The Kennedy Kick," *Vanity Fair*, July 1983.

170

Billy's parents paid the priest : McTaggart, pp. 241ff.

170

"The stricken face of old Joe Kennedy" : Alastair Forbes, "Upper Classmates," *Times Literary Supplement*, March 26, 1976.

170

Mass card with plenary indulgence : McTaggart, p. 245.

170

"It seems a strange" : Clipping of obituary shown to the authors by John White.

170

"The sudden death" : JPK to Beaverbrook, July 27, 1948. Beaverbrook Papers.

171

Eunice lashed out : Authors' interviews with John White and Patsy White.

171

"For her that airplane" : Authors' interview with Lem Billings.

171

"Kathleen and Joe [had] everything moving" : Cited in Burns, p. 54.

171

He told Joe Alsop : Authors' interview with Joseph Alsop.

171

"Tell me, Teddy boy" : Authors' interview with Ted Reardon.

171

George Smathers, who saw Jack : Authors' interview with George Smathers.

171

"He wanted to know" : Ibid.

172

"There was something about time" : Authors' interview with Charles Spalding, April 22 and 23, 1980. These sentiments are echoed in one form or another by almost everyone who got to know Jack at this time, although many did not know his personal circumstances well enough to connect this intensity with his precarious health. Columnist Rowland Evans, for instance, says, "Jack was simply the most appealing human being I ever met. He loved people—not in the intimate sense perhaps, but he loved their humanness. He loved conversation. The more personal and gossipy the more he loved it. Whenever you had inside, salacious stuff, he wanted to hear it. It was part of the human comedy.'' Authors' interview with Rowland Evans, July 22, 1980.

172
"Well, I guess if you don't": Authors' interview with Eugene McCarthy, March 28, 1980.

172
"I don't think": Cited in Blairs, p. 534.

172
FDR and Yalta: "A sick Roosevelt, with the advice of General Marshall and other chiefs of staff, gave the Kurile Islands as well as the control of various Chinese ports, such as Port Arthur and Darien, to the Soviet Union." *Congressional Record*, February 21, 1949.

172
"Our policy in China": Ibid.

173
McCarthy "may have something": For an account of JFK's appearance at the Graduate School of Public Affairs, see John P. Mallan, "Massachusetts: Liberal and Corrupt," *New Republic*, October 3, 1952. Mallan, a student at the time, took notes on Kennedy's speech. When he published his controversial report about the appearance two years later, Kennedy tried to deny he had said these things, but historians have since determined that the article was "essentially accurate." See Parmet, *Jack*, pp. 211ff.

173
"I think time was heavy": William O. Douglas Oral History, JFK Library.

173
Jack always inveighed about "psychologizing": Authors' interview with Charles Spalding.

173n
The chief problem: For lengthy discussions of these therapeutic efforts, see the Blairs, pp. 595ff.

173
"The father and husband": See Conrad Arensberg, *The Irish Countryman*, New York, 1968 (paperback), p. 63.

174
"This is going to be something": Authors' interview with Charles Spalding.

174
"Be sure to lock your door": Authors' interview with Patsy White.

174
"Your husband is just a two-bit politician.": Cited in Blairs, p. 364.

174
A young woman named Edie: Authors' interview with Red Fay. Fay was amazed at the flagrant nature of this relationship. "Jesus, Jack, what's going on with this woman Edie?" he once asked his friend. Jack shrugged, making it clear this was a subject he didn't want to discuss: "He says she's a friend of his."

174
"For an instant": Authors' interview with Jewel Reed.

174
"Jack loved his mother": Authors' interview with Lem Billings.

174
"Do you really want": Authors' interview with Priscilla McMillan, April 23, 1980.

174
"My mother is a nothing": Authors' interviews with Mary Gimbel, July 11, 1980, March 15, 17, and 19, 1981, and April 28, 1981.

175
Jack often didn't bother: Authors' interview with Gloria Emerson, March 23, 1981.

Emerson roomed with one of Jack's girlfriends of the time and double-dated with him.
175
"He was as compulsive": Ibid.
175
One such date: Authors' interview with Jane Blodgett.
175
"Jack really wasn't": Ibid.
175
"Bobby, look at this fine chick": Bobby Baker with Larry King, *Wheeling and Dealing: Confessions of a Capitol Hill Operator*, New York, 1978, p. 77.
175
"He had absolutely no idea": Authors' interview with Jewel Reed.
175
"He knew he was using women": Authors' interview with Lem Billings.
175
"He'd read everything about him": Authors' interview with Charles Spalding.
176n
"In what way?": Authors' interview with Lady Diana Cooper, October 26, 1982.
176
"The whole thing with him": Authors' interview with Priscilla McMillan.
177
"We're just worms": Burns, p. 93.
177
"I've decided": Authors' interview with Lem Billings.
178
"I said, 'For Chrissakes, Jack' ": Authors' interview with George Smathers.
178
"Why should they take risks": Statement to the U.S. Senate Committee on Foreign Relations, February 22, 1951.
178
"Bobby felt he was weak": Authors' interview with Charles Spalding.
179
Research paper on Yalta: After surveying the background and decisions of the conference and saying that it was incumbent on the United States to place itself on the "right side morally" regarding the Eastern European sphere FDR had conceded to the Soviets, Bobby wrote: "This he failed to do and it will be to our everlasting dishonor." A copy of "A Critical Analysis of the Conference at Yalta, February 4–11, 1945" was made available to the authors by the University of Virginia Law Library.
179
"He is just starting out": JPK to Beaverbrook, March 23, 1948. Beaverbrook Papers.
179
"My friends soon burst into": Authors' interview with John Magnuson, January 27, 1983.
179
Bobby was "heavy in the water": Harold Ullen Oral History, JFK Library.
179
Skakel backgrounds: Lester David, *Ethel, The Story of Mrs. Robert F. Kennedy*, New York, 1971. "I once got an idea of exactly how rich the Skakels were," Tom Bilodeau recalls. "Jack was on the road making political appearances. He had an impossibly tight schedule. We were all standing around wondering how he'd ever manage to get where he was going on time. The Ambassador finally looks at Jack and says, 'Well, why don't you get Bobby to ask Ethel to find out if we can borrow one of the Skakels' *fast* planes.' " Authors' interview with Tom Bilodeau.

180
"Un paquet de nerfs": David, p. 25.
180n
In another legendary family ritual: Ibid., p. 6.
180
"An excited hoarse voice" Ibid., p. 36.
180
"I like films such as *South Pacific*": Cited in Margaret Laing, *Robert Kennedy*, London, 1968, p. 18.
180
"Bobby, *you* tell it": Authors' interview with Anita Fay, April 2, 1980. Rose would use Ethel in her sales pitch for Manhattanville over Wellesley and the other of the "seven sisters." She told one of her nieces that the Catholic school was far "safer" and also better preparation for the future: "If you're worried about getting a husband, just look how well Ethel made out." Cited in Gail Cameron, *Rose*, New York, 1973, p. 52.
180
The Ambassador drove up from New York: Authors' interview with Mary Lou McCarthy.
180
George Skakel, Jr., threw pennies: Authors' interview with Robert F. Kennedy, Jr., December 28, 1980.
181
"A pain in the ass": Authors' interview with Lem Billings.
181
"Must give the same aura": Cited in Schlesinger, *RFK*, p. 91. In a letter from Beirut, Bobby described the Mideast situation to his father in grim terms: "There is no question but that the Arab world is lost to the west. Where three years ago there was not an Arab Communist, now they are a large vocal force.... It is not that the people know anything about the ideas or principals [sic] of Communism, but they just repeat the old Arab belief that 'the enemy of our enemy (Israel) is our friend.' And they feel because of the work of Communist agents Russia is the enemy of Israel." RFK to JPK, October 10, 1951. RFK Personal File, JFK Library.
181
A "very, very major impression": Ibid.
181
"The formative experience": Authors' interview with Walt W. Rostow, September 30, 1982.
181
Gullion cautioned him: Authors' interview with Edmund Gullion, October 2, 1982.
181
In twenty years: Ibid.
181
"Because of the great U.S. war aid": RFK to JPK, October 28, 1951. RFK Personal File, JFK Library.
182
An abrasive interview: Authors' interview with Edmund Gullion.
182
"The fires of nationalism": Cited in Parmet, *Jack*, p. 227.
182
"Now, Paul": Garrett Byrne Oral History, JFK Library.
182
"Sat in an office": Authors' interview with Tommy O'Hearn. "If it hadn't been for Mark Dalton on a given Saturday afternoon in 1951, Jack might not have been President. He and Dever were fencing around as to which would run for Governor and which for Senator. Jack was getting mad. At one point he said, 'That guy's not

going to hang me up any more.' We went out from his place at 122 Bowdoin and took a walk. We passed in front of the State House. I could tell he was thinking about it. He went to a booth and called Mark Dalton and asked him if he could beat Lodge. Dalton said, 'Yes, but it will be a close race.' Jack said, 'Prepare the announcement for the Senate.' " Authors' interview with Tommy O'Hearn.

182

"We've got the race": Larry O'Brien, *No Final Victories*, New York, 1974, p. 26. Mark Dalton remembers: "We wrote out a statement of candidacy and called the Ambassador and read it to him. The old man said to call Jim Landis and Arthur Krock and clear it with them and then put it out to the papers." Authors' interview with Mark Dalton.

183

"All I ever heard": Joseph P. McCarthy, *The Remarkable Kennedys*, p. 25.

183

Lem Billings was working: Authors' interview with Francis H. McAdoo, October 22, 1981. McAdoo was vice president of Emerson Drug.

183

One was Kenny O'Donnell: Authors' interview with Robert Ajemian, September 25, 1981. Ajemian was a classmate of O'Donnell's.

184

"Had thought and questioned": In Edward M. Kennedy, ed., *Bough*, p. 28.

184

JPK's control of 1952 campaign: John T. Burke, who was in charge of advertising, says: "I met frequently with Mr. Joseph P. Kennedy in [his] apartment.... As a matter of fact, most of the time I would meet with Mr. Kennedy prior to meeting with our own little group [of campaign directors]. I would see him first and show him the material we had in." John T. Burke Oral History, JFK Library.

184

The Ambassador attacked Dalton: "It was rough," recalls Larry O'Brien, who joined the campaign that day. "There was a fairly large group in the room and it was a heavy scene. I saw a broken Mark Dalton." Authors' interview with Larry O'Brien, November 7, 1979.

184

Jack shrugged impotently: Authors' interview with Mark Dalton.

184

The Ambassador discovered anti-McCarthy ad: Burns, p. 109.

184

"I'll just screw it up": Cited in Schlesinger, *RFK*, p. 94.

184

JPK arranged RFK's Justice Department job: Authors' interview with Ted Reardon.

184

O'Donnell persisted: See O'Donnell and Powers, p. 84.

184

"It was Bobby's first ... opportunity": Authors' interview with Ted Reardon.

184

Before and after the revolution: John Droney Oral History, JFK Library.

185

"My brother Jack couldn't be here": Cited in Laing, p. 97.

185

JPK sat high in the balcony: Damore, p. 115. Also authors' interview with Larry O'Brien.

185

JPK loan to *Boston Post*: See Richard Whalen, *The Founding Father*, New York, 1964 (paperback), p. 419. The Ambassador had had an interest in the *Post* for some time. According to James Landis, he had considered buying the paper in the late 1940s, when it was sold to John Fox. Worried that Jack's health would make it

impossible for him to keep up with the rigors of political life, he had thought to give
him the editorship of the *Post* as another way of wielding power. See Whalen, p. 402.
185
"From 1952 on": Tip O'Neill is quoted in Burton Hersh, *The Education of Edward
Kennedy*, New York, 1972, p. 155.
185
"Greetings, you have made a political contribution": Authors' interview with Leo
Racine.
185
"I don't want my brother": Authors' interview with John E. Powers.
186
"Don't give in to them": O'Donnell and Powers, p. 100.
186
"I know you're an important man": Nick Thimmisch, *Robert Kennedy at Forty*,
New York, 1963, p. 113.
186
"Look at what a Christly mess": Authors' interview with Tommy O'Hearn.
186
Ted Reardon had spent weeks: Authors' interview with Ted Reardon.
186n
"While he terms himself": Ted Reardon showed his personal copy of the "Black
Book" to the authors.
186
"He has been much closer": the "Black Book," Ted Reardon's copy.
187
McCarthy checked size of JPK contribution: Roy Cohn, *McCarthy*, New York, 1968,
p. 66.
187
"How dare you couple the name": Robert Amory Oral History, JFK Library.
187
"Just another shanty Irish": Authors' interview with Charles Spalding.
187
"Up here this anti-communist business": Quoted in John Bartlow Martin, *Adlai
Stevenson of Illinois*, New York, 1976, p. 683.
187
"I certainly didn't want him": Parmet, *Jack*, p. 250.
187
The Ambassador suspect in the Jewish community: Authors' interview with Phil
Fine, April 11, 1981. Fine was a pro-Kennedy leader in Boston's Jewish community.
188
"Would you forgive me": O'Brien, p. 35.
188
"The blueberries are *out*": Authors' interview with Ted Sorensen, October 30, 1979.
188
"I'm sure they are quite pleasant": Cabell Phillips, "Case History of a Senate
Race," *New York Times Magazine*, October 26, 1952.
188
An eight-page tabloid: Shown to the authors by Phil Fine.
188
"Joe was smooth": Authors' interview with Ted Reardon.
189
"I will work out plans": Edward M. Kennedy, ed., *Bough*, p. 127.
189
"At last the Fitzgeralds": Laing, p. 100.
189
"Sonofabitch": Larry O'Brien, p. 37.

189
JFK sang "Sweet Adeline": John Droney Oral History, JFK Library.
189
"The robber baron is still his highest ideal": Cutler, *Honey Fitz*, p. 200.
189
"The first Irish Brahmin": Cited in Schlesinger, *RFK*, p. 97.
190
"We were all sitting": Authors' interview with Dinah (Brand) Bridge, October 19, 1982.
190
"From the beginning": Authors' interview with Lem Billings.
190
"Her eyes are so far apart": Authors' interview with Mary Gimbel.
191
"He saw her as a kindred spirit": Authors' interview with Lem Billings.
191
The Bouviers were immigrants too: Background data on the Bouvier family from John H. Davis, *The Bouviers*, New York, 1969.
191
"Bouvier was unusual": Authors' interview with a confidential source, July 15, 1982.
192
"Lee was the pretty one": Kitty Kelley, *Jackie Oh!*, New York, 1979 (paperback), p. 18.
192
"A chubby little thing": George Carpozi, Jr., *The Hidden Side of Jacqueline Kennedy*, New York, 1967 (paperback), p. 13.
192
Junior year in Paris: Davis, pp. 351ff.
192
Wins Prix de Paris: Ibid, pp. 354–355. She chose Baudelaire, Oscar Wilde, and Sergei Diaghilev as the subjects for the "People I Wish I Had Known" essay which made up the most important part of the contest.
192
Jackie's fey questions as inquiring photographer: Kelley, p. 18.
192
"Jackie's great talent": Authors' interview with Mary Gimbel.
192
Michael Canfield rowing them around lake: Ibid.
193
Men born to drive, women to be driven: William Manchester, *Controversy*, Boston, 1978, p. 10.
193
"If I want any photos": Susan Sheehan, "The Happy Jackie, the Sad Jackie, the Bad Jackie, the Good Jackie," *New York Times Magazine*, May 31, 1970.
193
"Don't pay any attention": Kelley, p. 5.
193
Jackie did one of her interviews with Jack: Parmet, *Jack*, p. 260.
193
She translated reports: Authors' interview with Daniel Ellsberg, September 9, 1979.
193
"Rhymes with queen": Kelley, p. 30.
193
Ethel "more Kennedy than thou": Authors' interview with Lem Billings.
193
"With those feet of yours?": Kelley, p. 30.

193
"Fell all over each other": Ibid.

193
Lem Billings took her into a corner: Authors' interview with Lem Billings.

194
"She wasn't sexually attracted": Authors' interview with Charles Spalding.

194
"All I want to do": Authors' interview with a confidential source, July 18, 1982.

194
"I couldn't visualize him": Authors' interview with Lem Billings.

194
"They talked about sports": Davis, p. 308.

194
"She has a tendency to think I'm not good enough": Fay, p. 160.

194
Jack delayed the announcement for the *Saturday Evening Post:* Parmet, *Jack,* p. 260.

194
JFK bachelor party: Authors' interview with Red Fay.

195
Jackie's father provided the melodrama: Stephen Birmingham, *Jacqueline Bouvier Kennedy Onassis,* New York, 1978 (paperback), p. 80.

195
"He would build empires": The poem appears in its entirety in Rose Kennedy, pp. 351–353.

195
"No perceptions": Authors' interview with Mary Gimbel.

195
A very private manuscript: Authors' interview with a confidential source, April 24, 1981.

195
Oil painting episode: Authors' interview with Lem Billings.

196
"You might remind her": Cameron, p. 249.

196
"Jack went crazy": Authors' interview with Lem Billings.

196
Jack and Winston Churchill: Sir William Douglas Home Oral History, JFK Library. Also authors' interview with Sir William Douglas Home.

196
"They were so much alike": Authors' interview with Lem Billings.

197
"In the pictures of all of us": Authors' interview with Anita Fay, April 2, 1980.

197
"Jack appreciated her": Authors' interview with Charles Spalding.

197
"I don't think there are any men who are faithful": Kelley, p. 67.

197
She found herself stranded at parties: Authors' interviews with Priscilla McMillan and Gloria Emerson.

197
"Jack liked to go": Authors' interview with George Smathers.

197
"Jack kept assuring us": Authors' interview with James A. Reed.

197
"After the first year": Authors' interview with a confidential source, April 24, 1981.

198
Jack and Werner von Braun: Werner von Braun Oral History, JFK Library.
198
Sorensen background: Theodore Sorensen, *Kennedy,* New York, 1965, p. 17.
198
First interview with JFK: Ibid., p. 12.
198
"You've got to remember": Authors' interview with Theodore Sorensen.
198
"Jack Kennedy wouldn't hire": Sorensen, p. 11.
198
Sorensen submits articles under JFK by-line: See Parmet, *Jack,* pp. 269ff.
199
He could impersonate Jack: Sorensen, pp. 60–61.
199
Sorensen eclipses Reardon: Jean Mannix Oral History, JFK Library.
199
"You couldn't write speeches for me": Sorensen, p. 31.
199
Sorensen and JFK cabinet choices: Ibid., pp. 17–18.
199
William O. Douglas and Diem: William O. Douglas Oral History, JFK Library. Diem was touring the country as part of an effort to rally the "Catholic lobby." He spent time at Maryknoll College, in Lakewood, New Jersey, where his older brother, a priest, was studying. Diem left Maryknoll allegedly to become a member of a Benedictine monastery in Belgium.
199
"To encourage through all means": Cited in John Galloway, ed., *The Kennedys and Vietnam,* New York (Facts on File), 1971, p. 7.
199
A Communist takeover imperiled Burma. Ibid., p. 9.
200
"The war can never be successful": *New York Times,* July 2, 1953.
200
"To pour money, matériel and men": Galloway, ed., p. 11.
200
"Issues which he and I don't discuss": Authors' interview with Charles Spalding.
201
"It's true": Ibid.
201
"Jesus, Jack": Authors' interview with Red Fay.
201
"Don't worry": Kelley, p. 41.
201
Reardon asked about JFK health problems: Ernest Warren Oral History, JFK Library.
201
"I'd rather be dead": Authors' interview with Priscilla McMillan.
201
"This is the one that kills you or": O'Brien, p. 44.
202n
"Hey, Frip": Authors' interview with Ted Reardon.
202
Jack had been furious: Ibid.
202
Kennedy's first chore: Victor Lasky, *Robert F. Kennedy: The Myth and the Man,* New York, 1971, p. 83.

202
"Did somebody see me": Cohn, pp. 69–70.
202
"He felt he was getting nowhere": Authors' interview with Lem Billings.
202
Bobby in Soviet Union: Schlesinger, *RFK*, p. 126.
203
Confrontation between RFK and Cohn: Damore, p. 140; Schlesinger, *RFK*, p. 121. It was something Bobby never forgot or forgave. In 1955, invited to a testimonial dinner for Cohn, he replied in a scornful letter: "Regarding the dinner for Roy Cohn, it is my feeling that being an anti-Communist does not automatically excuse a lack of integrity in every other facet of life." RFK Personal Files, JFK Library.
203
"How could I demand": O'Donnell and Powers, p. 110.
203
"The public isn't the slightest bit": JPK to JFK, July 19, 1954. JFK Library.
203
Bobby's letter to the *Times:* Laing, p. 84.
203
Schlesinger reply: Ibid.
204
Jack had Sorensen draft a speech: Parmet, *Jack*, p. 305.
204
"He used to get in touch": Kenneth Birkhead Oral History, JFK Library.
204
The scene in Jack's hospital room: Authors' interview with Priscilla McMillan.
204
"He'd be on his stomach": Ibid.
204
"Jack's dying": Arthur Krock Oral History, JFK Library.
204
Evelyn Lincoln and others: Evelyn Lincoln, *My Twelve Years with John F. Kennedy*, New York, 1965 (paperback), pp. 45ff.
205n
"The responsibility": Sorensen, p. 49.
205n
Kennedy "was sufficiently conscious": Parmet, *Jack*, p. 310.
205
"Do you know": Charles Spalding Oral History, JFK Library.
205
"Is it still open?" Authors' interview with Lem Billings.
205
"It was a terrible time": Ibid.
205
Jackie asked Grace Kelly to dress up as a nurse: Authors' interview with Priscilla McMillan.
206
He met Dr. Janet Travell: See Blairs, pp. 600ff.
206
"There wasn't so much talk": Authors' interview with Lem Billings.
206
Origins of *Profiles:* For a detailed and original discussion see Parmet, *Jack*, pp. 323ff.
206
Jack poured the money back into ads: Ibid.
207n
Joe Kennedy asked Hoover: See Joseph P. Kennedy FBI File.

207n

Jack asked Neuberger: Richard Neuberger Oral History, JFK Library.

207n

Sorensen not forthcoming enough: James MacGregor Burns Oral History, JFK Library.

207n

Blair Clark comment: Parmet, *Jack*, p. 330.

207

"If you are chosen": Ibid., p. 363.

207

Jack had Sargent Shriver write: SS to JPK, July 18, 1956. JFK Library.

208

"Whew! Is he mad!": Rose Kennedy, p. 328.

208

JPK tried to pull strings: Authors' interview with Morton Downey.

208

"Do you know anyone in Nevada?": Jackie did not know anyone. But eventually Bobby contacted Peter Lawford in Santa Monica, and Lawford contacted Wilbur Clark of the Desert Inn in Las Vegas, who said later on: "Peter tracked me down by phone at three o'clock in the morning to make sure Nevada went for Jack." (Cited in Lasky, p. 241.)

208

On the second ballot: The core of his support came from the South. When the balloting was over, he went to see Arthur Krock, who was also staying at the Drake Hotel. "His face was bright and shiny. He was a very happy-looking boy. He said to me, 'I'm going to sing "Dixie" for the rest of my life.' " Arthur Krock Oral History, JFK Library.

209

"Well, I see Dad's roughing it": Authors' interview with Sir William Douglas Home.

209

"I guess it's the only thing I can do": Ibid.

209

"God is still with you": *New York Post*, January 9, 1961.

209

Jack went off to meet: Authors' interview with George Smathers.

209

"Unique among them": Authors' interview with a confidential source, April 23, 1980.

209

Smathers insists that Jack return: Authors' interview with George Smathers.

209

"He was just not": Schlesinger, *RFK*, p. 136.

210

"If he had lived": Cited in Rose Kennedy, p. 329.

211

A "prematurely aged twenty-year-old": Authors' interview with Morton Downey.

211

A "stomach condition of rather suspicious origins": JPK to Beaverbrook, June 15, 1955. Beaverbrook Papers.

211

A series of operations: JPK to Beaverbrook, October 27, 1956. Beaverbrook Papers.

211

Pinning notes to the front of her dress: Authors' interview with Frank Saunders, November 19, 1982. Saunders was the Kennedys' chauffeur and handyman for several years.

212

"I suddenly thought of your slippers": Rose to RFK, March 16, 1959. RFK Personal Files, JFK Library.

212

Rose as papal countess: Cameron, p. 66.

212

"The phone was his instrument": Authors' interview with Morton Downey.

212

He placed two-dollar bets: Ibid.

212

He golfed for up to $10,000 a match: Authors' interview with George Smathers.

212

Caravan to Harvard-Yale game: John Droney Oral History, JFK Library.

213

"You failed me": Henri Soulé in Edward M. Kennedy, ed., *Bough*, pp. 166ff.

213

Gallup Poll: Burns, p. 162.

213

"If an Irish Catholic can get elected an Overseer": O'Donnell and Powers, p. 147.

213

"I don't want them to inherit my enemies": Authors' interview with Morton Downey. During the 1958 Senate campaign, JPK told Myer Feldman the same thing as a reason for maintaining a low profile. Authors' interview with Myer Feldman.

213

JPK lunches with Hoover: See Joseph P. Kennedy FBI File.

214

Eunice as observer in a women's reformatory: On January 19, 1949, James Landis wrote to Eunice to help her prepare for this experience. He urged her to study "the character of the crimes...the circumstances of the person who committed it...the manner of conviction...the concern over the rehabilitation process..." James Landis to Eunice Kennedy. Landis Papers, Library of Congress.

214

"He's not marrying anybody but me": Authors' interview with a confidential source, April 23, 1980.

214

"I searched all my life": Liston, p. 59.

214

She also kept in touch with Rosemary: Authors' interviews with Eunice Kennedy Shriver and Herbert J. Kramer.

214

Pat first met Peter Lawford: Authors' interview with Peter Lawford, February 23, 1980.

215

"Wait until you get a few lines": Authors' interview with Milton Ebbins, January 14, 1982. Ebbins was Lawford's manager and agent.

215

They ran into each other again: Authors' interview with Peter Lawford.

215

"If there's anything I'd hate": Dineen, p. 134. Also authors' interview with Peter Lawford. "One night we were at Frescatti's restaurant and I said, 'You know, one day I'd really kinda like to think about getting married.' And she said, 'What about April?' I said, 'You're pulling my leg. April what?' And she said, 'Next April.' I went home and said, 'My God, what have I done?' I was Charley bachelor, and had always been." Authors' interview with Peter Lawford.

215

A Malibu house once owned by Mayer: Authors' interview with Milton Ebbins.

215
The Kenlaw Production Company : Ibid.
215
Stephen Smith background : Dineen, p. 135.
216
He was the afterthought : Teddy was self-conscious about his place in the family. On the 1980 campaign trail he talked to T. R. Reid of the *Washington Post* about "the sense that he came so late, when his parents weren't expecting any other kids. He told me that when there were eight kids, Joe Kennedy bought a yacht which they called the *Tenovus,* because they thought the family was over. Edward came along and they bought a new yacht called *One More.*" Authors' interview with T. R. Reid, March 25, 1981.
216
"Teddy was the shining light" : Authors' interview with Peter Lawford.
216
Teddy's Spanish final : This incident is discussed in Hersh, pp. 79ff.
216
He impulsively enlisted in the Army : Hersh, p. 82.
216
"Don't you even look at what you're signing?" : JPK was so upset that he asked Landis to start researching the legality of Eisenhower's extension of enlistment periods on July 9, 1951, in case that statute should be retroactively applied to Ted. Memo, July 18, 1951. Landis Papers, Library of Congress.
216
"I'd like to see Teddy" : John Droney Oral History, JFK Library.
216
"He just wanted to get through" : Anne Taylor Fleming, "The Kennedy Mystique," *New York Times Magazine,* June 17 and 24, 1979.
216
Rose called Mother O'Byrne : John Corry, *The Golden Clan,* Boston, 1977, p. 172.
217
"Someone who would put a slipcover on a Louis Quinze sofa" : Kelley, p. 31.
217
"Really, Joan" : Authors' interview with Myra McPherson.
217
"Boy Scout" : Authors' interviews with Fred Dutton, November 2 and December 6, 1979, and April 29, 1980.
217
"Inside brother-in-law" : Ibid.
218
"This is the most exclusive club" : Authors' interview with Lem Billings.
218
"My, he is unassimilated" : Cited in Milton Viorst, *Hustlers and Heroes,* New York, 1971, p. 224.
218
Conflict with McCarthy over Bob Greene : Authors' interview with Clark Mollenhoff, September 9, 1982.
218
"Joe McCarthy, you're a shit" : Ibid.
218
Bobby stalked out of a ceremony : Schlesinger, *RFK,* p. 115.
218
"I liked him" : Robert E. Thompson and Hortense Myers, *Robert F. Kennedy: The Brother Within,* New York, 1962, p. 121.
218
Proposed investigation of Nixon and Chotiner : Authors' interview with Clark Mollenhoff.

219n
"First of all": JPK to RFK, July 21, 1955, RFK Personal Files, JFK Library.
219
"Who the hell": Authors' interview with Clark Mollenhoff.
219
"If you do your job": Ibid.
219
"Well, goddamn it": Ibid.
219
In touch with Ed Guthman: Ibid. "Who is Bobby Kennedy?" Guthman asked. "The son of the Ambassador," Mollenhoff replied. He explained later that he identified Bobby through his father "because that was the most prominent thing about him then: Jack Kennedy had not been a very distinguished member of the House and was simply fluttering around in the Senate, where he was not really greatly respected except as a playboy." Authors' interview with Edwin Guthman, March 23, 1981.
219
One case which had a particularly strong impact: Robert F. Kennedy, *The Enemy Within*, pp. 17ff.
220
"The old man saw this": Authors' interview with Lem Billings.
220
"The worst we ever witnessed": Jean made this statement to Arthur Schlesinger, who repeated it to the authors. Authors' interview with Arthur Schlesinger, May 28, 1981.
220
"He feels it is too great an opportunity": Schlesinger, *RFK*, p. 142.
220
Bobby vs. Beck: Robert Kennedy, pp. 36ff.
220
Bobby almost sorry for Beck: Ibid., p. 38.
220
Taken the Fifth 140 times: Dan Moldea, *The Hoffa Wars*, New York, 1978 (paperback), p. 71.
220
"He was dead, although still standing": Robert Kennedy, p. 43.
221
Hoffa background: James R. Hoffa, *Hoffa: The Real Story*, New York, 1976, pp. 30ff.
221
"A wicked conspiracy": *Investigation of Racketeering in the Detroit Area*. Joint Subcommittee Report, U.S. Senate, 1954, pp. 2–4.
221
"Damn spoiled jerk": Schlesinger, *RFK*, p. 184.
222
"There were times": Moldea, p. 177.
222
Hoffa and Sylvia Pagano: Ibid, p. 25.
222
Beck's attitude toward his son: Robert Kennedy, p. 49.
222
"I do to others": Ibid., p. 50.
222
"Maybe I should have worn": Ibid.
222
"I'm still alive, dear": Schlesinger, *RFK*, p. 153.
222
Hoffa later claimed: Hoffa, p. 75. According to Hoffa this was just the climax of

several physical confrontations, all of which he won: "I let him strain for a couple of seconds. Then, like taking candy from a baby I flipped his arm over and cracked his knuckles on the top of the table. It was strictly no contest and he knew it."

222
"When a grown man": Robert Kennedy, p. 50.

222
"A man who always made a big thing": Hoffa, p. 70.

222
"Want to spend the summer": Robert Kennedy, p. 52.

223
"I'll jump off the Capitol": Ibid., p. 62.

223n
A few weeks later: See Walter Sheridan, *The Fall and Rise of Jimmy Hoffa*, New York, 1972, p. 36.

223
"You can tell Bobby Kennedy": Pierre Salinger, *With Kennedy,* New York, 1967 (paperback), p. 43.

223
"Get your feet off ": Robert Kennedy, p. 76.

223
"To the best of my recollection": Ibid.

223
"Told him I did not": Schlesinger, *RFK,* p. 157.

224
"Am very pleased with myself ": Cited in Schlesinger, *RFK,* p. 150.

224
Bobby on the UAW and the Kohler plant: See Robert Kennedy, pp. 254ff.

224
"My brother's name was Joe": *New York Times,* March 5, 1958.

225
"Although Reuther was an honest trade unionist": Authors' interview with Clark Mollenhoff.

225
"We don't want you on the opposite side from us": Schlesinger, *RFK,* p. 177.

225
"For the first time": Authors' interview with Lem Billings.

225
"In heaven": John Jay Hooker Oral History, JFK Library.

225
"My first love is Hoffa": John Bartlow Martin, "The Struggle to Get Jimmy Hoffa," *Saturday Evening Post,* June 8, 1959.

226
"They are sleek": Robert Kennedy, p. 78.

226
Glimco interrogation: Senate Select Committee on Improper Activities in the Labor and Management Field. *Hearings,* p. 17848 (August 20, 1958).

227
"I thought only little girls giggle": Ibid., p. 18681.

227
"So you're Joey Gallo": Cited in Laing, pp. 106–107.

227
"What is that": Laing, p. 111.

227
"I felt that he and his people": Authors' interview with William G. Hundley, July 22, 1980.

227
"You admit": Ibid.

227

"He'd be up in the morning": Authors' interview with John Seigenthaler, March 27, 1981. Getting the "truth" out about Hoffa became something of an obsession for Bobby Kennedy. Early in 1959, Jim Bishop asked Kennedy's office for a response to a newspaper series he had done that put the Teamster boss in a somewhat favorable light. Kennedy had Pierre Salinger write out a seven-page single-spaced letter criticizing Bishop's "factual errors." (Salinger to Bishop, January 21, 1959. RFK Personal Files, JFK Library.) When Bishop did not respond, Bobby sent a copy of Salinger's letter to Frank Coniff, national editor of the Hearst papers and in charge of syndicating Bishop's series. (RFK to Coniff, February 11, 1959. RFK Personal Files.) At that point Bishop angrily replied to Bobby, "There is nothing in the book of journalistic ethics which says I must consult you on any story. Whatever truths have been adduced regarding Mr. Hoffa are, I suggest, not your private property but rather the property of the people of the United States . . ." (Bishop to RFK, February 19, 1959.) Bobby ended the correspondence a couple of weeks later with a final letter to Bishop: "I cannot, with equanimity, look upon the prospect of Hoffa and his ilk dominating the economy of this country. Your articles would tend to further his ambition towards this end . . . The series was a dishonest piece of reporting, as your letter, obviously written for the benefit of Mr. Hearst, was a dishonest piece of writing." RFK to Bishop, March 5, 1959, RFK Personal Files.

227

"The will to fight what is evil": Robert Kennedy, p. 307.

228

"You're not to speak"; Authors' interview with Lem Billings.

229

"Frankly, I've got some apprehensions": Authors' interview with Clark Mollenhoff.

229n

"Before the hearings": Ibid.

230

Eisenhower Administration politics against Kennedy-Ives: See Parmet, *Jack*, pp. 429ff.

230

"Jimmy Hoffa can rejoice": *New York Times*, August 8, 1958.

230n

"The Kennedys have met": Authors' interview with James Rowe, January 16, 1981. Also authors' interview with J. William Fulbright, December 15, 1982. Johnson selected Kennedy for the prized committee seat ahead of Estes Kefauver, just as he had supported JFK over the independent Kentucky Senator for the vice presidential nomination in 1956. Jack Bell, who covered the Senate for the Associated Press, says, "Johnson ran the Senate and Kefauver ended up a kind of lone wolf, pulled off the crime investigation, and Johnson was jealous. He didn't like anybody sticking his head up above Johnson's. Kennedy was not exactly tractable, but he had not stirred up Johnson. Johnson had hopes for making Kennedy a Johnson man and eventually bringing him into the inner circle . . ." Jack Bell Oral History, JFK Library.

230

American Friends of Vietnam: See Galloway, p. 13.

231

"What we must offer": Ibid.

231

"Shape a course of political independence": Cited in Parmet, *Jack*, p. 403.

231

Stevenson denounces speech: Ibid., p. 403.

231

"The struggle against imperialism": John F. Kennedy, "A Democrat Looks at Foreign Affairs," *Foreign Affairs,* October 1957, p. 44.

231
Rockefeller Brothers Panel Studies: See Peter Collier and David Horowitz, *The Rockefellers: An American Dynasty,* New York, 1977 (paperback), pp. 324ff.
232
"We may be as much as several years behind": Parmet, *Jack,* p. 445.
232
Against "Fortress America" approach: *New York Times,* December 8, 1957.
232
Reported loss of America's "superiority": John F. Kennedy, *The Strategy of Peace,* New York, 1960, pp. 34ff.
232
"Export the revolutionary ideas": Ibid.
232
A radicalism of the status quo: "I saw JFK as a conservative Democrat, right of center like myself." Interview with Joseph Kraft, July 23, 1980. Kraft joined the campaign and wrote speeches for Jack.
233
Less than forthcoming on the Civil Rights Act: Jack backed the bill but got caught in the crossfire on an amendment concerning jury trials for defendants charged with violating an individual's civil rights. Black leaders charged that it would allow whites to be tried before southern and presumably all-white juries. Although liberals were opposed to the provision, Jack, citing the civil liberties issues it raised, voted with the majority for the jury trial amendment. His supporters suggested that it was a "dilemma" caused by his regard for constitutional guarantees. If so, it could become a benefit as well. In 1959, when he sent Bobby south to talk to party leaders who had supported him at the convention in 1956, he reminded his brother to point out to them that Humphrey and Symington, two potential rivals for the nomination in 1960, had been against the jury trial provision while he had voted with the South.
233
"By 1958 all those men": around: Authors' interview with Lem Billings.
233
"Cowardice rationalized": Arthur Schlesinger, Jr., in *Partisan Review,* May-June 1947.
233
"S is a much richer": Cited in Schlesinger, *RFK,* p. 203.
234
"I intend to be as brave as I dare": Senator Joseph Clark Oral History, JFK Library.
234
"I'd be very happy to tell them": Paul Healy, "The Senate's Gay Young Bachelor," *Saturday Evening Post,* June 13, 1953.
234
Superman coming to supermarket: See Norman Mailer, "Superman Comes to Supermarket," in *The Presidential Papers,* New York, 1963.
234n
Burns's possible involvement in Senate office: Burns to Sorensen, December 6, 1958. Burns Papers, JFK Library. Burns first met Kennedy in 1951. In 1955 he was one of the first to float the trial balloon for a Stevenson-Kennedy ticket in 1956. In 1958 Burns had himself run for Congress in Massachusetts and Jack offered help. "During the campaign I went to Boston and he and I made a short TV film together. He also slipped me $500 after the filming. I had a prepared script which made a nice human interest reference to Jackie. He took it out without comment." James M. Burns Oral History, JFK Library.
235
Changes in the Burns MS.: Burns to Sorensen, November 11, 1959. Burns Papers, JFK Library.

235
Letter from Jackie and call from JPK: James M. Burns Oral History, JFK Library.
235
"Like a method actor": Authors' interview with Lem Billings.
235
"Jack is the greatest attraction": Cited in Ralph Martin and Ed Plaut, *Front Runner, Dark Horse*, New York, 1960, p. 461. JPK had always seen politics and films as related. (It was in fact his only original and far-reaching insight into the new era.) Late in life he said to Jimmy Roosevelt: "There are only two pursuits that get into your blood, politics and the motion picture business." Cited in Whalen, p. 455.
235
"We'll sell him like soap flakes": Ibid.
235
"All right, Jack": Cited in Fay, pp. 76–77.
236
"How would you like looking forward": Ibid.
236
Bobby was the spectral presence: Authors' interview with Charles Spalding. And as always, behind the scenes was Joe Kennedy: "Joe Kennedy reached into amazing places, the Church, business... He had friends in Chicago, in New York, in Florida, in California, and up on the Lakes too. I remember going up to Wisconsin for the primary. Joe used to own those loaders on the Lakes that carry coal and ore off the docks." Authors' interview with Robert Healey, December 1, 1981. Healey was a reporter for the *Boston Globe*.
236
"You're too soon, my boy": Authors' interview with Charles Spalding.
237
Bobby exploded to Walter Cronkite: Schlesinger, *RFK*, p. 197.
237
"Is it true": William O. Douglas, *Go East, Young Man*, New York, 1974, p. 101.
237
"I think it's so unjust": O'Donnell and Powers, p. 92.
237n
Lisagor and Jackie: Peter Lisagor Oral History, JFK Library.
237n
Niebuhr and Jackie: John Cogley Oral History, JFK Library.
237
"Nobody asked me": O'Donnell and Powers, p. 191.
238
The finest impromptu speech: To H. White, *The Making of the President 1960*, New York, 1964 (paperback), p. 107.
238
The Ambassador was active: And not just at the political level. "When I was traveling with Jack alone in '59 through Oregon and California and West Virginia, before the national campaign gained intensity, the old man would call almost every night. It was not a call to inquire about how the campaign was going. The only thing he wanted to know was how Jack was feeling, how his health was. Was he 'behaving' himself. It was a fatherly call: how's the kid doing?" Authors' interview with Robert Healey.
238
"And the states *you* have": Hersh, p. 123.
238
Call to Burton Wheeler: In Edward M. Kennedy, ed., *Bough*, p. 85.
238
"He knew instinctively": Authors' interview with Eugene Keogh, May 6, 1980. The Ambassador also wooed New York party boss Mike Prendergast. "Mr. Kennedy

arranged a meeting at the Sheraton Plaza with some New York bankers and myself. He wanted me to come out for Jack before the West Virginia primary, but I said I couldn't, we had our own problems. He was hard-headed, but we got along afterward. He sent a lot of people in to donate money to the state organization, which we used for Jack's election.'' Authors' interview with Mike Prendergast, July 10, 1980.
238

''Mr. Kennedy had flown this man'': Authors' interview with Thomas (''Tip'') O'Neill.
239

Flattering letters to FBI: See Joseph P. Kennedy FBI File.
239

FDR, Jr., endorsement postmarked at Hyde Park: Rose Kennedy, p. 369.
239

''In a certain sense'': Charles Peters Oral History, JFK Library.
239

''Just look at him'': Authors' interview with Charles Spalding.
239

''It's amazing'': Ibid.
240

''Well, that's it'': Authors' interview with Eugene Keogh.
240

''Why didn't you tell me'': O'Donnell and Powers, p. 203.
240

Bobby worried about Stevenson: Kennedy delegates had their own concerns. ''Jesus, the Stevenson operation in L.A. had hookers trying to entice our guys. I used to go around the Ambassador Hotel, where I had all our delegates, and say, 'You sons of bitches, who got laid last night?' I'd find out, and then I said, 'I'm gonna tell your wife, if you don't vote for Jack.' '' Authors' interview with Mike Prendergast.
241

''She hated my father'': Gore Vidal, ''The Holy Family,'' *Esquire,* April 1967. To counter the charges of Eleanor Roosevelt and former President Truman that he was too young, Jack asked Sorensen to do some research. The assiduous aide came up with the fact that Jefferson was younger when he wrote the Declaration of Independence, Washington younger when he commanded the Continental Army, Columbus younger when he discovered America. Sorensen also had Jesus Christ on the list, pointing out that he was younger than Jack when he was crucified, but was persuaded to delete that entry. Sorensen, p. 152.
241

LBJ comments to Sidey: Hugh Sidey Oral History, JFK Library.
241

''A scrawny little fellow with rickets'': Peter Lisagor Oral History, JFK Library.
241

''I knew he hated Jack'': Ibid.
241

John Connally's whispering campaign: Sorensen, p. 156.
241

The man ''who held Chamberlain's umbrella'': *New York Times,* July 15, 1960.
241

''You've got your nerve'': Baker, p. 118.
241

''I remember the second day'': Bernard Bouton Oral History, JFK Library.
242

''But, Daddy, how can Jack'': Authors' interview with John Seigenthaler, March 27, 1981.
242

''Don't worry,'': O'Donnell and Powers, p. 214.

242
"You have in your grasp": Fay, p. 49.
242
"It was the first time": Hugh Sidey Oral History, JFK Library.
242
Tip O'Neill offer to LBJ: Thomas ("Tip") O'Neill Oral History, JFK Library.
243
"I'm forty-three years old and I'm the healthiest candidate": O'Donnell and Powers, p. 221.
243
What he apparently thought was carte blanche: See Rowland Evans and Robert Novak, *Lyndon B. Johnson: The Exercise of Power*, New York, 1966 (paperback), p. 302. Bobby and several of the other principals in the vice presidential offer to LBJ later gave interviews which put "his side" on the record. O'Donnell and other of the secondary figures in the matter also left accounts of the offer.
243
"Shit!": Herbert Parmet, *JFK: The Presidency of John F. Kennedy*, New York, 1983, p. 29.
243
"Bobby's been out of touch": Schlesinger, *RFK*, p. 210. For the Phil Graham memo, see Theodore H. White, *The Making of the President 1964*, New York, 1965, p. 408.
243n
Bobby's reaction to Graham memo: RFK Oral History, JFK Library; also Katharine Graham Oral History, LBJ Library.
243
"That little shitass": Cited in Baker, p. 113.
243
"I didn't want him to take it": H. L. Hunt Oral History, LBJ Library.
243
"I'll be goddamned": Ibid.
244
Scene at Marion Davies' house: Charles Bartlett Oral History, LBJ Library.
244
"Yesterday was the best day": Charles Bartlett Oral History, LBJ Library. See also Arthur Schlesinger, Jr., *A Thousand Days*, Boston, 1965, p. 58.
244
"Don't worry, Jack": Schlesinger, *RFK*, p. 211.
244
"There was no respect": Authors' interview with Henry R. Luce III, July 9, 1980.
244
A phrase conceived by Rostow: Rostow, a professor of government at MIT who had been traveling the country for Kennedy for almost a year, later wrote: "As I met and talked with people I found widespread concern. Some were worried about missiles, others about the state of American education; many were worried about our slow rate of growth . . . I told [Jack] I knew what the first sentence of his acceptance speech should be: 'This country is ready to get moving again and I'm ready to lead it.' " Walt W. Rostow, *The Diffusion of Power*, New York, 1972, p. 111.
245
The tv debates: The best account is in White, *Making of the President 1960*, pp. 335ff. See Also O'Donnell and Powers, pp. 243ff.
245n
Jack refused to be captured: Stanley Tretick Oral History, JFK Library.
245
"Drop dead, Fatso": Ibid.
245
Joe Kennedy's call to Levin: Donald Larrabee Oral History, JFK Library.

246
"Listen, you worry about financing": Authors' interview with Franklin D. Roosevelt, Jr., January 24, 1980.

246
Jack and Bob will run the show: Cited by Whalen, p. 444.

246
"God, if I hadn't cut you off ": Fay, p. 33.

246
JPK's meeting with Gibbons: Authors' interview with Harold Gibbons, October 25, 1979.

247
"All I can say is": JPK to Beaverbrook, September 9, 1960. Beaverbrook Papers.

247
JPK complains to Cushing: John Henry Cutler, *Cardinal Cushing of Boston,* New York, 1970, p. 220.

247
Kennedy refused to speak to Spellman again: RFK Oral History, JFK Library.

247
"Quit the dull line": Aide-mémoire, October 20, 1960. Krock Papers.

247
Krock defended himself: AK to JPK, October 20, 1960. Krock Papers.

247
"What I asked you to do": Krock later said of his relationship with the Ambassador: "I've often reflected since those days that he probably never liked me at all, but found me useful and thought he might be able to make use of me." See Blairs, p. 9. On November 21, 1961, Krock wrote to a Kennedy aide: "This is to request that you see my name is eliminated from the Washington list to which Mr. Joseph Kennedy sends Christmas wishes in the delicious form of a case of Haig and Haig..." Krock Papers.

247
"Look, I can't control my father": Authors' interview with Charles Spalding.

247
Goodwin and Cuba statement: Peter Wyden, *The Bay of Pigs,* New York, 1979, pp. 65ff. Also authors' interview with Richard M. Goodwin, June 1, 1980.

248
"Get back on high ground": William Attwood Oral History, JFK Library.

248n
"Eunice was a little stodgy": Authors' interview with Robert Ajemian, September 25, 1981.

248
"Is it possible that anything can equal this?": Authors' interview with Charles Spalding.

248
"Well, we all have fathers": Authors' interviews with Harris Wofford, February 2 and March 22, 1981.

249
Talking with Cornelius Ryan: White, *Making of the President 1960,* p. 25.

249
The primitive IBM computer: Ibid. p. 16.

249
As the night wore on: Ibid., pp. 413ff. At 3:00 A.M., with the results swinging in Jack's favor, Lem Billings, who had been watching the returns with Bobby, decided to make one last trip across the lawn to Jack's house. Before reaching the door, however, he was stopped by Secret Service men who made inquiries about him inside. When Jack sent word back that nobody had ever heard of anyone named Billings, the frustrated Lem had to give up, recognizing that whatever the election results, some

aspects of his old friend's character were not going to change. Authors' interview with Peter Kaplan, January 24, 1981.
249
"All right, let's go": White, *Making of the President 1960,* p. 416.
249
JFK goes back for JPK: Rose Kennedy, p. 377.
250
Loaded his car with dynamite: O'Donnell and Powers, pp. 278–279.
250
JFK tried to get agents to change uniform. Ibid., p. 262.
250
"Are they expecting Castro to invade": Ibid.
251
"It was just as well": Ibid., p. 263.
251
"I'm never there when she needs me": Ibid., p. 268.
251
"There are no accidents in politics": Cited in Whalen, p. 457.
251
"There! Now he's doing it": Cited in Hugh Sidey, *John F. Kennedy, President,* New York, 1964 (paperback), p. 31. Also authors' interview with Charles Spalding.
252
Neustadt submitted memos: Authors' interview with Richard E. Neustadt, January 11, 1983.
252n
He had taken: Authors' interview with Lem Billings.
252
Neustadt on presidential greatness: See Richard E. Neustadt, *Presidential Power,* New York, 1964 (paperback).
252
FDR "wanted mastery": Neustadt, p. 155.
252
"Fascinating stuff": Authors' interview with Richard E. Neustadt. Neustadt says that Bobby called him several times during the transition with ideas about the White House staff. "These were things he wanted to recommend to his brother and wanted to know what I thought of them first. He obviously didn't know who the hell I was but his brother had talked about me so I must be important." Ibid.
253
"Yeah, we're pushing it": Ibid.
253
Jack asked Neustadt to prepare: Ibid.
253
"From the very beginning": Authors' interview with a confidential source, March 23, 1981.
253
A line in the Inaugural Address: Sorensen, p. 242.
253
"Wild-eyed ADA people": O'Donnell and Powers, p. 270.
253n
Jack had appointed: Ibid., p. 280.
254
"In many ways": Authors' interview with Lem Billings.
254
"How many other automobile executives": Harris Wofford, *Of Kennedys and Kings,* New York, 1980, p. 70.

254
McNamara asked about *Profiles:* O'Donnell and Powers, p. 272.
255
"Bobby we'll make Attorney General": Fay, p. 11.
255
"Chasing bad men": RFK Oral History, JFK Library.
255
"I had to do something": Schlesinger, *RFK*, p. 229.
255n
Jack had originally intended: Authors' interview with Phyllis MacDonald, July 13, 1980.
255
Douglas advises Bobby: Schlesiner, *RFK*, p. 229.
256n
"Thank you very much": Parmet, *JFK*, p. 64.
256
"He felt that the President": RFK Oral History, JFK Library.
256
"Don't tell me now": Authors' interview with John Seigenthaler.
256
"Well, Johnny, what about me?": Ibid.
256
"Well, I guess we'd better go": Ibid.
257n
"If you announce me": T. H. White, *In Search of History*, p. 496.
257
"The guts of a burglar": Thompson and Myers, p. 23.
257
Inscriptions in *The Enemy Within:* Schlesinger, *RFK*, p. 232.
257
Jack had told Sorensen to study Gettysburg Address: Sorensen, p. 240.
258
"An early draft of FDR's Inaugural": Ibid., p. 243.
258
Meeting with Eisenhower: Parmet, *JFK*, p. 81.
258
"How can he stare disaster in the face": Sidey, p. 44.
258
Jack would bring up the subject: RFK Oral History, JFK Library.
258
"Jack doesn't belong any more to a family": Sidey, p. 30.
259
"Who are these people?": Letitia Baldridge, *Of Diamonds and Diplomats*, Boston, 1968, p. 153.
260
"You know what this reminds me of?": Authors' interview with Lem Billings.

PART 3: BROTHERS WITHIN

263
Galbraith at the White House: Kay Halle Oral History, JFK Library.
263
JFK's desire to achieve "greatness": Authors' interview with Lem Billings.
263
"Before my term has ended": *New York Times*, January 31, 1961.

264
"The junior officers of the Second World War": Cited by Peter Wyden, *The Bay of Pigs,* New York, 1979, p. 306.
264
Like an extended family: Herbert Parmet, *JFK: The Presidency of John Kennedy,* New York, 1983, p. 87.
264
Lem reminded of the Kennedy family: Authors' interview with Lem Billings.
264
"You know how many people": Authors' interview with George Smathers.
264
"I know how they are at the State Department": Robert Monagan Oral History, JFK Library.
264
"I know this outfit": William Manchester, *Portrait of a President,* Boston, 1962, p. 35.
264
"I don't care what it is": Cited by Wyden, p. 95.
265
The missile gap a fiction: Edgar M. Bottome, *The Missile Gap,* Rutherford, New Jersey, 1971, pp. 179–184. "During the 1960 presidential campaign, I wrote many of Kennedy's speeches on the missile gap. But I did not believe there was a missile gap and we were in trouble." Authors' interview with Joseph Kraft, July 23, 1980. But cf. Arnold L. Horelick and Myron Rush, *Strategic Power and Soviet Foreign Policy,* Chicago, 1966. Horelick and Rush claim (p. 35) that "Beginning in the late summer of 1957, the Soviet leaders, and chiefly Khrushchev, undertook to deceive the West regarding their strategic capabilities."
265
"Who ever believed in the missile gap": Maxwell Taylor, *Swords and Ploughshares,* New York, 1972, p. 205. A few years later, in 1967, Robert McNamara admitted that it was not necessary "to build as large a number as we have today." See *The Essence of Security,* New York, 1968, p. 58. And by the mid-1970s it would become clear that the fictive missile gap justification for a huge buildup had effectively ended the possibility of a freeze in strategic weapons and prompted the Soviets to remedy the very real gap they suddenly faced, triggering a new phase of the arms race.
265n
"Do we have a chance": Werner von Braun Oral History, JFK Library.
265
Jack distributed Khrushchev's speech: Robert Kennedy Oral History, p. 22, JFK Library. The Khrushchev speech had been delivered on January 6, 1961.
265
"He seemed to regard these people": Authors' interview with James Rowe.
265
"Let us once again": Cited by Theodore Sorensen, *Kennedy,* New York, 1965, p. 534.
266
"We need to develop a doctrine": Cited in Parmet, *JFK,* p. 137.
266
Jack had been reading Mao: Hugh Sidey, *John F. Kennedy,* New York, 1964 (paperback), pp. 75–76.
266
Lansdale's report: See David Halberstam, *The Best and the Brightest,* New York, 1973 (paperback), pp. 158–159.
266
Rostow looks into counterinsurgency: Walt Rostow Oral History, JFK Library.
266
FDR's hundred days: The very first position paper that Neustadt prepared for

Kennedy "told him there isn't going to be any 'hundred days.' " In addition to the lack of any sense of emergency, Neustadt pointed out, "the midwestern/southern coalition on domestic affairs was still in existence as it had been since '38." Authors' interview with Richard Neustadt.
267
Bissell was point man for the Cuba action: Wyden, pp. 10ff.
267
"I'm your man-eating shark": Ibid.
267
Bissell's plan: Ibid., pp. 30ff.
267
Jack vetoed Trinidad Bay landing: Ibid., p. 100.
267
"You know, I've reserved the right": Ibid., p. 152.
267
"He kept telling Kennedy": Robert Amory Oral History, JFK Library.
268
"Everyone's trying to grab their nuts on this": Wyden, p. 165.
268
"Do you know anything about the Cuba proposal?": Dean Rusk Oral History, JFK Library. In keeping with Bissell's mania for secrecy and bureaucratic control, CIA Deputy Director Robert Amory, in charge of the Agency's intelligence gathering operations, was not informed of the Bay of Pigs operation. Authors' interview with Robert Amory, June 9, 1980.
268
Bowles and Rusk: Chester Bowles Oral History, JFK Library.
268
Bobby wasn't told: Arthur Schlesinger, Jr., *Robert F. Kennedy and His Times*, Boston, 1978, p. 443.
268
Chuck Spalding was told: Charles Spalding Oral History, JFK Library. Also authors' interview with Charles Spalding.
268
Jack orders Bissell to reduce planes: Wyden, p. 170.
269
JFK calls JPK: Cited in Rose Kennedy, *Times to Remember*, New York, 1974, p. 400.
269
"I don't think it's going as well": RFK Oral History, JFK Library.
269
"The most brilliantly staffed department": Cited in Schlesinger, *RFK*, pp. 238–239.
269
The Organized Crime Section an elite group: See Victor Navasky, *Kennedy Justice*, New York, 1971, pp. 53ff. Ramsey Clark felt that Bobby "focused almost exclusively on crime from the beginning of the administration." Wiretapping was a notable example. "He was intolerant of any criticism of it. He was convinced that it was an essential instrument in the pursuit of evil and he was unwilling to examine some of the ramifications of its use." Authors' interview with Ramsey Clark, October 26, 1979.
269
Target list: G. Robert Blakey and Richard N. Billings, *The Plot to Kill the President*, New York, 1981, p. 196. Blakey was a special prosecutor in the Justice Department under Kennedy.
270
Marcello was rumored: See Dan Moldea, *The Hoffa Wars*, New York, 1978, p. 108.
270
Federal agents arrested Marcello: Blakey and Billings, p. 243.

270

RFK calmed by Rostow: Walt W. Rostow, *The Diffusion of Power*, New York, 1972, pp. 210–211.

270

"The shit has hit the fan": Cited in Wyden, p. 269.

270

"Burke, I don't want the United States involved": Ibid., p. 270.

271

"The guerrilla option": Ibid., p. 271.

271

"We've got to do something": Sidey, p. 129.

271

"They can't do this": Marquis Childs, "Bobby and the President," *Good Housekeeping*, May 1962.

271

JFK at Glen Ora: Diary of Lem Billings, Billings Papers. There are dated entries for April 29, and 30, May 6 and 7. Billings apparently began the diary this weekend after the Bay of Pigs, but gave it up after these initial entries because the Bay of Pigs had become a debacle rather than a triumph for his friend. From April 29 entry: "At dinner [JFK] told us of his meeting with MacArthur. He felt MacArthur was very pleased that the President had talked to him. He admires MacArthur a lot, and feels that although he is a little out of touch, his mind is as good as ever. MacArthur advised him strongly against sending troops to Laos. He said the Chinese would eat us up. That we had one opportunity to crush the Chinese during Korea, but now a war in Laos would be a terrible mistake. He said MacArthur hates Eisenhower and thinks he has no brains at all. The President told us he knew both Eisenhower and Truman were furious he had called upon MacArthur." From April 30 entry: "No one called Mr. President for church this morning until about 10 minutes before Mass time. He burst into my room and asked me why I hadn't wakened him, which of course was silly. During lunch after church he told us that he was exceedingly unimpressed with Eisenhower. That Eisenhower was completely misinformed but that he was rather pleased that all the troubles inherited from him had come to roost with the new Administration, because it makes Eisenhower look better."

271

"That was even more fucked up than Cuba": Herbert Parmet interview with Robert Donovan, April 11, 1977. From a transcript kindly given to the authors by Parmet.

271

"No, go ahead": Arthur Schlesinger, Jr., *A Thousand Days* (paperback), New York, 1967, p. x.

271

"I should have had him involved": Authors' interview with Lem Billings.

272

"He would have taken a bolt of lightning": Authors' interview with John Seigenthaler, March 27, 1981.

272

A "political loser": Authors' interview with Ramsey Clark. "His brother's presidency was his consuming passion. It wasn't important to him whether he was considered a great Attorney General except insofar as it meant a great Kennedy presidency. If something didn't serve his brother's presidency, he would dismiss it." Ibid.

272

"As far as this administration is concerned": Robert F. Kennedy Oral History, JFK Library. See Also Harris Wofford, *Of Kennedys and Kings*, New York, 1980, p. 369.

272

"This is worthless": Sidey, p. 145.

272

Jack asked RFK to take over the CIA: RFK Oral History, JFK Library.

272

The Cuba Study Group: The group met regularly for some six weeks, ultimately interviewing over fifty witnesses. Dulles and Burke were put on the committee to keep the CIA and Joint Chiefs, respectively, from "feelings of persecution." Bobby was there to guard "the Presidential interest." And Taylor's objective was to secure a unanimous report. Schlesinger, *RFK*, p. 448.

273

"You're the kind of guy": RFK Oral History, JFK Library.

273

Taylor found a "shocked administration": Maxwell Taylor Oral History, LBJ Library.

273

"There can be no long-term living with Castro": U.S. Senate Select Committee to Study Governmental Operations with Respect to Intelligence Activities, *Alleged Assassination Plots Involving Foreign Leaders: An Interim Report*, 94th Congress, 1st Session, Report No. 94–465. Washington, November 20, 1975, p. 135. (Hereafter cited as *Senate Interim Report*.)

273

"I think we would have sent large numbers": RFK Oral History, JFK Library.

273

Jack looked at logistics: Former Secretary of State Dean Rusk observed: "Most of the critics of our Vietnam policy overlook the Laos experience. The only specific recommendation to Kennedy from Ike was to put troops in Laos—with others if possible, alone if necessary. When we took office, we looked at it. It seemed too difficult logistically. Laos was landlocked. The people were peaceful. We got a report that the troops of the opposing armies once left the battlefield for ten days to celebrate a water festival. So we thought we would try to get everybody out." Authors' interview with Dean Rusk, July 26, 1979.

274

"If we have to fight in Southeast Asia": Authors' interview with Dean Rusk.

274

"Lyndon, you've just to go out there": On the way home from the visit, after Johnson announced a new military aid package and called Diem "the Winston Churchill of South Asia," the party stopped over in Honolulu. Pointing to NBC correspondent Nancy Dickerson, who was traveling with the party, Jean Smith kept teasing the Vice President: "Tell us, Lyndon, which do you think is sexier, Nancy or myself." Johnson dodged the issue as long as possible and finally replied, "Jean, you know I never mess around with Catholic girls." Charles Bartlett Oral History, LBJ Library.

274

Second State of the Union address: *New York Times,* May 26, 1961.

274

"It really is true": Richard M. Nixon, *Memoirs,* New York, 1978, pp. 234–235.

274

"Stop them!": Authors' interviews with Harris Wofford, February 2, March 22, 1981.

275

JFK sprains back: Schlesinger, *A Thousand Days,* pp. 343–344.

275

"He's been my house guest since I was married": J. B. West Oral History, JFK Library.

275
Lem and Jack at the White House : Authors' interview with Lem Billings.
275
"Jack was against her going" : Ibid.
275
The Ambassador cut out pictures of women : Edward M. Kennedy, ed., *The Fruitful Bough*, privately printed, 1965, p. 264.
275
The Ambassador went to bed in annoyance : Authors' interview with Frank Saunders. Saunders was the Ambassador's recently hired chauffeur. The visit was his introduction to the President. Jack and Lem lounged in the house drinking milk and making small talk with Saunders. Jack turned to him : "Are you a Catholic, Frank?" The chauffeur nervously answered that he was. "Good! Good, Frank," Jack replied. "You'll be driving my mother to church. You'll be in a constant state of grace, Frank." Frank Saunders, *Torn Lace Curtain*, New York, 1982, p. 44.
275
"I go as the leader of the most revolutionary country" : *New York Times*, May 30, 1961.
275
Lem and Khrushchev's gift : Authors' interview with Lem Billings.
275
"Maybe Dad will buy it" : Ibid.
275
"Oh, Dad, I don't have a cent" : Edward M. Kennedy, ed., *Bough*, p. 264.
276
"You look very nice, dear" : Sidey, p. 169.
276
"I want all mine to be originals" : Kitty Kelley, *Jackie Oh!*, New York, 1979 (paperback), p. 105.
276
"For you, intervention" : Charles De Gaulle, *Memoirs of Hope: Renewal and Endeavor*, New York, 1971, p. 256.
276
"We had just had a fiasco" : Chester Bowles Oral History, JFK Library.
276
"Am I Acting Secretary" : Ibid.
276n
"The President snuck up" : RFK Oral History, JFK Library.
276
Khrushchev at Vienna : Sidey, pp. 188ff ; Schlesinger, *A Thousand Days*, pp. 360ff.
277
"I would say that there was only one mistake" : Charles Bohlen Oral History, JFK Library.
277
Michael Forrestal and others : Authors' interview with Michael Forrestal, October 26, 1979.
277
"The meeting began to go very badly" : Ibid.
277
"He regarded this as plunder" : Authors' interview with Lem Billings.
277
Like "dealing with Dad" : Ibid.
278
"Joe, I want you to know" : Authors' interview with Joseph Alsop, July 22, 1980.
278
"We have a problem" : Halberstam, p. 97.

278
Taylor suggested an insert: Sorensen, p. 591.

278
"Go get my brother!": *Time*, February 16, 1962.

278
"The President felt strongly": RFK Oral History, JFK Library. Later on, Bobby estimated the odds of nuclear war as having been one in five. Ibid.

278
Robert Amory recalled: Robert Amory Oral History, JFK Library.

278
"Get off your ass about Cuba": *Senate Interim Report*, p. 141.

279
"An insult which needed to be redressed": Cited in Taylor Branch and George Crile III, "The Kennedy Vendetta," *Harper's*, August 1975.

279
"To use our available assets": *Senate Interim Report*, p. 139.

279
"A solution to the Cuban problem today carries top priority": Ibid., p. 141.

280
Gilbert Harrison was amazed: Gilbert Harrison Oral History, JFK Library.

280
Ben Bradlee found himself banished: Ben Bradlee, *Conversations with Kennedy*, New York, 1976 (paperback), p. 21.

280
JFK got first copy of *Time:* Authors' interview with Henry Luce III, July 9, 1980.

281n
"Now there's an impartial man": Hugh Sidey Oral History, JFK Library.

281
Gentleman's Quarterly incident: Ibid.

281
Jackie living inside a fishbowl: She used the analogy in a conversation with Kennedy chauffeur Frank Saunders. See Saunders, p. 68.

281
Air Force One sent back for Chubby Checker record: Authors' interview with Mary Gimbel.

282
"There's something bad about you": Herbert Parmet interview with John Hersey. Parmet kindly made his files available to the authors.

282
"So that's what you look like, you old rascal you": Authors' interview with Sir William Douglas Home.

282
Antique wallpaper from Maryland house: Letitia Baldridge, *Of Diamonds and Diplomats*, Boston, 1968, pp. 269–270.

282
"When the Eisenhowers were here": A. L. Karitas Oral History, JFK Library.

283
"It was an indication": *New York Times*, November 15, 1961.

283
Jack, Sinatra, and starlets: "Part of the appeal [of Sinatra] was the women, stunning, aggressive girls who were always around, always available, many of them dancers or starlets or simply pretty faces. And it was no secret to Sinatra and the rest of the Rat Pack that Kennedy never ran the other way when they came out of the woodwork, and the Pack went out of its way to make sure they were there." William Brashler, *The Don—The Life and Death of Sam Giancana*, New York, 1977, p. 194.

283

JFK and Mary Meyer: See *Newsweek*, March 1, 1976. See also Philip Nobile and Ron Rosenbaum, "The Curious Aftermath of JFK's Best and Brightest Affair," *New Times*, July 9, 1976.

283

Fiddle and Faddle: See Parmet, *JFK*, p. 111.

283

"Here, would you find who these belong to": Kelley, p. 130.

284

"If you had a current event": Authors' interview with Mary Schreiner, April 24, 1983. Schreiner, a classmate of Kathleen Kennedy, rode in the car pool.

284

The kids gave charades and recited poems: Authors' interview with Kathleen Kennedy, February 15, 1980, and Victoria Lawford, June 14, 1982.

284

"Christmas Seals" and other Skakel practical jokes: Authors' interviews with Robert F. Kennedy, Jr.

285

"Dear Jack, I am so glad": Rose Kennedy, p. 407.

285

He asked Steve Smith if his sons "wanted him": Schlesinger, *RFK*, p. 587.

285

"The old man saw": Authors' interviews with Fred Dutton, November 2 and December 6, 1979; April 29, 1981.

285

Huntley got accustomed to the Ambassador calling: Chet Huntley Oral History, JFK Library.

285

Kennedy used his Hollywood connections for *PT 109* and *The Enemy Within:* See Richard Whalen, *The Founding Father*, New York, 1964 (paperback), pp. 255–256. Teamster officials used the union's crucial role in film production and distribution to keep Bobby's book from getting to the screen. But Jack's was more successful. From the time *PT 109* began production, Jack took a major interest in it. Robert Donovan, author of the book version of *PT 109*, recalls: "Joe Kennedy reached agreement with Jack Warner that any contract they would sign with me would have to have certain provisions, and one of them was that the President would have the right to veto whoever represented him in the movie.... The President ... said to me, 'I want Warren Beatty to play the role.' So I went back to the Warner Brothers people and there was some to-do in Hollywood over that ... [They] said the only way Warren Beatty will play the part of Kennedy is if Kennedy is a pacifist and doesn't go to the South Pacific. So Warren Beatty was out. Then they came up with the idea of Cliff Robertson ..." Herbert Parmet interview with Robert Donovan, April 11, 1977. From a transcript kindly given to the authors by Parmet.

285

"Take care of yourself": Edward M. Kennedy, ed., *Bough*, pp. 262ff.

285

Teddy his "sunshine": Authors' interview with Charles Spalding.

285

"How's my girl?": Authors' interview with Mary Lou McCarthy.

285

"He thought his place in the world": Anne Taylor Fleming, "The Kennedy Mystique," *New York Times Magazine*, June 17, 1979.

286

"Lookit—get this straight": Garrett Byrne Oral History, JFK Library.

286

Teddy "should have the right to run": RFK Oral History, JFK Library, p. 254.

286

"I don't want him to run": Authors' interview with John E. Powers, May 26, 1982. *Boston Globe* writer Robert Healy says: "They thought Jack was risking his own presidency. I'm talking about Kenny O'Donnell mainly, but even McBundy and Arthur Schlesinger. O'Donnell simply didn't think that Kennedy should risk his presidency for his younger brother." Authors' interview with Robert Healy, December 1, 1981.

286

"We're having more fucking trouble": Authors' interview wiwith Robert Healy.

286n

"It won't go over with the WASPs": Bradlee, p. 69.

286

The Senate seat bought and paid for: "I heard them all say 'That's our seat,' or 'That's the Kennedy seat.' " Ibid.

286

"[Mr. Kennedy] wants to be sure": James Fayne to JFK, December 4, 1961. JFK Personal Files, JFK Library.

287

"There's nothing I can do but pray": Saunders, p. 121.

287

"One breath away": Authors' interview with Lem Billings.

287

"It was awful to have these one-way conversations": Authors' interview with Leo Racine, February 12, 1980.

287

Rehabilitation at the Rusk Institute: Authors' interview with Dr. Howard Rusk, October 22, 1979.

287

"He was ... easier to deal with": Authors' interview with Charles Spalding.

288

She told Beaverbrook: Rose to Beaverbrook, August 1, 1962. Beaverbrook Papers.

288

"Before he had been the Supreme Being": Authors' interview with Frank B. Saunders.

288

"I don't want to be like that": Authors' interview with Lem Billings.

288

"Uncle Joe's stroke": Authors' interview with Mary Lou McCarthy.

288

"He's got high moral standards": Bradlee, pp. 142–143.

288

"It was strange to hear them": Authors' interview with Lem Billings.

288

Comic drawing of Hickory Hill: Harrison Rainie and John Quinn, *Growing Up Kennedy*, New York, 1983, p. 77.

288

"Whenever we came back": Authors' interview with Paul B. "Red" Fay.

289

"I think it is the Second Most Important Man": Authors' interview with Lem Billings.

289

"He's probably all choked up": Authors' interview with Charles Spalding.

289

"It's not McNamara": Merle Miller, *Lyndon, An Oral History*, New York, 1980, p. 305.

289

Greeting a tour: Baldridge, p. 201.

289
Jack on presidential greatness: Charles E. Bohlen Oral History; see also Donald Wilson Oral History, JFK Library.

289
Weekending with Jim Reed: Authors' interview with James Reed.

289
Swimming with Red Fay: Authors' interview with Paul B. "Red" Fay.

290
"That's not my face": Authors' interview with Lem Billings.

290
He asked Averell Harriman: Authors' interview with Rowland Evans, July 22, 1980.

290
Bobby the "moving spirit" behind Mongoose: *Senate Interim Report,* p. 160.

290
"We should ... do more": Ibid., p. 160.

290
"My God, these Kennedys keep the pressure": Thomas Powers, *The Man Who Kept the Secrets: Richard Helms and the CIA,* New York, 1979, p. 138.

291
"Had the agents landed?": Ibid., p. 139.

291
"Hey, where are you going with that?" Ibid., p. 141.

291n
RFK in conflict with Taylor: Ibid., p. 135.

291
"Chasing bad men" on a global scale: "Bobby saw counterinsurgency as a kind of very elaborate Boy Scout effort with guns." Authors' interview with Michael Forrestal.

291
Sargent Shriver refused to let his children watch: Authors' interview with Harris Wofford.

291
"This is a new kind of war": Cited by William V. Shannon, *The Heir Apparent,* New York, 1967, p. 113.

292
"The extreme kind of reaction": Robert Amory Oral History, JFK Library.

292
Bobby received a memo from Hoover: *Senate Interim Report,* pp. 129–130.

292n
Campbell introduced by Sinatra: Judith Campbell Exner, *My Story,* New York, 1977, pp. 86ff.

293
Bobby and Gore Vidal: Schlesinger, *RFK,* p. 594.

293
Bobby and Ellen Romesch: Bobby Baker, *Wheeling and Dealing: Confessions of a Capitol Hill Operator,* New York, 1978, pp. 79–80.

293
"Jack and Teddy put their arms around Bobby": Authors' interview with Mary Gimbel.

293
"About someone I knew or a member of my family": RFK Oral History, JFK Library.

294
"If you had seen [his] eyes": *Senate Interim Report,* p. 133.

294
Contact with Johnny Rosselli: Ibid., p. 134.

294

According to William Harvey: Ibid.

294

Richard Helms later noted: Ibid., pp. 148ff. In his book on Helms, Thomas Powers, who interviewed the former CIA director and other top Agency officials, discusses the question of presidential authorization of assassination plots and the bureaucratic policy of "plausible denial" frustrating the Senate committee's efforts to pinpoint responsibility, and concludes: "The available evidence leans heavily toward a finding that the Kennedys did, in fact, authorize the CIA to make an attempt on Castro's life." Powers, pp. 120ff, 143ff. Arthur Schlesinger, disputing such conclusions, notes that Kennedy "took care to send CIA his statement of May 29, 1961, that the United States could not as a matter of general policy condone assassination . . . a statement he never thereafter withdrew, qualified or amended." But Kennedy's remarks, issued the day before forces armed and—until the Bay of Pigs disaster—encouraged by the CIA and the State Department assassinated Dominican dictator Rafael Trujillo, are perhaps more reasonably seen as a cover statement of "plausible denial" than a strong injunction against assassination. See *Senate Interim Report*, pp. 191ff.

294

Bissell had created "Executive Action": *Senate Interim Report*, pp. 181ff.

294

"What would you think if I ordered Castro": Ibid., pp. 138–139. Also authors' interview with Tad Szulc, February 14, 1980. According to Szulc's notes of his conversation with the President, "JFK said he raised the question because he was under terrific pressure from advisers (think he said intelligence people, but not positive) to okay a Castro murder, said he was resisting pressures." *Senate Interim Report*, ibid. Senator Howard Baker, a member of the committee, commented: "This conversation raises a number of questions on the issue of authority [for the assassination attempts]. The central question, of course, is who, in November 1961, was putting pressure on the President to authorize Castro's assassination?" Baker noted that all the top CIA and administration officials had testified before the Senate committee and "everyone has uniformly denied ever even mentioning assassination to President Kennedy, let alone 'pressuring' him to approve it." Ibid., p. 325.

294

Szulc always wondered if this conversation: See Tad Szulc, "Cuba on Our Minds," *Esquire*, February 1974.

294

"It was the obvious consensus": *Senate Interim Report*, p. 162.

294

Lansdale's new plan: Ibid., pp. 161–162.

295

Harvey exploded at the indiscretion: Ibid.

295

RFK ordered harassment of Giancana: Schlesinger, *RFK*, p. 533. Hoover recorded his version of the conversation in a memo dated May 10, 1962, two days after he had met with the Attorney General: "Stated as [Kennedy] well knew the 'gutter gossip' was that the reason nothing had been done against Giancana was because of Giancana's close relationship with Frank Sinatra who, in turn, claimed to be a close friend of the Kennedy family. The Attorney General stated he realized this and it was for that reason that he was quite concerned when he received this information from CIA about Giancana and Maheu." Ibid., p. 133*n*.

295

"Johnny, you just can't associate with this guy": Authors' interview with Paul "Red" Fay.

295

Peter Lawford got the job: Authors' interview with Peter Lawford.

295

February 20 meeting: *Senate Interim Report*, p. 143.

295
August 10 meeting: Ibid., p. 147.
295
NSC memo 181: Ibid.
296
"Detailed plans": Ibid., p. 144.
296
Soviet buildup in Cuba: David Detzer, *The Brink: The Cuban Missile Crisis, 1962,* New York, 1979, p. 58.
296n
"Of course the odds are": Authors' interview with Joseph Alsop. Also communication from Alsop, January 17, 1984.
296
RFK and Bolshakov: Schlesinger, *RFK,* pp. 537ff.
296
September 4 meeting: Robert F. Kennedy, *Thirteen Days,* New York, 1969 (paperback), p. 25.
297
Bobby suggested a presidential statement: Robert F. Kennedy, *Thirteen Days,* p. 26.
297
"The matter of attacking": *Senate Interim Report,* p. 147n.
297
"Consideration will be given": Ibid., p. 147.
297
Jack "concerned with the progress of the Mongoose program": Ibid.
297
"All efforts should be made": Ibid.
297
"I now know how Tojo felt": Robert F. Kennedy, *Thirteen Days,* p. 31.
297
JFK's "dissatisfaction" with Mongoose: *Senate Interim Report,* p. 146.
298
Dean Acheson found the informality distressing: See Dean Acheson, "Dean Acheson's Version of Robert Kennedy's Version of the Cuban Missile Affair," *Esquire,* February 1969.
298
Harvey bluntly told Bobby: Powers, p. 142.
298
Acheson demolished Bobby's Pearl Harbor analogy: See Dean Acheson, "Dean Acheson's Version of Robert Kennedy's Version of the Cuban Missile Affair," *Esquire,* February 1969.
298
Adlai fit the requirements: "The Kennedy circle hated Stevenson. He wasn't their type. They were always putting him down, making fun of him. It came from Jack." Authors' interview with Marian Schlesinger, April 12, 1980.
298
Stevenson referred to the President as "Kennedy": Authors' interview with Michael Forrestal.
298
"Adlai wanted a Munich": JFK later denied inserting the remark, a position aides such as O'Donnell continued to maintain. See O'Donnell and Powers, p. 374.
298
"He's not strong or tough enough": Ibid., p. 373.
299
"I never knew Adlai had it in him": Ibid., p. 387.
299
"The 1930s taught us a clear lesson": Sorensen, p. 703.

299

"Inexplicably I thought of when he was ill": Robert F. Kennedy, *Thirteen Days*, p. 69.

299

"A very near thing": Dean Acheson, "Dean Acheson's Version of Robert Kennedy's Version of the Cuban Missile Affair," *Esquire*, February 1969.

299

"Thank God for Bobby": O'Donnell and Powers, p. 327. (The authors introduce this anecdote with the following remark: "Dave Powers remembers [JFK] speaking warmly of Bobby only once, on the black Saturday of October 27, 1962, at the height of the Cuban missile crisis.")

299

"This is the night": Robert F. Kennedy, *Thirteen Days*, p. 110.

300

"To finally win his manhood": Authors' interview with Joseph Kraft.

300

RFK complained to Seigenthaler: Authors' interview with John Seigenthaler.

301

Bobby insisted that the trip would assuage the "guilt": RFK Oral History, JFK Library.

301

"He's still too young": Haynes Johnson, p. 344.

301

"I can assure you": Ibid.

301

Miro Cardona accuses Kennedy brothers of "breaking promises": *Cuba, the U.S. and Russia*, New York (Facts on File), 1964, p. 131.

301n

"The U.S. must do something": *Senate Interim Report*, p. 172; "to nourish a spirit of resistance": ibid., p. 173; sabotage operations: ibid; AM/LASH: ibid, pp. 174ff.

301

Trying to practice containment on black aspiration: "We didn't begin serious efforts at civil rights legislation until about March 1963." Authors' interview with Ramsey Clark.

302

"Their attitude was 'don't do anything' ": Theodore Hesburgh Oral History, JFK Library.

302

JFK's housing order: Wofford, pp. 124ff. Also authors' interview with Harris Wofford.

302

"I hope that every drop of blood": Cited in Schlesinger, *RFK*, p. 355.

302

Hesburgh told about the Alabama National Guard: Theodore Hesburgh Oral History, JFK Library.

302

"Can't you ask them to fly?": Authors' interview with Harris Wofford.

302

RFK, Harold Cox, and federal judgeships: Navasky, pp. 244ff.

302

"Tell your brother": Robert Sherrill, *Gothic Politics in the Deep South*, New York, 1969(paperback), p. 212.

303

Bobby didn't "lay awake nights": RFK Oral History, JFK Library.

303

"One of the most violent, emotional verbal assaults": Cited in Schlesinger, *RFK*, p. 333.

303
"Children of wealthy [white] parents": RFK Oral History, JFK Library.
303
"It is brother Bobby": Cited in Schlesinger, *RFK*, p. 303.
303
"Now let's get Hoffa": Navasky, p. 347.
303
"See that?": Authors' interviews with Robert F. Kennedy, Jr.
303
Orrick was struck by the fact: Navasky, p. 411n.
303
"It burned my ass": Navasky, p. 404. Also authors' interview with Edwin Silberling, July 11, 1980.
304
"Flimsy as hell": Authors' interview with Ramsey Clark.
304
"Questions of procedure and due process": Ibid.
304
Partin contacted Sheridan: See Walter Sheridan, *The Fall and Rise of Jimmy Hoffa*, New York, 1972, pp. 216ff.
304
"I've got to do something about that son of a bitch": Ibid., p. 217. The U.S. House of Representatives Select Committee on Assassinations later considered evidence that in his discussions of "hitting" Bobby, Hoffa had discussed "the possible use of a lone gunman equipped with a rifle with telescopic sight, the advisability of having the assassination committed somewhere in the South, as well as the potential desirability of having Robert Kennedy shot while riding in a convertible." *The Final Assassinations Report*. Report of the Select Committee on Assassinations, U.S. House of Representatives, New York, 1979 (paperback reprint), p. 218.
305
"Here I am helping the government": Michael Hellerman, *Wall Street Swindler*, New York, 1977, p. 86.
305
"With Kennedy, a guy should take a knife": G. Robert Blakey and Richard N. Billings, *The Plot to Kill the President*, New York, 1981, p. 237.
305
"Hitting Hoffa, a man who is a worker": Anthony Summers, *Conspiracy*, New York, 1980, p. 284.
305
"Don't worry about that little Bobby": Ibid., p. 287.
305
"Let us reexamine": John F. Kennedy, *Public Papers of the President 1963*, Washington, 1963, pp. 459ff.
306
"There are some who say communism": Ibid., pp. 524–525.
306n
"You have to understand": Authors' interview with Daniel Ellsberg, September 9, 1979.
306
The incarceration of peasants in strategic hamlets: According to Kennedy's Assistant Secretary of State Roger Hilsman: "We were telling the President [at this time] that the strategic hamlets were not strategic hamlets, but were concentration camps." Authors' interview with Roger Hilsman, October 23, 1979.
306
"We've got to face the fact": Charles Bartlett Oral History, LBJ Library.
307
A split in the administration: See Halberstam, pp. 317ff.

307

He brought in Henry Cabot Lodge to share responsibility: Later, historians would have conflicting opinions about the extent of Lodge's liability. They would contend not only against each other on the issue but sometimes against themselves. For instance, in Arthur Schlesinger's 1965 account of the administration, Lodge is portrayed as a hero of the occasion: "The White House doubters were mistaken about Lodge. We had forgotten his patrician's preference for fair play and his patriot's pride in the dignity of his country....By 1961 choices had already fatally narrowed; but still, if Vietnam had been handled as a political rather than a military problem ...if a Lodge had gone to Saigon in 1961 instead of a Nolting..." See *A Thousand Days*, pp. 990, 998. But thirteen years later, after Vietnam had become a national debacle and the Kennedys' responsibility for it was an issue of hot debate, Schlesinger's view of Lodge shifted. Lodge becomes something like the villain of the piece. While the President is characterized as a man leaning toward disengagement and withdrawal, Lodge is portrayed as thwarting these intentions by forcing coup attempts from the field: "In Saigon Lodge was determined to overthrow Diem." See *RFK*, p. 771. In revising his interpretation, Schlesinger was following the post-hoc argument of Robert Kennedy: "The individual that forced our position really at the time of Vietnam, was Henry Cabot Lodge.... The President would send out messages and he would never really answer them." RFK Oral History, JFK Library. However, White House cables made public by the Church Committee show that despite the ambivalence that typified JFK's response to such dilemmas, he gave his support to both coup attempts during his administration. See *Senate Interim Report*, pp. 217ff.

307

"For us to withdraw from this effort": John Galloway, ed., *The Kennedys and Vietnam*, New York, 1971, p. 40.

307

Cable to Lodge: See "The Untold Story of the Road to War in Vietnam," *U.S. News & World Report*, October 10, 1983. This special report, based on extensive interviews with participants, cites several documents which had not been published before, among them this cable.

307

"My God, my government's coming apart": Schlesinger, *RFK*, p. 770.

307

"The only time the government was broken in two": RFK Oral History, JFK Library.

308

"To be successful, this operation must be": *Senate Interim Report*, p. 219.

308

Nhu talks of accommodation with Ho Chi Minh: In May 1963 Nhu had proposed that the U.S. start withdrawing its troops. During the ensuing period there was secret diplomacy between Saigon and Hanoi, with a tentative agreement for a South Vietnamese coalition government headed by Diem. See Mieczyslaw Maneli, "Vietnam '63 and Now," *New York Times*, January 27, 1975. Maneli, then a Polish diplomat, was the intermediary. As Arthur Schlesinger notes, both pro- and anti-Diem factions in Washington saw these secret negotiations not as an opportunity to extricate the United States from Vietnam but as a threat to victory—and hence an added reason for the coup. See *RFK*, p. 720.

308

"If we have concluded that we are going to lose": "The Untold Story of the Road to War in Vietnam," *U.S. News & World Report*, October 10, 1983, p. 10.

308

"What I am concerned about": Galloway, ed., p. 43.

308

"Push us toward a reconciliation": "The Untold Story of the Road to War in Vietnam," *U.S. News & World Report*, October 10, 1983, p. 16. The proposed withdrawal of "advisers" has been used by Kenny O'Donnell, Arthur Schlesinger, and others who argue that Kennedy was moving toward a withdrawal from Vietnam. Such a theory ignores the purpose of this token withdrawal: pressure on Diem to make policy changes, including the exile of his brother-in-law—"reforms to which [as Schlesinger himself admits] Diem would not conceivably accede." *RFK*, p. 771. Former Secretary of State Dean Rusk told the authors, "I personally am convinced that Kennedy had not made a decision in 1963 to take the troops out in 1965. I had talked with him about Southeast Asia hundreds of times and on no occasion did he breathe a word of such an idea... The withdrawal of 1,000 troops out of 17,000 is nothing." Authors' interview with Dean Rusk, July 26, 1979.

308
"While we do not wish to stimulate a coup": "The Untold Story of the Road to War in Vietnam," *U.S. News & World Report*, October 10, 1983, p. 18.

308
"We certainly cannot be in the position": *Senate Interim Report*, p. 221.

308
Bobby felt his "hands were tied": RFK Oral History, JFK Library.

309
"[The President] leaped to his feet": Maxwell Taylor, *Swords and Ploughshares*, New York, 1972, p. 301.

309
"No, they were in a difficult position": Authors' interview with Mary Gimbel.

309
"The issues were clear in FDR's day": George Herman Oral History, JFK Library.

309
A "narrow and constricted view": Peter Lisagor Oral History, JFK Library. Speaking of the presidential news conferences, Lisagor says that JFK made reporters into "spear carriers for a televised opera. We were props in a show, in a performance. Kennedy mastered the art of this performance early, and he used it with great effectiveness. We were simply there as props. I always felt that we should have joined Actors Equity. Those of us who asked questions should have charged that much extra for speaking lines." Ibid.

309
Arthur Krock's attack: The article appeared in *Fortune*, March 1963. It was inserted into the *Congressional Record* on February 26, 1963.

309
Hanson Baldwin complained: "Managed News: Our Peacetime Censorship," *Atlantic Monthly*, April 1963.

309
"I thought I had become such a liability": RFK Oral History, JFK Library.

310
Jack speaking "September Song": Authors' interview with Charles Spalding.

310
"Come on, Jack, let's go": Richard Cardinal Cushing Oral History, JFK Library.

310
"How do you think Lyndon would be": Charles Bartlett Oral History, LBJ Library.

310
"Oh, a gun": Herbert Parmet interview with Phyllis MacDonald. Parmet kindly made a transcript available to the authors.

310
"A series of exercises which would do credit to a gymnast": George Bulkey Oral History, JFK Library.

310
JFK's tenderness toward JPK: Authors' interview with Lem Billings.

310
"There are two naked girls": Authors' interview with a confidential source, April 21, 1980.
311
"We better get out of the way": Stanley Tretick Oral History, JFK Library.
311
"Don't leave me!": J. B. West Oral History, JFK Library.
311
Caroline and the White Whale: Authors' interview with Lem Billings.
311
Jack's speculations about 1964: O'Donnell and Powers, p. 12. Jack found Romney's strict, abstemious Mormonism amusing. "You have to be suspicious of someone as good as Romney," he told Red Fay. "No vices whatsoever ... Imagine someone we know going off for twenty-four or forty-eight hours to fast and meditate, awaiting a message from the Lord whether to run or not to run. Does that sound like one of the old gang?" See Paul B. Fay, Jr., *The Pleasure of His Company,* New York, 1966, p. 240.
311
Bobby to be enticed back: Shannon, p. 8.
311
"Not particularly thrilled" about Bobby succeeding him: Charles Bartlett Oral History, LBJ Library.
311
"I know why you're against me": Authors' interview with John Seigenthaler.
312
"If only he were a Negro": Charles Bartlett Oral History, LBJ Library.
312n
"As soon as he spotted me": Baker, pp. 76ff.
312
"I really feel sorry for Lyndon": Ibid., p. 116.
312
Warnings about Jack's Dallas trip: O'Donnell and Powers, p. 19.
312
"Jack's been shot": Schlesinger, *RFK,* p. 609.
312
"I thought they'd get one of us": Edwin Guthman, *We Band of Brothers,* New York, 1971, p. 244.
313
"Joey, you should read more": Gail Cameron, *Rose,* New York, 1972 (paperback), p. 261.
313
Joe Kennedy after the assassination: Rita Dallas, *The Kennedy Case,* New York, 1973, p. 19. Also authors' interview with Rita Dallas, private nurse to Joseph P. Kennedy, September 11, 1979.
313
"Daddy, there's been an accident": Ibid.
313
JPK tries to go to JFK funeral: Authors' interview with Frank Saunders.
313
JPK awakens and screams: Dallas, p. 253.
314
Joe Kennedy had a wetness: Authors' interview with Frank Saunders.
314
"He didn't really bother": Ibid.
314
Rose spent long hours: Ibid.

314
"The whole family was like a bunch of shipwreck survivors": Authors' interview with Lem Billings.

314
"He seemed to be everywhere": Ibid.

314
"How do I look?": Authors' interview with John Seigenthaler.

315
Bobby wouldn't say "assassination" or "death": Authors' interview with Mary Gimbel.

315
Bobby couldn't bear the visual reminders: Ibid.

315
"Sure I've lost a brother": Richard Goodwin, "A Day in June," *McCall's*, June 1970.

315
"'Well, you're young and you're going to be productive'": Authors' interview with Mary McGrory, July 23, 1980.

315
"Hackett and I have so much experience": Richard Goodwin, "A Day in June," *McCall's*, June 1970.

316
The Greek Way: Bobby's underlined copy is in the possession of Mary Gimbel, who kindly allowed the authors to examine it.

316
"God, whose law it is": Edith Hamilton, *The Greek Way*, pp. 52, 108, Gimbel copy.

316
He was actually reading: Authors' interview with John Seigenthaler.

316
"Because he knows the secrets of the deep": Authors' interview with Mary Gimbel.

316
Jack's old garments: Authors' interview with Ronnie Eldridge, July 14, 1980. Eldridge is a New York political figure who worked with RFK in the post-assassination period.

317
"Did the CIA kill my brother?": Walter Sheridan Oral History, JFK Library.

317
The answers he might get: Fifteen years later a congressional committee concluded that both Lee Harvey Oswald and Jack Ruby had substantial connections with organized crime figures such as Carlos Marcello and Santos Trafficante. "The Committee's review of the [FBI] surveillance transcripts and logs, detailing the private conversations of [national crime] commission members and their associates, revealed that there were extensive and heated discussions about the serious difficulties the Kennedy administration's crackdown on organized crime was causing ... [including discussions of] possible violent courses of action against either the President or his brother, Attorney General Robert F. Kennedy ..." (*U.S. House of Representatives Select Committee on Assassinations Report*, New York, 1979 (paperback), pp. 201–202.

317n
Sheridan sent to interview Garrison: Authors' interview with Frank Mankiewicz, March 24, 1981.

317
"He had been so involved with Jack's destiny": Authors' interview with Ramsey Clark.

318
"President Kennedy was more than just President": Cited by Shannon, p. 17.

318
"It was Camelot": Theodore H. White, "For President Kennedy: An Epilogue,"
Life, December 6, 1963. See also White's *In Search of History*, New York, 1978, pp.
518ff.
319
"Can't you wait?": Cited in Schlesinger, *RFK*, p. 627.
319
"He'd just deluge me": Authors' interview with Rowland Evans.
319
Qualities of sibling hatred: "Did you ever see two dogs come into a room and all of
a sudden there's a low growl, and the hair rises up on the back of their necks? It was
like that. LBJ got along quite well with Jack, but somehow he and Bobby took one
look at each other and that was it. Johnson attributed to Bobby some extraordinary
powers. He became really childish about it. I remember one day reading an *Esquire*
article by Gore Vidal about Bobby that I thought was one of the nastiest hatchet jobs
I'd ever seen. Johnson called me in my office and and said, 'Did you see that article
about Bobby Kennedy in *Esquire?* Who do you think planted it, George?' I said, 'I
don't think anybody planted it, Mr. President. Gore Vidal is a well-known writer; he
can get anything he wants printed.' Johnson said, 'Nah, nah, somebody planted it.
Do you suppose it was Bobby Kennedy who planted it? It's an outrageous puff
piece.' " Authors' interview with George Reedy, July 1, 1980.
319
An LBJ voodoo doll: *Life*, November 18, 1966.
319
LBJ's "generosity of spirit": Jacqueline Kennedy Oral History, LBJ Library.
319
"Bobby gets me to put on my widow's weeds": Charles Bartlett Oral History, LBJ
Library.
319
Jackie and the renaming of Cape Canaveral: Jacqueline Kennedy Oral History, LBJ
Library. Yet months later, when Rowland Evans was at dinner with Jackie, "She
told me what worried her more than anything was that the Johnson Administration
would clear the record of any allusion to the success, victories, and policies of the
Kennedy Administration. That these would be wiped off the slate and there would be
no record." Authors' interview with Rowland Evans.
320n
Schlesinger "declared war": Ralph Dungan Oral History, JFK Library.
320n
"Find something for him": Authors' interview with Joseph Alsop.
320
"There are a hundred men": Cited in Schlesinger, *RFK*, p. 631.
320
Bobby bitterly accused them: RFK Oral History, p. 477.
320
"His general demeanor ": Orville Freeman Oral History, LBJ Library.
320
LBJ's emotional contact with Jack: The climactic moment in the LBJ-JFK relationship had come when Johnson was about to go to Scandinavia on a good-will tour and
wanted a preflight meeting with the President to give his trip stature. From his
position as appointments secretary, O'Donnell had blocked the meeting, saying
Jack was too busy, but Ted Clifton, the President's military attaché, circumvented
O'Donnell by arranging for LBJ and Lady Bird to come to Hyannis for an
hour, during which time Jack treated the planned tour as an event of great importance. LBJ, moved, said to Clifton as he was leaving, "Tell that young man
that what he did today was a good and generous thing." Ted Clifton Oral History,
JFK Library.

320
"Johnson used to tell Kenny": RFK Oral History, JFK Library, p. 470.
321
"A bitter, mean conversation": RFK Oral History, JFK Library.
321
"Bobby Kennedy's just another lawyer now": Sheridan, p. 300.
321
"There's nothing to celebrate": Cited in Schlesinger, *RFK*, p. 637.
321
"I have influence because": RFK Oral History, JFK Library, pp. 448ff.
321
"We were making more of an effort in August": Ibid., pp. 410–411.
321
Bobby offered to go to Saigon: RFK to LBJ, June 11, 1964. Johnson Papers, LBJ Library.
322
"I'm not just a senator": RFK Oral History, JFK Library, pp. 448ff.
322
"I can't hang around here": Authors' interview with Robert Ajemian, September 25, 1981.
322
"Somebody up there doesn't like us": William Nicholas, *The Bobby Kennedy Nobody Knows,* New York, 1967 (paperback) (unpaged).
322
"The Kennedys intend to stay in public life": Burton Hersh, *The Education of Edward Kennedy,* New York, 1972, p. 202.
323
"Like a kind of stunned semi-idiot": Stewart Alsop Oral History, LBJ Library.
323
"Unctuous calls" from Steve Smith: John Bartlow Martin, *Adlai E. Stevenson and the World,* New York, 1977, p. 812.
323
"The avarice of the Kennedys": Ibid.
323
Bobby felt he "was being pushed forward": Authors' interview with Ramsey Clark.
324
"They're for *him*": Guthman, p. 294.
324
"Steve, I just want to tell you": Richard Reeves, "Goldilocks May Not Be the Most Exciting Fellow in Town, But He's the Only One Who Can Win This Year," *New York Times Magazine,* June 14, 1970.
324
"He was terrible": Authors' interview with Lem Billings. RFK's use of television in the 1964 campaign is examined in Terry Smith, "Bobby's Image," *Esquire,* April 1965.
324
"If my brother was alive": George Plimpton and Jean Stein, *American Journey,* New York, 1970, p. 182.
325
"Let's go for a ride": Authors' interview with John Seigenthaler.
325
He had been fearful: "Bob Kennedy told me he was frightened himself on that climb. He said to me, 'Don't do it,' when we talked about it afterwards." Authors' interview with John Seigenthaler.
325
"After they'd been blessed": Authors' interview with Lem Billings.

327
"When you have older brothers": Hersh, p. 132.
327
"I've got to take second spot": David Burke Oral History, JFK Library.
327
Newsweek cover: William Honan, *Profile of a Survivor*, New York, 1972 (paperback), p. 132.
327
Bobby took "the President's chair": Authors' interview with Dun Gifford.
327
"Little brother" to be "sent right home": Hersh, pp. 216–217.
327
"Very good in committee arguments": David Burke Oral History, JFK Library.
327
"The chairman or some other senator": Ibid.
328
"Being who he was": Authors' interview with Senator George Smathers.
328
Edelman and Walinsky: Authors' interview with Fred Dutton.
328
"The President was most fond": *New York Times*, November 23, 1965.
329
Bobby and Ian Robertson: Shannon, p. 137.
329
"My brother believed": The full texts of Robert Kennedy's speeches in South Africa were published by the *Rand Daily Mail* under the title "Robert Kennedy in South Africa."
329
"I could be smoking a cigar": Schlesinger, *RFK*, p. 786.
329
The model for this effort: Authors' interview with David Hackett, November 1, 1979.
330
"Ah, why am I going": Authors' interviews with Peter Edelman, November 2, 1979, February 14, 1981, and June 15, 1982.
331
"What shocked me": Authors' interview with Prudence Weatherby, July 18, 1980.
331
"Lots of white men": Authors' interview with La Nada Means, January 28, 1971.
331
"Sooner or later": Cited in Schlesinger, *RFK*, p. 698.
331
Bobby and rhino: Nicholas (unpaged).
331
Bobby diving over the side: Authors' interview with Mary Gimbel.
331
Family skiing trips: Authors' interviews with Robert Kennedy, Jr.
332
Family river trips: Ibid. Also authors' interview with George Plimpton, March 19, 1981. Plimpton accompanied the family on the Colorado River trip.
332
"It was like he was thumping his chest": Authors' interview with Lem Billings.
332
"If I wasn't a United States Senator": Authors' interview with Jack Newfield, March 16, 1981.
332
"I wish I'd been born an Indian": Fred Harris Oral History, JFK Library.

332

"If I hadn't been born rich": Margaret Laing, *Robert Kennedy*, London, 1968, p. 32.

332

"I'm jealous of the fact": Jack Newfield, *Robert F. Kennedy: A Memoir*, New York, 1978 (paperback), p. 90*n*.

333

He dismissed it as a "zoo": Ibid., p. 171.

333

"Bored out of his mind": Authors' interview with Barbara Coleman, March 24, 1981.

333

Men he privately scorned: Bobby used his ineffectuality in taming New York state politics as a subtle way of challenging the popular image of him as powerful and ruthless. Democratic Party ally Ronnie Eldridge recalls him in Buffalo during the 1966 convention which selected O'Connor as the party nominee. "He was wandering around disheveled in his shirtsleeves saying, 'Do I look like the power behind the throne? Do I look like someone who's calling the shots? I don't even know what's going on.'" Authors' interview with Ronnie Eldridge.

333

Bobby and Red Fay's book: Authors' interview with Paul "Red" Fay.

333

Jackie chided Fay: Ibid. Fay says that in a long-distance phone call she indicated "ten or twelve things" she wanted deleted or changed, in particular that she be called Jacqueline and not "Jackie" in the book, and that her son be called John and not "John-John."

333

He demanded that Fay cut out two-thirds: Ibid.

333

"I'm going to keep your book": Ibid. "They put the screws on me. I said to Bobby, 'Nobody loved your brother more than I did. There's nothing here in my opinion that would jeopardize him. You point out the things you think might demean your brother as a human being. But just don't go through and slash the whole thing.' He answered: 'I told you what you should do, and that's it.' I said, 'Well, Bobby, I'm not going to do it.' And he said, 'Then I'm going to stop your book from being published.' And he went to Harper and Row, and he got ahold of Evan Thomas, and Thomas told me that he couldn't publish it." Fay then wrote a letter reiterating his offer to compromise, but with an ultimatum ("I said 'If you block this book, I'm going to make twice as much on it'") and an agreement was reached.

333

Bobby and Manchester's book: For a discussion of the controversy from Manchester's point of view, see Manchester, *Controversy*, Boston, 1976, pp. 6ff.

333n

"I will not talk to you": Jim Bishop, *The Day Kennedy Was Shot*, New York, 1968, Introduction.

333

Jackie on Manchester: Jacqueline Kennedy Oral History, LBJ Library.

334

"Bobby and his political advisers": Manchester, *Controversy*, p. 37.

334

The passages Jackie worried about: Ibid., p. 30. Also authors' interview with Frank Mankiewicz, who was Bobby's press secretary at the time.

334

The passages Bobby worried about: Manchester, *Controversy*, p. 30.

334

Of the 69 percent of the public: Ibid., p. 63. See also William Manchester, *The Death of the President*, New York, 1967.

334
"The United States has made a commitment": RFK Oral History, JFK Library.
335
"Victory in a revolutionary war": Cited in Schlesinger, *RFK*, p. 730. Also authors' interview with Adam Walinsky, October 25, 1979.
335
"I'd be willing to give blood": Transcript of press conference of November 5, 1965. RFK Papers, JFK Library.
335
"A share of power and responsibility": *New York Times*, February 20, 1966.
335
Attacks on Bobby: Bundy quoted Jack's axiom about popular-front governments— "I don't believe that any democrat can ride that tiger"—in an attempt to discredit Bobby, who was outraged at the "cheap trick" of using his own brother against him. See Newfield, p. 132.
335
"The last time I spoke out": Ibid., p. 134.
335
"The President felt": RFK Oral History, JFK Library.
336
"These are very complex problems": Cited by Newfield, p. 133.
336
The European "peace feeler": See David Kraslow and S. H. Loony, *The Secret Search for Peace*, New York, 1968 (paperback), pp. 202ff. The "leak" was reported in the *New York Times*, February 6, 1967.
336
"I'll destroy you and . . . your dove friends": Cited in Schlesinger, *RFK*, p. 768.
336
Time reports RFK called LBJ a son of a bitch: *Time*, March 17, 1967.
336
"Three Presidents": *New York Times*, March 3, 1967.
337
"Its own Bonapartism": Max Ascoli, "Two USA's," *Reporter*, March 23, 1967.
337
"He looks like a damned Beatnik": Hersh, p. 365.
337
Robert Lowell on Bobby: Robert Lowell, "Robert Kennedy, 1925–1968," in *Notebook*, New York, 1970, p. 197.
338
"I always felt that her love for her father": Authors' interview with Peter Lawford.
338
"Frank wouldn't even talk to Peter": Authors' interview with Paul "Red" Fay. Also interview with Milton Ebbins, January 14, 1982.
338
"We're getting out of here": Authors' interview with Christopher Lawford.
339
"One of the walking wounded": Authors' interview with a confidential source, September 22, 1982.
339
Shriver as an ornament of the Great Society: Eunice had been primarily responsible for Shriver's acceptance of the OEO job. Reflecting on her ambition, long-time Kennedy aide Fred Dutton says of Eunice, "If there's a hot pie in the window, you can bet Eunice is for taking it." Authors' interview with Fred Dutton.
339
JPK gives up on rehabilitation efforts: "He wouldn't wear leg braces for long. He wouldn't let our speech therapist stay with him longer than ten minutes at a time. He

was used to doing things his own way." Authors' interview with Dr. Howard Rusk, head of the Rusk Institute, October 22, 1979.
339
Fitzgerald relatives hide from JPK: Authors' interview with Frank Saunders, November 19, 1982.
339
"I'll make changes, Dad": Cited in Dallas, p. 288.
340
"Bobby didn't know": Authors' interview with Lem Billings.
340
Bobby held the family together: Authors' interviews with Bobby Shriver and Chris Lawford. Journalist Robert Ajemian, a close friend of Kenny O'Donnell's, says: "I heard Kenny say many times, 'Bobby really held the family together.' Since 1952, he was the one who made sure that they didn't stray, that they showed up for family get-togethers, birthdays, and all family things that held the clan together. If they didn't, they'd hear from him." Authors' interview with Robert Ajemian.
340
Bobby's trips: Details of skiing and river trips from authors' interviews with family members (Bobby Shriver, Bobby Kennedy, Jr., David Kennedy) and family friends (George Plimpton and Chuck McDermott), who went on these outings.
340
Hickory Hill football games: Authors' interview with Jim Boland, May 18, 1981. "When you intercepted a Jurgensen pass you thought you should be out there Sundays!" Boland was a friend of Bobby's son Joe III.
340
Bobby's ad hoc decisions: Authors' interviews with Chuck McDermott, February 28, and April 24, 1981; April 17, 1983. McDermott was a friend of Joe III.
340
"Hear ye, hear ye": Nicholas (unpaged).
340
"Except for war": Ibid.
340
"If you dropped one of his passes": Authors' interviews with Bobby Shriver, February 10, 1980, January 28, 1981, and May 16, 1983.
340
Bobby's kids underfoot at Justice: Esther Newberg, one of the "boiler room girls," who worked first in the Justice Department and later in the communications center of RFK's 1968 campaign, was not as charmed by the children as other Kennedy secretaries. She remembers the day Bobby brought two of his younger sons, Christopher and "Max," into the office. They were eating crackers and he brought them to Newberg's desk saying, "Show the lady how you learned to whistle." Christopher and Max did, spewing crumbs everywhere. Authors' interview with Esther Newberg, January 25, 1980.
341
They called him "Mama's boy": Authors' interview with Gustavo Paredes, December 7, 1981. Paredes, the son of Jackie's maid, Provi, grew up with Caroline and John.
341
"You're not Kennedys": Authors' interview with Bobby Shriver. "I would answer back, 'I wouldn't sit next to a Kennedy if my life depended on it!' " Ibid.
341
Keepsakes on the wall: Authors' observations.
341
A child-oriented atmosphere: "It was all very endearing, very much the way to live, provided you could afford to get your sofa covered every year." Authors' interview with Anita Fay.

341

"If any of us had done that": Anne Taylor Fleming, "The Kennedy Mystique," *New York Times Magazine,* June 17, 1979.

341n

"Bobby was much more openly loving": Authors' interview with Lem Billings.

341

A literal interpretation of the Flood: Manchester, *Controversy,* p. 41.

342

RFK tried to make the dinner table a classroom: Authors' interviews with Kathleen Kennedy and Robert Kennedy, Jr.

342

"You are the oldest": Cited in Schlesinger, *RFK,* p. 612.

342

"He was the one": Authors' interview with Lem Billings.

342

He skewered his older brother: "Bobby Junior around Joe was like a hound dog around a bear, running in and biting and running off. He just absolutely drove Joe out of his mind when they were growing up." Authors' interview with Lem Billings.

342

"Who is Ho Chi Minh?": Authors' interview with Chuck McDermott.

342

Joe trying to spell: Authors' interview with Robert Kennedy, Jr.

342

"That boy is just like Jack": Authors' interview with Lem Billings.

342

"What should I do with it?": *Boston Globe,* March 12, 1961.

342

His father teased him: Authors' interviews with David Kennedy.

343

He hugged the boy: "I remember vividly David holding on to his father and hugging him a lot. When the Attorney General came home from his office late in the evening and we were downstairs watching television in the study, it was David who immediately went to sit in his lap." Authors' interview with Barbara Kirby, March 12, 1983. "There was some level on which David tapped his father's sensitivity. You would find him walking with David or with his arm around David. David just seemed to need it." Authors' interview with Chuck McDermott.

343

"It doesn't seem like much of a world": Authors' interview with Lem Billings.

343

"He felt we were living in a crazy, poisonous time": Authors' interview with Adam Walinsky, October 25, 1979.

343

"Too precious a commodity": Schlesinger, *RFK,* p. 825.

343

"I don't believe it": Newfield, p. 205.

343

"I don't think Bob in his wildest imagination": George McGovern Oral History, JFK Library.

343

Bobby at Marymount: Galloway, ed., pp. 101–102.

343

December meeting: Hersh, p. 294.

343

"He felt he should have been the first": Newfield, p. 203.

344n

"Well, Joe": Authors' interview with Joseph Alsop.

344

"I'm not so sure": Cited in Schlesinger, *RFK*, p. 846.

344n

"They felt that Bobby running": Authors' interview with David Hackett.

344

"I agree with you, Benno": Benno Schmidt Oral History, JFK Library.

345

Bobby listened to O'Donnell and O'Brien: Authors' interview with Fred Dutton.

345

"You sonofabitch": Frank Burns Oral History, JFK Library.

345

A climactic meeting at Hickory Hill: Ibid. Also authors' interview with Fred Dutton.

345

"What have I got to lose": Authors' interview with John Seigenthaler, who later headed RFK's Northern California campaign.

345

"The country is in such difficulty": Cited in Schlesinger, *RFK*, p. 849.

346

"What the hell's the point": Hersh, p. 297.

346

Bobby's meeting with Clifford: In the memorandum of the meeting that Clifford later dictated he summarized Bobby's offer as follows: "Senator Robert [Kennedy] said he wished to devote the conversation mainly to a discussion of the President's policy in South Vietnam. He felt that the policy was a failure and both because of his conscience and pressure from others, he felt compelled to action in this regard. He stated that one way to correct the policy would be for him to become a candidate for the Democratic nomination, and if elected he could then change the policy. The other alternative was for him to find the means to persuade President Johnson to change the policy. He said that he had talked to Dick Daley in Chicago and had also talked to Ted Sorensen and his brother, and they thought consideration should be given to a plan that he had evolved. Sorensen said that if President Johnson would agree to make a public statement that his policy in Vietnam had proved to be in error, and that he was appointing a group of persons to conduct a study in depth of the issues and come up with a recommended course of action, then Senator Robert Kennedy would agree not to get into the race..." Memorandum, March 14, 1968, LBJ Library.

346

Dutton as go-between: Authors' interview with Fred Dutton.

346

"Bobby's therapy": Hersh, p. 290. For his part, Eugene McCarthy continued to believe that Bobby had yielded to internal pressure caused by the Legacy: "He didn't really want to run. I think he believed we really had a chance to win and he didn't want the line of succession cut off. It was like Robert Lowell said to me: 'the family tartan was involved.'" Authors' interview with Eugene McCarthy, March 28, 1980.

346

"Kennedys don't act that way": Schlesinger, *RFK*, p. 856. Also authors' interview with Fred Dutton.

346

"At stake is not simply the leadership": Cited by Lewis Chester, Godfrey Hodgson, and Bruce Page, *An American Melodrama: The Presidential Campaign of 1968*, New York, 1969, p. 125.

347

"Try to understand, Dad": Cited in Dallas, p. 295.

347
"Bobby's trouble": Authors' interview with Jim Weighart.
347
A cost of $3 million: Hersh, p. 300.
348
"Well, I guess I'll start out by saying": Authors' interview with Fred Dutton.
348
"Won't it be wonderful": Cited in Dallas, p. 298.
348
"Well, what are you going to do": Richard Lee, "Ethel Kennedy Today," *Washingtonian*, June 1983.
348
"If they want to get me": Authors' interview with Hays Gorey, March 26, 1981. Gorey covered the campaign for *Time*.
348
"Don't worry, everything is going to be all right": Authors' interview with Leonard Duhl, August 29, 1979.
348
"Bobby felt he was in Jack's shadow": Authors' interview with Lem Billings.
349
Violence "slower but just as deadly": Newfield, p. 273.
349
"If I was really ruthless": Newfield, p. 292.
349
"Dad, I'm going to California": Cited in Dallas, p. 303.
349
Bobby calls for debate: During the debate, Bobby accused McCarthy of wanting to move ten thousand Negroes from Watts to Orange County, a reference to McCarthy's proposed "dispersal" solution to the problem of the ghetto (Bobby himself had advocated a "reconstruction" solution). Years later the memory of the charge still rankled the former Minnesota Senator: "I think he got desperate. He figured he had to do it in order to win, and he'd take the consequences after that. What he said were really lies. About the plan to move ten thousand blacks from Watts to Orange County. It was purely calculated to intimidate the Orange County people." Authors' interview with Eugene McCarthy.
350
"My only chance is to chase Hubert's ass": Chester, Hodgson, and Page, p. 351.
350
"You know, Ken": Lester David, *Ethel*, New York, 1971, p. x.

PART 4: THE LOST BOYS

353
Chris Lawford was struck: Authors' interviews with Chris Lawford, January 31, February 26, April 8, May 14, December 1, 1980; January 25, March 1, 27, 29, April 23, July 22, September 16, 29, November 25, 1981; March 29, May 12, July 15, 31, September 6, 7, 1983.
354
Sixteen-year-old Joe: Authors' interviews with Chuck McDermott, February 28, March 2, April 24, 1981; April 17, 1983.
354
When death came: Authors' interviews with Robert F. Kennedy, Jr., November 5, 7, 1979; February 20, May 31, December 1, 28, 1980; January 25, February 19, March 3, September 27, October 29, 1981; June 10, 11, 1982; February 27, May 11, 1983.

355
David, who had been alone: Authors' interviews with David Kennedy, July 1980;
March 7, 8, April 4, 10, 26, May 1, 3, 6, 10, 14, 23, June 20, July 9, 16, September 15,
1983.
355
Phil Kirby asked along: Authors' interview with Philip Kirby, March 10, 1983.
355
"I'm Joe Kennedy": Authors' interview with Chris Lawford.
356
"Kennedy sand"... "Kennedy questions": Authors' interviews with Pam Kelley,
May 5, July 15, 1983.
356
"It means that we're exactly the same": Authors' interview with David Kennedy.
356
"We were all, every one of us": Authors' interview with Chris Lawford.
356
"Thank you for inviting me": Joseph Kennedy III to JFK, n.d. RFK Personal
Papers, JFK Library.
357
"Joe's after me": Authors' interview with Chris Lawford.
357
"Put that junk down right now": Authors' interviews with Robert Shriver, Febru-
ary 10, 1980; January 28, 1981; May 16, 1983.
357
"America has been very good": Authors' interview with Robert Kennedy, Jr.
357
"God gives us no more": Authors' interview with Chris Lawford.
357
"Sometimes Grandpa would look at us": Ibid.
358
"It was so different from Jack's death": Authors' interview with Robert Shriver.
At the same time this "splitting apart" was taking place, however, the Robert Kennedy family was being held up as an example of disciplined, stoical suffering. Writing in *McCall's*, psychiatrist Gerald Caplan analyzed family reaction to Bobby's
death and funeral and called his children "models for our own ways of handling
bereavement." See "Lessons in Bravery," *McCall's*, September 1968.
358
David's birthday scene: Authors' interview with Philip Kirby.
358
She told Joe he must be: Authors' interview with Barbara Kirby, March 12, 1983.
Kirby, the sister of David's friend Philip, was present during the scene.
358
Joe sang the "Battle Hymn of the Republic": Authors' interview with Mary
Schreiner, April 24, 1983. Schreiner, a schoolmate of Kathleen Kennedy's, was
present.
358
"Get out of here!": Authors' interviews with Philip and Barbara Kirby.
358
"I can't stand it any more": Ibid.
358
Joe in Spain: Authors' interview with Chuck McDermott.
359
Joe's travails at Milton: Authors' interview with Caroline Casey, February 25, 1981.
Casey, granddaughter of Congressman Joseph Casey, who defeated Honey Fitz in
the 1942 Massachusetts primary for the Democratic nomination for the Senate, was a
classmate of Joe's at Milton.

359
"That had been the big thing in his life": Ibid.
359
Memorial mass scene: Authors' interview with Philip Kirby.
360
Bobby's interest in animals: Authors' interview with Bobby Kennedy, Jr.
360
"Just like the President": Ibid.
360
Lem takes Bobby to Africa: Ibid. Also authors' interview with Lem Billings.
360
"Lem could have chosen any of us": Authors' interview with David Kennedy.
360
"If we ever go broke": Doris Connelly, "Wilderness Trip with the Kennedys,"
McCall's, May 1966.
360
He was the only one: Authors' interview with David Kennedy.
360
"He feels very badly": Authors' interview with Hays Gorey, March 26, 1981. Gorey,
in the Washington Bureau of *Time* during this period, has the original copy of the
note.
361
RFK saves David: Authors' interview with David Kennedy.
361
Ethel hustled David off: Ibid.
361
"Some seventeen-year-old girl": Authors' interviews with Chris Lawford and David
Kennedy.
361
"It was like watching": Authors' interview with Chris Lawford.
361
Scene back home: Authors' interview with David Kennedy.
361
Seven months pregnant: *Time,* April 25, 1969.
362
"It's not a subject": Authors' interview with David Kennedy.
362
"Oh, has our sister hurt his knee?": Authors' interview with Mary Schreiner.
362
"How can you ever expect": Ibid.
362
Bobby, Kelley, and LSD: Authors' interview with Philip Kirby.
362
"Don't do that, David": Ibid.
362
"You're dying": Author's interview with David Kennedy.
363
"Daddy would have done it": Authors' interview with Mary Lou McCarthy.
363
"Daddy got in fights": Authors' interview with Bobby Kennedy, Jr.
363
"Daddy was very funny": *Time,* April 5, 1969.
364
"Now that Bobby's gone": William H. Honan, *Ted Kennedy: Profile of a Survivor,*
New York, 1972 (paperback), pp. 129–130.

364

"I can't let go": Burton Hersh, *The Education of Edward Kennedy*, New York, 1972, p. 330.

364

"The moment Bobby died": Authors' interview with Jim Weighart, May 5, 1981.

365

"All I want if someone's going to blow my head off": Anne Taylor Fleming, "Kennedy: Time of Decision," *New York Times Magazine*, June 24, 1979.

365

"We shall honor him": *Time*, June 18, 1968.

365

He was also drinking heavily: Hersh, pp. 334ff.

365

One day he took his father's power boat: Authors' interviews with Timothy Haydock, January 24, November 18, 1981. Haydock, a close friend of Joe Kennedy III and Bobby Kennedy, Jr., spent the summers of 1967 and 1968 with the Kennedy family.

365

Drinking party with Green Berets: Hersh, p. 334.

366

"The nautical metaphors": Authors' interview with a confidential source, April 19, 1981.

366

A midsummer Harris Poll: In *Newsweek*, August 5, 1968.

366

A call from Richard Daley: Hersh, pp. 338–339.

366

"Like my brothers before me": Honan, p. 133.

366

It was "Bobby's year": Honan, pp. 130–131.

366

"He recognized that he had always been pushed": Authors' interview with Dun Gifford, March 30, 1981.

366

"You know, someday": Authors' interview with Tom Oliphant, April 13, 1981. The aide was David Burke.

367

"For God's sake, Jackie": Fred Sparks, *The $20,000,000 Honeymoon*, New York, 1970, p. 26. Jackie first met Onassis when he visited Joseph Kennedy in the South of France in the late 1950s, bringing Winston Churchill with him as a yacht guest. In early 1963 there had been another Kennedy-Onassis connection, when Jackie's sister Lee began to spend so much time aboard the *Christina* that the international gossip mill began to claim she was on the verge of leaving "Stash" Radziwill for Onassis. That fall, after two-day-old Patrick Bouvier Kennedy's death, Onassis wrote a note to the White House inviting Jackie to join him, Lee, and other guests in the Aegean. Her participation in the cruise caused considerable comment, but the fact that Onassis left Europe the day after Jack's death and was one of the few nonofficial, nonfamily acquaintances to pay respects to Jackie in the White House after the funeral went virtually unnoticed.

367

"All very married": Ibid., p. 21.

367

"I hate this country": Cited in Kitty Kelley, *Jackie Oh!*, New York, 1978 (paperback), pp. 294–295.

367

"I like seeing all these politicians": Authors' interview with Gloria Emerson.

367
"The Kennedy women had always flaunted": Authors' interview with George Smathers.
367
Cardinal Cushing threatened to resign: John Henry Cutler, *Cardinal Cushing of Boston,* New York, 1970, p. 358.
367
Teddy remarked bitterly to Lem Billings: Authors' interview with Lem Billings.
368
"These are many of the programs": Hersh, p. 362.
368
"He'd always been the spoiled kid brother": Authors' interview with a confidential source, June 22, 1979.
368
"It was the perfect solution": Authors' interview with a confidential source, December 3, 1981.
369
Muskie wondered about Teddy and alcohol: Hersh, p. 381.
369
EMK fulfills RFK's promise: Authors' interview with John J. Lindsay, April 29, 1980. Lindsay, a Washington Bureau reporter for *Newsweek,* accompanied Kennedy on the trip.
369
He began to unwind with frightening velocity: Hersh, pp. 378ff. Also authors' interviews with Hays Gorey, November 21, 1979, and John J. Lindsay, April 29, 1980. Gorey of *Time* was also on the Kennedy trip.
369
"Es-ki-mo Power!": Hersh, p. 380.
369
"They're going to shoot my ass": Authors' interview with John J. Lindsay.
369
"Hey, Cassie!" Ibid.
369
"Under terrible stress": Authors' interview with John J. Lindsay.
369
The facts of Chappaquiddick: See Jack Olsen, *The Bridge at Chappaquiddick,* New York, 1970; Robert Sherrill, *The Last Kennedy,* New York, 1976. Among the many peculiar theories about Chappaquiddick was one disseminated by a nephew of Teddy's and allegedly based on conversations overheard among Kennedy advisers which explained the events as follows: Mary Jo Kopechne, who was not a heavy drinker, became drowsy from alcohol and Joey Gargan suggested to her that she sleep it off in the back of Teddy's Oldsmobile. Later, not realizing that Kopechne was asleep in the back seat, Teddy drove off with another of the "boiler room girls" at the party. After the accident at Dike Bridge, Teddy and the other woman escaped from the sinking car, swam to shore, and returned to the party. Gargan realized that Kopechne must still be in the car. The two then went back to the scene to try to rescue her from the submerged vehicle. Authors' interview with David Kennedy.
370
Goodwin argued for making a clean breast: Anne Taylor Fleming, "The Kennedy Mystique," *New York Times Magazine,* June 17, 1979.
371
"I will never follow": Ibid.
371
"Diving into the strong and murky current": Ibid.
371n
Burton Hersh compared the galleys to the published book. See Hersh, p. 415.

371
"Never would have happened": Cited in Hersh, p. 411.
371
"Nobody said a word": Authors' interview with Chris Lawford.
371
"We all felt a lot of bitterness": Authors' interview with Chris Lawford.
371
Raft trip down the Green River: Details of the trip based on authors' interviews with Chuck McDermott, David Kennedy, Chris Lawford, and Bobby Kennedy, Jr.
372
The adults "wanted to float along": Authors' interview with Chris Lawford.
372
"We were all upset": Ibid.
372
Visitors were appalled: Authors' interview with Mary Gimbel.
372
"On your feet!": Ibid.
372
"I never witnessed": Authors' interview with Molly Haydock, May 4, 1983.
372
Joe hanging out in the graveyard: Authors' interview with Caroline Casey, who was a member of the group.
373
"In one sense he liked": Authors' interview with Tom Cleveland, April 30, 1981.
373
John found him to be an odd collection: Authors' interview with John Cleveland, February 6, 1983.
373
"He didn't have anybody he could lean on": Ibid.
373
"I can get any girl": Rita Dallas, *The Kennedy Case,* New York, 1973, p. 179.
373
The Hyannis Port Terrors: Details based on authors' interviews with Bobby Kennedy, Jr., Chris Lawford, David Kennedy, Bobby Shriver, Philip and Paul Kirby, Patrick Butler (April 12, 1983), and Gustavo Paredes (December 7, 1981). All were members of the HPTs.
374
Ethel was "like an ostrich": Authors' interview with Duff Pacifico, September 23, 1981. Pacifico, a girlfriend of Bobby's, was present when Lem made this comment.
374
Lem arranged for Bobby to go to Colombia: Authors' interview with Bobby Kennedy, Jr. The trip was reported in the *New York Times,* March 14, 1970.
374
Ethel banished Kim: Authors' interviews with Pam Kelley, May 5, July 15, 1983.
374
Bobby climbed a tree: Ibid. Kim Kelley's mother and father discussed this episode in an interview with the *National Enquirer,* May 17, 1972.
374
"If you can't live by the rules": Authors' interview with David Kennedy.
374
He set up a tent: Authors' interviews with Philip Kirby and Pam Kelley.
374
David would be depressed: Authors' interview with David Kennedy.
374
"Don't pretend to understand me": Authors' interview with Charles Spalding.

374
"A miracle!": Authors' interview with David Kennedy.
374
"You've killed a Kennedy!" Ibid.
375
"Fuck them": Authors' interview with a confidential source, January 21, 1981.
375
He had brought a human skull: Authors' interview with Philip Kirby.
375
The HPTs made Molotov cocktails: Authors' interview with Patrick Butler.
375
"Funnilators": Authors' interview with Gustavo Paredes.
375
"A competition of guts": Authors' interview with Chris Lawford.
375
"What have you got in there?": Ibid.
375
Bobby made LSD and "black beauties" part: Authors' interview with a confidential source, January 21, 1981.
376
The girls came to JPK's room: Authors' interview with Victoria Lawford, June 14, 1982.
376
The big boys had come to watch the Red Sox: Authors' interview with Bobby Kennedy, Jr.
376
"Dad, I'm in some trouble": Dallas, p. 338.
376
The old man had stopped eating: Authors' interview with Frank Saunders.
377
"It made me wonder what my grandfather had done": Authors' interview with Chris Lawford.
377
"Oh, Grandpa, I want to tell you": Cited in Dallas, p. 345.
377
JPK deathbed: Dallas, p. 346ff.
377
"Even though he had been sick": Authors' interview with Mary Lou McCarthy.
377
"If he just could have lived": Authors' interview with Lem Billings.
378
"As close as you could get to being a Kennedy": Authors' interview with Eunice Kennedy Shriver, December 1, 1981.
378
"This is a good time": The photograph was examined by the authors.
378
He had become especially close: Authors' interviews with Eunice Kennedy Shriver and with Fred ("Josh") Billings, November 2, 1981. Details of Lem's career based on authors' interviews with him and also with Francis H. McAdoo, Sr., October 22, 1981.
378
He kept the Billingses compartmentalized: Authors' interview with Francis ("Bucky") McAdoo, Jr., October 21, 1981.
378
"If I had, I never would have had": Authors' interviews with Peter Kaplan, January 16, 24, March 1, 18, May 13, September 25, 1981; February 28, April 9, 1983.

A friend and contemporary of Bobby Kennedy, Jr.'s, Kaplan was also close to Lem.
379

He had become important: "John F. Kennedy Center for the Performing Arts," *New Yorker*, September 28, 1981.
379

He defeated moves to rename Pennsylvania Avenue: Ibid.
379

"Do you want to hear my father?": Authors' interview with Mary Gimbel.
379

"Killed just like my father": Cutler, *Cushing*, p. 322.
379

"He knows more about whales": JBK to LB, October 23, 1969. Billings Papers.
379

Muckers' Club pin: Caroline Kennedy to LB, n.d. Billings Papers.
379

Outing to see *Henry V*: JBK to LB, n.d. Billings Papers.
380

"It was my cousin Bobby Shriver's": "Bobby Jr. in Africa," *Life*, February 14, 1969.
380

"Some animals are smarter than others": Ibid.
380

$25,000 from *Life*. Contract examined by authors. Billings Papers.
380

A collector's paradise: Lem's apartment was visited by the authors.
380

Massive notebooks of snapshots: They have been reviewed by the authors.
380

"You listened to him": Authors' interview with Peter Kaplan.
380

Bobby's troubles at Pomfret School: Authors' interview with Bobby Kennedy, Jr.
380

He did not go home on his six free weekends: Authors' interview with Bobby Kennedy, Jr.
381

"It was like growing up with the President": Ibid.
381

"He seemed like such a lonely kid": Authors' interviews with Doug Spooner, January 13, 1981; April 10, 1983.
381

"Naturally the guy said": Ibid.
382

Bobby went home to the Cape: Ibid.
382

"John and I are seated": Rainie and Quinn, p. 176.
382

Bobby Shriver had tried to keep pace: Authors' interview with Bobby Shriver.
382

Andy Moes: Authors' interviews with Philip Kirby and Bobby Shriver.
382

"He was whining that he had this girlfriend": Ibid. Philip Kirby, who was also present, confirms this account. See also *Boston Globe* interview with Moes, September 16, 1971.
382

Bobby Kennedy's favorite hawk: Authors' interview with Bobby Kennedy, Jr.

382
Arrest scene: Authors' interviews with David Kennedy and Bobby Shriver.
382
"We never had any *cannabis*": Ibid.
382
"You've dragged your family's name": Ibid.
382
Court appearance: See *New York Times,* August 7, 1970.
382
"I have no control over you": Authors' interview with David Kennedy.
383
She called in Robert Coles: Ibid. Also authors' interviews with Bobby Kennedy, Jr., and Chris Lawford.
383
Bobby took six hundred dollars: Authors' interview with Bobby Kennedy, Jr.
383
'I had no contact with home": Ibid.
383
Ethel's kids were being systematically isolated: Authors' interviews with Bobby Shriver, Chris Lawford, and David Kennedy.
383
"That's okay, you can go ahead and cry": Authors' interview with Harris Wofford.
383
"He made me see": Authors' interview with Bobby Shriver.
383
"It was almost on general principle": Authors' interview with David Kennedy.
384
Pat decides to go to Paris: Authors' interview with Victoria Lawford. ("We were in Southampton in August and all of a sudden mummy kept playing these Berlitz French records. I didn't understand why she was doing that, and was saying to myself 'What is going on here?' And then Mammie—that's short for Ma'moiselle, what we called our maid—came in one morning and said, 'You're going to France.' And I said, 'Thanks.' ")
384
"I don't want anything to do with this family": Authors' interview with Chris Lawford.
384
David and Chris decided to hitchhike to New York: Authors' interviews with Chris Lawford and David Kennedy.
384
"It was great being just ordinary": Authors' interview with David Kennedy.
384
Heroin was selling for two dollars a bag on Dope Hill: Ibid.
384
The scene at Pat's vacant apartment: Authors' interviews with David Kennedy and Chris Lawford.
384
David often slept in the hedges: Authors' interview with David Kennedy.
384
David transferred to Middlesex: Ibid.
384
David on the breakwater: Authors' interviews with Philip and Paul Kirby, March 10, 1983. ("The rule of the breakwater was that once you started, you had to go to the end.")
384
He made a small reputation for smoking marijuana: Authors' interview with David Kennedy.

384

Hippies vs. neofascists: Authors' interview with Chris Lawford.

384

David rarely heard from his mother: Authors' interview with David Kennedy.

385

"My father had been involved": Ibid.

385

"She was standing there looking at me": Ibid.

385

Bobby at Pomfret: Authors' interview with Bobby Kennedy, Jr.

385

"Like all the rest of us": Authors' interview with Chris Lawford.

385

Bobby visited by Kim: Authors' interviews with Bobby Kennedy, Jr., and Pam Kelley. Pam, Kim's sister, occasionally hitchhiked to the school with her.

385

Bobby had run afoul of the law again: Authors' interview with Bobby Kennedy, Jr. See also *New York Times*, August 24, 1971.

385

"What's that thing": Authors' interviews with Bobby Shriver and Bobby Kennedy, Jr.

385

Bobby spat: *Boston Globe*, August 23, 1971.

385

Taken to court: Ibid.

385

"The officer is lying": Ibid.

385

Lem arranged for him to live with the Brodes: Authors' interview with Joey Brode, April 13, 1983.

385

"He looked like a bird": Ibid.

386

"They were on the phone constantly": Ibid.

386

"We'd be sitting in his apartment and a call would come": Authors' interview with "Bucky" McAdoo.

386

"Bobby put him through some very tough times": Authors' interview with Fred Billings.

386

"He was very anxious to impress": Authors' interviews with Andy Karsch, July 27, 1980; January 7, February 10, 23, March 18, December 1, 1981; September 6, 1983.

387

"By the end of that year": Authors' interview with Joey Brode.

387

"He was yelling about our irresponsibility": Authors' interview with Andy Karsch.

387

Bobby sold David a pound of marijuana: Authors' interview with three confidential sources, among them two classmates and a member of the Kennedy family, who asked not to be named because of their relationships with and within the Kennedy family.

387

"Your father felt he was one of the most moral men": Authors' interview with David Kennedy.

387

"I knocked on the door": Ibid.

388

"He was out for freshman crew": Authors' interview with Peter Kaplan.

388

"The Bhutto leap,": Ibid. Also authors' interviews with Bobby Kennedy, Jr., and Doug Spooner.

388

"It was like someone who wants a massage": Authors' interview with a confidential source, August 12, 1982.

388

Kim Kelley broke her leg: Authors' interview with Pam Kelley.

388

In Portillo they met Fleetwood: Authors' interviews with Blake "Harvey" Fleetwood, January 5, September 23, 1981; March 2, 1983.

389

The *Times* story: "Skiing the Andes—and Drawing Fire from the Border Patrol," by Blake Fleetwood. *New York Times,* November 11, 1973, Section X, p. 33.

389

"That's how Jack got started": Authors' interview with Lem Billings. See also Robert F. Kennedy, Jr., "Chile," *Atlantic Monthly,* February 1974.

390

Steve Smith in New York state campaign: Authors' interviews with Ronnie Eldridge, July 14, 1980, and Peter Fishbein, February 19, 1981. See also Richard Reeves, "Goldilocks May Not Be the Most Exciting Fellow in Town, But He's the Only One Who Can Win This Year," *New York Times Magazine,* June 14, 1970.

391

"Tell me, what do you *really* think": *Newsweek,* August 14, 1972.

391

"*Shriver!* Who wants him?": Ibid.

391

"A way of giving to others": Authors' interviews with Bobby Kennedy, Jr., and Chris Lawford.

391

Bobby Shriver's catering business: Authors' interview with Bobby Shriver.

392

"I'm like a BB rattling around": Authors' interview with Chuck McDermott.

392

Robert Coles was called in: Authors' interviews with Diane Clemens, June 25, August 8, November 9, 1979. The authors talked with both Coles and Brenner, who refused to discuss the Kennedy grandchildren, noting that all communications between them and any of their patients must remain confidential. Coles further stipulated that this statement was not to be taken as a tacit acknowledgment that any Kennedy grandchild had seen him on a professional basis.

392

Joe at MIT: Ibid.

392

"I hate academics": Ibid.

393

"Like all the other Kennedys": Ibid.

393

"I'm through!": Ibid.

394

"This fantasy": Ibid.

394

Joe's job as coordinator: See *New York Times,* February 24, 1973. After news of his resignation had spread, Joe received a letter from Samuel Price, director of a poverty program in Harlem. "I personally commend you for taking an interest and wanting

to live and work among the poor. As a result of your courageous stand, I am offering you a position with the . . . Anti-Poverty Program in Central Harlem. . . . We will be able to secure safe, comfortable, clean and quiet living quarters for you, conveniently located around the corner from the job on West 139th Street.'' A copy of the letter was given to the authors by Diane Clemens.
394
''I thought that with the framework'': *San Francisco Examiner,* February 23, 1973.
394
Joe's erratic behavior: Authors' interview with Diane Clemens.
394
''God, it's so depressing'': Ibid.
394
Note: Described to the authors by Diane Clemens. (''Raúl'' and ''Linda'' pseudonyms.)
395
''I'll never forget it'': Ibid.
395
Joe's Berkeley accident: See *Boston Globe,* March 29, 1973.
395
''I'm going and nobody can stop me!'': Authors' interview with Diane Clemens.
395
Chris Lawford in Hollywood: Authors' interview with Chris Lawford.
396
Elizabeth Taylor meets Mae West: Ibid.
396
''Christopher, let's get the hell out of here'': Ibid.
396
''I ran after your car'': Ibid.
396
Peter Lawford's alienation from the Kennedys: The one person in the family with whom Lawford managed to keep a friendly relationship was Rose. He sent her little presents for her birthday and she wrote him little notes like this one in 1976: ''It was a joy and a pleasure to see you again, dear Peter, and I only regret that your visit was so short. I talked to Sydney last night and requested your address. She had just come back on Tuesday and she will not be here this weekend on account of exams. She as well as the other children speak of you with warmth and affection. I am so glad.'' Rose Kennedy to Peter Lawford, March 11, 1976. A copy of the letter was given to the authors by Peter Lawford.
396
''Peter and I would stay up all night'': Authors' interview with Christopher Lawford.
396
''I need you, Dad'': Ibid.
396
''You must be high'': Ibid.
397
''Joe had problems of his own'': Authors' interview with David Kennedy.
397
''I told him I'd had a terrible year'': Ibid.
398
''He didn't have the hardness'': Ibid.
398
''She went around complaining'': Ibid.
398
David's and Pam's ''honeymoon'' trip: Authors' interviews with David Kennedy and Pam Kelley.

398

"It was a Saturday night": Authors' interview with Pam Kelley.

398

"David was ecstatic": Ibid.

399

"His SuperKennedy act": Authors' interview with David Kennedy.

399

"We were all sort of standing": Authors' interview with Pam Kelley. For a news account, see *Boston Herald,* August 15, 1973.

399

Joe's appearance in court: *New York Times,* August 21, 1973.

399

"Everybody would gather there": Authors' interview with Pam Kelley.

399

David read Hunter Thompson in hospital: Authors' interview with David Kennedy.

399

"That fucking bitch friend": Authors' interview with Pam Kelley.

399

"He'd come in and see me": Ibid.

400

"You finally find someone to love": Authors' interview with David Kennedy.

400

"It felt great": Ibid.

400

Chris and Bobby using heroin: Their drug use during this period was described in detail to the authors by four individuals in separate interviews, including members of the Kennedy family. Because of their relationships with and within the family, all four people interviewed on this subject asked that their names not be used as sources.

400

"I was swallowing Percodans": Authors' interview with David Kennedy.

400

He shot the drug all during his senior year: Ibid.

400

"David looked at himself in those pictures": Authors' interview with John Seigenthaler.

401

"David was the skinniest": Authors' interview with John Warnecke, Jr., May 12, 1983.

401

Hickory Hill scene: Authors' interview with David Kennedy. Also authors' interview with Elaine Shannon, June 15, 1983. For background see Bo Burlingham, "The Other Tricky Dick," *Esquire,* November 1975.

401

"Should I vote to impeach": Authors' interview with David Kennedy.

401

"This kid's going to the edge": Ibid.

402

"Go into the eye of the storm": Authors' interview with Lem Billings.

402

"If you see your limits": Authors' interview with Bobby Kennedy, Jr.

403

Lem and drugs with Bobby: Lem Billings's drug use was described in considerable detail to the authors after his death by six individuals, including members of the Kennedy family. Because of their affection for Lem and because of the role his memory continues to play in the Kennedy family, all six asked not to be cited as sources. (Lem's godson, Francis H. "Bucky" McAdoo, Jr., who was not one of these insiders, told the authors: "He had been a terribly conservative man all his life. When I was growing up, if I had sideburns that stuck out a quarter of an inch below my earlobe, he would personally shave them off. He was just very much into 'the way things should be.' But then he made a complete switch, adopting all of Bobby's habits and his friends' habits including drugs. He got into drugs, tried it all. He'd say, 'Hey, ma-a-n,' and get in there with all that hip talk.

403
"Bobby and some of the other kids": Authors' interview with confidential source, July 8, 1982.

403
"Lem was lying on the bed and complaining": See note above on Lem and drugs. This particular scene was described to the authors by an individual who was present.

403
"There was one time when Bobby got burned": Ibid.

403
Cunnilingus contest: The authors interviewed the woman involved, who has requested that her name not be used.

403
"Joe would soon get very antsy": Authors' interview with Phoebe Sheldon, October 2, 1983.

404
"You'd pass him somewhere": Authors' interview with Francis H. McAdoo, Sr.

404
Details of the Apurímac River trip: Background comes from interviews on the subject with Lem Billings, Bobby Kennedy, Jr., Chris Lawford, David Kennedy, Doug Spooner, and Harvey Fleetwood, who kindly gave the authors a copy of the detailed diary he kept of the trip.

404
"I was really shaken": Authors' interview with Harvey Fleetwood.

405
"During the time": Ibid.

405
One couple had tried it: See Helen and Frank Schreider, *Exploring the Amazon*, Washington, D.C., 1969.

405
"Here you have it": Authors' interview with Harvey Fleetwood.

405
Bobby's dare to swim across the river: Authors' interview with Doug Spooner.

405
"Stopped at Cativirini": Fleetwood diary.

406
"Bobby would get one": Authors' interview with Harvey Fleetwood.

406
"He was the opposite of Bobby": Authors' interview with Chris Lawford.

406
"Caught 180 pound catfish": Fleetwood diary. Fleetwood took a photograph of the fish, which was shown to the authors.

406
Dynamite incident: Authors' interviews with Bobby Kennedy, Jr., Chris Lawford, and Harvey Fleetwood.

407
"Epifenio would lie on the raft": Authors' interview with Harvey Fleetwood.

407
Bobby climbed for his sweater: Ibid.

407

Bobby's "frightening facility with language": Authors' interview with Peter Kaplan.

407

Bobby's tricks: Ibid.

407

Lem's obsession with comparisons between Bobby Junior and Jack: Authors' interviews with Peter Kaplan and Andy Karsch.

407

"I used to do it for Jack": Authors' interview with Andy Karsch.

407

"He had filled several albums": Authors' interview with Chris Lawford.

408

"Jack had all the charm in the world": Authors' interview with Lem Billings.

408

"Dear Mr. Billings": The letter, which is part of the Billings Papers, was copied by the authors.

408

Lem talks about Bobby's future marriage: Authors' interview with Duff Pacifico, September 23, 1981.

408

"South Pacifico, you say?": Ibid.

409

"Lem used to tell Bobby": Ibid.

409

He talked for hours: Authors' interview with Peter Kaplan.

409

Bobby Shriver's thesis: Authors' interview with Bobby Shriver.

409

Maria Shriver's thesis: Ibid.

409

Conversations with Kaplan and Breindel: Authors' interview with Peter Kaplan; also with Eric Breindel, December 21, 1980.

409

"I feel that it is my destiny": Authors' interview with Mary Schreiner.

409

"Where Is the Idealism of Youth Now?": The speech was also published in the *Boston Globe*, May 26, 1975. In one perhaps unconsciously revealing passage, after a discussion of the problems faced by poor and disillusioned youth, Bobby said: "Also the well-to-do and privileged youth of this country, so many of whom have their own troubles and fears and confusions. Whereas millions their age have virtually nothing, they have everything, it seems, except a sense of who they really are and what they believe in. . . . They are the privileged in many ways, but the deprived in others. They have more, but they feel, I suspect, at loose ends."

409

"RFK Jr. Like Father": See *New York Sunday News*, September 7, 1975.

409

Bobby's involvement in Shapiro campaign: Authors' interviews with Peter Kaplan and Chris Lawford. Shapiro was a friend of Kaplan's; Chris worked in the campaign with Bobby.

410

Bobby on sociobiology: Authors' interview with Bobby Kennedy, Jr.

410

Advice from Robert Coles: Authors' interview with Bobby Kennedy, Jr.

410

Bobby in Alabama: Authors' interviews with Bobby Kennedy, Jr., and Peter Kaplan; also interview with Governor George Wallace, March 29, 1982.

410

"Wallace received us": Authors' interview with Peter Kaplan.

410

"There was an air": Ibid.

411

Bobby and Frank Johnson: Authors' interviews with Peter Kaplan and Bobby Kennedy, Jr.

411

"You don't know Bobby": Authors' interview with confidential source, March 26, 1982.

413

"To me he was Jack Kennedy": See Judith Exner, *My Story*, New York, 1977, p. 13.

413

"The only Campbell": Exner, p. 231*n*.

413

"Well, Eunice recently asked": Authors' interviews with Harris Wofford, February 2, March 22, 1981.

413

David Eisenhower article: "Another Generation Heard From," *Saturday Evening Post*, April 1976.

413

Teddy's office urged Bobby to reply: Authors' interview with Bobby Kennedy, Jr.

413

"I would say to young Mr. Eisenhower": *Saturday Evening Post*, April 1976.

414

"Iron had gone into Edward Kennedy's soul": Cited in Hersh, p. 383.

414

Teddy's political identity: For a detailed examination of Edward Kennedy's legislative activity in the post-Chappaquiddick period, see Theo Lippman, Jr., *Senator Ted Kennedy, The Career Behind the Image*, New York, 1976.

414

"I just thought we'd tried enough": Anne Taylor Fleming, "Kennedy: Time of Decision," *New York Times Magazine*, June 24, 1979.

414

One journalist friend: Reported in Burton Hersh, *The Education of Edward Kennedy*, New York, 1980 (paperback), pp. 606–607. The incident is described in an epilogue written especially for this edition.

414

"One must not be defeated": Cited in Rainie and Quinn, p. 223.

414

Family problems and Teddy's decision not to run in 1976: Authors' interview with John J. Lindsay. ("The weekend before Kennedy's announcement, I had come back from L.A., where I was doing a piece for *Newsweek* on Nixon, and by sheer coincidence was on an airplane with Joan. She had been in a drying-out tank in Point David, which was just four or five miles up the coast from San Clemente. She was coming back and was in a really awful condition. Whatever she'd been out there to have done had not been done. She was vague and she was on tranquilizers. We got down to Dulles terminal that Saturday night. It was raining and miserable. All the kids were there. Teddy Junior had just got off from his chemotherapy. He looked like an owl, purple, ghastly. Little Patrick was wheezing like an old brewery horse [as a result of asthma] and the girl Kara was looking overweight and distraught. But Ted wasn't there. I went home and said to my wife, if this guy takes this family through a presidential campaign, there is no pain in hell that is enough for him. The next day I got a call from Dick Drayne, Teddy's press secretary, who said, 'You better get up to Boston tomorrow morning, we're going to have an announcement.' Everybody in town thought it was the announcement to go. I was the only reporter

who said he's not going to go. I thought: 'This is the best thing this man has ever done in his life, as a human being: to take himself out of the race.' ")
415

"And I intend to claim that Legacy": *Newsweek*, January 26, 1976.
415

Shrivers as center of gravity: Authors' interview with Chris Lawford.
415

Eunice bringing Rosemary home: Authors' interviews with Bobby, Timmy, and Eunice Kennedy Shriver.
415

Eunice's role in Special Olympics: Authors' interviews with General Robert Montague and Herbert J. Kramer, both involved in the Joseph P. Kennedy Jr. Foundation. ("Eunice's monument will be the Foundation and the Special Olympics. You can go through the whole Kennedy family litany of values—sports, competition, excellence, excelling, family, publicity—it's all embodied in Special Olympics. And there's no macho in it. It's Eunice urging people on to their limits. Saying to a mentally retarded kid: 'You can do better.' " Authors' interview with Herbert J. Kramer.)
415

Party leader called him "Eunice": *Newsweek*, January 26, 1976.
415

"You've got to spend some time with Ted": Authors' interview with Harris Wofford.
415

"Poor Sarge": Ibid. (Tsongas told Wofford about the incident.)
415

"Teddy didn't do shit": Authors' interview with Bobby Shriver.
415

Joe as 1976 campaign manager: Hays Gorey, "Joe Kennedy Comes of Age," *New York Times Magazine*, May 29, 1977.
416

Pat Lawford and French designer: Authors' interview with Victoria Lawford.
416

The Smiths had more or less withdrawn: Authors' interview with Bobby Shriver.
416

"The fact that you write": The letter is in one of Lem's albums. Billings Papers.
416

Onassis marriage: The best account of the vicissitudes of the marriage can be found in Arianna Stassinopoulos, *Maria Callas: The Woman Behind the Legend*, New York, 1981.
416

"Can you believe that *voice?*": Rainie and Quinn, p. 75.
416

"You're the richest woman in the world": Authors' interview with Mary Gimbel.
416

"Roses are red": Ethel's valentine is in one of Lem's albums. Billings Papers.
416

"How could I": Richard Lee, "Ethel Kennedy Today," *Washingtonian*, June 1983.
416

"There are cherished memories here": A copy of *Words Jack Loved* is in the Billings Papers.
417

"The presidency is in our system": Authors' interview with Chris Lawford.
417

Half a Kennedy: His mother had emphasized rather than diminished this fact by formally changing Chris's middle name to "Kennedy."

417
''Before, everything I did'': Authors' interview with Chris Lawford.
418
'' At times, when it was just the two of us'': Authors' interview with Chris Lawford.
418
Chris and Jennifer: Authors' interviews with Jennifer Jacobson, December 15, 1981, September 19, 1983.
418
''Like all the Kennedy kids'': Ibid.
418
''Christopher and Bobby liked heroin'': Ibid.
419
Activities in Lem's apartment: Four people involved in these activities, including members of the Kennedy family, described these sessions in considerable detail. Because of their continuing relationship with the family, they have requested that their names not be cited as sources.
419
''What he'd do was interpose himself '': Authors' interview with Jennifer Jacobson.
419
''Chris would take me'': Ibid.
419
Chris's illness: Ibid.
419
''He came to the door'': Ibid.
419
''I never saw him'': Cited in Anna Quindlen, ''The Kennedy Who Went Wrong,'' *McCall's,* April 1980.
420
'' He'd bring papers'': Authors' interview with Tom Oliphant, April 13, 1981.
420
David following Bobby at Harvard: Authors' interview with Gustavo Paredes, December 7, 1981. (''Bobby preceded David by a year at Harvard, so everybody figured David would be just like Bobby. Bobby would get them into places. He would call up an exclusive discotheque and say 'I'm Bobby Kennedy' and get everybody in. David would be self-conscious about doing that sort of thing.'')
420
The Kennedys in Aspen: Authors' interview with Harvey Fleetwood.
420
''She just tore into David'': Authors' interview with Gustavo Paredes.
420
''Bobby came over one night'': Authors' interview with Bob Rafelson, July 20, 1979.
421
David on a forty-day binge: Authors' interview with David Kennedy.
421
Kaplan and Breindel found David: Authors' interviews with Peter Kaplan and Eric Breindel.
421
David's endocarditis: Authors' interview with David Kennedy.
421
'' At first, there was the usual outpouring'': Authors' interview with David Kennedy.
421
''They said I needed activity'': Ibid.
421
Trip to Pakistan: Authors' interviews with Doug Spooner and David Kennedy.
421
''We were in helicopters'': Authors' interview with Doug Spooner.

421

"My father was concerned about blacks": Authors' interview with David Kennedy.

421

David mugged in Roxbury: Ibid.

421

"I was modeling myself": Ibid.

422

David's o.d.: Authors' interview with Doug Spooner.

422

"The Committee to Keep David Out": Authors' interview with David Kennedy.

422

"It looked like the Ritz": Ibid.

422

"The others say not to trust you": Ibid.

422

David and Patterson therapy: Ibid. See also Kathleen McAuliffe, "Brain Tuner," *Omni*, January 1983.

422

English evangelicals: Authors' interview with David Kennedy.

422

David and Rachel Ward: Ibid.

423

"We had good times.": Ibid.

423

"Rachel wanted to get an apartment": Ibid.

423

David in Harlem: Ibid. See also *New York Times,* September 6, 1979, and *Boston Herald,* September 13, 1979.

423

"I should have just said": Authors' interview with David Kennedy.

424

As Steve Smith was telling reporters: *Boston Herald,* September 13, 1979.

424

David at Massachusetts General: Authors' interview with David Kennedy.

424

"I was hooked to an IV": Ibid.

424

"I have watched him overassert himself": LB to A. E. Howard, November 26, 1976. Billings Papers.

425

"There are oversights":See *New York Times Book Review,* July 30, 1978.

425

Bobby at LSE: Authors' interviews with Bobby Kennedy, Jr., and Eric Breindel.

425

Joe's stabilization: Authors' interviews with Andy Karsch. Karsch roomed with Joe and worked with him in Teddy's 1976 campaign.

425

"He had just gotten to the point": Authors' interview with Chuck McDermott.

425

"He began to challenge my commitment": Authors' interview with Grace Olivera, June 1, 1980.

425

Citizens Energy Corporation: Authors' interviews with Steve Rothstein, March 12, 1983, and Michael Kennedy, March 3, October 23, 1981. Rothstein is general manager of Citizens Energy. Michael Kennedy has worked for it. *Boston Herald* columnist Peter Lucas speculated about Joe's future in an article titled "Will

Joe Kennedy Run for Lieutenant Governor?'' After noting that Joe had been getting considerable publicity for his plan to have Citizens Energy purchase oil from Venezuela, Lucas wondered if perhaps young Kennedy might step into the Lieutenant Governor's job currently occupied by Thomas P. O'Neill III: ''Joe Kennedy came close to running against State Treasurer Robert Q. Crane in the last Democratic primary, but pulled out at the last minute. Still it is clear that Kennedy, who lives in Brighton, has ambitions to run for statewide political office.... Joe Kennedy's ambitious oil project may be grounds to base such a candidacy on. Many candidacies in Massachusetts have been based on much less.'' *Boston Herald,* January 30, 1980.

426
''I'm different from Bobby'': Authors' interview with Andy Karsch.

426
''I'm getting the shuttle'': Ibid.

426
''If you've got a problem'': Authors' interview with Bobby Kennedy, Jr.

426
Duff had read about Rebecca: Authors' interview with Duff Pacifico.

426
Trip to Haiti: Ibid.

427
''I was right'': Authors' interview with confidential source, September 9, 1983.

428
JFK Library opening: See *Boston Herald,* October 21, 1979. Also authors' interviews with Bobby Kennedy, Jr., Chris Lawford, and John Seigenthaler.

429
''I don't plan to say or write'': Authors' interview with Bobby Kennedy, Jr.

429
''My father'': Authors' interview with David Kennedy.

429
''The Unfinished Business of Robert Kennedy'': See *Boston Herald,* October 21, 1979.

429
Joe threatened not to take part: Authors' interview with Bobby Kennedy, Jr.

430
''The heart of the Democratic Party'': Cited in Jeff Greenfield, *The Real Campaign,* New York, 1982, p. 56.

430
''I tried to talk about it'': Joan Braden, ''Joan Kennedy Tells Her Own Story,'' *McCall's,* August 1978.

431
Mudd interview: Mudd had been close to the family for years. It was he who forced a path for Ethel through the crowd in the Ambassador Hotel where Bobby lay mortally wounded.

431
''Well, it's, um'': Teddy's inarticulateness had become an issue even before the Mudd interview was broadcast. *Time* did a cover story on him quoting him thus: ''The case we, uh, that has to be made, and I'd like to see what each of you has to say on this, is, wh, why should we do it for Mexico, and why not the others?'' (''The Kennedy Challenge,'' *Time,* November 5, 1979). When *Washington Star* reporter Judy Bachrach asked Teddy why he talked so oddly he said somewhat illogically that it was because he was the last child in a large family. See the *Washington Star,* October 15, 1979.

431
Southwick told reporters: Authors' interview with T. R. Reid, March 25, 1981. Reid covered the Kennedy campaign for the *Washington Post.*

431

The Kennedy campaign: The authors traveled with the Kennedy campaign during the 1980 campaign season. Also interviews with journalists T. R. Reid, John J. Lindsay, Bob Ajemian, Tom Oliphant, and Walter Isaacson, and Kennedy political advisers Carl Wagner, Fred Dutton, Doris Kearns Goodwin, Peter Edelman, Dick Donahue, Andy Karsch, and John Gage.

431n

"He said to me, 'Bella!' ": Authors' interview with Ronnie Eldridge.

432

Teddy seemed disoriented: Authors' interview with Peter Edelman.

432

"The tv reporter asked him what he could do": Authors' interview with T. R. Reid.

432

"I feel embarrassed": Cited in Greenfield, p. 72.

432

But now, when he wanted to make headlines: Authors' interview with Carl Wagner.

432

"Fuck the fat rich kid": David Broder et al., *The Pursuit of the Presidency*, New York, 1980 (paperback), p. 107.

433

Joe in Iowa: Authors' interviews with Carl Wagner, John Gage, Chuck McDermott, and Andy Karsch.

433

"Somewhere along the line": Authors' interview with Chuck McDermott.

433

Joe and Tully: Ibid.

433

"If my father was alive": Ibid.

433

"Listen, you and your guys": Ibid.

433

"Okay, listen, pal": Ibid.

434

A pleasure "to see a chastened man": Cited in Greenfield, p. 76.

434

"Regardless of what happens": Authors' interview with T. R. Reid. (Reid elicited this comment during one of his campaign interviews with Kennedy.)

434

Teddy's security: Authors' interview with campaign aide John Gage.

435

Media playfulness: Authors' interview with T. R. Reid.

435

"He ate alone": Authors' interview with Walter Isaacson.

435

One of the pieces of journalism: Suzannah Lessard, "Kennedy's Women Problem, Women's Kennedy Problem," *Washington Monthly*, December 1979.

435

The press watch at Tunney's: Authors' interview with Walter Isaacson.

435

"It *was* the course he cheated on": Authors' observation.

436

"There he is": Authors' interview with John Gage.

436

"And here we have": Authors' interviews with John Gage and Tom Oliphant.

436

"Where's the FRK taking us": Authors' interview with John Gage.

436

Pat as chaperone : Ibid.

436

Eunice's "kid brother" attitude : Authors' interview with Peter Edelman.

436

"Eunice, you know" : Ibid.

436

"Do you Bobby guys still hate" : Ibid.

436

Steve Smith's inadequacies as campaign director : Authors' interview with Tom Oliphant.

437

Meeting with grandchildren : Authors' interview with Chris Lawford.

437

"He does not deserve" : Rainie and Quinn, p. 9.

437

"You know your father killed" : Ibid.

437

Chris tried to get on board : Authors' interview with Chris Lawford.

437

"It was the old Kennedy runaround" : Ibid.

438

Chris's toast : Ibid.

438

Darvon bust : Ibid.

438

Bobby in Alabama : Authors' observations.

438

"Black people are worse off " : Ibid.

439

Looking for an appropriate district : Authors' interview with Andy Karsch.

439

"It's getting stupid" : Ibid.

439

"Naturally, I chose" : Authors' interview with David Kennedy.

439

"Therapy by humiliation" : Ibid.

439

"What's the matter, David?" : Authors' interview with Nancy Narleski, March 20, 1983. Narleski was David's girlfriend during this period.

440

"I feel they should have done something" : Authors' interview with David Kennedy.

440

"Having a mental breakdown" : Ibid.

440

He rarely ate : Authors' interviews with Nancy Narleski and David Kennedy.

440

"I thought I was in the Mafia" : Authors' interview with David Kennedy.

440

Narleski called Barbara Kirby : Authors' interviews with Barbara Kirby and Nancy Narleski.

440

"Don't you call the Kirbys!" : Authors' interview with Nancy Narleski.

440

David remained in exile : Authors' interviews with David Kennedy, Timothy Haydock, Craig McNamara, and John Warnecke, Jr. Haydock, McNamara and Warnecke

were friends of David and the Kennedys and were living in California at the time.
440
David's phone call to Pam Kelley: Authors' interview with Pam Kelley.
440
David stayed off drugs by drinking: Authors' interviews with David Kennedy and John Warnecke, Jr.
440
David's job interview: Authors' interview with David Kennedy.
441
"She had a new pair of white shoes": Ibid.
441
"For the most part": *Sacramento Bee,* August 26, 1980.
441
"He kept saying that the presidency": Authors' interview with Tom Oliphant.
441
Family conference at Hilton: Authors' interview with Jim Weighart, May 5, 1981. Weighart was present at the meeting.
442
"The end of the entire Kennedy time": Garry Wills, *The Kennedy Imprisonment,* New York, 1982, p. 7.
442
Teddy's speech sent to supporters: Authors' interview with Dun Gifford.
442
"My God, why does he have to do it?": Authors' interview with Peter Kaplan.
442
A whole new generation had discovered Lem: Authors' interviews with Michael Kennedy and Timothy Shriver.
443
"He always knew what was proper": Authors' interview with Michael Kennedy.
443
"Our lives have not been as extreme": Rainie and Quinn, p. 132.
443
Drinking at Trader Vic's: Authors' interview with "Bucky" McAdoo. McAdoo occasionally went along on these excursions.
443
"He was fun to be with": Authors' interview with Timothy Shriver.
433
He telephoned Eunice every day: Authors' interviews with Lem Billings and Eunice Kennedy Shriver.
433
"Why wasn't I seated on the right?": Authors' interview with Timothy Shriver.
443
"What is this?" Authors' interview with Harvey Fleetwood (who was present during the conversation).
444
"We'd talk for a long time": Authors' interview with Duff Pacifico.
444
He was short of breath: Authors' interviews with Timothy Haydock and "Bucky" McAdoo. Haydock, who had become a doctor, had to revive Lem after he passed out at Courtney Kennedy's wedding. McAdoo accompanied Billings on his last trip to Haiti, where he had a "crisis" that appeared to be a heart attack.
444
Lem insisted on bringing a body bag: Authors' interview with Chris Lawford.
444
Now it took on a more serious, morbid aspect: Authors' interview with "Bucky"

McAdoo. ("He told my father in a candid moment, 'You know, I really don't have anything much to live for.' His life had taken a big turn downward.")
444

"I'll be here all through eternity": Authors' interview with Timothy Haydock.
444

He changed his will: Authors' interviews with Bobby Kennedy, Jr., Peter Kaplan, and "Bucky" McAdoo. McAdoo says, "He would even tell you. He would say, if I made some comment he objected to, 'Well, I'm striking you off the will.' "
444

"Lem was very upset": Authors' interview with Harvey Fleetwood.
445

"It was hilarious": Authors' interview with Michael Kennedy.
445

"Do you think I've wasted my life": Authors' interview with Duff Pacifico.
445

"I'm taking all my Kennedy pictures off ": Authors' interview with Harvey Fleetwood.
445

Lem's autopsy: A copy of the report was examined by the authors.
445

"He felt pain for every one of us": A copy of the eulogy was given to the authors by Bobby Kennedy, Jr.
445

"I'm sure he's already organizing everything in heaven": Ibid.
446

Thanksgiving at Hyannis, 1982: Authors' interviews with Chris and Vicki Lawford; authors' interview with Dotson Rader, October 1, 1983.
447

"I want you all to remember": Authors' interview with Dotson Rader. Rader jotted down his recollections of the speech at Teddy's request—"He wanted it for 'history.' "
448

"Why don't we take a vote?": Ibid.
449

"Well, Daddy did it": Authors' interview with David Kennedy.
450

"A political boss": Authors' interview with Chris Lawford.
450

"We have to measure what we are": Authors' interview with Bobby Shriver.
450

"Joe has accepted the old way": Authors' interview with Chris Lawford.
450

He had been arrested: *Boston Globe,* September 16, 1980; authors' interview with Chris Lawford.
450

He had gone into a drug program: Authors' interview with Chris Lawford.
450

"We're so goddamned good": Ibid.
451

"I did it for politics": Ibid.
451

"I'm a bad person": Ibid.
451

David's overdose in Aspen: Authors' interview with David Kennedy.
451

"It's weird, the way you're standing": Ibid.

451

Everyone half expected David to kill himself: E.g., "I was scared to death for David. There wasn't a day when I was not expecting someone to call me and tell me David's overdosed." Authors' interview with John Warnecke, Jr.

451

"Mummies for dummies": Authors' interview with David Kennedy.

451

"At the beginning my shrink": Ibid.

451

"My Uncle Jack and my father always used to quote": Ibid.

452

"You're a junkie too": Ibid.

452

Breindel arrested: *New York Times,* May 19, 1983.

452

Ethel boasted that she had tipped officials: Authors' interview with a confidential source, September 15, 1983. Also authors' interview with Winston Proude, September 15, 1983.

452

Proude attempted suicide: *Washington Post,* May 28, 1983.

452

Bobby got a lawyer: Authors' interview with Winston Proude.

452

Events in Republic airliner: Authors' interview with Greg Madson, attorney for Republic Airlines, September 30, 1983. See also "The Tragedy of Bobby Kennedy, Jr.," *People,* October 3, 1983.

453

At first he said his name was Bobby Francis: "The Tragedy of Bobby Kennedy, Jr.," *People,* October 3, 1983.

453

"He was the best and the brightest": Authors' interview with David Kennedy.

453

"If you think of it as one movement": Authors' interview with Chris Lawford.

453

Chris and Bobby's telephone conversation: Ibid.

INDEX

PICTURE CREDITS

The following credit lines refer to the seven-page photo section at the beginning of this book. The credits are listed in order of their appearance, from left to right and top to bottom.

PAGE *1*
Courtesy John F. Kennedy Library
Courtesy John F. Kennedy Library
The Bettmann Archive, Inc.
Courtesy John F. Kennedy Library
Collection Mary McCarthy
The Bettmann Archive, Inc.
F. W. Owen/Black Star
F. W. Owen/Black Star
F. W. Owen/Black Star

PAGE *2*
F. W. Owen/Black Star
F. W. Owen/Black Star
F. W. Owen/Black Star
Pictorial Parade
Pictorial Parade
Pictorial Parade
The Bettmann Archive, Inc.
The Bettmann Archive, Inc.
AP/Wide World Photos

PAGE *3*
Pictorial Parade
Pictorial Parade
Collection John White
Courtesy John F. Kennedy Library
UPI
AP/Wide World Photos
Collection of The Lady Lloyd
Collection of H.N. Sporborg
AP/Wide World Photos

PAGE *4*
AP/Wide World Photos
AP/Wide World Photos
AP/Wide World Photos
AP/Wide World Photos

Henri Dauman/Magnum
UPI
UPI
UPI
AP/Wide World Photos

PAGE *5*
© Elliot Erwitt/ Magnum
UPI
AP/Wide World Photos
UPI
AP/Wide World Photos
UPI
UPI
UPI
UPI

PAGE *6*
AP/Wide World Photos
UPI
UPI
UPI
UPI
UPI
UPI
UPI
UPI

PAGE *7*
UPI
UPI
UPI
UPI
AP/Wide World Photos
UPI
Collection Pam Kelly
UPI
AP/Wide World Photos

"Architect of Their Lives"—F. W. Owen/Black Star
"The Stand-In"—Marcus Adams/Courtesy John F. Kennedy Library
"Brothers Within"—Henri Dauman/Magnum